THE PRAGMATIC REVOLT
IN POLITICS

THE PRAGMATIC REVOLT IN POLITICS

SYNDICALISM, FASCISM, AND THE CONSTITUTIONAL STATE

BY

W. Y. ELLIOTT

With a New Preface
and
Three New Appendices
by the Author

NEW YORK

Howard Fertig

1968

First published in 1928
by the Macmillan Company

HOWARD FERTIG, INC. EDITION 1968
published by arrangement with the author

Library of Congress Catalog Card Number: 67-13632

PRINTED IN THE UNITED STATES OF AMERICA
BY NOBLE OFFSET PRINTERS, INC.

To
A. D. LINDSAY
MASTER OF BALLIOL

PREFACE

In shaping this book as a presentation of the modern tendency away from the dominance of rationalism in politics, I have had certain objectives in mind which have necessarily imposed definite limitations upon its scope and its form. It seems best to indicate these objectives and their consequences at the outset.

As a study of contemporary political thought and its immediate context of fact, this volume does not attempt an exhaustive survey. It is not itself an outline and it does not attempt to outline still other outlines. Consequently I have selected references in the notes and I have appended no other bibliography than the Index. It is my aim simply to run a thread of unity through the chief modern theories and experiments which are in revolt against political rationalism. Although many of the chapters have been printed as separate studies, they were originally written and they now stand as parts of an inquiry into a central problem. Since that problem, like all fundamental problems, has its roots in the development of ideas as well as facts, I have tried to set it in this historical context in the Introduction.

The particular form of revolt upon which this study is focussed is the attack now taking formidable shape in practice as well as theory, over a great part of Europe, against the constitutional and democratic state. After the Great War this form of state seemed to be the assured type to which all the larger Occidental powers must come. The triumph of the Allies, for a few short months at least, seemed to mean the triumph of the rational Wilsonian principles of national self-determination, of representative and democratically responsible government, and of the adjustment of political control by the liberal technique of counting heads rather than by breaking or by bowing them. Divine right, organic efficiency, the claim to a cultural superiority all seemed in a fair way toward being discredited as bases for political authority. To the more hopeful it had even seemed that the method of adjusting disputes by persuasion and common confrontation under a rule of law might be extended to the sphere of international relations. The hope remains, but contemporary facts seem to doom it to the status of hope, not actuality.

Although this is a selection rather than an outline, I may be allowed to venture the suggestion even at this point that the political products of the current revolt against rationalism are the most characteristic contributions of the period, and that pragmatism is the philosophy that gives them their ideology and their values. Whether the War simply assisted the development of political aspects of problems which were imbedded in the whole development of modern capitalistic industrialism or whether Reconstruction stress and strain snapped social bonds that might otherwise have held, it is certain in either case that democratic constitutionalism and the sovereignty based on it are being widely challenged by the Marxian labor forces, particularly by the Syndicalist and Communist left wing. At the other extreme, Fascist reaction, model of an alarming crop of dictators, although it attacks not sovereignty but the constitutional organization of responsibility for that sovereignty, is equally pragmatic in its savage onslaught on parliamentary futility.

The only serious omission that prevents this work from claiming to be a fairly complete critique of at least one side of the "isms" currently offered as social gospels is communistic Bolshevism. Insofar as that is not a sort of regenerative religion, and so far as it is a philosophy of political society, it is too dogmatically faithful to Marx and Lenin to be closely related to anything so skeptical of absolutes as is pragmatism. Its practice under the New Economic Policy may be increasingly pragmatic, but the core of the doctrine upon which it depends for its quasi-religious domination of the Communist *élite* is and must remain intellectualistic—springing from a faith in those Marxian prophecies which are correctly described as an inspired Hegelianism of the Left. I have attempted only to relate Bolshevism to Fascism and to Syndicalism by way of comparison. As a revolutionary Social Myth, a product of the Will to Believe, it is akin to M. Sorel's Romanticist pragmatism; but it goes further than that apostle of revolt would go by having a rationalistic technique to operate its New State.

With some temerity I have ventured to offer at the conclusion of this critical study an effort of modest pretensions at reconstructing the essential problem which is common to all these attacks on constitutionalism—the nature of the constitutional state as an association, and its relations to other associations, including other states. Pragmatism as a philosophy has forced a restatement of the problems of modern philosophy in terms that will meet its valid objections to the traditional concepts and methods. Political pragmatism ought to have at least as fruitful results in its application to theories of the state. With this aim I have summed up what seem to me to be the valuable results of the pragmatic revolt in politics under the theory of the nature of group life for which I have proposed the term *co-organic*.

This volume is necessarily, however, critical in its emphasis and limited in its constructive scope. I have had, for lack of space, to leave out a chapter on Professor H. Krabbe's interesting idea of the *Rechtsgefühl* (or non-rational "feeling for right") as the basis of law. Given the already too ample proportions of this work, I shall also be forced simply to indicate (by way of orientation) general agreements as briefly in the preface as I have indicated my disagreements at length in the body of the work.

First of all, I ought to put the theoretical works of Alfred Weber, whom I had neglected in favor of his distinguished brother Max Weber, until the courteous suggestion of my colleage, Dr. Carl Joachim Friedrich of Heidelberg University (now Assistant Professor of Government at Harvard), acquainted me with the theses of his recently published *Die Krise des Modernen Staatsgedankens in Europa* (1925) and *Ideen zur Staats und Kultur-Soziologie* (1927). I find many points of theoretical community in his general position, with which I was unhappily not acquainted before the completion of this work. The conceptions of (1) *culture* and (2) *civilization* in Professor Weber's later works seem to serve for his construction of social theory much the same use to which I have tried to put the idea of the co-organic nature of associations: that is (1) both socially purposive and (2) historically conditioned by their total institutional and environmental context. Professor Weber has obviously pushed his inquiries into the technique of social organization, particularly as to industrial society, much further than I have been able to do here, but without putting the operation of the two forces quite so definitely in individual groups. The reader is earnestly referred to the above works and to his *Über den Standort der Industrien* (1909), of which Dr. Friedrich is making an English edition.

It is a matter of regret to me that the following works, just published, came out too late for me to profit in any way from their contents: John Dewey, *The Public and Its Problems;* K. C. Hsiao, *Political Pluralism;* P. W. Ward, *Sovereignty, A Study of a Contemporary Political Notion.* Mr. Dewey's work, particularly, offers a nice comparison with Mr. Lippman's.

In order that this work, with its ambitious attempt to set political thinking in so wide a context of social philosophy and experiment, may be understood to be really less controversially biased than it is bound to seem, I should like here to indicate my realization of two facts of prime importance: (1) The theories of Mr. H. J. Laski with which I have largely disagreed have been my greatest stimulant. (2) In selecting certain tendencies that seem to me most important in the works of philosophers like Dewey and James and jurists like M. Duguit, it is inevitable that I should not do justice to the whole of their rich and various thought. Every great theorist has at least as many faces as Janus, often more. If I have emphasized the anti-intellectualistic aspect of pragmatism, and its Romanticist as well as its "scientific" values, it is because the political uses to which these value theories have been put have had too little notice. The practical working test of pragmatism which they afford ought, on pragmatism's own criteria, to be of first importance.

In order still further to show a smiling rather than a carping face at the outset, I own myself able to find little except admiration for the following works, which may serve to give the reader a general orientation as to my own philosophic per-

spective. For convenience sake I shall limit them to typical
books in English.

In sociological theory there are the works of Professor R. M.
MacIver, especially *The Modern State*, and of Professor Morris
Ginsberg, especially his useful *Introduction to the Psychology
of Society*.

In ethics, after the works of T. H. Green, I accept as outstanding the work of L. T. Hobhouse, whose *Rational Good* and
Morals in Evolution seem to me the most adequate basis of
ethics available in the works of a single thinker.

Though I cannot altogether agree with his statement of value
as purely a function of interest, Professor R. B. Perry's magistral treatise *The General Theory of Value* has enabled me to
leave out a chapter of exposition on "The Pragmatic Theories
of Value".

In Metaphysics I have derived great stimulation from the
work of Professor A. N. Whitehead, whose ideas (so far as I
profess to understand their often poetically obscure suggestions
of the organic nature of all reality) seem to me to afford a metaphysical basis for much that I have tried to say here. I am sure
of agreeing with L. T. Hobhouse's *Development and Purpose*.

In the Philosophy of the State on its ethical side, I accept
with few reservations at least one side of Professor Hocking's
Man and the State and *The Present Status of the Philosophy of
Rights and Law*, i.e., the rationally purposive nature of rights.
I have, however, tried to suggest the limits of his formal theory
by an analysis of the relations, actual as well as normative, of
the state with other associations.

For a judicious and historically illustrated statement of the
Foundations of the Modern Commonwealth, with especial emphasis on American constitutionalism, there is the work of that
title by my colleague, Professor A. N. Holcombe. The only
reason that I have not used his term *Commonwealth* throughout
where I have referred to the constitutional state is that commonwealth has been put to so many different uses as to blur the
ordinary meaning of the term. The British Commonwealth of
Nations, so-called, is not a constitutional state, but a co-oper-
ating group of states united by the formal symbol of the crown,
so far as the Dominions are concerned; and an Empire with the

most complex and various organization of dependencies for the rest.

For a brief picture of international realities, Manley O. Hudson's Calcutta lectures on *Current International Co-Operation* seem to me to be as just a statement as any.

In a book that has been growing since 1920 the list of my obligations is naturally, if formidably, long. I owe my greatest intellectual debt for this work and for anything I may ever do, to my old tutor at Balliol, Mr. A. D. Lindsay, now the Master. I have tried by the dedication to indicate something of the extent and the abiding nature of that obligation to one of the wisest of friends and counsellors. After the Master of Balliol, I should name that great scholar under whose kindly supervision much of this work was done, the late Sir Paul Vinogradoff, then Corpus Professor of Jurisprudence at Oxford. How still more short of its goal this work would have been but for the critical guidance of his vast erudition, only the author can know, and any expression of gratitude is at best feebly inadequate. Valuable criticisms were also made by my examiners, Mr. A. J. Carlyle and Mr. John McMurray. No list of my indebtedness for this work would be complete without acknowledgment of the truest assistance of my friends and my fellow students in the golden days at Oxford just after the war—Professors W. R. Dennes of the University of California, and R. K. Gooch of the University of Virginia, and Basanta K. Mallik of India, to all of whom I would acknowledge what I owe for the stimulus of their own ideas as well as for their criticism of mine. As this work grew, in a way, out of an attempt to answer some of Professor Alexander Meiklejohn's questions to the Lotos Club at Oxford, it is fitting that I should thank him here and at the same time apologize for the inadequacy of the answer.

My debt to my colleagues at Harvard is a collective as well as an individual one, that of one to whom support and good counsel has been freely given by his seniors in a great fellowship. If I single out for special thanks Professors Allyn A. Young, R. B. Perry, Ernest Hocking, Irving Babbitt, W. B. Munro, A. N. Holcombe, C. H. McIlwain, Carl Friedrich, and John Dickinson (the latter now of Princeton University), it is simply because I have most imposed upon their generous willingness to criticize helpfully. It goes without saying that they can hardly be held responsible where I have failed to profit by their counsel.

An almost equal debt of gratitude is due from me to my former colleagues at the University of California, first of all to Dean R. G. Gettell, but hardly less to Professors E. M. Sait, D. P. Barrows, Carl O. Sauer, George Adams, W. R. Dennes, David Prall, and Stephen Pepper. I have further profited by helpful suggestions on juristic theory from Professor Max Radin of the Law School and from Professor C. G. Haines of the University of California in Los Angeles.

For reading parts of the proof and for many useful corrections I wish to thank Professor F. W. Coker of Ohio State University and Dr. Rupert Emerson, my colleague at Harvard, and the following Rockefeller Fellows, now Research Fellows in Government at Harvard: Drs. J. Lambert, M. Einaudi, E. Hula. Mr. Joseph Wright, Superintendent of the Library for Municipal Research at Harvard, has prepared the index and re-read all the proof—a service of the greatest value, as every scholar knows. I shall be grateful to those who point out any remaining errors.

To my students I owe the usual debt of any teacher, perhaps the greatest of all where the final shaping of one's ideas is concerned. And to my uncle, Edward Graham Elliott, formerly Professor of Politics in Princeton University, there is due an acknowledgment for criticism and guidance of a very intimate sort, for which no thanks are expected, but for which I should none the less like to render them here. If I have sometimes differed from his own theories and those of his late master in theory, Professor Georg Jellinek of Heidelberg, it has always been with real respect.

A final acknowledgment is due to the editors of *Economica*, of the *Political Science Quarterly*, the *American Political Science Review*, and the *American Economic Review* for permission to reprint with the necessary alteration portions of this volume that appeared as separate studies in these journals.

W. Y. Elliott.

Cambridge, Massachusetts.
April, 1928.

PREFACE TO THE 1968 EDITION

This earliest work still seems, at least to its author, the most important (if not the most influential or most read) which he has contributed in a long list of books and essays to a deeper philosophical understanding of political thought's main currents in the first half of this century. It has become a rare and, alas, a very expensive book to own. Many copies have disappeared from libraries where they were once in continuing use and availability.

I welcome, therefore, this publisher's willingness to reissue it as it first came off the press under Macmillan's imprint in 1927, several years after much of it had served as part of a longer thesis for the Oxford D. Phil., fruit of some pleasant postwar (World War I) years at Balliol College. I should like to add Mr. Fertig, therefore, to my original list of acknowledgments. I should also like for this late fruit to acknowledge the great debt I owe to many wise colleagues, especially to *Fugitives* at Vanderbilt and to those who helped me as friendly critics first at Berkeley, then for nearly forty years at Harvard, and now at American University (Washington, D.C.). At least an equal debt is due to my students over these forty-odd years, to hundreds of undergraduates who worked with me as a tutor, to many more in my classes, especially Government I, and to the nearly one hundred Doctors of Philosophy whose theses I have directed at Harvard, plus some others at those other universities. I have been helped by students to grow at each new academic home.

The added appendices, particularly the concluding one, will serve, I hope, not only to review some growth of my own understanding of the chief concepts reflected in the original and seminal volume, but also to show a reshaping of some of its emphases as well as its basic ideas and values.

The necessity of balancing "organic" needs (the data of our surrounding political and cultural environments) with the deeper dynamics of moral ideas and purposes in human development looms larger in its importance as sweeping revolutions of human technology impinge on every political system and all human institutions. "Behavioralism" of the current vogue is not only "not enough"; it is mostly a lot of noisy giving tongue on false trails.

The rapidity of social adjustment already demanded of our political responses may outstrip the capabilities even of our most developed social systems and defy the conditioning also of the professedly totalitarian regimes. Computers cannot themselves think, or "program," or establish priorities. They can do systems analyses only if and where the mind, commanded by true logic, finds real systems in the nature of things. Even to try to revert to the finished evolution of insect societies based on habit and instinct, like those of the ants and the bees, could fatally involve a bankruptcy destructive of all future *human* growth. Yet without public purpose, always geared to individual moral responsibility and personal, even if divinely guided, freedom, this bankruptcy is inevitable. Equally without socially stable communities in which force and law can be responsibly limited and exercised, apocalyptic doom seems probable if not inevitable. That is why a review of love, justice, and reason in the service of mankind needs restatement for this and every area of evolution. Epic myths and real heroes (not antiheroes) are still our greatest teachers, as all the world's true religions can prove.

Perhaps this reprint, with some rather summary new appendices, may serve usefully to that larger end.

                                             W. Y. ELLIOTT

CONTENTS

PART I. PRAGMATIC THEORY

PART II. PRAGMATIC POLITICS

PART III. PRAGMATIC ETHICS AND THE FASCIST
STATE-ORGANISM

PART I

PRAGMATIC THEORY

"If a philosophy of society is to be effective, it must be as mobile and realistic as the forces which it would control."

R. H. TAWNEY, *Religion and the Rise of Capitalism.*

INTRODUCTION

THE RELATIONS BETWEEN MODERN PHILOSOPHY AND POLITICS

No problem of modern politics presses for solution, theoretical and practical, with more insistence than does the many-sided revolt now aimed at the constitutional state. In England and Continental Europe constitutional sovereignty has been again and again, of late, challenged by syndicalistic labor movements which aim at reducing its authority through the tactics of what Mr. Laski calls "contingent revolution". Labor's attack on the state's authority varies all the way from protests like those of our American Federation of Labor against court injunctions, through scattered sabotage, up to a revolutionary general strike of national proportions. As for the state's constitutional responsibility, it is at the other extreme disparaged, or completely dispensed with by dictatorships that range from Communistic Bolshevism on the left to Capitalistic Fascism on the right. Even among the friends of constitutional government there are those who see no real possibility of a rule of law in a world whose major issues are controlled only by the armed truce of egoistic and legally absolute nationalism. Many of the most internationally minded of them are bent on limiting the sovereign authority of the constitutional Nation State by erecting a constitutional World or Super State.

Both the pluralist syndicalism which would discredit the state and the Fascist syndicalism which would regiment humanity under a functionally organic and a politically irresponsible state profess to (and actually do) spring from the same pragmatic impatience with the Liberal gospel of representative government.

What both syndicalism and Fascism most dislike about liberal constitutionalism is the assumption that rational solutions along the lines of government by discussion and voting are possible.

3

They demand action and they insist, equally, that the solution of social problems demands either a revolutionary violence or a repressive force which scorns constitutional restraints.

A study of pragmatism, as it crops up in the dominant issues of contemporary politics, requires in spite of its theoretical and practical importance, more than the usual apologia. This is so, if only for the reason that the ruling spirit of American political science is itself too pragmatic to take much thought about the relation between ideas and facts where the start is made from ideas. One is tempted to say that the general preoccupation of political thought in this country with descriptive studies of institutions and with attempts to formulate and apply an objective and purely scientific method to political studies may be intimately related to the fact that there is not a single contemporary political theorist in America who is to be counted among those of the first order—with the possible exceptions of Dean Roscoe Pound, W. W. Willoughby, and Mr. Walter Lippmann. We have had, and we have now, historians of political ideas: W. A. Dunning, V. Louis Parrington, C. H. McIlwain, R. G. Gettell, C. E. Merriam, F. W. Coker, and from different angles thinkers like A. M. Schlesinger and Irving Babbitt. We have, due to the influence of political scientists, like A. F. Bentley, Charles A. Beard, W. B. Munro, and C. E. Merriam again, an increasingly fruitful study of political behavior and political motivation as well as of the actual working of democratic institutions. We have significant contributions to economics, to psychology, and to sociology as they affect politics—the last heralded in somewhat extravagant terms by H. E. Barnes. In this generation there have also been a small number of outstanding contributions such as those of Professor Hocking to the ethical aspects of politics. But of creative and even of critical studies of the interweaving of contemporary political ideas and political practice, with which European political literature abounds, we have had almost nothing of a creative sort except the writings of Walter Lippmann and of Miss M. P. Follett, and in jurisprudence of Dean Pound.

Perhaps for that very reason, a theorist like M. Léon Duguit, or Herr Hugo Krabbe, or Mr. H. J. Laski, who attracts for one reason or another the attention of our scholars, immediately attains a large and in part an uncritical following for an idea like that of the Public-Service State, or the *Modern Idea of the State* as based on the *Rechtsgefühl* ("feeling for right"), or for the Pluralistic State. The whole context of controversy out of which these theories have emerged is generally ignored. Happily the awakening of American scholarship once more to the importance of theoretical orientation is manifested by the increasing number of competent critical studies from such scholars as Professors F. W. Coker, Morris Cohen, Norman Wilde, George H. Sabine, Walter Shepard, H. R. Spencer, R. K. Gooch, and E. D. Ellis, and some of the younger scholars among whom one may partly claim English sojourners like G. E. G. Catlin and L. J. Rockow.

This study of the revolt against the rationalistic theories and the actual control of the constitutional state is aimed at supplying at least an approach to the central problems of contemporary political theory where they intimately affect political practice. It is devoted to an examination of the most important pragmatic political theories and of something at least of their economic and cultural contexts. It is undertaken with the conviction that facts can not be separated from ideas with any more fruitful results than attend the complete abstraction of ideas from facts. Its temper is pragmatic to the degree that it is willing to set all the problems of politics in their historical, their economic, and their cultural environments—instead of trying to work out a "Science of Politics" based on abstractions. It accepts man as a biological creature, functioning in a context of economic needs and at different stages or in different types of cultural development.

But it insists as against the extremists of the revolt against reason that there is a much neglected fact of a validity quite equal to the *given* of man's cultural, economic, biological, and geographical setting: the fact that he is a purposive animal, even in politics, endowed for his further perplexing with moral needs and a speculative reason. It insists further that *facts are shaped and used as they are interpreted.* If *"le coeur a ses raisons que la raison ne connaît pas"* one ought not to forget the addendum: *"mais la raison a aussi ses raisons."* The problem of political values, too, must be critically approached.

A. Pragmatism as a Political Philosophy of Both Revolt and Reaction

It would be relatively easy to fasten upon pragmatism all the evils which one might view with alarm in our present civilization. What Professor Moritz Bonn has rightly stigmatized as "a cheap pragmatism" is no doubt characteristic of much contemporary vulgarity, particularly evident in an impatience with serious matters, with "moral" principles and attitudes, or with anything other than cultural dilettantism. Pragmatism, because of its impatience with reason (as reason is expressed in metaphysics and logic) has been hailed as the ally of this vulgarity. Some such popular interpretation of pragmatism is expressed by revealing phrases of current slang like "getting by", "putting it over", "a good front", etc. Pragmatism, with this connotation, is an absence of principle, and of moral or other standards, with a resultant gesture of cynical acceptance for the current views and values as to what is called "success"—what William James himself wrathfully called the "worship of the bitch-goddess Success".

Nothing would be more easy but few things could be less profitable. Why do we need to fasten these eternal vulgarities upon modern pragmatism? What is pragmatism *as a philosophy* in the hands of men like William James and John Dewey really trying to say? What in the social context has called forth the overpowering evidences of its popularity among thinkers as a way of looking at things, among agents as an apology for their ways of acting?

In politics, particularly, why do the currents of syndicalist revolt and of Fascist reaction each claim genuinely pragmatic inspiration? Is pragmatism a sort of revaluing of values that will destroy the old rationalized systems of liberal and representative constitutionalism? Is it the strongest current in the larger flood of anti-rationalism which has set against metaphysical doctrines of all sorts?

There is, by all evidence, a revolt in process and of alarming proportions already against the democratic and constitutionally unified State: to what degree is this due to the two main pragmatic ways of interpreting the forces of history—as myths or products of a will to believe, on the one hand, by those whose thinking is fortified by William James; as determined by the specific economic and social context and capable of highly scientific formulation and control, on the other hand, by those who take Mr. John Dewey as a model?

Or is any such inquiry into the ideology of social movements mere waste of energy? That attitude has characterized the dominant aspects of contemporary American political science, as a branch of social study. It has been due, no doubt, to students of "actual government", to use Professor A. B. Hart's term, having been so painfully impressed with the emptiness involved in the manipulation of the typical concepts of "sovereignty", "natural rights", "civil liberty" which are the stock in trade of the scholasticism of constitutional dogma in the United States. It has turned by way of reaction toward the pure description of institutions and of political machinery, or it has attempted forays into social psychology such as the "scientific" measurement of public opinion; or it has busied itself with endless statistical studies of problems of administration, comparable, as T. R. Powell puts it, "to counting the man-holes on sewers".

Some of these preoccupations of the political scientist are genuinely fruitful and produce useful results other than the mere piling up of monographs. The utility of the statistical method, properly directed and interpreted, is not to be doubted, particularly in those political problems where groups take on something like an organic regularity of behavior. Professor Holcombe's remarkable economic study of *The Political Parties of To-day* is a case in point. But many of them have been sadly lacking in a sense of direction, in a methodology that would bear criticism, and consequently in any results worthy of the term "scientific". At least one side of pragmatism, with its insistence upon the concrete and the immediate, is an encouragement to this much business, a defence of the assumption that general theory is irrelevant, and an apologia for the method of purely scientific description as the only approach to politics. It is, in short, behavioristic in terms of psychology and positivistic in terms of philosophy. And this has been the main stream of American political science.

But if it is useful, even necessary, to have values as well as facts, then we have too few political theorists and too many technicians, engineers, scientists or artists in America.

On the other hand, the philosopher who does not know the relevant facts is apt to be very wide of the mark in his theories of political values. Pragmatism is perfectly sound in insisting upon the relevance of the context to all ideas about politics.

Given the departmentalization of our modern academic disciplines, a book that attempts to talk politics to philosophers is in almost as dubious a case as a book that tries to talk philosophy to politicians. Any one who listened to the Sixth International Congress of Philosophy must have felt that. Lip service is paid Aristotle, but the unity of his philosophy and his politics is hardly ever attempted. The philosopher has usually regarded his own job as completed when he had furnished logically self-consistent systems of metaphysics to a world that might conform or not at its own good pleasure or dire peril. Naturally the politician, even more than the political scientist, has had scant regard for these intellectualistic constructions. The "practical" politician has had a more immediate urge to muddle through with the present difficulties of getting votes and keeping power. The "scientist" has, for his part, contented himself with describing the way political phenomena actually occur and the manner in which political animals habitually do behave. They seemed to him best treated without ethical or metaphysical bias if he were to qualify as a true scientist. Politician and "scientist" have shared (of late more than ever) a fine pragmatic contempt for the abstract solutions of philosophy. They have been interested only in the matter of technique,—the politician as an artist, the political scientist quâ scientist. But to have no principles is surely as socially dangerous as to have too rigid ones.

Students of politics, envious of the *éclat* with which the physical sciences have been set to the control of natural forces, have imitated the purely quantitative methods of physical measurement with the hope of securing some measure of control over social forces by applying the same technique. They have rightfully claimed that those who strive to know social facts objectively have as much right to the term scientist as any servant of science in the realm of inorganic matter. In such cases as those of Robert Michels, Vilfredo Pareto, Max and Alfred Weber, they have gone far toward methods which make good their scientific pretensions. But most of them have attempted to treat their own realm of social phenomena as if reason and a normative human will did not exist in it. They have outdone the politicians in their attitude of pragmatic skepticism. To what extent is this skepticism of rational purpose in politics only a current of the tide which has everywhere set against intellectualism?

It does not require a profound historical perspective to observe that the balance between anti-intellectualism and intellectualism has swung perpetually backward and forward throughout the development of human thought. The reason finds the best of reasons for distrusting itself, and does not need the insistent clutch of the emotions or the urge of will to chasten its rationalistic presumption. From the contradictory claims of intellectualistic system-builders, Babel-tower emerges once more, with every man speaking his own tongue and understanding no other.

Yet if, armed with logic alone, Reason has wounded itself, the Doubt of consistent skepticism is even more suicidal. Life demands an affirmation from those who would keep it. One is a voluntarist by the mere fact of living. To treat the tough world of fact as one of mere appearance is itself the greatest illusion. This realism is the first premise of the anti-intellectualism which, under a variety of names, makes common cause against the metaphysical abstractions of absolute Idealism. The modern Pragmatists, whose name is legion in the circles of lay philosophy and whose number is formidable among those who are philosophers by profession, are all enrolled under this banner. Naturalism, too, with something of the same anti-intellectualistic tenets and under the poetic inspiration of Mr. George Santayana, has concluded that intellectualism must issue in skepticism, and has therefore reasonably embraced "animal faith". As a reaction all this is both natural and wholesome. As a philosophy it suffers the penalty of extreme revolt: it goes too far and destroys its own usefulness where it approaches the constructive problem of explaining and applying its values.

Led in America by William James and John Dewey, the

pragmatists have conquered a foothold of the strongest sort in the academic life of the nation. What is more important, they have laid claim to being the true interpreters of that new spirit which the vast promise of America has led the world to expect and of which Walt Whitman was an earlier prophet. One may find journalists, authors, politicians, jurists, all speaking of pragmatism as "the American philosophy". A literary artist like Waldo Frank thinks that he discerns in pragmatism the dominant attitude of *Our America*.

Of course this would be absurd if it were put forward as a proprietary claim. They are not mere repercussions that we remark in other lands, but part of a deeply rooted anti-intellectualism from which pragmatism itself is but an offshoot. Consciously or unconsciously the same, it is still the spirit of pragmatic anti-intellectualism which informs movements in thought and in act whose social import it would be hard to overestimate. It is this spirit which offers a philosophical apologia for all the revolt against the sovereignty of the personalized state and against parliamentarism. It marks alike syndicalism, the more chastened pluralism of Mr. H. J. Laski, the *droit objectif* of M. Léon Duguit, and the Fascist "efficiency" gospel of Mussolini.

That apostle of strenuous imperialism, whose only consistent rule is a contempt for rules, professes to have a new pragmatic philosophy for the corporative and functional state. The ideology of Fascism contains a very queer *potpourri* of a sort of Machiavellian Pragmatism, Gentilean Idealism, Sorelian myth-making and violence, and even the functionalism of the Guild Socialists and Syndicalists of Italy. Mussolini's schemes for a functional state have been compounded of these elements. Through Papini, Pantaleone, Pareto, and Sorel he has sucked up his ideas of pragmatism. It is interesting to notice that since he has adopted a dogma for his state he has ceased talking of pragmatic solutions and begun appealing for faith in the greatness of Italy under organic and hierarchical discipline. He is, of course, exploiting the Will to Believe as well as the *Wille zu Macht* in his constant theme of a revived Roman grandeur for his new Empire.

Even if one took only the most openly professed pragmatists

among those who are trying to find new channels for the powerful groups growing up within the Nation-State, and often striving
to remain independent of its existing legal structure, one would
still have to do with an important body of modern political
theory, almost all of it bent upon pluralizing the units of political authority in accordance with the proper doctrines of pragmatism. Mr. H. J. Laski and M. Georges Sorel themselves
acclaim William James as the philosophic way-shower for their
own social theories. The whole vaguely syndicalistic grouping
of thinkers who repudiate the state as a moral agent and legal
overlord draw strength from James' robust contempt for the
absolute, either in a Platonic heaven or *ici-bas*. All of the efforts
of the pluralists at doing justice to the real life and spiritual
nature of groups have drawn upon the doctrines of pragmatism
to show that the Hegelian State, with its absorptive unity, is a
falsification of the actual nature of political society.

At the opposite pole of the problem of authority is the functional philosophy of Fascism, also based upon an attack on
rationalistic theories of the state, but a rabid defender of nationalistic reaction and absolutism. Along with Bolshevism, it is
the most important of contemporary political novelties. Post-
war misery and class struggles have produced similar dictatorial
reactions against parliamentary dallying, springing up like mush-
rooms over continental Europe as if to verify Oswald Spengler's
picture of the West declining into Cæsarism. Fascism puts its
great emphasis on the will to power, rather than the *rationale*
of power. As far as it attempts a defence of its authority it
rests upon the efficiency of its functioning as a national organism
for industrial and agrarian production and the greatness of Italy.

After the movements, both nationalistic and anti-nationalistic,
which surged up like true Leviathans in the turmoil of world
readjustment following the war, destroying the bonds of rationalized social conventions with the thresh of their upheaval, there
have followed the movements of reaction, striving in turn to
replace smashed institutions with still stronger chains. Russia
has passed through one colossal political overturn, the result
of an elemental disruption perhaps comparable in historic importance to the French Revolution. Its masters are now firmly
in the saddle of the old *régime*, with a better solution of the

federal problem of uniting nationalities in the U. S. S. R. than was ever possible to the Czar of all the Russias. But who will say that the *status quo* of modern Russia is permanently fixed? Even the British Empire, dependent as well as autonomous, is undergoing an evolution whose future course few dare predict with certainty, solid as the constitutional foundations of that Empire are. Continental Europe, despite the promise of Locarno and Thoiry, is still terribly shaken and dazed from a struggle whose economic aftermath cannot fail to affect the political organization of Europe more radically than has appeared at the present time. Asia appears to be slowly rousing to the fury of nationalism at the very time that within the western nations nationalism is being challenged by internationalism of various types. Struggles between classes and racial groups or between conflicting social creeds have never, perhaps, been more universal or more acute than they have on the world stage of the past decade (1917-1927).

Given this condition of human society, whirled along as it is by the fantastic change of the ordinary conditions of living which has been wrought in a brief century by the magical industrialization of the world, it is hardly a matter of wonder that there is no general confidence in the powers of broad rational solutions for the social problems with which governments are faced. Like John Dickinson in the Constitutional Convention of 1787, one may well exclaim, "Reason may mislead us; experience must be our only guide." Yet experience itself is not more provident of new solutions now than it was then. And new problems demand new solutions.

There is, on the one hand, where nationalistic centralization is an old story, a wide-spread feeling, evidenced by the growth of "regional" movements for political administration, by the growth of federalism in favor with both statesmen and theorists, and by the "syndicalist" trend in the labor movement[1] that the

---

[1] *Cf.* the study which Professor J. W. Scott has made of *Syndicalism and Philosophical Realism* in which the author points out very acutely some of the connecting links in theory particularly with the philosophy of Bergson. but does not think it relevant to consider the actual practice of syndicalism as it exists in the labor movement. On the other hand, there have been numerous suggestive studies of the application of anti-intellectualism to social problems which have an illuminating value when one approaches the practical questions raised most acutely by the political

State-Idea as it is realized in the modern Nation-State is becoming an empty concept, devoid of the vivid meaning that it had when the national areas were taking shape by the definition of language and royal centralization, shaking themselves free from papal control and feudal lawlessness. The experience of men holds the great state to be alien to their daily control, remote, gigantic, capable of being moved only by the pressure of great interest groups, in which the individual is almost as much lost as he is in the state.

At the opposite end of the scale of magnitudes the pragmatic test of the concrete benefits which the state can confer, when it is set for weighing alongside the economically vital concerns that are represented by international trade and finance, or by the international labor solidarity of the trade unions, places the "ringed-fence" national state in the balance and finds it wanting. The national state remains, perhaps, the formal framework for present society under law. But the rule of law is itself a concept, and one whose truth is to be tested by its utility in the given instance. The League is trying to give that concept a vigorous stretching beyond its traditional power to include only a national community. Is political reality in international matters as brittle and rigid as the Austinian concept? Syndicalism and Sovietism in this respect reach out to join hands with the Internationalists.

Yet there is an even more overwhelming reaction against the Romanticism which is represented by the more extreme pluralistic movements of revolt against the sovereign state. Syndicalism and the disruptive pluralistic efforts at direct action culminating in the strategy of general strikes are encouraged usually by the General Staff of Marxian labor in order to discredit the capitalistic state. These tactics have been met by dictatorship and by the revival of the most extreme form of state absolutism which the world has possibly ever seen, if only because the state now touches human life at more points. Inter-

theories arising from "the Greater Unionism" as Mr. G. D. H. Cole has called the syndicalist movement. Such a study was presented by Mr. J. E. Boodin, before the Oxford Congress of Philosophy of September, 1920. (*Cf.* the short summary given in the *Journal of Philosophy*, March, 1921.) Most of these studies, however, have remained too exclusively content with tracing spiritual genealogies, not facts.

nationalism, too, receives a vigorous challenge to battle from the same source. Italian Fascism has assumed a control over the life of individuals within the power of the Italian government which puts to shame the mild bureaucracy and the strutting militarism of prewar Prussia. And the international limit of its control it will measure only in terms of the force at its disposal. Mussolini and his imitators, like good pragmatists, urge in their own defence that dictatorship *works* and that parliamentarism does not. They treat the League with a very thinly veiled contempt wherever it touches their vital interests, and fear it not as a super-state but as a machinery for directing powerful alliances of their natural enemies against them.

There is thus a twofold conviction, actually at work and issuing in quite opposite political ends, that the rationalistic efforts of democratic liberalism to create a political vehicle such as parliamentary government, which strives to provide for social evolution under law and to extend that machinery gradually from constitutional nationalism to a World League, are foredoomed to failure. The place of reason is after the fact, according to this view. Men have needs which they realize experimentally. Truth itself is such a need, and reason is a tool in the service of evolutionary adaptation. The efforts of that great rationalist, Wilson (and of his collaborators at Versailles who really collaborated) to fit the nations of the world into the formal framework of a League which would provide them with the unifying constitutional sovereignty necessary for an international rule of law simply show by their results that any such conceptual framework will be burst by the pressure of facts. No one takes Article Ten seriously now, and the sanctions of force written into the covenant are useful only to police minor clashes.

The facts, they say, are hardly less brutally disruptive of the fictitious parliamentary sovereignty of the state than they are of that of the Society of Nations. It must be, say the anti-intellectualists of a thoroughgoing sort, either Syndicalism, Bolshevism, or Fascism, in the future. In the end purpose must conform to economic necessity, and to the "facts." Anti-intellectualism finds in contemporary events, including the apparent eclipse of democracy in a large part of Europe, good grounds for a profound skepticism as to the power of collective reason. It is a philosophy well fitted for the service of a period of disillusion following one of high hopes.

B. The Age of Skepticism

Is it not an illuminating commentary on the temper of the age to note with what fine scorn we describe an era not two centuries gone as "The Age of Reason"? We pronounce it as who would say, "Alack, what blessed innocence! No doubts as to the adequacy of human wisdom to cope with human problems came to trouble the dogmatic slumber of those fortunate days. But for us the glass is cracked. We have seen the mirror, and the image itself is shattered."

Reason in the age even of Franklin and Doctor Samuel Johnson was enjoying the fullest measure of its credit through the conquests it had made. The same Science which now abandons, through the high priests like M. Jules Henri Poincaré and Professor Eddington, most of its high claims, abdicating every kingdom save that of convenient manipulation, seemed then about to inaugurate the absolute reign of causality. Kant could look with envy at the noble structures reared by mathematics and by physics, and set them up as examples of the method philosophy must emulate.[2]

Theism gave way in that generation not to skepticism but to rationalistic Deism. The faith in a Law of Nature upon which all human laws and rights must rest is pathetically evident, for instance, in the original American state constitutions and in the philosophy which inspired the Declaration of Independence. The same logical zeal, too, inspired the men of the French Convention of 1791. After the amazing progress of science which had given Newton's conceptions of the astronomical laws that govern the universe, it is no wonder that God came to be thought of as *deus in machina*, a principle rather than a person. Knowledge

---

[2] The complete change of emphasis from the *Critique of Pure Reason* to the *Critique of Practical Reason* shows, however, how little Kant's later thought on moral philosophy found it possible to carry the method of the natural sciences into ethics. Even the *Critique of the Judgment*, for all its efforts to marry the two into a more systematic unity, is as far as ever from returning to the original program.

had proved itself to be power; therefore knowledge, certain and scientific, *a priori* rather than Baconian in its method, was the ultimate aim of human life. From the tone of certainty which pervaded the pronouncements of the sages of that age, it is clear that they felt the door to the Mysteries so superstitiously guarded by the ancients to be already more than half ajar. The Perfectionists, the Necessitarians, the Godwinites, shared the exalted mood of the fathers of the French Revolution. In America the same confidence inspired the Revolutionary States. Natural rights could be divined by right reason and enshrined forever in unalterable or very rigid constitutions.

Not that there was no protest, "in erring reason's spite" against this 18th century flood of reasonableness, even before its full tide. But the very voices raised against the omnicompetence of rationalism in every sphere were, like Pope's, hardly the less for that the chief celebrators of its triumphs. Or else how approve that arch-rationalism which proclaimed, "Whatever is, is right"? Divine Perfection found its prophet in divine Reason; wherever Faith had gone, there Reason could follow. There were, to be sure, the beginnings of the Romantic Revolt already in the air. They spoke, even earlier, in such voices as that of the Earl of Rochester, that odd sensualist and wit:

> Were I (who to my cost already am
> One of those strange prodigious Creatures, Man,)
> A Spirit free to chuse for my own share
> What case of Flesh and Blood I'd please to wear,
> I'd be a Dog, a Monkey, or a Bear,
> Or anything but that vain animal
> Who is so proud of being Rational. . . .
> The Senses are too gross, and he'll contrive
> A sixth to contradict the other five;
> And before certain Instinct will prefer
> Reason, which fifty times for one does err.

The doggerel sentiments of the noble earl found many echoes even in his own time, none, however, powerful enough to waken the drugged emotions and make them cry out for their birthright. It was not until Rousseau had bathed them with his tears that they were refreshed to life. At once the greatest Rationalist and the greatest Romanticist of his age, he ministered to *la civi-*

lisation malade not only with the heroic potions of emotional unrestraint, but with calculated doses of a rationalized distrust in reason's self and in all its artificial fruits. True enough the apostle of the "Natural Man" strove to force humanity to be free within the civilized chains of the Social Contract in the most rationalistic fashion; but his appeal in the beginning had been to an order sanctioned by its pre-rational character, at once "natural" and perfect.

When at length the full flood of the Romantic Revival had come to sweep the Age of Prose and Reason from the printed page, from the canvas, and the scene, in the domain of philosophy there remained a final asylum for exiled logic—an absolute monarch in the detached realm of Ultima Thule left him. There it was not until long after Kant in his search for a sure foundation for the laws of thinking had dug deep enough in the gaping pit left by Hume and Berkeley to undermine the whole position of traditional philosophy that Logic's throne began visibly to totter. To the very end Kant himself was busied with repairing the destruction wrought by the *Kritik der Reinen Vernunft*. He had compared his work with the Copernican revolution of astronomic laws from the geocentric to the heliocentric system; yet the critical problem with which he forced philosophy to concern itself from thenceforth really introduced the egocentric predicament in a more complex guise, one from which the succeeding generation of German philosophers escaped only by adopting the Absolutism of Hegel, the moral Voluntarism of Fichte, or the Romanticism of Schlegel, Tieck, Novalis, or Schelling. Kant himself had made his compromise with the human need for faith as a basis for morality; in Fichte the primacy of the practical reason was almost all that remained of the Kantian structure; in the German philosophical Romanticists, not the ethical but the esthetic bases were retained for a new edifice of values: by poetic intuition alone might man hope to pierce that veil which had been drawn over the eyes of pure reason with such impenetrable finality by the master.

On the other hand Pan-logism and the gigantic efforts of Hegel contrived to give the intellectualist constructions for a long while the appearance of an imposing bulk and solidity. But it was trowel-work to cover the cracks and to fill the breaches that widened unceasingly. Not even the casting away of the logic of identity and the radical reconstruction offered by the Hegelian dialectic could save the ruin from its crumbling, though Croce has shown brilliantly how much of Hegel's own building must remain so long as noble thought is a human legacy.[3] From this time forward, Hegel's followers and Hegel's opponents divided the field between them. Voluntarism, finding strength in Schopenhauer and in von Hartmann, turned upon rationalism and rent the garment of its logic to show how bare and poor a thing was the Absolute that it concealed. Evolution as a biological doctrine came along to put reason in its place, found itself translated into terms of philosophy by such a sonorous voice as Nietzsche's and by so mellifluously clear a voice as Bergson's. It was broadcast throughout the world, and accepted as the solution of all those philosophic puzzles with which formal logic had long wrestled with the vigorous impotence of Scholasticism. To utter the word *survival* was now deemed the key to the Mysteries.

Perhaps it was this broader aspect of evolutionary doctrine, which philosophy found itself forced to face and take into account, that revealed with finality the destruction which Kantian criticism had begun. Kant himself in the *Kritik der Urteilskraft* had shown the place of value in the judgments of men, had seen the development in time which reaches the world of history—the organic evolution which transcends mechanism. The intellectualist doctrine that explained being as fixed within a hierarchical caste-system of types was forced to yield more and more ground to the evolutionary conception of changing laws, evolving with the living spirits whose needs they expressed.

It was no more than natural, then, that the form of permanence should be stripped from the concepts which logic had created. The psychology of knowing demanded a reinterpretation of the cognitive process, one consonant with its place among the other functions of biological adaptation. Evolution turned back in the pragmatic accounts of knowing from the a-priorism of Kant to the empiricism of Hume. Let it be remembered that Hume himself turned neither to the poetic Romanticism that followed his day, nor to the pragmatic Romanticism of ours. He

[3] *That Which is Living and That, Which is Dead in the Philosophy of Hegel*, Benedetto Croce. English Translation of D. Ainslie.

fell back, as Mr. Dewey and kindred empiricists have been doing of late, upon the character of habit and custom in human experience. If he interpreted "habit" more conservatively than Mr. Dewey does he may not be farther from the psychological truth of the matter.

So far as the rational element of conduct was concerned axioms themselves were treated as postulates by the more thorough-going of the later anti-intellectualists [4]—postulates whose survival was determined by their utility in the evolutionary adaptation of man to his environment. The fact that ideas have a genesis and development led easily to the conception that knowledge itself is functional. Truth began to be set in terms of biology, and of biology alone.

The will, through such an interpretation of knowing as an active adjustment on the part of a self with desires and organic needs, became the central creative agent in the construction of truth. No longer as a passive "re-actor" to the deterministic pressure of an external universe, but as a co-creator of reality, it laid claim to a share in the legislation of God. It took the van left leaderless by slain dogma and discredited science, and chose for device the Heraclitean $\pi a\nu\tau\grave{a}$ $\rho\epsilon\hat{\iota}$ which intellectualism had renounced for the fixed noumenal reality of $\tau\grave{o}$ $\check{o}\nu\tau\hat{\omega}s$ $\check{o}\nu$. Pent up for a time by a Positivism which had attempted to dam back the emotional sources of the will's strength, anti-intellectualism burst all the flood-gates of reason and went roaring along as unresisted and unmastered as the *élan vital* it celebrated.

Professor Bosanquet, whose recent death deprives contemporary philosophy of one of the few outstanding great thinkers of the time, and whose loss to the Idealistic philosophy is especially

[4] *Cf.* Dr. F. C. S. Schiller's early statement of "Axioms as Postulates" in the volume of the six Oxford essayists called *Personal Idealism*. Dr. Schiller criticizes the empiricist psychology as being "at bottom quite as much infected with intellectualism as that of the a-priorists. It conceives, that is, the experience which yields the elements of our mental structure as cognitive ('impressions,' 'ideas,' etc.) ; it does not place the central function of mental life in volitional striving and selective attention. Now intellectualism, though it may lend itself to many descriptive purposes in psychology, and hence will probably never wholly disappear, is ultimately a misdescription of mental life even as psychology while it is essentially incapable of connecting itself with the wider biological context, in which the organism is conceived as reacting on its environment, or with the higher ethical plane, on which it is conceived as a responsible person" (p. 65).

heavy at a time when it is being so widely challenged, had called
attention in the latest of his books to *The Meeting of Extremes
in Contemporary Philosophy.* Both neo-realism and neo-ideal-
ism, he showed, were in agreement in rejecting that ideal Absolute of which he and Mr. Bradley have shown themselves stout
champions. The general temper of the extremes in modern
philosophy was to insist on the reality of time and the essential
plurality of beings. Some of the excesses, particularly of the
pragmatic attack upon "the block universe", as James called it,
have been characterized by a juvenescent impetuosity that has
drawn rebukes from many others than Mr. Bradley, but none
more adequate.[5]

Certainly, though, there must be some lack in the intellectualistic constructions of Absolutism which calls forth this wide-
spread unity of front among the anti-intellectualists. If their
excesses have been great, it is conceivably because there was
great excuse for them in the temper of thought against which
they are in revolt. Of all the contributory currents in this
voluntaristic reaction, the part played by the thinking of the
American pragmatists, Dewey and James, will be the special object of this investigation.

What do we find as characteristic of the philosophic mood at
the close of the nineteenth century when pragmatism enters upon
the scene? Is it not something of the same *fin du siècle* lassitude
which marked the end of a period of intense creative activity
here as in the arts? In nearly every field of human expression
there was a slackening of activity, a period which can be best
described by saying that artists and philosophers alike were "fed
up" with the methods in use, and were beginning to quit the old
fields like miners who leave an exhausted bonanza. In science,

---

[5] Mr. Bertrand Russell, in his *Philosophical Essays*, has called attention
to the failure of James to provide any other than a subjective criterion for
truth, and the practical translation of "making one's truth prevail" into the
gospel of violence and the appeal to force. But no one has so thoroughly
showed the critical defects of pragmatism as Mr. Bradley in his *Appearance
and Reality* and in the "Terminal Essays" to the last edition of his *Logic*
(2 vols., 1923). Mr. Bradley is, perhaps, too unsympathetic a critic to
render justice to all the aspects of pragmatism as a part of the general revolt
against just such an Absolute as he has given us, which has and can have no
intelligible or fruitful relations with the world of "Appearances". Yet he
has certainly shown the bankruptcy of the anti-intellectualist sides of
pragmatism when it approaches construction.

too, there was beginning to be evident what later became unmistakable: a growing distrust among its servants of the ability which they had once predicted for it—the power to attain a universal synthesis of all knowledge under a single discipline. Religious dogma, too, shaken to the core, had to fight for existence in the midst of a general skepticism that extended beyond positivistic bounds to a distrust of all human ability to cope with the confusion and complexity of civilization. Tchekov, in a memorable bit of his *Note Book* has described the numbed daze in which men's minds wandered:

"So long as a man likes the splashing of a fish he is a poet; but when he knows that the splashing is but the oppression of the weak by the strong, he is a thinker; but when he does not understand what sense there is in the chase or what use in the equilibrium which results from destruction, he is becoming silly and dull as he was when a child. And the more he knows and thinks, the sillier he becomes."

The twentieth century began with a fear of the monstrous complexity with which it was faced hanging in the air like a heavy pall. Life had lost forever, men seemed to think, the poetic simplicity and untroubled confidence with which the youth of Western civilization had faced its problems. Eucken said of this time: "A paralyzing doubt saps the vitality of our age. We see a clear proof of this in the fact that with all our achievements and unremitting progress we are not really happy. There is no pervading sense of confidence and security. . . . Alternative systems; alternative ideals, *fundamentally different in kind*, solicit our adhesion." And Croce, too, has given words to the same thought: [6] "In face of the future of society, in face of the path to be pursued, we have occasion to say with Faust 'Who can say "I believe?" Who can say "I do not believe!"'" The prophet of this period is old Henry Adams whose final conclusion was that "Silence is best".

If these were the changes in men's ways of thinking, with how much greater changes were they not faced in their ways of acting? The industrial revolution, which had brought with it the most complete change in men's lives that had ever marked their

[6] Eucken, *The Meaning and Value of Life,* and Croce, *The Historic Materialism of Karl Marx*, p. 104.

history as users of tools, now sent out a series of pyrotechnical displays of the inventive genius; the automobile, and the various other power-engines, including an undreamed conquest of electricity and radio-activity as an agency of converting not only darkness but space and time themselves into more feeble tyrants over man's life. Within a generation the whole life of humanity has been altered out of all recognition. Wire communication which once seemed so magical, yielded the place of novelty to wireless. The world has suddenly become integrated in its communications, and thought life, in its industry and commerce. How was the rationalistic individualism of Godwin or even of the Utilitarians to cope with this collective complexity?

If we go back only to the beginning of the twentieth century, the impact of cultures (hitherto fairly self-sufficient) upon each other had begun to shake the complacency with which philosophy had habitually spoken as the apologist of the standards of a particular culture. Standards of all sorts were being revised to fit changed modes of life, and compared with yet other standards to demonstrate their relativity to the desires of men and to their settings. Comparative philosophy ended by finding the cultural values involved simply incommensurable.

This was the stage set for William James when he pronounced the manifesto of pragmatic anti-intellectualism in his memorable lecture on "The Will to Believe", with its flat declaration of the rights of the passional side of human nature to affirm the truth of options beyond the competence of reason. The Benthamite conception of reason as a sort of passionless and infallible arbiter guiding man to the realization of the pleasure which motivated existence had already been generally condemned as a rationalistic simplification of human conduct—simplified to the point of falsification. When Mr. Leslie Stephen came to chronicle *The English Utilitarians*, for example, so much had the philosophical temper turned toward anti-intellectualism that he could write: "Men are not governed by their abstract principles, but by their passions and emotions." [7] And Bryce quotes that "cynical old statesman in Disraeli's *Contarini Fleming*" speaking over half a century ago the wisdom of experience and sophistication to an "ardent son who wished to get away from words to ideas: 'Few

[7] Quoted by Bryce, *Modern Democracies*, Vol. II, p. 329.

ideas are correct ones, and what are correct no one can ascertain; but with *Words* we govern men!' " [8]

Psychology, modern to whatever degree it can claim to be scientific, has echoed these criticisms of intellectualism and elaborated them. James himself came to philosophy by this route, and to psychology *via* physiology, facts that are perhaps not without psychological significance to the understanding of his own "habit of thought" as he called pragmatism. It was from a study of the psychology of thinking that he came to feel the necessity of turning his back on the parade of logical concepts which passed for philosophic discipline, and getting at the root of what actually takes place in making choices and in believing "truths". His philosophy was aimed against the idea that truth could be attained by formal logic, for he saw into what a confusion of tongues the system-builders had fallen. He proposed pragmatism, "a new name for some old ways of thinking", as the way out of the intellectualist impasse. Absolute truth he renounced cheerfully in favor of that "working" truth which his psychological insight showed him that men accepted and lived upon in all the issues of their daily existence. No one can question the fresh and at times profound insight of James as a psychologist. His *Principles of Psychology* are acknowledged, even by the most acrimonious critics of his pragmatism, to constitute one of the really classic contributions to the study of the active self in its "minding". What it is necessary to determine, however, is the adequacy of a description of the psychology of *the way we do think* if that description be taken as the sole principle by which to ascertain the logic of *how we should think if we are to think truly*. The same descriptive psychology applied to ethics leads finally to the same result: the way we *do* act habitually is taken as the criterion for the way we *should* act, with the result that anti-intellectualism is continually approaching more and more closely the very attitude of determinism in which individual responsibility and purpose are lost that it set out to leave behind. It can, with this purely "scientific" method, offer us no norms of value beyond survival or fact. It has no normative program.

This progress from the Romanticism of desire back to the

[8] Bryce, *op. cit.*, Preface, p. ix. Vol. I.

positivistic Instrumentalism which shows how desire is determined by its conditions, and which issues ultimately in a purely
"survivalist" view of value and of truth is almost inevitable to
pragmatism that takes itself seriously as philosophy. It is impossible to stop short as James did, most of the time, with the
acceptance of desire or interest as the ultimate determinant of
truth. If value is a function of interest, one must inquire further
into the nature of interest itself. Pragmatism may still avoid
introducing a normative element or a coherent groundwork of
logic into its system, but it can do so only by accepting the full
implications of a positivistic method, *i.e.*, by the attempt to find
a completely satisfactory account of knowledge and of value
in a description of what are called "the facts" of a given specific
situation. It adds nothing to this method to propose a scientific
criticism of consequences, as Mr. Dewey does, if that scientific
method does not become philosophic method, based upon logical
consistency and normative values.

With this tendency of pragmatism to restrict itself to the descriptive method most proper to the natural sciences, the tendencies of "behaviorist" psychology and of positivistic social
psychology run parallel. The "Instrumentalist" pragmatism of
Dewey, in particular, finds a resounding echo in the whole
school of "anti-metaphysical" social theorists on the Continent,
notable among them M. Duguit. The fact-loving empiricist temper is regnant to such a degree that a *science des moeurs* is proposed alongside the other sciences. And the political scientists
have turned to calipers and statistical studies for their salvation.

At least a partial corrective of this so-called scientific method
is found in what may be called the historical approach to the
problems of value. To seize upon that objective spirit of institutions of which Hegel spoke in the *Phänomenologie des Geistes,*
a large school of modern thought finds it necessary to leave the
method of purely logical analysis for the spirit of history which
alone can inform the shapeless mass of fact with relevance and
individuality. Windelband and Rickert have given great promi-
nence to such a treatment of the value problem so central to
modern thought; but it is Croce, again, who has taken over from
his early master, Labriola, a conception of the living force of
History almost mystic in its scope:

"If," he has said in the *Historic Materialism of Karl Marx*, "from abstract laws and concepts we pass to observations of historical facts, we find, it is true, points of agreement between our ideals and real things, but at the same time we enter upon those difficult calculations and conjectures, from which it is always impossible to eliminate, as was remarked above, the diversity of opinions and propensities.

". . . Not indeed that we wish to advocate a vulgar skepticism. But at the same time we need to be sensible of the relativity of our beliefs, and to come to a determination in practice where indetermination is an error. This is the point; and herein lie all the troubles of men of thought; and hence arises their practical impotence, which art has depicted in Hamlet. Neither shall we wish to imitate that magistrate, famous for miles around the district where he officiated for the justice of his decisions, of whom Rabelais tells us that he used the very simple method, when about to make up his mind, of offering a prayer to God and settling his decision by a game of odd and even. But we must attain personal conviction, and then bear always in mind that great characters in history have had courage to dare. '*Alea jacta est*,' said Cæsar. '*Gott helfe mir, amen!*' said Luther. The brave deeds of history would not be brave if they had been accompanied by a clear foresight of consequences as in the case of prophets and those inspired by God.

"Fortunately logic is not life and man is not intellect alone. And whilst those same men whose critical faculty is warped are the men of passion and imagination, in the life of society the intellect plays a very small part, and with very little exaggeration it may be said that things go their way independent of our actings. Let us leave them to their romances, let them preach, I will not say in the market places where they would not be believed, but in the university lecture rooms, or the halls of congresses and conferences—the doctrine that Science (*i.e.* their science) is the ruling queen of life. And we will content ourselves by repeating with Labriola that 'History is the mistress of all us men, and we are as it were vitalized by History.' " [9]

Croce, even though he has proposed that his own philosophy be called the "New Pragmatism", has as a systematic philosopher

[9] Croce, *op. cit., loc. cit. supra.*

very little claim to that dubious honor. Yet this is a passage which might well have come straight out of James, *mutatis mutandis*. And it is not necessary to call to witness any number of similar citations which one might make from the works of philosophers radically opposed to pragmatism in order to show a general agreement about the insufficiency of logic as a complete method of social science. Professor Bosanquet himself drew the distinction between the logic of "Implication" and the logic of "Linear Inference" in his last work on logic, in a master's effort to reconstruct for Idealism an adequate mental tool. But more than in any single field, the growth of the anti-intellectualistic attitude may be traced in the chastened humility with which philosophers of all schools now approach their problems. To propound a dogmatic solution to any problem in these times is equivalent to a *naïveté* which mature thought has outgrown. Even among the Theologians only the Catholics and Fundamentalists stand fast. And not the least of the measures of anti-intellectualism's prestige and success may be found in the changes which the Absolutists of all sorts have been driven to concede in their position, a re-statement often in terms very far away from the original in their spirit, at least.

But pragmatism has been the *enfant terrible* of anti-intellectualism, taking a position among the schools as Whitman did among the poets, proposing to carry democracy into metaphysics, even, and to end by reducing all values not merely to individuality but to individualism. In the hands of James it was as much a gospel of optimism as it was a philosophy. He refused to accept the skeptical leading of his own doctrine, although it was almost exactly the "every man the measure of his own truth" that the Sophists had taught. Instead he received all beliefs into the pragmatic fold, without partiality, almost without discrimination. His amiability has been described by Santayana as coming from a conscience like the Diet of ancient Poland, in which all laws had to be made *nemine contradicente*.[10]

How great was his debt to Hodgson, to Peirce, and to J. S. Mill his own grateful acknowledgment tells us; the central parts of the pragmatic doctrine as to the empirical and practical nature of the test of truth, its relativity and its particularity, James took

[10] *Character and Opinion in the United States,* "William James."

out of the *atmosphere circumambient* of his time, but he made
them known as no less charming personality could have done.
He had a respect for the lay mind in philosophy which endeared
him to a very wide audience, all the more because of the familiar
and untechnical form in which he set his problems. He addressed
himself, it is hardly too much to say, to that lay figure whom the
academic professors of philosophy have treated with so little
respect—"the man in the street". And the man in the street
heard—what was a great wonder even though philosophy offered
to champion him—and heeded, what was an even greater wonder.
So that presently "pragmatism" became quite respectable enough
to champion over teacups, or to discuss at clubs—all through
the efforts, one might almost say, of a single very unacademic
Harvard professor who had succeeded in making his "truth"
work.

But the growth of pragmatism as a philosophy which must
be taken into account in professional circles owes perhaps even
more to the early adherence of Mr. John Dewey to what may be
called "the movement". James, always ready to find an ally
rather than make a foe, welcomed Mr. Dewey and his colleagues
of "the Chicago School" as pragmatists because they made common cause with him in his war on formal logic and had stressed
the "working" test for truth.[11] Mr. Dewey accepted the alliance
with certain reservations. In his hands pragmatism has changed
character radically from the individualistic and romanticist "way
of looking at things" that it had meant to James. Later on it
may become clear that for pragmatism to walk the same road
with what Dewey has called Instrumentalism is a case of the
lady and the tiger all over again. James, the enemy of scientific
determinism applied to human conduct, would have cast off the
alliance had he been able to foresee Instrumentalism as it appears
in *Experience and Nature*. It is not without significance that
Mr. Dewey came to pragmatism by way of logic, though it was
a logic very largely psychological in its nature and origins. Although his writings have never been systematic in the sense that
system seems anathema to pragmatists, they have none the less
developed in a logical fashion from the implications of the

[11] Shortly after the publication of *Essays in Experimental Logic* by "The
Chicago School."

premises with which Mr. Dewey started in *The Logical Conditions of a Scientific Treatment of Morality*. The *Reconstruction in Philosophy* of which he has been a prophet and a way-
shower has been consistently interpreted by his Instrumentalism
as leading away from contemplation toward operation. And his
own development has been, one may suggest, in thorough conso-
nance with that dictum. Of late Mr. Dewey has interested himself in the very practical affairs of education in America and in
China, and has devoted the bulk of his time to useful propaganda in the *New Republic* and other American journals. But
his philosophy has gone on working out its behavioristic presuppositions until *Human Nature and Conduct* and *Experience
and Nature* assume that the sciences, without aid, are the key
to all philosophy.

What most antagonizes Mr. Dewey in the traditional philosophy which concerns itself with problems of metaphysics and
epistemology is what he would call its irrelevance to the concrete
problems of human conduct. There is a character in Tolstoi's
great novel, *Anna Karenina*, who shows, I think, what is the *bête
noire* of Dewey's anti-intellectualism. He is Sviajsky, marshal
of the nobility for the district of Levin, Tolstoi's protagonist.
Sviajsky is clever and logical, but utterly impotent to deal with
the real issues which his position calls upon him to decide. He
is an intellectualist of the sort Dewey meant when he wrote
"Historic intellectualism, the spectator view of knowledge, is
a purely compensatory doctrine, which men of an intellectual
turn have built up to console themselves for the actual and social
impotency of the calling to which they are devoted. Forbidden
by conditions and held back by lack of courage from making
that knowledge a factor in the determination of the course of
events, they have sought a refuge of complacency in the notion
that Knowledge is something too sublime to be contaminated by
contact with things of change and practice. They have transformed knowing into a morally irresponsible estheticism." [12]
Tolstoi painted the picture of this intellectualism with subtle
strokes in a brief sketch of the character of Sviajsky:

"Sviajsky belonged to the type of men so surprising to Levin,
whose consistent, though never independent thought, goes on of

[12] *Reconstruction in Philosophy*, p. 117.

itself, while their lives, extremely fixed and definite in their tendencies, also go on of themselves, as a rule diametrically opposed
to their reasoning. Sviajsky was very liberal in his views. He
despised the nobility and accused the majority of them of being
secret adherents of serfdom, too timid to express their opinions
openly. . . . He looked upon the Russian peasant as in the
transitional stage between monkey and man, yet at elections was
the first to shake a peasant by the hand and listen to his opinions.
He believed neither in God, nor the devil, nor in death, but was
much concerned about improving the conditions of the clergy,
interested in the division of parishes, and used all his influence to
retain the church in his own village."

Yet to Levin, Sviajsky seemed very happy. His life appeared
singularly clear and definite by contrast with Levin's own, full
as that was of hesitation and tentative experiments in the direction of applying his thoughts to the improvement of the peasantry. The younger man was filled with what the Germans
called *"Scherz und Ernst"*, forever trying new plans, never satisfied to pursue his reflections into a metaphysical vacuum, critical
of the practical aspects of every program. The marshal, on the
other hand, considered opinions as a sort of luxury to be indulged
in privately, entirely set apart from his daily life. "Every time
Levin attempted to penetrate into the inner regions of Sviajsky's
mind, he would always draw into his shell. It seemed as though
he feared that Levin would really understand him, and he kept
him off in a jocular, good-natured way. . . ."

"Levin gave up all hope of finding the connection between this
man's life and thoughts. It was a matter of utter indifference to
him where his reasoning led him; all that interested him was the
process of reasoning itself, and whenever that led him to a blind
alley he grew annoyed and changed the subject for something
more pleasant." [13]

This man who would not suffer the intrusion of fact and practice upon his world of theories is typical of the intellectualism
that stirs up the bitterness of Mr. Dewey's spirit. Like Levin,
Mr. Dewey wants to batter down the blank wall of indifference
to matters of conduct which intellectualism interposes. There is
(on the other side of pragmatism) a manifest tenderness in

[13] *Anna Karenina*, Vol. I, p. 320, Everyman Edition.

James' writings toward a certain side of Sviajsky's character, to be understood only in the light of the emotional satisfaction which "The Will to Believe" puts at the bottom of "satisfactoriness". In *The Varieties of Religious Experience* he has dealt with a gentle hand with the freaks of belief. Wherever, that is to say, intellectualistic abstractions or beliefs of any sort come to have a reality in the emotional life of the individual, they became true, as he once said of the Absolute, *"in so far forth"*. The refuge they afford is a holy asylum, not to be touched by the profane violation of reason in the shape of logical analysis.

There is nothing of this temper (which I have ventured to call Romanticist—a much abused term) in Dewey. Knowing is only a special sort of tool in the service of organic adaptation, and its test is not so much the subjective satisfaction it affords as its ability to master circumstance, to survive. His pragmatism is much more the social utilitarianism of the later John Stuart Mill, with, however, the individualism disappearing into an organic conception of group interaction, pluralistic in name still, but increasingly *"solidariste"* in tendency. If James' philosophy, pushed to an extreme, lies at the base of all the modern emphasis on the power of auto-suggestion that can blind the eyes to ills it can not cure, Dewey's philosophy may be pushed to the other extremity of supposing that the intelligence has no other function than the ordering of what may be called man's economic life, the satisfaction, *i.e.*, of materially determined needs and desires. The former is apt to adopt the attitude which is popularly if perhaps incorrectly attributed to Christian Science; the latter to that materialistic interpretation of life which underlies the economic interpretation of history,[14] and finds the cure of social

[14] Not all of the economic interpretations of history follow the orthodox Marxian dogma. There is, for example, a school of growing importance in America which may be studied in the writings of such exponents as Mr. Dewey's former colleagues, Mr. E. R. A. Seligman, author of *The Economic Interpretation of History*, and Mr. Charles A. Beard, whose writings on American history include *The Economic Interpretation of the Constitution of the United States*, *The Economic Origins of Jeffersonian Democracy*, *The Economic Interpretation of Politics*. Mr. Beard is a historian of the first importance, whose clever setting of the facts of history in the light of the economic motives of the actors in the drama is based on an anti-intellectualism not very different from Mr. Dewey's own. It is interesting to find him quoting Pascal, "The will, the imagination, the disorders of the body, the thousand concealed infirmities of the intelligence conspire to reduce our discovery of justice and truth to a process of haphazard in which we more

ills in external organization. Not that either James or Dewey ever follows the logical leadings of his theories to any such points—though the tendencies may appear as clearly present in their respective doctrines under the examination we shall make of them. But theories, more especially theories of an anti-intellectualist order, have a way of translating themselves queerly into their extreme terms in the use to which disciples put them. M. Berthélot has recently examined the use to which theologians in France have put the side of James' pragmatic doctrines which he calls *Un Romantisme utilitaire*. It will be the object of this study to examine some of the uses to which pragmatic anti-intellectualism (Romanticist and Instrumentalist) has been put in political practice, and in the theories which have grown up with it, centering the problems about the nature of the "group self" that forms the issue on which the modern theory of sovereignty is being worked out.

It may seem a curious thing to find in the solution of the nature and the function of groups in political life the test of the value of pragmatism to political theory. Yet a little reflection will show several reasons for the choice. In the first place, the problem of the nature of groups is a case, as Mr. Ernest Barker has pointed out of the nature of universals. The reality of group selves, including the state, forms the rock upon which Idealism and pragmatism have alike gone aground with their ships of state. If Idealism tends to create an omnicompetent unitary state as the synthesis of all group life, so Romanticist pragmatism tends to treat all groups except the state as real moral persons, and hence to pluralize authority and to refuse all value to the conception of the constitutional sovereignty of the state, or to yield to the state any place other than it accords to the actual government. Instrumentalism, starting with the same denial of corporate personality to the state, extends the conception of the organism to all association. In the end its functionalist attitude re-enthrones the state as an organic necessity, stripped of other than economic restraints,—in short, Fascism.

often miss than hit the mark." Quoted, *Economic Interpretation of the Constitution of the United States*, p. 5. The epic *Rise of American Civilization* (1927) in which he has collaborated with Mrs. Beard is less economic in emphasis, but hardly less skeptical of the historical effectiveness of rationalistic programs.

Thus, different as their practical applications are, the point of real divergence in syndicalism, pluralism, guild socialism, solidarism, and Fascism begins in their ideas of the nature and political functions of social groups, including the state. It is by these paths of divergence that theories, all anti-intellectualistic, achieve goals so diametrically opposed.

The difficulties in the way of a just estimate of theories and their bearing on events so largely contemporary are obvious at the outset. Times that shift rapidly have many currents; and he who traces only a few must guard against the assumption that these alone shape the course of the stream. Judgments of connection between facts and theories are risky affairs enough, even when they are applied to periods already crystallized, and with rich historical remains. How much greater must be the caution with which one ought to approach the living body of the present, and how carefully must the scalpel of analysis be used! Yet unless we are to fall into that pit of anti-rationalism which, through distrust of human reason, closes its eyes and surrenders either to the subconscious, to so-called "instinct", or to the Mephistophelian promptings of the senses, it is inevitable that we should try to understand the forces of all sorts that are at work in our time; not least, those forces of thought that do shape human conduct through institutions and ideas, whether they attribute to ideas that power or not.

To what extent is it ever possible to unravel the twisted connections of a philosophy with its historical setting? What possible bearing has pragmatism as a philosophy on politics as a fact? What priority of logical causality may be attributed to each? This last is itself the question upon which thinkers lean to one side or the other as they are more or less rationalistically inclined. Whatever the answer, it is certain that thought and act form a unity in history, as they do in human beings, not to be dissevered without mutilation.

Pragmatism (which in our consideration of its purely theoretical side we must limit for obvious reasons of scope to its chief American exponents, James and Dewey) is at once the voice of its age and an echo blent with many others. It is a reverberation, though, which has magnified its sources of sound, assumed a certain unity of tone, and increased to clangorous proportions. The *Zeitgeist* forms itself in this one of its Protean shapes, the logos is made flesh, and assumes the power of conscious activity.

It is only through their ideas of facts that men can grapple with their problems. Economic interests themselves have to be conceived and stated in terms of some units. The pragmatic conception of the groups which serve as the "facts" of economic interest and political loyalty will determine the course of events where pragmatism rules the thoughts and acts of men. That it does rule a large realm in modern politics, practical and theoretical, we have the witness of facts. What do those facts mean?

We have had too recent witness of the reality of the hold of the "general strike" idea not to recognize that the pragmatic counsel to direct action in the service of loyalty to a class is a fact of prime importance in the modern state. On the other hand, its counterpart of nationalist reaction—the effort to stamp out all opposition to the "Fascist" state—may be seen in practice in Italy and blazoned forth in the press of much of the rest of the world. Facts are shaped by ideas, out of material at hand.

C. Social Implications of the Revolt Against Intellectualism

Has the purely speculative anti-intellectualism of the pragmatic philosophy any real connection with this very evident revolt in social theory and political act? My suggestion is that pragmatism is receiving a pragmatic test by being put into practice in the realm where ideas take on what Hegel called "hands and feet". Its values are those actually aimed at by syndicalism and Fascism. Something really useful can be gained if it can be shown that there is such an intimate connection between the anti-intellectualistic doctrines that are so much in the air and their social applications in politics and law that neither of them can be understood without the other. At least one truly pragmatic value to be attained in this fashion is a juster estimate of pragmatism as a method, for it claims only the test of "results".

On a wider stage, one cannot help noticing the universality of an anti-intellectualist temper in all that vague movement

called "modernism". It has been too often and too well shown
to be at the basis of the revival of religious faith in the movements called "modernism" in theology, as well as in Ritschlian-
ism, and in the Catholic mysticism of M. Leroy and others in
France, to need proof here. Indeed M. Berthélot has termed
this religious movement *Un Romantisme utilitaire*. There must
be very few Protestants who are not to some degree familiar
with James' *Varieties of Religious Experience* if they are interested either in theology or in the psychology of religion. From
many a modern pulpit one may hear, too, the pragmatic gospel
that counsels belief on the terms of Pascal's wager: believe and
you will be saved, doubt and you will be damned—if Christian
doctrine be true. In any case you will not gain anything but
unhappiness—even if it is not. There is such a chaos of conflicting dogma that belief on grounds of reason has been rudely
shaken; now one hears faith advocated because, as Kant thought,
it is the necessary basis of morality,—a truly pragmatic counsel:
Protestant fundamentalism is an absurdity, not even of respectable antiquity; if dogma is to be worshipped, go learn its essence
from Catholicism, or the Buddhists. Hence a notable drift of
the disillusioned skeptics to Catholicism, reminiscent of some
sides of the Oxford Movement.

And what has been the case in art of all sorts? One need not
be really expert in order to testify to the anti-intellectualistic
nature of the earlier phase of the revolt there. Schools upon
schools have followed each other in painting and poetry, in
music and sculpture, in all the arts, each bent on revolution, on
jettisoning the whole burden of tradition, on freeing art from
the trammels of rationalistic conventions of every sort. The
trail, for a time at least, led with curious singleness of direction
back toward the primitive. Instinct has been exalted at the
expense of reason and we have heard talk of the regression of
the artist to savagery in his creative or gestative period. His
music and his sculpture hark straight back to the jungle in
jazz and dadaism and *l'art nègre*, while his painting loses even
the significance of Cro-Magnon drawings, and his poetry sur-
passes the most barbaric yawp of the savage in its exaggeration
and unintelligibility. In every one of the arts there are these
rebels against coherence in expression who push the individualism

of their work as far as philosophic solipsism. It is the sensuous formulation, if form of any sort it possess, of the extreme anti-intellectualism which the artist is at all times ready to follow a long way in the name of creative intuition.

Unless the evidence of the critics is of no account, there is here too, as in religion, an unmistakable swing back to the formal and secure. Revolt has begun to exhaust itself. Now the tide of reaction has set in, among the revolutionists themselves, toward abstraction and "pure form"; in the more naturally conservative, toward "the old masters"; toward Palestrina, Bach, Scarlatti, and Mozart, for example in music, toward the most rigid classicism in all arts. Not that the reaction holds the field, any more than in religion. Yet it may certainly claim the support of numbers—of the leaderless many to whom revolt has offered so confusing a wealth of paths—and no final direction.

Is science in a less chaotic condition? Certainly yes, if we look to the substantial agreement of scientists on observable facts, and on the solid conquests that have been made in the direction of bringing the material forces more and more under control. But hardly less chaotic, on the other hand, if we look to find the basis of some unity of theory for the construction of our universe. Even before relativity had become a name with which to astound the vulgar, M. Jules Henri Poincaré and other scientific high priests had begun to question the significance of scientific law as anything but the most convenient conceptual shorthand to note similarities and recurrences in the behavior of the physical world. M. Poincaré long ago stated in *La Science et l'hypothèse* (1902) that in sciences "we are led to act as though a simple law, when other things were equal, must be more probable than a complicated law. Half a century ago one frankly confessed it, and proclaimed that nature loved simplicity. She has since given us the lie too often. To-day this tendency is no longer avowed, and only as much of it is preserved as is indispensable so that science shall not become impossible.

"Doubtless if our means of investigation should become more and more penetrating, we should discover the simple under the complex; then the complex under the simple; then anew the simple under the complex; and so on without ever being able to foresee the last term. . . . How should I answer the ques-

tion whether Euclidian geometry is true?   It has no sense!
. . . Euclidian geometry is, and will remain the most convenient."

It is noteworthy, though, that M. Poincaré, in opposition to
that complete indeterminism which M. Leroy wished to attribute
to him, found room for "just enough determinateness to require
the physical hypothesis and method for their explanation. . . .
Experiment is the sole source of truth.   It alone can teach us
anything new; it alone can give us certainty."

Nor is M. Poincaré out of the general trend of the scientific
thought of his time.   As Henry Adams pointed out, science has
moved far from the faith it once held with almost scholastic
fixity in Tennyson's

> One God, One Law, One Element,
> And one divine, far-off event
> Toward which the whole creation moves.

Stallo, Adams thought, treated the world beyond sense impression as a chaos; Langley popularized the revolution wrought by
radium and the Roentgen rays, and Sir William Crookes and Sir
Oliver Lodge turned to psychical research for a superscientific
certainty.   Karl Pearson's *Grammar of Science* in its earliest
edition was dogmatically skeptical, one might almost say, carrying the first Kantian *Kritik* to where logic led it:

"In the chaos behind sensations, in the beyond of sense-impres-
sions, we cannot infer necessity, order, or routine, for these are
concepts formed by the mind of man on this side of sense impressions. . . . Chaos is all that science can logically assert of
the supersensuous." [15]   And Dr. J. Hjört writing a recent work
on *The Unity of Science* had to admit that, *a priori*, no reasons
exist for believing science can ever prove the continuity of the
universe, or reduce to one ultimate entity the entities of its
different branches.   All that Professor Eddington can offer us in
Space, Time, and Gravitation, even though his closing remarks
are strangely like the opening ones of Schopenhauer's *Die Welt
als Wille und Vorstellung,* is the elusive Einsteinian interval,
ultimate enough perhaps, but a very dubious entity.   Relativity,

---

[15] Quoted in *The Education of Henry Adams,* chapter on the "Grammar
of Science."   For the best modern statement see *The Logic of Physics,* by
P. W. Bridgman.

in fact, seems to be the only absolute law left in the contemporary scientific world.[16]

The former dogmatic certainty in such formulations as the second law of thermodynamics which produced the magnificent pessimism of Henry Adams, or the heroic mood of Mr. Bertrand Russell's *A Freeman's Worship*, can hardly remain unshaken by the phenomena of radio activity. Read Mr. J. B. S. Haldane's *Daedalus* alongside Mr. Bertrand Russell's *Icarus*, and then, if you feel venturesome, lay a wager on the basis of probability. For the higher reaches of scientific speculation can lay claim only to probability. The metaphysics of the scientific frontier differs from poetry only in its more objective aim and the control which may eventually be brought to bear on its verification.

If we turn to such a broad and important field of social practice as it is represented by education, in America we find pragmatism at is strongest. The classics threatened for a time to go by the board because it was generally accepted that they yielded no practical return commensurate with the outlay of time and effort required for their mastery. Some of the fruits of pragmatic method may be seen in the ascendency of Mr. Dewey's theories in all the normal schools or teachers' colleges of the country, with considerable benefit to the psychological aspects of teaching as a profession, but of dubious cultural benefit. Method, "scientific pedagogy", seems to be all that teachers need know.

When the practical side of pragmatism is pushed so far as to introduce vocational education into the public school system in such a way as to supplant the possibility of the equal opportunity to all citizens to as much of cultural education as they can assimilate, then we may begin to see a phase of anti-intellectualism at work which is shortsighted and dangerous.[17] The extremes of liberty in the elective system of choosing the curriculum to be followed by the student have been in harmony with the pragmatic emphasis on the democracy of evaluative

[16] Lord Haldane's *The Reign of Relativity* has linked up the philosophic meaning of the general theory of Relativity to metaphysics, especially from the standpoint of the necessary logical and epistemological applications it involves. See also *Die Philosophische Bedeutung der Relativitätstheorie* by M. Geiger, Halle, 1920.

[17] As Mr. Dewey himself has said several times, notably in *Human Nature and Conduct* and in *Democracy and Education*.

judgments, with no objective standard of reference, but they have resulted in a very undisciplined type of education, and in thrusting responsibility upon shoulders too young to be expected to bear it with ripe wisdom. There may be some question, even, as to the complete efficacy of the case-system, the method of pragmatic empiricism in legal education unsupported (as it often is) by any comprehensive study of legal theory. If the object of a legal education be no more than turning out efficient lawyers who know the law and how to go about its practice immediately upon leaving law school, then the case-system is beyond question a huge pragmatic success. But if the object of legal training is to equip the graduate with a mind broadened beyond the scope of ordinary practice to view the law in its relations with the organized society in which he lives, then something more than the case-system seems necessary. The Harvard Law School, which was the first to demonstrate the unquestionable advantages of the case system, has also, under Dean Roscoe Pound, been among the first to supplement that training with a more philosophical setting for the law.[18]

Consider, too, the rise in importance of social psychology and the corresponding decline of the importance of metaphysics. There is something more than Comtean positivism at the roots of this change. It is not intellectualistic sociology which is gaining in importance, but the psychological and finally biological approach to the problems which were treated formally under the traditional sociology. Of this tendency in sociology the powerful theoretical works of Professor T. N. Carver stand out, aiming, as he says, at a "biological ecololy". Dean Pound, again, has pointed out the necessity for a sound sociological foundation for modern jurisprudence. He and Justice Holmes of the Supreme Court have given a new impetus to American jurisprudence in this direction, although the latter is perhaps more justly than the former credited with having introduced pragmatism into jurisprudence. The work of Dean Pound has gone beyond pragma-

[18] Northwestern University Law School, under the influence of its great dean, Wigmore, has especially led the way toward the study of statute-law as well as case-law. There is a very full bibliography on the method of legal instruction known as the "case-system." It may be found in compact form in the appendix which Dean Pound has added to *The Centennial History of the Harvard Law School*, 1817-1917, and in the scholarly labors of M. Edouard Lambert, *Le gouvernement des juges*, pp. 24 ff.

tism as a legal philosophy to a social utilitarian philosophy which uses eclectically the best of the comparative, the historical, and the analytical methods.

May not this turning away from analytical and metaphysical method in the social sciences such as jurisprudence mean that the pragmatic criteria of truth and goodness and values of all sorts —stated in terms of effective difference to the concrete situation rather than ideal self-consistency—have been widely accepted? But is there not wide-spread on all the winds of doctrine the pragmatic attitude toward matters as well of theory as of practice, a sort of voluntaristic escape from such a skepticism as Mr. (now Lord) Arthur Balfour popularized years ago in his *Foundations of Belief,* and restated in his Gifford lectures at Edinburgh (1923)? Something of the skepticism and emotional impotence of intellectualism had been portrayed by Henry Adams in his *Education.* It was as terrifying in its way as the ineffectuality which Dostoieffsky had painted in such morbidly fascinating colors in his portraiture of the sick soul of Europe—the spectator at a play whose scene was laid in a madhouse.

But the answer to Adams' philosophy of history, with its cumulative complexity gradually outstripping man's power of organic adjustment, was given by his own colleague at Harvard, William James.[19]   James, like Goethe's *Faust,* interprets the doctrine of the Logos to mean "In the beginning was the act". Intellectualism, he had noted, led to quietism in the West just as it had in the contemplative East.   Activism, which he saw fermenting in the social turmoil of his America, was the answer he proposed.   And as modern thinkers accept anti-intellectualistic leanings, they increasingly tend toward the "action for action's sake" which Mr. Ralph B. Perry has shown to be the gist of some important modern philosophies, and their translation into act.[20]

[19] It is interesting to note that James and Adams became friendly correspondents, though there is no direct evidence, so far as I have searched in James' collected letters, that the two ever joined issues in argument of any sort.   But it was precisely the intellectualistic attitude of Adams, "the spectator view of knowledge," that James was attempting to answer.   He was intent on restoring a healthy optimism to his generation, for he felt that its "native hue of resolution" had been "sicklied o'er with the pale cast of thought".

[20] *Cf. The Present Conflict of Ideals,* pp. 335 ff., an application of the earlier *Present Tendencies in Philosophy.*   Renouvier, de Biran, Bergson lead to French "spiritualism" and Blondel's *L'Action.*

It is natural that such a change in thought should accompany its transformation in the world of idea by kindred movements in the world of act, since there lay the testing grounds which pragmatism itself proposed. Activism, pluralism, survivalism, have shaped the ideological programs of movements in which the group formed a common social denominator, have meant syndicalism, guild socialism, and "droit objectif", finally Fascism. The theory of sovereignty of the constitutional state, in the unitary legal statement that was given it by Dicey in England, by Burgess and Willoughby in America, by Jellinek in Germany, and by Esmein in France, for example, has been dismissed by a very large school of political writers as either an idle abstraction, or as positively vicious. The syndicalists and pluralists, among them, say it does not fit the facts. The Fascists say, "We are the state." The legal sovereignty of the national state thus finds itself between two fires: it long ago was beset by the intellectualist critics because it did not afford the embodiment of that all-absorptive unity required by the state-idea with its logical requirements leading to the world state; from the other side it now meets the anti-intellectualist attack of the upholders of group federalism in its various forms. These latter, indeed, accuse it of having retained too much of the absolute monism of Hegel, or of protecting the abstract rights of individuals, laid down by eighteenth-century rationalism, against the organic needs of groups. The restraint which it imposes belongs to a traditional organization of society which has been, they think, outgrown. The life of certain groups within the state, notably the trade unions and professional associations, has become a more real thing in men's experience than the common political life represented by the state. One section of the anti-intellectualistic philosophy develops the Jamesian idea of applying the pragmatic test to the so-called "group self" by finding that practically it may be treated as a person. McDougall and Dr. Rivers have treated the group as possessing a "group mind", agreeing in curious fashion with Gierke's idealistic doctrine of the *Gesammtperson,* which Maitland had so brilliantly applied to English law. Mr. Laski, in his earlier works, applied the notion of corporate personality to the problem of sovereignty, claiming autonomy for all real corporate persons within the state, and a consequent necessity to pluralize authority and to discredit the state.

Another section of the anti-intellectualistic school follows Mr. Dewey in denying reality to the corporate self, treating it as M. Duguit does, as a metaphysical abstraction. The sovereignty of the state is attacked by this side of pragmatism (which we may roughly identify with Instrumentalism), not because it interferes with the free growth of groups within the state, but because it is an abstraction which does not correspond to the realistic view of political power. It merely proposes, as M. Duguit has, to strip sovereignty of idealistic connotations. Power of government, seen from that viewpoint, is force, and force which needs no justification except that it can get itself obeyed. If force be applied to assuring national solidarity and the public services it gets itself obeyed as a fact. Witness the program and performances of Italian Fascism, which organically stifles all groups except its own. The "corporative" state tries to forestall all chance of divided loyalty.

The traditional theory of parliamentary sovereignty is really justly described as rationalistic by its pragmatic opponents. It rested upon the assumption that the deliberative body, under the division of powers, controlled and directed the functions of government with the same absolute power which rationalism attributes to the human reason. To think of government in such simplified terms may be necessary to a theory of legal sovereignty, but it is quite evidently not adequate to a political theory which would look behind the mask of legal fiction to see the social significance underlying it. In McDougall's words, so long as philosophers have gone on "describing society or the nation as wholly the work of reason or free will, [they] have been guilty of the intellectualist fallacy of regarding man as a rational being; they have ignored the fact that all men, even the most intellectual, are largely swayed and moulded by the processes of suggestion, imitation, sympathy, and instinctive impulse, in quite non-rational ways; and they have ignored still more completely the fact that the operation of these non-rational processes continues to be not only of immense importance, but also inevitable and necessary to the maintenance of that organic unity of society upon which as a basis of contract unity is superimposed as a bond of a higher, more rational, and more spiritual quality." [21]

It is the balance of these two elements, the non-rational (or organic) and the purposive (or contractual) which we must seek in order to evaluate the contribution of anti-intellectualism to modern political theory and practice. It is in the nature of the "group self" that that balance is to be found, if at all, a balance which may then be tested by applying it to the legal and political problems that actually depend for their treatment upon discovering the parts really played by the state and the groups within the state.

The study of this problem of corporate personality may serve to show the inadequacy of anti-intellectualism, however, when it approaches the necessary task of construction. In this brief introductory survey of a very broad field, the attempt has been simply to indicate suggestively the importance of the pragmatic attitude to the attempts that are being made to reconstruct society. But its real import can only be made clear through a study of its pragmatic application, i.e., through watching its development in practice. Here it is only possible to sketch expectations; their fulfillment cannot be anticipated without the appearance of arbitrary dogmatism. What one might risk suggesting at this time, though, may be very briefly stated:

The anti-intellectualistic attempts at supplying a theoretical test for truth and goodness result either in mysticism, in intuitionalism, or in pragmatism. Mysticism is either above or below the realm of critical consideration, and intuitionalism usually offers the same difficulty.[22] Pragmatism professes to accept a single test: "By their fruits shall ye know them." The fruits of the pragmatic attitude have only the criteria of arrival and survival, however, to tell us what it is lawful and good to eat. Eventually, wherever it does not make its peace with necessary logical coherence, pragmatism can offer no normative program, *before the fact*. Evidently this is to treat morals in terms of the descriptive method of the natural sciences. "Fact" becomes a fetich, without our having any applicable

[21] *The Group Mind*, pp. 241-242.
[22] For a criticism of mysticism, intuitionism, etc., from the viewpoint of philosophy, *cf.* Aliotta, *The Idealist Reaction against Science*, pp. 147 ff., and Benedetto Croce, *Logic*, pp. 10-22, "The Pure Concept."

criteria to distinguish fact from fancy. Instrumentalism with its
test by consequences has no test for consequences themselves
except that of post-mortem analysis. Even this coroner's attitude must accept survival as the only criterion: *De mortuis nil
nisi malum.*

The expression of this philosophy in the attitude which, under
the broadly used name of syndicalism, attacks the "right" of
the state to command, translates itself first of all into Romanticist terms of instinctive revolt, what we shall have occasion
to study in M. Sorel's "Myth of the General Strike". But the
actual evolution of violence is toward the enthronement of
force through the degeneration of anarchy, just as pragmatism
itself tends through chaotic tests toward an organic conception
of society, functioning biologically, with a resulting suppression
of individual moral responsibility. Instrumentalism thus lends
support to that conception of society through an impositional
morality which is known in France as *le solidarisme,* based upon
the conception of organic social interdependence made widely
known by the works of M. Durkheim, particularly by his *La
Division du travail social.* In Italy "scientific" social theories
have been popularized by Pareto and by Pantaleone. Social
determinism is M. Duguit's interpretation of this solidarism, a
determinism of organic necessity. Fascism is its realistic application in the functional state now being created by Mussolini.

By a curious route anti-intellectualism has reached the very
thing it condemned as determinism in the Absolute Idealist
school, just as anarchy sets up absolute depotism through its
failure to secure orderly society. If Hegel was the apologist of
Prussianism, Duguit is not less that of Fascism. I shall not
elaborate the point at this place; but it may suffice to recall
Mr. F. C. Bradley's "My Station and its Duties" and then to
put beside it these words of M. Duguit, in a lecture at Columbia
University on "The Solidarist Conception of Liberty": [23]

"Let each one do energetically and courageously the task
which is incumbent on him in the *milieu* and the conditions in
which nature has placed him, and the life of society (*la vie*

[23] *Souveraineté et liberté,* Lectures given at Columbia University, 1920-
1921, p. 151.

générale) will be by so much, the more active, the more fruitful, and perhaps the more happy.

"This idea has been expressed by a great French poet, Alfred de Vigny, in admirable verses which I cannot resist the pleasure of citing at the end of this lesson. Here they are:

> " '*Gemir, prier, pleurer sont également lâches.*
> '*Fais énergiquement ta longue et lourde tâche.*
> '*Dans la voie ou le sort a voulu t'appeler,*
> '*Puis après, comme moi, souffre et meurs sans parler.*' " [24]

Fascism preaches exactly this gospel to Italy, with the addition of Mussolini's myth of the new Roman Empire to palliate the harsh present.

This is a development of anti-intellectualism that we shall study in the conception of society to which it gives rise, and in its pragmatic test of application. Though M. Duguit himself remains an individualist by declaration, and one of the most determined opponents of the Germanic doctrine of the real personality of groups, he has followed a pragmatic development of his own, like that apparent in Mr. Dewey's later works, toward an Instrumentalism which finds in the ultimate moral responsibility of the individual conscience only "the last refuge of a non-empirical morality".

But this is to take away the possibility for the balance that was to be found between the organic and the contractual, the non-rational and the purposive. In order to restore it, it will be necessary to have recourse to a conception of human associations in terms of *moral* organisms, or "co-organisms" in the sense which that term will be given by this volume.

[24] It is hardly necessary to point out how closely this approximates that doctrine of conformity which many critics have read into Mr. Bradley's essay. How close it comes to the official version of Fascism one may judge from Mussolini's own words: "Fascism seizes individuals by the neck, and tells them 'You must be what you are. If you are a bourgeois you must remain such. You must be proud of your class.' " (From Mussolini as Revealed by Political Speeches 1914-1923. Collected by the Barone B. G. di San Severino, p. 317.)

CHAPTER I

THE CONTRIBUTIONS AND THE LIMITS OF PRAG-
MATISM AS A PHILOSOPHY AND AS A METHOD

A. PRAGMATISM VS. CONCEPTUAL LOGIC

The essential community of interest in the pragmatism of
William James and of John Dewey, different as their philosophies
are, lies in a common protest against that intellectualism which
regards the real world as the consummation of reason. In
Kantian terms, the choice of pragmatism is the "Primacy of the
Practical Reason" as against the Hegelian development of the
Pure Reason into a metaphysical idealism or pan-logism. But
it is not a temper like that of Fichte's moralism alone that gives
pragmatism its anti-intellectualist character. Thought for
Fichtean voluntarism is indeed a contrivance employed in the
interest of the moral will, but that moral will is itself subject
to a necessity, the necessity of doing its duty. For pragmatic
voluntarism, the word necessity, either moral or logical necessity, means intellectualism, and all the train of absolutism which
follows the "block universe".

Along with their complete repudiation of absolutism, both
types of pragmatism attack the logic that inheres in the idealist
view of things as a totality. To be consistently pluralistic pragmatism must deny Bosanquet's assertion: "Logic, or the spirit
of totality, is the clue to reality, value, and freedom. . . . The
logical spirit, the tendency of parts to self-transcendence and
absorption in wholes, is the birth-impulse of initiative, as it is
the life-blood of stable existence. And the degree to which this
spirit is incarnate in any world or system is one with the value,
the satisfactoriness, and reality by which such a system must
be estimated, as also with the creative effort, by which it must
be initiated." [1] Pluralistic pragmatism is as nearly as possible

[1] *The Principle of Individuality and Value*, pp. 23-24.

45

the exact contradiction of this attitude. It insists that the parts are ultimate, and that they defy all efforts to relate them into a whole. For idealism, Bosanquet puts it, "A world or cosmos is a system of members, such that every member, being *ex hypothesi* distinct, nevertheless contributes to the unity of the whole in virtue of the peculiarities which constitute its distinctness."[2] But "things as they are" form, not a cosmos, nor a universe, but a "multiverse", for James' philosophy.

And so far as James is condemning system when system is a logical trick leading to the Absolute, Dewey would agree with him. Not pragmatism alone, but the prevailing trend of modern philosophy, has condemned a-priorism of this character. The term intellectualism is often applied loosely to cover the temper of mind which especially characterized the philosophy of the early sages of Miletus and their successors in Greek thought: the spinning out of metaphysical conjectures as to the nature of things on a background of final cause, a spider's web construction of the universe, often subtly and delicately woven, but as easily brushed out of existence by the hard hand of fact. Against a logic and a metaphysic so completely *a priori* the face of the times is set. Save for Mr. Bradley and a few kindred spirits, there are few who have so cavalier a disregard for the facts commonly accepted as the most immediately given elements of experience as to set them down as mere "appearances" over against that reality which is the ideal absolute.

But the common temper of modern philosophy, with its respect for happenings as against "projectings", can not bring together on ground really mutual the two great pragmatists. Dewey is not a romanticist by temperament, and only a romanticist can follow James as far as he leads in the direction of the irrationalism and pluralistic individualism that finally laid "The Will to Believe" open to the charge of being merely credulous. James himself, for all the claims which he put forward for his position as a radical empiricist, was the least "tough-minded" of men wherever the accepted moral values of his

---

[2] *The Principle of Individuality and Value*, p. 37. One of the most adequate expositions of the coherence theory in its general outlines, in spite of the modest scope of the volume and its consequent limitations, is Joachim's *The Nature of Truth*. See also Bosanquet's *Implication and Linear Inference*.

Protestant upbringing came into question. His faith in democracy and in democratic equality of value in the beliefs of each individual led him to the most tolerant and sympathetic interpretation of religious experience of all shades and sorts. There is apparent throughout his own writings a faith at once profound and uncriticized in the morality of liberalism in which his breeding and education had grounded him. It is worth while noting that he, the most unflinching champion of the ultimate indetermination of the moral will, is an example to which determinists might point as illustrative of the impositional character of all morality, the perfect product of the non-conformist conscience grafted upon a nature full of artistic insight.

It is only worth while noting this, though, if one is prepared to admit that similar *ex post facto* charts may be constructed of any man's activity, all about equally inadequate to explain the man himself, as James once noted in his essay on "Great Men and Their Environment." The real value of the observation is the contrast in temper which it helps to illumine between James and Dewey: for the latter, after offering the most radical exposition of a morality of social imposition, a science of morals, turned out to be himself in noteworthy revolt against the accepted interpretation of the self as morally ultimate which used to be imposed in American academic circles—a belief that James may be said on the whole to maintain. For Dewey laid down quite early the general lines of the future development of his treatment of social ethics: in the "Logical Conditions of a Scientific Treatment of Morality" [3] he had said that the attempt "expressly disclaims any effort to reduce the statement of matters of conduct to forms comparable with those of the physical sciences. But it also expressly proclaims an identity of logical procedure in the two cases." . . . "The system of science (employing the term 'science' to mean an organized intellectual content) is absolutely dependent for logical worth upon a moral interest: the sincere aim to judge truly." It follows that the logical value of every intellectual proposition depends upon moral or practical considerations. "Universals of science can take effect, in a word, only through the medium of habits and

[3] *Decennial Publications of the University of Chicago* (1903), Vol. 3, Part 2, p. 115 ff.

impulsive tendencies of the one who judges. They have no *modus operandi* of their own." [4]

The study of the "medium of habits and impulsive tendencies" constitutes the latest contribution made by Mr. Dewey to the social psychology which he had proclaimed as a necessity to moral judgment in that early work just cited. In *Human Nature and Conduct* (1922) he elaborates the theme which has run through all his ethical writings: "The energies and forces which animate man differ in organization but do not differ in kind from the energies and forces discovered and described by science" [5] is the summary which Mr. W. T. McClure used in reviewing the volume, very sympathetically. Apparently, then, whereas Mr. Dewey set forth with the idea of reducing all scientific method, so far as its logical worth was concerned, to "a moral interest; the sincere aim to judge truly", the logical nature of true judgment has turned upon him and devoured the moral. At least the two have become so identified that we find Mr. Dewey completely absorbed in a science of morals like the physical sciences in its method, in which one may suggest there is a little more of "science" than of morality. To substantiate such a suggestion requires not only a critique of the position held, but to some extent also a statement of the critic's own position; but as that will be the work of later chapters, it may suffice here to call the reader's attention to the early but acute criticism, from a somewhat unsympathetic European viewpoint, of the "Case of Dewey", in M. Schinz' *Anti-Pragmatism*, in which he points out that Dewey's method, if it be conscientiously applied, leads not only to the "reciprocal determination" of the judging subject and the situation judged, which Dewey proclaims, but to the very attitude of ultra-positivistic *"science des moeurs"* which Mm. Durkheim and Lévy-Bruhl have taken; an attitude which leaves little room for any but the social determination of all morality, the imposition of conventional or customary norms by the group upon the individual: "collective representations", as we shall see, do not offer responsibility to the person. The difference is, of course, that Mr. Dewey reserves his pragmatic privilege of not being conscientiously at the disposal of the logic of his method. He agrees as to the

[4] *Ibid.*   [5] *The Nation*, July 6, 1922.

social nature of morality, as we shall see later: but he would not agree with Lévy-Bruhl in saying that "a science can not be normative in so far as it is theoretic" for it is his avowed object to show the normative nature of all theory, and to reduce science as well to normative or pragmatic judgments. It is not greatly to be wondered at, perhaps, that the progress one may trace throughout Dewey's development is one that he strives in vain to prevent from a bifurcation in two directions which threaten to part company forever: the one lip-service to the anti-conceptual and particularistic philosophy of pragmatism, with its continual harping on the anti-intellectualist string; the other, a growing need to fasten upon some firm ground, and a consequent seizure upon "fact" and descriptive science as a way to the pragmatic heart of things, always farther and farther along the road that leads toward regarding the method of the physical sciences and its objective treatment of phenomena as the valid procedure of moral philosophy.[6]

With this latter tendency, it is obvious that the philosophy of James was in complete disagreement, though one might urge that it was because of his steadfast refusal to be bound by logical implication that this was so. James to the end remained the enemy of *"scientisme"*, going over to Bergson and to intuition for support of his "Right to Believe". Something of Idealism, of its moral fragrance, lingered about his thought always. He was a devotee—and a constant one—at the shrine of the moral personality in the individual. It was in no small degree due to the obstinacy with which he clung to this and other ideas which did not jibe with the main implications of his philosophy that gave him, perhaps, his contempt for logic as a factor in the creation of beliefs.

Dewey, on the other hand, retains the objective cast that he gave to Instrumentalism from the very first statement of his

[6] M. Shinz has traced this development in the work cited. *Cf.* his interesting notes, pp. 90-99, on Dewey's refusal "to draw a rigorous line of separation between philosophy which is purely normative and the sciences which are purely descriptive." It is a refusal which, as may appear later, is at the bottom of the failure of Instrumentalism to be of any practical or theoretic assistance as a normative philosophy. Even though one may not accept the completely immaculate separation of method advocated by M. Schinz, there is clearly a vast difference in methodological emphasis in the two disciplines.

ideas. The particularity upon which he insists is always that of the situation, the concreteness of experience which regards the self as a sort of reagent whose activity is shaped into habits and impulsive tendencies by the content of its social setting.

In *Experience and Nature*, his most recent bow to the necessity of a metaphysics (at least of attitude toward the world we live in) Mr. Dewey has come to the consideration of the "most far-reaching question of all criticism: the relationship between existence and value, or as the problem is often put, between the real and the ideal." His conclusion embraces once more what seems to be an impossible solution. He states what few would contest, that the object of philosophy is the conscious criticism of values by means of reflective thought. But at the same time he will not admit that the method of reflective thought in determining "*de jure* from *de facto* knowledge" is a "wholesale" in quiry into the nature of thought or reality.[7] It can not depend, he thinks, upon "analysis and definition"; for the relation between thought and things is not a wholesale relationship, nor is nature a "block universe" susceptible of being compartmentalized, if I may use such a word to sum up Mr. Dewey's "watertight-compartment" idea. Where philosophy transcends literary discourse (a legitimate use of it to heighten our appreciation of values) it must take on scientific method. He differs from Mr. Santayana in believing the scientist a more serious philosopher than the poet or artist.

The test of the whole of Instrumentalism comes, then, in its conception of scientific method, and the nature of the "nature" which must be understood. The valid contribution of Instrumentalism lies in its naturalistic insistence that thought must be provisional and .actively concerned with experiments. But the method of experiment is itself wrongly, or at least only partially conceived. Granted that reasoned criticism takes place in a world of trial and error, that "if its eventual concern is to render

[7] *Op. cit.*, p. 343, and pp. 410-411. Nevertheless he speaks of "an organon of criticism," of the needs of—"a generalized instrument of criticism" (p. 409)—which, however, Instrumentalism leaves it to science to supply. In his address to the Sixth International Congress of Philosophy in September, 1926, at Harvard, he reproached American philosophy with being too "fact-loving," too obsessed with scientific method, and too timorous in forming metaphysical and speculative hypotheses. See *The Proceedings of the Sixth Congress*, especially pp. 541-542 (1927).

goods more coherent, more secure, and more significant in appreciation, its road is the subject matter of natural existence as
science discovers and depicts it",[8] one must remember that the
"eventual concern" is the function of philosophy, not the method
of scientific discovery. For that method itself does not give a
clue to value judgments. Scientific discoveries are entirely
neutral in their contribution to a theory of value.

What is more, the method of science itself, the working
hypotheses which it frames, the analysis and interpretation of
its results, all depend upon logical processes as well as imaginative construction. They require "a generalized instrument of
criticism" not possessed by scientific method itself. The fruit-
fulness, the richness, etc., of scientific results is so largely a matter of logical interpretation that instead of making logical procedure depend upon science, as Mr. Dewey does, the scientist
himself tests his own results by logic.

And as for the "block universe", which our pluralists assail,
James was correct in attributing it to science. If the scientific
specialization which resulted from this "block universe" conception has to some degree undermined the old assumptions of the
"unity of science" of James' day it has not done so in the most
advanced scientific method. More and more the linkages between fields of scientific inquiry are being made: physics and
chemistry become closer allies; biology and physiology and
botany rely on both; astronomy and geology find community of
an unsuspected nature in the presence of chemical methods, and
all the social sciences derive their modern inspiration to a tremendous degree from biology and genetics, as these affect
psychology.

The whole method of science in its newest speculative and
critical reaches is increasingly metaphysical; perhaps it is not
too much to say that it is Hegelian rather than Einsteinian in
its relativity, and increasingly ·monistic. Although its monism
is one that is purely tentative and hypothetical, it is the result
of a new and very recent recrudescence of interest in the leadings
of scientific experiments which point to the universal extension of
a causality apparently teleological and purposive which science
must recognize, if it cannot explain. It is not indeed a "block

[8] *Ibid.*, p. 408.

universe" but it is still a *universe* with causal continuity. The excesses of anti-intellectualism appear to be passing in the world of science.

This is admittedly speculative. The actual results of science, though, flow in great measure from the introduction of hypotheses based on the assumption of a natural coherence in the systems under investigation.

As for consequential tests, the scientist who discovers poison gas, or a new method of immunization does not by scientific method arrive at a value judgment. The values attributed by critical philosophy to either result are in terms of human life and standards. What the consequences will be, either of poison gas or of immunization, depends upon one's whole scheme of human values—in short upon philosophy, not upon scientific method. For a society in which increase in numbers is considered the great end of living, humanitarian motives dictate the suppression of poison gas and the application of immunization. But science itself has no judgment either on poison gas or immunization. It is the business of philosophy to criticize the *probable* consequences, and even to control the use of scientific inventions. Scientific method will not help it where that method has no relevance.

Science, Dewey thinks, is simple in principle: "We know an object when we know how it is made, and we know how it is made to the degree we ourselves make it." [9] The same thing is true of knowledge and of value, he says. They are not in any way the product of an "immaterial reason superior to and independent of the body". This is true if reason is thought of an immaterial substance or a transcendental absolute. It is not true if reason is thought of as a method of discounting psychological error, proper to men, and grounded upon a logical relationship in thinking that is discovered, not created. The addition necessary to Instrumentalism, both as a method and as a philosophy, is the acknowledgment that our entire attitude toward the universe, whenever we introduce reflective criticism into it, must be an acknowledgment of the necessity of conceptual logic and the coherence of truth in an ideally self-completing system. The "scientific method", to become a fruitful critique

[9] *Experience and Nature*, p. 428.

of moral values, must approach consequences themselves with this spider's web of coherent logic and normative values. Otherwise it remains merely positivistic, behavioristic, descriptive— and morally blind.

If nature is not to be conquered except by being essayed, she must also be obeyed. And obedience here implies the recognition that experience, like nature's self, forms a relational unity; that man's knowledge, as a tool, has discoverable laws of use and improvement.

It is apparent that pragmatism is essentially a philosophy of revolt (1) against abstractions, taken as exhausting the nature of reality; (2) against metaphysical monism and the Absolute (with a capital A) that takes all things to itself; and (3) against the logic of ideal coherence in a system as the method of thought applied either to facts or to values.

With (1) we can perfectly agree, with only the reservation that concepts are nevertheless the only tools for scientific discourse. Literary and artistic symbols may pioneer in search of truth, beauty, and goodness; they may seize the imagination to increase these values. With (2) we can say that metaphysics must always make its peace with monism. Even while it holds most strongly to the fact of individuality, it can never remain ultimately pluralistic. With (3) we must disagree completely. Truth is not exhausted either by the coherence or the correspondence theories. But as an active adjustment it must use both.

B. Pragmatism as Romanticism or Instrumentalism

Two attitudes are characteristic of anti-intellectualism as a whole: from logical a-priorism the appeals of James and Dewey respectively have customarily taken the form of (1) a more or less mystic Romanticism (even when that Romanticism has called itself "tough-minded") or (2) of a positivistic empiricism which parades what it designates as "facts". The latter refuses to see facts themselves as in any sense theoretical, or as it prefers to call them, "metaphysical". The attitude which our proposed study of the anti-intellectualist theories of the State in its relations to Society will take, on the other hand will be one of admitted compromise, insofar as it is neither willing to reject the validity of the categorical forms which render a systematic ordering of experience possible, nor to extend the universality which may be validly posited of them as *forms* to the *concrete content* of any system formed with their aid, since that can have only the full truth of its historical setting. A-priorism, in other words, will be held to be the necessary fashion in which the instrument of knowledge must be used, but it will not be held that the categorical nature of the demands thus framed demonstrate an absolute validity for the knowledge content with which they are forever being filled by human experience. Each individual has an experience that is relative to a self not ultimately reducible to any Absolute super-self, and it is experience into which enter qualitative differences of content that are not further reducible to terms of any absorptive unity. To this extent one may agree with the pluralistic tenets of pragmatism. On the other hand the significance and the value which attach to any individual experience are relative not only to the particular event but to a totality, always ideal but gaining in meaning to the extent in which its systematic coherence emerges from obscurity and contradiction into the realm of *"idées claires et distinctes"*, a region where unity makes for the pilgrim an ideal horizon which never closes about him. It is this that makes the philosopher, like the rest of mankind, "hopelessly religious" insofar as he never descends into the Slough of Despond that holds the weary skeptics.

A deep and abiding sense of this pilgrimage shines through all of James' philosophy, most of all perhaps in *The Varieties of Religious Experience,* but in brilliant gleams in all his occasional essays, and even in the scientific works on psychology. It is this unflagging courage of the spirit and debonair bearing among many who were either long-faced or "Jeremian" that so endears James to his age. His philosophy, like his life, was one continuous curve of indignation, moving away from the flat plane of determinism to which scientific method seemed to condemn human beings as well as inorganic nature. James himself, had he been more self-conscious, or fuller of himself than he was of his work, might have commented with a smile on the radical empiricist of his later days, a sympathetic interpreter of mysticism and psychic phenomena, in contrast with the lecturer on biology, and the scientific psychologist of his early career. Or he might have gone back even farther to the very youthful efforts as a painter and artist for the enduring key to his revolutionary zeal against the sciences that he had deserted.

Both as artist and as moralist, in any case, James would have none of any such view of the world as that of his friend Henry Adams, who had managed by dint of taking thought to reduce the universe to a sort of monstrous mother of complexity, begetting children with frames too weak to hold the explosive poison of mechanical power with which they were forever drunkening themselves. Nor would he make either genuflections or breast-beatings according to the ritual of the "Free Man's Worship", to man's position as a slave tied with a short tether, in a land where he must forage widely afield or die. His refuge was in a moralistic repudiation of the intellect *qua* reason, and an exaltation of the desires that use reason to attain their ends. Obviously the desires themselves can be criticized only by their continued failure or their continued success in attaining satisfaction, and we are reduced to the exaltation of the "natural" as opposed to the "artificial", the "instinctive" as against the "rational". But it would be unfair to say that James ever accepted any such solution. He held onto reason with one hand, and allowed it its uses within a biocentric circle of ends. His underlying presupposition, though it was one that he never took the trouble to make explicit, was that the morality of universalism was the one which actually did work best; and it seems never to have occurred to him that so far as the tests he offered went in the direction of logical implication, it was not this morality, but a thoroughgoing Nietzscheanism, or an evolutionist "survivalism" which should be adopted. His spirited diatribe against "the bitch-goddess, success" is a case in point of this unwillingness to allow pragmatism its own test.

If James himself did not see this, he does not lack disciples who do. There are the "romantic" individualists who find that James, properly interpreted, means Nietzsche, or perhaps the rebel whom Mr. Laski feels Athanasius to have been. They appeal to the psychology which says every self must determine for itself what works best, and they point to the lack of any standard of values in pragmatic ethics by which individual actions are to be judged. Those of the romanticists who are not individualists are still pluralists, for they merely substitute the group for the individual. They have recourse to the same "intuition" of rightness which is not susceptible to rational consideration, though in their philosophy of action they would substitute the class, or a grouping religious or occupational, for the individual, maintaining not unjustly that the class is the real unit of social activity and of evolutionary survival or decline. It is this interpretation which has inspired the revolutionary syndicalism of M. Sorel, and much of the "functionalist" theory of Guild Socialists and their ilk.

What we may call the "activism" which inspires James' conception of the moral life becomes, in the hands of his followers, an apologia for the appeal to force, since it is only by force that the final test of survival can be applied. This, at least, is the pragmatic gospel of M. Sorel, and the other syndicalist apostles of violence, as we shall see when we come later to examine the anti-intellectualist bases of syndicalism. The case of Mr. Laski, involving the repudiation of the unitary state in favor of a pluralism as yet a little contradictory in its actual outlines, is another interesting illustration of the uses to which the philosophy of James has been put, for Mr. Laski time and again proclaims his own discipleship, and appeals to pragmatists to understand what he means by denying the legal right of the state to impose its commands. For pragmatists, he feels, are qualified to know what it is that is involved in making each separate demand the state addresses to other "group persons" within it prove a right to claim obedience by "working".

If the subjective romanticism of James is characteristic of one of the two generally prevalent tendencies of anti-intellectualism, the objective cast which Dewey has given to his instrumentalism, tending toward the empiricism of scientific method, but refusing to form "metaphysical" theories, is the other. It ought then to be possible to establish the same relationship between certain philosophies of the state with the doctrines of Mr. Dewey as the disciples of James admit in their own cases. Mr. G. D. H. Cole, who speaks for Guild Socialism and functional representation, stands between. But in coming to consider the typical system of *"droit objectif"* proposed by M. Léon Duguit of Bordeaux University, such an affinity is quite evident. The philosophical position of both M. Duguit and Mr. Dewey becomes clearer through its examination, though there is of course no question of discipleship here; indeed there is room to doubt that either of these influential gentlemen has ever examined seriously the bulk of the other's work. Between them they have prepared a philosophy whose logical criteria are fit for Fascism's deeds. Finally there is the highly important body of jurisprudential theory of writers like Demogue and Geny in France, and of Dean Pound and Justice Holmes in America which owes its admitted inspiration to the pragmatism of which Dewey and James are common champions. Pragmatism for these jurists, however, has meant merely a fertile interest in *all* the sources of law—a salutary influence.

In the course of the examination of certain theories of the state and of the nature of law to which this pragmatic philosophy has given rise we shall come again and again to the problem about which most of the questions of modern public law and many of private law center: the nature of the so-called "corporate person" which stands in law for the entity created by association for a common purpose. These questions will make necessary a consideration of the *"moi commun"*, the group self, which Mr. Laski, for example, so strongly championed in his earlier works; but which M. Duguit, with whom he is otherwise in sympathy, so completely and scornfully rejects. The difference in attitude between James and Dewey, not always clearly defined in their own writings, will become clearer as their positions are developed by their disciples and by the practical dialectic of their application, the pragmatic test that they have themselves required for every theory. Does a group, because it acts like a person, possess the reality of moral personality? Is "working" a sufficient test?

It is, above all, through this vexed problem of the nature of moral and of legal personality, and the degree to which those terms are applicable to the state and to associations within the state, that it may be possible to make clear the viewpoint from which this criticism of the implications of anti-intellectualism through the study of its application to concrete problems has been undertaken.   It is with the belief that theory and practice, like most other things that we are in the habit of studying in their causal relationships, are intimately united in the reciprocity which the mind learns to use by understanding, that these suggestions are offered.   Obviously if theory is all *ex post facto* rationalization of uncontrolled acts, all social theory is at best the mere satisfaction of a craving to reason about matters in which reason has no real interest, for upon them it can have no real effect.   And yet this is, I am inclined to think, the *reductio ad absurdum* to which the irrationalist types of anti-intellectualism are eventually brought.

Still, it is reasonable to suppose, where reason has a place at court, that the bad odor into which intellectualism has got itself is not without some justification.   Ideas have too often been supposed to have "hands and feet", in true Hegelian fashion, where they went maimed for lack of will.   That they have lives of a sort is demonstrated by the stubborn way in which the oldest of them refuse to give up the ghost.   But that they can by some esoteric magic that is to be found only in names and symbols produce their appropriate genii, and mould the world of phenomena instead of distorting man's vision of it—that is medievalism.   It should be one ghost that Francis Bacon laid, if he created others in its place.   "God forbid," said he, "that we should give out a dream of the imagination for a pattern of the world."

C. The Pragmatic Contribution to a Useful Philosophy

The usefulness of pragmatism, paradoxically enough, does not lie in its claims to being either a *philosophy* or a *method* of the practical, but in its being an exhortation to practice.   The pull that it has exerted has been felt by philosophers of every description—the persistent way in which it has seized them by the trousers leg to pluck them back from the contemplation of the bodiless regions of pure thought into which they were ascending, back to lands in which very impure thought exists and acts.

Not that the protest was either new or novelly stated.   In its exaggerated forms, from which pragmatism can hardly be said to be free, it has been the weapon of attack upon any such as felt the call to teach or question, ever since Aristophanes pictured Socrates, dangling in a basket among "The Clouds".[10] Nor are its errors any more novel than its claims to truth. The Sophists, from whom Dr. Schiller does not hesitate to claim philosophic descent, had followed the psychological account of the true and the good to its logical end in the prostitution of philosophy into the art of special pleading, if their reputation as a group does not sadly belie the fact. As a rhetorician and demagogue, the Sophist had learned how to move man for his own ends, and he had forgotten how to apply any other test to those ends than the one pragmatists still propose. In consequence the Sophist was interested in men simply as means to ends: he learned the passions and desires of the state with which he had to deal, that "huge and powerful brute" to which Hobbes was to give later the unforgettable name of "Leviathan". As there was for the Sophist no universalized law of Nature dictated by reason to guide the use to which he essayed to put his great beast, and he had neither the desire nor the ability to play the Philosopher-King, he was only interested in it pragmatically, that is as it served his own desires to attain their uncriticized fulfillment. He learned "how to approach and handle it, at what times it becomes fiercest and most gentle, on what occasions it utters its several cries, and what sounds made by others soothe or irritate it." [11] His interest in it was "behavioristic", to apply a modern term.

There is no great difficulty in pointing out that this is the only attitude which a consistently descriptive account of social psychology, that declines to "account" for experience, or to examine its schematic logical nature, is bound to give of politics. It is not more difficult to point out that its morality is essentially Nietzschean, for nothing is unlawful. Its pragmatic justification lies in its ability to manipulate Leviathan successfully, or as American slang expresses it, "to put it over on the public". Nothing is easier to establish than this theoretical conclusion, one that goes a long way toward showing why pragmatism is identified (wherever consistency is valued) with opportunism,

[10] *Cf.* Graham Wallas, *The Great Society*, pp. 223 ff.
[11] Plato, *The Republic*, p. 493 (Jowett), cited by G. Wallas, *Human Nature in Politics*, p. 171.

and why its practical application should result in the degeneration of politics to the violence of actual anarchy, or the forcible
repression of Fascism. If there is no validity in .appealing to
reason in educating values, naturally parliamentarism is idle, and
force is the *ultima ratio*.

Nothing is easier, yet from the pragmatic point of view nothing
is more futile. "What earthly good is to be got," pragmatists
insist on knowing, "out of the parade of formal categories whose
content is filled by actual, concrete living, or out of ideal norms
of truth and value which remain forever unrealized *ici-bas?*
To escape to your unreal realm of norm is simply cowardly, so
long as there are evils and untruths to make life miserable for
those who have the courage to face and bear them out. Is the
Book of Job comforting to you? Well that is how things often
are. And do you find a survey of politics and politicians in the
flesh morally invigorating as examples of the marching feet of
Absolute God? Aren't you making myths of democracy, representative government, constitutionalism? Do the facts not more
often stir you to curse politicians and go off to live comfortably
in the Metaphysical State? You reproach us with being 'merely
descriptive,' etc., because forsooth we are courageous enough to
face the facts which you flee. But is not our entire program one
of finding the best possible solution under the circumstances by
a process of continuous experimentation as long as life is in us?
What more can any man?"

The Idealist who is honest enough to apply his own criteria
of truth to the processes of his own mind is forced to admit the
justification of much with which the pragmatists have reproached
him. It needs but little psychological insight to remark how
often the ideal is a refuge wherein to escape from a distracted
world, rather than a norm for creative activity. Indeed that
Idealism of the Absolute which is arrived at by transferring the
aimed-at ideal of significant totality everywhere necessarily
present in thinking, to the realm of ontological reality, and which
then forces all human facts into this monistic scheme, merits
just the reproach that pragmatism has put upon it. James
showed logical as well as psychological insight in equating the
source of all that is repugnant to our moral natures to a conception of a "block universe", "dead and done for". So long as

he restricted the meaning of intellectualism to this deterministic conception of system, one might heartily agree with him in being an anti-intellectualist. The norms of truth and goodness by which we expand and relate our experience with every judgment never exist apart from thinking, and even in thinking they become clearer and more sharply defined in a continuous progress of becoming conscious of selfhood. Coherence may be and often is posited by intellectualistic hedonists as characteristic of ideal reality, simply in order to escape facts. To set up a metaphysical Absolute because ideals tend indefinitely toward perfection is to miss the meaning of relativity and relevance, to leave knowledge, as Kant would have put it, for faith. James, at least, would have admitted the part that this faith plays in human experience; indeed he would sometimes almost have claimed that all knowledge is faith. But from the point of view which has been set forth in this examination of pragmatism, faith begins where knowledge leaves off.[12] The Absolute must be left in the realm of faith. Our experience is relative; but knowledge has a demonstrable validity different in kind from matters of faith.

Experience is relative, though, to an ideal system of logic and of value in human thinking. While logic in our actual thought never escapes the passional setting of the emotional natures, or the necessity of acting that truncates reflection, it is never absent from any part of our activity. It is this formal character of consistency aimed at as a systematic ideal which gives meaning and value to the world of contemplation. It aims, as Dewey says, at enriching the given world of the immediate data of experience by criticizing its parts. But its method, if it is indeed to be scientific, must be scientific in more than a descriptive and empirical sense. It must *aim at* logical coherence, and work through conceptual analysis if it is to achieve the "enriching" of consequences which Instrumentalism desires. The *method* of Instrumentalism simply is not instrumental to this end.

As for Dewey, he, like James, is by temper an Idealist in the moral sense of the term, not an absolutist, certainly, in spite of some of the implications of his treatment of the individual in

---

[12] There is a clear distinction drawn between Kantian and pragmatic postulation in Leslie Walker (S.J.), *Theories of Knowledge.*

other terms than selfhood—but an Idealist in the sense that he believes that there is an ethical postulate of universal human validity: "What is really good for me *must* turn out good for all, or else there is no good in the world at all. . . . Moral self-satisfaction means social self-satisfaction . . . such faith or conviction is at the bottom of all moral conduct." [13] " 'Idealism' must indeed come first," he says in another place,[14] where he defines it as "the imagination of some better state generated by desire." He, just as much as James, must finally take the ability to decide what is better from what is worse for granted, leaving off his analysis where Idealistic logic begins. "But," he qualifies his admission, "unless ideals are to be dreams and idealism a synonym for romanticism and phantasy-building, there must be a realistic study of actual conditions and of the mode of law of natural events, in order to give the imagined or ideal object definite form and solid substance—to give it, in short, practicality and constitute it a working end." This insistent demand that philosophy shall not become a dull and muddy John-a-Dream is Mr. Dewey's real contribution to modern thought.

When the pragmatic movement ceases to be merely a protest against metaphysical rationalizations that cover up psychological motives into which investigation would be painful, it must treat satisfaction, emotional and psychological as ultimate or it must of necessity develop from mere Romanticism into an Instrumentalism. As Instrumentalism it must meet the test it proposes, that is, its program must be of practical value in operation. It can not remain forever content with repeating its admonition to test theories by their consequences, for it helps nothing at all to know the bare aims of a method, unless that method is given significance and logical consistency. The consequence test of pragmatism is as formally empty as any other abstract concept, and its application illustrates just those vices of which it had accused the intellectualism that dwells in abstractions. Pragmatism no more than other philosophies can escape "the double urgency" of which James talked: the urgency to account scientifically for facts and at the same time fit them into the total scheme of values which every self acts upon. To

[13] *Critical Theory of Ethics*, pp. 127-128.
[14] *Human Nature and Conduct*, p. 70.

describe practical "satisfactoriness" as whatever does fulfill this double urgency "felicitously", and then to urge one to strive to obtain such fulfillment, is to define by tautology, and to preach a mistaken hedonism. Pragmatic theory, *quâ* pragmatism, wanders hopelessly between subjective satisfaction of desire and the test of survival: it ends by embracing both in a behavioristic description of the fact that men do form a continual compromise in order to act. But the description does justice neither to the Promethean nor to the Epimethean elements in thought. Thinking is happily neither a blind leap in the dark nor an autopsy performed on the corpses of dead acts; it projects continually, actively; but its projection is a process of education which uses the past to shape the future. Indeed, one could not wish a better statement of this aspect of activity than Dewey has given in the later chapters of *Experience and Nature*.

The Romanticist revolt against reason took philosophic form (if form it can be called) first in the protest philosophy of James. But reason has its revenge; because headlong rebellion against conceptual logic led him into urging the rights of belief where conviction could not be, James came in his later philosophy to destroy the very foundations upon which belief may rest with satisfaction. For by reducing all knowledge to faith created by desire, he left no room for a knowledge which is intrinsically desirable because it is true. The effort of Instrumentalism to give some content to the practice of pragmatism has led to really useful experimentation in educational and social psychology, and its insistence upon concrete activity as opposed to passive reflection upon the nature of the ultimate has been of value in a democratically organized society in which thought must be active in order to become effective, all the more active by reason of the immense thoughtlessness which is always active there. But Instrumentalism, in its constructive phase, is an economic interpretation of philosophy. It can talk only descriptively so long as its logic is that of psychology, or of a false interpretation of thinking in terms simply of supply and demand.[15] Its test, as

---

[15] The best logical demonstration of pragmatism as the economic interpretation of philosophy may be found in F. H. Bradley's "Terminal Essays" to the second edition of his *Logic*. See especially "On Theoretical and Practical

I have suggested, must either be taken for granted from the beginning, or applied only when the act is a *fait accompli*. Even in the latter case, its method is apt to be a *post mortem* inquest which is prejudiced in favor of *de viventibus nil nisi bonum*, for survival value is all that Instrumentalism has as a check upon the interest value upon which judgment is to be passed. Nor can this *impasse* be escaped by an appeal to the method of science, unless that method be admitted to imply the necessity of something like a philosophy of science itself.

When pragmatic theory is applied to the fields of thought where the problems of philosophy take on that practical character which is their pragmatic test, it may be expected that one may trace the same development from a Romanticist revolt against attempts at systematic construction, to a more scientific and positivistic trend which still contemns the logic of concepts and systematic coherence, which still scorns as metaphysical all efforts to analyze the *a priori* conditions of human association on a moral plane; but which at the same time is forced to introduce in the guise of very dubious "facts" the metaphysics that it has banished. Just as political anarchy goes for individual protection through feudalism to a final state of national absolutism, with small place for the practice or the theory of liberal democracy or constitutional morality in politics during its survivalist phase of national consolidation, so anti-intellectualistic pluralism begins with individualism, goes through groups, and finally ends up in force as an abstract power, in the organically absolute state of Fascist theory with no place for a morality in which the individual shares the good of the communities of which he is a member by helping freely to create it. The culmination of the pragmatic dialectic, where it leaves off being revolutionary Romanticism and becomes constructive, is a social theory that conceives individual relationships as simply organic, as functional, as parts of a socially interdependent whole, a Fascist state in which the only divisions possible of determination are along the lines of the intensity of "real" social forces. Purpose, having been omitted from the beginning, purposeful society can

Activity," pp. 721-22, Vol. II. His criticism has caused me to omit much of this critique of pragmatism as otiose, in view of the incisive strokes with which he has sketched its shortcomings as a theory.

never be. The effort to impose the purposes of individuals upon it through force is the surest means of preventing the spontaneous development of a community of purpose, a constitutional morality, binding because it is freely shared.

PART II

PRAGMATIC POLITICS

"History has shown that the application of the ideals of democracy to a large and complex society is a difficult matter; that the proper methods and machinery of democracy vary with circumstances, and can only be slowly evolved by experiment—that in this process of experiment the belief that the task is simple or that there is any ready-made method is a hindrance and not a help to success. In the working out of practical machinery, success has been the reward of the English temper, with its distrust of far-reaching schemes, its concern with the immediate practical problem, its instinctive dislike of speculating as to where it is going, its readiness to deal with the concrete, and its entire disregard of the abstract grievance. But when the practical Englishman congratulates himself upon his supreme capacity for politics, and contrasts his practical efficiency with the abstract impossibilities of continental ideologues, he is making a mistake. Esmein is right when in his great text-book on constitutional law he attributes the achievement of modern liberty to the French philosophers of the eighteenth century as well as to English constitutional practice. The man who will not look beyond his immediate grievance will probably find an effective solution for it, but he will also, the solution found, probably then go to sleep contentedly till some spur from without comes to disturb his complacency. . . . Democracy has developed wherever the abstract appeal of the ideologue and the concrete experimentation of the practical man have worked together."

A. D. LINDSAY, *Karl Marx's Capital.*

CHAPTER II

PRAGMATIC POLITICS

A. ANTI-INTELLECTUALISM IN POLITICS

Graham Wallas has attributed the modern distrust of intellectualistic solutions to a factor that has changed the whole aspect of modern thought: one to which Dewey has devoted his book: *The Influence of Darwin on Philosophy.* "Before Darwin," says Mr. Wallas in *Human Nature in Politics,* "most political speculators used to sketch a perfect polity which would result from the complete adoption of their principles, the republics of Plato and of More, Bacon's Atlantis, Locke's plea for a government which should consciously realize the purposes of God, or Bentham's Utilitarian State securely founded upon the Table of the Springs of Action. We, however, who live after Darwin, have learnt the hard lesson that we must not expect knowledge, however full, to lead us to perfection." After the prophetic Mr. H. G. Wells, for instance, had sketched *A Modern Utopia* he found it necessary to add a completely pragmatic appendix called "Skepticism of the Instrument".

But this skepticism as to rational solutions has been accompanied by a change in political psychology which is perhaps worth remarking. Professor J. T. Young, in *The New American Government and its Work,* has called it "the demand for quick government". Parliamentarism of the Victorian era at least pretended to look for carefully worked-out principles of settlement, based on the assumption that if one found the reasonable solution, the problem was solved. One can not help being impressed with this characteristic of Lord Oxford and Asquith's *Fifty Years of Parliament.* That is not the present temper of our changing politics, either in England or the United States.

"An interesting change in the political psychology of the American people," says Professor Young, "is the nervousness and impatience of delay that we now show towards public questions. Instead of the meditation and reflection on political problems that marked our early history as a nation we now think in sudden gasps, spasms, and outbursts of emotion. Whether it be the hysterical outbreak of a lynching mob, or the serious, earnest efforts of a city improvement club, we are inclined to rush matters and we are impatient of obstacles, once it is known that an evil exists and demands a remedy. The age of oratory, eloquence, and prolonged discussion has almost passed. The people want action, immediate action. Doubtless it were better that more deliberation be exercised, that in the quaint phrase of a former state governor 'celerity should be contempered with cunctation'; but such is not the view of the people as a whole."[1]

That quick-on-the-trigger, "try-it-and-see" temper is partly imported from our industrial and commercial processes, where rapid shifts in technique make speedy adjustment and a pragmatic willingness to experiment the great virtues. We have not displayed the same inventiveness in the machinery of social control, although there is real need to recognize that the machinery of government adequate to a pioneer, or to an agricultural, or even to a nineteenth century manufacturing community, can not be applied without radical changes to the urbanized maëlstrom of the newer industrialism. But we have, in the United States been extremely impatient *of* results and *for* results in politics, even though we have not devoted to that art (or science, if such it be) one-tenth of the invention or the attention that has gone into industrial growth. Such adaptation as we have made in our necessarily cumbrous federal structure has come quite as much through parties or through courts as through legislatures or amendments or conventions.[2]

The empirical side of pragmatism is devoted to social inventiveness. It is therefore the proper mother of a brood of revolutionary theories of the state. The point of view from which this critique is written is that most of these pluralistic and romanticist theories of syndicalist revolt, or solidarist and organic theories of reaction toward the Fascist state, lack historical per-

[1] *Op. cit.* "Introduction," pp. 7-8.
[2] See Walter Thompson, *Federal Centralization*, C. G. Tiedeman, *The Unwritten Constitution of the United States;* and H. W. Horwill, *The Usages of the American Constitution.*

spective. Like their philosophical mother, these political scions
of pragmatism overlook the abiding and universal elements
of human experience. Pragmatism, Romanticist or Instrumentalist, holds that conceptual logic is vicious because concepts are not "reality". But concepts are realities. Pragmatism
is so impressed with the truths of psychology, that it denies the
validity of logic, and the usefulness of metaphysics. Its method
is for that reason positivistic and behavioristic. It has no use,
as Mr. Dewey puts it, for "wholesale views" of truth or reality.
Because of the limitations of this method it has no really useful
information to give as to the proper use of knowledge as a tool.
It blithely advises the philosopher, as all others, to learn by
trying.

That is sound advice, up to a point. One must always learn
by trying. But trying is only valuable if learning be method-
ically possible. There is, too, a deal of human effort already
available for learning from. In philosophy, whether or not
axioms are postulates in the beginning as a matter of genetic
psychology, in the course of human development their universal
logical validity has been pretty thoroughly demonstrated. No
scientific method would be fruitful that did not follow them.
They have proved to be necessary rules for using the tools
which we have, not merely because we have preferred them on
esthetic or economic grounds, but because, as Bacon said, *Natura
non nisi parendo vincitur*. They are *a priori* conditions of truthful thinking. That is why they are fruitful; not truthful, as
pragmatism says, simply because their consequences have
seemed to fit our organic needs better than several more-or-less-
good but possible alternatives. Alternatives to usable logic are
not, like rival systems of mathematical postulates, all equally
self-consistent. The very use of logic is to establish self-
consistency.

But, the objection is always raised, Is it not merely a matter
of convenience, as is the case with our use of the system of
Euclidean geometry, that we do follow them? Since Einstein
we have had to add time as another dimension to our universe.
Are not your laws of thought as relative to your hypotheses as
any other calculus is to the axis of temporal reference? Does
not activity enter, *real* adaptation in a spatial and temporal con-

text that can never be reduced to your conceptual scheme, any more than the motion of stars can be correctly reduced to a three-dimensional space calculus?

That is very true, and well taken, so far as pragmatism is merely a protest against a static idealistic monism that tries to fix the activity of human beings within the confines of some "block-universe" conception of a rigid metaphysics. On the other hand it is very misleading to make the pragmatic induction from the fact of a developing and active human self, that there can not be moral purpose involved in that activity, or laws of thought which shape experience and give coherent meaning to its value judgments.

Pragmatism in politics manifests the same virtues and vices of method. A way of thinking, even distorted and warped as pragmatism in politics gets to be by the applications of disciples of the most diverse character, shows to a remarkable degree the pervasive spirit of the general "way of looking at things" that has inspired it. Less than other philosophies has pragmatism the rights to demur at what it might, if it were left to the original proponents, regard as historical misapplication of its doctrines. For pragmatism has only one test of philosophies, as of all things else—consequences, results, what Mr. Dewey calls "endings". It can not bitterly protest that Fascism or Revolutionary syndicalism are logically inconsistent with its own reservations. The only logic recognized by pragmatism is the logic of events. What has been its connection with those events?

It is even possible that M. Sorel is not philosophically incorrect in finding pragmatism the most congenial of philosophies, any more than is M. Duguit, or Signor Mussolini himself. There is a certain consistency of temperament and of logic among these anti-intellectualists. A study of its political application may serve to show a dialectical coherence between the method of pragmatism and the results in political preaching and practice. Rather, it may appear, it is James and Dewey whose liberal ethics and politics are inconsistent with their doctrines. The latter particularly, as we shall see, develops an impositional "social" morality that badly accords with his own liberal democratic ideas.

If there are no tests but consequences, and we have no universally valid aspects of experience, any of the prophets of "the new state"—or of no state at all—may be right. If he can "make it work", he is pragmatically sanctioned. Mussolini asks no more. What, though, are the tests by which one shall know consequences for good or bad? Romanticist and hedonistic satisfaction? Or Instrumentalist survivalism? Or is it possible to arrive at more objective standards?

If there are some *a-priori* conditions of morality, derivable from the fact of morally responsible personality, and verifiable by an examination of actual historical development, then we may be justified in laying down an ideal norm of political activity toward constitutional government; and we may use these criteria to test the consequences themselves. It may appear that political pluralism is in too great pragmatic haste to discard constitutional for direct action, and that the attack upon the constitutional state and the concept of sovereignty are either misdirected against the constitutional state (being aimed at irresponsible autocracy) or utterly inconsistent to their own construction. It may appear, also, however, that a solidarism like that of M. Duguit's "public-service state", or of Fascism, intent upon creating the organic state of economic necessity through fear and force, is equally mistaken in overlooking the purposive and free elements in human association.

The "consequences", the "facts" on which they ask judgment to be made of their pragmatic success may turn out to be too ephemeral, or too mistaken as facts or even when valid as facts, of too negative moral value to point the way to a new ideal of political organization. Through the repudiation of that "wholesale" method of linking up all experience into as consistent a whole as is possible to human effort, pragmatism in politics may turn out upon examination to be retailing short-run views that are fatal even from economic criteria alone.

That is frankly my own opinion. I shall try not to load the dice, but the reader is forewarned of what may well be my prejudices, so that he may discount what follows if he disagree with this estimate of pragmatism as a partial psychology of politics and a poor ethics. Because it has been thought by many to be impossible to see philosophy in naturalistic terms without accepting pragmatism, there is a natural bias toward the pragmatic attitude in this, a scientific age. But pragmatism has had its own test. What are its fruits?

Among the most important fruits of any philosophy are the social attitudes which it induces. Pragmatism ought profitably to induce an adventurous empiricism characteristic of the radical temper. But does it not by its exaggerated anti-intellectualism induce a complete skepticism of any common standards of value, attainable through reasonable discussion? Does it not thereby argue for force rather than consent to cement community? Does it not further promote the tendency to regard economic motives as the most tangible factors in human behavior, and hence introduce an economic interpretation of morality that denies purposive control of economic forces through co-operative effort? Does it not, finally, as the Sophists did, offer the philosophic bulwark for stressing clashes of interest between groups as reconcilable only through force, not by constitutional arbitrament at the hands of a legal community in which they all share equally? Greek democracy went to pieces, among other reasons, because of its sophistic attitude toward clashes between Hellenic cities and toward class struggles. Let us in a nationalistic age be advised and seek to apply an Aristotelian remedy.

A way of looking at things, while it is partly the result of historical forces, is not simply determined by them. The philosophy of men is not automatically produced by the times. It results from their efforts at understanding the times. Quite as much it reshapes the times, as e.g., Benthamism did in England through the first half at least of the nineteenth century. Economic interests themselves appear only through the conceptions which men have of them—more or less adequate. The economic man finds himself superseded by a variety of other interest groups. A critique of these conceptions of pragmatism may show some ways of acting upon a more coherent and fruitful political philosophy.

B. Some Outlines of a Constructive Theory of the State

Any pragmatic application and test of pragmatism must start out with an admitted working hypothesis; put to the test that it itself proposes for political "working", pragmatism will show its defects as well as virtues as a philosophic method. Such a study must, if it is to fulfill its critical possibilities, have implications of its own; they are here set forth in order to clear the ground. They are simple, but they must be clearly understood at the outset.

Constitutional government represents the same effort at political synthesis that conceptual logic does for thought synthesis. It must shun alike pluralism and absolutism; it must admit the ideal character of its coherence, without abandoning logical coherence as a working method. A philosophy of constitutionalism is not so much a mere description of facts as it is a normative philosophy of the state. It tries to describe only the mature constitutional state and describes that as an ideal rather than a completed achievement. No state is *ideal* as it actually exists, although some states clearly approach the ideal of constitutionalism more nearly than others. Constitutionalism means an accepted rule for fixing political responsibility.

The coherent structure of law, shaped under a constitution, implies of necessity some accepted method of legal unification and determination for the solution of pluralistic forces which, if left to themselves, develop either the centrifugal tendencies of anarchy or the repressively centripetal tendencies of dictatorship. There is, wherever the organization of a people under law has achieved statehood, an habitual although not an absolute constitutional morality. This morality may be described as the active recognition of a relatively permanent community of purpose in the enforcement of law that has taken organic shape in a constitutional system. The constitutional system is accepted as the necessary presupposition of ordered human intercourse. If the consent and the participation of a culturally homogeneous population is invoked through constitutional means, the laws under which they live represent a working basis for moral freedom. Therefore, there is a moral presupposition in favor of obeying law, as long as one accepts the constitution of the state as a fair basis of social adjustment, and the best *practicable* means of institutional development. As opposed to Mr. Laski's idea of moral obligation to obedience depending upon each act of the state as it affects every individual or group, this theory maintains the moral validity of obedience as long as the constitutional system as practiced is accepted by the individual and not violated by the government.

If revolution is genuinely thought to be a better means than political activity within the sphere made possible by the existing constitution, there is an ultimate moral right of revolution. But any analysis of the comparative efficacy of persuasion and violence would suggest a presumption in favor of persuasion as a means, given the possibility of a free hearing and of free association to political ends. It is, as a rule, only where persuasion is not constitutionally possible, where there is an attempt to marshal force to the regimentation of human thought through educational perversion and the repression of free press and speech, that revolution by violence has a moral justification.

Convinced communists and crusaders for a new motivation for our economic life think that the whole basis of capitalism vitiates the reality of political freedom and equality before the law, no matter what the constitution of the state. They approach the practical issue with a religious fervor that brooks no argument. Experience with direct action toward these ends suggests that the overthrow of constitutional government or its sabotage by degrees is not the best practicable means of attaining the ends of freer economic life. If the state in a capitalistic society refuses enemies of capitalist economy the means of being heard, they have no recourse but violence—that is clear. But where they are given constitutional scope to win political power by persuasion, violent means (including the "contingent revolution" of political general strikes) lead to a repressive Bolshevism; or are more likely to draw the harsh rebuke of Fascism. Unless communists are prepared for an open test of strength it is not wise to undermine the state. Nor need they be surprised if piecemeal revolution provokes slightly more consistent repression.

The whole case comes down to the modern attack on representative control of government—"anti-parliamentarism" as it is called, where parliamentary institutions rule, anti-constitutionalism under more rigidly separated systems of distributing governmental powers. If the cleavage in society justifies the ruthless Marxian antithesis between classes, then the persuasive methods of parliamentarism and constitutional responsibility are indeed vain. There is no basis for a community of purpose sufficiently strong to support the state. The solution is, indeed, force —whether that of Bolshevism or of Fascism.

On the other hand, if we eschew the pragmatic attitude toward values—i.e., that there is no rational basis for preferring some to others, except by pitting them like gamecocks for a test of consequences,—we may escape the destruction of constitutional government and of the method of social settlement which it represents. Parliamentarism rests upon the assumption of idealistic ethics that values achieve coherence and real meaning through criticism. There is always a presumption that a great group interest meets a real need. It must be canalized by the state into its voluntary sphere of activity.

Sovereignty by this interpretation is a reality (which is idealistic only in recognizing the value of ideals) just as other fundamental concepts are realities, valuable because it describes within practicable limits a state of facts. Included among these facts is one overlooked by pluralism; that of the utility which such a unifying conception of the legal order presents to the society constitutionally organized by it. The state which holds together against outside forces and internal disruption shows an abiding constituent community of loyalty at its base. Its constitutional form is the attempt to deal with the grounds of this loyalty—a statement of accepted rules of co-operation toward a common and socially pre-eminent group purpose—the regulation of clashes of interest through laws.

This active community, that has taken historical form in national states, though neither a fixed quantity nor forever enduring, is relatively more permanent than other communities of interest and purpose within it, and more intense than those without it, under the present conditions of occidental society. It is more permanent because it is more indispensable to the collective life of its citizens than other groups are. Its ancient rival, the Church, has yielded place, at least temporarily, in most Occidental nations before the economic as well as the cultural pressure of modern industrialism. This is the normative basis upon which its legal sovereignty is accepted—that the rule of law is the *a priori* condition of any moral freedom.

Legal sovereignty, under modern conditions, simply implies that each developed state possesses *a unifying method of legal reference*, a constitutional system which includes a definite center or a determinate process for arranging the hierarchy of laws and for altering them. The analysis of this concept, for the present, need go no farther than the statement that the government so constituted can be shown in fact to possess the ultimate coercive powers of a state, so long as that state commands the loyalty of its citizens to the degree of remaining able to survive as a political unity. That is not to say, however, that coercion is the normal procedure or the wisest method of giving effect to legal sovereignty. Forcible coercion of considerable groups within itself is characteristic not of the normal, but of the pathological state. Nor is it to say that the exercise of coercion, even within the constitutional channels of normal state activity, does not meet, on occasion, with resistance. The constitution is a working symbol of unity, not a logical universal. Where the life of the state is threatened through a breakdown in the legal means of settling vital issues, the issue must be met by the force at the disposal of the state. But normally a constitutional state depends upon political settlement, relying upon the fact that the minority, too, is part of the constitutional community which is the state's self.

Clearly these general outlines of a theory of the state must be filled in and tested by seeing to what degree they are compatible with the coercion of facts. Pragmatists in politics we must all be to that point. But when we describe the behavior of political societies, our interpretation of that behavior can not select merely part of the facts by rejecting the part that ideals and moral ends play in shaping facts. We can not, indeed, slight the economic setting which so largely determines the organic needs and the actual survival of the industrialized states typical of our time. But we must also do justice even to the Platonic Myths upon which political actions often rest. Even Mussolini's myth of the new and grander Roman Empire as a propagandist force is also a fact of a certain order. So are the tenacity of faith and good sense with which England clings to political action as opposed to violence or Fascism. If we are to be real "realists," instead of parading a "tough-minded skepticism" of the effect of principles and moral values upon human conduct, we shall try to understand these ethical as well as the economic phases of activity. Social ideals and individual moral choice are also "facts".

While we are describing the facts we can hardly fail to notice how various they are and how little self-explanatory. Syndicalistic doctrines have less survival value as a matter of fact —so far as our pragmatic method takes us to date—than the absolutistic reaction toward Fascism and dictatorship. The nation-state reaches in Fascism its apotheosis as an organic unity attempting to gain self-sufficiency and complete subordination of the groups within it. Read in terms only of present consequences, unitary Fascist sovereignty has overthrown, it seems, alike the pluralism of the syndicates, the revolution of the communists, the impotence of parliamentarism and the liberal ideology of the constitutional state. The example of dictatorship has seduced a large part of Europe that found "government by talking" too exacting and too expensive for hard times. But if we criticize these consequences in the light of values and facts of longer standing than Fascism, if we transcend the immediate-consequence theory of pragmatism for what has been condemned as a "wholesale" view of the nature of the relation between thought and things—thinking activity, perhaps we may gain a view ultimately more useful and more true.

The value of the pragmatic attitude lies in its refusal to accept as universally valid the conceptual logic applicable to the constitutional state; or, better, in refusing to apply this logic where the constitutional state is not a fact. Its error lies in the refusal to accept the value of the concept where the ideal of constitutional sovereignty—i.e., representative government that sums up the constitutional restraints and the institutional procedure necessary to freedom—is substantially realized in practice, as it is, say, in the government of the United States or of modern England. It is indeed necessary to draw the attention of Idealistic theory to its irrelevance to, e.g., some of the actual Republics of Central America, except as Idealism upholds a normative direction of progress. The state about which Idealism is talking does not exist there, *in fact*, to a degree that permits constitutional morality.

Mr. Laski has rightly stated that it is the actual state which must compete for our loyalty with other groups. Actual states manifest the widest variety of departures from the ideal of constitutional government here held to be necessary to any moral imperative to obedience. A citizen of Italy might claim with a show of justice that the state does not offer to him the guarantees of freedom, either in political or civil liberty; and he might reject the pretence of such a state to moral pre-eminence over the groups within it. In order to make good his security, however, he must constitutionalize his state, not destroy it. The same challenge may be directed to Bolshevism as to Fascism. Force can not, as Mr. Laski has eloquently shown, create moral consent. Why invoke it, then, as sovereignty in a constructive and normative theory of the state?

There is a challenge directed at every state to some degree, as Mr. Laski holds. But the conditions which justify those challenges on ethical grounds are matters of importance, and so is the motivation of the challenge. In the constitutional state, the condition justifying challenge is reached *when the constitution no longer offers a basis of community wider, deeper, and more permanent than the communities of interest which are at strife.* When that condition is reached the issue is frank revolution; until it is reached constitutional morality demands lawful action. Every civil war may be interpreted as a choice of evils as well as of goods.

If the state does not offer in fact the basis of constitutional freedom through representative government or the prospect of successful revolution, the individual may choose another state or completely outlaw himself as anarchist or criminal. But Aristotle has shown how dangerous is the position of the man who lives outside of all political community. By his denial, he refuses fellowship, with its good as well as its ill. He becomes "a beast or a god". It is given to very few to become gods.

Mr. Laski advocates, it is true, neither frank revolution nor outlawry, nor real martyrdom, but sabotage by degrees and piecemeal disobedience. Can he hope for peace after his "Labor State" has gained the day by pursuing such methods? Are not such tactics precisely destructive of constitutional morality?

The morally inspired revolutionist does not aim at outlawry. He wishes with his fellows to remould a state that will command obedience through justice. Violence may be a necessary method to meet force. Unless it aims at creating a new state that uses force not to repress opinion but to prevent actual crime, violence is a vicious circle.

Granted the moral case for resistance, and the ultimate residence of choice in the conscience of the individual; granted, too, the actual and the frequent employment of direct action by groups of individuals—on what grounds ought the ethical case for the constitutional state to rest?

In the first place, as no community of moral purpose can be absolute, so long as there is any truth in our hypothesis of individual moral responsibility, neither may the state's claims to moral infallibility be taken seriously. What we can say is that the norm toward which any state should, ethically considered, be developing is the substitution of political action and constitutional morality for violence and coercive repression. States in fact vary in the degree of their legal absolutism. No form of state can put its government beyond the reach of all resistance. No government dare do things that fly in the face of the economic possibilities, the institutional life, and the deepest traditions of its people. None can permanently fail to fit the character of a race—and survive. History documents the lesson too thoroughly to make it necessary to point to the overturns and the oscillations of French governments from the Grand Monarch to the Third Republic; or to point a modern moral with the struggle of Bolshevism with the peasants, or with the battle of Fascism against the toughly resistant elements of the Italian economic situation and national temperament. Mussolini may exhort and drive, may inspire and command. There are some things not even Fascist absolutism can accomplish—among them the creation of a stable and favorable trade balance as long as there is no limit to the multiplication of consumers in a land naturally unfitted for diversified industry. His Roman virtues of stoic silence and discipline under hardship can only be temporarily imposed upon a pleasure-loving race, one may guess. The ultimate solution must lie rather in decreasing rather than increasing the birth-rate and in finding peaceful outlet for Italy's normal overflow of population and her trade needs.

The fact is indisputable, that resistance to Fascist commands in Italy is so dangerous as to be extremely rare. Fascism may

eventually overreach its firm control; at present the Fascist
state is sovereign in fact. As such it is a living disproof of Mr.
Laski's *Grammar of Politics* as a complete description of political
usage.

Fascism is one fact. But there are other facts, too. The Pre-
Fascist Italy of the War's aftermath must be numbered among
them. Resistance was then the rule, coercion the exception.
Modern China is in a similar state. There is not in that vast
geographic and historical area even a passably enforced general
community of law, unless Canton and Peking succeed in dividing
China between them, and organizing order in each sphere.

The pragmatic view of politics can only describe in behavioristic terms. All these "facts" are ultimate to its method. It has
no norms, except survival values, and consequently no constitutional morality to aid free development.

An idealistic view, taken as implying a normative estimate
of political development, must start from these facts, too, but it
can point beyond the facts to tendencies in facts. One such
tendency seems to be the lack of any abiding sense of moral
obligation in unconstitutional states, and its presence in states
where the basis of community rests upon an accepted means of
constitutional settlement. Machiavelli himself recognized this
in the *Discorsi*. The presence of a degree of constitutional
morality sufficient to protect political freedom insures resort to
law.

The degree to which resistance to acts of a constitutional
government have moral validity is a delicate question, permitting no universal statement, because constitutionality varies in
degree. It is safe to say that wherever the nation sums up in
its form of government the abiding loyalty of its people, the
presumption is always in favor of obedience to law. The State
may survive sporadic and temporary resistance by groups within
it, so long as the challenge is not organized against the basis of
the state itself. It can hardly permit general strikes for political
purposes without abdicating its rôle of umpire. Resistance must
not be chronic, for resistance by direct action has the effect
of continually widening the breach in legal community. One
act of resistance brings on a train of others and a reactionary
resort to force. Ultimately the only choice left by direct action

is between an impotent and disrupted state and Fascist or Bolshevist dictatorship. Constitutional government, *obeyed legally*, *resisted politically*, is the type presupposed for the state, as the state is defended in this study. It may be said to exist wherever the state commands the enduring loyalty of its citizens, under a form of government constitutionally determined to political and legal responsibility.

To political pluralists this seems a timid and conservative view of society. It is inspired, however, not by the fear of the contingent anarchy which they think the state will bear, but by fears for the rebuke of Fascism with which pluralism is actually being met. Its solicitude is for the slender realm of moral freedom which constitutionalism preserves. It proceeds from the conviction that political pluralism in practice goes through precisely the evolution of Mussolini and his Fascist groups: from revolutionary action, usually inspired by ends like those of the Socialist left, through conquest of power to repressive dictatorship in favor of nationalist ends of the imperialistic right.

The thesis of this critique, constructively, is that any theory, of the state which attempts to evaluate political consequences must be normative. It must try to do justice to *all* the facts, including the purposive and moral aspects of the state, as well as the economic and psychological limits of morality. Its ideal state is the constitutionally responsible state, not the "discredited state". It assumes the necessity of legal organization and an element of coercion in modern industrialized society. On the basis of the facts, it finds that the nation-state of occidental society is the most enduring and tangible synthesis of law and of loyalty, though the nation is being forced, in its own interests, to secure an international rule of law.

What I shall call, by a terminology later to be explained, the co-organic theory of the state accepts the pragmatist's insistence that no such state is final in its form or morally absolute. Politics must begin with the instrumentalist method in the description of facts of political behavior and return to it for its empirical application. But the reflective criticism of values, which Mr. Dewey admits to be the business of philosophy, must in politics as elsewhere follow a method which instrumentalism does not furnish. That method is normative in ethics, and must be based upon a coherence theory of values, as well as of truth, which gives to logic its rightful place.

The state, in the significance here assigned to that term, serves as a working concept of social integration under law. Its law must be self-completing and systematic. Its relations to other states and to groups within itself will depend upon its own nature as a moral community, able in some degree to control economic necessity and to improve the cultural ideals which are its abiding foundations. But the existence of an ideal of constitutional statehood is necessary to any effort of actual states to make possible the conditions of the good life to their citizens. Without this ideal norm Hobbes and the Fascists have the last word.

To sum up, political theory, like any social philosophy, must fulfill a double urgency: it must first of all be adequate through an understanding of facts, that is, it must have a scientific and positive side which talks in terms of actual states, not simply of *the* state; and of actual human behavior, not simply of men as moral abstractions. But there is also a legitimately normative side to political theory without which this description remains useless for judgments of better or worse; this second need in political thinking is the Aristotelian description of the moral end of the state which must be criticized in terms of the ideal purpose served by political association. The first aspect of politics may be said to concern itself with technique, with the limits of the entire cultural context presented by a particular political group—state, party, etc., with what may be called, after Croce, "the economic aspect of the practical activity", or what I have preferred to call the organic side of a political problem. The second involves the statement of ethical principles: it is the purposive or moral aspect, and stands in relation to the economic activity as end does to means.

It is the business of the statesman to combine ends and means as best he can in the light of the whole situation with which he is confronted. The "pure" political scientist, so-called, often professes to deal only with the first mentioned aspect of politics. The political philosopher has generally remained content with a formal statement of the second. Yet it seems clear that the political theorist must attempt to combine both methods. While he is not forced to *act* the part of statesman, he must none the less *understand* that rôle if he is to be adequate to his task. For politics is not a purely formal science like mathematics, nor a purely mechanistic science like physics. The philosopher must understand the practical limits of his normative principles; the scientist must allow for the fact that the political animal man is also a purposive creature.

CHAPTER III

SOVEREIGN STATE OR SOVEREIGN GROUP? *

The late Professor William A. Dunning, for so long the dean of American political theorists, is reported to have said of the recent political theories which attempt to replace the conception of state sovereignty by some pluralistic grouping of social forces that they were "radically unintelligible". It is hard for political philosophers of a juristic turn of mind, who have been accustomed to regard the conception of sovereignty as a foundation stone and a sort of "rock of ages" for their faith, to be told (as one is every day, more or less) that the anti-intellectualistic type of sociological description is the only valid one for juristic structure. For that, according to the old rationalistic conceptions of analytical jurisprudence, is indeed to base sovereignty upon shifting sands and to deprive law of any special significance of its own by equating it with social reactions of the most indeterminate character. But the anti-intellectualistic trend of modern political theory indignantly denies this charge. The assumption, it counters, that any legal center of reference can be final in its actual authority or in its moral right to command is an outworn Hegelianism, discredited by practice and theory alike. Law is too much a thing of fictions to be taken seriously in its claims, when it pretends to be giving an accurate description of facts in the abstract terms of a pretended right on the part of the state to be the sole author of enforceable commands and the only rightful claimant of men's ultimate loyalty. To a scientific view of "social forces", sovereignty is no more than an antiquated relic of that barbarous and monistic rationalism that could see in the state *"der Gang Gottes in der Welt"*. The fact is, they say, that in the actual conflict of loyalties the state is

* Reprinted with alterations from *The American Political Science Review*, Vol. XIX, No. 3. August, 1925.

not a *"communitas communitatum"* but among other groups merely *prima inter pares*.[1]

One may admit that the absoluteness of legal supremacy, internally and externally,[2] which formed the essence of the Austinian conception of sovereignty, is a conception that hardly accords with the facts of political life, either in intra- or international relations. And yet one may be entirely unwilling to jettison the whole notion of sovereignty as the pluralists suggest we should. If it turns out to be to some extent a fiction, that is, the hypostatization of an ideal for the sake of systematic coherence in law, it may yet be a necessary fiction to any society that wishes to take or keep organic form under law. Upon its existence as a fact accepted by what Austin called "the bulk of the people" depends constitutional government.

But obedience is not capable of the rationalistic synthesis offered by the theory of sovereignty, say its critics. Like the universe itself, the state is ultimately a pluralistic arrangement of grouped forces, among which government, at its most absolute, can arrange but a temporary and tolerable resolution. This is a contention often enough reiterated, and with enough truth in it, to demand searching consideration from political theorists.

Why is it that anti-intellectualism in politics should fasten on the doctrine of state sovereignty as the point of its attack? It is, on this reading of its theory at least, simply because the suspicion of all that is rationalistic, all that is the fruit of conceptual abstraction, attaches with peculiar force to the idea of unitary sovereignty.

The idea of sovereignty, like the idea of the state itself, is a conceptual abstraction. What we actually deal with, think

[1] See the excellent essay contributed by F. W. Coker to the memorial volume contributed by the students of Professor W. A. Dunning, to complete his *History of Political Theories* by adding a fourth volume on *Recent Times:* "Pluralistic Theories and the Attack Upon State Sovereignty," for an extensive bibliography and a very considered critical appraisal of the whole pluralistic movement (pp. 80-119, *op. cit.*). Miss E. D. Ellis has considered the juristic significance of this effort to restate the doctrine of sovereignty in a very interesting article "Political Science at the Cross Roads" in which she very soundly insists that the doctrine of legal sovereignty must be properly related to political sovereignty. *Am. Pol. Sci. Rev.*, Vol. XXI, No. 4, November, 1927.

[2] E. M. Borchard has done the same good service (that Mr. Coker did for political pluralism) for "Political Theory and International Law" (pp. 120-140, *op. cit.*).

these realists in politics, is not a single determinate force which we may term sovereign, nor a collective spiritual entity which we may term the state. In fact, they say, we must recognize the reality of many unrelated social forces which are never resolved into unity; and in place of the state, only the rule of the actual government—those in control of the force of government.

Naturally, then, they will not accept as real any manipulation of the concept, "sovereign state". That conception in politics has gone hand in hand with rationalism in philosophy. Sovereignty for political theory has served the same purpose that the concept has for traditional logic and for epistemology. To anti-intellectualism, the method in the one is as vicious as in the other. "Reality" the "strung-along, flowing reality", of which James wrote, is not so constituted, either in thinking it truly or thinking it politically. It can not be crammed into concepts. "Everything you can think of," said James, "however vast or inclusive, has on the pluralistic view, a genuinely 'external' environment of some sort or amount. Things are 'with' one another in many ways, but nothing includes everything or dominates everything. The word 'and' trails along after every sentence, something always escapes. The pluralistic world thus is more like a federal republic than an empire or a kingdom. However much may be collected, however much may report itself present at any effective center of consciousness, something else is self-governed and absent and unreduced to unity." [3]   To pluralists, as much as to Hegelians and absolutists in general, the state remains a sort of mikrokosmos of the makrokosmos that is the universe; the difference is now that the universe and the state become pluralistic instead of monistic; the universe becomes a multiverse, and unitary sovereignty, "polyarchy".

The analogy of the importance of sovereignty in political theory to the place of the concept in logical theory suggests at once the reason that it has become the point on which the most varying types of the pragmatic revolt converge in attack and at the same time, something of the general strategy under which that attack must be conducted. At a period in world history when all the possible changes are being rung on the forms of

[3] William James, *Pluralistic Universe*, pp. 321-322.

government under which political societies can come, it is natural that the stereotyped conceptions of representative democracy should undergo critical examination, examination at the hands of friends as well as by those who have no prepossessions in favor of democracy as an ideal. The notion of sovereignty has accommodated itself to the growth of democratic institutions by developing into the idea of popular sovereignty of the general will, expressed through representative agencies of government. Are we now to speak simply of the divine right of the people, instead of the king? And can parliament or government be substituted as the equivalent for people? [4]

If sovereignty be restricted to its formalistic aspects, to its purely Austinian outlines so to speak, our pragmatists will claim that it is as empty of meaning in real politics as the concept is in real thinking. In each case the important element of psychology is left out. Pragmatists will have none of the conceptualistic logic of rationalism or the manipulation of the abstractions which are called concepts. Pragmatists in politics say that the juristic logic which is built up about the concept of sovereignty is equally empty of real use or meaning. The psychology of politics means that here, as in everything else, *real* obedience is a matter of degree, and *real* sovereignty is a complex of accommodation between conflicting groups.

Now, the error of pragmatism may lie in its refusal to notice that the world of logical concepts, including the juristic notion of sovereignty, is a world so necessary as to be practically indispensable. Granted that to talk of *absolute* sovereignty in human affairs is to talk nonsense, it does not follow that we can dispense with the notion of sovereignty as the basis of law. The validity of psychology is unquestionable, for psychology includes all that gives individuality to any particular thought or act. Still to talk of sovereignty, for example, in general terms is as necessary as to talk of thinking itself, in terms of thought in general, as formal logic does. On the other hand, the purely legalistic notion of sovereignty must be supplemented by the effort to see what is really meant by the "general will", to use the

---

[4] The hopeless confusion into which Rousseau fell in these questions, he attempted to escape by the device of an ideal legislator. Apologists of the General Will theory as the basis of law have usually followed his steps, more cautiously, but to the same end.

phraseology that is commonly dated from Rousseau; and only an adequate psychology can keep that conception from being turned by a logical *tour de force*, as Rousseau turned it, into a bit of empty sophistry. Pragmatism, which may be called the new nominalism, will not accept a word for an "essence" that does not exist—and in this respect its criticism has been of the utmost value to political theory.

Political pluralism first attempts to show the uselessness and the inadequacy of the formal conception of the sovereign state that serves as the basis for most of the jurisprudential systems arrived at analytically: its method is to show that this conception does not touch the changing political reality underneath. In the second place, it rejects the whole psychology of the general will, used ordinarily to justify on moral grounds the exercise of unitary sovereignty; it holds this psychology to be vitiated by the same rationalistic method of arriving at a conceptual synthesis that is displayed by absolutistic systems in general. In politics, its attack derives especial strength from the discredit lately attached to absolutism as the peculiar contribution of Germany.

Some pragmatists push this advantage so far as to declare that the solution is to be found only in the pluralistic state, in which sovereignty is to be shared by many groups, instead of being monopolized by the state alone. In the hands of exponents like Mr. Laski, pluralism is the transformation of sovereign state to sovereign group.[5] A general agreement to this effect may be found among thinkers so widely separated in methods and aims as M. Georges Sorel, the syndicalist priest of the myth-cult of violent revolution through the general strike, and the eminent French jurist, M. Léon Duguit, whose whole effort is to establish the "rule of law" based upon the assurance of the public services and social solidarity. Their common theme is the passing of the state as the author of commands, and the rise of the group as the new political unit of autonomy. It is this theme that gives a further unity to the political theory of anti-intellectualistic pluralism.

[5] This hardly applies to the Mr. Laski of the constructive part of *A Grammar of Politics*, although it still applies to his *theory* of group rights. See *infra*, Chapter V-B.

Let us set our stage for this battle of the group against the state by a general survey of the field of action, which we may then be able to develop in detail in later chapters.

Perhaps the most authoritative summary of this whole movement has been given by Ernest Barker at the conclusion of his brilliant little volume in the Home University Library Series on *English Political Thought from Spencer to To-day*. After having traced the sources of modern anti-intellectualism in politics as far back as their nineteenth century origins, he sums them up in a passage worthy of quotation even at some length: [6]

"Among the new sources of thought we have to reckon social psychology, the new economics, and the new aspect of legal theory which has been emphasized by Maitland. Social psychology tends to issue in a criticism of the machinery and methods of representative government. Intentionally or unintentionally, it allies itself with a certain trend of anti-intellectualism which is one of the features of the age. In reaction against what they regard as the false intellectualism of the utilitarians, and the equally false if very different intellectualism of the idealists, many of the thinkers of to-day are returning to the cult of instinct, or at best of subconscious thought. They find unexpected allies. The new economics, in some of its phases, is also intuitional and anti-intellectual. If social psychology tends to base the State as it is on other than intellectual grounds, syndicalism is prone to expect that nonintellectual forces will suffice to achieve the State as it should be. Both may find themselves in the issue, however paradoxical the prophecy may seem, the allies of Conservatism. Conservatism, with its appeal to sentiment, and its antipathy to doctrinaire Radicalism, is the residuary legatee of all anti-intellectual movements."

That this is a prophecy which is borne out by the historical development of sovietism into the most repressive communist dictatorship is now too commonplace an observation to be characterized as paradoxical or to excite comment. Fascism could not be better described in a sentence. But the same development in the theory of group autonomy that is lumped together under the miscellaneous heading of Syndicalism, or "The Greater Trade-Unionism," as Mr. Cole calls it, is perhaps

[6] *Op. cit.*, p. 248.

less often remarked, though no less worthy of comment.[7] Mr. Barker himself noted the direction of the anti-intellectualistic drift toward the pluralistic Syndicalism of group rights. "If we are individualists now," he had said in his discussion of federalism, "we are corporate individualists." Our "individuals" are becoming groups. "No longer do we write *Man versus the State*, but we write *The Group versus the State*. There is much talk of federalism in these days. Behind the talk lies a feeling that the single unitary state, with its single sovereignty is a dubious conception, which is hardly true to the facts of life. Every state, we feel, is something of a federal society, and contains within its borders different national groups, different churches, different economic organizations, each exercising its measure of control over its members."

The most imposing manifestation of this federalistic feeling is, he thinks, the development of the newest socialism toward guild socialism. "In this new Socialism the claim of the Trade Unions to be free groups, freely developing their life in pursuit of their own purposes—the claim urged during the reaction against the Taff Vale judgment, and largely recognized by parliamentary legislation since 1906—finds its apogee. The same movement which appears in the new Socialism economically appears politically in the new Liberalism. The core of that Liberalism would appear to be a new federalism, not directed, as federalism used to be, toward the integration of several small States into a larger whole, but rather toward the disintegration of the great State into small national groups on which large powers are to be conferred by way of devolution. Such at any rate is the lesson which the policy of Liberalism in Ireland, in Wales, and to some extent in Scotland, would seem to suggest." [8]

---

[7] Syndicalism may claim to have furnished Italian Fascism both with its original leaders and with much of its ideology. Even after it was swallowed up by the nationalist maw of Mussolini's imperialism, it left its mark on the new "Fascist-Syndicalist State." See Chapter XI, *infra*.

[8] *Op. cit.*, pp. 181-182. The reaction against the Liberal extension of the widest special privileges to the Trade Unions came after the General Strike of 1926 with Tory legislation aimed not only at sympathetic strikes, but at picketing, union levies of political funds, and at the participation of civil servants in the Trade Union Congress. The Unionist Party has gone back toward the Osborne Judgment, and taken hints from the American Supreme Court on Labor Law. See L. B. Ferguson, *The Trades Disputes and Trade Union Act*, 1927.

Had Mr. Barker written in 1926 instead of just before the war, he might have drawn additional confirmation from the existence of an Irish Free State, from an India started along the road to responsible self-government and Dominion status, perhaps complete *Swaraj*, and from the actual assumption by the Dominions, under the Peace Treaty and the League of Nations covenant, of the legal status of equal states, coöperating toward the accomplishment of a common end that men still call the British Empire. And what is stranger still, he might have witnessed an effort on the part of British statesmen to fit the law logically to the new order of facts, instead of priding themselves on the quaint discrepancy between the two.

Even at the time Mr. Barker wrote, there were tendencies visible, which he was among the first to remark, of revolt against the formalistic conception of the state as power. "At present, however, the current which acts against 'intellectualism' sets also against the State. A certain tendency to discredit the State is now abroad. The forces which combine to spread this tendency are very various. There is the old doctrine of natural rights, which lies behind most of the contemporary movements that advocate resistance to the authority of the State. But there is also the new doctrine of the rights of groups, which is to-day a still more potent cause of opposition to the State. In the sphere of economics this doctrine assumes the form of Guild-Socialism. In the sphere of legal theory it assumes the form of insistence on the real personality, the spontaneous origin, and (with some of its exponents) the 'inherent rights' of permanent associations. In this latter form the doctrine has been urged, on the one hand, by the advocates of the rights of trade unions and, on the other hand, by the champions of the rights of churches and ecclesiastical bodies. In both forms it has tended to produce a federalistic theory of the State, whether the State is regarded as a union of guilds, or as a 'community of Communities' which embraces groups not only economic but also ecclesiastical and national." "The State in England is passing Home Rule Acts, and Welsh Disestablishment Acts to meet the claims of the national groups. All Europe is convulsed with a struggle of which one object at any rate is a regrouping of men in ways which will fulfil national ideals and accord with national aspirations. Trade unions have recovered from Parliament more than the ground they have lost in the law of courts." [9]

The upshot of all this ferment of new grouping, politically speaking at least, is interpreted by Mr. Barker as a federalism of fact which is gradually being clothed in legal form. He is himself neither an anti-intellectualist nor a pluralist in these matters. He insists that "we must be quite clear what we mean by our groups; and we must not content ourselves with a hazy intuition that they are somehow real personalities or have somehow inherent rights"; and he has laid it down quite finally that the state cannot abdicate the rule of law where its purpose is challenged by a group of any sort whatever. "Whatever rights such groups (guilds, national groups, and churches) may claim or gain, the State will still remain a necessary adjusting force; and it is even possible that if the groups are destined to gain ground, the State will also gain, perhaps even more than it loses, because it will be forced to deal with ever graver and ever weightier problems of adjustment." [10]

But the leading exponent of that guild socialism in which Mr. Barker has seen the most evident sign of the working of federalism, Mr. G. D. H. Cole, challenges the sovereignty of a state which he treats as no more than the actual government. Not, indeed, that he denies the necessity of retaining a final power of adjustment which turns out in the end to be very much what Mr. Barker means by the state; but that he challenges the whole idea of representative parliaments as the organs of the state will. Parliamentary institutions based on the intellectualistic assumption that the community will can be determined by selecting a group of persons to represent the wills of all (representing them for all sorts of questions merely by majority rule within the miscellaneous group that is the House of Commons, for example), do not seem to Mr. Cole "to be democracy at all", though it was so understood by the Victorians. "The challenge to existing institutions which is implicit in this book goes considerably deeper," he says in *The Future of Local Government*, "than any mere criticism of the unwieldiness, because of its size

[9] *Op. cit.*, pp. 249-251. For the present qualifications to this statement made necessary by recent changes in Labor Law, see note 8, *supra*.

[10] *Op. cit.*, p. 250, and p. 183. By way of confirmation see "The Return of the State," by Kingsley Martin, *Economica*, March 1926, No. 16.

and the magnitude of its duties, of the present State organization. There is implicit, not only the desire for decentralization, but also a challenge to the theory of representative 'democracy', worked through parliamentary institutions, which gained almost universal acceptance during the last century." [11]

Mr. Cole's remedy, which he has set forth in a number of books, is "the substitution for the universalized representative system which has prevailed during the past century of a system of *functional representation*. . . . The essence of my contention is that, in order to get a healthy Society well administered and responding effectively to the will of its members, it is necessary to do at least two things. In the first place it is necessary to organize Society throughout, on functional lines and to make the form of organization designed for the fulfilment of each social purpose, appropriate to that purpose; and in the second place it is necessary, within the organization set up for each of these purposes, to adopt the basis of representative democracy, which only under these conditions, that is when it is combined with the idea of function, becomes a real instrument of effective popular control. In other words, what is wanted is a merging of the ideas of mediaeval functionalism with those of Victorian 'democracy'. Out of this union will spring the real *functional democracy* of the future." [12]

The "commune", however, which Mr. Cole promptly reintroduces in place of the state, seems hardly better than an alias for the sovereign parliament he has just ushered out. It is a body "in every area, local, regional, national . . . . in which all these various groups of elected persons will be brought together for the common determination and discussion of vital questions of policy in which they are all concerned." [13] The present parliament of England is not constituted in just the way that Mr. Cole would have his national "commune" chosen; but it occupies exactly the place that the highest of the hierarchy of communes does in his theory of the "new state". If he

[11] *The Future of Local Government*, p. 177. For similar criticisms see S. and B. Webb, *Constitution for the Socialist Commonwealth of Great Britain;* H. Belloc and G. Chesterton, *The Party System;* and H. Delbrück, *Government and the Will of the People.*
[12] *Op. cit.*, pp. 178-179.
[13] *Op. cit.*, p. 181. See also *Guild Socialism Restated*, chapters on the "Commune."

prefers to change the name to "commune", no one will quarrel with him except those captious persons who insist that the word *commune* has already acquired a determinate usage in a different sense, and those who do not see the good of offering the same thing by another name. They might insist that Mr. MacIver's *Community* cannot be so translated into politics.[14] Parliament, as the sovereign policy-forming organ of the British Empire, has undergone many changes in the method of selecting its membership, without changing its name or its function. Unless Mr. Cole proposes to reject the finality of its decisions, as a high court as well as the sovereign legislature, there is little use to call it a commune. It will differ from the other representative bodies (or communes) that are local and regional, in the finality of its decisions, the supremacy of its laws. And even under the dyarchy of producers' and consumers' parliaments of his earlier guild-socialist theory, Mr. Cole was sufficiently bound by the logic of things to institute a court of last resort, made up of an equal number from each body, to solve disputes between the two.

His real point in his latest writings does not seem to be that there is any possibility of ultimate pluralism in political authority, within the state, although he still speaks of deconcentration and of decentralization as if he meant some such irreducible federalism. What he is aiming at is rather in line with Mr. Dewey's idea of the vicious quality of abstractions: he insists that representational bodies, whether they be called parliaments or communes, must not be selected on the basis of representing "interests or purposes in general", but for a particular "piece of work or group of duties".

Now it is true that there are many disadvantages in the practice of electing men to "represent" whole communities on every conceivable question. The growth in the complexity of the problems with which the modern legislator is confronted renders it impossible that he should accurately register "the will of his constituents", even if there were such a thing. Troubled political scientists propose the short ballot, and more power to the executive. Rousseau's general will and Rousseau's ideal legislator

[14] Mr. MacIver's notion of *Community* is full of the most fertile suggestions; but to translate every possible community of interest or even every "area of common life" (as Mr. Cole would do) into political structure is to put an intolerable burden on citizens.

exist alike in the realm of pure idea; but for that matter it is only in that realm that Plato's Philosopher was King. The modern legislature of any state you choose, harried by the necessity of placating every conceivable type of interest-bloc, bargaining for such combinations of votes as will enable the majority to keep "rule without power", is a sorry spectacle enough. Those who are patient hope for better things, or trust the veto power of the executive or of the courts. The impatient of every persuasion, have been won over to "direct action", though they may not all be classed as communists or fascists. "Parliamentarism" is assailed on every side.[15] Labor forces resort to the use of economic power quite as often as the "capitalists" whom they accuse of exploiting the community by more devious methods; under modern conditions of social interdependence the strike in the public services is a forthright bludgeon, whether it be used for offense or defense. Mr. Cole's solution for this pass of affairs is to render the legislator a special instrument, to avoid the blunt edge of party control by specializing the functions for which the representative must represent, that is, to "functionalize" representation. He thinks this will provide a constitutional basis for a more flexible and more acceptable legal sovereignty.

That is an excellent suggestion, no doubt, so far as administrative decentralization is in question. And under modern conditions, administrative bodies carry an increasing burden of quasi-legislative and quasi-judicial functions, as we have called them in order to preserve the fiction of the separation of powers. As a matter of fact, they form policies and decide issues, as well as administer; and some of their decisions, for example, those of the Inter-State Commerce Commission of the United States,

---

[15] F. W. Coker, *loc. cit. supra*, (note 1) also gives a comprehensive bibliography for this attack on parliamentarism. The works of Mr. H. J. Laski furnish some interesting studies and very valuable bibliographical notes. Bertrand Russell's *Proposed Roads to Freedom* remains the classic criticism of the more extreme views of this nature. See also P. H. Douglas' chapter on "Proletarian Political Theory" in *A History of Political Theories, Recent Times.* For the narrower meaning of parliamentarism see R. K. Gooch, "The Anti-Parliamentary Movement in France," *Am. Pol. Sci. Rev.,* Vol. XXI, No. 3, Aug., 1927. See also Carl Schmitt, *Die Geistgeschichtliche Lage des heutigen Parlamentarismus* (München und Leipzig, 1923) and *Die Diktatur* (1921) ; M. J. Bonn, *The Crisis of European Democracy* (1925) ; H. Heller, *Die Politischen Ideenkreise der Gegenwart* (Breslau, 1926).

are of the most far-reaching importance.[16]   But in the end, it seems impossible to escape the maintenance of a central policy-forming organ, a central court of last appeal, a central executive to enforce responsibility, whether they be united in the way these three branches are in the English parliament and ministry, or more dubiously united under the terms of a rigid constitution, as they are in the United States.   As long as governments are faced with general problems of policy, some men must be vested with general responsibility to the political community as a whole to face those problems and settle them.   Representative government, as Henry Jones Ford has so adequately shown, can hardly escape the terms of a general mandate of power, limited only by the law and custom of the constitution.   The particular "piece of work or group of duties" which the responsible ministers of parliament must face is apt to be general enough to try the wisdom even of the Philosopher King, and it is so by the very necessities of organized government, within the nation as well as in foreign affairs.

And what particular interest or purpose is it which is capable of guiding our selection of the men who are to be so empowered? The instrumentalist philosophy of government, looking in the direction of their functions, has said: "They must be specialists, chosen by special community groups of interests."   Well and good, so far as specializing is compatible with the necessary simplicity of democratic control.   But someone, some body, must also be responsible for the coördination of services, and the fitting together of policies into a "government", as the parliamentary term goes, or into an "administration" as we say in the United States.   With the President going one way, and Congress balking, or actually going in another, the difficulties that lie in the way of getting a responsible "administration" are the chief concerns of our contemporary politics in the United States. Politicians and party leaders, then, may well stand aghast before

---

[16] See "The Expansion of American Administrative Law," by A. A. Berle, Jr., 30 *Harvard Law Review* (1916-1917, pp. 430 ff.) which gives a typical statement of the extent to which administrative commissions use all three types of power in fact, and the limits set upon them by the jurisprudence of the Supreme Court of the United States. *Cf.* Ernest Barker's article on English administrative law, "The Rule of Law," 1 *Political Quarterly*, No. 2, May, 1914, and Léon Duguit, *Traité de droit constitutionnel*, for French *droit administratif.*

the flat claim that, because it is impossible to represent interests in general, or purposes in general, there must be the selection of representatives by specific interests (professional, occupational, and so forth) and for specific purposes (functional representation). "All very well," they would probably rejoin, "but someone must run the country as a whole, and join foreign to domestic policy in such a way that the two things fit together." [17] The separation of powers makes this already difficult enough.

The case for proportional against occupational representation has been excellently put by Mr. Paul H. Douglas in the September 1923 *Journal of Sociology*. He has well established the disadvantages connected with purely occupational representation. As for proportional representation, it would certainly have the advantage of giving political status and legal character to a number of groups that now make raids on the legislatures, through lobbies or through the balance of power they hold between the two parties. That is, proportional representation would accomplish this end, if they chose to use it. But most of the associations who form blocs without responsible majority control, or without actually electing candidates on their own tickets, seem content to use the weapons presently at hand. The farmers prefer the farm-bloc to a farmer's party, apparently. Labor, so far as it is controlled by the American Federation of Labor, had declared for a like policy until Mr. La Follette's candidacy and the political success of the British Labor Party seduced the A. F. L. The convention at El Paso on November 24, 1924, voted a return to its old policy. Neither the "veterans" nor the prohibition forces could use their potential strength if they diverted it to electing congressional candidates by proportional representation. And there are other practical

[17] This is the difficulty to be found with the proposal recently made by the Webbs in their *Constitution for the Socialistic Commonwealth of Great Britain* to cure the present hypertrophy of Parliament by dividing it into two halves, so to speak: a Social and a Political Parliament. The scheme is seductive enough until one reflects that it destroys the one virtue Parliament has retained, unified responsibility and simplicity in its enforcement. The German experiment of a subordinate and advisory Industrial Parliament seemed at first more hopeful. See H. Finer, *Representative Government and a Parliament of Industry*. See also his "Case against Proportional Representation," *Fabian Tract* No. 211. On the other hand, Mr. Laski in *A Grammar of Politics*, has made out a strong case against even advisory economic parliaments. He believes that the same function of expert advice may be served by consultative commissions as parliamentary adjuncts.

objections from the point of view of the country at large to an unqualified system of proportional representation in a nation so vast as the United States, federal in its form of government, and already harassed to its full share by the difficulty of getting any stability in the control of all the organs of government at one time by a party strong enough to put through its program. The experience of Italy, before *Fascismo* cut the Gordian knot into which many parties and proportional representation had tied its government, may be an extreme case, but it is one in point.[18]

In any case, proportional representation and even occupational representation do not really signify political pluralism. They still treat the state as sovereign, and try to fit legal to political sovereignty as justly as may be. The only thoroughgoing pluralism is that of syndicalistic theory: it amounts to a feudal anarchy among contending occupational groups, and rejects the state entirely. The experiments so far undertaken with that theory lead one to hope for little more than reënthroned despotism, as was the case in Russia, or for failure to make more than a gesture of futility, as was the case when the workers in Turin and other Italian cities seized the factories in 1920.[19] The more chastened pluralism of modern political theory is merely interested, as Mr. Dewey and Mr. Cole are, in pointing to the inadequacy of sovereign parliaments to the needs of modern society, and in suggesting the spreading out of authority among newly recognized legal groupings,—in short, turning unions into units of political authority. Mussolini allows such political power as he wishes to grant to be exercised by the corporations.

This criticism of "representation in general" is not an isolated cry nor an unheeded one. Even Lord Bryce in *Modern Democracy* fell to musing on the pathology of modern legislatures; and so profound a conservative as Dicey went so far as to find

---

[18] The impotence of a parliamentarism in Italy was due in no small part to the *bloc* system of majority-forming that seems to be necessary where there are more than two strong parties, and no party has a clear majority.

[19] Odon Por, himself a Guild Socialist, in *Fascism* (translated by Mrs. Emily Townshend), has given an unbiased picture of this failure of syndicalism in its revolutionary phase in Italy. See especially pp. 41-55. See also E. A. Mowrer, *Immortal Italy*, (1922)—"The Revolution that Never Was." But see Don Sturzo, *Italy and Fascismo*, for a different view of the seizure. supported by William Bolitho, *Italy Under Mussolini*. and Gaetano Salvemini, *The Fascist Dictatorship in Italy*.

hope in the referendum, though he made a strong case against proportional representation.[20]

The possibility of recording through government a real general will finds very few defenders in modern theory, outside of the Hegelian rear-guard so stoutly led by the late Dr. Bosanquet. The paradoxical aspect of the matter is that, along with the increasing drift in actual law and government toward collectivism, traced in English law by Dicey's *Law and Opinion in England in the 19th Century*, has gone an attempt to escape the consequential centralization through all manner of schemes for federalizing authority in various degrees, from those which look only to regionalism and a more vigorous local government, all the way to proposals like Mr. Cole's for a redivision of political society along lines occupational as well as territorial; or like the Webbs' for dividing work between a Social and a Political Parliament.[21] Leaving out of account, then, the extreme pluralism of the revolutionary, and almost anarchistic syndicalists, such as M. Sorel, one may still say that the pluralistic critique of the sovereign state has had a great impact on political theory, in so far as it has forced a reconsideration of the part groups play in making law.

In France, M. Duguit has taken the same general doctrines enunciated by Mr. Dewey as long ago as 1894 (in an article in the *Political Science Quarterly* on "Austin's Theory of Sovereignty"),[22] and has erected one of most formidable of the modern reconstructions of juristic theory, pluralistic to the degree that it recognizes in federalism, in the new legal status of trade unions, and in regional and representational reforms, a complete break with the older and classic doctrines of sovereignty. In England, too, "the Metaphysical Theory of the

[20] A. V. Dicey, *The Law of the Constitution*, 8th Ed., Introd., p. xci, *et seq.*
[21] G. D. H. Cole, *Social Theory*, and *Guild Socialism Restated;* also *The Future of Local Government*, especially the chapter criticizing "Webbismus". For criticisms of Mr. Cole's theory in detail see the essay of F. W. Coker, *op. cit.*, and the following articles: E. D. Ellis, "The Pluralistic State," 14 *American Political Science Review*, (1920) ; "Guild Socialism and Pluralism," *ibid.*, Vol. 17, (1923) ; G. H. Sabine, "Pluralism, a Point of View," *ibid.*, Vol. 17, (1923) ; and P. H. Douglas, "Proletarian Political Theory" —*loc. cit. supra.* Note 15.
See also Odon Por. *Guilds and Coöperatives in Italy.*
[22] Mr. Dewey's "instrumentalist" pragmatism contained in germ the philosophy of "*Solidarisme*" upon which M. Duguit bases his decentralized theory of the functional state.

State", as Mr. Hobhouse has called it, has fallen into sad disre-
pute. Mr. Ernest Barker, and the present Master of Balliol,
Mr. A. D. Lindsay, have joined forces with those who, like
Maitland and Figgis, pointed out the theoretical as well as the
practical limitations of state sovereignty,—though they have by
no means gone so far as Mr. H. J. Laski in the pragmatic point
of view that sees no good in the theory of legal sovereignty
because it cannot be sustained, in practice, in its formal purity.[23]

The case against "the discredited state" is one whose strength
cannot and ought not to be underestimated. At the same time,
one must not misunderstand what Mr. Barker meant in that
article, in the *Political Quarterly*, which has been hailed by Mr.
Laski and others as the classic statement of the grounds for
political pluralism. The "discredit" which he felt attached to
the state was rather aimed at discrediting the all-absorptive,
supermoral state of Hegelian idealism, that offered so excellent
an apology for the *Goose-step*.[24] One ought not to forget that
his article was written before the war, at the heyday of the
great to-do which was being made by the apostles of the new
"greater unionism". Professor R. G. Gettell, in his recent *History of Political Thought*, has pointed out what a change Mr.
Barker's ideas have undergone since that date.[25] Even when
The Discredited State was published, its author found it necessary to append a footnote: "It is curious to reflect how differently one would have written in January 1915. We have
forgotten that we are anything but citizens, and the state is
having the high midsummer of its credit."

His point, though, he did not forget in those times of flurried
judgment, as many others did; and his point was simply that the
"problem of resistance is always a problem of groups". The
reality of groups, was, he noted, not that of a "general will",
or of some mystic group mind or corporate personality but
simply the reality of the hold their "organizing idea" had upon
their members. The hold of the state idea was not always so

[23] Mr. A. D. Lindsay, the present Master of Balliol, has given his own
views of "Sovereignty", a classic statement, in *The Proceedings of the
Aristotelian Society*, June 16, 1924.
[24] *Loc. cit.*, Vol. 2, (Feb., 1915).
[25] *Loc. cit.*, p. 462, note. The whole chapter on "Pluralistic Theories of
Sovereignty" is an excellent summary of the relation of the modern doctrines
to the development of political theories in their historical continuity.

intense or so exclusive as to prevent loyalty to other groups, for the hold of ideas upon men's loyalty varies with time and circumstance. When he wrote, home rule for Ireland had brought the Liberal government to the verge of a despairing admission of its impotence to coerce Ulster—nor has the problem disappeared with the creation of the Irish Free State. It was not only that trade unions and the Church had enforced their claims on the government; the whole empire was a standing example of the truth of Mr. Barker's claim that loyalty was capable of degrees of intensity, even of division against the claims of the state, as the state was defined by existing law.

In times of political transition when the very basis of the state, its "organizing idea", in Mr. Barker's phrase, is in dispute, it is reasonable to demand that the power of government shall not be used to enforce the *status quo* merely to prevent change. The political genius of the English has rested just in a willingness to recognize that there are times when legal sovereignty does not command a sufficient acceptance to make it worth while to force the government's point. When the threat is aimed at the very life of the state, government commands as of right—as it did in the general strike of 1926, or again even earlier when the threatened general strike was inaugurated by the strike of the English coal miners in the Spring of 1921, or as it did during the war. But in most instances it is properly chary of even the display of force—unless that is made necessary by violence.

In troubled times the body politic is in a pathological condition, one which it often requires a skilful physician to deal with. Is it best to operate or to wait? That is the question that always faces politicians when revolution is in the air. And the English are notorious homeopaths in their medical persuasions when it comes to dosing for political ills. They are convinced that the genius of free government lies in persuasion, not in force.

But in such times political pluralism is not so much a philosophy of the state, as a description of its pathological symptoms. The normal condition of the constitutional state is one in which obedience to the law is a matter of constitutional morality. Where law can neither be agreed upon nor enforced, where the decision is thrown into the arena of what Mr. Laski proposes as "negotiation" or "group competition", the illness of the body politic ceases to be slightly chronic, and takes on an acute phase. Its demise is not so probable as its recovery after a crisis, and a period of such heroic dosing as Mussolini has prescribed to his Italy.

Internally, England too has been undergoing a crisis whose issue is not yet clear; externally from the war-time intensity of its unity, the whole British Empire has slackened to a sort of international coöperation characteristic of a league of nations, rather than of a state. Some of its members have shown a notable unwillingness even to coöperate. The legalistic aspects of the former constitution of the Empire have been for several years simply in abeyance. The constitution has changed insensibly to that of a league of nations, and statesmen are casting about in vain for a more satisfactory government than that by conferences, after which there is always the possibility that a change in the member governments (either in the Dominions or in England) may undo whatever has been done. Gestures by the Foreign Office, like that of Lloyd George in making his appeal to the Self-Governing Dominions over the Turkish trouble in 1922, show that the prestige of the British Empire, in which they are all interested, may be involved to such an extent by an English minister despite the formal disclaimer of responsibility in the Imperial Conferences of 1923 and 1926, that they may be drawn into difficulties without wishing to be. The loyalty of all the Empire "in a pinch" has been too sternly and too recently proved to admit of any doubting, when the issue is the life of the whole. But the Dominions' loyalty to decisions in which they have no voice is too important a matter to England herself to be endangered by any but the most thoroughly considered actions. A feeling of this sort was certainly not the least of the factors which operated at that time to the overthrow of Mr. Lloyd George's government—and to weaken General Smuts in South Africa later. The great emphasis placed upon the necessity of general consultation in international treaties by the Imperial Conference of 1926 shows how informal but how real the coöperation of the units of the commonwealth must be.

These are matters of contemporary and practical import. As such they serve to show that it is idle to consider adequate the formal or intellectualistic conception of legal sovereignty for the solution of problems in which law is actually in the making, and sovereignty is being newly delimited. Yet it is not less idle on these grounds to attack the conception of the unitary state in its legal sovereignty, within those limits where such a unifying principle is present and actually operative in law; and that is what pluralism proposes we should do. Even within the limits of territorial federalism, the concerns which affect the purposes of the whole call for a unified power of decision and jurisdiction. The Imperial Conferences of prime-ministers, and the Judicial Committee of the Privy Council still furnish a working basis for the necessary unity, with some prospect either of enlarging the scope of their activity, or of forming instead some more adequate method of expressing the responsible will of the governments concerned in matters touching the common purpose of the Empire. If no such basis of unifying legal agreements does arise, the application of the term *state* to the Empire will simply have ceased to fit the facts. New areas of sovereignty will have arisen, whose community of action will be limited to specific agreement, in the same manner that international matters are treated by members of the League of Nations at the present time. And while one may see in the heroic proposals to outlaw war by compulsory arbitration a consummation devoutly to be wished, its fate up to the present suggests that the League is apt for some time to come to remain a league, and not become a super-state.

The point is, surely, that there is a real significance in the term "sovereign state", derived from practice as well as theory. The history of federal government in the United States is proof of that fact. Pluralism accurately described the period immediately before our Civil War, yet the pluralistic conception of the nature of the federal union has yielded to the conception of unified sovereignty not of the federal *government,* but of the federal *state,* wherever national concerns are at stake. And this has occurred through the dialectic of historical facts, and is continuing to change constitutional theory to fit those facts. Federalism can hardly be irreducible and ultimate. If there is to be accepted law, there must be the possibility of determining finally what is law, and of amending the constitution itself where the law is outgrown. The position of the Supreme Court of the

United States presents the spectacle of a power of juristic unification unique in the history of political institutions. Ever since Chief Justice Marshall and his associates brought the Supreme Court to the rescue of a Federalist Party defeated at the polls, the sphere of federal jurisdiction has increased, not without being challenged, but without being stayed in its course. The "due process" clause of the Fourteenth Amendment, the interstate commerce clause of Article I, Section 8, and the continued enactment of nation-wide amendments to the Constitution, all prove the essential unity of the rule of law, and of the sovereignty of the nation over the states. It is true that the federal *government* is possessed only of limited sovereignty but that is not true of the federal *state* created by the Constitution.[26] And to the degree that we continue to become a nation and cease to be a federation, national powers will be expanded to national control. The uses (and the proposed uses) to which we are putting the amending power are proof of the reality of such a need. One may deplore it, yet admit the fact.

The concept of sovereignty, in the sense of the constituent basis of the state, is in no danger from either syndicalism or the pragmatic attacks of Mr. Laski and his allies, for the very good reason that it is, in the form of an ultimate willingness among a given people to make law in certain ways and accept laws when so made, the condition of a society under law. The legal sovereignty of government is another matter; but it, too,

[26] The Eighteenth Amendment to the Constitution of the United States, and proposed Amendments such as that authorizing the passage of nation-wide child labor laws, are evidence that the amending process may be turned to statute making, as it has in state government within the nation, if the rigidity of the Federal Constitution blocks this national spirit. For an excellent criticism of the dangers inherent in pushing this centralizing tendency too far see Walter Thompson, *Federal Centralization*.

The platform of Mr. La Follette's party in the election of 1924 demanded that Congress be constitutionally empowered to override the decision of the Supreme Court. Such a provision would naturally make for putting the guardianship of the principles of the Constitution ultimately in the hands of Congress, and would undoubtedly render the Constitution "flexible" in practice to the point of destroying its really federal character.

If the proviso that no State may be deprived of its equal representation in the Senate without its own consent is actually to be construed as a perpetual limitation on the power of amendment, then the federal state is limited, and we are to that degree a confederation still. But it is unthinkable that this provision should limit three-fourths of the states should it ever become dangerous or galling.

must be capable of being determined constitutionally, though its locus may be widened or narrowed. Matters which transcend the purpose which government exists to realize under the constitutional mandate from the state may be referred to an arbitrament outside the bounds of a narrowly conceived Austinian doctrine, and matters which are the special concern of local areas or specific interests will properly be left in their hands. Government is the creature of the political community and is limited by the limits of the purpose that creates that community.[27] Where, however, the unified purpose of a community, partly resultant from historical heritage (even more, no doubt, from economic interdependence), but also partly the creation of an active and normative purpose expressed through constitutional agencies, is at stake, it cannot be suffered, in the words of the Master of Balliol, "to go by default".[28] This is the area of the fundamental law, private as well as public. Resistance here means attack upon the state. When labor unions, for example, propose to attain political ends by the rude persuasion of force, any pluralism of powers or division between the state and the parties to social strife, means an end to the rule of law. M. Duguit, for all his pluralistic bias, has recognized that, if Mr. Laski has not.[29]

And so does Mr. Barker, for that matter. "Years of ordered life," he said: "have permitted the germination of other ideas

[27] The real point that is being made by pluralists is that the acceptance and enforcement of laws (statutes, ordinances, etc.) is a matter of degree, and that even the constitutional bases of legal sovereignty do not command a loyalty from citizens that is undivided with other groups within the state. If one grants, however, that legal sovereignty is a pragmatic matter, to be tested in the working, one may also point out that constitutional unity still remains an *a priori* as well as a pragmatic necessity to the limitation of the resort to force by groups of any sort, and to the enforcement of responsibility against government itself, as the agent of that particular community of purpose which can be reduced to legal terms.

[28] *Loc. cit. supra*, note 23. See also his articles on "The Political Theory of Norman Angell," 1 *Political Quarterly*, no. 1, Feb., 1914), "The State in Recent Political Theory," *ibid.*, no. 4, (Dec., 1914), his contribution to *Recent Developments in European Thought* (edited by F. S. Marvin), "Recent Political Theory" (pp. 164-180), and *Karl Marx's Capital* in the World's Manuals series.

[29] M. Duguit, both in the *Traité de droit constitutionnel*, and in *Sovereignty and Liberty* recurs again and again to the manner in which the French government broke the general strike of May 1, 1920 (launched first on the railroads) by calling out troops. See also Appendix A, reprinted from *Pol. Sci. Qu.*, Vol. XXXIX, no. 4 (Dec., 1924).

than the indispensable minimum idea of law and order. . . .
If that basis is not secure, if the building of our common life
shows cracks and signs of subsidences, if the enemy without
should see a gaping opportunity for his battering ram, the cry of
'Back to law and order' will be great and will prevail. Perhaps
the hour is not yet. [!] But if it should strike there is no fear
for the State, or for the idea of law and order. There is rather
fear for other societies, other ideas. The idea of law and order,
when it is roused is one of the cruellest things in history. Think
of the suppression of the Parisian Commune of 1871." [30]   The
hour was, it turned out, even then (1914) at hand; and Mr.
Barker may have the melancholy pleasure of one who correctly
prophesied dire things in watching the state exhaust its credit in
other lands by a most unholy zeal for law and order in a period
of repression which may go far to explain recent conditions in
Ireland, in the specific case of the British state.

That Golden Age in which the ancients loved to steep their
imaginings of the ideal perfection can hardly be thought of as
existing without an accompanying race of innocents.   The
Metamorphoses sang it as forever vanished, living only in the
poet's dream:

> Aurea prima sata est aetas, quae vindice nullo
> Sponte sua sine lege fidem rectumque colebat.
> Poena metusque aberant, nec verba minantia fixo
> Aere legebantur, nec supplex turba timebat
> Iudicis ora sui.

Whether men have degenerated from the happy age of spontaneous goodness that Ovid celebrated, or whether they have
risen from as thick a slime as Huxley's generation believed,
they are at any rate so far below the angels, and so little above
the beasts, that the view Hobbes took of "the state of nature"
seems to justify itself in times of civil strife.

When all men take the view of the state which characterizes
the political pluralism of Mr. Laski, for example, that every
command of the sovereign is called upon to justify itself before
the moral conscience of the individual as right in itself, then the
majesty of law is rendered a thing of shreds and patches. Constitutionalism is the necessary context of single laws. "Plural-

[30] *Loc. cit.*, 2 *Political Quarterly*, no. 1, (Feb., 1915).

ism" puts an impossible demand upon such laws. The essence of the morality of "law-abiding" people lies in the recognition of the necessity for a delimitation of "rights" by an accepted rule of law. And when the individuals who call the right of the state to command into question are "corporate persons"— whether church, business, or labor unions—the matter is even more impossible of the solution Mr. Laski proposes. Then the rights of personality become the corporate interests which know no limits (in the case of economic groups) except those imposed upon them by necessity. To speak of the "moral personality" of the United States Steel Corporation or of the A. F. of L. smacks of a *mauvaise plaisanterie*. A feudal régime of pluralistic sort among such "moral" persons brings us back to Hobbes; for life under it, if it be not solitary indeed, is nasty, brutish, and short, enough and to spare, as the early days of the oil companies' feudal competition in the United States may prove. Weak as the state sometimes is, unless it breaks down sufficiently to permit open resort to force it hardly merits the term "discredited." And when it genuinely attempts to control unfair competition and does regulate monopolistic public services, the day of industrial feudalism is passing. *Homo homini lupus est* applies in an even greater degree to corporate persons, employers or employees, than to human ones, for there is a certain "soullessness" about bodies whose *raison d'être* is economic gain that is hardly to be found even in tyrants. Truly they have "neither soul to save nor body to kick".[31]

[31] In the interesting Scopes trial under the "anti-evolution law" the Fundamentalism of Tennessee asserted its claim to group rights in an extreme degree, even to the control of state education. It did so, however, by legal methods, asserting through a legislative majority its control over the public-school teacher group. On the other hand, the recent decision of the Supreme Court extending the protection of the First Amendment (through the Fourteenth) over the state of Oregon, has protected the group rights of religious sects against compulsory state control of all education.

See *Pierce v. Society of the Sisters of the Holy Name of Jesus and Mary*, 268 U. S. 510 (1925).

The Scopes case was cleverly disposed of by the Supreme Court of Tennessee so as to prevent it from being appealed to the Supreme Court by determining that the defendant had been wrongfully fined $100.00 through a technical error of the trial judge in naming the exact sum to the jury. Thus the defendant was deprived of the chance of an appeal through writ of error, and the law stands. See 289 Southwestern Reporter 363 (1927). It would probably not have been held unconstitutional by the U. S. Supreme Court in any case, the issue not being analogous to *Meyers v. Nebraska*, 262 U. S. 390 (1923).

So that, while we may approve the "discredited state" of which Mr. Barker talked, so long as that discredit is .paradoxically "greatly to its credit" (like being an Englishman in Gilbert's immortal song from *H. M. S. Pinafore*), and because, forsooth, it is as uninterfering and as kindly as a London Bobby, we may take alarm when it is proposed seriously to discredit the state and the law. The English attitude of "grousing" at the government deceives no one who understands how firmly the roots of English liberty are planted in respect for law, and in the willingness to wait its slow education at the hands of public sentiment rather than to force radical changes upon it by minority violence, or majority repression. One may suspect that the Labour Party, even more really in power than it has been so far, would not be so revolutionary as in its opposition days. "Direct Action" appeals perhaps more strongly to the Latin love of the "sublime" because it is more dramatic. But the attempt to introduce it, even under the genial auspices of William James' pluralism, into the political atmosphere of responsible government, destroys the genius for political liberty which characterizes the free peoples who make and maintain law. It is an appeal to that violence which M. Sorel has eulogized, whose only immediate issue is the reappearance of a sovereign equally despotic whether he be black-shirted or red.

CHAPTER IV

M. GEORGES SOREL AND THE "MYTH" OF THE GENERAL STRIKE

A POLITICAL APPLICATION OF ROMANTICISM *

Had William James, the most amiable and tolerant of philosophers as of men, lived to see his doctrines hailed by the
apologists of social violence and war to the knife between the
classes, he might have been more than mildly surprised. Yet
just such an acclaim has been rendered him by M. Georges
Sorel, who had previously made his philosophic homage to the
philosophie nouvelle of M. Bergson. M. Sorel has long been
known as the chief of those anti-intellectualistic *intellectuels*
who have called themselves *"La Nouvelle École"* of Socialism,
and who have preached the gospel of revolutionary syndicalism
through the numbers of *Le Mouvement Socialiste,* and the equally
sympathetic organs of Italian Socialism.

M. Sorel's doctrines have really had a vogue which makes them
of sufficient importance as theories to deserve consideration. He
has had the insight to push to their logical conclusions the anti-
intellectualistic philosophies of "activism", and the unrestrained
fashion of expressing himself that is fitting to an apostle of
violence. Add to this a very wide range of historical information,

* Reprinted with alterations from the *Political Science Quarterly* (Vol.
XXXIX, No. 2). The term political romanticism has been applied even to
a type of parliamentarism—the precise reverse of my own usage—on the
grounds that the Romanticists of the 19th century believed in endless talk
and esthetic rhetoric but not in action, by Professor C. Schmitt, in *Politische
Romantik.* I cannot agree with Professor Schmitt, remembering Byron as
an actor, and the revolutionary passion for action of Wordsworth, Shelley,
et al. It is true that there was a faith in Nature, in perfect Nature, in
Reason, etc. But the emotional outlet was the thing. I point to a use of
the term similar to my own by M. Berthélot, *Un Romantisme utilitaire*
(Paris, 1922).

It must be said, however, that Professor Schmitt in terming romanticism
"ein subjektivierter Occasionalismus" has exactly expressed the side of
Pragmatism which derives from William James. See especially the interesting *"Vorwort,"* op. cit.

and a certain detachment which leads him to counsel others to actions where he is patently sceptical as to the value of any activity, and you have the qualities which give him the literary flavor, at least, of that line of intellectualistic and pessimistic anti-intellectualists among the French thinkers whose writings always have a curiously Mephistophelian flavor. It is perhaps as much for his literary as for his philosophic oddity, brilliant but unbalanced, that M. Sorel has enjoyed so wide a popularity.

As a propagandist his works have been of real importance in the development of modern socialistic theory on the continent, as may be evidenced by the number of editions through which *Réflexions sur la violence* has passed, as well as the fact that it has been translated, along with two or three of his other writings on Marxian doctrine, into Italian (*Saggi di critica del marxismo,* and *Insegnamenti sociali della economia contemporanea,* the translation and prefaces by V. Racca). The practical application which has been made by the proletariat of his *Matériaux d'une théorie du prolétariat,* even more than the general recognition accorded to M. Sorel by political writers as the spokesman of the theorists of Syndicalism and Marxian Revolution, makes him peculiarly fit for an examination of political anti-intellectualism, under the acceptance of the pragmatic test of application I have set down as a method.

Mr. Cole, in the pre-war *World of Labour,*[1] was of the opinion that the real impact of the "Social Myth" of the violent General Strike as a means of social regeneration had been greater in Italy than in France, and the post-war developments of the two labor movements have gone far toward bearing him out, as we shall see. The impact of the doctrine has been met at length by something more than inertia. As Mr. Ramsay MacDonald said very early in the struggle, "The answer to Syndicalism is Fascismo."[2]

But how is it that M. Sorel should find in the essentially kindly and ethically naïve doctrines of William James anything to serve as a prop to his own *Réflexions sur la violence?* True enough he had barely heard of pragmatism when first he set about reflecting upon the nobility of proletarian violence. At that time he found that the philosophy of action and of intuition which M. Bergson had begun to make prevail so widely could be in-

[1] *Op. cit.,* pp. 166-168.   [2] *Socialist Review,* June, 1923.

terpreted in a Nietzschean sense to fit the regenerative revolution of the workers for which he was trying to enlist the active
support of the *syndicats* of the French C. G. T.[3] But only so
recently as 1921 he found that James, with his gospel rendered
according to the sophisticated theological interpretation of "a
European brain", had supplied him with the really useful philosophy for which he had been searching. That, at least, seems
to be the significance of *De l'utilité du pragmatisme*, taken in
connection with his earlier works. For although M. Sorel had
become an apostle of violence before he professed the pragmatic
faith, he had manifested his predilection for it clearly enough in
its generally anti-intellectualistic aspects, and had shown himself an unconscious disciple of the "Will to Believe" by his
doctrine of Social Myths,[4] and in particular the Myth of the

[3] Before his accession to the pragmatism of William James, M. Sorel, in
common with the entire group of theorists calling themselves *"La Nouvelle
École"* and writing in the *Mouvement Socialiste*, claimed to be philosophical
disciples of Bergsonian anti-intellectualism. M. Sorel time and again professes the same faith, e.g. *Refléxions sur la violence*, pp. 9, 40 *et seq.*, 219
et seq., and the chapter devoted to a critique of *L'Évolution créatrice* in
De l'Utilité du Pragmatisme. However he derives many of his philosophic
premises from Hartmann (*Réflexions sur la violence*, pp. 13, 22, 289, 112 *et
seq.*), among others that capitalism of the Marxian Myth plays a rôle analogous to that which Hartmann has assigned to the unconscious in the world of
nature. But as Bergson has carefully refrained from interpreting his doctrines as to their ethical implications, it is to Nietzsche that he goes for
ethics. The American captains of industry, completely dominated by the idea
of success (p. 115), are really the best modern example of the "Master Morality" of which Nietzsche had written. M. de Rousiers had described the
Yankees as all willing to "take a chance", each one "to try his luck". "To
be and to remain an American, it is necessary," he had laid down, "to consider life as a struggle, and not a pleasure, to seek in it the effort for victory,
energetic and efficient activity, rather than agreement or leisure embellished
by the culture of the arts, and the refinements proper to other societies"
(quoted *loc. cit.*). This delights M. Sorel as a sign of national vigor and the
same heroic qualities possessed by the freebooting Greeks, but not less because
he feels assured of the proper Marxian evolution where industrial conflict is
so frankly conducted, and so bitter.

[4] When M. Sorel wrote *Les Illusions du progrès* (first edition, 1908, two
years after the appearance of *Réflexions*, etc.) he had the following to say
about pragmatism: "a new philosophy . . . called pragmatism," "the last
term to which bourgeois thought had come: this philosophy admirably suits
every *parvenu* who wishes to get himself received in a very indulgent world,
thanks to his supple truckling, his bragging, and to the cynicism of his
success." In a note (which could not have been written before the second
edition, as the work of Schinz to which it refers was not published until
1909) he adds: "In the United States pragmatism must have been given a
more decent appearance than it has taken on in Italy: one of the books of
the Italian pragmatists has been called *The Liars' Manual*. but it seems
they have taken from the new philosophy, *with good right*, the Machiavellian
consequences that it carried [*sic*]. A professor of an American University

General Strike. This is the kernel of M. Sorel's contribution to Syndicalist theory, and it has had such surprising applications in fact that one may be justified in examining its relations to pragmatism at some length.

In the first place let us note briefly the nature of the General Strike, reserving a more detailed consideration of its implications for later. In Syndicalist theory generally, the General Strike has been conceived as the means by which society will pass from capitalism to socialism; it is the catastrophic revolution of the Marxian prophecy; and it has been put before the C. G. T. at its Congress in Tours by M. Guerard as long ago as 1896: [5] "The conquest of political power is a chimera . . ." he said by way of preface. "Partial strikes fail because the workingmen become demoralized under the intimidation of the employers protected by the government, and succumb. The general strike will last a short while and its repression will be impossible; as to intimidation, it is still less to be feared." The reasons which M. Guerard offered for this last statement are particularly interesting in view of the character the General Strike assumes as a myth. In the latter case it is left purposely as indeterminate in character as possible, in order that it may partake of the true character of myths as opposed to intellectualistic utopias. But M. Guerard, as a practical man, felt it necessary to go into detail as to the probable success of the program he was putting before French labor. He felt that intimidation by the employers and repression by the government would alike be rendered impossible by the fact that the strike

has recently written, as a matter of fact, that pragmatism is an exaggerated individualism authorizing every extravagant caprice. . . . He compares its destiny to that of the Epicureanism which in the hands of Epicurus had originally nothing offensive about it." One wonders whether the doctrines M. Sorel derives from pragmatism are "Machiavellian consequences" drawn "*with good right*" from his newly adopted philosophy, and whether they, too, like the later developments of Epicureanism, might not have something offensive to the genial and tolerant spirit of James.

[5] Louis Levine, *Syndicalism in France*, quoted p. 82 *et seq.* This study, revised under the title, *The Labor Movement in France*, remains the most complete and accurate exposition of the origins and early history of the Syndicalist movement, as an actual labor movement. The modern literature on actual Syndicalism is of enormous extent. See the bibliographies in Cole's *The World of Labour* and *infra*, p. 244, note 1. The modern aspects of the movement are best gathered from C. W. Pipkin, *The Idea of Social Justice*, which contains an extensive analysis of social legislation and literature in both France and England.

would be general, extending over the entire country, whereas the army would be scattered and dispersed. He even went into such minutiæ as the probable difficulties of the army in guarding the railroads. There were 39,000 kilometres of railway lines, and only 300,000 soldiers at most; that made one soldier to every 130 meters—palpably a very difficult task! "The General Strike," he concluded, "will be the revolution, peaceful or not."

M. Sorel's conception of the General Strike is a very different one. For him it simply suffices that the idea of a General Strike as the means to the Marxian revolution exists widely as a belief which gives the proletariat courage and the will to revolt. In common with all the beliefs of a similar nature which have inspired men to sacrifice and even to martyrdom, it is mythical in its character, and not to be tested by critical analysis. The pragmatic essence of his thought follows a reasoning which may perhaps be put in something like the form of James' "faith-ladder" of inferences, by which men actually proceed to a determination.

As a general proposition from which to start, we may say that intellectualism and the "scientific" logic which it uses lead us only to the barren reconstruction of reality in the skeletons of concepts, which are slain, so far as the living reality is concerned, in the making. For this proposition we may thank M. Bergson, as well as for the corollary that intuition is the only means of laying hold upon the fugitive essence of truth. Upon this base M. Sorel's propositions are raised, about like this:

(1) The pragmatic test of truth is that which the historian must apply; what "History" (taken in the almost mystic sense given it by Labriola) has rewarded by successful survival may be taken as true.

(2) Belief in myths has strengthened races and nations and sects to acts of sublime heroism and enabled them to conquer.

(3) These myths were true, historically speaking, because of their survival value.

(4) The only consideration justly applicable to the General Strike Myth is: Does it, or can it, grip the proletarian imagination with the force of a great myth?

(5) All other questions, such as whether the General Strike can succeed in furnishing a positive basis for the new order, and

by what provisions, are meaningless ideologies. The future must be left to the *élan vital*. Science only pretends to provide, it really "has no way of foreseeing".[6]

It was in no small degree due to the fact that William James, too, had made war on the *"scientisme"* which pretends to predict the future course of events, that M. Sorel joins forces with him.

"People who take seriously what are commonly called the moral and political sciences owe great thanks to William James for the important part he took in the struggle waged against the servants of *scientisme* by the philosophers endowed with robust common sense. . . . *Scientisme* corresponds too exactly to the magic needs of the popular imagination ever to disappear . . . [but] if to-day someone still dares to boast the services which a sociology would be able to render coming generations, a sociology in which the doctors seek to *know* how the general lines of the past are organized with a view to foreseeing the future forms of civil order—which suit [their] present aspirations, why really cultivated people have about the same consideration for such an up-to-date scientist as they have for a compiler of almanacs." [7]

M. Sorel's Romanticism, it will appear, has about it the forced note of the thoroughly disillusioned intellectualist who distrusts

[6] The statement that "science has no way of foreseeing" occurs, paradoxically enough, in the work of M. Sorel's own "prophetic period," *L'Avenir socialiste des syndicats*, p. 54. After this work (1904), M. Sorel casts off the rôle of prophet and adopts that of Myth-maker, refusing to give utopian specifications as to the future course of society, beyond *der Tag*.

[7] *De l'utilité du pragmatisme*, pp. 1-2. For his *anti-scientisme*, cf. also pp. 38, 41 *et seq.*, and the chapter *"Observations sur la science grecque,"* *op. cit.*, especially, and in *Réflexions*, pp. 53, 203, *et seq.* The method of science is absolutely inapplicable to Myths. One who preaches Myths is *"à l'abri de toute réfutation"* (p. 49). Socialism is necessarily obscure and mystic (Bergsonian, one might say), but "one may say that this obscurity is only scholastic". The intuition can seize the Myth readily enough: "it [the necessary obscurity of Socialism] in no wise prevents it from being easy to represent the proletarian movement in a manner complete, exact, and striking, by the great construction that the proletarian soul has conceived in the course of social conflicts, and that may be called the General Strike. It must always be borne in mind that this perfection in the mode of its representation would vanish in a moment if one attempted to resolve the General Strike into a sum of historical details; *it is necessary to take it entire* [to swallow it whole?] *and undivided, and to think of the passage from capitalism to socialism as a catastrophe whose process escapes description"* (p. 217)—my italics. This is, in good sooth, very much like that ineluctable quality of experience itself, with which Mr. Dewey has made so much play (*Essays in Experimental Logic*, p. 9 *et seq.*, and in *Experience and Nature*, Chap. 1.).

reason on rational grounds. Proudhon he acknowledges as his master; and he has something of Proudhon's critical pessimism that escapes itself by transports of enthusiasm for the virtues of the men of the Revolution, and for instinctive revolt in general. Proudhon in *De la Justice dans la Révolution et dans l'Eglise* had weighed his France in the balance and found her wanting.

"France has lost her morals [he lamented]. From critique to critique we have arrived at this sad conclusion: that the just and the unjust, in which we formerly thought ourselves possessed of some discernment, are terms of convention, vague and indeterminable; that all these words—Right, Duty, Morality, Virtue, etc., about which pulpit and school make so much fuss, only serve to cover pure hypotheses, vain utopias, undemonstrable prejudices; that thus the practice of life, directed by I know not what human respect, by conventions, is an arbitrary bond." [8]

Yet Proudhon turned to the "clear conception of Justice of the men of the Revolution" as the basis of that *foi juridique*

[8] Proudhon, *op. cit.*, quoted by Sorel, *Réflexions*, p. 332. Justice, in particular, is dissolved into a mere bourgeois and intellectualistic concept by M. Sorel (*cf.* Lenin's famous "Democracy is a mere bourgeois superstition"). He notes that Pascal had penetrated the absurdity of a *lex naturæ*, as a system of law founded on a set of principles revealed by divine Reason to mankind: "Three degrees elevation of the pole upsets all jurisprudence, a meridian decides truth ; in a few years of use fundamental laws are changed ; law has its epochs ; the entry of Saturn into the Lion marks for us the beginning of some crime. A fine justice that a stream may bound ! . . . They say that we must go back to the fundamental and primitive laws of the State of Nature that an unjust custom has abolished. That is a gamble sure to lose all ; nothing is just on those scales."

The resultant state of ignorance as to what *is* just leads us, Pascal said, to fall back on what is customary—an anti-intellectualistic tendency worth nothing : What is customary is what has had force to survive. So the father of French anti-intellectualism set about the work his legitimate heirs have carried on, linking up justice to force, and showing the vassalage that puts it on its knees before might. "Justice is subject to dispute, force is easily recognizable and indisputable. So we have not been able to give force to justice, because force contradicted justice and declared that it was force that was just. And thus, not being able to make what was just strong, we have made that which was strong just." (*Pensées*, Fragments 294, 297, 299, 309, 312, ed. Brunschvicg, partially quoted by Sorel, p. 26 *et seq.*).

The incurably religious soul of the great mystic took refuge in the Justice of God. Positivism has no such refuge, and rests in the justice of Force, while Sorel's Romanticism comes to rest in the justice of Violence. His friend, the Italian sociologist V. Pareto, who thinks social sciences possible, proposes as his method the finding experimentally of non-logical "residues" in human institutions which are the basis of all attempts at "derivations" in every society. See *Sociologia Generale* (Three volumes, 1923).

in which he placed the hopes of social salvation. Similarly M. Sorel, after becoming disgusted with the proletariat for its spineless acceptance of capitalism, (on more than one occasion announcing his intention of leaving off his reflections on violence if others were going to do nothing but reflect, too)—apparently was so heartened by the Russian Revolution and the unstinted use of violence by the Bolshevik dictators that he issued a fourth edition of his *Réflexions* in 1919, with a very interesting *"Plaidoyer pour Lénine"* appended, of which more later.

A very important connection between pragmatism and violence for M. Sorel is that pragmatism opens up to him the philosophy of the American people whom he had previously praised as the only really heroic race in modern times capable of favorable comparison with the ancient and piratical Greeks. In all his writings—and he has been fairly prolific, even for an anti-intellectualistic *intellectuel*—M. Sorel has drawn attention to the commendable features of American life, as they were disclosed to him through a remarkable work on American morals and social habits, by M. de Rousiers.[9] Time and time again he quotes with approval some confirmatory evidence from this work to bear out his idea of what a properly behaved capitalistic society should be like. The stratification of society is what an orthodox Marxian has the right to expect: here are the hard-faced captains of industry ruthlessly grinding the faces of the poor, on the one side, and on the other are the workers, made increasingly class-conscious by the pitilessly conducted industrial warfare. One can expect great things in the way of violence from a people which has shown itself so handy with what M. Sorel eulogizes in Lynch law,[10] an institution in the national life for which he finds nothing but praise. Furthermore there is

    [9] P. de Rousiers, *La Vie américaine*, a Frenchman's impressions of America, not wanting in psychological insight into the economic motives of American society, but stamped with the characteristic French attitude that is powerless to see any of the larger background of idealism, to which de Tocqueville almost alone among his compatriots has had the perspicacity to do real justice, in the American character. Perhaps one ought now to add (1927) M. André Siegfried's *America Comes of Age*.
    [10] The pragmatic realism of the Americans is shown by the fact that they "regard the *jus gladii* . . . as imposed so imperiously by nature of things that they accept it even under the form of Lynch law" (*De l'utilité du pragmatisme*, p. 75). *Cf.* Mr. Waldo Frank's *Our America*, in which pragmatism is related to the same tendencies. Mussolini is an outspoken admirer and even an imitator of these "American" traits.

native to the American character, perhaps from its pioneer origins, the altogether praiseworthy temper of risk and adventure necessary to embark on such ventures as M. Sorel has in mind for society: "The Yankees not only 'consent to live on possibilities'," notes Mr. Sorel (quoting James), "but they even seek out the hazardous in their enterprises."[11]

So it is largely because pragmatism offers him a new point of approach to the problem of discrediting the false intellectualism which he had clearly discerned all along as the enemy of the sublime and the freely heroic, and as the friend of calculation and rationalism, that M. Sorel offers to enlist himself as a disciple of William James. He himself is like a disillusioned Mephistopheles counseling the pleasures of activity to the Faust-spirit of the age, and not at all the honest romanticist that was James. But his doctrine is romanticist, and his perception of the development of James' doctrine shows how the inherent determinism of a pragmatism which tries to pass beyond this romanticism into scientific description is sure to appear.

For it is always well to remember that M. Sorel, although he professes the creed of violent revolution, is still a Marxian, with the conviction that capitalism carries fatally within its own nature the seeds of its destruction. His conception of "artificial nature" is very interesting from this aspect: the mechanism of modern industry and the mechanism of the physical sciences are analogous in being the forms under which we handle this artificial nature. "The former furnish economic utilities under the hands of skilful workers, whereas the latter makes laws appear to him who knows how to interrogate them; but this difference of social employment cannot conceal from us the systematic identity of these two means of operation [*moyens de travail*]." Moreover, "the artificial nature of the *savants* and that of the producers are equally submitted to these revolutions which overturn every few years the finest contemporary inventions." These revolutions, like the Marxian catastrophe, are the facts, and the proper pragmatic method would be to proceed from them to scientific description, not from description in its fantastically ideological "scientific" form back to "historic creations". He reproaches James with having been misled in this respect by

[11] *De l'utilité du pragmatisme*, note, p. 20.

allies like M. Jules H. Poincaré, for the scientists who follow the ideological method miss the true determinism of history, or as M. Sorel puts it, "they can't come to the comprehension that history can explain itself historically; pragmatism is at one with the historic materialism of Marx".[12]

In order to sustain the thesis that his own interpretation of pragmatism is the correct one, he begins with the following declaration: "In this book there will be little enough question of the positions held by William James [les thèses organisées]; I shall set myself the task of treating some problems whose importance is universally recognized in the spirit of pragmatism; it is only in re-thinking, in a European brain, the philosophy of William James that one can give it the fecundity, the force, and the sureness of application that we exact of every classic doctrine." (Shades of the long-suffering James!) The proper method to follow in this interpretation would be, according to an earlier dictum of M. Sorel's which he repeats with some edification, "to learn pragmatism pragmatically", or as he had said earlier: "The true method to follow in order to discover the defects, the insufficiencies and the errors of any considerable philosophy, consists in criticizing it after its own proper principles." [13]

But instead of applying pragmatism to those concrete social ends by which its fruits could be tested pragmatically, the rest of the book is devoted largely to historical and critical "Observations on Greek Science", on "Experience in Modern Physics", and to a detailed "Critique of *Creative Evolution*" and M. Bergson's theories, with a final chapter on "Renan and

---

[12] *Ibid.*, p. 85 and note. M. Sorel has pointed out, however, the aptness of pragmatism to the democratic optimism in *"les forces novatrices"* of the American civilization to which the philosophy is indigenous (p. 168 *et seq.*). He thinks, with a good deal of justification, that the adventurous spirit of the Yankees finds its expression in pragmatism because that doctrine is "full of confidence in the *'forces mystérieuses de l'histoire'* " (p. 172). As a Marxian, he has faith in a particular form of the same myth, the degeneration of capitalist society.

[13] *Insegnamenti sociali della economia contemporanea*, p. 89. He had written in an article in the *Revue de métaphysique et de morale*, Sept., 1910: "Philosophy should renounce the pretence of bringing solutions. . . . A philosophy is only valuable by reason of the *results that it provokes indirectly*. . . . In a word, a philosophy is only valuable as a means of favoring invention." This was true pragmatic doctrine, in advance of any conscious conversion.

the Theology of Saint Sulpice", in the course of which even the
spirit of James's pragmatism vanishes utterly.

It happens, however, that all unconsciously M. Sorel has had a
practical application of pragmatic romanticism to syndicalist
problems before his very eyes—one which has been receiving for
some time a very searching pragmatic test. He had given a most
striking exhortation, in the spirit of his interpretation of the
"Will to Believe", to French and Italian Syndicalism, urging
the necessity of creating an heroic "Myth": the catastrophic
regeneration of society through the General Strike—a sublime
fanaticism of violence to revitalize the sick soul of Europe. The
"Myth" was already a stock-in-trade of the revolutionary Syndicalism which had captured the C. G. T. in congress after congress.[14] It had been preached by M. Berth, Griffuelhes, Pouget
and other disciples of the more rather than less anarchistic
branch of Syndicalism which Pelloutier had organized as the
real beginning of the C. G. T.[15] Lagardelle, as M. Bouglé said
in his *Syndicalisme et Démocratie,* had "furnished the theme for
young socialism, syndicalist and revolutionary", in his war-cry:
"Duel to the death between socialism and democracy." [16] The
same anti-democratic tendency characterized the syndicalism of
Panunzio and Mantica in Italy, and to a large degree the dominant attitude of Mussolini's youthful rebellion against the milk-
and-water social democracy of his own party. It explains the
later incoherence and impotence of Italian syndicalism when
it had the possibility of capturing political power. It distrusted
democratic means of success and yet democracy blocked its way
toward real grounds for revolution. Democracy was championed
by the Catholic social democratic or Popolare Party led by Don

---

[14] See Levine, *op. cit.,* note 5, *supra.* It has been noted and expatiated
upon at length by Cole, *World of Labour,* Russell, *Proposed Roads to Freedom,* M. Challaye, *Le syndicalisme révolutionnaire et le syndicalisme ré-
formiste* (1909), M. L. Jouhaux, *Le syndicalisme français* (1913), M. G.
Guy-Grand, *La philosophie syndicaliste,* and a host of others. A useful
bibliography of the older Syndicalist literature is given by Cole, *op. cit.,* and
of the more modern by R. L. Mott, "The Political Theory of Syndicalism,"
Political Science Quarterly, Vol. XXXVII, no. 1, March, 1922. The most
important works of recent date are M. Jouhaux's *Le syndicalisme et le C.
G. T.* (1920), M. E. Berth's *Les derniers aspects du socialisme moderne*
(1922), M. Maxime Leroy, *Les techniques nouvelles du syndicalisme* (1921).
See Pipkin, *op. cit.*
[15] *Cf.* Cole and Levine for the history of Syndicalism, *op. cit., supra.*
[16] Bouglé, *op. cit.,* p. 96.

Sturzo. It was repudiated by Sorel's followers who believed in an *élite* like that expounded by Pareto in *Les Systèmes socialistes*. Democracy is the bog in which the proletariat remains stuck fast. By reducing all men to an equal fineness, as if they had been ground by the mills of the gods, democracy "mixes the classes" into a single class, and takes away the only protection men find against economic slavery: the right to protection through association. Therefore, down with democracy, at its best a vulgar tyranny of the majority, at its worst, a hypocritical subterfuge, masking from sight the chains they .wear! The way out: the General Strike. Destroy the old, and the *élan vital* of living will take care of the new.

The Syndicalist doctrine M. Sorel seized upon to turn into Myth, a motive force for that belief which he saw with James that men must have in order to act, but which he went about creating in the same rationalistic spirit that had characterized his reinterpretation of the "Will to Believe". It is evident from M. Sorel's entire writings that he "thinks too much" ever to be anything but an *intellectuel* in the labor movement himself. "If one reflects too much, one never does anything," [17] says M. Griffuelhes, very aptly. But although M. Sorel quite evidently does not believe in the possibility of his social Myth's attaining anything but mythical reality, he has, true to the temperament of the man of thought, an exaggerated idea of the value of "heroic action". His effort, really, was to get people to believe in Violence and the mythical Strike because he thought it would be good for them to do so. Mr. R. L. Mott, in discussing "The Political Theory of Syndicalism" has noticed that: "In general the pragmatic test for goodness is accepted, and the attempts of philosophers to generalize regarding its nature are discountenanced." [18]

---

[17] Griffuelhes, *Bibliothèque du mouvement social*, p. 57.

[18] Mott, *op. cit.*, *Pol. Sci. Qu.*, Vol. XXXVII, No. 1, pp. 26-27; *cf.* also E. Dimnet, "Syndicalism and its Philosophy," *Atlantic Monthly*, Jan., 1913; and E. C. Fairchild, "Syndicalism and its Philosophy," *English Review*, Oct., 1919. See the extensive analysis and bibliography in C. W. Pipkin, *op. cit.*, for later titles.

Carl Schmitt in his *Die Geistgeschichtliche Lage des heutigen Parlamentarismus* has noted that while parliamentarism rests on "a relative rationalism" (*cf.* note under title of this chapter), syndicalism and Fascism both make their appeal to the irrational basis of a force that cannot be balanced or divided as can constitutional powers. His genetic treatment of Sorel's

The foundations of the Myth of the General Strike, then, are the same that the cloudy spirit of Pascal laid down in that famous wager on the existence of the deity; the truth of the belief can only be tested by the results it brings in; believe in God because you can't lose by believing in Him. Exactly the same *raisons de cœur* underlie James' "Will to Believe"; and it may be in each case the counsel of romanticism is equally unproductive of pragmatic results. Faith is not to be attained in any such fashion. Fanaticism is, though, even to the point of martyrizing those who do not accept your uneasy "faith". Renan noted with cynical insight that Giordano Bruno felt he must die to offer the supreme proof of martyrdom to the sincerity of his convictions, while Galileo submitted to the Holy Office of the Inquisition in the calm certainty of his scientific rightness—"and yet it does!" he added, after formally denying that the earth moved about the sun. "One is only a martyr for the sake of things about which one is not really sure," Renan concludes. There is something of the same spirit of fanaticism, *a tergo*, in beliefs founded upon myths which one wills to believe. The very insecurity of the conviction makes it necessary to "prove" it by forcing it upon others.

But the labor movement in France was fertile soil for the seeds of violence, and the Latin temperament of the Italian worker even more productive of the rank weeds of anarchy, their quickly sprung crop. M. Sorel himself has consistently avoided the pragmatic test for his myths, and has warned his disciples against the querulous attempt to test a "Myth" in terms of its actual consequences.[19]   In his despite, however, the C. G. T. and Italian Syndicalism hastened to a proof of the pudding—without finding it very much to their liking in the eating. No *élite* appeared to lead the workers, but the *élan vital* did produce, in Italy most notably, men with the master morality who dedicated their cudgels to disciplining labor, offering it a controlled syndicalism of a quite mythical nature.

One has to set M. Sorel's doctrines in their proper Latin background before it seems credible that enough importance should

Marxian doctrines and their relations to Proudhon and Bakunin is especially interesting : pp. 53-65.

[19] *Cf. supra*, note 6; also p. 33 *et seq., op. cit.*

have been attached to them to give them to the test of act. Mr. G. D. H. Cole, in *The World of Labour*, refused to take the General Strike Myth seriously; he could not believe that the real meaning of French Syndicalism was to be had "in copying the opinions of M. Sorel out of one book into another", because he believed, with great justice, that the C. G. T. was more opportunistic than romanticist.[20] He was prepared, though, even before the war, for revolutionary and communistic developments in the Italian labor movement, both because of its lack of stable and responsible organization, and because of the suitability of M. Sorel's doctrine to so excitable and ill-educated a proletariat as the Italian industrialized population comprised.[21]

Possibly one must have seen popular demonstrations in the Latin countries to appreciate the ease with which violence breaks out, and the general suitability of M. Sorel's doctrine to the *milieux* for which it is intended. It was my fortune once to watch the May First demonstration of labor in Paris. It was in the armistice period, 1919, and the threat of Bolshevism was being taken seriously. From the top of the big German "Bertha" that pointed its captive nose up beside the Obelisk in the Place de la Concorde—as if it were still ready to hurl defiance at the heart of Paris and at the Idealist in the Hotel Crillon opposite who was trying to create a Peace—from that point of vantage, I watched the Red Flag go hurly-burly down the Rue Royale, breaking the thick cordons of the *agents de ville* and the special police. *"Debout les damnés de la terre"* the marchers sang, hoarse voices lifting the *Internationale* as once they must have raised the Revolutionary hymns, gathering to pull down the Bastille. The mob debouching from the Place de la Concorde met others coming from the Place de l'Opéra to form a junction at the Madeleine. There had been "incidents": word flew about that barricades were going up in parts of the city, that there was fighting going on at the Place de la Bastille, that the Red Flag had been raised. The crowd swayed and surged uncertainly, its voice rising to a steady roar. The street was packed,

[20] Cole, *op. cit.*, p. 127.
[21] Among the important sociologists Sr. Vilfredo Pareto, a great friend of M. Sorel's, had in his *Traité de Sociologie Générale* (Paris, 1919), and his *Fatti e Teoria, Transformazione della Democrazia* (1919), prepared the way for Fascist theory.

and the herd was beginning to trample some under, it almost seemed, in order to make room for the others.

Suddenly there was a sharp bugle blast, and a series of staccato commands from the cavalry which had been waiting, massed along the open Place on the side of the Tuileries, as if in memory of the direction in which the mob had turned its wrath in the days of the Commune. The squadrons began to move, forming with admirable order and in compact array to clear the streets. The crowd saw. There was a moment of dead silence, then pandemonium. The troopers moved steadily forward, sabers drawn, faces set. Incredibly a way opened for the first of them; the crowd seemed to melt back, to shrink like butter under the direct sun. Then the possibility of giving way further ended and people began to be trampled by the cavalry mounts. Some began to seize bridles and try to force the horses back. The troopers used the flats of their swords. An officer ordered the red flag to be seized. There was a confused fight, and a great outcry—a trooper or two knocked or dragged from their horses, and some of the marchers with sabre wounds. The crowd was beginning to feel the thrill of combat run through it.

I watched from my post on the captive Boche gun, wondering whether I was seeing the beginning of another Quatorze Juillet—wondering, too, I confess, whether I had chosen a healthful spot of observation, and whether an American officer would be reckoned as a neutral—when the situation suddenly dissolved into pure comedy. From somewhere appeared the *pompiers,* more resplendent than the Greeks before Troy, or even the *Garde Républicaine* on a fête day—with their helmets agleam, and their business-like fire hoses playing powerful streams into the midst of the mob. It was literally washed away—spluttering, still full of incoherent wrath, but divided against itself by the Gallic laughter of those who were not being drenched at those who were. Who knows? Had Versailles been protected by *pompiers,* and had all the water in its fountains been brought into play, the Bourbons might have had nothing to forget, nor indeed, anything to learn. Alas for the stupidity of the *ancien régime* and its Swiss Guard, or perhaps their misfortune in not having survived to the day when water might be projected by steam-pressure, and when the sense of humor of Demos had been rendered automatically susceptible of stimulation by episodes which suggest the American "Movie Comic"!

At any rate I left with the feeling that the annual May First General Strike had in it the possibility of becoming, under favorable circumstances, something more than a mere demonstration. The same opinion seems to have led the C. G. T. to attempt the pragmatic test of the Myth in May, 1920, the very next year. M. Duguit, the distinguished French jurist, has summed up the attempt in these words:

"In France, in the month of May, 1920, the *Confédération Générale du Travail* attempted to provoke a Bolshevist revolution by launching first a general strike of the railroads, then a series of assault-waves in succession, a strike of the united transport services, a strike of the metallurgists, a strike of seamen and dockers. But the attempt was a lamentable failure. The French conscience revolted. The entire nation rose and fell in line against the enemy within, as it had fallen into line in August, 1914, against the enemy without, and it nailed the Bolsheviks on the spot, just as it had nailed the Boches on the banks of the Marne." [22]

That was the ordeal of the pragmatically taught Myth, tested in its own pragmatic terms. According to the *Temps* of May 9, 1921, the revolutionary control of the *syndicats* had suffered so great a blow that in the principal railway *syndicat* involved, eighty per cent of the membership had withdrawn within the year. There was a notable change in the attitude of the C. G. T. toward the Third International in the same year, one which resulted in a serious split within the ranks of the C. G. T., the power passing out of the hands of the most revolutionary element, and into the hands of those who refused any longer to do the bidding of Moscow.

The pragmatic test of the Revolution based upon the General Strike Myth which had been preached to them was applied even more thoroughly by the *Rivoluzione Mancata* of the Italian syndicalists. M. Sorel's teachings had proved very congenial indeed to the leaders of the Italian movement, who had, according to an Italian member of Parliament, "preached violence,

[22] *Souveraineté et liberté*, p. 189.

revolution, and a quantity of other things; but, on the other hand, did not give themselves the trouble of preparing the proletariat technically or politically for the coming revolution." [23] The result was a two-years interim of strikes and utter social disorganization. "The maximalist movement," says the same observer, "revealed itself to be one of incoherent verbosity, but essentially and typically impotent. Revolutionary in word, yet estranged from the economic reality of the country, it demonstrated its incapacity to prepare a rational movement, alienated the sympathies of the very middle classes in whom lay the only possibility and the indispensable elements of the success of a revolution, because of the fact that they furnished the technicians for all industry and commerce." In September the famous episode of the occupation of the factories occurred, just a few months after the complete failure of the C. G. T. in France.

All the elements which M. Sorel had thought necessary to the success of proletarian violence were present. The government, largely Socialist in its composition, behaved with the poltroonery which the Myth attributes to those in power, to the despised bourgeoisie, that is. But in spite of the fact that the workers were permitted to retain unmolested possession of the factories, the General Strike and the Social Revolution which was to accompany it simply "fizzled out".[24] The factories fell idle, because there were no skilled technicians to direct their operation. The "aristocracy of manual labor," inspired by the uncalculating fervor of the producers' morality of which M. Sorel had spoken, came to an abrupt halt before the problem of credit and of exchange. They accepted an increase of wages as a "sop," and vague promises of joint control in the metallurgical industry in which the chief operations of

[23] *Il Fascismo*, anonymous "*Deputato al Parlamento*" (*La Modernissima*, Milan, 1922), pp. 15-16. This political document contains a very good bibliography of early writings on Fascismo in French and Italian. Sorel is admitted by Mussolini to have been one of his great spiritual masters, along with Nietzsche, William James, and Machiavelli. Mussolini has been, after Lenin, the aptest pupil in the manipulation of a Myth.

[24] Ex-premier Bonomi, in his excellent study of the development of Fascism (*From Socialism to Fascism*, 1925) holds that the government refrained from interfering in order to let the syndicalists discredit themselves by unopposed failure. William Bolitho in *Italy Under Mussolini* (1925) attributes even more Machiavellian motives to Giolitti.

the seizers of factories had occurred and then subsided. The bubble of the General Strike Myth had to be pricked again, and Fascismo had found a *raison d'être*. As an observer of the pre-Matteoti phase of Fascism in Italy, I could not in 1923 wonder greatly at its acceptance by Italians.

But M. Sorel, for all his pragmatism, has insisted that the Myth is not to be tested in that way. That is the sort of condemnation which is passed on Violence by English Socialism and milksop parliamentarianism. It is English and Belgian Socialism, and that of Jaurès in France and Kautsky in Germany, against which the special wrath of the *Mouvement Socialiste* is stored up—the Socialism which has recruited "Reformist" leaders who straightway desert it when the chance of power comes their way: "Make an insurrection when we feel ourselves solidly enough organized to conquer the State, that's what M. Viviani and the *attachés* of his office understand," says M. Sorel in disgust at their want of the sublime: "but proletarian violence which has no such end can only be treated as folly and the odious caricature of revolt. Do everything that you please, but don't break the butter plate!" [25]

The character of the Myth can never appear to such pusillanimity. On the contrary, "the men who share in great social movements, represent their approaching action under the form of battle-images, assuring the triumph of their cause. I propose to call these constructions, whose recognition holds so much importance for historians, *myths;* the general strike of the syndicalists and the catastrophic revolution of Marx are myths. I have given as remarkable examples of myths, those which were constructed by primitive Christianity, by the Reformation, by the Revolution, by the Mazzinians; I wish to show that it is not necessary to analyze such systems of images as one decomposes a thing into its elements, that it is necessary to take them *en bloc* as historical forces, and that it is above all necessary to guard against comparing the accomplished facts with the representations which had been accepted before acting." [26]

He might now add Bolshevist World Revolution and Fascist Imperialism to this category.

[25] Sorel, *Réflexions sur la violence*, 4ᵇᵐᵉ ed. (1919), p. 32.
[26] *Ibid.*, p. 33.

The Myth, then, partakes of the nature of Plato's "noble lies"; its object is to stir men to the heroic and the sublime, to carry them "out of themselves," and it cannot be justly submitted to a "detailed critique" by such intellectualistic critics as "accumulate objections against its practical possibilities." It is a belief, and its justification is the effect it has upon men's lives. It is, in pragmatic terms, the result of willing, not of logical analysis. James himself had said, "Reality falls in passing into conceptual analysis; it mounts in living its own individual life—it buds and burgeons, changes and creates." And it is the romanticist test M. Sorel insists upon applying to his Myth, rather than the Instrumentalist test of Dewey's pragmatism. Good Catholics ask themselves no such questions about the exact nature of their Myth, he insists. They are never discouraged by the hardest trials because they represent life as one perpetual battle between Satan and the army of Christ in which they serve. Let the workers but embrace the faith of the General Strike and they will be preserved similarly from the black doubts that come with failure.

The greatest cross M. Sorel himself has to bear is the accusation that is sometimes made against him that his theory of myths is no more than "a false translation" which turns the real opinions of the revolutionary Syndicalists into a mere "intellectualistic sophism." On the contrary, he maintains, he "wishes to get rid of the whole 'control' of the intellectualistic philosophy" because that can only embarrass the historian who follows it.[27] As an anti-intellectualist and an historian he reproaches Renan for having shown too much respect for that "scientific opinion" which his historian's insight should have shown him was worthless. The sacrifices of the Napoleonic soldier to the glory of his *"épopée éternelle,"* of the Roman to the conquest of the world, of the Christian to his other-worldly faith—these are things which no intellectualistic philosophy may explain. History shows such faith rewarded by success, and it is a faith that does not go with intellectualism.

Renan it was who said this, yet could not see the escape from intellectualism through the creation of a sublime myth. "To have seen [the aimlessness of human affairs which he had said

[27] *Ibid.,* p. 35.

were almost without seriousness or precision] is a great result
for philosophy, but it is an abdication of every active rôle. The
future is to those who are not disabused."[28] One is tempted to
say that M. Sorel is so honestly convinced of this that he sets
about "abusing" the minds of the proletariat in order that they
may have the future. As against the upholders of a false
"*scientisme*" in human affairs he sets up the "Right to Believe"
in a Myth of one's own choosing. This Myth would lose its
moral and motive power if it were turned into an Utopia, an
intellectualistic construction. It partakes of the nature of in-
finity and of Bergson's *vraie* or *pure durée*, because it is "not a
description of things," but "an expression of the will." It will
not be satisfied, like Utopias, by granting it parts of its wants,
because its wants are not formulated. They simply "lead men
to prepare themselves for a combat to destroy what exists."[29]
The future will take care of itself: we have the assurance of the
prophet for it. Is it not written in *Das Kapital* that the working
class is being prepared for its sublime rôle by the development of
a new morality, engendered by that capitalistic régime which "is
borne, by intimate laws of its own nature, in a road which con-
ducts the present world to the gates of the future world, with the
extreme rigor that governs the evolution of organic life?"[30]

The only fear is that reformist Socialism may lull the world
into apathetic sleep. The mediocrity of the *haute-bourgeoisie*
alone serves to make that a danger. Their sociologists preach
a doctrine of conservative mediocrity and humanitarianism,
seek to correct the abuses of capitalist economy in a way that
the Marxian doctrine of catastrophic social revolution could not
foresee, so that the Reformist Socialists actually seem to be
gaining power. "Two accidents alone, it seems, are capable of
arresting this movement," wrote M. Sorel in 1906; "a great foreign war which would be capable of refreshing their energies,
and which, in any case, would bring, without doubt, men into

[28] Sorel, *Réflexions sur la violence*, 4ᵃᵐᵉ ed. (1919), p. 38, quoting Renan.
[29] *Ibid.*, p. 46.
[30] *Ibid.*, p. 112. Along with the organic rigidity of the evolution of capital,
one may well remark that M. Sorel's idea of *devoir*, like that of M. Duguit,
is one of social solidarity. But as social solidarity is a contradiction of the
Marxian class struggle there can be no *devoir* until the bourgeoisie is sup-
pressed. Then, however, the worker will have an obligation to outdo himself
in production.—*Op. cit.*, p. 89; *cf.* "*La morale des producteurs*," p. 331.

power who had the will to govern; or a great extension of proletarian violence which would make the bourgeois see the revolutionary reality and would disgust them with the humanitarian
platitudes with which Jaurès puts them to sleep." [31]   The first
of these M. Sorel was bad enough prophet to consider improbable
when he wrote; so that he turns for hope to the second, which has
likewise proved his contention true in the outcome.   After the
Russian display of "revolutionary reality," he can hardly com-
plain that the bourgeoisie has gone to sleep and refused to accept
the Marxian challenge.   Smelling out Bolshevism has been the
principal occupation of the social alarmists in every country
since that time.   The United States deported all those "agitators" suspected of "red" tendencies, and the State Departments
of Justice secured a number of convictions under statutes aimed
at "criminal syndicalism."   His own France, possibly through the
advent to power of men with "the will to govern" during the
war, has dealt very hardly with revolutionary spirits among
the Communists, witness M. Marty, M. Cachin, M. Peri *et al.*,
who have recently seen something of the inside of French prisons.
And as for Italy?

In short, M. Sorel would find to-day very little need to counsel the laborer "to pay with black ingratitude the kindness of
those who wish to protect the workers, to oppose abuse to the
homilies of those who defend human brotherhood, and to reply
with blows to the advances of those who would propagate social
peace."   All this was for the sole end of keeping the bourgeoisie
class-conscious, and forcing it to maintain the rigor of the Marxian class-struggle, without which "chance is introduced, and the
future of the world is completely indeterminate." [32]   The answer to Communist tactics is, as Mr. Ramsay MacDonald has
again and again pointed out to British Labor, Fascism.

Anti-intellectualism's answer is set in terms it can understand:
Violence begets force, as anarchy begets despotism.   *"Tu l'as
voulu, Georges Dandin!"*   In Italy the reign of violence, the

---

[31] *Ibid.*, p. 110.   M. Sorel may have had good reason before his death in
1922 to exclaim with Hamlet, "Oh, my prophetic soul!"   This essay was
written before I learned of that unhappy event. The following studies have
since appeared: P. L. Perrin: *Les Idées sociales de G. Sorel* (1925) P. Caylis
(Alger), and Gaetan Pironi, *Georges Sorel* (1847-1922), Paris, 1925.
[32] Sorel, *op. cit.*, pp. 116-117.

seizure of the factories, then the anti-communist dictatorship in Bologna; the perpetual strikes and petty civil wars, then the Black Shirt enthroned; all through Central Europe, White Terrors succeeded the Red: Bela Kun, then the Whites. In that nightmare land of Russia, violence is maintained in power by force, in a fashion so glaringly tyrannical, so Erastian, and so thorough that it is hard to believe anyone ever found it necessary to preach for violence in order to revive the nobility of the sleeping savage in Europe. With Germany convulsed more than once since the War by threats of dictatorship, with Rivera, Bethlen, Pilsudski, and Mussolini in power, it is not needful to go back to a history earlier than that of the third decade of the twentieth century to watch Napoleon climb to power on the shoulders of the Directorate, again, or to see Repression swing its punishing axe over the neck of the Commune. Nor need M. Sorel, in his pragmatic preoccupations with history, have gone farther afield to learn the lesson his France could teach him as to the outcome of violence. In the contest between Myths, the *Machtsstaat* myth has swallowed instinctive Revolt as a rock-python might an adder. Even with the most Nietzschean will to worship power, and the sublimity of violent might, one must have the temperament of an ostrich and its mythical habits of hiding the head in order not to see, if one finds a mystic freedom for the proletariat in revolt. Those who have plans and who have the will to mastery are not backward about putting a leash upon the self-destructive power of proletarian violence. And no one drives harder than he who fears the steed he has tamed. Witness Signor Benito Mussolini.

The lesson has not been lost on those radicals of the labor movement who are more interested in its success than in furnishing a spectacle of sublime futility through Myth-worship, and who remember how short a step takes the sublime to the ridiculous. Mr. Robert Hunter, who is one of labor's most sympathetic partisans, published in 1919 a careful study of *Violence and the Labor Movement* in which he developed with overwhelming wealth of instances the obvious thesis that anarchism in all its degrees simply strengthens the reaction against which it is aimed, just as reaction tends to develop violence through repression and injustice. The disciples of the General Strike

Myth in America, the I. W. W., or Industrial Workers of the World, by advocating non-participation in the political life of the community, and by a concomitant policy of direct action and revolution, have simply placed the means of repression within the hands of government, and given its use through the "Criminal Syndicalism" Acts the support of public opinion. No one can expect the unorganized rabble of casual labor that constitutes the American Syndicalist movement to deal with labor problems in the frame of mind of the British Labour Party, or even that evinced by the cohorts of the late Mr. Samuel Gompers. Instinctive revolt and violence are natural to them. But it is fairly Mephistophelian to strengthen this hopeless anti-intellectualism by an intellectualistic Myth of violence, as many of the *intellectuels* of the movement have followed M. Sorel in doing.[33] American labor of the unskilled and unorganized type is sufficiently prone to violent protests to make it certain that their very real wrongs will not pass unnoticed. A Herrin massacre, a miners' war in West Virginia—these show a native tendency to take the law into their own hands or to have recourse to lawlessness which it needs no Myth to rouse.

The Syndicalist trend in the labor movement, so far as it tends to violence, is only a proof of the unreadiness of labor for any such mastery as the Myth has led them to expect. There is another significance in Syndicalism as it means the broad movement toward industrial organization by occupational groups, one that has been interpreted by a radical like Mr. Tannenbaum in America as conservative in its tendencies. It is the Syndicalism to which M. Duguit looks for a new juridical basis for a social organization, and of which Guild Socialism and kindred doctrines are theoretical expositions. How conservative a movement this may become may be seen in the "Fascist-Syndicalist" state which Mussolini, an ex-revolutionary of the extreme stamp, has now imposed upon Italy by his imperial will. The "associationist" character of modern society is the key to an understanding of its problems, nor can there be any mistaking the importance of the "group movement" in every field of social

[33] Haywood. W. D. (imprisoned in 1918 under war-time Criminal Syndicalism Act) and Bohn. F.. *Industrial Socialism*, an apologia for the I. W. W. See Brooks, J. G.. *American Syndicalism, the I. W. W.*, for a critical study, and Dr. P. Brissenden, *The I. W. W.*

activity—in religion, in art, in industry, and in politics. Society, that *Great Society* of which Graham Wallas has written
with such a comprehensive view, is being forced to develop what
he has called "Organizations" in order that the will and thought
of groups with a community of purpose may find expression,
and may carry weight against the dead inertia of our complex
and intricately balanced civilization.[34]

Said Mr. J. A. Penty, in *A Guildsman's Interpretation of
History:*

"The danger that confronts us is precisely the same as confronted France on the eve of the Revolution. It is the danger
that a popular though unconscious movement back to medievalism may be frustrated by intellectuals whose eyes are turned in
the opposite direction, and revolution be precipitated by the fact
that the instinctive impulse of the people, instead of being guided
into their proper channels where they would bear fruit a thou-
sandfold, would be brought into conflict with doctrinaire idealists
who believe in an economic evolution as it is not." [35]

That is an accurate enough description of what actually took
place in Russia. Graham Wallas, again, has pointed out that
the origins of the Russian revolution were largely instinctive
and in response to the blind push of revolt that says to swollen
hearts, "Everything is wrong. Destroy!" He has taken for
his illustration the use to which the word *stikhjyny* was put by
the people in describing their revolt: *stikhjyny* means, according to Mr. Julius West (from whose article in *The New Statesman* of May 5, 1918, Mr. Wallas gets this information) "elemental" or "intuitive." "One finds Bolshevik leaders," he says,
"justifying most of the things for which they are responsible
by the statement that they result from elemental forces. Revolution is a matter of these forces rather than of deliberate
organization."[36] And so it is, no doubt; but the control of revolutionary force passes into the hands of those with whom organization is a part of a larger plan—into the hands of Lenin

[34] G. Wallas, *op. cit.*, chapters on "Thought Organizations" and "Will
Organizations"; *cf.* E. Frankel, "Germany's Industrial Parliament," *Political
Science Quarterly*, Vol. XXXVII, no. 3, September, 1922.
[35] Penty, *op. cit.*, p. 299. *Cf.* an article on "The Problem of Control in
Medieval Industry," Austin P. Evans, *Political Science Quarterly*, Vol.
XXXVI, no. 4, Dec., 1921.
[36] *Our Social Heritage*, p. 249.

and Trotsky, and the All-Russian Executive of the Communist Dictatorship. The Mensheviks waited for the situation to shape itself, in accordance with the doctrines of Liberalism, and because of their general futility before the forces of violence which the Revolution had unleashed. The Bolsheviks, believers in a fatalistic and doctrinaire Marxism, had a plan and put it into execution. No doubt Robert von Müller was right had he been speaking of the Revolution itself in saying "Bolshevism is not really communism. It is the argument that men suffer, therefore act.[37] But Bolshevism passed quickly into the power and control of those who had definite, even fixed, ideas about the way in which men should act; and Bolshevism became communism.

M. Sorel himself has seen and approved the development of his Myth. Previously his Myth had been free from any ideology, in particular that of the State: "Proletarian violence changes the aspect of all the conflicts in the course of which one observes it; for it denies the force organized by the bourgeoisie, and aims at suppressing the State which forms its central kernel." [38]   In 1919 he had come to see the sublime in force, in the force of repression, as well as in the violence of revolt. It had been suggested by M. Paul Seippels, the Swiss publicist, that Lenin had no doubt derived his ideas of the efficacy of violence from M. Sorel. M. Sorel modestly disclaims any knowledge of such an influence—"but if it were true, I should be uncommonly proud of having contributed to the in-

[37] *Bolshevik und Gentleman* (1920). A brief but comprehensive description of the seizure of power in the Soviets is contained in P. H. Douglas, "Occupational vs. Proportional Representation," *American Journal of Sociology*, September, 1923. See also Michael Farbmann, *Russia in Revolution*.

[38] *Réflexions sur la violence*, p. 29; cf. the chapter on the *"Grève générale politique"* where M. Sorel makes some pertinent observations about a General Strike which simply aims at a change of masters—observations especially applicable to Russia to-day. All the bourgeois education has tended toward social solidarity, says M. Sorel (pp. 267-268) ; "all the revolutionary effort tends to the creation of *free men;* but the democratic rulers set themselves the mission of realizing the moral unity of France. This moral unity is the automatic discipline of producers who would be happy to work for the glory of their intellectual chiefs." (*Cf.* also, *Décomposition du Marxisme*, p. 53.) But to copy the democratic ideology of the state in this fashion would be to suffer defeat at the outset. "Better to know how to content itself [Syndicalism] for a while with feeble and chaotic organizations than to fall under the domination of syndicates which would copy the political forms of the bourgeoisie" (p. 268). The experience of the soviets and their powerlessness before Communist organization might be of some pragmatic value in weighing such a theory.

tellectual formation of a man who seems to me to be at the same time the greatest theorist that Socialism has had since Marx and a *chef d'État* whose genius recalls that of Peter the Great.

"At the moment when the Commune of Paris succumbed, Marx was writing a manifesto of the International, in which modern socialists are accustomed to search the most finished expressions of the political doctrines of the master. The speech made in May, 1918, by Lenin on the problems of the power of the soviets has not less importance than Marx's study on the civil war of 1871. It may be that the Bolsheviks will end by succumbing under the blows of the mercenaries engaged by the plutocracies of the Entente; *but the ideology of the new form of proletarian state will not perish* [my italics] ; it will survive in amalgamating itself with the myths which will borrow their subject matter from the popular accounts of the struggle sustained by the Republic of the Soviets against the coalition of great capitalist parties." [39]

M. Sorel, like Minever Cheevy, was born out of his time. He should have been a troubadour to sing the sublimity of feats of arms. Gone all that aversion to the power of the State, now that its control rests upon might established by violence. His appreciation of *tours de force* is really medieval and thoroughly in line with the romanticist pragmatism he has called in as an ally. Let the dubious go to William James's essay on "Great Men and their Environment." M. Lagardelle had put forward the basic principle of Syndicalism in a way which had formerly commanded M. Sorel's approval: "To-day men believe less and less in the creative force of the State and the magic of Parliamentarism. . . . It is the business of Syndicalism to be self-sufficient." [40] But with the transformation of the State from the organ of bourgeois poltroonery to communist might, even the ideology of the State assumes a value, and an imperishable one. M. Sorel accepts the State which the genius of Lenin

[39] *Reflexions*, pp. 442-443. Violence had been the god in whom M. Sorel had put his trust to prevent the erection of a State founded on force. Now that his god has forsaken him, he worships the conqueror, accepting the pragmatic test of history. During the war he became "an admirer of the Italian monarchy." See James Oneal, "Extremists who deserted" in "The Changing Fortunes of American Socialism," *Current History*, April, 1924.

[40] Quoted by Cole, *op. cit.*, p. 85.

has created, or at least preserved. In his own person he has fulfilled the cycle of the Myth; starting with a defense of anarchy he has wound up with a defense of despotism. But how could a politics founded on the sublime do anything else, in the presence of Lenin, moved dramatically across the world-stage by a *"mysticisme têtu et illuminé,"* [41] and the spectacle of Trotzky and his Red armies beating against the gates of Europe.

For all M. Sorel's refusal to turn his Myth into a Utopia by any specifications beyond its content of destruction, he was not entirely a stranger to the idea of social discipline, and he had eulogized repressive force before—as he does now in the entirety of his "Defence of Lenin"—in the persons of those epic figures of history whose morality had been the Master Morality of Nietzsche. [42] Indeed the morality of the proletariat, he agrees with Kautsky, is only to be reckoned in terms of the sublime. [43] In a very left-handed way this morality of the sublime is very much the same thing which M. Duguit, the jurist, talks of in terms of "social solidarity." For it becomes, when M. Sorel considers it in the setting of production proper to it, the morality of class solidarity, and it knows no laws save the realistic ones of fear and force. It is of course necessary to make the reservation that M. Sorel is consistently a Marxian in his insistence on class solidarity as opposed to social solidarity, and a Romanticist in his anti-intellectualism, while M. Duguit is, in his *solidarisme,* the complete Positivist, with a pragmatic outlook that is Instrumentalist throughout. That is, the sublime gets the emphasis of M. Sorel because of its mystic and heroic side. The realistic and organic sides of society, on the other hand, are most stressed by M. Duguit. But the fact both cling to is force or power. M. Sorel's sublimity is that of Nietzsche's superman and of proletarian might so ruled. M. Duguit's solidarity is that of force of economic needs. Mussolini has tried to marry the two in Fascist wedlock.

[41] Taken by Sorel (p. 452) from Etienne Antonelli's description of Lenin in *La Russie bolchéviste,* p. 272,—with the remarkable observation *"Cette formule n'est pas très claire"* (!). This from the creator of the Myth of Violence!

[42] *Cf. Réflexions,* especially pp. 322-323, 358-359.

[43] For a more moderate and very brilliant estimate of the moral claims of socialism see Fernando de los Rios, *El Sentido Humanista del Socialismo* (1926), Javier Morata, Madrid.

Yet how rude a difference there is between the class morality of producers which M. Sorel had predicted, and that which actually exists in the Russia which has risen out of the application of his Myth! He had compared the worker in the factories with the soldiers of the Revolution, and the artist, and he had found that under the Syndicalist régime of the future the worker would consider himself a moral person, freely abandoning all idea of exact recompense, striving only to pass all exactly measured production, and solicitous only to be exact in his craftsmanship. The springs of this idealistic morality of service, which would assure the social solidarity of the future could come from only one source: the General Strike Myth, whose motive power, once started, apparently was to go on "impassioning" the souls of the workers forever. "Violence, illuminated by the idea of the general strike," that was to be the syndicalist end: "All the old abstract dissertations on the future socialist régime become useless; we pass to the domain of real history, to the interpretation of facts, to the evaluations of an ethical order of the revolutionay movement." [44]

But when we have actually passed to "the domain of real history" our "interpretation of facts" can only lead us to one evaluation of the position of the worker in Russia. There, if anywhere, Syndicalism was expressed by the Soviet, the Myth by violence. The law offers the worker under Bolshevism its protection only so long as he supports the dictatorship; otherwise he may expect the summary judgment of the Cheka. In this respect he is hardly better off than the worker of Italy under Fascism. According to the charges Trotsky had levelled at Stalin's government, the worker under Bolshevism is quite as badly off as under Fascism. [45] He is forced in both cases to work longer hours, and to accept any pay he is given, and is, to all practical intents, a slave, and without the "wage slave's" little area of legal liberty. The worker's morality as a producer under Fascism is a slave's morality. How much better is it under Bolshevism? And this is not to reckon that considerable part of the population which Syndicalism ignores in theory, the peas-

---

[44] *Reflexions*, p. 389; *cf.* also p. 331 *et seq.*
[45] See Trotsky's charges as given in the *New York World*, November 20, 1927. For these charges in the *Pravda* he paid with exile.

ants. In practice they have made their individualistic claims felt in Russia, where their economic position is stronger than it is in Italy.

Stripped of its trappery of the sublime and the violent, M. Sorel's Syndicalism does offer to us, it is still worth noting, the same optimism for a new social order to come out of the organization of society through occupational groups that is implicit in all the theories growing out of the greater Unionism, as Mr. Cole has called it. The attack on the State is in the name of a more vivid reality represented by the *syndicat*, the trade union. It is the State of Rousseau, the intellectualist and egalitarian State, consecrated in the American Revolutionary State Constitutions and in the *Declaration des droits de l'homme*, that he will have none of.[46] The "New State" of Sovietism, conceived in violence and dedicated to the proposition that force is the legitimate weapon of a class-conscious minority, he accepts. Is not the "New State" of Fascismo fathered by the same Myth, to the degree in which it rejects constitutional democracy?

Force is the *ultima ratio* of the pragmatic gospel of Syndicalism, at least, and it would be interesting to know whether the sublime quality of Fascismo justified it in the eyes of M. Sorel, after the demonstration of impotence which Italian Syndicalism furnished in 1920. He became an admirer of the Italian Monarchy during the war for less. Now that the war has brought to power in all Europe men with the will to govern, one may believe that the sublimity of dictatorship will supply the lost glory of the exploded General Strike myth. Signor Benito Mussolini, well schooled in the Sorelian doctrines of the sublimity of violence as he boasts, from his earlier rôle as a Socialist leader, simply turned the reverse side of the shield, and showed that the Myth of patriotism which the Syndicalist theories had considered only a war camouflage for national self-interest, could be used to enlist violence more successfully than the General Strike myth.[47] It remains to be seen how long Italy can be

[46] *Reflexions*, pp. 401-402.
[47] On the eve of the March on Rome, Mussolini in his famous Naples speech of October 26, 1922, proclaimed: "We have created a Myth, a Myth that is a Faith, a passion. It does not need to be a reality, it is a stimulus and a hope, belief and courage. Our Myth is the Nation, the grandeur

held together by such bonds, but for the time being it is certain that Fascism has a strong grip. Once more, the violence aimed at the State idea has rebounded to the injury of its initiators, succeeding only in establishing the rule of an unconstitutional dictatorship, based on popular reaction against lawlessness. Now that Fascismo is trying to swallow Labor in Italy, shall we see Fascismo swallowed in turn by the controlled syndicates that it has created?

Surely, too, something like the Fascist revolution that is gaining in Europe has happened in Ireland. The land is so weary of politicial murders and of violent methods of asserting political opinions that it has sanctioned repressive measures on the part of its own government that have hardly been equaled under English rule except when Cromwell ground order into the Irish with an iron heel. The moral of the story is not hard to guess: The answer to violence is force. It is not in that direction that the promise of Syndicalism lies. Tested by the pragmatic test of history, the romanticist doctrine of instinctive revolution translates itself into calculated despotism. The anti-intellectualist faith in intuition lends itself to the preachers of such Social Myths, just as the pragmatic criterion of the good is used to justify the Nietzschean gospel of force. But in the issue of fact, the myth of violence suffers a sea-change: slowly it turns to repressive force.

Force is the economic interpretation of morality. It ends by reducing anti-intellectualism to materialistic determinism, as M. Sorel has claimed, for force is the conception under which the physical sciences must construct their deterministic world. In theory and in practice, human conduct treated in these terms resolves itself into the satisfaction of organic needs, what we may sum up as economic interests. Into a world conceived only in these terms the morality of the ideal can never enter.

of the Nation, which we will make a concrete "reality." And he compared it with the inferior mythology of Socialism. Compare the translation of San Severino (*Mussolini Speeches*, 1923) in which "myth" is translated as "ideal" (p. 177). The original Italian is: *"Noi abbiamo creato il nostro mito."* See *Discorsi Politici "I Discorsi della Rivoluzione"* (Imperia, Milano, 1923), p. 58. *Cf.* L'*Italie vivante* by Paul Hazard (Paris, 1922), *Communisme et "Fascio" en Italie* by Jean Alazard, Paris, ed. Bossard (1922), and *Il Fascismo e i Partiti politici*, R. Mondolfo col., Bologna Cappelli), 4 Vols. See also, J. Murphy, "Fascismo, Reform or Reaction? the Development of Italian Syndicalism," *Atlantic Monthly*, Jan., 1924.

The ethical method proper to it is that of "scientific" positivism, which Romanticism set out to leave behind. Yet so long as it proceeds on the lines laid out by its pragmatic criteria of value, it can construct only in this way. Romanticism is forced into an acceptance of the Instrumentalist test of survival, because its own "subjective satisfactoriness", without more in it than "ability to work", leads no further than mysticism. And survival means Fascist, not Sorelian, syndicalism.

So far as man is an organism, and so far as society is organic, it is susceptible of pragmatic treatment. But the normative nature of man and of society is never content with the fulfilment of need alone. It is forever reshaping need into purpose, the necessity it finds into the moral necessity it creates. The actual never represents to it the limits of the possible, as Aristotle showed so finally. It is a future-building function, in terms that set it in relation to its real connection with the organic part of its nature; and it carries the germ of futurity into its every present act. Fascism, no more than King Canute, can command the tide of human purpose.

That is what gives so real an importance to the conception of justice in human societies. Those who set up Force as their god have created a jealous god that will have none other before him. Justice can not exist where he rules: As Pascal said, Force makes Justice in that kingdom. But neither can Force be worshipped where there is a common will to realize Justice through rights reciprocally admitted, and duties mutually assumed. That is, under an English conception, through the rule of law.

CHAPTER V

THE POLITICS OF MR. H. J. LASKI *

A. POLITICAL PLURALISM

The sensationalistic roots of pragmatic pluralism are sufficiently sunk in the soil of English thought ever since Hume to lead us to expect a fruit in political theory which would show at least the common stem. The old individualist *laissez faire* economic doctrines had such a derivation, it has been often said. And yet Benthamism was the very root of the Austinian philosophy of sovereignty! Truly here is a relationship so subtle as to defy casual examination. When we observe the reversal of theoretic positions in modern English political and economic thought, the thing is even more striking. Economic theory and its reflection in the legal organization of the community have, as Dicey has shown, increasingly tended toward what may be called "collectivism." And yet the dominant trend of modern political theory has, Dicey's juristic findings to the contrary, attempted to find in federalism the solution of the problem of the organization of power in the modern state. Even within the sphere of law there has arisen an increasing area of legislation by almost autonomous, professional and religious groups which tends toward so complete a division of powers as to escape the "rule of law", as the cognizance of the courts may be called.

Actually the main current of modern English political philosophy may be described as pluralistically inclined in revolt against the "Metaphysical Theory of the State" which the neo-Hegelian idealists had caused for so long to prevail in that sphere where theory is active in shaping practice. Hobhouse, Barker, Figgis, and to some degree, A. D. Lindsay, have all joined in pointing out the theoretical limitations of state sovereignty,

* Reprinted from *The American Political Science Review*, Vol. XVIII, No. 2, May, 1924, with additions and alterations.

142

where Dicey contented himself with showing the practical. Mr.
H. J. Laski has gone so far as to question the legal doctrine of
the unitary state, as he says himself, from a pragmatic point
of view which sees no good to be had from maintaining in theory
what can not be realized in practice. Let us see what is the case
which Mr. Laski, in particular, makes against the "Discredited
State," as Barker called it, and how far the pluralistic reaction
against it in the name of particular associations is capable of
such an extreme application.

In all the varied current of contemporary political theory
which seems to have set against the conception of unitary sovereignty as the basis of the structure of the state, the work of
Mr. Laski stands out sufficiently to command general attention.
Perhaps this is as much because of the arresting fashion in which
he has challenged the traditional doctrines of political theory as
it is from the positive content of his own theories. He has seized
upon the ideas centering about group rights which Figgis and
Maitland forced so brilliantly upon modern attention, and has
made forceful way with them in developing Mr. Ernest Barker's
idea of "The Discredited State." [1] Because of the radical implications of some of these theories as Mr. Laski has expounded
them, political theorists have for some time been waiting for the
promised exposition of Mr. Laski's ideas in more systematic form
than has yet been offered by any of the historical and critical
studies and the two brief introductory chapters of *The Problem
of Sovereignty* and *Authority in the Modern State*, or even *The
Foundations of Sovereignty*.[2] This promise he has fulfilled by the
exhaustive treatise which he has called *A Grammar of Politics*
(1925). As Mr. Laski is professedly a disciple of William James,
it is perhaps too much to ask that he throw even his *Grammar*
into any form that smacks of system and the rationalistic taint

[1] Mr. Laski has so often made grateful acknowledgment of his debt to Mr.
Barker and to Dr. Figgis that he has very nearly succeeded in crediting to
their account some implications of their ideas which are entirely due to him.

[2] After due acknowledgment is made for the debt we owe to Mr. Laski's
erudition, as shown particularly in the essays reprinted from the *Harvard
Law Review*, "The Early History of the Corporation in England," and
"Corporate Personality," his recent book, *The Foundations of Sovereignty*,
seems hardly to justify its title by its contents. It is worth noting that he
puts no more "economic interpretation" on political history than his
sophisticated little study of *Karl Marx* would imply. In this respect he is
a follower of Figgis.

which pragmatists seem to attach to system. To the end of his days William James never entertained seriously the idea of giving his "way of looking at things" any more logical arrangement than the form of a series of rather popular lectures—with vast benefit, no doubt, to the "readableness" of his essays, but with equal difficulty to an unambiguous interpretation of what he meant by his suggestions. The similarly casual nature of such connection as has yet bound Mr. Laski's ideas to a single unity may excuse one, then, for finding some difficulty in selecting a method of presentation. As the *Grammar of Politics* represents a considerable development from the earlier points of view, it may be useful to state and to criticize the main theses of the earlier works in order to understand how great a change some aspects of this doctrine of political pluralism have undergone. I shall deal, therefore, first, with the works of what may be called his critical period; then it may be easier to compare the ideas there suggested with the constructive principles which mark *A Grammar of Politics*.

To begin with, it is obvious, if Mr. Laski is to be taken at his word, that he regards the Austinian conception of legally absolute sovereignty as nothing more than one of those pompous fictions in which the men of the robe delight, but in which there is no meaning for a political realism that would seek the substance behind the shadow. Austinian sovereignty is a concept of the most vicious unreality when applied to the pluralism of actual affairs. It is a doctrine which partakes of the same absolutist temper that pragmatists hold to be discredited by all modern thought, and it engenders the same fetich-worship that Mr. Dewey excoriated so thoroughly in his war-time denunciation of *German Philosophy and Politics*. The day of the "Omnicompetent-State" myth is done, and to talk of its sovereign power is merely to fly in the face of facts.

These facts present themselves to Mr. Laski under two broad heads, closely related: first, every individual act of the state can be reduced simply to the act of those in power, and commands no especial moral sanction because it is the act of the state; second, as the acts of the state are to be tested in terms of the purpose they express or fulfil, they must of necessity compete for the loyalty of individuals with the purpose of other associations as real as the state. This, I take it, is tantamount to the assertion that the political framework under which law is made, interpreted, and administered, has no claim upon obedience *quâ* political framework, for it must eventually face the existence of other corporate bodies with autonomous wills of their own, with ends often distinct from its ends, and a hold on the lives of their members more secure than its hold.

In the earlier works, it is true, there was a tendency for Mr. Laski's attack on sovereignty to fall back on the juristic conceptions of M. Duguit, and the limitations upon sovereign power implied in the conception of *solidarité sociale*, and its positivistic sociology, rather than to stress the idealistic and individualistic ethics that hold suspect the absolute state. In the Translators' Introduction which he wrote for M. Duguit's *Law in the Modern State* he attempted, indeed, to graft the notion of real corporate personality and the idea of group rights upon M. Duguit's theory, which will itself have none either of corporate persons or of rights of any sort whatsoever.

From his earliest conception of the state as a purpose-organization, Mr. Laski's politics moved with some inconsistency toward the more *"solidariste"* notion of an organic society which M. Durkheim has furnished to M. Duguit.[3] This is not without its significance, when one remembers that the whole effort of M. Duguit is to substitute objective law for subjective right as the basis of a legal system. At the outset, Mr. Laski questions the sovereignty of the state in the name of the moral sanctions of rights. But his pragmatic conception of what is meant by rights leads him to define them in terms of functional relation to the social organism: "What I mean by 'right'," he puts it in *The Problem of Sovereignty,*[4] "is something the pragmatist will understand. It is something the individual ought to concede because experience has proved it to be good." From this "ought", it is no very long step indeed to the *"devoir"* of M. Duguit, an obligation not moral but necessary, imposed by reactions of the social organism.[5] It leads away from the start-

[3] M. Duguit has based his system of *droit objectif* throughout upon the positivistic sociology expounded in M. Durkheim's *La division du travail social.*

[4] *Op. cit.,* p. 18.

[5] *Cf. Traité de droit constitutionnel,* 2ᵇᵐᵉ ed., Introduction, Vol. I.

ing point of individual responsibility to the group morality of the so-called *science des mœurs*. And that is just where Mr. Laski winds up in these works of his critical period. Though he has banished authority in the name of the individual so far as legal sovereignty is concerned, he reintroduces the subordination of the individual in the name of the group. Corporate persons are real moral persons, he holds with Maitland. It is in the name of these larger persons within the state that its right to command is challenged.

The conception of real corporate personality serves Mr. Laski for a binding material for the elements of romanticist individualism and positivistic functionalism. He uses it to bring about so much of synthesis as he conceives to be a necessity to society. The state is merely one group among other groups: "It is clear that the sovereignty of the States does not in reality differ from the power exercised by a church or a trade union. The obedience the church or trade union will secure depends simply on what measure of resistance the command inspires."[6] If obedience is simply a matter of the degree of resistance a command inspires, then political organization has, indeed, no especial differentiating quality from other organization. In fact that is the sum of Mr. Laski's attack on the doctrine of sovereignty. Real sovereignty is to be found in society at large, "not in the coercive power possessed by its instrument, but in the fused good will for which it stands. . . . The power Parliament exerts is situate in it not by law but by consent, and that consent is, as certain famous instances have shown, liable to suspension."[7]

Mr. Laski cites as an instance Cardinal Wiseman's resistance to Gladstone in the controversy over the papal decrees of 1870. But the reality of power had so largely gone out of the hands of Rome that the cardinal's challenge could only assume political importance if it were rebuked by force, and thus put in the light of martyrdom for religion's sake. Had the medieval power of the papacy been behind the bull which claimed primary allegiance for the church in all matters, temporal and spiritual, Gladstone's action would have been necessary. Witness the long struggle of Church and State out of which emerged the sovereignty of the national state. Mr. Laski's hint that the unions,

The Problem of Sovereignty, p. 270.   [7] *Ibid.*, pp. 12-13.

too, can take matters into their own hands wherever there is a question of allegiance as between the state and themselves is meeting its pragmatic test in the present period of reconstruction. Perhaps it is not too much to suggest that the issue is being settled historically by the same rude persuasion Henry VIII employed against the claims of the papacy. Unions and corporations of all sorts may find freedom for their own ends within the state when, like the church, they cease to attempt political ends by nonpolitical means.

In any case, to argue that "the power Parliament exerts is situate in it not by law but by consent" is to miss the all-essential point Professor Krabbe has clinched, *i.e.*, that the "unity of legal rule," which is the form of law, is more important than particular content. It is this unity of legal rule which is made possible by Parliament as a sovereign legislature that commands consent, ultimately, and which is supported by a community "sense of right" as Professor Krabbe calls it (*vide: The Modern Idea of the State*, pp. 69-78). Man is sufficiently a political animal to be not so ready as Mr. Laski thinks he ought to be, to trust to "a ceaseless striving of progressive expansion," where the game is played without an umpire. And constitutions, to carry out the figure, are "the rules of the game."

Apparently it is his contention that, since the legal power of Parliament gets itself obeyed in historical instances only when it does not meet resistance strong enough to thwart it, the supreme sovereignty of the state, upon which law is based, is a concept devoid of reality. As he puts it: "Sovereignty is, in its exercise, an act of will, whether to do or to refrain from doing. It is an exercise of will behind which there is such power as to make the expectation of obedience reasonable. Now it does not seem valuable to urge that a certain group, the state, can theoretically secure obedience to all its acts, because we know that practically to be absurd." [8] Pragmatically speaking, therefore, law is whatever rules of conduct can get themselves obeyed in a given society. On these grounds there is no use in speaking of positive law as distinguished by a difference in kind from positive morality, to use the Austinian terminology. The difference is rather one of degree, of the distinctness with which

* *Ibid.*, p. 270.

the sanctions of social reactions are formulated and applied. This position, let us note in passing, is also that of M. Duguit.[9]

Is there not, though, a real distinction in kind between political activity and other organized action under authority? If the state has a purpose of its own, as Mr. Laski admits at times, is it not precisely that of establishing the rule of law, the law it makes? And does not the permanence of the end it serves provide a sufficient necessity to guarantee that positive law must assume the proportions of a self-completing system, distinct from positive morality by virtue of the determinate character of the organs for its declaration and enforcement? These questions bring up the reality of the legal conception of sovereignty. Is there any validity in the theory that the state can command obedience to the law it proclaims, and can demand absolute recognition of its sovereignty? Mr. Laski thinks not; and yet how can any system of law exist which admits the legality of resistance to its rules? It may envisage the possibility of resistance to its decrees; indeed its provisions of legal sanctions are admissions of the fact that law is rarely absolute, because it does not get itself automatically obeyed.

But unless the law is to be treated as no more than the sum of social forces, there must exist within any society an area within which the interests at issue must be submitted to arbitrament. Legal sovereignty is very far from being merely idle theory. The supineness with which men accept Fascist rule after a period of rulerless anarchy shows how fundamental a need it fulfils. A state in which this area is so unclearly delimited as to permit law to be made by "direct action," cases of which Mr. Laski cites for historical justification with considerable

[9] Esmein has said of this attempt to break down the bounds between law and positive morality, "Law as it is conceived by my esteemed colleague (M. Duguit) is nothing more than custom registered by the legislative will of the rulers; and yet he wants that to be law none the less. Isn't there in all this a confusion between what Montesquieu would perhaps have called the nature and the principle of legislative power?"

"That which causes the legislative power to act and that which leads it to legislate are indeed the given needs and the mean ideas of the population, and it is certain that the best laws are those which are made in advance by public opinion, mature and self-conscious. But that is not reason to mix up needlessly the categories of public law, and to confound the opinion which inspires the law with the authority which declares it. Let the proposal be made to return to the pure system of customary law: that would be clearer." (Introduction, *Eléments de droit constitutionnel*, 6ème ed.)

satisfaction, is simply a state in which legal sovereignty is in abeyance. If that be made an habitual condition of the body politic, respect for law is gone and a period of feudalistic strife among the interests ensues, with the cycle of degenerative force set up in full swing. As feudalism begot nationalism, so syndicalism begets Fascism.

For law, then, it is a theoretical necessity to regard sovereignty as of that "supreme, irresistible, uncontrolled authority," the *"jus summi imperii"* of which Blackstone wrote.[10] But Mr. Laski correctly questions whether indeed this is so formidable a power as the mere words indicate. One must, as a matter of fact, examine the sources of this authority in which to find its limitations. Now if, as John Chipman Gray has told us, "the real rulers of a society are undiscoverable," it is still necessary to look for some responsible sovereign in order to give stability to juridical principles. Mr. Laski himself recognizes this as a technical necessity: "It implies only that for the courts the will of the sovereign body, the king in Parliament for example, is beyond discussion. Every judge must accept unquestioningly what fulfills the requirements of the forms of law. But, for the purposes of political philosophy, it is not so abstract and *a priori* a definition we require. What we desire to know is not what has the legal right to prevail, but what does in actual fact prevail and the reasons that explain its dominance. Here, it is clear enough, the legal theory of sovereignty is worthless. Once we are in the realm of actual life it is upon the limitations of sovereignty that attention must be concentrated. What then impresses us is the wide divergence between legal right and moral right. . . ."[11]

This is really the gist of Mr. Laski's case against the state as sovereign. It is a question of where attention must be concentrated. And as theories inevitably reflect to greater or less degree the historic setting of the time and the *parti pris* of their author, it is well to notice that the pragmatic purpose of Mr. Laski's declaration, "the theory of legal sovereignty is worthless," comes from a background of judicial decisions like that in the Osborne judgment and the Taff Vale case, reflected by Mr. Laski's Labour-Party self. The pragmatists, with their

¹⁰ *Commentaries* I, 48.   ¹¹ *Authority in the Modern State*, pp. 40-41.

fertile emphasis on the necessity of considering the psychology as well as the logic of thinking, are always ready to show us the "reasons" for theories on other grounds than reason. It is fair, then, to bear in mind Mr. Laski's very useful affiliation with the Labour Party when we consider his claim that "in the realm of actual life it is upon the limitations of sovereignty that attention must be concentrated." One may wonder what the attitude of the Labour Party in power will be toward the same sovereignty some of its intellectuals have so often assailed as unjust.[12]

But, remembering that as often as not Mr. Laski's use of pluralistic theories advances the church and other institutions and associations in the state as stalking-horses for the unions of the world of labor, one may do well to weigh the proposal that we must discard the theory of legal sovereignty from political theory, in order to grapple with the substances of which it is but a shadow. This is to deny any special justification for the realm of law, any presupposition in its favor, so to speak. Mr. Laski draws the conclusion from his theory of real corporate personality that the state is only one association among many, not different in kind and therefore not possessed of a special right to command. This sort of reasoning not only involves a *non sequitur* among its logical fallacies—although that is perhaps no objection to it from the point of view of pragmatists: it is also the formal denial not only of the possibility of systematically accepted and applied law, but of the entire realm of political organization under law. It is all very well to say: "Such is the natural consequence that the personality of associations is real and not conceded them by the state"; it by no means follows that these persons all share the political character of the state. Unless there be one group among the many capable of enforcing law, the only means by which the group rights can be maintained is by the appeal to force. While Mr. Laski claims for his doctrine that "like Dewey's philosophy" it is " 'consistently experimentalist' in form and content," he says "it

---

[12] The men in England who have won the Labour Party its present power have no doubt about the permanence of the state and the necessity of its sovereign authority as the source of recognized law. See Ramsay MacDonald's pronouncements on *Syndicalism*, and Sydney Webb's *Proposed Constitution for the Socialist Commonwealth of Great Britain*.

denies the rightness of force." Yet in the same passage he says: "It dissolves—what the facts themselves dissolve—the inherent claim of the state to obedience. It insists that the state like every other association shall prove itself by what it achieves. It sets group competing against group in a ceaseless striving of progressive expansion." [13]   And expects, apparently, that the "progressive expansion" that will come out of this pitting of "Group against group in a ceaseless striving" will result from some Law of Nature. The state is to be made a combatant, and in order to show that one does not believe in "the rightness of force" (if it is the force of established law), it is to possess only the same force that the other strivers have. It is then to be measured for its success in terms of its achievement, which will necessarily be limited to its own survival, for it has by definition no superior power of regulation over the conduct of other groups.

It is curious that Mr. Laski can arrive at a conclusion which strips the majesty from law without seeing that he is rendering the very individuals helpless whom he set out to protect against the absolute sovereignty of the absorptive state. The authority he has taken from law he has given to the pseudo-individuals whom he calls corporate persons. It is true that the state is a corporation among other corporations, but its purpose is one which it alone can serve. A community in which there is a general unwillingness to accept the law arrived at by constitutional means, and in which the limits that are put upon corporate interests are those merely of survival in the general conflict, is a community not under law. That is what Mr. Laski's theories lead to in practice, with whatever pragmatic caution he refuse to push them to their logical conclusion as theories. And in such a community the individual grows less and less, the corporation grows more and more, until one, like the medieval church, tends to absorb all. Just as in the case among business corporations, the big fish swallow the little, until society becomes ill from this cannibalistic diet.

The sort of doctrine which denies the inevitable rightness of law is perfectly justifiable so long as that denial means that the individual conscience can not be coerced into ascribing moral goodness to acts of the state—or any other corporation—simply

[13] *Problem of Sovereignty*, p. 23.

because that corporation forms a community of interest and of purpose in which the individual reckons himself a member. But because the purpose that such a community, in particular the state, serves, is one larger than the individual act, a man may with good conscience obey laws which do not command his approval separate from their context in the larger purpose. It is this larger purpose that Mr. Laski, in effect, denies. So long as he maintains his denial on the ultimate moral responsibility of the individual, he is on safe ground; for the way of the absolute state is what James said of the absolute's self: it is like the lion's dens of Æsop's fables: *vestigia nulla retrorsum*. But when he passes from that moral ultimacy of human personality to the same ultimacy in corporate personality he is destroying the former in seeking to establish the latter.

The state, for instance, does represent a real corporate life; but its only claim to this reality lies in its moral purpose, the community of the will to the good life among individuals. It is true that the moral element of this shared purpose only exists as a controlling factor where states have reached a certain maturity of constitutional development toward free representative government. For it is a will which can be realized only by intelligent moral coöperation to delimit the blind play of economic interests.[14] Mr. Laski has claimed that the trade-union ideal of the workers "was a wider ideal than that which the state had attained," but in the light of trade-union practice this is a statement which can be challenged, particularly so long as the unions exist chiefly to further the economic interests of the members. The state has always existed to some degree as the *communitas*

[14] It was one of Sidgwick's most emphasized contributions to political theory, and after him Mr. A. D. Lindsay's, to insist that the state exists to take moral account of the blindness of economic forces in their deterministic play. T. H. Green's great service to English political theory was to recall it to the tempered idealism of Aristotle, and Aristotle's famous reconstruction of politics about the doctrine of the good life. The state comes into existence in order that man may live, that *Politics* held. But it agreed with Plato that the state continued in existence in order that man might live well.

Mr. Laski professes to take a deal of comfort from the idea that Aristotle was really anticipating the modern pragmatists in politics, interpreting that to mean an attitude of what he sometimes calls political realism. But Aristotle with his insistence on the superiority of the speculative over the practical reason (*Politics*, Book IV, Chapter 14, as well as Chapter 3, Book IV), and on the moral end of the state can hardly be claimed as a supporter for the view of politics, *positive et réaliste*, as M. Duguit has called it, which strips inquiry to the bare recital of facts.

communitatum, and for that reason it can and does command the moral adhesion of individuals more widely than any particular association because it serves a moral purpose more universal than that of any other. Liberty, in whose name men have so passionately died, can not exist where there is not a law to protect the individual against the enslavement of force. The liberty which Mr. Laski champions is a matter all of rights with no reciprocal obligations. It was this philosophy of group license which was put into practice by the Maximalists and Syndicalists in Italy after the war. The result was the destruction of all liberty through the provoking of Fascism.

The ideal of the legally sovereign state—let men's actions when that sovereignty is seriously challenged attest it—is an ideal both wider and more intensely cherished wherever races have attained to the political maturity of responsible government, than any other single ideal, wider, perhaps, than that of the liberty which it is the duty of the state to protect. To treat the state as *prima inter pares* is simply to deny to it any functional significance of its own. That is just what Mr. Laski would do, however. Accepting Gierke's demonstration that the state does not create that reality which is the group person of other groups, "We then give to this particular group (the state) no peculiar merit. We refuse it the title of creator of all else. We make it justify itself by its consequences. We stimulate its activities by making it compete with the work of other groups coextensive with or complementary to itself. As it may not extinguish, so it may not claim preëminence. Like any other group, what it is and what it will be, it can be only by virtue of its achievement. So only can it hope to hand down undimmed the torch of its conscious life." [15]

Either there is the expectation of the return of the Golden Age at the back of Mr. Laski's theories, or he is not particularly concerned with whether or not the lamb-like state will ever rise from where it has attempted to lie down beside these corporate lions. For the propositions that the state may not extinguish, as well as that it may not claim preëminence, are equally incompatible with the rule of law. It can not allow the groups within itself to be self-governing where the interests of the groups are

[15] *Harvard Law Review,* Vol. XXIX, "Problem of Sovereignty," p. 426.

pushed into the realm protected by the law. The rule of law can not exist side by side with, say, the Ku Klux Klan. The "torch of its conscious life" gutters or is trampled out if the state permits the law of the land to be thrown into the arena of social strife, for that law is the very breath of its flame. Law represents a certain area of agreement for the settlement of disputes, for the protection of generally recognized rights and the enforcement of duties corresponding to them. Truly enough, as Mr. Laski has demonstrated in the historical studies he has undertaken of clerical and political authority, the law is never static in its formal completeness. One may admit that the forces which ultimately give law its origin and its sanction lie outside the halls of legislatures and of courts. But it is a pragmatic error to forget the utility of the formal and systematic character of law, and to insist that because the final sources of sovereignty are extra-legal, there is no place for the theory of legal sovereignty in political science. Social solidarity, to which Mr. Laski's appeal has been made in order to hold society together, is an ideal, not a fact. The state exists to help the realization of that ideal. It can only do so if it represents a will of sufficient permanence and stability to abide by law, that is to accept the sovereignty of the state as the necessary condition of a government in which men may have confidence. Really, after all, the community of purpose which the state represents is only possible upon the basis of reciprocal obligation, and a common willingness to accept the rules of the game. That implies a certain trust in human goodness, and a mutual willingness to put that confidence to the test by voluntarily "casting in one's lot" with a political society.

Mr. Laski sees the matter from a different point of view from that of trust, however. The loyalties of men are various indeed, as he says. At times the basis for political agreement is so slight, as compared with the violence of disagreement, that the real ground for political settlement is lacking. But it is worth noting that this is generally the outcome either of continuous oppression of a part of the community by another part through an abuse of power which revolts men's feeling for justice in law, or of perverting power in order to establish law by force. Whether it be a numerical minority or majority that so acts, the balance generally is restored against it by the community of resistance that it meets from a society whose normal intercourse depends upon legal stability and constitutional procedure.[16]

The point which Mr. Laski really raises is, Can there be in the present state of human relationships any sovereign state capable of such unity that its law will be willingly accepted by the associations within it, where its interests conflict with their own? And on a realistic basis, certainly, no view of a cross-section of any actual society would show the modern state completely absorptive of all the lesser associations, their purposes or the loyalties of their members. He has put it in this way: "But sovereign your state no longer is if the groups within itself are thus self-governing. Nor can we doubt this polyarchism. Everywhere we find the groups within the state which challenge its supremacy. They are, it may be, in relation with the state, a part of it, but one with it they are not. They refuse the reduction to unity. We find the state, in James' phrase, to be distributive and not collective. Men belong to it; but they belong to other groups, and a competition for allegiance is continually possible." [17]

Gladstone's attack on the Vatican decrees of 1870, Bismarck's *Kulturkampf*, the long struggle of France with *"clericalisme,"* and the failure of the state to exact a complete loyalty to itself—these are matters of history. Mr. Laski points to the successful resistance of unions, notably the English coal-miners' resistance to the demands of the state even during the war, as offering a parallel. He would, no doubt, echo the words of Mr. Gompers, the head of the American Federation of Labor, with real approval: "The law must not interfere with labor," spoken as they were of the injunction issued by Attorney-General Daugherty against the striking railway crafts unions in 1922. As a matter of fact, Mr. Laski has cited the Adamson Eight-Hour and Wages Act of 1916, "railroaded" through Congress by the express threat

[16] Willoughby and Rogers in *An Introduction to the Problem of Government* have recalled Grote's phrase "constitutional morality" as descriptive of respect for law in a community really politically educated (p. 58, note). Grote, in speaking of the "Athenian Democracy in the time of Kleisthenes, emphasized the necessity for 'a perfect confidence in the bosom of every citizen, amidst the bitterness of party contest, that the forms of the constitution will be no less sacred in the eyes of his opponents than in his own.' Such constitutional morality he called 'a natural sentiment' as exists in the United States. Grote, *History of Greece*, Vol. II, p. 86."

[17] *Problem of Sovereignty, loc. cit. supra*, p. 425.

of a strike on all the railroads by the members of the "Four Brotherhoods," cited it, too, as an instance of the state's helplessness to enforce the so-called "general will" of law against the will of a really powerful "corporate person" within it. In the fact he is unhappily quite right. The growing power of great "blocs," possessed of both voting and economic power, over modern legislative assemblies, proves the fact to be that the state not only dare not act strongly against these interests, but that it is often bullied quite openly into placating them by special favors. The political observers in the American press, for example, are never tired of Jeremian lamentations on the passing of political power from the party leaders into the hands of ostensibly nonpolitical organizations: the Farmers' "bloc" through which Mr. Gray has been said to exert a much more real political power than its official spokesmen in Congress; [18] to say nothing of the "Prohibition" forces and the "veterans" organizations, standing whip in hand over the harried legislators. In general, the opposition of one of these bodies is sufficient to "kill" almost any candidate or any bill of at all doubtful strength; and only President Harding's

[18] A somewhat extreme presentation of this aspect of politics has been made by the anonymous author of *Behind the Mirrors* (1922), which aims at giving a realistic picture of persons and forces in national politics. The writer makes a very clever analysis of certain "peaks of reality" which are beginning to thrust themselves up out of chartless surface of the old party systems. He believes that these "interest-blocks" will largely dominate legislation, forming an opportunistic and somewhat feudal balance of power among themselves, which will gradually take the residuary significance out of the party system. The representation of economic interests, without necessarily commanding a legal sanction for their organization, will so undermine the old system of territorial representation as to make it meaningless.

The pronouncements of the late Mr. Gompers and the leaders of American labor seem to indicate that the Federation of Labor intends to push its political ends through this system of threats to the individual legislator or to the party at large. Perhaps that may explain why the United States Supreme Court has come into so much opprobrium with the labor leaders. It is not so amenable to this method of persuasion as are politicians looking to elections for good or ill.

A list of the interest groups maintaining lobbies at Washington includes all the important interests of the country. We can witness at any time the National Anti-Saloon League putting pressure on the Treasury Department to carry out its ideas of enforcing the Volstead Act; or of the U. S. Chamber of Commerce having its powerful say on the reduction of corporation taxes and taxes in general; or of the A. F. of L., or the rest of them speaking with the assumption of making a single voice for millions of throats. The most complete study of the activities of these national groups, particularly as they affect opinion, has been made by Mr. E. P. Herring, *Representation of Organized Groups Before Congress*, Johns Hopkins Doctoral Dissertation, 1928.

veto prevented a display of positive strength in the form of a raid on the national treasury for a bonus of several billions of dollars to be dispensed to the "veterans" for "compensation." The subsequent "paid-up insurance" plan of "adjusted compensation" was a necessary sop to these organizations.

These things are true. But does the distribution of "bread and circuses" to lobbyist organizations, or the impotence of the state before the combined power of either what is called "Capital" or what is called "Labor" constitute a hopeful political trend? May one not suggest that it is the pragmatic attitude of the "economic man" in all the purity of utilitarian individualism, and even more, the same attitude in "corporate persons," which goes far toward furnishing a psychological basis for the growth of a political pluralism founded on interests and not upon the protection of moral responsibility? If German philosophy and politics took one extreme is not this the other? Nor does it add morality to the purely economic character of the struggle to do, as Mr. Laski has done, transfer the unit of plurality from the individual to the corporation. If anything is changed, it is in the direction of a more and more deterministic attitude, one of pure survivalism in such ethics as remain. May not a part, at least, of the growing willingness of groups to exploit the state to their interest, and the corresponding growth in their power to do so, be the result of the growth of an anti-state philosophy, or perhaps the lapse of a real philosophy of the state, reflecting itself in the character of the actual sovereign—that intangible thing called public opinion? An escape from industrial feudalism can come only as the escape came from medieval feudalism—through the redevelopment of a sovereign.

Englishmen and Americans have insisted, correctly, that the actual government is the servant of the constitutionally defined state, not its master. But the servant of the law must be invested with its dignity, if the law is to be obeyed. It is not self-enforcing. Perhaps we could use fewer eulogists of the Constitution and more men of force and integrity in public affairs. Still it is certain men have not come to feel that the state purpose is weaker in its hold on their loyalty without good reason being afforded by actual circumstances as well as by theory. For one thing, modern business claims greater talents and more time than business did. Recent scandals seem to argue that it claims too many of those entrusted with the offices of state. Much of Mr. Laski's attack on the sovereign state strikes a universally responsive chord in our moral being, too, for we feel that any such absolute sovereignty as is literally set down by Blackstone would be a denial of our individual freedom of choice. If the state in its governmental practice is bad, we will not call it just. We are, as he says, "whether we will or no" . . . "bundles of hyphens" in our loyalties. "Where the linkages conflict a choice must be made." The absolute sovereignty of the state remains a necessity to law and to judicial interpretation, but as the state is "the community organized for law," [19] and community itself is a matter of degree, the state can only claim such power as the degree of community endows it with.

When all this is pressed home to its uttermost emphasis, however, it falls very far short still of "polyarchism" wherever a constitutional state actually exists. Where political issues, that is to say the sovereignty of the community of law, are vitally affected, the unity of the state-purpose is made clear. Mr. Laski thinks that, where this allegiance is in question "it is obvious that every great crisis must show its essential plurality." Surely this is not the judgment of modern history. The state-purpose varies in the intensity of its hold upon men's loyalty; but it needs no more than a knowledge of the facts of actual issues in the recent conflicts between, for instance, the general-strike idea and the idea of the rule of law to show where allegiance lies. Among the workers themselves, to a very large extent, the issue has been settled in favor of the state. Witness the Italian communists' fiasco of 1920, then Fascism; or more near Mr. Laski's concern, the breakdown of the great British General Strike of May, 1926.[20]

[19] See the magistral statement given to the relations between "Law and Political Theory" by Sir Paul Vinogradoff, *Outlines of Historical Jurisprudence*, Introduction, Chapter IV, Vol. I, especially the definition of the state.

[20] There is no longer any denial of the syndicalistic origin of important elements of the Fascisti in the earlier periods of the movement. See Paul Hazard, *L'Italie vivante*, an expansion of his "Notes sur Italie nouvelle," in the *Revue de deux mondes;* also *Communisme et "Fascio" en Italie* by Jean Alazard, Paris, 1922 (ed. Bossard), and *Il Fascismo e i Partiti politici*, Collection R. Mondolpho, Bologna, 1923 (Cappelli), 4 Vols. For its present

The dangers inherent in the absorptive personality of the economic group, for instance, are equally as great as those involved in the doctrine of what has been called by Hobhouse *The Metaphysical State.* The error involved is as old as steering toward Charybdis in order to escape Scylla. In *The Great Society* Mr. Graham Wallas has pointed out very fittingly the pits into which the anti-intellectualist advocates of group pluralism fall by failing to take note of the beams in their own eyes. The guild-spirit of the Middle Ages had much of the narrow spirit of "closed corporation" in it, as well as much that enlisted men's creative energies.[21] Perhaps it is only by weighing things in terms of their respective contributions to the good life that the right relation of the state to other associations can be established. And no matter how final be the individuality of this judgment, it is certain that the province of law must be respected if there is to be any protection for the right of choice.

The Kantian background of Mr. Laski's ethical individualism should have prevented him from taking the pragmatic leap to a pluralism in which ends are weighed in terms only of economic interest, with no escape from anarchy save through the appeal to functional solidarity. From there, is no return to the state as serving a common moral ideal. The path from thenceforth is toward what may be called broadly the Marxian doctrine of economic determinism, in which the state serves the interests of the prevailing power of blind force. And who will say that there are more footprints leading back from that cave of shadows than from the lion's den of the Absolute?

In Mr. Laski's works the incline toward this realm of shadows

relations to syndicalism see "Fascismo, Reform or Reaction," by James Murphy, *Atlantic Monthly*, Jan., 1924, and Chapter XI of this volume.

[21] *The Great Society* constitutes Mr. Wallas' effort to put the extremes of anti-intellectualism in their proper light, just as *Human Nature in Politics* had been an attempt at rebuking rationalistic idealism. See also Austin P. Evans, "Problem of Control in Medieval Industry," *Political Science Quarterly*, Dec., 1921, p. 603, for an estimate of the stifling influence of the gilds, shared to some degree by the canonists, upon industry and commerce. Contrast J. A. Penty's *Guildsman's Interpretation of History*, and G. D. H. Cole's attitude to medieval gilds, especially his Introduction to Renard's *Guilds in the Middle Ages*, with the facts collected by Mr. Evans, and the warning of *The Great Society* against the dangers of narrow professionalism seem borne out. The discussion of "Occupational *vs.* Proportional Representation" of Mr. P. H. Douglas, *American Journal of Sociology*, Sept., 1923, is also of interest.

is detected all along in his attitude toward the social context
of force in which the state is set. The will of the state "is a
will to some extent competing with other wills, and, Darwin-
wise [!] surviving only by its ability to cope with its environment." [22] On the other hand, the idea of sovereignty implied
by the sovereigns state (which Mr. Laski thinks is being supplanted by this "Get on who can" struggle of group-forces),
holds that the maintenance of a government capable of responsible expression of public opinion means the rule of law. But
it need not try to carry Austin's province of jurisprudence into
the extra-legal realm where opinion is being made. Austin
himself made careful note to the contrary.[23] The protection
of the freedom with which opinion may be developed and
expressed is itself the most cherished right which men require the
law to protect. And as for state responsibility, the doctrine
of auto-limitation under which the state submits its own acts
of government to judicial review is no more "meaningless" than
is the ability of the individual to act in accordance with accepted
moral norms which he freely chooses to follow. On pragmatic
grounds, on the ethics of survivalism, Mr. Laski would be equally
right in denying that freedom to each. As a matter of fact,
that is what the doctrine of real corporate personality does more
effectively to the individual than to the state, although Mr.
Laski accuses Jellinek of meaningless theory in talking of auto-
limitation on the part of the state. "For to be bound by one's
own will is not, in any real sense, to be bound at all," he thinks.[24]
How else than as auto-limitation can one explain the origin and
development of constitutional states, where the limits of ordinary

[22] *Problem of Sovereignty*, pp. 13-14.
[23] *Jurisprudence*, Sections 248-254. His description of legal sovereignty is
applicable only to parliamentary government under a flexible constitution.
Cf. Lord Bryce's *Studies in History and Jurisprudence*, Vol. I, Chap. 3,
"Flexible and Rigid Constitution." When Austin fell back upon the
electorate as the final sovereign he was really describing what Bryce calls
the "political sovereign."
[24] *Authority in the Modern State*, p. 41. For a statement of the classic
doctrine of the State-Person see Jellinek, *System der Subjektiven Öffentlichen Rechte* (Ed. 1892), pp. 12 ff., *"Die Rechtliche Natur des Staates."*
For the doctrine of Auto-Limitation see *ibid.*, pp. 201 ff., and Hauriou,
Principes de droit administratif, 6ème ed. (1906), pp. 393-395. Mr. Laski's
criticism of the doctrine is founded on Duguit's often repeated attack : See
Traité de droit constitutionnel, 2ème ed., Vol. I, Chap. 1 *et passim*, p. 307.
Law in the Modern State, p. 148, and *Souveraineté et liberté*, pp. 108-110.

law are determined by the fundamental control of a constitution?[25]

It is surely a more intelligible view of law to see in it the registration of community of purpose, the expression of an agreement among wills as to the conditions of their political association, than to treat it as the resultant simply of blind or at least non-moral social reactions. On the latter view, which Mr. Laski accepts in effect in his "Translator's Introduction" to M. Duguit's *Law in the Modern State,* it is completely impossible to talk of any other bonds than those of organic social necessity. Purpose has no place in social solidarity which is taken for granted as a fact, and which means only that the strongest rule by right of might. If the state be the expression of social purpose, on the other hand, the doctrine of auto-limitation means that law itself is the vehicle for registering the moral will men bring to bear on politics. Constitutions, whether written, or practiced in the way all its critics have shown that the English constitution is, alike present the safeguards of tolerance under which continuous political association is alone possible. To be preserved they must be respected.

That this is "idealism" does not prevent it from being as well an *a priori* condition of political association without which the mere facts to which Mr. Laski makes his appeal lead only to "a state of nature" in which the conscious direction of the moral will play no part. Mr. Laski, as well as M. Duguit, sees in government only power "exerted in the interests of those who control its exercise . . . . It is the habit of government to translate the thoughts and feelings and passions with which it is charged into terms of the event and deem them the achievement of the State-purpose." Yet he admits that this is "progressively less true." And if it is progressively less true, it is because politically minded societies are becoming more and more clearly conscious of the state-purpose, and more and more effectively able to realize it by constitutional means.

What M. Paul-Boncour calls *Le Fédéralisme economique,* "regional" movements, the rise of groups of a voluntary nature,

[25] In a footnote to *Law in the Modern State* (p. 76) Mr. Laski admits, however, that "This [the state's submitting its acts to the rule of law] is virtually possible under the doctrine of auto-limitation of Jellinek."

have, it is true, exerted a happy pressure upon government to conform to the degree of purpose which it must serve in the national state.[26]   There is hope even of translating the wider community of purpose into a substantial international organization of justice, to take national concerns out of that Hobbesian state of nature on which Lord Bryce made a sorrowful comment in his address inaugurating the Institute of Politics of Williams College in 1920.[27]   But this does not mean that the sovereignty of a people over affairs which concern them *domi* is not final as it operates through law.   To challenge it in the name of one set of interests (trade unions) is the same fault that Mr. Laski has condemned as its abuse by another ("capitalism").   "No political democracy can be real that is not as well the reflection of an economic democracy," he lays down as a maxim.   Yet no economic democracy can escape the necessity of a politically unified sovereignty of law, if it is not to degenerate into political tyranny by an autocracy of interests.

The "principle of federalism" to which Mr. Laski turns to establish this "polyarchism" of groups, sovereign in themselves, must find some common political sovereignty in an accepted state under law, or it must resolve itself into the feudal régime which his bolder speculations anticipate.   It is to James that he turns for philosophic justification, again: "The pluralistic world thus is more like a federal republic than an empire or kingdom.   However much may be collected, however much may report itself present at any effective centre of consciousness, something else is self-governed and absent and unreduced to unity." [28]

Federalism on this reading means ultimate pluralism, the

[26] Mr. A. D. Lindsay's excellent summary of "The State in Recent Political Theory," *Political Quarterly*, Feb., 1914, makes clear that the old division of society into state and individual can no longer serve as the basis for a modern theory which must take into account the reality of associational life of all sorts.   But that is, as he points out, not tantamount to denying a special sphere to the State, or to treating it as *prima inter pares*.   Political theory may discard what Dr. Figgis has set the fashion for calling "the Omnicompetent State," "the sum of atomistic individuals," and do full justice to "the inherent rights of associations" without concluding as Mr. Laski does that legal sovereignty is "a barren concept," "without practical utility" (*Problem of Sovereignty*, p. 269).

[27] "International Relations," an address to the First Institute of Politics.

[28] Quoted from James' "Pluralistic Universe" in *The Problem of Sovereignty*, p. 10.

absence of a singly unifying relation.[29]   So M. Laski continues, "We are urging that because a group or an individual is related to some other group or individual it is not thereby forced to enter into relations with every other part of the body politic. When a trade-union ejects one of its members for refusing to pay a political levy it is not thereby bringing itself into relations with the Mormon Church. A trade union may work with the State but it need not do so of necessity."[30]   Let us take this fling at the Osborne Judgment as a test case. Must a trade union "work with the State" wherever its acts assume political character, that is to ask, must it act in conformity with the rule of law, or is it a sufficient source of authority to act upon its own law in its internal affairs, even where those affairs have an external bearing? And suppose it forbid its members to belong to the Mormon Church, for example, while attempting at the same time to enforce "closed shop"? Has the state nothing to say in its character of guardian of rights and enforcer of duties?

The legal status of the individual, as long as law is sovereign, assures the members of all associations equal protection in all the plurality of their relations, so long as they are brought under the uniting bond of citizenship. The law cannot, without surrendering its entire usefulness, admit the claims of nonpolitical associations to create law in its despite. There may be—and

[29] Federalism which divides legal sovereignty by the terms of a constitution accepted by all the members of the body politic so created, in practice has tended to increasing unity, as is the case in the United States, or to a sovereignty in fact and in law, more and more completely absorbed by the constituent states, as is the case with the British Empire. The federal government of the United States has tended to gather legislative power to itself (see, for instance, Pierce, *Federal Usurpation*, and Thompson, *Federal Centralization*), whether through the interpretative powers which the Supreme Court exercises or through the more difficult method of nation-wide amendments to the constitution. De Tocqueville called our young republic "un gouvernement national incomplet" and pointed out the compromise in fact between two theories logically irreconcilable. Some critics go so far as to say that the Civil War and the exigencies of modern business have completed the nationalization of our law to such an extent that federalism means little more than administrative decentralization when it is not merely the survival of outworn forms. This is hardly adequate as a statement of fact. The evolution of the British Empire has been in the opposite direction, toward a federalism which in fact more and more approaches a confederation. See H. D. Hall's *The British Commonwealth of Nations*, and for the United States, "The Limits of Federalism," by Stephen Leacock. *The Proceedings of the American Political Science Association*, p. 37, Vol. V, (1908).   [30] *The Problem of Sovereignty*, p. 10.

there unquestionably is at times—what James would have called "a genuinely 'external' " moral character to the acts of trade unions which the law does not reach. The changes in the law of labor disputes in England, which Professor Geldart so well traced show that the opinion which makes law is not insensible to that side of the matter.[31]   But for the union to take matters into its own hands where common law rights are at issue is not to be tolerated, any more than governmental infringements of constitutionally guaranteed liberty would be. The strength that is in union may be justly and legally used to prevent the economic exploitation of labor; but when it is put to the use of exploiting the helplessness of a community dependent upon the functioning of essential services, what M. Duguit has given so prominent a place under the title of "the public services which it is the sole duty of the law to secure," then indeed it is M. Duguit and not Mr. Laski who has the right of the matter; the law can not remain indifferent. If it is called upon by such an actual challenge as Mr. Laski makes, it must establish its right to rule by the force with which it is endowed by the community will to law. M. Duguit's remarks on the *"quelques milliers d'égarés et de criminels"* who "wished, by fomenting a strike on the railroads, to starve out and to ruin the country," and "by creating misery and suffering, to realize some sort of Bolshevist revolution" [32] show that he at least has gone very far with the changing times from that syndicalist leaning of which he was once accused. He still interprets law in terms of social force, but he faces the fact that social force reacts ruthlessly against those who would meet it with force to overturn the stability of ordinary intercourse.

Nothing breeds antagonism like an antagonistic attitude. One need not document the history of the coal strikes in England and America to show that where lawlessness has been invoked, even to such a terrible extent as "the Herrin massacre," which filled the American press in the summer of 1922, the attitude of govern-

---

[31] See his "The Law of Trade Unions," *Political Quarterly*, May, 1914. For American conditions see *Principles of Labor Legislation*, by J. R. Commons and Andrews and *Labor Economics* by S. Blum.
[32] *Traité de droit constitutionnel*, 2ème ed., p. IX, Vol. I.   The occasion being the attempted general strike of May 1, 1920, engineered by the most radical elements of the French Confédération Générale de Travail.

ment has necessarily changed character. At the same time one must look behind the actual occurrences to see whether or not there was not such provocation, by legal inactivity or worse, in the face of intolerable labor conditions, as to make the events almost necessary. The idealist view of the state need never blind its eyes to the pitiable travesty of law that sometimes soils the robes of justice. The report of the Inter-Church Commission which investigated the Steel Strike of 1919 is proof of the danger that is as real in that direction as is the counsel to violence in the other.[33] And if one may trust the files of *The New Republic* for several years back one may trace a condition of legally winked-at terrorism in West Virginia that could hardly have had any other issue, after what has been described as "the murder" of Sid Hatfield, a miner, by the Baldwin-Felts detectives hired by the coal operators. It appears that these "gun-men," of whom a considerable force were in the employ of the companies operating the mines, enjoyed in some instances the anomalous legal position of deputy-sheriffs, while at the same time their ostensible purpose was "to preserve order" by terrorizing the union organizers who were attempting to "unionize" the coal region in West Virginia. Murders and retaliations developed into a dramatic march of several thousand armed miners on the stronghold of the operators and detectives. A pitched battle was narrowly averted by the governor's intervention, although for some time a state of what amounted to a localized civil war actually existed. The present (1928) investigation by the Senate of the reign of terror in the Pennsylvania coal fields has exposed similar conditions of industrial feudalism.

No theory of the state can overlook such incidents without remaining merely formal. Industrial conditions are increasingly the concern of the law, and must be. Yet it is throwing the baby out with the bath-water to find that the existence of such crying evils means that the remedy lies in recognizing their necessity and resigning oneself to the rule of no law. What Mr. Laski calls the realistic view in political theory amounts to this: It attacks not the evils themselves nor their cause, but the

[33] See "The United States Steel Corporation," "An analysis of the social consequences of modern business policies," by Kirby Page, *Atlantic Monthly*, May, 1922.

very sovereignty of law to which it must in the end appeal for
remedy, unless it is to rely on some solution like the "Social
Myth" of M. Sorel's syndicalistic general strike. Not in abating
the sovereignty of law, but in making it flexible to the increased
demands a wider state-purpose puts upon it, lies the hope of
good government. It is as little possible to contract the sphere
of government to that "best government which governs least"
of Jeffersonian democracy, as it is to do without government
entirely.[34] The pragmatic attitude of intense individualism and
distrust of office-bearers which characterized pioneer societies is
out of place in so closely knit a unity as is formed by the modern
state. And when that individualism is invoked in the name of
"corporate persons" with a threat at the back, it can become
socially dangerous.

When Mr. Laski himself comes to grips with the task of setting
up a constructive theory of the State, he is, as we shall presently
see, curiously but naturally divided against himself. As a
pluralist he wishes to retain his doctrine of "contingent anarchy"
and of the "Discredited State." As a more genuinely useful
pragmatist, however, he has elaborated a set of political and
economic institutions which demand the utmost constitutional
morality in the "new state" of the future. He is not quite
willing to term sovereignty the broad and highly unified powers
of coercion which he vests in the Laskian State, but the constructive features of his theory put the most Austinian demands upon
this power—whatever it be.

B.   An Ethics of Politics (Mr. Laski's *Grammar*)

Mr. Laski's restatement of the principles of political science
in pragmatic terms is apt to be one of the very few books on
contemporary political theory which have a sure future.[35] Despite

[34] No more striking proof of the changed attitude of government could be
asked than the decisions of the Supreme Court of the United States, upholding the validity of the Railway Transportation Act of 1920 on the one
hand, and, in the Coronado Coal Co. case on the other, holding "Capital"
and "Labor" equally to account. See E. S. Corwin, "American Constitutional Law, 1921-1922," in the *Am. Pol. Sci. Rev.*, Nov. 1922.

[35] H. J. Laski, *A Grammar of Politics*, New Haven, Yale University Press,
1925. Reprinted with alterations from the *Political Science Quarterly*, Vol.
XLII, No. 2, June, 1927.

its great length and despite a tendency to treat subjective wishes and opinions as if they were objective facts, it may well be the most important contribution that has been made to recent political theory. To this distinction it has several claims of a unique order, the chief being that it is the first sustained attempt on the part of the accepted leader of contemporary political pluralism to state an adequate basis for political reconstruction. Its claim may rest also upon the fact that it is the most ambitious survey of the essential problems of politics yet undertaken by any modern writer of English—and this in spite of the confessed omission of the whole bearing of the agrarian problem. Within the scope of a single volume Mr. Laski has managed to get in not only a treatise upon political ethics but a very richly suggestive outline of the political and economic institutions which he holds to be the best means of realizing an ethical world order, as well as of realizing the "new state" that will extend the area of freedom in industrial society.

His incidental criticisms of Communist, Guild Socialist, Syndicalist and "Sidney-Webbicalist" proposals reveal in the new Mr. Laski a brilliant and surprisingly conservatve defender of parliamentarism, whose pluralistic theory is notably at outs with his unitary juristic construction. The chapter on "Political Institutions" is a defense of English parliamentary methods with few radical changes. And the final chapter proposes to vest coercive power in the League of Nations, holding it to be in fact already a superstate. If Mr. Laski's theory in Part One still breathes "contingent anarchy" through direct action, his construction of political institutions in Part Two, even without his international superstate (pp. 588-638), vastly extends both the scope and the power of state action, with an obvious reliance upon constitutional morality to make the "new state" workable. The voice may be that of violent Esau, but the hands have become those of reasonable Jacob.

One may suggest, indeed, that the whole scope of the *Grammar's* Part One is an ethical elaboration of the opening quotation from Lord Acton: "The great question is to discover not what governments prescribe, but what they ought to prescribe; for no prescription is valid against the conscience of mankind." In carrying out this mission, Mr. Laski has written a

"Rhetoric" or an "Ethics", rather than *A Grammar of Politics*; or if it be a grammar, its preoccupation is too exclusively with the contrary-to-fact conditional subjunctive, and with the future more (or less) vivid.

The duty of good citizenship, Mr. Laski believes, lies in emulating Athanasius, and with as high moral motivation. "In relation to the modern state each man is, in this department [religion] or elsewhere ultimately, an Athansius. He will be broken by the world rather than yield to the world. . . . For that experience [of conscience], I suggest, makes law for him . . ." (p. 247). It is indubitable that where church and state clash, there the state meets its most formidable enemy, often because the state machinery has been captured by partisans in a religious struggle. It is interesting to note that it is precisely where labor rules (Mexico and Russia) that those clashes are most bitter. But in the light of contemporary phenomena of state absolutism such as Bolshevist Russia and Fascist Italy, to say nothing of the rising wave of Continental dictatorships, it is surely not political realism to insist that individual consciences are so tender on points of moral liberty that men will forego either bread or the comfort of social security in order to challenge each law for its moral validity. They do not pant with a martyr's rage to be broken by the state. They err, if anything, in the other direction of a too great complacency in the face of autocracy. Perhaps every man ought to follow Mr. Laski in his uncompromising discipleship to Athanasius, although conceivably such an attitude defeats its own ends. To suggest that many men do in fact act so is to overstress the active voice in one's political grammar, and to mistake the hortatory subjunctive for the indicative.

Part Two of the present *Grammar* abundantly proves that Mr. Laski thinks there will be small need for Athanasius, once Labor governs according to the grammatical rules laid down.

"The State protects the wholeness of men over and above those parts which express themselves through groups more specific in character. It does not do so by being something over and above them. It coordinates with them by associating itself with them, by becoming a means through which they reach a general medium of expression. To that end it seeks to embody the largest induction open to it. It speaks not for some, but for all. It decides, not for a few, but for the whole."

This, surely, has a most Hegelian ring, and brings us to figures of speech.

"In such fashion the State might become a genuine search for social integration. It might cease to be the organ of a few because its will would become instinct with the desires of the many. . . . It could be taken as suffused with good faith in a sense in which the State in our own day is void of such virtue. . . ."[36]

Such a state, integrative not pluralistic, he believes would command loyalty because it would no longer be what he assumes the present state to be: simply the government actually (and wrongfully) in power. Wipe out economic inequality of the present sort, and then you may build the unifying parliamentary state of Part Two. Although his pluralism would not permit that state to "impose a uniform rule," the actual institutions outlined all assume that Parliament will in fact suggest such a rule with complete confidence of having it enforced. If Mr. Laski supposes that the new state, plethorically institutionalized, will not coerce, he is erecting merely another Utopia.

The real points at issue between pluralism and its critics hinge on the value of constitutional morality, and on the adequacy of the political means now at the disposal of radicalism in states where representative government with constitutional safeguards of free speech and minority rights is a fact. Mr. Laski recognizes the impossibility of both the Syndicalist and the Communist methods of open violence and frank class revolution, because such states could not survive in a preponderantly capitalistic world society and because the application of revolutionary methods provokes "an attempt, which may be a successful attempt, at fascism" (p. 534). Curiously enough this is the only mention of what is perhaps the most portentous contemporary political phenomenon, the word *Fascism* not even finding a place in the index of a political *Grammar* published in 1925.

The handwriting of Fascism is upon the wall, for all that, so far as sabotage by general strikes and direct action is concerned, just as much as it is in the case of frankly Communist revolution. The futility of direct action serves simply to create an

[36] Pp. 281-282.

excuse for force. The way toward a freer state does not lie in repudiating the constitutional methods at hand, so long as they are observed by the government in power. Political revolutions obtained through parliamentary methods seem on the face of evidence such as the breakdown of the General Strike of 1926, to offer more hope to Labor than the policy of direct action and of contingent revolution.

Obviously the *Grammar* under consideration was written primarily for English political usage, with some applications to American variations. It is only by inference and the most occasional reference concerned with the Dominions, and with intra-Imperial relations, although both these fields would have afforded some interesting material for the thesis of "authority as federal." One could hardly ask that political grammar be internationalized to the degree of taking in Oriental usage, but there are certainly relevant grammatical principles, particularly for a pragmatist, in the present European reaction against the impotent state that post-war pluralism produced all over the Continent. Dictatorship is too obvious a political fact to be left out of account, even though it does not give the required pluralistic answer.

It is perhaps worth while to notice in this connection an interesting change of view: Mr. Laski has recognized that he can salvage from M. Duguit's theories only their idealistic conclusions as to functionalism as a doctrine of state responsibility, and that he can find little comfort in the positivistic "public-service" state which legitimizes any kind of law and order that keeps the state functioning with organic perfection. If one deny moral value to the state, however, one must accept the positivist's "fear and force." The uses to which Fascism has put M. Duguit's suggestions as to a state-controlled and regimented "syndicalism" are enough to scandalize any proper pluralist. They take away the right to strike, not only in the public services, but in practice throughout industry.

In omitting all reference to agriculture, Mr. Laski has simply followed the uniform precedent of writers who are preoccupied with "the great industry," and who have the natural bias of the Labour Party. "I have said nothing about agriculture and the land problem. That is because I know nothing directly of either," is the disarmingly frank confession of the Preface. The omission leaves, as he notes, "a great gap." It is a gap which is simply one of several in the Labour Party's effort to treat the varied occupational life of society in terms of the Marxian idea of the proletariat, lumping all social activity together in a single category, and offering for control a single technique. But for that matter the Labour Party with its ultimate hope of industrializing agriculture and its reliance upon producer's coöperation is not worse off than the Baldwinism which has only Imperial Preference to offer. Agriculture in every country depends for its economic health upon adopting scientific production and cooperation.

Perhaps it is the unacknowledged specter of Fascism, evoked by Syndicalist and Communist tactics, which has inclined Mr. Laski to his defense of parliamentarism and to his repudiation of the extreme proposals of the gentlemen from the mines, from the red Clyde, and their allies. He rejects vocational along with proportional representation, guild socialism along with advisory parliaments of industry, and the two parliaments, the political and the social, of *Sidney-Webbicalismus* (to use Mr. Punch's phrase). Although he recognizes the impossibility of England's survival as a Communist state, given her present commitments to a capitalistic world community of states, he seems hardly to realize that the same tough elements of nationalistic capitalism vitiate any proposals to make the League of Nations a coercive superstate. Yet unless his prophetic assumption that the League can really come to control natural resources, raw materials, tariffs, competition for markets, immigration, and colonial policies—and all the other non-justiciable issues of the present—be taken as a valid presupposition, the possibility of many of his economic reforms falls to the ground unsupported. An England struggling for her imperial and national existence in the present competitive welter of nationalistic finance and marketing—which the League regards helplessly—has demands that are prior to the "national minimum", "fit for decent citizenship", and adequate education. The first necessary fact, which Mr. Laski as the spokesman of the Labor intellectuals does not care (and the Tories do not dare) to deal with, is that England is too tight an island by many millions.

How much his proposals for economic reorganization owe to

the Webbs' *Proposed Constitution for the Socialist Commonwealth of Great Britain* appears by simply comparing the relevant
portions of the two works. Hardly more than leading indications of the solutions proposed for a complete economic (but
a very slight political) reorganization of society can be given
in such an attempt as this must be to reduce the nearly seven
hundred pages of the *Grammar* to brief statement. First of all,
both the political and economic institutions, and particularly
the latter, presuppose an intensely active and aggressive democratic citizenship. Mr. Laski is notably at odds with his fellow
anti-intellectualist in politics, Mr. Walter Lippmann, as to the
possibilities of a public opinion that demands the right to pass
moral judgment upon the intrinsic merits of important issues.
Mr. Laski has a mystic belief, as befits a labor "intellectual", in
the omnicompetence of the "conscience of mankind"—except
where it falls foul of the conscience of an Athanasius. His
faith accords not at all with Mr. Lippmann's insistence upon the
externality of public opinion to the merits of social conflicts or
"problems". One may not share Mr. Lippmann's pessimism as
to the absence of any consensus of opinion, even within the limits
of the national state, on the merits of large issues. The public
is not such a phantom as he is trying to persuade it to be, nor
are representatives or conflicting groups able to settle their
difficulties free from its "outside" pressure, as Mr. Lippmann
supposes that they are—or ought to be. A general election does
elicit at least the information that there is a decided unwillingness to increase the cost of food in England in order that imperial
preference may be afforded to the Dominions—let Mr. Baldwin
witness. On the other hand, the introduction of Mr. Laski's
scheme of voting into the whole process of economic organization, even allowing for the possibility of defining appropriate
spheres for determining the limits of community of opinion,
would put an additional and an impossible burden upon citizens
who already show signs of being hopelessly fuddled by the complexity of the relatively simple choices necessary to political
control through party government. Yet Mr. Laski, after a most
trenchant criticism of the political unwisdom of the complexities proposed by Mr. G. D. H. Cole in the "Commune", and by
the Webbs in their dualism of parliaments, purposes a plethora

of economic democracies almost fantastic in their demands upon the voter—with small consideration of the question of whether votes really afford either a dynamic of production, or an adequate means of social control in industry.

One must note, in the second place, that his entire economic program is based upon a socialization of wealth equal not only to maintaining the minimum subsistence level at present agreed upon by all parties in England and operated through the "dole", but upon a further increase of state assistance to create a standard wage capable of furnishing education and "decent" citizenship. It is worth remarking that Mr. Laski lays down his "standards" quite regardless of the conditions of the national economy or of individual effort.

In the third place, his economic proposals look to the nationalization of all vital public services such as railroads, mines, shipping and transport, into which there enters the element of natural monopoly. In other public services of a more localized or less monopolistic character he would depend upon consumers' coöperation. In non-essential industries he would permit private ownership under rigorous regulation. In general his solution may be described as state capitalism, varied by cooperatives and by private enterprise of a narrowly limited character. Theoretically the ground has been laid for this emphasis upon the socialization of wealth by a chapter upon "property" that is a very fine statement of the ethics of the program of British Labor. One may again suggest, however, that the context of economic recovery and the tendency of private capital to take flight from such conditions have not been faced.

Within all types of industrial activity and economic services labor is to be "professionalized", although it is not to assume complete control. The state, through a complex system of governing boards and administrative commissions, is to have the right to argue with labor (on equal terms) as to output, and as to conditions and hours of labor. Even in the nationalized services there are to be no laws against strikes and no power to enforce settlements; for such laws, Mr. Laski holds, are in fact useless. This is, of course, something of an assumption in face of the success with which most modern states prevent strikes by state functionaries and in face of the undoubted success of the Republic of Germany in extending the area of compulsory arbitration to a wide range of public services without resorting to Fascist methods.

Here as elsewhere, Mr. Laski is curiously *a priori* for a pragmatist. It was heretical enough to attempt a statement of political principles apparently intended for all states to aim at without regard to the concrete limitations in their cultural and economic contexts. But for a pragmatist steadfastly to ignore the evidence with which political experience has furnished the student, even within the range of British and Dominion practice, in favor of solution along lines of abstract principle, is to renounce the most valuable part of pragmatic method.

Little of the evidence at hand tends to support the view that civil liberties are really the better protected for being enshrined in a rigid constitution, and left to the judiciary to defend—unless the rights of property are in question. English regard for personal liberty is notoriously higher without this device than is Irish or American regard for liberty with it. Yet Mr. Laski favors such a rigid constitution with its bill of rights, even for a unitary state like England. The fear that the power of judicial review for the constitutionality of laws may lead to judicial absolutism constrains him to sanction constitutional amendment by two-thirds of his legislative body, which is to be single-chambered, modeled upon a more wieldy and a smaller House of Commons, "magnicompetent" in its powers, and with parliamentary control over the executive.

In the construction of his "New State" Mr. Laski has perforce vested legal omnicompetence in a determinate majority of his legislature, for he has put the constitution itself in the hands of this power. His conception of devolution is certainly not federal, for his central parliament still remains supreme. Indeed his remarks on devolution clearly apply only to such homogeneous countries as the United Kingdom, although they are very good so far as they go. No clear relation of the chapter on "Authority as Federal" to his single-chambered parliament, either from the territorial or from the functional point of view, appears from a study of the powers with which he thinks it necessary to endow that "magnicompetent" body. Federalism, like pluralism, turns out to be a weasel word. The juristic structure of the Laskian state does not offer that essential protection to his federal communities that consists in eliciting their consent to an amendment of their powers and in affording them representation not based purely upon numerical proportions. Federalism appears to mean only a willingness to pit group against state through direct action.

If the United States, on the other hand, were unable in fact, as Mr. Laski supposes it to be (pp. 49 *et seq.*), to change the composition of its Senate by means of amending the amending clause itself in respect to equal state representation, it would be a League of States under a covenant to that degree. Mr. Laski's own construction shows how impossible it is to escape the juristic necessity of vesting final powers in a constitutional majority. The "Fathers" may have thought of Article Five as embodying a contract perpetually binding. But it is no longer so conceived by many American jurists.[37] It is probably safe to say that the provision will not defeat a willingness of three-fourths of the states to change the composition of the Senate, should that ever be secured.

Mr. Laski becomes the pragmatist once more in his discussion of the judicial process. He finds that judges reflect the conservative legal tradition of their social background in their decisions, with the result that radical social legislation gets short shrift. Consequently he looks with mixed favor upon the judicial supremacy required to protect constitutional rights; and he even finds that the prosecution of criminal proceedings under a Public Prosecutor ought to be flexible enough to assume the political responsibility which can take bias into account (pp. 582-586). One of the most interesting applications of Mr. Laski's own experience is his analysis of the conduct of the judge in the famous *O'Dwyer* v. *Nair* case on which he acted as juror (pp. 552 *et seq.*). His allusions to the trial come from first-hand acquaintance.

[37] See, however, the interesting article supporting Mr. Laski's view as to the unconstitutionality of an amendment which would amend Article V in this respect without the consent of the state or states involved, by W. L. Marbury in *Harvard Law Review*, Vol. XXXIII, No. 2, p. 229. It would, certainly, not require a civil war to change this part of the constitution, as the abolition of slavery did. See also the interesting reply to Mr. Marbury's broad "Limitations on the Amending Power," contained in an article by Mr. W. L. Frierson, "Amending the Constitution of the United States."— *Harvard Law Review*, Vol. XXXIII, No. 5, p. 659.

An interesting discussion of the possibility of changing the character of the American Senate is to be found in Mr. W. S. Carpenter's *Democracy and Representation*.

To sum up, there is a changed attitude toward two essential problems: (1) The group is no longer treated, in discipleship to Maitland, as morally ultimate and possessed of a corporate personality which endows it with absolute rights. (2) The necessity of coercive and unifying sovereignty for a rule of law is recognized and defended, although the only appropriate locus of such sovereignty is held to be the League of Nations, not the nation-state.

For (1), we are told that the group possesses personality only in the sense that "it results in integrated behavior." "The group is real, I suggest, as a relation or process." (p. 256.) Its claims to loyalty are put on grounds of function, not absorptive personality. "Even industrial bodies can not coerce their members beyond the point of insisting on what might be termed mental conformity." (p. 258.) One would think the state might be justified, then, in insisting on these limits.

For (2), I need only quote: "It is necessary, Mr. Ramsay MacDonald has said, 'to empty our minds of those revolutionary, futile ideas that one nation by its strength of will and determination, can simply ride roughshod over the rest of the world.' But our minds will be emptied of such ideas only as the Council firmly decides upon intervention whenever such aggression is attempted." (p. 638.) Does such a declaration of the rule of law not fit direct action within the state, if applied to the relations between groups as well as to those between nations?

In *A Grammar of Politics*, when all is said, one can not help finding a book written in the great tradition. It belongs to the effort made by a few figures in each generation to reinterpret political phenomena in a way that is true to the prevailing philosophy of the times and prophetic of the direction which political reforms will take. No one, without being completely and dogmatically lost to reason, could fail to acknowledge the stimulus which Mr. Laski has given contemporary theory. The *Grammar* that he has offered us shows a side of political thought to which the old legalistic theory was a complete stranger. The theory of the future will be grateful for the avenues which he has opened up. The sovereign nation-state may have more life in it than Mr. Laski thinks; it cannot be a finally satisfactory solution in a world so closely interdependent as ours is becoming.

CHAPTER VI

FUNCTIONAL INSTRUMENTALISM IN POLITICS: GUILD SOCIALISM AND *ORGANOKRATIE*

If pragmatic Romanticism finds its test in Mr. Laski's attempt to pluralize the state, and in the syndicalist efforts to claim autonomous legal power for occupational groups, Instrumentalism has carried the same problems into a different stage of development in the Guild Socialist theories of which Mr. Cole is the foremost exponent, and in the juristic theories of M. Duguit. The Romanticism of M. Sorel, who would destroy the state idea by the myth of a general strike, with no other content than its destructiveness, proved really only a more thoroughgoing Latin version of the pluralistic doctrine of Mr. Laski. The difference is that the latter attacks the doctrine of unifying legal sovereignty on the grounds not only that it is noxious to the growth of trade union freedom, but also because it does not correspond to the moral claims which each group person may make as of right. In both cases the need of a unified system of law, as the ground of constitutional morality is scouted as an intellectualist abstraction, without practical value or ethical appeal, and in both cases the final appeal is to the sanction of force, though M. Sorel is not apologetic about calling his solution of conflict violence, while Mr. Laski puts forward the right of each group to attain its own interests by direct action, as proceeding from the moral rights, inherent in personality. But about the essential points, (1) that there is no moral obligation to obedience created by the existence of constitutional government, and (2) that class war is necessary, both Mr. Laski and M. Sorel are in some agreement. M. Sorel is more consistent in following political pluralism to its revolutionary conclusions in theory, and to its justification by violence in fact. Both types of syndicalism, British and French, differ from guild socialism.

The Guild Socialist theories in whose name the unitary state

177

is equally subjected to a hostile analysis, do not derive their own support from a proposal to substitute for it either the reign of violence or the rulerlessness of philosophical anarchy. They have no instinctive or intuitional morality at their base, such as Romanticist syndicalism implies, although William Morris' return to medievalism undoubtedly gave them original inspiration. They are neither Nietzschean, nor Jamesian, and their pluralism tends continually to the same compromise that Mr. Dewey's Instrumentalism has made, a definite unification finally of morality with fact. There is about guild socialism, too, the very wholesome effort to liberate the creative impulses in human nature which Mr. Dewey has so often stressed.[1] It is an attempt in the field of industrial organization to give the possibility of that "immediate satisfaction" without which the laborer, under modern conditions suffers from what Mr. Graham Wallas has aptly called "a balked disposition."

The theories of Guild Socialism differ in another radical particular from syndicalist and kindred theories, and differ in the same way that Instrumentalism does from Romanticism. Romanticist revolts against the sovereign state have stressed this "incompleteness" of the emotional life in all the activities of men and have claimed that only the abolition of repressive state sovereignty could free the voluntary groupings of society through which that life should find its normal outlet. In this they are at one with the anti-intellectualist starting point of Instrumentalism. But they go further and propose to substitute for the state under law the reign of something for which they themselves have found the Bergsonian conception of *élan vital* the best description. It seems to me that whatever it is which Mr. Laski had in mind as the basis for a state of society without sovereign states ultimately comes to a Romanticist conception of this sort, although his challenge to the "right to command" has been thrown down in the name of "morality", and not "violence". In *A Grammar of Politics* he has, it is true, abandoned syndicalism in favor of an Inter-National Super-State with coercive powers. The guild socialist theory, too, would make its compromise with the necessity for unified law, admitting the need of a determinate and ultimate arbiter. It places very little faith

[1] Dewey, *Human Nature and Conduct*, p. 271.

in the myth of proletarian omnicompetence, or in the *élan vital* to bring order out of the chaos of revolutionary destruction. Its position as regards syndicalism is very much like that of Dewey as regards the Bergsonian element of Romanticism: Anent the *intuition* and the *élan vital* of that philosophy, he says, "Concrete intelligence is concerned with the habits which incorporate and deal with objects. . . . Nothing remains to spirit, pure thought, except a blind onward push or impetus. . . . The net conclusion is surely the need of revision of the fundamental premises of separation of soul and habit."[2]

Indeed it is the program of guild socialism to offer a scheme for the reorganization of society along lines quite consonant with those suggested by Dewey, taking into account the necessity of giving the instinctive and emotional sides of men's natures a guided outlet through reshaping what Dewey broadly terms habit. There is much that it has to say about the autonomous and democratic control of industries divided occupationally that is suggestive and valuable. Further examination of its claims may lead us to question whether political organization by occupations can ever supplant territorial organization as the basis for making law, even to the extent of Mr. Cole's modified claims, and whether, in any case, such law does not demand unity of legal sovereignty. We may also look, in passing, at the probability that the political democratization of industry can ever satisfy the real need for an outlet for the creative impulse; and see, further, what the meaning of the necessary entry of economic organizations of all sorts into the political life of the state really means, if it be possible to treat so vast a topic suggestively in outline.

At the outset of our proposed survey, however, let us frame the Guild Socialist movements in its relations to the rest of what we have called the anti-intellectualist revolt, and set it in its particular position in the general philosophy of Instrumentalism. Already its divergencies from syndicalism have been briefly commented on, but they can only attain real significance against the background of the general impatience with what Mr. Cole has, in *The World of Labour*, called defining "the perfect society

[2] *Ibid.*, pp. 73-74. In *Reconstruction in Philosophy* Mr. Dewey himself has likened the State to the conductor in an orchestra (p. 203 ff).

in vacuo." He tends as a Socialist of sorts to equate this sort of definition with the efforts to establish a millennium through the power of a collectivist state. The State of orthodox collectivist Socialism, because it extends its activities like an octopus over the whole life of men, and because it is an intellectualist construction *par excellence,* is anathema to Syndicalists and Guild Socialists alike. What Mr. Punch has called *"Sidneywebbicalismus"* is their particular *bête noire.* There is something ironical, though, in the gradual reapproach which the Guild Socialists make to their old intellectualist enemy in trying to escape the dubious premises of syndicalism, just as there is in Mr. Dewey's conversion of Instrumentalism into a philosophy whose anti-conceptualist bias grows less and less, in trying to escape the vagaries of Romanticist pragmatism. Mr. Cole has come nearer and nearer to the program of the Webbs in their *Proposed Constitution for the Socialist Commonwealth of Great Britain,*[3] except in his theory of representation.

To begin with, however, there is no question of the agreement between Guild Socialists and Syndicalists on one fundamental point that has been concisely stated by Mr. Bertrand Russell: "The glorification of the State and the doctrine that it is every citizen's duty to serve the state, are radically against progress and against liberty."[4] But where Mr. Russell (like Mr. Laski) sees in a state whose authority is limited "by means of groups which are jealous of their privileges and determined to preserve their autonomy, even if this should involve resistance to laws decreed by the State—when these laws interfere in the internal affairs of a group in ways not warranted by the public interests"[5] —a state none the less for that, a necessity for social order, the syndicalist conceptions amount to anarchism very thinly disguised. Guild Socialism holds with Mr. Russell that there is a necessity for a state, and that political organization is a sort of necessary evil which must be counterbalanced by industrial organization along the lines of powerful guilds, capable of protecting their autonomous sovereignty over their own purposes. But

---

[3] See Cole, *The Future of Local Government,* however, for a significant difference. He proposes functional instead of "Globe-Wernicke" representation. Nor does he think politics can be made "scientific."

[4] Russell, *Roads to Freedom,* p. 145, 3rd ed.

[5] *Ibid.,* p. 144.

its guild spirit sometimes leads it to a "labor solidarity" which Mr. Russell is far from sharing with it. He remains first and last an individualist in his moral doctrines, using whatever social movement or institution appears to him to have the greatest chance to promote "the free growth of the individual" which he rightly says "must be the supreme end of a political system which is to refashion the world." [6] Mr. Laski, too, in *A Grammar of Politics* puts ultimate control in the State organized to protect individuals as consumers and in its "magni-competent" parliament, territorially selected.

The emphasis on what Mr. Laski called a "realistic" interpretation of society and politics in terms of social "forces" leads much of the Guild Socialist doctrine of Mr. Cole, to construct the classic antithesis of the Marxian class war as the background of all political fact. Further he divides the sphere of consumers from that of producers. Sovereignty then becomes a sort of "resultant of forces", as Brooks Adams called it: "If law were the will of the strongest it would be logical and direct. Law is not the will of the strongest, for the will of the strongest is always deflected somewhat from its proper path by resistance. Sovereignty, therefore, is a compromise, as the earth's orbit is a compromise." [7] The best practicable compromise of sovereignty, therefore, suggests itself to Mr. Cole as a division of power between the state as the representative of the community of consumers politically considered, and an organization of all producers along similar lines, including a Guild Congress. *In Self-Government in Industry* he explains the division of power along lines of functional difference: "Where the State now passes a Factory Act, or a Coal Mines Regulation Act, the Guild Congress of the future will pass such Acts, and its power of enforcing them will be the same as that of the State." [8]

It is evident that this division of power must require some higher tribunal of settlement on the issues where the State, representing men organized as consumers, differs from the Guild organization of the producers, if there is to be a stable rule of law. Mr. Cole, in fact, accepts this necessity by proposing a

---

[6] *Ibid., loc. cit.*
[7] Brooks Adams, *Centralization and the Law*, p. 52.
[8] *Op. cit.*, p. 52.

divided representation of both bodies united in a sort of Supreme Council (or Court). It is hard to say how this body would differ from the sovereign Ministry of present parliamentary organization except that it would necessarily have wider and more final powers, and that it would bring the pressure of labor questions and industrial issues to the fore in a way that would hardly be possible without the return of the Labour Party to power at the present time. Obviously such proposals as these are aimed at extending the sphere of political machinery into a realm which the state has up to this time invaded only from time to time for more or less extensive Fabian experiments, or for purposes of regulation. Though Guild Socialists may declare that there is no peace with the present order of political might, they are merely aiming at a better expression of the will of the entire community than is at present afforded by merely geographical representation. Mr. Cole's own sympathies have never been noticeably with the Syndicalist myth, and his work on *The Future of Local Government in England* indicates that the organization of powers in the state presents more and more important problems to the type of socialism upon which he hopes to engraft the guild idea. So that he differs from orthodox "Marxism" (if there is any such thing) only by wishing to restrain the power of centralized bureaucracy through devolution of functions, and through a new principle of representation—that of the functional *commune*.

In spite of this fact, he never ceases to chide Socialism, Fabian Socialism, with being "as fantastically fatalistic as the worst of the later followers of Marx." [9] The divinely necessary evolution of society under a Fabian "State-Providence" proves only another cloak for what Mr. Belloc has called the *Servile State*, and so English Labour is, according to Mr. Cole, more and more turning away from Fabianism. The continued presence of Mr. Ramsay MacDonald as leader of the Labour opposition in Parliament, the

[9] Mr. Cole himself notes a tendency in the labor movement to become intensely "practical" because "so far as the end in view was concerned" it was "as fantastically fatalistic," etc. (*World of Labour*, p. 3). It is a criticism he applies to the Fabianism imposed as a creed on the movement by its intellectuals, chiefly the Webbs. Yet it applies with even more force to the uncritical attitude of Romanticism, from the Social Myth theory to Mr. Laski's "ceaseless striving of progressive expansion" among groups all equally a law to themselves.

influence of Mr. Laski and of Sidney and Beatrice Webb, taken in conjunction with Mr. Philip Snowden's repeated motions—through which the Labour Party almost solidly endorsed Socialism as a general doctrine—throw some doubt upon the present truth of Mr. Cole's observation, made in 1913. "The vague uprising of Syndicalism, which is in itself much more an instinctive process than a new philosophy," [10] failed, in spite of the efforts of *The Syndicalist Railwayman* of that period, and Mr. Fabian Ware's acclamation of the instinct as manifested in syndicalism against the reason of the political State, to provide any "working philosophy" for the liberation from Parliamentarism which many prophets within the movement had predicted.[11]   But Mr. Cole had himself predicted as much, while he attempted to estimate the real weight of the anti-intellectualist revolt. Fabianism, not syndicalism or communism, still rules the Labour Party, despite the General Strike.

"What, at bottom, does all this worship of instinct mean?" he asked. "It is clear that there is a widespread breakdown of the old reverence for law and order, a readiness not merely to disobey, but to give theoretical justifications for disobedience.

[10] *The World of Labour*, p. 4. For the debate on Mr. Snowden's motion in the House of Commons, see the *Times*, March 17-23, *Parliamentary Reports*, 1923.

[11] *Cf.* Fabian Ware, *The Worker and his Country*. The political General-Strike idea has never taken very effective root in England, however, in spite of the fact that it was invented by a Londoner, Benbow, in 1830. Possibly this is because English labour has learned from the failure of all the really important political general strikes, the Swedish, the Dutch, and later the French C. G. T. strike on the railroads of 1920, as well as from the failure of the other allied Federations of trade unions to come to the aid of the English coal strikers in 1921, and of its own great strike of May, 1926. Even the extremists now recognize that it must only be attempted again as a revolution. And in France, M. Berth has denied that the General Strike may be taken as M. Sorel has said it should, as a Social Myth : "The catastrophe, according to the syndicate, will not be the mystic Revolution, automatic and idle, but the supreme effort of working class action coming to crown a long series of patient and toilsome efforts." (Quoted by Cole, *op. cit.*, p. 93.)

As for the English Labour Party's attitude toward syndicalism, it may be deduced from the articles of the leading intellectuals of the Labour Party, as well as from the failure of syndicalism to make any headway in organizing the trade unions along its own lines. See, for instance, J. Ramsay MacDonald's *Syndicalism* (1912), Graham Wallas, "Syndicalism" in *Sociological Review*, July, 1912, and the Webbs' "What Syndicalism Means," and Mr. Cole's own chapter on "The Control of Industry" (*op. cit.*, pp. 344 ff.) for pertinent criticisms. Mr. Russell's *Proposed Roads to Freedom* contains what is still the best criticism of the theoretical defects of Syndicalism.

There is a feeling that the great State has got out of touch with the people, and that no more democratic machinery at elections will be able to bring it back again. . . . And there is a claim, on behalf of the individual, for a greater measure of effective self-government than can be given by the ballot-box and the local constituency." [12] In consequence we find the *Daily Herald*, the official news organ of the Labour Party, treating the House of Commons as the "House of Pretence"—an attitude, one may remark, which has undergone some moderation since "direct action" in the General Strike of 1926 proved disastrous, and since the Labour Party has once acted as His Majesty's Government albeit somewhat under restraint by the Liberal partners in the coalition.

[12] *World of Labour*, pp. 4-5. Mr. Cole finds that "all these protests are mainly negative; they point to something wrong without indicating the remedy. The worship of instinct is, in form, a worship of the indeterminate, when what is wanted is a new determination." The negative evil exists: "industrial questions have come to absorb so much of his (the individual's) energies that he can hardly regard himself as concerned with the State or Society in any save industrial relations . . . for the worker the State has come to represent merely 'a justice' that either holds its hand or miscarries" (p. 25). But the remedy which Mr. Cole proposes is not the instinctive destruction of what is feared by the worker in the power of the State, but rather the bringing back of a "general will" in which he may really share through the democratic control of industry. The growth of the Labour Party is evidence of the reality of the political interests which the Greater Trade Unionism represents. But insofar as the policy of that party is not purely Socialistic, its relations with Liberalism present one of the most curious anomalies of current politics. Mr. Cole's feeling that Labour "Parliamentarism" would be obviated by the organization of a Guild Congress is very dubious if one recognizes as he does the many points at which the State must intervene with the power of ultimate decision. But it might have the effect of clarifying the purely political issues which suffer such confusion in the minds of the electorate at present. The present Labour Party pulls in two directions: one toward a national political policy closely akin to that of the advanced Liberals, usually identical in matters of foreign policy: the other toward a purely "Labour-interest" point of view.

Perhaps the view of Mr. Austen Chamberlain, expressed in an important speech (see the *Times* of March 17 and 18, 1923, for his position as put in a Letter, with Editorial comment) is justified as a prognosis of political development in the party system. He declares that the old lines of party division on which Parliamentary stability was built up are vanishing through the introduction of a majority of "independent" voters into the electorate. Only part of the change can be accounted for by the suffrage of women newly enfranchised. The same tendency toward rapid shifts in power is marked in elections in the United States to a degree that has caused very widespread comment. Some have attributed it to the intensity and variability of the problems created for politicians by the "reconstruction period." Mr. Chamberlain thinks it is a condition which must be reckoned with, however, from this time forth, owing to the failure of any political program along party lines to command continuous loyalty.

But Mr. Cole was certainly in line with the forces operating in *The World of Labour* when he estimated the potential strength of Syndicalism (outside the Latin countries) to lie in its effective ability to organize men as producers where Collectivism thought only in terms of consumption. This necessarily means that the Trade Unions occupy themselves with other questions than the purely economic ones of wages and shorter hours, and begin to set the whole problem of labor in the community in the light of its broader moral issues and its organic relations with a state that is increasingly forced to take cognizance of the relation of men as workers to men as citizens. As Dewey, in the fields of education and social ethics, has striven to turn the pragmatic movement aside from mere Romanticist protest, and into a concrete and adequate Instrumentalism, so Mr. Cole and his associates in the Guild Socialist movement[13] are attempting to guide the Syndicalist revolt into paths where Trade Unionism may become a reconstructive factor in social evolution. Just as Mr. Dewey still engages in a polemic against intellectualism which prevents him from attempting the analysis of some of his fundamental assumptions, such as the adequacy of "the test of consequences" as the only criterion of truth, so Mr. Cole, by accepting the Syndicalist damnation of the state as an end, forgets that the state remains as essential means to any social end, and wastes much of his ammunition on a barrage laid down in that empty no-man's land supposedly occupied by the Idealists' State-concept. It is interesting to note in both Mr. Dewey and Mr. Cole, a gradual restriction of the attack on intellectualism to a condemnation of solution by abstractions, and a parallel

---

[13] A very useful bibliography of the earlier Guild Socialism is contained in Mr. Cole's own *World of Labour*. The works of Mr. A. J. Penty and Mr. S. G. Hobson, and Mr. Orage, and the files of the *New Age* show completer aspects of the movement as does also Mr. Cole's *Guild Socialism Re-stated* (1922). There are also Mr. G. R. S. Taylor's *The Guild State* (2nd ed., 1920) and *Guild Politics* (1921). Niles Carpenter's *Guild Socialism* is a useful critique, and (from the purely ethical viewpoint) Professor Norman Wilde's *Ethical Basis of the State*. The most recent critiques are those of Mr. Laski in a *Grammar of Politics*, and Mr. L. Rockow in *Contemporary Political Thought in England*. R. de Maeztu, in *Authority, Liberty, and Function*, accepts guilds but not real socialism. A remarkable critique and bibliography is to be found in Fernando de los Rios, *El Sentido Humanista del Socialismo* (Madrid, Morata, 1926). In *Pour Gouverner* (1918), and in *Les techniques nouvelles du syndicalisme* (1921) of Maxime Leroy a typical French interpretation is given.

development away from a pluralistic to an organic notion of society.

But Mr. Cole does not start from any such point of view as that of organic unity in society. He condemns it as vigorously and as specifically as Mr. Dewey has done,[14] although the dialectic of their ideas leads both of them back to it. Mr. Cole accepts "the class-struggle . . as an awful fact of social structure", and he strives to work out "the relation between the class and the group" in such a way as to show that "the group-principle . . is the true principle of working-class solidarity, and is alone able to substitute, for the disorderly discontent and unrest of the mass or mob, the organized protest and formulated demand that are essential to all movements that Society need recognize."[15] "It is the right of such groups, called in France the new 'droit proletarien', that the philosophy of Syndicalism (which is after all in origin only the French name for Trade Unionism) has arisen to assert. In this it is not too much to say that we have the germ of the political philosophy of the future."[16]

The real failure of the state lies in its externality to the life of the workers, according to the Guild Socialist theories. But the remedy does not lie in Syndicalism, "an idea done to death", for there remains a province for the state, once the trade unions have taken over the control of industry, and secured their own sphere. The program of Industrial Unionism, of the I. W. W. in America, of the old C. G. T. in France, of Tom Mann's Industrial Syndicalist Education League, all alike fail to recognize that man's industrial setting is not his complete background.[17]   Mr. Cole's

[14] *World of Labour*, pp. 20-21.
[15] *Ibid.*, p. 19.
[16] *Ibid.*, p. 22.
[17] *Cf. From Single Tax to Syndicalism*, of Tom Mann ; and his *The Industrial Syndicalist;* also M. Bouglé's *Syndicalisme et Democratie*, and J. G. Brook's *The I. W. W., American Syndicalism*, as well as the more recent work, *The I. W. W.* by Dr. P. Brissenden. Haywood, W. D., and Bohn, F., have put the case for the "one Big Union" in *Industrial Socialism*. But the movement of the I. W. W. in America, although it has attempted to carry out faithfully M. Sorel's counsel to violence, has generally represented far more the anarchic protests of unorganized labor against what was instinctively held to be social injustice than any considered theory of anti-state action. In the States along the Western Coast its program of "Don't Vote" and "Don't Fight," and its acts of lawless destruction (starting forest fires, bomb outrages, etc.) have amounted to a declaration of war on society, and have been treated in kind. The activities of "the Wobblies," as they are called, have been so connected with lawlessness and sedition that their

Social Theory has here taken a valuable hint from Mr. R. M. MacIver's *Community, A Study in Social Integration.* Nations have a real life apart from the mere productivity of industry. Were that not true, Fascism would be a defensible philosophy. It is the fallacy of the materialist philosophy, of Marxian doctrine in particular, to think they have not; but if Marxian materialism were true, it would tend to produce Fascism rather than more humane Bolshevism. Mr. MacIver has put it, "It is not possible that the state alone should effect a fairer and happier equilibrium, but it might well be—surely in fact it must be—the agency through which is finally expressed whatever form of readjustment an awakening social sense and the pressure of economic organization have made practicable." [18] If the adjustment is not to be the simple one of force, it must be that of the constitutional state.

There seem to me to be two Mr. Coles when it comes to a clear-cut attitude toward the real function of the state in its relation with the guilds. Perhaps, though, he seems Janus-faced in this matter because (again like Mr. Laski), at one time he is viewing society from the point of view of the present order, in which the class war is an awful fact and there is no place for the state as an impartial arbiter; while at the next moment he is giving the state its due in the new order. In his chapter on "Social Peace and Social War" in *The World of Labour,* for instance, he says: "A public that acquiesces in exploitation has no rights against workers who are up in arms against it; the State has no right to intervene *as an impartial person.* The State should represent the moral sense of the community, and for the moral sense of the community to be 'impartial' in the great war between justice and injustice is for it to forfeit its right as a community." [19] On the other hand it is a poor way for the justice-dealer in any dispute to rule the issue by the method of *parti pris* in the way Mr. Cole

industrial unionism has been hardly taken seriously by the bulk of American labor. They are, so far as they have any program, a syndicalistic combination of anarchy and socialism after M. Sorel's own heart; but their importance to the anti-intellectualist tendency of the labor movement is even greater because of the fact that they represent in its purest form the blind revolt of those who feel themselves oppressed, against the "jusfice" of the democratic political organization in a country where real control is so largely oligarchic.

[18] *Elements of Social Science,* p. 90.
[19] *Op. cit.,* p. 288.

assumes to be the only just one. "The overthrow of capitalist society," which he says is the only condition of social peace, is an ultimatum to a very large part of the community, and one which can hardly be put into force by the state without the very suppression of a convinced majority, or in any case, a very considerable minority, which cleaves to the "injustice" of the present social order—the rights of private property.

It may be possible that the cleavage between the classes will result in social war in England, in which case the state will naturally cease to furnish any basis of legal community, and the final appeal for the immediate issue will be to force.   Overpopulation, underproduction, unemployment, war debts help the Marxians along.   But so long as the state exists to give justice under law, it must strive to act as a politically responsible arbiter. Mr. Cole himself believes that "ultimate power must reside in the democratic State", though the unions must fight to the death until social justice is secured, resenting any interference of the state in their war on capitalistic control of industry.   Nevertheless he concludes his chapter on "The Future of Trade Unionism" with the sentence: "The Trade Unions must fight in order that they may control; it is in warring with Capitalism that they will learn to do without it; but it is the State that, in the end, will set them free." [20]

In the end, then, it is difficult to find any difference in the "Joint Council" to which Mr. Cole in *Social Theory* (or his "Great Commune" in later works) proposes to hand over the work of co-ordinating the state and the "Greater Unionism", and the sovereignty of the King in Parliament of English law. The name is different, the functions may be extended further than those of any existing body, and it is to be chosen very differently; but the power is the same.   The justice which is to be dispensed is still a justice under law, administered by a body which attempts the reconciliation of interests where that is possible, and the safety of the community interest in constitutional procedure, where it is not.

Let us look at Mr. Cole's attack on the present state, organized for territorial representation.   His claim is that it can never interfere equitably through compulsory arbitration, however the

[20] *World of Labour*, p. 392.

compulsion be disguised, for to interfere is inevitably to take sides, owing to the element of time involved in the issue of strikes. Owing to its lack of really intimate connection with the conditions of industry, it intervenes as an outsider, but an interested outsider because it represents the consumer's interest in stopping strikes as quickly as possible. The history of compulsory arbitration in Australia, New Zealand and in Canada largely bears out the statement that the government dare not interfere in labor disputes in the guise of the arbiter of justice of the issues involved, and fixer of the awards without carrying its industrial program much farther than the interventionist awards in question. In Canada, notably, there have never been any serious efforts to enforce the absolute character of the legislation establishing compulsory arbitration insofar as the sanctions against stoppage of work during the progress of the statutory period (in which the board of arbitration was still considering the case and its own recommendation) were concerned.[21] In modern Germany, always congenial to state regulation and to a degree of collectivism beyond the rest of European practice, the Reich under the German Imperial Republic was early forced to intervene in wage and labor questions, just as it has over the entire range of the country's economic life, because of the chaotic exchange rates of the mark. Railroad labor in particular has been forced to accept compulsory wage awards, and strikes against the awards were met with all the force of government, including troops for train service on essential lines. The situation created by the rapid fall of the mark had rendered government supervision of prices as well as wages

[21] Perhaps the best theoretical discussion of English *Conditions of Industrial Peace* is the book of that name (1927) by J. A. Hobson. There is also Mrs. E. M. Burns' *Wages and the State*, and L. L. Price's *Industrial Peace*. W. O. Sells' *The British Trades Boards* is an objective study. For American conditions see W. J. Lauck and C. S. Watts, *The Industrial Code*, and H. Feiss, *The Settlement of Wage Disputes*. See the monograph in the Columbia Studies, of Mr. Ting Tsz Ko, (No. 271), *Governmental Methods of Adjusting Labor Disputes in North America and Australasia*. W. Pember Reeves, *State Experiment in Australia and New Zealand*, unfortunately leaves off twenty-five years ago. For a Labour view see Cole, *op. cit.,* pp. 291 ff. The Judicial Committee has recently held the Lemieux Act to be *ultra vires* the powers of the Dominion of Canada, so far as it affected the compulsory arbitration of disputes *within* a province. See 41 *Times Law Reports* at 238 *sub nomine Toronto Electric Commissioners* v. *Snider et al.* in Appeal Cases to Privy Council for 1923.

necessary, however, so that the workers have accepted the situation as necessary, with all the better grace since the Socialist majority in the Reichstag (for a part of the period) constituted practically a labor government.[22]

But apparently, even with the stabilization of the mark, the industrial courts continue to function with marked success and to get their decrees enforced. Italy, under Fascism, has been able to abolish both strikes and economically avoidable lock-outs up to the present time, by the simple expedient of forbidding all but the Fascist labor unions (over which the government has so far an absolute control) and by favoring employers to stimu-late production. Since the revalorization of the lira unemploy-ment had grown through the industrial stagnation of 1927 (even according to Fascist figures) above a quarter of a million. How long it will remain true that labor can be controlled by Mussolini's decrees, now that the Fascist syndicates have begun to function to some extent in the interests of labor, under the Turati and Rossoni régime in the Fascist party, of course remains to be seen. Fascist absolutism has raised up a dangerous enemy to itself, as Rocco, Minister of Justice, has not hesitated to say.

In the United States, the courts have drawn the teeth from such experiments as the Kansas Industrial Court, and the Repub-lican Party has allowed the Railway Labor Board to be abol-ished by Congress and supplied in its place a Mediation Commis-sion. There is no escaping the fact that the continuance of perennial coal and rail strikes may change the attitude of gov-ernment toward intervention, by creating boards of arbitration that have real teeth in their awards. President Harding, under stress, demanded as much, but his successor has preferred to depend on conciliation and mediation, feasible enough during a period of great national prosperity.

Generally speaking both employers and employees in capital-

[22] Rathenau's assassination presumably put an end to his own program of social reform but the Socialist majority even during his tenure of office was largely responsible for the very firm hand used in the settlement of the strikes on the Prussian and Rhenish railway lines. The *Volkspartei* of which Rathenau was nominally a member often holds the balance of power in the German government, and it never hesitates to throw it against the more radical Left. The political power of a general strike for political purposes and to prevent the usurpation of power by a minority employing armed force was amply demonstrated, however, by the overthrow of the Kapp *"Putsch"* in 1920.

ist countries insist on the method of conference rather than upon compulsory award, and they have proved strong enough in England and America to hold the ultimate resort to the strike or lock-out, with the government merely intervening to "assist" a settlement. The real assumption underlying the refusal to submit to a compulsory award is that there is no ethical standard of appeal common to both parties.[23] Each protests that its rights are such as cannot be submitted to judicial procedure; they partake of the nature of absolute rights, based on the employer's side on what he is pleased to call "the law of supply and demand", and on the worker's side usually upon something closely akin to the same philosophy, expressed in terms of the right to strike. The attitude of the labor unions in a period of boom is precisely that of the capitalists. Each is out to squeeze the market for what it will bear, and by judicious pressure at the right place and time it can be made to bear a surprising amount. The only difficulty about prolonging the squeezing is that it may choke off the prosperity it is exploiting. In hard times the method of industrial warfare is even more disastrous. The attitude of the labor unions usually undergoes a marked change in periods of industrial depression. The A. F. of L. has demanded for labor its share in the increased productivity of industry, basing its demands upon a quite Marxian labor-value theory, and neglecting to consider what proportion of increased productivity arises from capital investment in fixed plant. We shall, in periods of depression, very probably hear little about labor's proportionate share in the *decreased* productivity of industry. Deprived of their economic weapon because of the ineffectuality of strikes, they turn to a different conception of their function and begin to talk of the duty of the community to the worker, and to exert political pressure toward that moral end. Surely, though, the time is rapidly approaching in the more essential industries and means of transport when state intervention in industrial disputes must assume some different character from the opportunist one followed in the conferences in which the state participates simply as another interested party, on an equal footing with the other two.

[23] *Cf.* Small, *General Sociology*, pp. 657 ff., and MacIver, *Community*, p. 303.

The nature of the conference itself precludes the hope usually of any real or permanent success. In a conference men sit as representatives of certain interests. They are conscious of the eyes fixed suspiciously upon them by their own side if they show a conciliatory mood, and they go through their parts with a histrionic care to seem loyal to those whose interests they are to protect if possible. The only hope of reaching a settlement lies in a compromise, and the compromise each tries to force is one based upon the other's fear, extorted through threat. The idea of an equitable settlement of the differences at issue is completely absent in fact, although it is much paraded in the speeches of both sides, each holding that its own view is the only possible just one. The procedure is very much like that of nations at a conference where their economic interests are closely involved. None of them probably desires war; yet each is conscious of the other's military and naval forces as the final argument on all questions. It is the atmosphere of war which breeds armaments, which in turn beget a still more warlike atmosphere. And the same psychology was at work in the conferences such as the one Mr. Lloyd George called between representatives of the coal operators and the miners before the great strike of 1921, and in the succeeding train of conferences. Inevitably the stronger party, economically, uses its strategic position to overawe the weaker, and the weaker sometimes retaliates by the resistance of despair, feeling itself oppressed; or waits for its own turn for revenge. The matter is not a purely economic one, for emotions and the differences of two widely held social beliefs come in as well, just as economic nationalism always colors the issues of international conferences.

What happens when the state enters this arena of conflict as a combatant? Of course, to begin with, it was never as a combatant that it proposed entering. The "representatives of the public" chosen, for example, on the labor dispute commissions appointed by Wilson and by Harding, sat with the declared purpose of facilitating settlements by constituting a sort of go-between interested in permanent industrial peace, therefore in peace with justice. But it was thought that if they participated as equals in the discussion, with no powers of award, the antagonism of both parties to compulsory arbitration might be allayed and common ground be found. What really proved to be the outcome was the introduction of another set of interests for consideration. The interests of the public had theoretically been identified with the sovereignty of the rule of law, operating to protect the larger community involved in such disputes, although the practical limitations of that sovereignty in its powers of coercion had also been recognized. Now, on the other hand, the public interest was treated as possessed of no real difference in kind from the private interests at stake, to a degree that pleased all political pluralists.

Take the first Industrial Conference called together by President Wilson in October, 1919.[24] It had the usual composition, the three groups we may call for convenience's sake Capital, Labor, and Public. The first was represented by members of the National Chamber of Commerce, the national Investment Bankers' Association, and national farmers' associations; the second, by high officials of the American Federation of Labor and of the Railway Brotherhoods, led by the patriarch Gompers; the Public, finally, was represented by a group of sufficient heterogeneity to include all possible interests without really representing any one interest in particular. Some queer contrasts in extremes found themselves stable-mates under the banner that bore the Public for its device: there was John D. Rockefeller, Jr., amiably representing the same "interest" as John Spargo, the best-known, perhaps, of the Socialist writers of the country. But there was also Charles Edward Russell, another Marxian to counterbalance Wall Street insofar as it was present in Bernard M. Baruch. There, too, was Mr. Bert M. Jewell, President of the Railroad Employees Department of the A. F. L., seated on the same side of "interest" as Judge Gary of the Steel Corporation. And the late Charles W. Eliot, president-emeritus of Harvard, lent the academic prestige of his presence to the entire proceedings.

This is the description John Corbin gives of the Conference in the *North American Review* of October, 1920:

[24] *Cf. Report*, "First Industrial Conference," Washington, D. C. For later developments see "Proceedings of the Conference on Government in Industry," December 10-11, 1925, Washington, D. C.; "Trade Associations: Their Economic Significance and Legal Status," National Industrial Conference Board, Inc.; and E. P. Herring, *Representation of Organized Groups Before Congress* (shortly to be published by the Institute of Government Research), 1928, *passim.*

"This motley assemblage had much ado to agree among themselves; and they had the still stiffer task of calling down the dove of peace upon the other two groups.

"The inevitable happened—*c'est son métier!* Much was said of 'collective bargaining' but the conference proved unable even to define it. Judge Gary was derided in his capacity as a representative of the public, and ultimately quit the conference in disgust. At the first opportunity the labor group fell upon the capitalists in the old familiar manner, evading every clear issue and endeavoring to twist the Conference, which was to have brought the industrial millennium, into an engine for winning a single strike—the steel strike, otherwise hopelessly lost. Failing in this, Samuel Gompers walked out with his cohorts, threatening to join up with the farmers—except of course the three 'capitalists' present—and work universal destruction. 'The time will come when they will be glad enough to bargain collectively with labor!' And so the dove of peace moulted one more feather." [25]

Even when one discounts the sprightly style of Mr. Corbin, the facts of the conference bear his interpretation out. And is there any great change in setting, substituting coal for steel, *mutatis mutandis,* when one approaches the Conference which preceded the English Coal strike of the following Spring? The Government was equally afraid of the mention of Commissions, or Awards. Out of its position as an equal participant in the struggle came Mr. Lloyd George's offer of a subsidy to bribe the miners back to work in hope of better times, without any effort at determining the principle upon which a just settlement of the permanent difficulties was possible. "Black Friday" was his present reward; the General Strike of 1926 was the later fruit.

Mr. Cole thinks labor stands to win more by reserving its independence of action than by any appeal to the public conscience: "The public's chief use for its conscience is to send it to sleep; but a very rude shock will sometimes wake it up," he says.[26] The disillusioned Mr. Lippmann calls it *The Phantom Public.* The employers, too are willing to accept this state of affairs because they are well organized, and can afford to tighten

[25] *Loc. cit.,* "The Forgotten Folk," by John Corbin.
[26] *Op. cit.,* p. 289.

their belts in a period of industrial depression for a longer time than either labor or the community whose prosperity as a whole is affected. Surely there is a necessity for some more intelligent method of coping with the incessant social warfare involved in this appeal to "conference." It works so long as wages are high and can be kept high. Or the state may adopt the attitude of benevolent paternalism during periods of great unemployment as it is doing at the present time in England. In the end, however, it is sure to be driven to some more permanent method of dealing with industrial disputes than can be found in conferences called by the government to consider disputes already in progress, with industrial warfare staved off by subsidies designed to postpone the evil day.

That is not at all to say that the state must of necessity turn the attention of the ordinary legislative bodies, already overburdened as they are, to the specific development of labor-dispute settlements. Adamson Acts are the results, or the Baldwin patchwork for the miners. Parliamentary bodies are finding it increasingly necessary to adopt a devolution of their functions through the extension of committees and commissions with practically legislative powers. There seems to be no really adequate reason why the economic bodies which Mr. Cole's *Social Theory* envisages might not come into existence gradually and in slightly different form through the adoption of some such proposals as those considered in the Whitley Committee Report. That Report reads:

"It appears to us that it may be desirable at some later stage for the state to give the sanction of law to agreements made by the councils (the joint councils of capital and labor of a relatively permanent character), but the initiative in this direction should come from the councils themselves." This is simply to take into account a growth which may be actually remarked in industrial organization toward a unity of coöperation. The legislation passed by such bodies would have a political as well as an economic character, even though division of function separated it from the sphere of the national parliament. It would be enforced by the sanctions provided by law, and brought into the rule of law by the cognizance of the courts. Yet it seems certain from what we know of the history of political experiments that devolution along these lines does not mean such an ultimate pluralism of autonomous groups as pluralists talk of. That is a trap which Mr. Cole at least partially avoids. "The future of Trade Unionism," he says, "accordingly depends on the spirit with which it approaches the task of working out for itself a status in Society, of changing gradually from a fighting to a producing body, as the conditions of society are modified. The class-structure of Society necessitates the class-struggle; but the class-struggle is by virtue of its object, only a phase." [27] "The 'Sovereignty' towards which we wish to see the unions moving will be in the one case a 'political sovereignty' coextensive with all common action that requires co-ordination and control, and in the other a purely 'economic sovereignty' aiming solely at the control of industry and recognizing in other spheres the paramount right and authority of the State." [28] The difficulty, as Mr. Laski and the Webbs recognize, is that the state can not abdicate the control of industry, although they join Mr. Cole in refusing regulation by Parliament. They all hope for control through agreement; they all balk at force.

Pluralism of this "devolutional" type is the keynote of the solution generally offered for the jangled disharmony into which the law finds itself forced by the facts of modern economic life. It is not only Mr. Cole and Mr. Penty and the *New Age* who are advocating its adoption. In actual practice in Australia and in New Zealand, as well as in England, the Wages Boards and Conciliation Councils are tending to become more and more permanent instruments of law, although their general outlines are necessarily matters of Parliamentary legislation. Mr. Churchill's Act of 1908, setting up Trade Boards, was a step in the direction of bringing about a common legal meeting ground for "interests" under the delimitation of law. The Board of Trade Report shows its success when applied to 'sweated' industries,[29] and there seems to be no valid reason why it should not be extended gradually to other industries as well as those brought in during and after the war. The findings of the Industrial Council under the Chairman-

[27] *World of Labour*, p. 392.
[28] *Ibid.*, p. 393.
[29] *H. C. Reports* 134, cited by Cole, *op. cit.*, p. 304. *Cf.* Lord Milner's sympathetic treatment in *Questions of the Hour* (1923), Chapter II, "Towards Peace in Industry."

ship of Sir George Askwith are interesting from this point of view: while it does not favor compulsory arbitration, it holds that, "in order that the interests of the community may be adequately safeguarded . . . it is desirable that before a cessation of work takes place there should be a period of time (after the existing procedure has been exhausted) sufficient to admit of (a) the further consideration of the position by both parties, and (b) the opportunity of the introduction into the discussion of some authority representing the interests of the community." [30] The importance of the "authority" so introduced is of course the vital point to the sovereignty of law. If collective bargaining is to attain the status of contract in law, as it seems inevitable that it must, the time agreements arrived at must be enforceable alike against the employers and the unions. And in order to assure a sufficient flexibility to the changing economic conditions, the machinery for arriving at these agreements and for changing them must assume legal character and permanency, if the strike and the lockout are not to remain the habitual method of settlement.

The difficulty of the present rôle of the state is that it intervenes and can intervene only negatively. It waits upon the issue of threats of war to develop into real war in industry, and then throws its sword into the scales of justice—almost uniformly against Labor, because Capital is harder to lay hands upon under the law as it stands, and because ordinary courts are hopelessly reactionary in their personnel.

"A sufficient excuse for distrust of the operation of law in fields of clashing social opinions," says Mr. John Dickinson, "is afforded by the actual experience of the failure of law in these fields, or . . . by its occasional perversion into an instrument of injustice. The trouble, it is submitted, does not go so much with the applicability of the law as to the improper manner of its application—on the one hand a rigid artificial and mechanical application of rules and concepts without regard to their intent and meaning; on the other, an application of the uninformed personal bias of judges in place of that carefully reasoned de-

[30] Quoted, *World of Labour*, p. 308.

velopment of opposing considerations which the novelty of the cases calls for." [31]

A case in point is a recent serious strike (July, 1926) of the Interborough Rapid Transit workers in metropolitan New York. The company protested, perhaps justly, that it could not pay larger wages even though the present wages were inadequate, because it was allowed only a five-cent fare by the New York City laws which regulate it. The strikers were beaten, because they struck "against the public," and because they could not command a solid strength, lacking the support of the organized unions. Perhaps they deserved to have been beaten on the merits of the immediate situation.

But now, after permitting this recourse to open war, the state is asked by the Company to intervene and punish the vanquished strikers. Suit is filed in the Supreme Court against sixty-two of the striking members of the Consolidated Railroad Workers Union of Greater New York, asking for $200,000 damage, and a permanent injunction against the union from interfering with "the business of the company." Obviously the company relies upon the Danbury Hatters' cases and the Hitchman case against the United Mine Workers. The state has not tried to prevent war. Shall it punish the conquered?

Instances of this sort of unequal intervention tend to strengthen the position of labor leaders in all countries that there is no sufficiently common ground between employers and employees under the wages system to permit labor to give up the strike weapon. But their contention is valid only so long as the ordinary "law" courts are used. Mr. Cole proposes "democratic control of industry" as the basis of a new common ground, with the State playing the part of the nationalizing and expropriating agency. Justice Sankey's *Report* on the federalized national control of the English Coal Industry points in the same direction. One may not accept so socialized a rôle for the state, except in unusual emergencies, and still admit the necessity for a more coöperative control of industrial conditions than is afforded by

---

[31] *Administrative Justice and the Supremacy of Law in the United States* (Harvard Univ. Press, 1927), p. 216. Mr. Dickinson thinks that judicial conservatism in labor law proceeds not so much from "class consciousness" as from James' maxim, "No one sees further into a generalization than his own knowledge of detail extends." *Ibid.*, p. 228.

the present cleavage between capitalistic control and labor resistance. Not, indeed, that government ownership and operation of railways has proved any more conducive to a complete *rapprochement* between the state as an employer and the workmen under it than it has to economic efficiency of management. The position of civil servants under the present governments of France and the United States, for example, does not lead one to hope too much from the initial stages of state control, at least. But a new machinery for hearing all labor issues would help to give justice to civil servants, too.

It seems obvious that society is moving toward a condition of social interdependence, based upon the economic facts, which will make necessary the development of new legal methods of social control. Our institutions are inadequate to the task in their present form. They must take into account the rise of group life which is so apparent a fact of modern social structure. In particular the state must accommodate itself to the diversity of function which its agents are called upon to perform if its government is to prove responsive to social need and equal to framing social purposes. The rule of law, as Mr. Barker in England and Dean Pound in America have shown,[32] is in danger of being lost in the development of agencies of law outside the cognizance of the courts which the chronic need for flexible machinery to deal with concrete problems has created. No one has more acutely pointed this moral than Mr. John Dickinson in his *Administrative Justice and the Supremacy of the Law in the United States.*

The German administrative law and the New Zealand methods of arbitral awards in the settlement of industrial disputes, seem to me best calculated to attain this flexibility. Fascism is

[32] See Mr. Barker's article "The Rule of Law" in the *Political Quarterly* of May, 1914, and Dean Pound's *Spirit of the Common Law*, especially the Preface. Mr. Dickinson in commenting upon the often repeated claim of the pluralists that the rule of law can not be extended to labor disputes because it would be an abstract and artificial limitation of the free play of natural forces says aptly: "This view . . . would banish law from the fields of human relations which are the area of social attention and relegate it to be a sort of village constable watching over interests more or less secure or wholly trivial. . . . In fact to make the presence or absence of an issue of contested social policy the test of whether or not a field of human relations admits of the development of a body of law is to set up . . . a mistaken criterion. The question should be approached from a more pragmatic angle." *Op. cit.*, pp. 214-215.

flexible in its control to the degree of being able to be directed in its policies in almost any direction that the Minister of Corporations (Mussolini) and the Fascist Grand Council desire. For that reason it lacks the primary requisite of constitutional morality. Its control, being based upon force, has no moral sanction to obedience. Until the Syndicates of Labor of the corporations in which they theoretically act with the employers' unions, can enforce responsibility upon the Fascist rulers, Fascist "arbitration" will be like that of any other irresponsible monarch. It is apt to be controlled at present by Signor Benni and the bankers and industrialists who are the real powers behind the throne. Yet it is clear that if the political representation of the labor unions in the new Chamber, on equality with the federations of employers, ever becomes a fact, and has any real political significance, Italy will have constitutionalized a type of guild socialism. The actual functional representation will be that suggested by Mr. Cole, even in the new organization of the local communes. The only difference will be in the centralization of powers in Rome, rather than Mr. Cole's regionalism for local government.

The theories which Mr. Cole has advanced obviously suffer from the difficulties of all social theory, in that they do not completely interpret either social fact or social purpose. Yet they seem to me to constitute the sort of chart of the future which is socially very necessary to the adventurous spirit that initiates experiment and change, and the same thing may be said of Mr. Laski's *Grammar*. In this respect, they both partake of the real virtue of the pragmatic Instrumentalism which we have previously considered as a social philosophy. The pioneer spirit of James' philosophy is in them. For their test, however, they must meet the requirements of something more considered than the mere willingness to "take a chance" on them. Guilds must be proved to be economically feasible as a means of production; they must also be brought into a relation of legal consistency with the State, and of practical consistency with the possibilities of free economic development. To embark on a reconstruction of society so radical as that proposed by the Guild Socialists will necessarily demand more than formal schemata. Probably it would demand international acceptance to limit competition. The pragmatists have justifiably warned against expectations based on the realization of formal principles, and have insisted rightly on the necessity of conducting social experiments like others of a nature more rigorously scientific, with an open mind and an observant eye.

None the less a program such as Mr. Cole's offers a real instrument with which to attack the problem that modern industry forces the state to consider, whereas the pure Syndicalist doctrines, appealing only to the Romanticist gospel of instinctive or intuitive action, offer only the bludgeon of force, to be applied indiscriminately in the destruction of all the existing order, the state along with the rest. The latter produce, in practice, the rebuke of Fascism.

Despite the importance of the problem which human activity in production assumes for modern political theory, it seems to me that the real difficulty in Mr. Cole's position lies in an exaggeration of the rôle of the functional organization of producers along lines that are roughly parliamentarian. Industrial organization is being forced to centralize control by a more and more extended corporate form of administration that tends to form a possible basis for the first really solid internationalism that the modern world has known, not excepting the aspirations of labor. The United States of Europe is a dream; the European Steel Cartel is not. Yet the state itself has been forced to model its administrative agencies of control more upon the lines of business corporations in order to avoid bureaucracy, and the tendency is more and more to remove its civil servants from the realm of elective politics on a general suffrage.[33] The proposal to reintroduce into industry the "politician" as administrator by a process of democratization comes very queerly from those who attack the present state for its incapacity to deal with specialized problems on account of the general nature of the qualifications expected of representatives in its sovereign parliament. Democracy, on the contrary, needs to insist on expert qualifications for its administrators in government. So long as the international markets are not controlled by a world federation of guilds, business men may well throw up their hands at the proposal to put

[33] See the interesting article of Mr. B. F. Wright, "The Tendency away from Political Democracy in the United States" in *The Southwestern Political Quarterly*, Vol. II, No. I, June 1926.

the control of industry into the hands of trade-union leaders whose survival depends to so large a degree upon the power of their demagogic appeal to the interests of their followers.

Mr. Cole has pointed out that the prosperity of the guilds would be a common economic aim of the utmost educative value in the selection of officials, under conditions very different from the organization for fighting which remains the central purpose of the present union structure. Both he and the Webbs insist on qualified candidates in industry. One may indeed see in coöperative production the ultimate solution, and in the introduction of morality into the economic régime the only escape from class war. This heritage from Saint Simon and Fourier one may share without being led to propose simply "the promptest and most complete possible amelioration of the moral and physical existence in the most numerous class" which Saint Simon held out as the supreme social end. There are other associations besides those of production and of government; other classes than the proletariat; it is only by a social structure that is flexible and simple at once that the state can be adequate to its needs. The life of the social whole which is humanity can not be exhausted by a division between the two spheres, even were the economic proposals involved of the soundest.

To meet this need, Mr. Cole has turned to the sociological theory elaborated by Mr. R. M. MacIver in *Community*. Community as a term is there described as "any area of common life." *Social Theory* is an effort to translate this protean stuff of social linkage into a political network of legal tissues in a way quite foreign to MacIver's own idea of *The Modern State*. Mr. Cole thinks that representation on the "one-man, one-vote" scheme simply doesn't represent. Individuals cannot be represented as wholes. No man can represent another. But one man can, according to *Social Theory*, represent another in a particular relation, or for one set of interests. "It is impossible to represent human beings as selves or centres of consciousness; it is quite possible to represent, though with an inevitable element of distortion which must always be recognized, so much of human beings as they themselves put into associated effort for a specific purpose." [34]

[34] *Op. cit.*, pp. 105-106.

This principle he proposes to apply through a scheme of functional representation, arranged to allow "one man as many votes as interests, but only one vote in relation to each interest." [35] This is a proposal calculated to turn the old-fashioned "pluralist" voter in England green with envy. Before 1918, a man might get in, with the aid of a good motor car, as many as four or five votes at a general election, one in each constituency where he was a rate payer or "occupant." Mr. Cole however, proposes to put a premium on being what Americans call a "good joiner." In the Commune, a really active citizen might have six or seven or more votes. [36]

If the experience of modern democracies has taught us anything, however, it is the lesson that the multiplication of voting duties tends to create apathy. Even allowing for a more active attitude toward representation by interest-groups, one could hardly hope to reduce the opportunity for machine politics and boss control by multiplying opportunities for voting indefinitely. [37]

The Commune, which is to be made up of the various larger communities of interest in the local, the regional, and national areas, with representatives for professions, occupations, consumer groups, education, sanitation, what-not, even some territorial representatives, is the real control group. [38] Outside (or inside?) these political bodies, productive industry is to be organized into guilds. The consumers are to be organized into classes such as "personal and domestic" or "collective," with councils for each type.

Even if one only took the communes into account, however, it is apparent that not only would an impossible load be put upon the most active citizenship conceivable, but also that functional representation no more represents men in the "mirror-reflection"

[35] *Ibid.*, p. 115.

[36] For a description of the new electoral law (Representation of the People Act of 1918) see W. B. Munro, *The Governments of Europe*, pp. 134 ff. This is quite the most useful text on general questions of European Governments. The text of the Act is given in Sait and Barrows, *British Politics in Transition.* For Mr. Cole's restatement of representative principles see *Guild Socialism Re-stated*, chapters on "The Commune," as well as his *Social Theory* and *The Future of Local Government.* For an adequate criticism see H. J. Laski, *The Grammar of Politics.*

[37] See *Non-Voting* by C. E. Merriam and H. Gosnell, and *Short Ballot Principles* by R. S. Childs.

[38] See *Social Theory*, Chapter VI, and *Guild Socialism Re-Stated*, Chapters III-VII.

fashion that Mr. Cole wants than does territorial. Any co-ordinating body must consider a wide range of problems from the standpoint of a unifying policy. There is no possible means of reflecting directly the views of individuals without direct democracy. All representation implies a mandate to act within discretionary limits. Trade unions have tried to enforce a limited delegate theory of representation upon their spokesmen without success—sometimes disastrously with success.[39] Party control, organized on territorial lines, remains the best expedient so far found for holding representatives to an accepted policy, and for enforcing responsibility. And even party control must often be relaxed to get men of any personality to stand for office. "Cannonism" in the House of Representatives killed initiative. The Senate has fortunately been spared because of its originally ambassadorial character and its present regard for its own deliberative function, as Mr. Lindsay Rogers has shown in his brilliant analysis of The American Senate.

Nor can functional representation plead that it is not only functionalizing the sources of political opinion but also the foci. If it attempts the former, it gets a delegate for a narrow set of interests, who cannot in any case represent his constituents on broader issues of policy. If it tries to combine the second by saying that it chooses only specialists for specialized work, it is evident that the "commune" wants not specialists but synthesists, if I may be permitted the term. Its business is to reconcile differences, not to represent them. Functional representation suffers in an exaggerated form all the ideological and practical ills produced by occupational or exaggerated proportional representation.

But there is still another aspect of Guild-Socialist theories to be considered: do they offer the best technique for that reconciliation of an industrial dynamic of efficient production and distribution with industrial freedom that modern society demands? Where any serious dislocation of the complex system of production in a world of competing states throws millions out of employment and produces misery, does Guild Socialism offer a

---

[39] This is remarked by the Webbs in their History of Trade Unionism, in A Proposed Constitution for the Socialist Commonwealth of Great Britain and in Industrial Democracy.

workable solution? What England, for instance, needs most vitally just now, is a dynamic of production that will permit her to sell in new markets. Otherwise she must continue exhausting her capital until her population by Malthusian or Neo-Malthusian checks has reached a level supportable by a modest share of the world's trade. For it is largely her decrepit capitalism that makes labor willing to listen to Marxian remedies.[40]

Mr. Cole (and with him to some extent, both the Webbs and Mr. Laski) thinks that workers' control of industry through voting, will supply a new dynamic. They are, apparently, not deeply concerned about competition from other states where Labor is not self-governed in industrial processes. Nor do any of them offer any help on the problem of maintaining the standards of living fit for education and decent citizenship where the economic resources of the nation and the world market do not afford such a possibility.

It is true that Russia throws no real light upon the applicability of these theories, because Communism is a very different doctrine from Guild Socialism, and because Russia was the last possible country in which a Marxian revolution could have been economically successful, owing to the primitive stage of its capitalistic development. But other European countries clearly show that a strong and integrated state with power to introduce arbitral order into industry is the necessary condition of economic soundness—not the "state-as-adjunct" of pluralistic theory. Furthermore, these countries display—as England does—the fact that labor is not mystically inspired to produce as much as possible by the mere increase in its economic power. Mr. Cook and his coal miners were just as unwilling to face the necessary economic facts as were the coal operators, in the Coal Strike that touched the match to English industrial warfare. What England really requires is a government that will apply the findings of the Coal Commission on coal owners and miners alike, on the Duke of Northumberland as much as on "Czar" Cook and his cohorts. Such a government will eventually be created by misery if it does not come out of democracy.

[40] See *Britain's Economic Plight* by Frank Plachy, Jr. Also the author's review of Philip Kerr's *England's Industrial Dilemma* in the *Christian Science Monitor*, January 7, 1927.

Mr. Cole believes that the situation would be completely changed when labor ran the mines, in a guild system, with indirect representative control over labor policy, even technical policy and management. But would miners actually in complete and equally shared control welcome the introduction of labor saving methods that might make still fewer of them necessary? Or would they be less tenacious of wage rates beyond the economic possibilities of profitable operation—even allowing for the soundness of the policy of nationalizing the mines and its probable benefits? Perhaps. But the introduction of a doctrinaire democracy into the operation of industry would not, even Mr. Laski agrees, help its technical and productive efficiency.[41] There is already a too marked tendency to seek "political" prosperity.

England may require much more the dynamic of economic solutions than of political in the actual management of her industry. As for a country like the United States, it has a need for a much greater use of governmental powers to prevent the wasteful anarchy of unregulated production and distribution.[42] But this is to be obtained more by collectivist than by pluralist

[41] *A Grammar of Politics*, chapter on "Economic Institutions" and criticism of Guild Socialism, pp. 82 ff. and 444 ff.

[42] Even the timid report of the Federal Oil Conservation Board appointed by President Coolidge annoyed the interests who demand that government leave business entirely alone. And when Secretary Work, of the Department of the Interior, in an official pamphlet entitled *Then and Now* (1926) permitted himself the liberty of interspersing in his optimism the statement "We are advised that ten years from now we will realize a timber shortage and fifteen years later a lumber famine" he drew down on his head the smoking wrath of the lumber barons. The latter, having cut more timber than the market could absorb, are even now engaged in a furious campaign of advertising to stimulate the consumption of lumber. What right had government to interfere? Has not even the reliable Hoover slipped up and hurt sugar prices? Senator Caraway is not the only Southern politician who is urging the abolition of the Department of Agriculture because its crop forecasts ruined the cotton market in 1926, and broke a good market by some gratuitous advice in 1927.

As even Mr. Coolidge's administration has not been able to keep the government from hurting business, is it not evident that the federal government must be endowed with powers of control adequate to give real regulation, of a type that will protect not only our national resources, but the legitimate types of business that do not depend upon exploiting tariff-protected monopolies or chain organization? The personnel and the traditions of our great commissions are the most vital spots of democratic control. And the present method of holding-company control of public utilities that escapes state control has been referred to the Federal Trade Commission for a hearing instead of to the Senate Investigating Committee on Power Companies called for by the resolution of Senator Walsh of Montana. There is now a proposal to add a Federal Coal Commission.

methods. We have found an apparent dynamic of efficient production in high wages coupled with installment buying, and a remarkable stabilizer for industrial prosperity in "hand to mouth buying" instead of seasonal buying in our greater industries.[43] Even making allowances for the probability that it may hurt us to collect our European debts in the only way that we can —through equipping Europe to supply us and the rest of the world with competing goods; making allowance for a probable dislocation through overproduction of automobiles, and through the shaky structure of the abuses of installment buying—still we are more nearly in a position to achieve Professor Carver's ideal of distributive prosperity through high wages and employee investment than any other country. That we owe this to the tremendous natural resources and the almost self-sufficing domestic market created by our national area, is partly true. But we also owe it to the fact that American employers have come to the conclusion that wages are not really high to the point of economic unsoundness until they fail to get an equivalent productive return. They have had forced upon them the value of high wages as a productive dynamic and as a means of increasing the strength of their own market.[44] Henry Ford's theorem that high wages mean rapid consumption of goods seems proved.

The real question is this: Will guild socialism show virtues of control or production that state regulation of a diversified system of private and public industry will not? In any modern system the question of finance is the ultimate question of control. Guild socialism, in Mr. Cole's theory, proposes to vest the substantial features of this in the Commune, which is to say in the

[43] The series of articles running in *The Saturday Evening Post* (September and October, 1926) give some of the pros and cons on the question of hand-to-mouth buying. Installment buying and selling, one of the most important economic phenomena of the present age, has been given a comprehensive analysis by Professor E. R. A. Seligmann in an economic research problem subsidized by General Motors Corporation, in a work called *The Economics of Installment Selling*.

[44] Professor Carver's *Present Economic Revolution in the United States* is a statement of figures that are at least indicative of a real movement toward employee stock ownership, even if one disagree with some of his analyses. *The Secret of High Wages*, by two British engineers, Mr. Bertram Austin and Mr. W. Francis Lloyd, is too simple an analysis of the causes of prosperity to be taken as more than economically naïve; but it does indicate a truth that England's own textile operatives should have taught her as to the virtues of high wages. See also, H. L. Moore, *Laws of Wages*.

Political State.[45] There is a very real necessity to develop institutions of financial control in the hands of every modern state.
Corporate risk no longer equates with corporate control. Even if
Professor Ripley's crusade against non-voting stock control and
the prestidigitation of accounting in corporate finance succeeds
in denting the protective apathy of government to business
anarchy, the question is far from solved.[46] The most intelligent
stockholders' meeting can hardly control financial policy. The
real control is vested in the hands of investment bankers and
depends to a terrifying degree merely upon their personal or
business ethics. The Federal Reserve System and the Inter-
State Commerce Commission, the Federal Trade Commission
and their like in the states, offer some protection. But, too often,
they can only perform post-mortems.[47] Holding companies and
managing companies largely escape control.

We have not yet developed any political machinery adequate
to this task. The risk is widely distributed. Stockholders' protective associations may offer a partial way out. But a great
part of the risk falls also upon the citizen, so interdependent is
modern society economically. Undoubtedly the state will have
eventually to fortify the voluntary features of business control
by normative acts and by an extension of state regulation. That,
however, will not take us much if any nearer to Guild Socialism.
It may take us considerably nearer a national industrial or eco-

---

[45] Even in the division of powers between two parliaments proposed by
the Webbs, provision is made for joint committees to work out financial
adjustments. Vesting responsibility is a political necessity, and would
eventually involve putting the real control in the party system which could
insure agreement between the two through control of both.

[46] J. M. Clark, *Social Control of Business*, W. Z. Ripley, *Main Street and
Wall Street*, and E. W. Crecraft, *Government and Business*. See for
Germany G. Weiss, *Die Beziehungen der Bankkreise zur Industrie* (1921).
For an outline English view see D. H. Robertson, *The Control of Industry*,
and J. M. Keynes, *The End of Laissez-Faire*.

[47] See Ripley, *op. cit. supra*, and G. C. Henderson, *The Federal Trade Commission*, and John Bauer, *Effective Regulation of Public Utilities*. There
is no really adequate analysis of the problems presented by the modern
organization of corporate finance through holding and managing companies
as the problems presented are too new and too complex. J. A. Hobson
and D. H. Robertson, Todd, Keynes, and Pigou have written on the
problems involved from the English point of view. American literature is
confined to special studies and M. W. Watkins' *Industrial Combinations and
Public Policy*. In Germany one may cite V. Liefmann *Kartelle und Trust*,
5th ed. (1922) and in France, *La concentration des entreprises en France*,
1914-1919, by Pierre Cambonne, *Rev. d'Economie Politique* (1920).

nomic council such as Mr. J. A. Hobson proposes in his *Conditions of Industrial Peace.*

We shall approach the problem of labor's share in this general problem of control perhaps best by the indirect method that Professor Carver has shown to be operative.[48] The direct share of labor control of management must always be limited to co-operation and representative councils, even in nationalized industries, unless we are to discard productive efficiency. In small and unusually flourishing units like the Hapgoods', labor councils may pursue a more direct method of democratic control. But that is hardly possible in large scale and fluctuating businesses.

In many ways Mr. Cole's development from *The World of Labor* and *Self-Government in Industry* to *Guild Socialism Restated* indicates that he has followed the Instrumentalist's progress away from the finally pluralistic world with which he started, with the dualism of political and economic organization, merely "brought together" in a Joint Council. In *The Future of Local Government* he spreads his problem on a broader background, one which gradually assumes the form which Walter Rathenau in Germany proposed to call an *"Organokratie."* The doctrines of Rathenau, starting, too, from an anti-intellectualism almost mystic in its intensity, developed into the conception that "The Kingdom of the Spirit" could only find its realm on earth through an organization of society like that to which he had given practical, though partial, form in the *Allgemeine Elektrizitäts Gesellschaft.* It is worth comparing his ideas, briefly summed up by Gaston Rafael,[49] with those of the Guild Socialism which Mr. Cole has proposed:

"From Marxian Socialism he [Rathenau] separates himself by his conception of capital, of the spiritual setting free of the work-

[48] The system of employee stock control put into effect by Mr. Thomas E. Mitten, who operates over $500,000,000 worth of street railway, motor bus, taxicab, and air lines as chairman of the board of Mitten Management, Inc., is proving effectively the worth of profit-sharing on a real scale of partnership. The employees of the Philadelphia Rapid Transit Company, operated by Mr. Mitten, own nearly one-half of that company's $30,000,000 of common stock. For a description of Mr. Mitten's plan for industrial democracy see *The Christian Science Monitor,* Vol. XVIII, No. 255 (Sept. 25, '26). However, the Mitten interests have been vigorously assailed for an undue and unethical control of Philadelphia politics.

[49] Gaston Rafael, *Walther Rathenau, ses idées et ses projets d'organisation économique* (Payot et Cie., Paris, 1919).

ing class, and by his relative respect for individualism. He does not fall into pure *étatisme*. Such intervention of the State as he advocates is not equivalent to seizure. The State neither exploits nor regulates itself; it entrusts powers to men of each profession or trade, who preserve all initiative, and administer the enterprises for the best interests of all. His syndicates and federations differ essentially from existing trusts whose monopoly creates a profit only for a little group of individuals or even for a single one. Far from resembling the guilds and corporations of the middle ages, the new syndicates will be as much distinct from them as the German Federal Empire is distinct from the conglomeration of small States that once it was; they will be neither associations created for the protection of particular interests nor despotic corporative groups of isolated artisans or small employers, but associations of production in which all the elements are commanded and ordered mutually, the ones by the others, each [group] forming a living whole, endowed with organs of perception, of judgment, of force and of will, and which are in a word organisms and not their simple association." [50]

This would serve very well, indeed, as the description of the hopes of the Fascist Syndicalists like the present secretary of the party, Turati. The great distinction, however, is that Fascism has no place for other organisms within the state organism, where there is a possibility of pluralizing authority. The Fascist groups, in their present form, are used and suffered to exist so long as they raise no questions of discipline, and do not strive to control their master, Mussolini. But will not the future be rather to Rathenau than to Mussolini? The State cannot absorb all groups into a single corporate life, although it can and must delimit the areas of group life and activity. It can regulate and control, it cannot create and inspire the whole associational life of a nation.

The *"Organokratie"* must assume a character of political unity through the state. What then will be the relations of the members of guilds to the law? In the end, that of citizens, although no longer merely of atomistic individuals. The organization of *syndicats professionnels* to take over the management of industry tends significantly toward a conception of society in which the

---

[50] *Walther Rathenau etc.*, pp. 271-272.

group is the unit. That is the direction in which Mr. Cole has followed the anti-intellectualist development. Nor is he alone, or in the company simply of Mr. Laski, M. Duguit and the others whom I have mentioned. The whole burden of such song of hope as there is in the pluralistic efforts to reconstruct society is that of the group-chant. *Solidarisme* in France, with its off-shoots in syndicalism and regionalism, *Organokratie* in Germany, with Rathenau's conceptions of a federalized organization of groups finding practical political and economic expression, Miss Follett's *New State* of community groups in America, Guild Socialism and kindred efforts in England, the "Fascist-Syndicalist" state that is being born in Italy,—are all searching for the reintegrating principle in the rise of group life.[51] One of Mr. Dewey's students, Mr. Tannenbaum, who has written a book on *The Labor Movement* in addition to having worked with the most important elements of the radical labor "strike-organizers," has this to say of the change:

"The first and most immediate influence upon government structure and function implied in the development of the labor movement is the change from individual to group responsibility. Our political government rests upon the individual. In theory the defense of the rights of the individual, the duties of the individual, the relations between individual and individual, constitute the chief concern of contemporary political government. The structure of political democracy is built on the assumption of the essential equality of man and man, and upon the assumption that the function of government is to regulate men's relationships with one another. This description of the individual as the basic unit of community organization, however, has become and is becoming daily less true of the actual state of affairs in the community.

"The labor movement has been, if not the only, certainly one of the chief factors in shaping society away from individual self-sufficiency, individual responsibility, and toward functional group solidarity. The labor movement has differentiated the community into its organic industrial elements, and the function of

[51] See L. Duguit, *Law in the Modern State* (translated by Harold and Frieda Laski) and Miss M. P. Follett's *The New State*, as well as Odon Por's *Fascism* (translated by Mrs. Townshend).

government, even at present, is becoming more and more a function of harmonizing the conflicting interests of groups rather than of individuals. All one has to do to convince himself of this fact is to examine the activities of any legislative body. He will find associations of all kinds, as associations, as groups, demanding and receiving legislative attention. The railroads, the railroad workers, the mine owners and miners, the interstate commerce commission and the chambers of commerce, educational associations and organizations of civil employees, groups upon groups of all kinds are subject to the legislative activity. We must, therefore, be prepared to admit that the tendency has been and still is for government to become more constantly concerned with the development of the technique of group relationship. The organic unit rather than the individual, one might say, is to-day the actual if not the theoretic basis of governmental function." [52]

This is the crux of the whole pluralistic effort to restate the organization of society in terms of "economic federalism" as Mr. Cole and others have called it. The assumption is that the corporate personality of industrial groups has absorbed the legal personality of individuals to such an extent wherever the two meet that "the Trade Unions are tending to establish a sovereignty of their own, limited no doubt in its sphere, but real and

---

[52] Frank Tannenbaum, *The Labor Movement*, pp. 195-197. Mr. Tannenbaum begins his introduction by a quotation from Dewey, *Reconstruction in Philosophy*, to the effect that "notions, theories, systems, no matter how elaborate and self-consistent they are, must be regarded as hypotheses. They are to be accepted as bases for actions which test them, not as finalities . . ." and says that he quotes this passage "so that it will not be assumed that the kind of community suggested as a consequence of the growth of the labor movement is presented as an absolute and definitely predictable type. The labor movement is obviously on its way and this book attempts to indicate where it is seemingly going to come out." In carrying out this program he builds up the Congress of producers theoretically along the lines of functional representation. The theories of Guild Socialism he criticizes for separating the representation of men as producers and consumers (cf. the chapter on "Producer and Consumer"), on the grounds that the system of checks and balances which Mr. Cole has pointed to as operative in the United States Government is really a hindrance to political effectiveness in the expression of the community will. Functional organization he believes would provide a single congress capable of "a complete synthesis of the community" (p. 237). "It would include its territorial representation, its consumers' interests, its productive interests, and also those which are concerned directly with the production of what are called immediate consumer's goods." Pluralism has thus been swallowed up in Instrumentalist Functional Unity by a thoroughgoing disciple of Mr. Dewey. Mr. Tannenbaum now greatly admires the Mexican C.R.O.M.

absolute within its proper competence," in Mr. Cole's words. This means complete "closed shop" with no state supervision of unions. The "actual, if not the theoretical basis of government function," Mr. Tannenbaum reminded us, was concerned with the real claims that great interest groups made upon the state—a position familiar to political science since Bentley's *The Process of Government* appeared. It is clear that my underlying assumption in this critique is that the *ultimate* legal relationship between their members and the state could, however, only be one of citizenship made effective by political parties, although this citizenship is now "filtered" by group life. Political parties based on territorial representation must be the final means, on this reading, of enforcing responsibility and registering public opinion. The rule of law, though it must recognize the reality of group life and group purpose, must still enforce the possibility of a voluntary relationship between the individual citizen and the group of any sort—religious, occupational, economic or other.

On the other hand the claim is advanced by pluralists that the real corporate personality of the groups intervenes finally. This is the basic presupposition of Mr. Laski's older theories (though not of the *Grammar*), and it tends to develop in all the doctrines which share Instrumentalism's functional interpretation of society. I have suggested that if the personality of individuals is to be attributed "writ large" to corporate groups one may not stop short finally of the conception of an organic society, functioning with laws which are hardly a degree removed from those of biology—in short with Duguit's final conception of solidarism, or Mussolini's Fascism. "Syndicalism"—in the broad sense in which Mr. Laski and Mr. Cole both accept the term to cover "Trade Unionism in the light of the theory we have outlined, seeking in it the realization of the new group-personality which is the central fact of modern society"[53]—can hardly evade the eventual development, dialectical and actual, into *Solidarisme* or *Organokratie*. Syndicalistic guild socialism is a theoretical half-way house on the road toward those conceptions of society and government which appear most clearly in the theory of M. Duguit, and the practice of Fascism, just as M. Sorel's anarchistic Myth proved in application to be Sovietism in its develop-

---

[53] Tannenbaum, *op. cit.*, p. 28.

ment from group federalism to Leninism. Fascism is, *par excellence*, the result of this progress away from disintegration to absolute functionalism.

Before we can estimate the value of the contribution which "economic federalism" has to make toward a new basis of representation or toward the devolution of functions in government, it is necessary to consider the pragmatic interpretation of the organic nature of group life and of group personality, with its claim that the personality of a corporate entity is a "social fact" of the same order as the personality of individuals. And to do that it will be useful to consider the Instrumentalist interpretation of morality as imposed by the group, even where that doctrine stops short of locating a super-personality in the group. The "impositional" treatment of morality, the interpretation of law as the product of organic social reactions rather than the community of purpose arrived at by common willing toward the same end, is characteristic of Mr. Dewey's latest writings, and of the system of *droit objectif* proposed by M. Duguit. No theory of the state can adequately meet their challenge that does not do justice to the relation of the state to other groups.

PART III

PRAGMATIC ETHICS AND THE FASCIST STATE-ORGANISM

"Fascism seizes individuals by the neck and says to them you must be what you are; if you are a bourgeois you must remain such; you must be proud of your class."

BENITO MUSSOLINI.

"The nation is . . . an organism embracing an indefinite series of generations in which each individual is but a transient element."

THE PROGRAMME OF THE NATIONAL FASCIST PARTY (December 1921).

"To a temper so permeated with the conception that society is an organism compact of diverse parts and that the grand end of government is to maintain their co-operation, every social movement or personal motive which sets group against group, or individual against individual, appears, not the irrepressible energy of life, but the mutterings of chaos. The first demon to be exorcized is 'party,' for government must 'entertain no private business,' and 'parties are ever private ends.' "

R. H. TAWNEY, *Religion and the Rise of Capitalism* (speaking of Arch-Bishop Laud).

CHAPTER VII

THE IDEALISTIC VIEW OF THE STATE AS A COMMUNITY OF PURPOSE

In order to understand the protest of pragmatism against the ethical side of the Idealistic theory of the state, it may be worth while to examine what is one of the best modern statements of the Idealists' position, that of Professor Norman Wilde in *The Ethical Basis of the State*, which carries on, critically, the tradition of T. H. Green.

Politics, in the sense assigned to the word by Aristotle rather than in the *sens péjoratif* of American usage, is an ethical study— that is, if one approach it in the Platonic frame of mind which is bent on finding a justification for *the* State, rather than in the carping spirit of those tough-minded persons who are always pointing to the "cussedness" of some particular state. Most of our professors of politics would disdain the term *theorists;* they prefer to call themselves political "scientists." Your philosopher, even though he lay no claim to Plato's kingship, ventures among them at his peril. They sneer at his world of norms, and talk with fine scientific detachment of Tammany Hall, or of the psychology of politics.

The Ethical Basis of the State is an attempt to restate the case for philosophy. Although Professor Wilde is a philosopher, he is no neglector of the essential social studies which are termed sciences. Indeed he combines in an unusual degree the perspective of humanism and the thorough acquaintance with the modern point of view championed by Mr. Dewey. He is not hopeful of pointing out a way to social or political salvation, of finding it through scientific administration, or even via proportional representation or the short ballot. He does, however, hope to clear the ground so bitterly fought over by theorists (and the air as well) by "an untechnical exposition of the principles more or less clearly recognized since the time of Plato and Aristotle."

217

The modern critique of the state has issued in a general attempt to discredit the idealistic notion of a "general will", that is somehow summed up by the actual political community called the state. In the name of syndicalism, of sovietism, of guild-socialism, the attack has been carried on by boring from within. From without there are cosmopolitans as well as internationalists who demand a more inclusive ethical community than the nation-state. One may hear "Citizens of the world, unite!" preached with moral fervor, and a vehemence equalled only by the economic exhortation which has customarily been addressed to "Workers of the World". The ways of the smugly self-sufficient nationalism that blazoned the doctrine of state sovereignty on every page of constitutional and international law seem to have fallen on evil times, even if they are not drawing to so rapid an end as these defamers of the state may hope.

Mr. Wilde is bent on recapturing for the state its due meed of credit. He has scant consideration for either internationalism or cosmopolitanism, honoring them by consideration of only the most indirect sort. He assumes, apparently, the pragmatic impossibility of any moral community of purpose larger than that in which law is laid down with the indisputable sanction of force. That focuses his view on the nation-state as a unit.

The concern of modern ethical theory, idealistic and pragmatic, is largely with the State's rôle among the associations within itself. Abjuring any of the pompous manipulations of man as an economic or a political abstraction, Mr. Wilde proposes to find what it is in the nature of the human society that gives the state any moral claim upon the ultimate loyalty of its citizens. Now that the state has found a sphere for itself which, generally speaking, the church cannot successfully dispute, it must turn its attention to the claims of economic organizations, never before so numerous or powerful.

One can be grateful that here a chastened Idealism has shunned the Æsopian Lion's Den of the Absolute. He has not taken refuge in a mythical "general will," even in that hypostatized with such great sophistication by the late Dr. Bosanquet. But the solution offered by his "community of purpose" in things political must have clearer limits drawn for it than are here offered before it gives any convincing basis for our loyalty to the state. Does the state incorporate values absolutely superior to those offered by other associations? Mr. Wilde has refused to confuse it, as Idealists often do, with the whole organic context of social relations. What then are the peculiar ethical values in the political community that he defines as "an all-inclusive, non-voluntary, territorial association"? Has the state a real moral claim to be the sole trustee for society of all the organized force at society's command?

The justification offered is "that men in carrying out their settled purposes necessarily or naturally build for themselves a State, and that it is no external, artificial or accidental thing, but an essential condition of human excellence." The limits on the power of this community rest in fact upon the general recognition of an area of freedom for the individual sufficient to insure his contribution to the common good. Rights remain ideals, however, to be discovered, not socially created. They are "natural" in the sense that they are grounded "upon the deeper implications of human nature itself."

This is, it seems to me, the line which ethics must follow. But where does it lead us? The ethical basis of the state must somehow rest upon a sense of moral obligation; and that sense seems to vary in theory and in fact, both as to its intensity and its area of community. Obligations must, one would think, be relative to the values involved. In concrete instances, Mr. Laski rightly holds that the justification of the state must depend on the particular claims advanced by the state—with the admission that ultimate conflicts of moral values are inevitable. As Doctor Johnson had it, "The State had a right to martyr the Early Christians, and they had a right to be martyred."

But Mr. Wilde is searching for community, not conflict. Consequently he lays it down that "Out of wealth-seeking individuals we cannot build a free community." He sees no hope of an ethical synthesis to be arrived at by occupational representation, or by Mr. G. D. H. Cole's functional representation (to be obtained by giving one vote in each interest-group to which the citizen belongs). One may be of the same mind about the particular proposal, and yet find nothing hopeful in the group "interpenetration" to be achieved on a territorial basis by the integration of neighborhood communities—a process almost lyrically described by Miss Follett in the *New State,* and here accepted by Mr. Wilde. The unhappy party system, scepticism counsels, must remain our chief hope—under any scheme of representation—of enforcing and forming public opinion on national issues; though it may sound like a counsel of despair to say it. Garbage disposal *inter alia* may, as Miss Follett has suggested, form a real basis of neighborhood community; but it is hardly a criterion for national issues, unless the term "garbage" be used with unseemly levity.

As for the representation of interests, we can hardly escape the fact of powerful lobbies and blocs all bent on that very purpose. Unless community is to remain a pious wish we must somehow make bricks with the straw at hand: bankers' and manufacturers' associations, chambers of commerce, farm bureaus, labor unions. A really ethical community for the settlement of their differences must provide a machinery that offers some hope of expert and deliberate evaluation of their claims—in the light of a genuine desire for justice. Outside of our realm of ideas we insist on testing the state not only in terms of its constitutional morality, but in the fitness of its actual form of government. This hope of justice can be felt only in a state so organized as to provide for fair play on a common and public field. In this respect the German Industrial Parliament, or a similarly functioning if smaller and differently chosen advisory economic body, may offer the concrete beginning of a solution which advances the notion of workable community beyond a mere categorical imperative. Some consideration of advisory economic councils might conceivably have had a positive ethical value, both for hopes and fears.

Professor Wilde commands our thanks for recalling to the skeptical realists and pluralists of our modern political theory the necessity for looking well to their ends. He has not, perhaps, sufficiently considered his own problem in the light of means. With the main outlines of his formal ethics this critique of pragmatism is in accord. But it feels, as he apparently does not, the necessity of meeting the truth of the pluralistic and pragmatic contentions: (1) that the nation-state with its unitary sovereignty does not in fact command an absolute moral loyalty, nor is it always in fact the final unit of coercion, and (2) that the community of purpose attained by the state varies in extension and in intensity.

There is also a further, and a more vital issue raised as to the Idealistic ethical basis of the state from a quarter which Professor Wilde has not found it worth while to notice. Fascism is not an attack upon the moral value of the state-purpose. Rather it is an attempt to outdo the most absolute Hegelianism or Platonism in insisting that the state sums up all values, and is hence superior to any other or all other groups in its ethical claims. Fascism merely differs from idealism in deriving the source of the general will not from constitutional democracy but from an hierarchically organized and functionally integrated nationalism under efficient dictatorship.

As a contemporary challenge to the ethics of a philosophy of rights that would assert both individual, group, and state rights, Fascism is a more real danger than pluralism. It interprets syndicalism as merely a means to the end of social solidarity, organizes its state functionally to promote efficiency, not to protect group rights, and subordinates every moral value to the maximum production of which the disciplined nation is capable, under the integrating will of a "super-man." It is necessary, if we are to cherish constitutionalism as the ethical basis of our normative state, to meet this new issue.

CHAPTER VIII

PRAGMATIC ETHICS, POSITIVISTIC LAW, AND THE CONSTITUTIONAL STATE *

Pragmatism, according to William James, is rather a method than a philosophy. But in his own hands it remained so unmethodological as to create a scandal, even among the pragmatists who took their philosophy seriously. When Mr. Dewey brought his Instrumentalism to their aid, there was great rejoicing. For a logician to turn upon logic its own weapons, to break with the conceptualistic schemata offered by tradition, was almost too much to have hoped. He came, to the eyes of the pragmatists, arrayed as an angel of light. To the logicians as a whole, however, it is hardly too much to say that he seemed like the devil quoting scripture.

Now Mr. Dewey's impact upon contemporary thought, in America at least, is too easily perceived in any direction one turns to admit of discussion. He is the only figure, with the possible exception of Mr. Santayana, that stands out in several different fields of philosophy among the minds of the first rank; he has influenced our ideas of education profoundly; he has made distinguished contributions to the political literature of the times, theoretical and polemical, scientific and propagandist; and all this is to say nothing of his influence upon a legion of students who have sought him out.

In his philosophic career proper, many critics have thought to discern a sort of rake's progress of the pragmatist: the turning of his own thought more and more away from universals, principles, and the like, and more and more toward those concrete, specific, and occasional writings which have latterly contributed his peculiar brilliance to the columns of the *New Republic*. But, even though that would be hardly more than to practise what he has so often preached, it is not fair to charge Mr. Dewey with a

* Reprinted with alterations from *Economica*, No. 19, March; 1927.

neglect of the larger outlines of his philosophy. In fact, the more one examines a book like *Human Nature and Conduct* (1922), or even *Experience and Nature* (1925), the more the conviction grows that Mr. Dewey's proposed *Reconstruction in Philosophy* (1921) is a bit of rebuilding architecturally familiar enough. The outlines assume a striking similarity to those of the so-called *science des mœurs*, the work of the positivistic "social realists" in France, MM. Lévy-Bruhl and Durkheim.[1] The same approach to a science of society has led Vilfredo Pareto to much the same conclusions in Italy. His theory of the various rational "derivations" from non-rational "residues" has much in common with Durkheim's "collective representations." Both Durkheim and Pareto represent the positivistic and scientific attitude that is the heritage of European thought from Auguste Comte. M. Duguit himself gratefully acknowledges his debt to positivism. By placing social forces almost entirely in group coercion, M. Durkheim, e.g., has attempted to remain within the rigid stays of scientific method, as Mr. Dewey has insisted that the social philosopher must.[2] Social interdependence he interpreted as binding men into an organic, though not a mechanical, solidarity, and the morality that resulted from this organic interdependence had its socially compelling force upon the individuals within the groups merely because it existed as a fact. The fact was the pressure brought to bear by the group. As opposed to the morality of Kantian individualism, and the conception of individual rights which it enthroned, this positivistic philosophy of

[1] M. Albert Schinz had indicated quite clearly that Mr. Dewey's earliest programme in *The Logical Conditions of a Scientific Treatment of Morality* (1903) led him straight to Positivism. "La méthode consciencieusement appliquée ramène aux idées de Lévy-Bruhl, dans *La morale et la science des mœurs*, marchant lui-même sur les traces de M. Durkheim dans ses *Règles de la méthode sociologique*." (*Anti-Pragmatisme*, 1909, p. 89 et seq.) Mr. Dewey, at first, has pragmatically refused "to draw a line of rigorous separation between philosophy which is purely normative and the sciences which are purely descriptive" (*Logical Conditions, etc.*, p. 13, note). *Experience and Nature* finds him appealing to a scientific description for norms. M. Lévy-Bruhl has admitted that "a science cannot be normative in so far as it is theoretical" (*La morale et la science des mœurs*, p. 14), although, of course, one may reject the whole positivistic assumption on which "theoretical" is so limited to description.

[2] A remarkable analysis of their work is to be found in *The Method and Presuppositions of Group Psychology*, W. R. Dennes (University of California Press, 1924). For their relations to Comte see W. H. George, "Auguste Comte: Sociology and the New Politics," *The American Journal of Sociology*, Vol. XXXIII, No. 3, pp. 371-381.

society found no use for any other notion than that of "obligation" (*devoir*), not moral in any ideal sense, but actual and compelling through the pressure of group reactions. It is this sociology, denying the utility of either metaphysics or ethics, and planting itself squarely upon a description of social "facts" that is proclaimed by M. Duguit as the basis of his whole jurisprudence. It offers the theoretic basis for the rule of law that he has founded upon a social solidarity secured through assuring the public services. Legal theory can once and for all dispense with metaphysical constructions such as the legal personality of the state, the notion of sovereignty, and that other heritage of French jurisprudence from Rousseau, individual rights secured through a general will. Dean Pound and Justice Holmes in America, too, have gone far in this pragmatic direction.[3]

There is in this theory of law based on social facts, with its correspondingly "social" morality of pressure and conformity, a genuine affinity with the Instrumentalism of Mr. Dewey, in the recent phases of the latter, particularly. Not only in its general anti-intellectualism, but in its specifically positivistic qualities, the sociological jurisprudence of M. Duguit sees very nearly eye to eye with the pragmatic philosophy of Mr. Dewey. Underlying both is the assumption of society functioning to the limit of its organic (or economic) capacities. Instrumentalism does not look to an evaluation of moral ends. It takes these ends for granted, as the "datum" of the specific social situation of every act. The acts themselves are to be tested only by the efficiency with which they attain the given ends (or the equally given desires). Mr. Dewey's metaphysics is entirely summed up by scientific criticism of consequences. It has no norms, and it claims that none are needed except those which arise as facts out of experience; these are not logically classifiable.

In *Human Nature and Conduct* Mr. Dewey has attempted to

---

[3] In addition to the collections of the essays and writings of Dean Pound, such as *The Spirit of the Common Law*, *An Introduction to the Philosophy of Law*, and *Interpretations of Legal History*, his chief contributions to various Law Reviews, notably the *Harvard*, may be found in the bibliography given in *An Introduction to the Philosophy of Law*. Justice Holmes' philosophy has been set forth in a pragmatic light by Mr. Felix Frankfurter, "Constitutional Opinions of Justice Holmes," *Harvard Law Review*, Vol. XXIX, p. 683. His own books confirm this interpretation. See *The Common Law*, and *Collected Legal Papers*, and *Speeches*.

state that scientific social psychology whose need he has so long felt as the primary requisite of any useful system of ethics. In producing his psychology he derives the entire equipment of creative intelligence from something that he calls *habit*, assisted in coping with experience by the active biological impulses of man, and conditioned by the social setting of his every activity. The apparatus, thus simplified, is capable of turning morals to scientific account, and reducing the ethical notion of "rightness" to something like the description of organic reactions. The Kantian conception of human personality as morally responsible is simply left out of this equation altogether, as it is a disturbing factor in any attempt to reduce ethics completely to the terms of such a method as is used by the physical sciences. The appeal is to "facts," and these facts, *ex hypothesi*, rule out considerations of an *a priori* "ought." The doctrine is very succinctly put by Mr. Dewey:

"These two facts, that moral judgment and moral responsibility are the work wrought in us by the social environment, signify that all morality is social; not because we *ought* to take into account the effects of our acts upon the welfare of others, but because of facts. Others *do* take account of what we do, and they respond accordingly to our acts. Their responses actually *do* affect the meaning of what we do. The significance thus contributed is as inevitable as the effect of interaction with the physical environment. . . .[4]

"There is a peculiar inconsistency in the current idea that morals *ought* to be social. The introduction of the moral 'ought' into the idea contains an implicit assertion that morals depend upon something apart from social relations. Morals *are* social. . . . "[5]

In lamenting our lack of a scientific social psychology Mr. Dewey says that "at present we have no assured means of form-

---

[4] *Human Nature and Conduct* (1922), p. 316. How far Instrumentalism has led Mr. Dewey away from the ethics of Personalism and toward Positivism may be judged by contrasting this work with his early (1888) "The Ethics of Democracy," University of Michigan *Philosophical Papers*, Second Series, No. 1.

[5] *Ibid.*, p. 319. Mr. McDougall in an interesting critique of Habit, in the use to which Mr. Dewey puts it, asks "Can Sociology dispense with the Instincts?" *American Journal of Sociology*, May, 1924. One ought to add, "or with normative intelligence?"

ing character except crude devices of praise and blame, exhortation and punishment." The fact that there is disagreement as
to the principles of ethics, he thinks, is attributable to isolating
the facts of moral activity from the concrete interactions of
human beings, "an abstraction as fatal as was the old discussion
of phlogiston, gravity, and vital forces apart from the concrete
correlation of changing events with one another. . . ." One may
be very heartily in accord with this critique of the danger of
"empty" abstractions, without confusing abstractions, as it seems
that Mr. Dewey does continually, with the universals absolutely
essential to thinking. And certainly one of these universals
which has claims to being something more than a "crude device"
is the concept of *right,* or rightness, with its implication of responsible moral personality, for whose choice it is a necessary
presupposition and a frame.

Yet this conception is the one Instrumentalism must destroy
if it is to build up a scientific "social" morality. For "rightness" is an evaluation achieved by the individual. The stuff he
works with he receives; but the activity of reshaping it is creative in the true sense of that word. Mr. Dewey calls all this
"the last resort of the anti-empirical school in morals;" [6] so it is—
and likewise the last resort of morals of any sort that can be
differentiated from biological responses of an organism to appropriate stimuli, or mere tropisms. He asks how much would be
lost by dropping out this conception of Right and being "left face
to face with actual fact": no more would be lost, certainly, than
the actual fact itself, a fact without which experience itself
would be no more than inscriptions on that *tabula rasa* empiricism has always taken dogmatically for granted. "The answer to
the question, 'Why put your hand in the fire?' is the answer of
fact. If you put your hand in the fire it will be burnt. The
answer to the question 'Why acknowledge the Right' is of the
same sort. For Right is only an abstract name for the multitude
of concrete demands in actions which others impress upon us,
and of which we are obliged, if we would live, to take some
account. Its authority is the exigency of their demands, the
efficacy of their insistencies . . . in fact it signifies the totality of

[6] *Human Nature and Conduct,* p. 324. See also his *The Public and Its
Problems* (1928).

social pressure exercised upon us to think and desire in certain ways." [7]

It would be unnecessary to labor the point by quotation at such length were it not for the fact that Mr. Dewey is cheerfully unconcerned with the logical consequences of his own doctrines. He has insisted ever since his early *Logical Conditions of a Scientific Treatment of Morality* that "it is futile to insist that psychology cannot 'give' the moral ideal, and that consequently there must be recourse to transcendental considerations, to metaphysics." [8] Yet he has repeated in a variety of forms that "The social saturation is, . . . a matter of fact, not of what should be, not of what is desirable or undesirable." In spite of having just said that Right is only another name for "the social pressure exercised upon us to think and desire in certain ways," he proclaims that "it [the social saturation] does not guarantee the rightness or the goodness of an act" and that "there is no excuse for thinking of evil action as individualistic and right action as social." [9] To that one can only agree, given the premises, by saying that there is no such thing as rightness in the sense of a thing desired *against* social pressure. But Mr. Dewey meets his difficulty by one of those ingenious and astounding leaps that leave his readers breathless: "The difference [between evil and good] lies in the quality and degree of the perception of ties and interdependencies; in the use to which they are put." And with this bit of legerdemain he is ready again to talk of individual effort as creative!

Now it is not a little confusing, to minds not gifted with a pragmatic twist, to talk of Right as social pressure, as if that exhausted the facts, and then introduce a subjective calculus (whether in the individuals or the group, it remains subjective) of ties and interdependencies, and of utility. Utility for what and to whom? Whose vote is to decide those perplexing problems of "the quality and degrees of perception of the ties and interdependencies" that now differentiate evil from good—and, one would think, right from wrong—had one not been told spe-

[7] *Ibid.*, p. 326.
[8] *Op. cit.* (University of Chicago Decennial Publications, 1903), p. 115, Vol. III, Pt. 2. See also "The Need for Social Psychology," *Psychology* (revised), Vol. XXIV, 1917.
[9] *Human Nature and Conduct*, p. 317.

cifically that Right and "the totality of social pressures" were interchangeable terms? The answer to this question brings the pragmatic ethic once more back to "social" morality. "If the standard of morals is low it is because the education given by the interaction of the individual with his social environment is defective." Passing by the difficulty of finding how the totality of social pressures (which is always Right) *could* be defective, one arrives finally at the conclusion that the place to attack moral obliquity is in the adjustment of social forces. If, somehow, the proper "interaction" could be secured, the world and the individuals in it would be morally perfect.

Are we advanced on our road a whit by this sort of generalization? Unquestionably the individual does not operate *in vacuo* as a moral agent, nor does rightness grow up in a realm of pure idea, unspotted and immaculate. The doctrine of the social setting of every moral act is surely as old as Aristotle, perhaps older; so is the experimental nature of human activity. But unless we are to think of the individual merely as a sort of test-tube or retort, in which social forces work out their chemical reaction, we must do justice to the normative character of creative intelligence. It is the very "forward-looking" quality of the mind (whose preoccupation with the future to the detriment of the concrete and living present Mr. Dewey so deplores) that none the less prevents the "habit" of which he talks from growing solid—from "caking hard," as Bagehot would have said. The pragmatism of William James clung to individual moral responsibility even at the cost of giving up logic—"fairly, squarely, and irrevocably," as James put it. Mr. Dewey, by finding no facts except "social forces," can only retain moral responsibility at a similar cost.

His pseudo-scientific selection of facts with which to construct a scientific social psychology and a social morality, is so very like that of M. Duguit that to give an exposition of the latter's sociological foundations for law would be hardly more than repetition. In several respects that are illuminating, M. Duguit pushes the conclusions implied by Mr. Dewey to their logical conclusion, and is even willing to give them pragmatic application. If society is organic in its functioning, social solidarity will enforce its own criterion of rightness. Consciousness does indeed exist in human beings, but it cannot be shown to play any creative role. It is merely registrative of the decrees of social forces. He is even more impatient than Mr. Dewey with the attempt to go behind sociology and psychology to metaphysics. His system is built upon a positivistic description of facts, not "metaphysical theories." All theories, according to M. Duguit, are metaphysical which try to construct anything (and particularly law or morality) upon a will of any sort, or rights of any sort. One must not be misled by the use of such words as *devoir* or *lois normatives*. They have no connotation of moral obligation, or normative valuation. They are the product of social pressure, just as Mr. Dewey's obligation to act rightly is. M. Duguit would, I think, cheerfully accept the metaphysics of Mr. Dewey, which turn out upon analysis to be mere criticism in terms of facts as consequences, with no "wholesale standards of reality" implied.

It is interesting enough to note that, not only in ethics and metaphysics, but in law as well, Mr. Dewey is in substantial agreement with M. Duguit. As long ago as 1894, in the *Political Science Quarterly* of that year, in a critique of "Austin's Theory of Sovereignty," he had sketched what might have served M. Duguit for the germinal conceptions of most of his theories of law. There is nothing that I know of in the works of either Mr. Dewey or M. Duguit that would indicate anything more than the most casual acquaintance of either with the works of the other, but their "way of looking at things" (which James called the essence of pragmatism as a philosophy) is essentially the same. The similarity is readily apparent in the attack which both have launched upon the conception of legal sovereignty that has served analytical jurisprudence more or less satisfactorily since Austin's time, despite the criticism of the Historical School, and the sociological jurists.

Mr. Dewey quite fairly points out the injustice done to Austin by insisting, as Sir Henry Maine, Cornewall Lewis and T. H. Green had, that his doctrine "considers the essence of sovereignty to lie in the power . . . to put compulsion without limits on subjects, to make them do as it pleases." [10] Austin fully realized the extra-legal restraints upon rulers: he took the habit-

[10] T. H. Green, *Works*, Vol. II, p. 401, quoted by Dewey, *loc. cit.*

ual obedience of the bulk of the people for granted, however, in the normal state.

Austin's contention had merely been that, in order to define the province of jurisprudence, one must separate positive morality from positive law. The latter was the command of a determinate person or persons accustomed to habitual obedience from the bulk of a given society, and not rendering obedience to any other person or persons.[11] That put legal sovereignty squarely in the organ of government that had the final say as to what should be called law. But the identification of sovereignty with government, according to Mr. Dewey, is a mere fiction. The real sovereign can only be found in the complex of social forces that actually get themselves obeyed at a given time. Government itself is under law, in modern times: it must conform not only to the law, but to the custom of the constitution. To talk of this constitutional law as auto-limitation is as unsatisfactory to Mr. Dewey as it is to M. Duguit.[12] Neither of them will hear of a special domain for "public law," for all law is ultimately enforceable only by what Austin would have called "positive morality."

To both Mr. Dewey and M. Duguit, the group represents just as real a political unit as does the state. Group relations manifest the same pluralism that Lord Bryce remarked in international relations.[13] Laws of authority are enforced upon the individual by the family, the church, the occupational or professional group. They have plenary power within their own range of control. M. Duguit, indeed, looks to these associations within the state for an ultimate pluralism of authority upon which to found a system of law interested only in enforcing functional duties and securing the operation of the public services. Mr. Dewey talks of pluralism, too, as the modern practice of political authority. Yet both alike insist upon a rule of law to be enforced by determinate agents much as Austin did. Social solidarity demands it. It is difficult to see what "pluralism" can

[11] *Jurisprudence* ("The Province of Jurisprudence Determined"), p. 170. See for Austin's recognition of the trusteeship of Parliament and the binding character of the Constitution, p. 203 *et seq.* (Edition of 1861).
[12] See Jellinek's classic statement, *Allgemeine Staatslehre*, p. 357. (Edition of 1905.)
[13] *International Relations*, Inaugural Address of the First Institute of Politics, Williams College, 1920.

mean which is unified, as Mr. Dewey says, by a regulatory state, operating through "definite organs," "determinate forms of exercise." As long as one is talking of government as existing only for "utility," it is difficult to escape Austin's Utilitarian logic. The point Mr. Dewey is making, though, is not that Government does not demand determinate bodies to say what is law, and to apply it to specific instances, but that this determinate body or bodies of persons cannot be called really sovereign either in law or fact. Austin insisted that lawyers were not, could not be, interested in the complex forces that made for habitual obedience. Law must stick to the arrangement of the simplest available facts. Obedience was such a fact, and superiors issuing commands were other facts of the same sort. For law, then, the sovereign was the person or persons ("determinate superior") who commanded as of right. To admit that sovereignty was vested in society at large, as Mr. Dewey does,[14] would, from Austin's point of view, have been simply to fail in his central endeavor, which was, as the title of his book suggests, to determine the province of jurisprudence. Austin insists that laws "properly so-called" can only be "positive law," the commands of the determinate superior. Mr. Dewey, on the other hand, insists that all that law need insist upon is "determinate forms of exercise."[15]

Nor would he limit these "determinate forms of exercise" to constitutional procedure, as it seems to me that he should. His case against Austin, up to this point, is clear. Not only does Austin's theory fail to take into account the modern constitutional state, in which sovereignty rests ultimately in the habitual willingness of the "bulk of the people" to accept authority under law, and not merely the authority of a given person or persons. It fails as well, according to Mr. Dewey, to take into account the true nature of law even in absolute monarchies like, say, that of France in the late seventeenth century. He insists that we must "extend the operation of sovereignty and of the recognition of its authority clear through from constitutional law to the working of institutions like the family—wherever there is authorised control on one side and subjection on the other." In short, his

---

[14] Article cited (*Political Science Quarterly*, 1894), p. 48.
[15] *Loc. cit.*, p. 50.

own view of law is that it is equivalent to what Austin would have called "positive morality," the realm, i.e. in which authority does not command the special sanction of organized force which is at the beck of the state in enforcing what Austin called "positive law."

Let us make a special note in passing of this part of Mr. Dewey's reconstruction of the doctrine of sovereignty. He is impatient with Austin's attempt to make a special sphere for legal sovereignty to the exclusion of all other types of authority. He is all for admitting the genuine pluralism of authority which exists because there are many other social institutions and associations besides the state. Law cannot be reduced to the mere command of government without overlooking the source of law itself. Yet was not Austin facing a real difficulty in admitting into the consideration of the *legality* of laws this inquiry into their ultimate or sociological source? Was he not quite correct in insisting that *legal* sovereignty must be restricted to the commands of "determinate" bodies, bodies which were habitually obeyed because of what he called the "utility" of fixing on organized government as the sole power capable of saying what is law? How can Mr. Dewey find in a sovereignty extended to all group authority "the determinate forms of exercise" which he has agreed were necessary for government?

His objection is clear: "If this complex [authority in society] exists for the sake of what Austin calls 'utility,' then the operation of sovereignty cannot be reduced to the imposition of commands by a certain portion of society upon another portion, the part which imposes being itself exempt." [16]   The answer is that if Austin be brought up to date by agreeing that "determinate" shall mean *constitutionally empowered,* then the agencies of government must possess exactly the right of command with which Austin endowed them. Otherwise the lawyer is to be left groping for his law in sociological theories, and the judge must apply, not statutes or the common law, but his own evaluation of conflicting interests. This is a conception of jurisprudence by no means foreign to the Sociological Jurists, at their head perhaps M. Geny of France, and it finds an unmistakable echo in M. Duguit. Is it not tantamount to the assertion that there is

16 *Loc. cit.*

no real need for differentiating *legal* sovereignty from what I venture to call *constituent* sovereignty? And is even the latter, which we may define as the agreement among a given social grouping to become a state and to remain one, capable of the pluralistic treatment offered by Mr. Dewey? *Can political authority be dispensed with, and social morality substituted, in determining what is law, to begin with?* That is what our first question will require us to answer. The second will sum itself up about like this: *Can political authority be shared by the State with other associations?*

To answer the first we must determine what the nature of social morality is, whether human conduct can be pragmatically reduced to specific reactions to the forces which bear on it, and what the nature of these reactions is. Can ethics be reduced to a science like in kind to the physical sciences? What is the meaning of individual moral responsibility and of personality? Only after we have found satisfactory answers to these questions can we find the relation of morality to law.

To answer the second, we must agree to use the term *sovereignty* with the circumspection which it demands. If it proves to be a fiction, let us by all means discard it from the vocabulary of politics in any other sense. If it proves, like many another word, to be slippery in its meanings, let us try to lay fast hold upon the distinctions between them. The test will come in its application to certain problems of the nature of law and of the modern state which, though theoretical, are by no means idle, for they have the most immediate practical importance.

But to return to our first problem: what is the nature of social morality? Is it the product of a society completely organic in the subordination of the individual to its functioning groups? If that is the case, the psychology of obedience to any authority whatever is that of Hobbes: men obey because they are afraid not to; rulers are limited in their turn by the fear of provoking social reactions. Like Mr. Dewey's burnt child, they each dread such fire as they have experienced. "If sovereignty is what Austin says it is," says Mr. Dewey, "then we must not stick at saying that the whole organisation of society is based upon the fear of the commands of a certain part of society." [17] This is

[17] *Loc. cit.*

not entirely fair to Austin, as the present Master of Balliol, Mr. A. D. Lindsay, has shown in a considered essay on "Sovereignty" that deserves to become the classic modern statement.[18]   But, putting aside the question of whether Austin's theory implies the subordination of the many who are ruled because of their fear of the few who rule, Mr. Dewey's own interpretation of social morality implies the fear-theory of political obedience in an even more thoroughgoing fashion.   For not only do the many obey, but the few actually rule out of fear.   He attempts to supply the same escape from this implication of his impositional system of morals by speaking of social needs, just as Austin spoke of utility.   But what this interpretation of social morality as the product of the organic interdependence of societies amounts to is not needs, but necessity.

For the frankest possible recognition of this fact one has only to go to M. Duguit.   He agrees perfectly that the rulers, as well as the ruled, are bound by law; and he has the consistency to see in this law not anything morally obligatory (as it is imposed by social reactions), but simply the ruthless demand of social solidarity that the public services function.   He recognizes, further, that this activity under law is in response to social needs comparable to those of an organism, and accepts the purely economic interpretation of morality that fits these conditions:

"The cells composing an organism are subordinated to the laws of that organism.   Everyone recognizes that: the law of that organism is that which governs its formation and development. In the same manner the individuals composing a social group are submitted to the law of that group, a law which governs its formation and development.   The one and the other of these laws are laws of co-ordination.   We don't call the law of the organism a norm because we cannot affirm the cells composing it are conscious; the law of social group we do call a norm because the individuals who are its members act consciously, will a thing they have in view in virtue of a motive of which they are conscious." [19]

[18] *Proceedings of the Aristotelian Society*, June 16th, 1924.
[19] *Traité de droit constitutionnel*, Vol. I, pp. 18-19 (2eme ed.).
    M. Duguit has accepted the current *Solidarisme* which M. Léon Bourgeois popularised from Durkheim's conception of organic solidarity: "The Solidarist doctrine," says M. Duguit, "considers that individuals are like the cells

But consciousness, according to M. Duguit, cannot be affirmed to play any active rôle. The action of the group depends upon law, not a creative purpose.

Once we accept an organic social morality, fear is the only possible basis of obedience. Let Mr. Dewey remonstrate with the age that moral sanctions are "crude devices of blame, praise, exhortation, punishment." His own exhortation will remain equally futile until he can offer some more adequate foundation for true morality than social pressure. It is as difficult in practice as in theory to dissociate fear from force—a fact that M. Duguit admits unblushingly: "This fear [of ruled for the rulers and the rulers for the ruled] is always a product of the greatest force, and I can hardly be accused of slighting it, since it is on the contrary the point of departure of all my developments." [20] Mr. Dewey can only escape the implications of his own ethics in the same direction by turning his back upon them—as he does, in fact, in his extremely liberal exhortations in the *New Republic*.

Neither of them really have much to quarrel with Austin about in the matter of limiting the consideration of jurists to facts. Austin, however, wished to stop with the simple fact of political obedience. He did treat that as habitual (as Mr. Dewey does), and he did enter into utilitarian explanations of it in terms that were very much like those of Mr. Dewey, e.g., in his explanation of "utility" as the reason that men accepted government. But the moral problem did not concern him, as it does Mr. Dewey. It had, however, previously absorbed the attention of his countryman Hobbes, who furnishes him with the notion of legal sovereignty. Hobbes had, with something like the Gallic unconcern of M. Duguit for individual personality and moral responsibility, taken the Utilitarian conception of imposed morality to the fear-theory from which it can hardly escape, as indeed Plato's creature, Thrasymachus, in the *Republic*, and a line of others like Polybius

composing a living body. . . . From this interdependence is born the natural law which imposes on each one of them (the duty) of working in its sphere of activity, in order to assure the vital activity of the body which they compose. It is exactly the same with individuals, members of the social body." (*Souveraineté et liberté*, 1921, pp. 145-6.) Fascism has adopted this philosophy bodily for its new state, with very different views on state responsibility, from those either of M. Bourgeois or of M. Duguit.

[20] *Traité*, Vol. I, p. 498. (*2ème* ed.)

and Machiavelli, had found. Mr. Dewey, however, is bent upon having his cake and eating it too. He contemns fear, but he enthrones force; he wants moral responsibility, but he would have no morality but that of imposition.

Curiously enough, both he and M. Duguit agree with Austin on the necessity of "determinateness" in the organs of government, although they at once render that agreement nugatory by saying that the conception of legal sovereignty is valueless, and by going on to set law adrift on the uneasy groundswells of social reactions. The appeal from the old to the new Utilitarians has not had happy results, either from the practical or from the logical viewpoint. The pragmatic effort to make law and morality equally impositional and coterminous quite misses the real nature of both.

The pseudo-morality of pragmatism offers an ethics of necessity founded upon social interdependence in societies conceived to be quite organic in the imposition of group law upon the individual. Positivistic law accepts this foundation, with its fear psychology, and builds upon the force brought to bear by the social organism in assuring the functioning of its public services. Nothing can stand in the way of functioning—not human rights, nor any "metaphysical" abstractions such as the guarantees afforded by law for the free exercise of moral choice. This differs from the absolutism of *German Philosophy and Politics*, which Mr. Dewey trounced so thoroughly during the war, only in substituting for the Goose-Step (*"der Gang Gottes in der Welt"*?) the March of the Machine (*machina ex deo?*). It is the perfect apology for Mussolini's Fascist corporative state. Human conduct is looked upon as a purely economic activity, in the Crocean phrase. Morality concerns itself only with the means to the accepted end of organically determined social solidarity. The demands which it must fulfil do not raise the moral question, the question of the end *sub specie universalis*. They relate only to the conditions of fact under which the individual finds himself, and those facts are interpreted in terms of group wants, the satisfaction of which is economically imperative. They are necessities of survival only, not of improvement or moral progress.

Croce has shown well enough the relation of the economic to the moral as two phases of practical activity to make it hardly necessary to repeat him here.[21] Within the realm of the economic, pragmatism is an accurate description of conventional morality and conventional law. M. Duguit's *droit objectif* has seized upon the trend Dicey termed "collectivist" in modern legislation and jurisprudence, and given it an accurate translation. The part the public services play, the conception of "public interest", may be read most clearly in the decisions of the American Supreme Court, in a long line of cases dealing with the Police Power, with the regulation of interstate commerce, and the like. But it is as false to give an economic interpretation to all activity, and rule the moral activity out of consideration, as it would be to refuse to admit any but a moral activity to the human spirit.

Moral activity is the effort we make to lift ourselves above the infinite progression of individual economic ends by inserting into them universal value. In many cases of "social" morality and conventionally necessary laws, the moral question is not raised, because conflict is unnecessary. We accept the traffic conventions of turning to the right or the left as we pass from one country to the next, without question. We penalize violations of a minor nature, without imputing any particular blame of a moral sort to the car owner, e.g., who parks too long uptown. Even in traffic regulations, however, moral issues can really be raised, for upon the habitual observance of the most important of them depends not only our safety, but the whole possibility of modern transport. In the ends of groups, as well as of individuals, there are always issues not possible of decision on the basis of a purely utilitarian and quantitative analysis. Ends must be weighed, in short, not from a calculus of economic interests, or from fear of punishment of one sort or another, but in the light of a purpose that transcends the economic realm and attains to Kant's "good will."

Obviously this is more hortatory than descriptive. Men singly, or in groups, are most apt to "calculate their chances" in a fashion thoroughly pragmatic. "Business is business," the saying is. Granting that choices are not often made against economic pressure, and that the economic interpretations of history is often sound history—even as history it is not the whole story. Man-

---

[21] *Filosofia della Pratica*, Pt. 2, "*L'attivita pratica nelle sue forme speciali*," p. 211 *et seq.*

chester cotton-factory workers, on the point of starvation, sided with the anti-slavery North during our Civil War, though their economic interests and England's were those of the cotton-growing and blockaded South. The constitutional morality which has staved off revolution, communist or fascist, in an England battling against misery and lowered standards of living is also noteworthy. It is certain, in any case, that ethics holds up *ought* as well as *is* for our thought.

The function of the moral intelligence, according to Instrumentalism, is merely the criticism of means toward uncriticized ends. The process of attaining them is purely economic, and the criterion for testing the means is the efficiency with which the ends are attained. The end itself is accepted as part of the specific situation, arising from a desire that is the product of the *milieu* and the circumstances, in their effect on given impulses, which are usually treated as instinctive; culminating in a specific goal, which is the desire plus what happens to it in the course of its attainment. Pragmatism of the Jamesian type implied a somewhat robustious hedonistic calculus of satisfaction as its test; but, on the whole, Mr. Dewey's logical preoccupations have accepted the survivalist philosophy that has desires, indeed, but that is chastened enough to leave the end to fate. Perhaps it is not quite accurate to say that the end is uncriticized.[22] It is only uncriticized before the fact. Instrumentalism, in addition to picking out efficient means, can enter on an *ex post facto* analysis of the success of its ends by seeing whether they are still "alive" or not. But even then its criterion of successful survival is reduced either to the hedonistic calculus before mentioned, or to the survivalist critique in terms of self-fulfilment. Its attitude is necessarily descriptive, for it has no normative values to apply. It can only perform a *post mortem* on the ends themselves, in spite of Mr. Dewey's latest talk in *Experience and Nature* of criticizing them in the light of their consequences. For his Instrumentalism offers us no help toward an intelligent criterion for testing the value of those consequences themselves.

Elsewhere I have set forth at some length how close a resemblance the moral implications of M. Duguit's theories bear to this

---

[22] *Cf.* M. Fouillée, *La pensée et les nouvelles écoles anti-intellectualistes,* especially the chapter on "*La néo-sophistique pragmatiste.*"

same deterministic limitation of ethics to the realm of an economic calculus.[23] Pragmatic instrumentalism and positivistic realism turn out to be so closely allied as to be indistinguishable in their application as well as their implication. They have an undoubtedly valid application to what I have called the organic in society: the "economic" interests can be described and calculated, even translated into terms of law, by pragmatic theory. This is true only so long, however, as the pragmatic philosophy of the law does not do what its exponents immediately set it to doing—forbid the really moral consciousness of the individual, which is the ultimate selective and directive force in human societies, its rightful place. For it is that selective agency which addresses itself, not only to the problem of how to live, but also to the problem of how to live the good life. Aristotle's *Politics* show us that in the beginning of societies the pragmatic calculus was the only possible one; the state existed that men might live. But one ought never to forget what Aristotle added: the state continues to exist that they might live *well*. Once bare survival is assured, and the state has emerged from the tribe, the play of the moral consciousness, the good will, comes in to determine the conditions under which men shall continue to survive, and, as a surplus to organic needs, shall live in accordance with values that put an increasing responsibility and dignity upon individual personality. Tribal morality was very nearly organic; but the morality of the modern state admits of a degree of moral purpose in which its members may freely share. Description of social reactions, even as bare description, must include facts not to be explained merely in terms of fear and force, in M. Duguit's despite. He has half-heartedly recognized this by introducing into the last edition of the *Traité de droit constitutionnel* the "sentiments" of what he calls "*justice et socialité.*" Is not this very much like Mr. Dewey's attempt to add to his assets "the quality and degree of the perception of ties and interdependencies; . . . the use to which they are put," in order to determine bad action from good? The addition is too much for pragmatism, but too little for an adequate philosophy.

It is the business of ethics to clarify those values and to criticize

[23] *Infra*, Chapter IX.

them, and that not merely as "instruments" toward whatever economic ends press upon a given group, but in the larger context of "the good life," as Aristotle called it. If they are "instruments" they must be used to further or to attain ends which in themselves are not alone economically judged, but morally approved, as well. It is true that the determination of what is truly ethical is not always so simple as Kant's examples would have us believe. Mr. Dewey recalls to us the necessity of decision as a concrete, not an abstract matter. But the moral choice must utilize as nearly universalized norms as it can attain; it must aim at self-coherence in the same way that logic must. That is to say, its system of values is not set up by the economic calculus in its Utilitarian or pragmatic purity, even where the locus of choice is transferred from "economic man" and put in "economic group". On the contrary, moral values create a world of ends into which the economic enters but as a means. For while it is true that "Bread is the staff of life," it is also written "Man does not live by bread alone."

If we reject "social" morality in the name of responsible human personality, though, what place does it leave for the relations between law and morality? Impositional morality claimed law as its own, for both were alike impositional, the results of economic necessity and fear. If human personality retains moral responsibility by permitting the individual to play the rôle of an active and creative agent in the moral scheme of things, how does that affect the status of law? The fallacy of the general will has been so thoroughly and so often exposed since Rousseau's time that not even Dr. Bosanquet's heroic effort to revive it could inspirit it with new life.[24] You cannot compound the freedom of moral choice, it is urged by pluralists like Mr. Laski, into the necessity of obeying law. That is a necessity founded, according to M. Duguit, simply upon force. To Mr. Laski it is not a necessity. To say you choose to obey law freely is to be like the ox whom Tolstoi pictured as loving his yoke. Nor is it more helpful

[24] Mr. Hobhouse's strictures on Dr. Bosanquet's *Philosophical Theory of the State* are perhaps not entirely deserved. But the *Metaphysical Theory of the State*, as the former has termed it, depends altogether too much upon something like a super-personal state will, that absorbs mundane difficulties in the fashion of a divine absolute. For a criticism of the analogous German theories see R. Emerson, *The State and Sovereignty in Recent German Juristic Theory*. Yale U. P. (to appear 1928).

to talk of the state as itself a moral person; your own personality is then absorbed.

The moral personality of the individual is ultimate; but that is by no means to admit that the state is founded on force. The state represents a moral ideal, not a general will. That ideal is best put by saying that the existence of the state is the necessary condition of moral freedom for the individual, because without it he is delivered over to the rule of force. Just as he freely accepts the common moral standards without which life would not be worth living, so he accepts the state, because only through it can he preserve his freedom. "The theory of the sovereignty of the constitution which I have been advocating," says the Master of Balliol, in concluding his memorable essay, "maintains that the unit between the social and the juristic aspect of the state is the adherence by the great mass of the members of a society to a definite principle of settling differences." [25] I ask only to substitute *constituent* for "social", *legal* for "juristic", and *sovereignty* for "aspect of the state", to put the solution in the terms we have been using.

The second question that arises out of the joint efforts of Mr. Dewey and M. Duguit to pluralize the political authority of the state by dividing it between the state and other institutions, involves in its answer finding out exactly to what use they put the term *sovereignty*. Once we have agreed that "social" morality cannot be substituted for law, and that the constitutional state fulfils a function *sui generis* among human institutions, we are better able to proceed to the second step of our proposed inquiry. For it follows from a study of the ethical side of the question that impositional or "group" morality can only give an economic interpretation of human conduct. The only way in which conflicts of interest can be resolved on this basis is by the rule of the stronger, the right of might. That makes law no more than the arbitrament of superior force, with only such checks imposed upon the rulers of a given society as exist from fear of other force, what M. Duguit would call "social reactions." Now it seems probable from what we have seen of the relations

[25] *Loc. cit. supra* (Note 18). An important addition to the literature of the theory of sovereignty is the article of C. H. McIlwain, "Sovereignty Again," *Economica*, No. 18, November, 1926.

between law and morality, that this explanation leaves out of account the real moral nature of the state, wherever the state is based upon a generally accepted constitution. Men attempt to control through an organized force, operating under agreed upon rules, the blind lash of economic wants and conflicts of interest. The morality which they seek to realize through the rule of law is not ordinarily imposed upon them by their economic circumstances, or the rule of force—though such states exist. Witness Italy. But in a constitutional state men may attempt, by reasoning together and by taking common counsel to transform blind necessity into conscious direction of events, to impose their will to justice instead of accepting the imposed play of purely economic determinants. He would be something of a fool who would close his eyes, full of this vision of the ideal, and say that the will to justice is the whole story of human government and the rule of law. But is he not equally foolish who can see in the whole growth of the constitutional state no more than the reactions of an organism bent upon survival? Does not the "seeing will" play a part in changing the conditions of survival from those under which the tribe alone counts to those under which the growth of moral personality in the individual is the criterion of success? Relapses there are indeed; during war time, always; and in the impoverished aftermath of war, often. But the existence of constitutional states in which civil liberty survives shows that this is not a fatal rule.

If it be granted, then, that the organization of the sanction of force in the hands of the state alone is the condition not only of the harmonious functioning of economic interests, but of the realization of the "good life" itself, we are already well under way in our approach to the answer to political pluralism. But in order to set the stage for a more detailed critique of the division of political authority among non-political associations, let us resume briefly Mr. Dewey's case against the sovereignty of government: His quarrel with the Austinian conception was that it put sovereignty in the agents of authority as if they were the masters of the power with which the complex institutions of society invested them. Even though he admitted the necessity of definite organs and determinate processes to declare law, he insisted that *real* sovereignty rested in the complex of institutions, not in the government. M. Duguit's whole system is hardly more than an exhaustive elaboration of this theme.

It seemed, from the first, highly probable that they were both looking for something which we may call *constituent* sovereignty, and were bent on reducing *legal* sovereignty to the same terms in Austin's despite. For the sake of clarity, let us return to Austin's classic definition: "If a determinate human superior, not in the habit of obedience to a like superior, receive habitual obedience from the bulk of a given society, that determinate superior is sovereign in that society, and the society (including the superior) is a society political and independent." Putting aside the obvious tautology of superior, which has often been noted to involve a circular definition, and substituting "person or persons" as the context shows Austin intended, we still have a description of legal sovereignty that is inapplicable to any type of state in which the power is not vested finally in some unitary body (like the British Parliament) to say what is law. That is a claim that has been sufficiently often made, at least, and with considerable justification. How is one to fit Austin's description, even for legal purposes, e.g., to governments in which there is a constitutional division of power, as there is in the United States, not only functionally, by departments and branches of government, but federally as well, by territorial divisions, each sufficient in its own sphere? American theorists have held that legal sovereignty rests in any agency of government which is using in a manner not *ultra vires* the powers with which it has been constitutionally endowed. That is obviously a correct statement of fact. Yet the point remains that there must be some determinate body vested with final power to decide upon what is *ultra vires*, and ever since Chief Justice Marshall succeeded in carrying the day for the principle laid down in Marbury *v.* Madison, the Supreme Court has fulfilled that function. So long as the Constitution is left *in statu quo* the Supreme Court is the "determinate" body to which the law must look for its unification. In so complex a system as that of the federal state, with its functional separation and territorial divisions of power, that effort sometimes requires a veritable *tour de force*. Still it is necessary, and it has been accepted. Austin himself could not rest content with that, though. A legal system must provide the means of its own alteration by legal means if it is to escape the appeal to revolution. Many of the early state constitutions enshrined the right of revolution from Locke's *Essays on Civil Government*, as the only means of change in fundamental laws. A constitution, however, does not maintain itself like the laws of the Medes and the Persians, invariable. So Austin looked to the power which law recognized as having power to change all laws, even to the overriding of decisions from the highest tribunal. In England he found it in the electorate; in the United States he found it in the bodies capable of amending the Constitution. Out of the four possible combinations offered by Article V, in practice those bodies have been limited to a two-thirds majority of both houses of the Congress of the United States, for proposal, and to a ratification by the majorities of both houses of three-fourths of the state legislatures.

The objection has frequently been made that here is a legal sovereign who has acted only nineteen times in the history of the nation, and who does not concern himself with statutes, but with the terms under which they may be made. Yet that is no real objection to finding in that all-powerful force Austin's determinate superior. Even the most absolute monarch hardly did more, for all the high sound of *quod principi placuit, legis habet vigorem*. And there is nothing more to prevent this sovereign exercising his good pleasure than there was to hinder Louis XIV; the extra-legal limit of all power rests, as Hume showed, with the governed. Constitutional amendments are limited in our national existence to matters of principle, as much because of the inconvenience of turning such unwieldy machinery to legislation as from any question of principle itself. But the XVIIIth Amendment, and the proposed Child Labor Amendment are ominous signs that we in the United States may be about to embark on the venture of overriding the Courts' constitutional decisions to which our State Constitutions are already committed. If we are not to turn the amending process to statute-making, we must make our national government capable of expressing the real national unity which has come upon us all unawares, while we were still talking in terms of "an indestructible union of indestructible states." Is there anyone who seriously imagines it would take a revolution to override the proviso of Article V, which forbids any power under heaven to deprive any state of its equal representation in the Senate without its own consent? From the legal point of view such an act would be revolutionary. But quite probably the ultimate necessity of making the states conform to more real areas of economic and cultural community will some day force us to have recourse to a constitutional convention, called at the request of two-thirds of the states, in order to satisfy the tradition that since the convention of 1787 has held conventions to be the peculiar depository of federal sovereignty. It is worth while noting, too, that most of our federal amendments, after the original ten, have been aimed at arming the nation with national powers denied it by the Supreme Court.

The existence of an accepted constitution, written or practised, is quite necessarily bound to provide the unification of legal sovereignty upon which Austin insisted, though that must rather be accomplished by providing determinate means of *finding* and *putting into operation* the proper bodies to say what is law, or what shall be law, than by seeking for determinate individuals.

That, however, does not cover the case so far as Mr. Dewey and the pluralists are concerned. They would insist that we are still in the realm of convenient fictions. One would think that pragmatists must accept the fiction as truth, if it be convenient. But no, the realism of their doctrines demands its own share of satisfaction, and that is not to be attained short of finding those "real rulers of a society," whom John Chipman Gray declared to be "undiscoverable." Let us agree, then, that the legal sovereign is by no means the ultimate sovereign of a society, though that is not at all to admit that legal sovereignty is a mere fiction. The point is that law suffers the same limitations that formal logic does. It is necessary to political activity to bring things to a working synthesis through a constitutional unification of authority, just as we use a conceptual shorthand in thinking. But in neither case is that the whole story. In politics, too, we must go into the psychological bases of our state, just as we do supplement the formal outlines of concepts in concrete thought.

What is that constituent sovereignty by virtue of which we

continually talk of "sovereign nation" or "sovereign people," implying that all just governments derive their powers from the active participation as well as the consent of the people? Austin was content to let the matter go by taking "habitual obedience of the bulk of the people" as a fact, on utilitarian grounds. For the purposes of law, it is impossible to do otherwise, because law is in its nature a formal summary of facts. But M. Duguit, for instance, while he insists stoutly that he is not going beyond the "facts," finds that the latter include the fact of social solidarity, and accepts social interdependence as his explanation, as Mr. Dewey did. What are the limits of this social interdependence? Are they territorial? Are they racial? Are they economic? Are they cultural? Are they moral? Or, are they a complex of all these factors, out of which emerges the phenomenon of the nation-state? And are the areas of community in each case susceptible of variations in extension and intensity?

That there are such limits to the willingness of men to submit common concerns to arbitration and final settlement, let the present status of the League of Nations witness. Yet the existence of a League at all is a further witness that these concerns are not to be formulated rigidly and forever in the categories of purely national laws. The existence of the British Commonwealth of Nations, or of a Federation such as our own country was before the Civil War, affords ample proof that the limits of habitual obedience or social solidarity depend upon variables in human loyalty. The fluctuations of states give us more proof that the foundations of authority, like the foundations of belief, are psychological things. They vary, whether they be economic or moral communities of interest, both in degree of intensity and in scope.

Within the state, as well as without, associations claim our loyalties in certain directions. Who dare say that the state lays a more secure hold upon certain parts of its citizenship than the church or occupational associations? And if that authority, extra-legal as it is, be recognized as real, and frequently more powerful than the authority of the state in its hold upon certain groups, where there is a conflict of purposes, is it not true that to claim all political power for the state is to slight the facts?

The genuineness of these claims cannot be doubted in the face of class-warfare more or less openly conducted all over Europe, and the revival of the seriousness of religious cleavage through such issues as "Evolution" or the Ku Klux Klan, over which the last Democratic convention went very nearly on the rocks, not to mention similar struggles in other countries at the present moment. The state has normally to put up with associations within itself which can challenge its authority with some prospect of success, if it attempt to deny them their own right to existence. Mr. Laski has documented this thesis amply enough.

The only thing that one can urge in favor of holding on to the notion that the constituent sovereignty of the state exists as long as the state exists, and that it is not seriously impaired in its character of being the *sine qua nihil* of law, is that all these challenges to political authority ultimately result, not in lessening the province of law, but in extending it. I do not mean an extension into fields not properly political; but where *political* issues are raised political action has to be developed in one way or another to cope with direct action, if we are to avoid anarchy. The legal forms are often enough like old bottles unable to contain the newly fermenting spirit of the times. But containers must be found, if the value of that spirit is not to be dissipated entirely. Community of any sort depends in the long run upon agreement; although, as Mussolini says, consent may be aided by force! The moral agreement of free consent, however, is hardly to be reached by allowing the matters which properly can be the concern only of the political community in their settlement to go by default, because the present machinery of political settlement is so intolerable or so inadequate that groups of considerable importance force the issue by direct action. Presently direct action itself becomes so intolerable as to force more adequate means for political and legal arbitrament. That, it seems to me, means that constituent sovereignty exists in any society which aspires to be ruled by law and not by an unorganized and uncontrolled plurality of forces or by irresponsible Fascism. Law means that organized constraint may be and will be, if the issue is forced, put upon forces that challenge the community of purpose that is the state.

Granted that this community is not a fixed quantity, that it changes its forms and its organization in response to economic needs as well as moral purposes, that states are, in a word neither perfect, immutable, nor eternal—the state-idea holds a unified purpose before it, and the acceptance of a constitution by the bulk of the people is, after all, the test of statehood. Let us take a case very much in point. The British Empire is groping its way to a new form of association, in which parliamentary sovereignty by a body responsible only to the British electorate is an antiquated constitutional device. Like the United States of America before the Civil War, perhaps, better, like those same states under the Articles of Confederation, it is in a transitional stage. The lawyers must look on while the facts are reshaped into law. Dicey is already out of date, when the Dominions claim and receive equal partnership in the order of things. The *Law of the Constitution* of which he wrote hardly contemplated separate ministers for the Dominions in foreign countries, or the claim to ratify for themselves all treaties concerning them. Indeed, the Governor-General and the Judicial Committee of the Privy Council were, in Dicey's time, quite real partners in the law-making of the so-called Self-Governing Dominions. All that is rapidly passing, may be said in most instances already to have passed. The actual limits of loyalty to the old Constitution are not yet clear, and the "Empire," so far as the Dominions are concerned, is not *a state*, but *several states*, cooperating, or not, in various matters to varying degrees.[26]

Yet it seems fairly probable that out of this transitional stage a new and more flexible imperial unity will emerge. It will quite possibly reverse the parallel to the United States in being a greater decentralization of authority, instead of the steady growth of centralization that was well under way even before our

[26] Mr. H. D. Hall's book, *The British Commonwealth of Nations* (1920), although it is already outstripped by the facts, presents the best account I know of in brief scope of the genesis and tendencies of the new status of the Colonies and the Empire. The survey is brought to date by Richard Jebb's *The Empire in Eclipse*. To this list may now (1928) be added W. P. Hall's *Empire to Commonwealth*.

The November resolutions of the Imperial Conference of 1926 gave explicit recognition to Dominion equality with Great Britain, in the hope of more real coöperation now that legal control by the Imperial Parliament is no longer insisted upon. See President A. L. Lowell's article, "The Imperial Conference," *Foreign Affairs*, April, 1927.

Civil War and the XIVth Amendment. Constituent sovereignty, the acceptance of a constitution as the rules of the game of politics, is the precise negation of pluralism. Pluralism of political authority means a transitional stage of the state to a new normal. From the point of view of abstract theory, that is of legal theory which must find some rules generally accepted in order to apply them, pluralism is no doubt pathological. But that is far from meaning that it is an unhealthy state. The body politic, like the human body, renews itself by changing. So long as a sufficient continuity of purpose exists to prevent absolute disintegration into anarchy, things are probably not so bad as the lawyers think, though social and economic intercourse may suffer.

Within the state, so far as its relations with other associations are concerned, the situation is somewhat different. If the state intrudes upon what they consider to be their spheres, it does so with reluctance, and only when the issue is forced upon it by demands on their part for power which it cannot yield without allowing its whole purpose (which is to establish the rule of law) to go by default. It cannot suffer them to make law in the same sense that it does. It must maintain law as its own province, if there is not to be a conflicting welter of regulations of human conduct. It will not, on the other hand, attempt the regulation of the internal discipline of associations of any sort if it is wise. Cases in which that discipline interferes with civil liberty, it cannot brook; but civil liberty is not to be secured entirely by guaranteeing civil rights. Its very existence depends upon associations which are on the alert and are powerful enough to protect those rights if they are challenged by the perversion of force, either in the hands of government or of other associations. Syndicalism and Fascism are alike pathological symptoms, indicating illness in the political organism.

In the end, however, it is always to just laws that men must look for redress of legal grievances. There are many forms of social injustice and petty oppression which law cannot reach. But its utility as the guarantor of an increasing area of freedom, and the establisher of standards of life which make possible real moral freedom, depends upon its making legal sovereignty the true expression of constituent sovereignty. Public opinion, difficult as it is to define, does exist as something more than Mr. Lippmann's *Phantom Public* in a state like England, and does succeed slowly in moulding its institutions in its own image. If it is unenlightened, uninterested, incapable of intelligent formulation, or if it is intolerant, oppressive, and prejudiced, its institutions will be shaped to fit it. And if it is torn asunder by internal dissensions, by bitterness, and hatred bred of greed or injustice, the state can hardly escape a like disruption. There is no short cut to a Christian millennium, whatever Utopias promise.

Neither Mr. Dewey nor M. Duguit is interested in Utopian proposals. The latter particularly stresses the hard realism of force and fear. And yet there is something oddly Utopian about any proposal to improve human nature and conduct without the aid of moral personality, by scientific social psychology and ethics, and by fitting men into their functions in an organically "moralised" society. Ultimately, it results in an apology for the Fascist ideal of a "disciplined" national organism.

CHAPTER IX

THE "FEAR-THEORY" AS A FACT: M. LEON DUGUIT'S PRAGMATIC *DROIT OBJECTIF* *

"The strongest is never strong enough to remain forever master unless he transforms force into law and obedience into duty" said Rousseau,[1] a truth which every subsequent system of jurisprudence has implicitly accepted, and explicitly attempted to account for. As a broad base for the rest of their building, the most successful of these systems generally accepted Rousseau's doctrine, too, of a general will toward the protection of natural rights always in a form more or less absolutistic, according to the purposes which the systems were to serve. German jurisprudence, for example, on the whole arrived at an apologia for an absolutism as rigid as Rousseau's own, through its derivation of the force of law based on a theory of individual rights none the less rigid for having been obtained at second-hand through Kant. The classical French jurisprudence started with the assumptions of the Declaration of the Rights of Man only to find itself led by an irresistible logic to the unquestionable and legally final sovereignty defined by the Constitution of 1791. In England the Benthamite theory took authoritative form in Austin with something of the same logical rigor, though British practice and British theory have ever been two different things altogether.

Until the latter part of the Nineteenth Century, however, the sovereignty of the state, based on the representative relation in which it stood to the general will, was considered to be a dogma necessary to any juristic system. No other explanation of either the origin of rights or the bases of political obligation found any wide-spread acceptance. With the rise of the historical school of jurisprudence, however, the idea of what may be roughly called

* Reprinted with corrections from "The Metaphysics of M. Léon Duguit's Pragmatic Philosophy of Law," *Pol. Sci. Qu.*, Vol. XXXVII, p. 632 (December, 1922).

[1] *Du contrat social*, Chap. 2, Bk. I.

251

the Social Compact theory was subjected for the first time to a searching critique which was able, through a new approach to the problem, to force reconsideration of the ideas both of natural individual rights and of absolute sovereignty. At least the beginnings of sociological jurisprudence were laid when the emphasis was shifted from the *a priori* derivation of laws to their historical origins. The attack there begun on the metaphysical school of jurists has taken several very interesting directions in modern theory and has grown in strength as much as in complexity. It is worth while noting, however, that most legal systems in present application retain the theory of sovereignty as the basis of the coercive power to command and that the greatest jurists of the last decades have numbered among them those who like Jellinek, Ihering and Stammler sought to give a sound philosophical (what M. Duguit derides as metaphysical) base to the superstructures they have reared. Whether realistic or idealistic in temper, these systems agreed upon the necessity of accounting for legal phenomena by a method which contained *a priori* as well as descriptive elements.

But just as in eighteenth-century France and in the doctrines of Rousseau the intellectualist explanation of the nature of law found its classical statement, so in modern France once more and in the theories of M. Léon Duguit these doctrines meet their most elaborate rebuttal. They are attacked, so to speak, from top to bottom. The classical French jurisprudence rested its entire weight on two pillars and an arch: on the one side natural rights and on the other absolute sovereignty joined together to support the entire political structure by the arch of a social compact. M. Duguit says the pillars form an unreal and inadequate support, and he boldly sets about pushing them over without evidencing the least fear of bringing the state in ruins on his own head. Not content with his work of destruction, he goes so far as to attack the foundation of every such system by declaring that a jurisprudence which rests on any metaphysical assumptions whatever is built on sand and cannot in the nature of things remain long standing. The particular metaphysical foundation which he spends most of his energy in wrecking is the doctrine of some sort of general will which expresses itself through the acts of a state-person.

His own doctrine he characterizes as *"positive et réaliste."* In place of any and every metaphysical conception of rights deriving from relationship of wills, he proposes the fact of obligation (*devoir*) necessitated by another fact, social solidarity (*la solidarité sociale*). These notions are not abstractions of an intellectualistic order but, according to M. Duguit, scientific descriptions of social phenomena which act under laws in some respects analogous to those of the biological organism. Not, indeed, that these laws are biological, for they exist only through individuals "conscious of their acts and of the motives which determine them."[2] Still, as biological laws are founded on "the fact that constitutes the organism," so are social norms based on "the fact that is society."[3] Scientific jurisprudence must ground itself on these facts as ultimate and not seek for them a metaphysical apologia about which endless dispute is possible. Social interdependence, with its roots in an organic division of social functions such as M. Durkheim has described in *De la Division du travail social,"* exists as a state of fact independent of our will. That is, at least, in so far as we can treat it scientifically; the ultimate nature of the will about which the philosophers wrangle so tediously and so vainly is completely outside the possibility of scientific enquiry; the most that we are justified in asserting about our acts is that we are conscious of the ends toward which they are directed.

From the outset M. Duguit's effort is to stay within the bounds of scientific method which he has set for himself. This method, as he interprets it, will not permit him to set up ghostly essences

---

[2] *Traité de droit constitutionnel* (2ᵇᵐᵉ ed.), Vol. I, pp. 14-19.
[3] *Ibid.*, pp. 18-19.

"The cells composing an organism are submitted to the laws of that organism. Everyone recognizes it: the law of that organism is that which governs its formation and its development. In the same manner the individuals composing a social group are submitted to the law of that group, a law which governs its formation and its development. The one and the other of these laws are laws of coördination. We don't call the law of the organism a norm because we cannot affirm that the cells composing it are conscious; the law of a social group we do call a norm because the individuals who are its members act consciously, will a thing that they have in view and in virtue of a motive of which they are conscious. But apart from this difference there is none other between the law of a living organism and the law of a human society; and if one admits that the biological organism is founded on the fact that constitutes this organism, there is no reason why one should not look at the social norm as based on the fact that is society."

behind actual phenomena. The state-person has no more real existence than any other such abstract concept; all alike are qualified by what he calls "the inanity of the doctrines, whatever they be, which wish to give a philosophical justification of political might. The truth is that political might is a fact which has in itself no character of legitimacy or illegitimacy. It is the product of a social evolution." [4]

On such a reading of the facts of human society it is apparent that the question of an ideal morality not only does not arise; it is ruled out of court in advance. Consequently, when M. Duguit attacks all subjective rights and proposes to substitute for them the notion of *devoir* as the ground for the *règle de droit*, of *droit objectif*, he is not to be misconceived as meaning by *devoir* moral obligation in any sense. He himself is very anxious to avoid this fundamental misconception because it would obviously introduce the very metaphysical difficulties which he believes he escapes through a positivist treatment of social norms. "Likewise," he says, "I part company (*j'écarte*) with the notion of duty (*devoir*) conceived as creating a character proper to certain wills, a sort of negative power which would make of these wills subordinate wills. . . . The notion of duty so conceived is a notion of a metaphysical order just as much as the notion of right (*droit*)." [5] The true nature of the obligation which causes the rulers as well as the ruled to submit to the rule of law is to be found in that same *solidarité sociale* arising out of the organic interdependence of the social structure which equates itself in his view with the necessity of natural laws assumed by all scientific generalizations as fixed and determinate. Men obey juridical norms because they have to.

"For us, to speak of a norm as obligatory as a juridical norm

---

[4] *Manuel de droit constitutionnel* (3ᵉᵐᵉ ed.), p. 23.

Durkheim, who furnishes M. Duguit with the *Solidarisme* for his sociological and positivistic method, wrote :

"A social fact, a social situation is recognizable by the external coercion that it exercises or is susceptible of exercising on individuals, and the presence of power is recognizable in turn either by the existence of some determinate sanctions, or by the resistance that the fact opposes to every individual enterprise which attempts to do violence to it." (*Les règles de la méthode sociologique*, p. 15) Quoted by Duguit, *Traité*, Vol. I, p. 25.

Is not this a sociology apt for Austinianism? We shall not be surprised if M. Duguit's more practical proposals lead in that direction.

[5] *Traité, cit.* p. 18.

means simply that at a given moment, in a group under consideration, if this norm is violated the bulk of the people (*la masse des ésprits*) understands that it is just, according to the feeling (*sentiment*) of justice that it forms for itself at this moment, that it is necessary for the maintenance of social interdependence, that what there is of conscious force included in the group intervenes to repress this violation. To give another meaning and another value (*portée*) to the obligatory force of a rule of law, is to leave reality in order to enter into metaphysical hypothesis." [6]

I have gone to some length to show the anti-intellectualist bases of M. Duguit's doctrines, not only because of their obviously pragmatic temper, but because any shorter exposition of them would, I feel, be an unfair point of departure for such later criticisms as I might venture. If it be possible to formulate laws for society as it is for biology, as M. Duguit maintains, while remaining strictly within the limits of descriptive generalization from observed facts, he may fairly claim to rule out metaphysical consideration and ethical notions. On the other hand if any analysis of human action which leaves these latter out of the reckoning can be shown for that very reason to fail to account for the facts, we may fairly reject its claim to scientific adequacy.

I propose in this connection to consider several of the social "facts" which M. Duguit offers as requiring and indeed permitting no further explanation than is given by "social morality" and by the methodology of the French Social Realists so-called; [7] then to notice very briefly the account he gives of certain problems of constitutional law treated in the light of *droit objectif*. Among the facts he accepts as such, let us examine the notion of the basic *solidarité sociale*, its relation to the other fact of rulers who hold power *de facto* but are "bound" to act in the interests of social solidarity, and finally in the factual category, the "fear" which motivates obedience. Among the general problems offered by the *droit objectif* theory, let us look into the denial of "rights," specifically the state's right to command, and proceeding from

---

[6] *Ibid.*, p. 65.
[7] Which may be reduced to an Instrumentalism of the most strictly positivistic nature. *Cf.* Part 1, *supra.*

the treatment of sovereignty involved in this, to the nature of the responsibility of the state under law.

When M. Duguit presents us with the fact of social solidarity as a sufficient juridical stem to support all the branches of government and keep them growing and bearing lawful fruit, it is only fair to ask what he means by the nature of such a fact. It is evident that if society were completely organic in its functioning, social solidarity would operate ruthlessly toward the suppression of any disruptive influences operating within it. The social reactions in which lie M. Duguit's ultimate punitive sanctions would operate with the sureness of the responses of any nervous organism to unpleasant stimuli, and would suppress the disturbances or perish through failure. But an examination of the historical development of our own society or of a slice out of any particular period of the past will serve to convince us, I believe, that quite as good a case might be made out for the laws of social disruption as for those of social solidarity. The fact of forces working toward the breakdown of the rigidity of the *status quo* is on a par with the fact of forces working for its maintenance, and might be shown to be just as necessary to what we call its normal development or progress. In the society of a world order, nationalism is at the moment so powerful a factor militating against solidarity as to make some observers despair of the possibilities of economic reconstruction. Are the class struggles within the nation less disruptive in their results?

Now it is true that *droit objectif* need not equate the preservation of the *status quo* with social solidarity any more than it need speak of progress.[8] It remains none the less true that though social interdependence may make men realize the need for social solidarity it does not create that desideratum as a state of fact. The fact surely is that social solidarity is precisely one of those ideal ends which at the same time exist as great needs of which men are conscious and as consummations all the more devoutly to be wished because they can never be even approximately realized. In the light of what we know of the nature of such ends, our "fact" turns out to be one of the most metaphysical

---

[8] Speaking of progress and decline: "A scientific social theory can find no meaning in such terms. It can only point to significant difference." *Law in the Modern State,* Author's Introduction, p. xxxvi. Even the significance of the difference may be questioned.

order imaginable, leading us straight on to all the moral issues
it was claimed we should avoid by its admission.

M. Duguit's own treatment of this convenient "Open, Sesame"
is a tacit recognition of the ideal character of his so-called fact.
If the obligation to act always in the interests of social solidarity
were actually binding on the rulers who hold the force simply
from the organic nature of society, there would not be the necessity M. Duguit so strongly feels to exert his efforts toward bringing about government in France, or elsewhere, *"sous la règle de
droit."* That, too, would exist as a fact. Evidently the rule of
law is actual only in so far as it is an ideal realized through
human exertion—by M. Duguit's efforts and those of all the rest
toward attaining it and maintaining it.

When we are told too, and on almost the same page, that
"political power has no character of legitimacy or illegitimacy, it
is the product of the social evolution"; and yet that "like individuals the rulers have juridical obligations founded on the social
interdependence" [9] we may think that social solidarity has assumed a significance more mythical than metaphysical. The
rulers are simply those who possess for a variety of causes the
power to impose their wills, and this, as M. Duguit reiterates
time and again, is "a unique fact that one finds always . . . in
all the social groups which are qualified as states-individuals
stronger than others who will and who can impose their will on
the rest." Still these rulers who "possess, by definition, the
greatest force existing in a given society . . . are then obliged,
by the rule of law to employ this greatest force at their disposal
for the realization of social solidarity.[10]

Unquestionably the rulers of a constitutional state do find
themselves obliged to use the power they possess *de facto* in a
de jure manner. But it is because political power is constituted,
contrary to M. Duguit's assumption in a manner which gives it
a legitimacy in the eyes of the governed as political power. From
a juristic standpoint it is surely a jejune explanation of the character of government under law to offer in complete explanation of
its origin and character the so-called fact of social solidarity and
then to offer as the possibility of that social solidarity the assumption of government under law as still another fact. The

[9] *Manuel*, p. 23.   [10] *Ibid.*, pp. 32-33.

process savors of the conjurer's bag of tricks. By a brilliant *tour de force* one may indeed produce almost anything at all from this simple combination for into *la règle de droit* and *la solidarité sociale* have been put all that may be subsequently required of them, including an *a fortiori* obligation upon the holders of the greatest force never to misuse it.[11]   The possibilities of this *petit jeu* are at least equal to those of Rousseau's manipulation of *la volonté générale*, which, indeed, it suspiciously resembles.

Let us, if we are to accept M. Duguit's "facts," admit of them at least that they are facts of a highly metaphysical order.   M. Duguit thinks that his rulers are bound by functional necessity, but rulers have had a most curious way of interpreting their functions and that necessity.   They have at times appeared to believe they have served as a directive intelligence and will for the social organism and have manifested a remarkable conviction in freedom of this will to choose the worse alternative. Governments that hold force *de facto* have either been forced, as Rousseau said, "to transform force into law or obedience into duty" or they have made the most of the brief interval in which they were left in possession of force to make hay before the storm broke.   The latter alternative has been chosen just as much as the former.   Admittedly if the rule of law become a fact, the rulers must act in a general way in the interest of the social groups they govern.   But the rule of law, as I have pointed out, is at best only a very imperfectly realized ideal aim, a moral end, and not a fact.

If it were merely of a factual order and as such were our only criterion, we could offer no criticism of any specific legislative or judicial action, for each one would be on a basis of absolute equality as fact.   Like the chorus in a Greek tragedy (a chorus, however, which was stripped of even its privilege of moralizing), we might describe; we might wonder; but until we could offer more useful explanations of the social norms at the back of laws than simply the declaration that they are, they have been, and they will be, we should never be privileged to adopt any attitude of critical regulation.   The very basis common to all modern law, continuity of principle combined with flexibility of

[11] *Manuel, Loc. cit.*

concrete application, would vanish in an empty attempt to give judicial interpretation to every social norm whose character was that its violation would produce a *"réaction sociale."*

We must, I believe, seek the reasons that underlie the reactions of a given society even at the risk of being dubbed metaphysicians, though I should hold that our search is only in the interest of a scientific adequacy not content to be put off with words. Into the nature of these reactions themselves M. Duguit does not offer to inquire, but he does vouchsafe an explanation why men obey the norms which they sanction. It is possible that we may derive more than a hint of what the implicit nature of the sanctions is from the character which he gives to the reasons for obeying them. The explanation takes this form: first of an attack on the traditional conception that implies the existence of a political power imposing its commands because it represents a will superior to the wills of individuals. This will is non-existent because, *ex hypothesi*, it is a metaphysical abstraction. Even were it a real will it would not have the right to impose itself upon other wills, for all wills (says M. Duguit) are equal, an assumption for which he no doubt would invoke the all-compelling power of facthood. There is, then, no such really existent political power. On the contrary, "that which is a fact is on the one hand the belief that this political power exists, and on the other hand the material possibility in a given group for certain individuals called government to impose their will by the employment of force." The only new thing in this statement is the admission that there is at least a myth which remains tolerably obstinate as a part of the general faith, a myth that such a political power as M. Duguit has discredited does nevertheless exist. But his point is that it is on a par with other exploded myths, which men still cling to. The fact is always *"la plus grande force"* "which imposes itself by material acts of constraint or by the fear which it inspires."

Here we have baldly stated the nature at least of obedience. M. Duguit talks at length elsewhere of *le sentiment de la socialité,"* and of *"le sentiment de la justice"* as sanctions or as elements from which social reactions are derived. There is no mistaking them now, to be sure, for those vulgar and ancient metaphysical claims of rights, for the true nature of their application is force,

naked and no whit apologetic, and the reason men obey them
is simple fear. "This fear is always a fact of the greatest force
and I shouldn't say that I slight it, since it is, on the contrary,
the point of departure of all my (succeeding) developments." [12]

One would say that such a commitment must be conclusive.
Here is the "fear theory" in as unabashed statement as ever it
was given by Thrasymachus or hard-reasoning old Hobbes; acts
of government are acts of force, and men obey because they must.
Political power is amoral, even unmoral. This is parlous close
to metaphysical and moral anarchy, and from the pen, too, of the
champion of the rule of law. Some of Duguit's French colleagues
who can see no possible reconciliation of the two doctrines have
not hesitated to call him *"l'anarchiste de chaire,"* but he is not
one to be frightened by words. If his use of facts smacks of the
conjurer, his *volte-face* here is not less worthy of the acrobat.
"Soit" he rejoins to their pleasantry; anarchist, if an act of
government is to take its legitimacy from its origin; but jurist
if it is to be tested by its end, i.e., by its conformity with *"droit
social."* In whatever hands power resides, its use is legitimized
only in so far as it secures *solidarité sociale* or, as he is now

[12] *Traite*, Vol. I, pp. 45 ff. :
"In speaking of the sentiment of justice," says M. Duguit (*ibid.*, pp. 49-
50), "I only have in view the more or less vague notion that men form in a
given epoch and group of what is just or unjust. The notion of what is
just and unjust is infinitely variable and changing. But the sentiment of
the just and the unjust is a permanent element of human nature." Is this
the Law of Nature under a new form? Do we not also encounter the same
idea in Prof. Krabbe's *Rechtsgefühl?* "I say : sentiment of justice, as I have
said sentiment of sociality, and not notion of justice, no more than notion
of sociality, in order to show that my thought, no more here than formerly,
has in it nothing of a notion *a priori* [*sic*], of the conception of a superior
principle. Man has the feeling that he is *solidaire* with other men because
he is a social being ; that is the sentiment of sociality. . . . Justice is not
a rational idea, revealed by the reason. It is a sentiment proper to human
nature."
In so far as justice is not submitted to a rational critique, however, it
tends to be purely Romanticist and to serve only as the motive for violence.
The "notion" of justice which men form, however, in spite of its infinite
variety of content, implies the idea of reciprocity, of fairness. And it is not
until this idea has attained a tolerable development that men really expect
justice from others or render it to them. The virtues of the "many-wiled
Odysseus" are praiseworthy in a society where justice is only a sentiment.
Men of the Homeric age accepted injustice from their heroes as a matter
of course because, although there was a sentiment of justice, the idea of
justice had not a sufficient hold upon the mind to become clearly reflected
as a social check on strength or cunning.
For his statement of the "fear-theory," which he is apparently able to
reconcile with the sentiment of justice, see *Traité*, Vol. I, p. 498.

prepared to state it, in so far as it assures the public services. A legal act is one that performs a social function, a juridical act is one that secures this performance.

Surely this is very dubious sociology; it is even more certainly not helpful jurisprudence. It is hopeful, of course, that M. Duguit at last recognizes the end as a moral norm, even in this left-handed manner; but it is equally hopeless to attempt a system of jurisprudence apt for modern society without giving its declarative and interpretative organs a definite locus. Who, pray, is to decide whether an act of government is in conformity with an objective social law, unless it be a power legitimized as to its own existence by community consent to its arbitrament? Otherwise social reaction may follow social reaction in a headlong, violent descent to the *bellum omnium contra omnes,* sanctioning not the rule of law but rulerless anarchy. Were there space, it would be interesting to examine M. Duguit's little apologia for the violence of feudal ages, as à propos.[13] The essence of it is that society was bound together by the notion of feudal obligation in spite of violence, which in itself was a rather healthy manifestation of vigorous group life. But even on the test of a pragmatic ethic of survival, a political system which failed to give the necessary power of command and decision to any one arbiter is *démodé,* to say the least of it.

So long as government assures the public services, however, any acts its agents (who are, in M. Duguit's view, its very self) may perform are legitimate. In spite of his protest against giving a special character to the acts of government through a public law, he recognizes that these acts must remain outside the reach of direct legal sanction—which to my mind is almost the entire case for a separate province of public law, as no modern jurisprudence envisages government not responsible under its own organic law. It is noteworthy that for M. Duguit, however, the

---

[13] *Cf. Law in the Modern State,* p. 118 *passim.*

M. Esmein has made the following criticism of Duguit's feudalistic leanings to Syndicalism, as well as those of M. Charles Benoist in his *La crise de l'état moderne:*

"But if these associations, these corporations, these classes, which are the organs of social life, have no power above them, one falls back into a system comparable to feudal anarchy. What triumphs is no longer the *law* inspired of human reason, but *force:* the strife of forces and of classes is substituted for the empire of law." (*Éléments de droit constitutionnel,* etc. Introduction to the 6th ed., p. 45.)

mere lack of an ultimate legal sanction for acts of government makes no real differentiation between public and private law, for all legal sanctions may be reduced in the end to social reactions; and whenever government violates the norms of social solidarity it provokes a social reaction. Therefore, it is under law.

The logic of the matter is that so long as those who possess force do not so abuse it as to provoke violence, their acts *ipso facto* are within the law. The *solidarité sociale* stands flatly upon the fact of force and is kept standing by the fact of violence. Slavery itself could be legitimately imposed by the rulers if it assured the public services, and if the force which imposed it were sufficient to defeat the violence of the reaction it might arouse. One does not wonder at M. Esmein's exclamation apropos of Duguit's proposal, "Why not propose a return to customary law? That would be clearer!" The only question that arises is whether the return has not gone still further back along the scale of historical evolution to the law of the ant-hill and of the beehive.[14]

All along, it has been evident that M. Duguit is bent on exorcising the demon of a morally responsible will. It is not to the state alone that he would deny personality. It is to the individual as well, for let this fell spirit but once get no more than his toe into the door-jamb of M. Duguit's lumber room of fact and strictly non-metaphysical fancy and he would play hobgoblin with the carefully arranged and selected contents! M. Duguit doesn't believe that there really is a moral will, any more than he believes in ghosts. Still he is scrupulously careful not to offend the shade if it should exist, merely contenting himself with the recitation of a positivistic *ave* or two in the form of *ignoramus, ignorabimus.* Even if such a will did exist, he assures himself, it could not conflict with a fact and the social norms are, by definition, facts.

"This norm is a rule which leaves all the wills what they are, a rule whose violation brings about a social reaction and nothing else, a rule which must not be violated, because if it is, the life of society (*la vie sociale*) of which the individuals are at the same time the agents and the beneficiaries, is troubled and then the

[14] *Cf.* Note 3, *supra.*

social organism reacts against the author of the violation. This rule, however, is not a biological law because the individuals to whom it applies are conscious of their acts and of the motives which determine them." [15]

Very well! But what can be the function of consciousness in a world where the social organism subordinates the individual ruthlessly to its own ends? Certainly no different part from that which it plays in the complex nervous systems of other organisms; and the laws of society, for all the difference it makes in the total result, might be biological. Obviously this will not do. Whatever the nature of the conscious will, it does produce in human society not the laws of an ant-hill, nor yet those which govern, for example, the digestive processes of an organism. The effort at simplification of consciously directed social experimentation into mechanical or into biological adaptation simply results in leaving out the significant factor, that is, consciousness itself. M. Duguit recognizes this even though he will not concede any creative power to the consciousness he admits into the pale of scientific respectability.

Indeed I suspect M. Duguit of adopting on the whole a position not unlike the very one he has set up and then knocked down so often to his great content. In spite of his somewhat robustious parade of sticking to the tangible facts—force and the rest of them—he is always haunted by the ghost of a force behind the actual force which rulers control. Perhaps it is this ghost that tortures him on to reslay the slain once more with more than one sidelong kick at the mutilated fallacies contained in Rousseau's exposition of the *volonté générale*. But these have long been corpses without laying the stubborn ghost which once gave them life, and whose spirit still walks: that spirit is a will common to all πολιτικὰ Ζῷα to coöperate for a good recognized as common within the limits of an actual community. That will, which M. Duguit adumbrates by the remarkably fertile shades of obligation falling from his *"solidarité sociale,"* remains, I venture to say, the necessary presupposition of any form of political association, and its abiding character finds its expression in the relative permanency of principles of law, and the existence of determinate bodies to give them application.

[15] *Traité, cit.* p. 24.

The same curious result may attend a careful examination of M. Duguit's fierce onslaught on the concept of rights in law, i.e., he may turn out in the end to be attempting to safeguard just what modern English jurisprudence would regard as rights, by denying all rights in favor of a law absolutely objective, that is built up on the sole conception of social obligation. To understand his attempt we must remember the abstract nature of the absolute individual rights which the *Déclaration des droits de l'homme et du citoyen* had made the basis of French law. Let us admit at once a very old and often-repeated truth: a right against society is a contradiction in terms. The only meaning which rights can have is that well stated by the late T. H. Green: "A right is a power claimed and recognized as contributory to the common good," "a right, not against society, but a right to be treated as a member of society." [16] Right in this sense is the complement, not the converse, of duty. If groups and governments and individuals comprising them have duties, those duties derive their meaning from reciprocal relationships with each other, not with some abstract social solidarity. And out of these relationships spring reciprocal rights to claim the performance of reciprocal duties. Either right or duty, taken as a separate concept and divorced from its actual social context, is an abstraction of the most vicious unreality, and one that will ultimately reduce any system founded upon it to absurdity.

The obstinate fashion in which men hold to the notion of certain individual rights which every citizen may claim to have assured him by good government, life, liberty, and secure possession of lawful property, does not mean that these rights are felt to be innate in every human being as such and that from the very beginnings of society. The slow growth of these conceptions shows that they are the hard-won fruits of the whole development of social justice and of its incorporation into law. It may be said that before they were written into the fabric of legal security, men had no guarantee that they might lead what Green has recalled for us from Plato and from Aristotle as the end of all

---

[16] See Green's magistral treatment of this problem, the central one of political philosophy in "The Grounds of Political Obligation," *Principles of Political Obligation.*

action, "the good life." The rights which are assured to men by
law are the negative condition of realizing this moral good,
conceived by the individual as the same for others as for himself; and in this sense they form the only basis of connection
between law and morality. That is to say, law cannot force a
man to be morally good in the true sense of moral goodness, because that good can only be attained *sponte sua;* on the other
hand law can remove some of the hindrances to free choice, those
repressive influences which make the exercise of his rights to
become a morally responsible member of society virtually impossible. It is under such a conception of the province of law
that legislators have banned or regulated the use of narcotic
drugs and of alcohol in so far as these matters may be controlled
by control of their sale and manufacture. The extension of the
police power increases with the complexity of the context.

The idealistic conception of the state finds in consequence that
a government derives its power—the force which makes its own
use of coercive force possible—from a will which sanctions and
maintains that force. It sees in the political power so created an
instrument whose use is to assure the rule of law. For it is only
through the rule of law that any rights take their origin or keep
their existence. It is, I think, clear that governments do in this
sense have the right to command, for the use which government
serves demands it; it is just as clear that a government which
is responsible to the will behind this rule of law will act under
law. It is with this meaning that Jellinek and Ihering have
spoken of the limitation of public powers as auto-limitation on
the part of the state, i.e., on the part of the politically organized
community.

The limitation imposed on the acts of government is other in
kind according to M. Duguit. It is a limitation proceeding from
an external social necessity, which registers itself more or less
automatically in laws which are in turn mere norms for the integrating forces of social solidarity. The rulers do not tyrannize
for the same reason that the ruled obey; because they fear to
provoke a social reaction.

But it is a truth which needs little more than suggesting to command acceptance, that any such simplification of the nature of
law is a mutilation of fact. Men consciously adapt their laws to

their needs, and envisage these needs as ends.[17] Their success is never more than partial, and their procedure is always experimental. An endless history of experimentation has gone into the state as we know it, in its capacity of law-declarer and law-enforcer. The wisdom which we have derived from this social heritage is that the rule of law is not assured by leaving its declaration to the parties to conflict, to groups or to classes, but to the umpire created and sustained by the expressed will of a given community that such an umpire exist.

I do not pretend that M. Duguit in his system of *droit objectif* makes no provision for such an umpire. On the contrary, for all his efforts to show that his doctrine is an attack on the irresponsible state of traditional theory, he has gradually put the emphasis in each succeeding work more and more on the duty of the rulers to stick at nothing—coercion of any type, unrestrained by notions of individual rights—to assure the public services. Public services he equates with all the forces necessarily employed to assure functional interdependence in industrial nations. He has thus repudiated his earlier leaning toward a real pluralism of lawmakers. In order to carry out logically his conception of social reactions reflecting themselves in group-made laws, he seems to have come more definitely in the last edition of the *Traité* to feel that law as *une disposition impérative*—although it is still called a constructive norm—is for all practical purposes the rules enforced by those in actual power—a thoroughly Austinian position when it is supplemented by the concept of organic nationalism which shines from every line of *Sovereignty and Liberty*. State absolutism of the Fascist type turns out to be the most dominant of all his array of uncriticized facts, as we might have expected when he embraced the fear-theory as a "fact."

Such a state, restrained by no constitutional rules and limited only by the fear of provoking social reactions which not even organized terrorism could put down, has reached its apotheosis in Mussolini's Italy. Fascism illustrates both the vices and the virtues of the realistic side of M. Duguit's *droit objectif*. It

[17] Ihering has based an entire system of jurisprudence on the conception of *Der Zweck im Recht*, translated as *Law as a Means to an End*, Modern Legal Philosophy Series, Vol. V.

owns no moral necessity except that of pragmatic efficiency and the logic of survival. Its apology derives from a Romanticist myth of a superman leading an imperialistic nationalism to Roman glory, but its chief practical hold is based upon the claim that it has "assured the public services." Its theory of the state, now that it is in power, becomes more and more that of the organic functionalism which M. Duguit has hymned so lyrically. Mussolini, too, sees beauty in the Fascist philosophy, taught in a highly regimented system of state education, that the nation is an organism in which the individuals are only functioning cells, whose duty is to produce, and obey without complaint whatever the rulers judge fitting in the interests of efficiency.

In a great social crisis these ideals proved their attraction to the Italian people. Are they now to be turned to imperialistic ends? Revolutionary methods and the violence natural to them may be rendered necessary by the absence of constitutional morality and by the lack of democratic leadership in a country so new to democratic methods and discipline as was Italy. On M. Duguit's theory of the state, the ruthless repression which Fascism still employs to prevent any criticism of its aims and methods will be justifiable as a permanent philosophy of government, so long as its ends are those of keeping the state geared up to its maximum functioning as an organism. All consent is equally valid so long as it makes for conformity to this organic smoothness, with no lost motion through strikes or interruptions of production, whether it be the consent of a constitutionally organized nation to its responsible government, or whether it be consent that results from helplessness in the face of politically irresponsible force. From M. Duguit's point of view, force is always justified so long as it can inspire fear great enough to maintain itself in power. Its survival as a government is the test of its moral adequacy.

The wide acceptance of such a philosophy of the state, congenial enough to times in which the slackness of antiquated state machinery is a source of real social distress, will have an important bearing on men's practical attitudes toward the future of constitutional democracy. In order to understand and to criticize this new political *mythos* it will be necessary to get at the theoretical characteristics of *droit objectif*, and then examine their adequacy in practice to the development of a form of organic state that claims to have found in Fascism the solution of the political difficulties which beset industrialized nations.

CHAPTER X

THE STATE AS AN ORGANISM

A. DROIT OBJECTIF AS THE APOLOGY FOR THE FASCIST-SYNDICALIST STATE

The state, according to M. Duguit's *droit objectif*, is no longer to be conceived as a sovereign power issuing its commands, but as individuals who must use the force they hold to supply public need. Or, as he says in *Law in the Modern State*, "Government and its officials are no longer the masters of men imposing the sovereign will on their subjects. . . . They are simply the managers of the nation's business. . . . Their business increases, their duties expand, but their right of control is extinct because no one any longer believes in it." [1] One may no longer, indeed, use the word *right* in legal terminology. The proper word is duty (*devoir*).

Now one may ask whether the business which is the state's especial care is not of just the duty that makes control imperative to its fulfillment. How can it guarantee the operation of its "institutions of objective law" without a control, i.e., without asserting a right to arbitrate and even to coerce, which arises from its duty to safeguard the public services? This safeguarding of public services is a duty on which M. Duguit is never tired of insisting. It is apparent that he is attacking the metaphysical shadow of the Eighteenth Century conception of right—a right which has no corresponding duty. But granted that "the power to command . . . is the obligation in a practical fashion to supply needs," it by no means follows that the right itself to assert that power "is no longer a need." [2] Fascism learned early that it could not "manage" without commanding. Based upon no theory of sovereignty except its duty to "keep the trains

[1] *Law in the Modern State.* Translated by Frida and Harold Laski, p. 51.
[2] *Op. cit.* Author's Introduction, p. xliii.

on time" and the factories running it soon shed all restraints and ideas of rights in its efforts to assure social solidarity.

If M. Duguit's system has claims to being more than a proposal to strike out *right*, and insert *duty* where the former has occurred in past legal systems, i.e., to escape a misguided individualism by an equally erring collectivism, the test will come in his treatment of the concrete problems presented by the nature of statute in constitutional and in public law, involving as these legal categories do, the nature of sovereignty in its relations to the so-called "principle of federalism," and the locus of legislative power. As these are the points of attack generally chosen by pragmatism (witness Mr. Dewey and Mr. Laski), it will be instructive to see how M. Duguit develops his offensive.

I. Statute and Law

Nowhere more certainly than under the conception of statute as the expression of the general will through the representative legislature does the traditional doctrine of sovereignty manifest its strength; yet it is just here that M. Duguit has chosen to attack that doctrine most strongly. It is clear that here he is, like Mr. Dewey, a pluralist in his sympathies and strongly anti-Fascist.

The first difficulty and perhaps the greatest which has to be met by what M. Duguit terms the "imperialist" theory of sovereignty is the existence of organic laws which the sovereign state itself must obey, either in the form of a rigid constitution or of judicial review of legislation which may be refused application because it conflicts with the extraordinary body of law that determines in what fashion ordinary law may be passed. It is worth noting at once that this limitation exists only in constitutional states, and not in states where the rulers are simply those who control power through fear and force. In England, it is true, and to only a slightly lesser extent in France, parliamentary sovereignty is rightly summed up by Dicey: "The principle of Parliamentary sovereignty means neither more nor less than this, namely, that Parliament thus defined (the King in Parliament of English constitutional law) has, under the English Constitution, the right to make or unmake any law whatever; and further, that no person or body is recognized by the law of England as having a right to override or set aside the legislation of parliament." [3] At first sight this sovereignty seems to conform to the strictest Austinian dogma, and to be subject to no such limitations as those imposed on legislation in the United States by the power of judicial review and constitutional interpretation vested in the Supreme Court. The strict legal fact has found humorous expression in the saying, attributed to de Lolme: "Parliament can do everything but make a woman a man, and a man a woman." And yet Parliament itself must act in a legal way, i.e., under the organic formal laws and the mass of extra-legal conventions as binding as those laws, that govern its procedure, just as the rest of the government must operate under the law of the land. In France it is noteworthy that a school of jurisprudential theory increasingly favors the establishment of a Supreme Court along the lines proposed in the Chamber of Deputies by M. Charles Benoist (one of the steadfast enemies of parliamentarism) in 1903 as an addition to the constitutional law of Feb. 25, 1875, with the charge of "passing upon the claims of citizens for the violation of their constitutional rights by the legislature or the executive power." [4] In the United States statutes are reduced by judicial review to a legally subordinate position. Under several of the newer constitutions of Europe there is a possibility of a similar development.

Even statute, then, as a power of the sovereign is limited by the rule of law. The government itself must act under law: its will is not irresponsible and arbitrary. How is it possible to explain this fact under the doctrine of a sovereign will? "If we admit the personality of the state-person, and define law as the command of its sovereign will, it is absolutely impossible to understand how organic laws can be really laws since the state cannot address a command to itself." [5] There is great force in this criticism of the general will of the

---

[3] *Law of the Constitution* (8th ed.), p. 476.
[4] *Recueil* (1907), p. 913, and *Journal Officiel*, Proc. Parl. Chambre (1903), pp. 95-99, quoted by Duguit, *op. cit.* pp. 93-94, and footnotes. M. Duguit has, after some hesitation in earlier works, given it his blessing in the last edition of the *Traité*, Vol. III (1923), p. 779 *et seq.*
[5] *Op. cit.* p. 76. See notably for the ideas of M. Ch. Benoist, *La crise de l'état moderne,* and his recent article on the breakdown of parliamentarism in *La Revue de deux mondes, 1925.*

state person as the basis of law. The state can not be conceived as a person without entering the realm of legal fiction. But if "will" be conceived not as a general will but as a consensus of wills, his conclusion is only valid if one accepts M. Duguit's morality of necessity, and sees in will no more than the conscious response of an organism to external stimuli. No will, according to this reading of morality, is capable of self-limitation.[6] Auto-limitation, either for the individual or the state, is equally un-meaning. If, on the other hand, human purpose selects its alter-natives with a creative development in its scale of values, the constituent state may represent only a limited community of purpose. The constitution may be properly treated as an act of auto-limitation by the state, taking the state to mean a citizen-ship created by a community of wills. It is even difficult to see the possibility of a rule of law on any other basis—providing always that human society is something more than a mechanism, or a biological organism.

M. Duguit's real confusion arises first of all from treating the state as no more than the government actually in power. Gov-ernment in constitutional states is controlled by law. If the state in its present complexity of form is truly seen as the product of men's conscious effort to establish the reign of law, that law is best viewed as the terms of a mandate under which the powers of government are administered; but it is a mandate which de-mands for its own formulation the existence of a national pur-pose capable of representative expression. A long history of painful social experimentation in securing government responsible to that "will" lies behind the modern *Rechtsstaat*, and the con-temporary political welter of dictatorships testifies to Europe's precarious hold on it. Imperfect as the present system of repre-senting that "will" may be in parliamentary and constitutional governments, the determinate organs of government (and a con-stitutional convention is no more) still are the only means by which it has been found possible to announce the legal limits it puts upon the agents holding its power.

A second difficulty comes from the use of "will" where an abiding community of purpose is really meant. Ultimately, of course, that intangible but sovereign thing called public opinion

[6] *Cf.* Jellinek. *Gesetz und Verordnung* (1887), pp. 197-198.

acting within the constitutionally determined areas of political community determines the application of sanctions where the action of the government in power is in question—wherever the holders of power are answerable to a popular suffrage. But public opinion is a shared purpose, not the general will of a super person.

In his denial of the force of statutes as commands, M. Duguit is actuated by the same logic that Mr. Dewey used in his discussion of "Austin's Theory of Sovereignty" to rebut the theory "which, placing sovereignty in a part of society, makes government an entity *per se*, whose operations are all commands" in favor of a theory "which finds the residence of sovereignty in the whole complex of social activities, thus making government an organ—an organ the more efficient, we may add, just in proportion as it is an entity, not *per se*, but is flexible and responsible to the social whole." [7] Such a theory can not admit that commands which come from a part of society have any binding force on the whole, for it cannot see in that part (which not even Austin insisted was an entity *per se*) the empowered representatives of the community. Their possession of force is a fact for M. Duguit; but that fact has no moral significance because it is only a fact of accident or necessity. For that reason it is natural that he should put sovereignty in the whole. A sovereign people may miss the flexibility, though, that Dewey has hoped to find unless its government does become an entity, although not an entity *per se*. States without constitutional governments have tended to the rigidity of theoretic principles. Even Fascism falls back on the divine right of the superman to preserve the nation.

All social institutions are means, of course, as well as ends. Government under a constitutional system, because it is the agent through which the state makes good its claim to being a *communitas communitatum*, serves as a means whose central importance is so great to the safeguarding of so many means to ends (among them the external setting without which the good life is itself impossible), that it assumes the meaning, not indeed of an end in itself, but of an end necessary to the realization of all other ends dependent on social order. As such an end it must have a secure life of its own. To be flexible is not to be form-

[7] *Political Science Quarterly* (1894), Article cited, p. 53.

less. Indeed, the practical tenor of much of the reasoning of M. Duguit on the State's duty to assure public services is in the precise direction of shaping the proper functional divisions for state regulation.

But on his conception of statute, the organ for forming law does not issue commands; it is merely registrative. "It may be added," he says, "that if opinion is the essential factor in the making of law, it plays this rôle only when men think that a certain rule is imposed by a social sanction. In other words public opinion only makes legislation when the individual minds that have formed it possess juristic content. There comes a moment when the clear necessity of certain rules is so profoundly and generally felt by men that every statute which enacts them is universally admitted as possessing for all an obvious character that is obligatory."

At a certain moment, the shadow-land of vague sentiment and opinions clears up so that all may recognize juristic outlines. The legislator has only to wait for this moment. Before it appears, any rules that he may pass will not carry a social sanction, in other words, will not be law in the significance assigned to that term by M. Duguit. The movement of society in its political organization becomes, once more, medieval; it awaits the mass feeling, the unanimity of consent, before it acts, because its control is not directive but registrative. And the only possible organ of such registration in modern states would be a dictator who could suppress all opposition.

M. Duguit insists that, although the idea of "the order of a superior imposed upon an inferior will" must be given up for the "fact" that the "social environment necessarily gives rise to a rule of social conduct," statute is still not to be confused on that account with custom. Custom often gives the rule of conduct (later expressed more precisely and completely in statute) its "first and imperfect expression"; "it is doubtless true that the compelling power of statute and custom is derived from the same source, but they represent different degrees of objective law." But both are for M. Duguit objective law. The difference is merely one of degree. Custom would be, apparently, the almost universal source of law.[8] To say that the rule of conduct which

⁸ *Law in the Modern State*, p. 73.

has not been enacted in statute or accepted as common law may have a very important ethical reality but has no legal character because no legal sanctions follow its violation, or to point out that acts which conform to the rule likewise have no legal significance, does not touch his point. All acts which involve social sanctions by being imposed on men through the needs arising from social interdependence are legal in character. "It is, of course, true," he admits, "that when there is no written statute or, at least, no formulated custom, there does not exist for that rule of law a definitive legal sanction. *But that does not involve the absence of obligation in that rule of law understood not as a command but as a way of life derived from the necessities of social existence.*" [9] These "ways of life" which contain "a rule of law every ruler recognized at a given time and place" are called, in the phraseology of *droit objectif* "normative laws" and it is difficult to see their precise relation to actual statutes unless we accept statutes as a sort of mechanical registration of these laws. Very evidently, however, statutes are nothing of the sort. To try to fit them thus arbitrarily into the frame of *droit objectif* is a Procrustean endeavor. Mutilation ensues. Statutes are generally attempts to create "ways of life."

Take for instance, such legislation (I use the term advisedly) as the Eighteenth Amendment to the Constitution of the United States and the laws contributing to its enforcement. It is, I believe, more than dubious whether such legislation could be classed under the head of "normative" law as defined above; certainly they are not "constructive" laws which are by definition "the way in which society organizes the sanction" to ensure the acceptance of normative law. They are not normative law within the meaning of M. Duguit's definition because the decision as to their social necessity conceivably issued from a majority only, not by an *"adhésion unanime"* from the social whole; nor were they "ways of life." They were, collectively, "prohibition" of a way of life. It is even possible that they were the result of the determined insistence of a minority, bent upon prohibiting the sale of alcoholic beverages completely. Granted that this minority, on the realistic interpretation which *droit objectif* has offered, be conceived as limited in fact to those indivduals

[9] *Op. cit.*, p. 74. Italics mine.

actually in control of the force of government; granted, even, that this minority acted for what were the best interests of the *solidarité sociale;* it must have acted so on its own interpretation of what were those interests. Quite probably that interpretation coincided with that of the representatives of the constitutionally necessary majority of the citizens of the United States; possibly it did not. In either case, *the fact,* in M. Duguit's despite, was quite clearly the organized wills of a part of the community imposing prohibitory rules of conduct upon another very considerable part—for no one can doubt the very real and extensive opposition to national prohibition of all alcoholic beverages. The law is enforced with varying degrees of success. But it is a statute and it is enforced. The determination of law is not a matter of the mere declaration of an already existing state of fact. It is in cases of this sort, and even more in cases of technical economic legislation, the effort to create a state of fact in human conduct.

It may be that where these experimental efforts run foul of the deepest and most ingrained human characteristics they fail. Nevertheless slavery has been abolished, opium trade and white-slaving have been outlawed, sanitation is more and more effectively enforced.

The strength of the position of *droit objectif* lies in the fact that such laws as the Volstead Act, applied to as heterogeneous a population and as vast an area as the United States seriously overestimate the possibility of creating a state of fact. They are apt to break down, eventually, the whole machinery of legal enforcement by attempting too much.

A much clearer example of the inadequacy of the conception of "normative laws" as the real basis of positive law, can be witnessed in the legislation of Fascist Italy. Mussolini, emulating the great lawgivers of the past, has not hesitated to attempt to change the whole political character and economic life of the Italian people. Doubtless Italians were predisposed to accept Fascist measures by previous disorders. But many of Mussolini's decrees would not have had the support of opinion. Do these Fascist decrees command acceptance as automatically produced by "the social environment," or because they are the commands of an accepted legal sovereign who enforces them?

Positive law must equally describe the facts of habitual obedience, even in the unconstitutional state.

The crux of the question resolves itself into whether law in the modern state is not more than custom carried a degree further by declaration, as M. Esmein so keenly noted in his critique of the system of jurisprudence proposed by M. Duguit.[10] If legislators are the agents of popular sovereignty, even a popular sovereignty conceived in terms so mechanical as those outlined by the positivist method under consideration, they have *quâ* agents the duty of determining what shall be called law and the right to command its enforcement. The possibility of enforcing laws will depend upon constitutional morality in constitutional states and upon fear and force and social reactions in unconstitutional states.

Constructive laws, which "are simply those that organize public services," offer to M. Duguit the opportunity to reconcile some of the difficulties which normative laws have left on his hands. "Perhaps," he says, "no great inconvenience is involved in the denial that normative laws exist; there would still remain the fact that every general disposition of government which aimed at the organization of a public service would be imposed on all under the legitimate sanction of material constraint. Indeed, in the issuance of such dispositions government only fulfils the social function incumbent upon it from the situation it occupies." [11] One could not ask a more complete admission of the

[10] Esmein finds that Duguit confuses two very different things :

"(1) la loi, commandement du souverain ; elle tire sa force obligatoire de l'autorité dont elle émane.

"(2) la coutume, l'expression tacite et unanime de la volonté des populations ; elle se fonde sur des précédents répétés qui constituent, pour parler comme M. Duguit, autant de situations juridiques subjectives. . . .

"La loi, telle que la conçoit notre cher collègue, n'est guère que la coutume enrégistrée par la volonté législative des gouvernants ; et pourtant, il veut encore que ce soit la loi. N'y a-t-il pas là une confusion entre ce que Montesquieu aurait peut-être appelé la nature et le principe du pouvoir législatif?

"Ce qui fait agir le pouvoir législatif est ce qui l'amène à légiférer, ce sont bien les besoins constatés et les idées moyennes de la population, et il est certain que les meilleures lois sont celles qui sont faites d'avance par l'opinion publique, murie et consciente. Mais ce n'est pas une raison pour brouiller, sans aucun besoin, les catégories du droit public et confondre l'opinion qui inspire la loi et l'autorité qui l'edicte. Qu'on propose de revenir au pur système coutumier : cela serait plus clair." (*Elements de droit constitutionnel. Introduction*, 6ème ed.)

[11] Duguit, *op. cit.*, p. 74.

main Austinian position, nor is there any great significance to be attached to the introduction of the term *function*. The conception was not foreign to Austin himself, though he found that "The Province of Jurisprudence Determined" (as he significantly called his lectures on Jurisprudence) did not require its elaboration. After the following admission on the part of M. Duguit, it becomes increasingly difficult to see why he has introduced the notion of normative law at all, whether, indeed, it has not a meaning on the same metaphysical plane from which he so often insists on pulling down other systems.[12]

". . . I have pointed out that it is not necessary to know if there is a rule of law earlier in origin and superior in force to government. For the same reason we need not enquire if normative laws exist, for if they do they are only the expression of this rule of law. For myself, it seems clear that this rule of law and the statutes that are its expression have an actual existence. They must be postulated because we can not do without them. The very condition of social life involves our organizing certain activities with public services, and it is from this that their operation has the social force and value involved in their general rules."[13]

The passage from the original French of M. Duguit has been very roughly translated; yet I can not escape the conclusion that the foregoing statement involves, on its face, an obvious contradiction and a very interesting one. For it shows the basic difficulty involved in the whole so-termed "realistic" position; if government fulfils an automatic function in its legislation (and indeed in all its other capacities), we do not need to go behind its force for a rule of law superior to government (that is always if we propose to stick only to the necessary facts). On the other hand, if we propose to find the rule of law superior in force to government, we can not stop short of the ultimate realm into which we shall be led by logic. As Laird has so happily phrased the matter, "He who trusts himself to logic must trust

---

[12] This attack on Ihering and Jellinek may almost be reduced to his positivistic dogma of "No metaphysics," so far as its bearing on the will is concerned. But there is a supplementary insistence on the organic context of law that is valuable, and that jurists of the formalistic school neglect. This would apply, e.g., to Hans Kelsen's "Pure Theory of Law."

[13] *Op. cit.*, p. 75.

himself altogether. He can not seriously like the instrumentalists of Mr. Bradley, step into the stream with one foot and keep the other on the bank. For the bank is not firm enough and the stream too masterful." [14] The logic of his argument would lead M. Duguit straight back to a system of a Natural Law of Economic Necessity.

The dilemma is so obvious that he can not himself escape it; but his attempt to bring the two horns together into unity begets so strange a creature—the unicorn of mythos, one is tempted to say—that I propose quoting his ingenious *abracadabra* somewhat at length:

"Of course a statute is universally admitted to possess an obligatory, even imperative, force. A statute, it may be, is no longer the order of a superior imposed upon an inferior will. But it still remains true that civil servants and private citizens must obey statutes. The power of compulsion at the disposal of government may necessarily and can legitimately be applied to ensure obedience to them.

"*These are not contradictory principles* [my italics]. It is clear, as I have pointed out, that there is an objective law superior to government. As soon as a human society exists, the indispensable condition of its maintenance is social discipline. While we reject metaphysical theory [*sic*] it is of course clear that the social environment necessarily gives rise to a rule of social conduct.[15] . . . We obey this rule not because it creates a superior duty, but simply because we are, for good or ill, members of society and therefore necessarily subject to its social discipline. . . . It is clear to all of us that it has an obligatory nature not transcendental and abstract but based on the facts of life." [16]

"Once that is understood it becomes clear why a statute compels us to obedience. It is not, technically speaking, a command.

[14] *A Study in Realism*, p. 91.
[15] *Op. cit.*, p. 70. The analogy to Dewey's doctrine, *supra*, is too obvious to require elaboration.
[16] *Loc. cit. et* p. 71. This is the obligation by imposition, or by psychological coercion, which Durkheim and Lévy-Bruhl have developed in their treatment of social psychology, based upon the notion of "collective representations." See W. R. Dennes, *Method and Presuppositions of Group Psychology* (Univ. of California Press, 1924). See also P. A. Sorokin, "Sociology and Ethics," *The Social Sciences* (Ogburn and Goldenweiser, editors).

It is yet compelling because it formulates a rule of law which is itself the expression of social facts." [17]

This is to put Mr. Dewey's social morality of fact, outlined in *Human Nature and Conduct*, to legal use. But a very slight familiarity with the psychology of persuasive composition serves to convince one that M. Duguit is conscious of skating here on an ice-skim of the thinnest, from the number of repetitions of "it is clear" that he makes each time he approaches the question of what, exactly, the technical nature of a statute is. Here is that very "law superior to the state" which he finds, as we have seen, unnecessary to invoke in order to justify the force of the rulers and it is this law itself, nevertheless, to which he has recourse when he would establish that the statute is not a command. One may suggest that on M. Duguit's own method of selecting facts, one can not go further into the nature of statute than to say it is a command, for that is the only conceivable reality by which "the possessors of force" can impose their wills upon the ruled. Any other interpretation of the force which the rulers possess must seek to explain the facts of government in terms of a purpose-relation that possesses the right to command because that right has been granted it by the general consent of an ordered society, in a given territory. This shared will to order is, I suggest, nothing very different from M. Duguit's *solidarité sociale* as a Natural Law (*jus naturale*) superior to the state.[18] It is better stated, I believe, in the formulation given it by Herr Stammler, or by M. Charmont, a distinguished compatriot of M. Duguit, in terms of form, and better still by Mr. Morris Cohen.[19] But nothing is to be gained by exorcising the will *ex rerum natura*, as M. Duguit has done, or by calling the

---

[17] *Law in the Modern State*, *cf.* p. 72 ff. Precisely the difference between a statute and a social custom consists in the fact that the former *is*, technically speaking, a legal *command*.

[18] Geny said of it: "In reality, this objective law is enough like the old natural law to be mistaken for it, like that universal, immutable law, the source of all positive laws which was spoken of in the plan of the civil code of the year VIII. Nevertheless, I have no doubt that M. Duguit would cry out and protest with all his might against such a comparison." (*La revue critique de législation*) 1901, p. 508, quoted by Charmont, *Modern French Legal Philosophy*, p. 132, note. Mr. Morris Cohen has called Duguit, aptly, a "crypto-idealist."

[19] Charmont, *op. cit.*, *supra*, translated and selected from *La renaissance du droit naturel*, *cf.* especially Chapter IX.

Stammler, *Die Lehre von dem Richtigen Rechte*, especially Introduction.

result social order. It is the machine without the god that is left.

Nothing remains of M. Duguit's attack on Jellinek's doctrine of auto-limitation, after all, except the highly metaphysical affirmation that the will is unknowable and, from this *a priori* consideration, consequently incapable of prescribing its own law. There is no difficulty half so formidable under the doctrine of auto-limitation (once we see that state "personality" stands for organized purpose) in seeing how statutes themselves may be made subject to judicial review under the interpretation of organic law, as there is in the notion of objective law which somehow imposes social needs automatically. The latter conception can never deal adequately with the power of a political community (a state) to alter its own organic law, for it must treat that experimental manifestation of popular will as the fixed decree of social necessity. It never does justice to the part volition plays in determining what it will recognize as social necessity. We must, however, equally reject the notion of the state person when that concept is used to imply a super-personal unity as the basis of the state, and a general will.

II. Federalism and Statutes—Legal Unity

But what are we to say of the statutes which M. Duguit describes as "not derived from the people or its representatives," statutes passed by districts and groups? And how reconcile the statutory power which clothes certain commissions with legislative and quasi-judicial attributes, with the doctrine that statutes can issue only from the determinate legislative body of the national assembly? Can the popular will be said to be represented by administrative ordinances that possess equal claims to execution by the courts with the ordinary statutes passed by legislatures?

The existence of such laws alongside of the laws emanating from the organ supposed to represent "the national will," M. Duguit contends is a clear disproof of the old notion of sovereignty that on a given territory only one law can exist and that all statute must derive its recognition and validity only from that law. "Obviously," he says, "the sovereign can not admit a federalist organization" and he points to the *saeva indignatio* manifested by the men of the French Revolution in the Constitution of 1791,[20] against self-governing areas or communities in the State. He might later have pointed to Fascism gathering even the threads of local government through prefect and podesta, into the hands of the head of the hierarchy in Rome. Obviously the facts of political life do bear M. Duguit out in his contention that all law does not emanate from the enactments of a single national legislative body. It was this aspect of the federal form of government of the United States, together, of course, with the existence of a rigid constitution, that led Austin to place sovereignty in the determinate body capable of revising the constitution. But is it obvious that "the sovereign can not admit a federalist organization," if by federalist is meant "what we to-day call decentralization"? Decentralization of administrative areas does not imply federalism, for federalism means the restraint of a rigid constitution on the changing of the distribution of powers. Decentralization is, it may well be, the key to most of the problems of detail in government. But decentralization, when it means the delegation of certain powers of self-government to geographical communities, or of special powers to commissions with expert knowledge, need not in the least conflict with the legal sovereignty of the nation state. Even in a truly federal state, it is the latter, ultimately, through the amending power or the power which created the constitution, that must limit both state and federal governments; or through its judicial bodies which maintain the constitution it must decide all questions of the legality of ordinances or quasi-statutes, and on the basis of whether they are or are not *ultra vires* the powers conferred. The Constitution of such a federal state as the self-governing Dominion of Canada is a clear illustration of this contention. All powers are reserved for the Dominion which are not specifically granted to the separate provinces. Technically the laws of the Dominion itself are still subject to review by the Privy Council of The Empire, through the Judicial Committee— though since the Imperial Conference of 1926 that review no longer rests on the prerogative of the British Crown (as had just been held in the Frank Nadan Case) but on the voluntary con-

[20] Duguit, *op. cit.*, p. 96.

sent of the Dominion. Federalism implies unification in a legal system, although it can not be explained by the "state-person" or the general will, as it is for example in Professor Willoughby's *Fundamental Concepts of Public Law.*

The United States, though it presents the reverse situation from Canada so far as residuary powers are concerned, illustrates the same unification of laws: technically its separate states reserve all powers not specifically granted to the Federal Government by the Constitution, which, historically, can only be seen as a compact agreed upon by the several states. A trace of this compact theory remains in the formal restriction in Article V designed to protect the equal representation of States in the Senate even from the amending power itself.

Probably there is no other instance in history of an opportunity, such as that which was created by Hamilton and his co-workers on the *Federalist,* to analyze the basis of a contemporary political association so clearly derived from specific agreement. Yet the historical evolution of the federation thus created has been always more clearly away from a confederacy of real states, delegating specific powers to a central government, and toward a central government which took away from the states all final power that it found necessary to assure its control. This is the significance which the Civil War assumes in the political history of the North American political experiment; and it is more than ever the juristic meaning of the Supreme Court decisions arising out of the Fourteenth Amendment and "Due Process," [21] as well as the gradual extension of powers of the Federal Government under the Constitutional authority to regulate commerce between the States,[22] and to extend the police power through taxation and other main grants of power. Most of all it is the meaning of the facility with which the Constitution is latterly amended. Federalism is coming to mean Hamiltonian Federalism. So long, however, as the amending clause requires consent from three-fourths of the states, nationalism has not entirely conquered federalism.

That Austinian sovereignty would indeed preclude a *really*

[21] *Cf.* Franklin Pierce, *Federal Usurpation,* and Walter Thompson, *Federal Centralization,* Rodney L. Mott, *Due Process of Law,* and Charles Collins, *The Fourteenth Amendment and the States.*

[22] *Cf.* Beard, *The Supreme Court and the Constitution.*

federal (i.e., a completely *confederate*)²³ form of Government from claiming to exist in a true state there is no doubt, for Austin denied that a true sovereign could render allegiance in turn to another determinate superior. The Articles of Confederation showed that a confederacy degenerates easily into an impotent League of States. It was on this logic that the advocates of "States Rights" prior to secession denied the sovereignty of the Union. The Union was itself the creation of the sovereign states. It existed for their welfare in a common direction, not they for its. The logic of John C. Calhoun was rigorously Austinian: save that he applied it to South Carolina rather than to the Union, it was precisely the same which had moved fiery "Old Hickory" (Andrew Jackson) to threaten Calhoun himself with the hemp. In effect, it proclaimed that the political community was sovereign within its borders, and would brook no interference from without, or from within. Calhoun's theory of "concurrent" majorities or the consent of three-fourths of the states as a brake on unconstitutional federal legislation never had the grip of reality in it; it could only mean disagreement and disruption when applied to a growing nation.²⁴

The obvious quarrel arose as to the locus of sovereignty, not as to its nature. To the Unionists the indivisibility of sovereignty meant that the powers of the separate states were subject to limitation and even to revision where they conflicted with those of the United States; to the Secessionists, *per contra*, the same indivisibility meant that the powers of the Federal Government were granted only conditionally, and they were for that reason subject, if abused, to revocation by any state which entered into the compact. But there was no quarrel as to their indivisibility. Lee, who refused the command of the Northern Armies, saying with dramatic simplicity "I am first a citizen of Virginia," would have had no doubt about any proposal to divide Virginia itself. That issue would have met the rebuke of armed force applied with the same sternness that made the entire South a four-years battle ground. In fact Virginians still speak bitterly of "the rape of West Virginia." The larger issue was decided for the nation by that bloody arbitrament. But it would, no doubt, have

²³ *Cf.* Arthur Heath, *Personality.*
²⁴ Calhoun's *Works*, ed. 1853, Vol. I, pp. 28 *et seq.*

been decided ultimately by the quietly inexorable movement of historical forces all making for nationalism, not Confederacy. De Tocqueville's *"gouvernement national incomplet"* moved always toward completion. Perhaps the courts will be eventually freed from the onus they now bear of stretching the constitution to obviate its amendment. In any case, national supremacy in national concerns is assured. Sovereignty in legal systems must follow the growth of new areas of political community. It need not move always to unification in a single state as the juristic break-up of the British Commonwealth of Nations shows.

The difficulty in assigning definite bounds to the sovereign state suggests that the sovereign state itself is no fixed and permanent geographical entity, and that the will to political community is itself a matter of degree. Historically, federal government. has been a compromise of constituent sovereignty. The unity which finds its expression in willingness to admit national sovereignty is elicited by a complex of forces by no means so easy to formulate as M. Duguit's *solidarité sociale* would make us believe. It demands the technique of checks and balances and extraordinary majorities. It is, maybe unluckily, not capable of a sort of economic summary, which would divide the kingdoms among men according to purely economic groupings, though under modern conditions it is safe to predict that the economic factor will become increasingly predominant. The unhappy fact is that this solidarity of interdependence is conditioned by determinants of past history that traverse it and sometimes disrupt it completely. Mr. Ernest Barker has amplified this theme in *National Character*.

Renan, in his celebrated essay, put down nationalism to a sort of mythos, a common purpose created by a common belief. Real nationality can not be created by the blue pencils of economic experts in conference, even granted the best will in the world and the possession of insight that would need to be almost prophetic in its character. It is a matter of community, partly determined by environmental forces, economic needs, and past history, but also a community of ideals, of education, of morals, of religion, as well as what we are in the habit of calling national temperament. Environmentally considered, a good but only a partial case may be made out for climatic, for geographical, and economic factors as formative of *"l'esprit des lois."* In any case it is certain that the spirit of nationhood is a slow historical growth, and a stubborn one.

McDougall in the *Group Mind* has defined the nation simply in terms of a "national mind," though he hardly rests content with the concept in his later works. Indeed the practical value of such a definition may be questioned; but there is some such ultimacy about the fact that is a nation. Where this spirit does not exist, or where it has ceased to exist, no mere legal cement suffices to create the edifice of a state, or to hold the cracking parts long together. Where it does exist already, or where it comes newly into being out of the intertwined forces of social growth, no outside force short of a catastrophe is capable of disrupting it. Out of such a nation-wide consciousness, often, it is true, very imperfectly expressed, comes a shared will to common ends which can only be attained through political community. This is a will that is in no way open to the reproach of being what M. Duguit calls the vague construction of metaphysicians. Metaphysical it is in the sense that all realities are metaphysical; but vague it certainly is not, for it may prove its claims to facthood in a way capable of far more immediate and practical demonstration than a mechanically or organically operative social solidarity. It is the only possibility of legally enforced social solidarity in the degree to which that is realizable in a world of individuals and groups consciously pursuing an infinite diversity of ends. For it is a community of purpose that manifests itself politically, not only toward the creation of a sovereign arbiter of the difficulties inevitable upon human association, but toward the maintenance of that arbiter as the condition of peace.

The enduring nature of national unity finds expression in the enduring frame of government constituted for this end. Let him who desires proof of the reality of this consensus of wills but consider the amount of unity elicited by any serious threat to the sovereignty so created, be the threat from within or without. The fell spirit of Nationalism appears not to have been exorcised in any sense by the League of Nations idea; rather it took a new lease on life through "self-determination." Let him consider further the amount of inconvenience, of positive coercion

which individuals and minorities accept without a feeling of re-
belliousness, tacitly recognizing the greater good of maintaining
a source of impartial justice. The fact that people do "back"
the government and are willing to submit to its law can only be
explained in terms of an abiding and shared purpose, not the mere
recognition of an already existing social solidarity, but an affirmation of the common aim toward a social solidarity that is
endurable and enduring, based on the protection of those rights
of individuals which the social experience has proved necessary
to the development of real personality. Even Leninism is preferable to Hobbes' State of Nature; and Fascism is welcomed after
anarchy.

I have aimed at suggesting the notion that the will to establish
a governmental base for the state is a real fact, but I have intended to suggest that it was not the "general will" of a super-
person, but the consensus of purpose among citizens who recognize
the necessity of constitutional morality. I have tried to suggest
at the same time that the expression of this purpose is a matter
of degree and direction because the community desired is itself
a matter of direction and degree. Where the ends of political
association are local, the authority for realizing these ends is
local; where they reach out and touch the interests of a wider
community, a broader frame of government results. Rigid constitutions recognize and protect communities of purpose from
simple majorities. The constitutional form clothes each area of
community with law.

Because, however, of the increasing interdependence of society
the relationships between groups tend increasingly toward
contact with each other and with all, while at the same time
a growing specialization of function has tended to make each
association qualitatively further removed from the other. The
result of this may be seen in the tendency, sufficiently discern-
ible in modern corporate life of every sort, to solve the
problems arising from differentiation in function and increase
in extent, by progressive federal deconcentration, by centering
authority, so far as the needs of the particular unit involved can
be adequately met, within its own limits, but by reserving control of those matters affecting the entire association for its supreme governing body. Nowhere is this more apparent than in

the state itself, through decentralization of administrative areas, through the creation of *ad hoc* bodies and commissions of permanent functions, as well as through the development of a real degree of international community which transcends the nation state.

Furthermore all types of social groupings have disciplinary laws of their own enforceable against their members, what M. Duguit has termed "the organic law of the service." "Obviously," he says, "this renders impossible the imperialist theory of a unified law, for all men in a given state. . . . The evolution of discipline, in fact, goes, step by step, along the same road as the public services towards autonomy. We see being built up a penal law by the side and yet outside of the national penal law. Public law is clearly no longer monistic in its imperialism." [25] In common with Mr. Laski he is inclined to call this decentralization "a federalizing of authority." [26]

Obviously, as M. Duguit has claimed, if all the laws of associations "so formed in the midst of the national life as to break its absorptive unity" are *law*, there is indeed no "unified law for all men in a given state." This appears to me to be rather a *reductio ad absurdum* of the criterion of law which he has urged than a death-blow to the conception of unified law. It is the stock-in-trade of political pluralism to point thus to the existence not only of a multitude of governmental agencies capable of declaring law, but to the laws of associations which the courts recognize, in order to prove that law is not one but many. "The law of 1901 on the right of association does of course insist that in theory an association is still governed by the principles of the civil code on contracts and obligations (Art. III, tit. 3). This is merely a legislative error. . . . The statutes of an association are not the clauses of a contract, but a definite law." [27]

If they are a definite law, however, it is because the state proposes to hold an association to its associated end, and to hold acts done outside the powers conferred, to be *ultra vires*—not because the power of declaring law is vested in the association itself. For M. Duguit, so long as he holds to the juridically

[25] *Law in the Modern State*, p. 107 ff.
[26] P. Deschanel, *La décentralisation;* H. J. Laski, *Foundations of Sovereignty*, "The Problem of Administrative Areas."
[27] *Op. cit.*, 113.

useless notion of law as derived from all social morality whatever—so long, that is, as he refuses to make the one Austinian
differentiation that remains indubitably useful: that between
positive morality and positive law—naturally all "law" is of
equal value because of its identity of origin. But that is merely
to end with a stroke all juristic possibility of reducing law to a
workable unity. The only possibility of coördinating law lies
in a government which can command because to command is
its function, in order to arrange a systematic hierarchy of law
and to assure the rule of law. Otherwise there is no escape from
the anarchic welter of group laws conflicting as interests conflict.
To coördinate is to organize into unity, and to unify implies a
definite location of the power to issue commands which all citizens recognize and accept. This end can only be achieved satisfactorily under a definitely organized constitutional system.

I am aware that this, to ears attuned to the chorus of modern
pluralistic theory, sounds naïvely old-fashioned. "Much water
has passed under the bridge," I shall no doubt be informed.
"Has it not swept along with it the archaic traditions of the
omnicompetent state-person?" Not as a matter of actual fact.
Dictatorship is the order of the day. Mussolini deifies the state-
personality of Italy and becomes its prophet. Furthermore, even
on the basis of moral *ought*, instead of *is*, wherever law exists
as a consciously developed means of administering justice, it must
be brought into a unified and self-consistent system so far as
the political intelligence of a people is able to accomplish it.
Otherwise constitutionalism gives way to civil disorder and
force. The federal idea has not, in practice, militated against
this unifying of sovereignty; rather it has made such systematic
unification possible over wider areas, because it has distributed
the functional arrangement of law to fit the areas of community
involved, reserving ultimate sovereignty to the amending power.
Constituent sovereignty represents, I have said, the willingness
of societies to establish a common arbiter for common concerns.
Legal sovereignty is the constitutional arrangement of power so
upheld. And if I point to the growth of the idea of the need
of an international sovereignty over international concerns, it is
not with any intellectualistic fallacy in mind of solution by the
provision of framework of ideas, but as a practical extension of

the idea that is already operative in the spread of bodies of law like the English and the Roman over vast areas of the world's surface, and a gradual *rapprochement* of the fundamental ideas of justice the world over. "To Cæsar the things that are Cæsar's," if justice under law among the nations is to remain more than the dream *"Zum Ewigen Frieden."* National constitutionalism must precede international constitutionalism—although the former demands the latter for completion.

But even here we must remark the limits of justiciable questions. The thing that has kept that conception no more than a dream is a feudal society of nations. Just as a feudal society of lords and underlings, each jealous of the surrender of any part of his power to his suzerain superior, made the king's justice so long a mockery, to-day the same feudal conception of law makes international law valid only for a limited field of agreement. Yet M. Duguit wishes avowedly to see applied within the nation the same notion, i.e., that the reality of government is force, of one sort or another; and that the ability of a given group to impose its demands by social reactions, of one sort or another, is the only realistic form of law. He admits the analogy to feudalism but has no fears for social solidarity, for he sees in feudalism, alongside its violence, a vast *régime* of contract based not upon intellectualistic meetings of wills but upon fear and force and social reactions—in short upon "facts."

III. Statute and Contract

In the appearance of statutory agreements in modern times, M. Duguit sees a renaissance of the feudalistic notion that all law represents a contract so arrived at. Statutes founded on agreement represent just this break-away from the idea of a unilateral act of will, particularly in the case of labor agreements: collective bargaining of the unions for the wages and conditions of labor which are to be in force over an entire field of industry. The agreements thus arrived at are enforceable at law within limits; yet they are evidently not commands of the sovereign power. There is about them the character of a feudal relationship, "based above all on a *régime* of contract," as M. Duguit puts it. He says that the state can not command; it must bargain. Yet a state like Fascist Italy founded upon *droit objectif* alone uses force to enforce these "bargains." If he looks to the extension of organization in industrial structure "to make the trades concerned almost a legally organized body, it is because then the collective agreement will so regulate the relations of capital and labor as to be the law of an organized profession. It will thus achieve the coördination of classes by a series of collective contracts—by a series of agreements between the different groups in which each class is integrated." [28] Mussolini uses the same language. The Fascist State takes this machinery in theory. In practice it enforces the awards of wages determined by Mussolini or his industrial advisers on the Fascist Grand Council. The syndicates and corporations are mere façades, imposing at a distance.

If the element of contract were genuine this would be in germ very much like the guild-socialist idea of society. It is an idea even more fertile with suggestive possibilities of extending the field of voluntary agreement through collective organization. But the reality of the state's control, in the interest of a nationally regimented social solidarity, reduces the voluntary element to a preliminary and rests the ultimate decision in a Fascist state.

Even when the initiation of the agreement is really contractual, it can only become statutory by the recognition accorded it by the state, as Whitleyism in England is finding out. Collective labor agreements are not always possessed of statutory force by the mere fact of having been arrived at between labor and capital in conference. From time to time a given state exerts its power to intervene even to the extent of regulating wages, not only where no agreement is possible because labor is unorganized, but even in industrial disputes in which the very strength of the contending organizations makes their struggle disastrous to the public interest. M. Duguit warns the legislative bodies from such intervention carried out under either the individualist notion of contract or mandate, and demands that it "be inspired in the action by the idea of a law of conduct based on agreement and applied to the relations of two social groups." No doubt his warning is generally sound, except that there are more than two social groups involved in every labor dispute of importance.

[28] *Op. cit.*, 121.

There is also the whole of the society of a given political community: it, too, is involved in a most important and interested manner in a solution the issue of which will depend, not on the force that the contestants can bring to bear, but on justice. Its intervention ought to be impartial, and politically responsible, not Fascist. How to make it so is the most important problem of modern government.

It has often been suggested that in the feudalistic ordering of economic matters, with no sovereign arbiter to prevent the resort of labor and capital to the weapons of strike and lockout respectively, lies the greatest danger to impotent constitutionalism which dares not extend the sovereignty of the responsible state. The greatest excuse for the methods of Fascism by the same token is the refusal or the powerlessness of government to protect the public services. If the responsible state dare not intervene, because representatives are politically endangered by taking a strong course, Fascism will be rendered a necessity by social crises. The want of common ground on which to bring labor and employers together for legal solutions leaves the way open only for Fascism, or for the compromise of conflicting forces. M. Duguit is perfectly correct in pointing to the field of industrial dispute as one in which the traditional doctrine of sovereignty is not applied. Modern industry is pluralistic—or feudal, if you choose—precisely because there does not yet exist in it the willingness or perhaps the possibility for a common arbiter. The State now bargains; *can* it command? Can its commands be constitutionalized to win general acceptance? There is not the degree of common purpose necessary for the so-called freedom of contract to furnish a workable scheme for industrial peace. For the basis of agreement, a will toward common ends is wanting. Can anything short of a working partnership of employers and employed furnish it? No merely mechanical solution, either collectivist or syndicalist, can supply this *sine qua non* of industrial health: some profess to see no possibility of a solution so long as men can feel no creative joy in the product of their labor, and they find little prospect of artistry in any industrial system so highly mechanized as that of our own day has become. But in actual practice where labor is buying stock control with its own wages it is becoming its own employer to a limited but still significant degree. By shortening hours it may achieve a creative leisure.

Fascism, seeking only the short-cut of "discipline" by force, is a true interpretation of the social necessity, the fear and force, which form the other side of Duguit's "objective law", founded on the assurance of social solidarity and the public services. But Fascism sees only the morality of necessity. Even for so hard-pushed an economic plight as that of Italy, this practical enforcement of industrial serfdom offers no permanent hope.

On the other hand, one may have small hopes for any Utopian solutions for this out-of-joint state of things. It is possible, as the medievally minded suggest, that some of the abiding industrial discontent does lie rather in the lack of an outlet for the natural craftsmanship of the laborer and in his feeling of being himself a part of the machine, not its master, than in a desire to control business policy. But we must accept industrialism as a fact and then seek a remedy to curb its vices.

In any case, the remedy does not lie in allowing the solution of the affairs which immediately affect what M. Duguit calls the public services to go by default; to hope, that is, that the parties to the struggle may somehow arrive at an unenforceable agreement. For that, on the face of the daily evidence of the times, is to hope the impossible; it is merely to watch helplessly the growing breach which this supine attitude helps to widen. "Labor" and capital are still in a state of nature toward each other for want of a sovereign. The situation is not difficult where employers recognize the laborer's stake by paying high wages and attempting to give him a sense of partnership. But where, as in Europe and many industries in the United States, no such feeling exists, the state of anarchy becomes unbearable. There is real danger that, failing a joint solution between, say, coal miners and operators, the sovereign will be created with Fascist powers of control.[29] The great danger of industrial

---

[29] The evolution of anarchy toward despotism is not difficult to trace in the attitude which Labor troubles have forced on the Federal Courts in the United States, confronted as they are with alarming phenomena such as the Herrin massacre of strike-breaking miners, and the state of civil war that prevailed in West Virginia between miners and operators' armed guards. In desperation at violence which is no longer sporadic, but general and sug-

anarchy is precisely this tendency to make despotism inevitable. Once Fascism is in the saddle, constitutional control is made impossible.

In his latest edition of the *Traité*, this is precisely the position into which M. Duguit has been forced: It is a satire of circumstance that puts into the mouth of the great celebrator of the promise of syndicalism, the jurist of the group law, this fulmination against the actuality of a law based on no more solid basis than a social solidarity to be arrived at by group agreement: he exalts now the employment of the force of the rulers of the national state against *"quelques milliers d'égarés et de criminels"* (the flavor of the French would of course be lost in translation) *qui "ont voulu, en fomentant une grève des chemins de fer, affamer, ruiner le pays, et en créant de la misère et de la souffrance, réaliser je ne sais quelle revolution bolchéviste"!* Nevertheless he takes comfort for his theory in the thought that *"ce n'est point la prétendue puissance souveraine de l'État qui a brisé le mouvement, mais encore ici, une collaboration agissante et résolue des volontés individuelles."* [30] Mussolini agrees frankly in stating that the state is Mussolini and his obedient black shirts: in Italy at least, *individuals under hierarchy.*

It is not the despotism which grows out of anarchy that will assure genuine social solidarity. Europe seems to be turning back to its old gods, in the hard days of reconstruction, but it is not they who can furnish ultimately the means of settling disputes between employer and employed. There is the possi-

gestive of organized intent, the courts attempted to lay the basis of a rule of law by the issuing of sweeping injunctions against the unions, and by rulings which fix responsibility for tortious and injurious acts during strikes on the unions in their quasi-corporate character: witness the recent *Coronado Coal Company vs. United Miners' Federation* (notes to "Conception of Corporate Personality," *infra*), and the injunction granted to U. S. Attorney-General Daugherty against the striking crafts union on the railroads. President Harding admitted his helplessness to cope with the situation brought about by national strikes of railway workers, and miners, and suggested that the awards of the U. S. Labor Board be made compulsory. Instead, under the Coolidge administration, dedicated to "keeping government out of business," the Board was abolished and a Mediation Commission established with merely advisory powers, unless both parties, after confrontation, agreed to accept mediation—quite adequate as long as wages can be increased with the Interstate Commerce Commission benevolently passing the charge on to railroad rates.

[30] The occasion being a strike by the Railway Syndicates C. G. T. in the *Chemins de fer de l'Est*, May, 1920. *Traité*, Introduction, p. lx, Vol. 1.

bility of "a Roman peace" through such a regimentation of the worker as Mussolini deems necessary; or through the decimation of the bourgeois employer, after the amiable fashion of Bolshevism. But the former means revolution, sooner or later, for revolution can not be staved off forever by imperialism or even war. The latter means starvation and anarchy and the whole circle of degeneration over again.

The function of government intervention, under most enlightened national legal systems, is held to be the protection of the common interests of its citizenship by preventing either party to the dispute from exploiting the force in its hands to exact an advantage. Our public service commissions are created to act this part by curbing the exploitation of monopolies. Sooner or later we shall have also to curb labor monopolies in vital services.

Under M. Duguit's "law of conduct based on agreement," so long as the agreement is not a matter for state arbitration, the exploitation of force is the only basis of agreement possible; the result is an agreement of compromise, founded on fear. But agreements reached where the two parties have an acceptable arbiter of the justice of their claims is a different matter. That is the only reality there is in freedom of contract, not a freedom to secure social injustice by force or fraud, but freedom to secure an obligation mutually binding because it was arrived at under law, not under threat of violence. If commissions fix rates in essential public services that enjoy a monopoly and are essential to the life of modern communities, why may they not also adjust wages? The State must assume the power of command, and abandon the futility of bargaining: England, for example, will not be able to regain industrial health until she has a government in power that can say to both coal owners and coal miners: "Quit as individuals if you like. But do not use your collective force against the state. We shall not support you at the expense of the community unless we make terms in the community's interest and name."

IV. State Responsibility

The whole parade of the growth of state responsibility in administrative acts, of the decisions of the *Conseil d'État* holding the charters of public service corporations enforceable, do not point, it seems to me in the direction that M. Duguit assumes, i.e., to the abdication of its sovereign power to command by the state. The state may agree to submit its acts to the courts, because, in non-sovereign administrative relations, the state is more and more assuming relations in the exercise of its functions which place it in the same status as any other party to a civil action, and because as the sovereign, it is the source of positive law: it is therefore to be expected that it will not refuse to administer justice in cases where its governmental agencies have infringed the rights or the interests of its citizens which are protected by its own law. As contracts are secured by its law, they are enforceable against the state itself, and their violation for any purpose demands a just indemnification.[31]

Yet in spite of all this it is obvious that the power which is itself the source of law—of positive law, that is—has the final word as to what shall be enforced as law. The ultimate responsibility of government for its acts must be political responsibility to an electorate, rather than judicial responsibility. The courts themselves, for instance, can hardly be controlled by still other courts. Where they form policies, they are apt ultimately to be brought to book by organized opinion just as are other legislative bodies. Where they misapply their trust of the law, impeachment must serve. The command of a constitutionally empowered branch of government is ultimately sovereign in any legal sense. It does not, and can not divest itself of this character in any case involving the exercise of governmental power, and this fact necessitates as a matter of course a separate domain of public law, whether it be explicitly so recognized or not. There are limits to legal responsibility (where governmental acts are not *ultra vires*) which even American courts recognize in the Police Power exercised administratively, and in the whole range of "political" acts into which no court will inquire.

In the field of statutory agreements, so-called, this appears clearly in the unquestioned right of the state to alter the charters

---

[31] The Petition of Right and principle of "Grace" extended by the Crown is proof of the Common Law recognition of this principle in England. *Cf.* Court of Claims (established 1855) in the U. S. A.

of public-service corporations at need,[32] or to regulate hours of labor, conditions, and wages in accordance with the notions of social justice which its lawmakers hold. That is sovereignty, and that is the right to command, whatever M. Duguit may wish to call it. No state can abdicate this without losing the power to protect not only the public services, but all legal rights, and the responsibility for its own task.

V. Conclusions

M. Duguit's construction of jurisprudence seems to me to suffer from two fundamental misconceptions which vitiate a large part of his conclusions. The first is that his positivistic and anti-intellectualistic bias leads him to banish from consideration many essential facts, and many even more essential analyses of facts merely with the general condemnation of being metaphysical. This is a tendency, too, that in its extreme form equates all complex analysis with metaphysical vanity, and falls in consequence into the error of "pseudo-simplicity." The resulting system as I have attempted to point out, frequently involves the very metaphysical difficulties it has striven to avoid by closing its eyes to their presence.[33] In the case of M. Duguit, it is evident that the keystone to the arch he has built, the *solidarité sociale* which creates the only *devoir* of law, and the acceptance of law, is only a restatement of the old doctrine of Natural Law in an economic form. It suffers from the very same faults that render the *volonté générale* which it is to replace, so treacherous a foundation to build upon. Abstract theory, like nature, though driven out with a fork, has a way of slipping back in and playing the hobgoblin with the inhospitable dwelling. Best accept it among the household gods with offerings of piety, and try to come to a clear understanding of its implications for politics.

In the second place, M. Duguit's denial of the sovereign char-

---

[32] *Dartmouth College vs. Woodward* was robbed of its teeth even in Marshall's time by *Ogden vs. Saunders* (1828).

[33] "Here are the dogmas of scientific Positivism and here are their consequence; they constitute the state of mind of a whole generation which has allowed itself to be duped by Spencer and Haeckel." Hauriou and A. Mestre, quoted by Charmont, *Modern Legal Philosophy Series*, Vol. VII, p. 131 *et seq.*

acter of the state's commands, and his efforts to reduce these commands, which emanate from the definite organs of representative government, to the mere acceptance of social reactions, results, I believe, from an error uncommon among jurists,[34] but common enough among sociologists and political theorists: I mean the effort to identify the state, when he is attacking it, with actual government, but when he is defending it, with society at large. Now the constitutional state, if my arguments have been rightly founded, is the political community which sums up the results of what may be called historic environment and a present and active will among its member citizens to the satisfaction of common needs through a common government. Government is, then, a specific political instrument, the changing expression of this political community. It is not, as a positivistic explanation would have us believe, merely rulers strong enough to gain and hold the greatest force, but responsible rule under a legally organized mandate by whose terms force may be applied to secure a community of justice. The formal outlines of the state are shaped through government; but the state's self is the constitutional grouping of all the citizenship that results from a political purpose as extensive as the limits of the state itself—insofar as it has attained to true statehood, i.e., to the status of a community organized for law. The Fascist state conforms to Duguit's realistic criteria; but it is not a responsible or a mature state.

If I have stressed the political nature of this purpose of the state, under law, however, it is because the limits of the state are something more than geographical. There are limits of degree to the political community of will, limits of degree to the purpose to which that will is directed. It is, first of all, a *political*

---

[34] Berolzheimer has well stated this:
"The exaggerated importance attaching to 'society' and to 'social ethics' resulting therefrom is due to the fact that too many non-jurists occupy themselves with the philosophy of government and law, and therefore are disposed to replace the definite, though complex and difficult conceptions of law by the more elastic and vague one of society. 'Society' is more readily managed; it is like a lay figure upon which any sort of garment may be neatly fitted. The definiteness of legal concepts gives way to the foggy conclusion of social-political, social-reformatory, and social-ethical discussions, fertile in proposals that prove to be valueless and ineffective when philosophically tested. A return to legal and economic philosophy remains the sole scientific procedure." *Modern Legal Philosophy Series*, Vol. II, p. 380.

will, and that in itself is a limitation of prime importance; politics no more exhausts the entire range of human activity than does economics, religion, or art; it is not an equivalent to the sum of social forces as M. Duguit makes it [35] in theory and as Mussolini attempts to make it in practice. On the other hand, it is an effort to take these forces, arising from interests that often conflict, out of the arena of natural strife and into the court-room of legal arbitrament and into the legislative chamber for representative settlement. The sources of all law are as various in origin as the complex of social forces, no doubt, but their formulation into juridical concreteness comes only through the government which represents the political purpose. The search for the sources of law beyond the determinate sovereignty of government may be necessary to an understanding of jurisprudence; but it is odd that so pronounced a positivist as M. Duguit can not see that it must lead him beyond the realm of the so-called science of law-as-fact, and into what he has been pleased to call metaphysics, i.e., into the explanation of facts, and even to their evaluation. One need only contrast the genuinely objective science of law of Hans Kelsen in his *Allgemeine Staatslehre* in order to see the distinction.

It is only fair to note that M. Duguit has in the last edition of the *Traité* to some extent altered his position, so far at least as to admit that the rule of law is not causal, but purposive, and that he has given up, partially at least, the doctrine of a purely biological social organism;[36] but, though he has accepted the "fact" of a conscious will, he has taken all meaning from his acceptance by denying to the rule of conduct which results

[35] ". . . police, law and culture, are one and the same thing; they designate the mass of positive and negative obligations which rest upon the State, or more correctly, upon all the individuals of a social group, the strong and the weak, the rulers and the ruled. The State is a material force whatever be its origin; this force is and remains a simple fact. . . ." Duguit, "Prevailing Misconceptions of the State," *Modern Legal Philosophy Series*, Vol. VII, pp. 250-251.

[36] *Cf.* M. Geny's hopeful prediction, "With the same genuine and disinterested sincerity which caused him to abandon the organismic doctrine and the identification of social phenomena with physical or biological phenomena, he will some day be heard to admit that metaphysics has its necessary place alongside the observation of facts, that duty cannot be derived from knowledge alone, and that laws find no truly objective basis except in the depths and moral consciousness." *La Revue critique de legislation*, 1901, p. 510. Quoted by Charmont, *loc. cit., supra*, note 18.

any ethical significance. The will is conscious, and chooses consciously, but it must still fit into *droit objectif*, with its conception of the controlling material forces of society as ultimate. The result is either negation of the value of the admission, or pure contradiction.[37] If the human will can not shape its ends except by "reactions," it is not purposive but organic—and so is Society.

"Of positive social morality," says Arthur W. Spencer in his Editorial preface to the seventh volume of the *Modern Legal Philosophy Series*, "unity and distinctness of form can not be predicated; it is rather an amorphous mass of contradictory and infinitely divergent natural 'rules of law'. Duguit's one 'rule of law' is accordingly a fiction; his doctrine founders on the rock of Scholasticism it seeks to avoid." [38]   And yet as Mr. Spencer is careful to note, the great mass of Duguit's work remains valuable, as illustrative of the way in which a system of jurisprudence may aim in the direction of a rational theory of the law, in spite of, rather than because of, the premises upon which it claims to rest. Like the Instrumentalist philosophy upon which it is philosophically based, its moral exhortation does not follow the leads of its logic.

The abuses to which the French *droit administratif* showed itself susceptible, in the last century particularly, furnish ample enough evidence that it is necessary from time to time to remind the government that its legal sovereignty is conditioned by its duty to maintain the *Rechtsstaat*, just where it is itself involved. The responsibility of the state's governmental agencies to the will it represents needs to be reiterated, for it is one of those fundamental conditions of good government which it is easier to accept in theory than to enforce in practice. Legal respon-

---

[37] There is, as I have already pointed out, this fundamental contradiction running through all M. Duguit's doctrine. It leads M. Charmont to say of Duguit that he is an "unconscious Idealist." "Duguit is a pseudo-positivist; if he censures arbitrariness, the tyranny of the violent, the oppression of the weak, the fact is due, in his case, to a faith as yet unconscious of itself, and destined perhaps to reveal its presence in the future" (*loc. cit.*). Might not the same thing be said of all the Pragmatic moralists, with the exception, perhaps, of Sorel and Mussolini, the declared apostles of violence? The humanitarian doctrines of James, for instance, depended far more upon his uncritical and complete acceptance of the ethics of Idealism than upon his own Pragmatic method. Volume V of Duguit's *Traité* shows the same quality.

[38] *Op. cit.*, p. xlvi.

sibility can and ought to be stretched as far as possible, before political responsibility begins. Otherwise, an impossible burden is put upon democracy by complicating its method of control.

In the same fashion, though we may not see the utility of an attack on the notion of subjective rights that commits itself to an equally abstract and one-sided objective duty, perhaps the very exaggeration of M. Duguit's polemic may serve the useful end of showing the necessity we are under to keep the correlation of right and duty clearly before our interpreters of the law. Though social solidarity offers no such absolute ground of law as M. Duguit's metaphysical positivism would use it for, it does represent increasingly the need for legal recognition of the growing interdependence of modern societies.

His protest against a representative government has led him to emphasize, perhaps unduly, the functional nature of the governmental organs through which the rule of law is registered.[39] The classic idea of representative government was that of a legal state-person, created by the general will to act for the common interests with legal finality. The organic or functional idea of government, on the contrary, sees the only ultimate sanction of legal acts in some "rule of law" which is the organic law under which all the parts of the social whole function. The state-person had a will of its own, and that will was legally final. Government as a function, properly speaking, is not describable in terms of will at all, but in terms of law, a law objectively organic, rather than mechanical, but one of perfectly scientific determinateness. In spite of all the concessions M. Duguit makes to the demands of fact, his principle of a rule of law, which limits the actions of ruled and rulers alike, which statutes affirm rather than create, means that this law is organic, or it means nothing.

The problem is evidently clearly defined in the question of the nature of the thing which has been called a State-Person; but the solution of that problem involves the general nature of the entities which are called "group-selves", "corporate persons", etc. A considerable pragmatic and positivistic school of thought follows Dewey in the denial of any reality to the self

[39] Though he from time to time denies that there is any such organic or functional implication in *droit objectif*, as noted *supra*, Note 36.

so created; another branch of pragmatism, accepting William James' test of the concept of the group-self as valid so long as groups *behave like* persons, treats corporate personality as a thing-in-itself as real as reality can be. Yet it is the Instrumentalists, not the Romanticists, who treat morals as imposed.

M. Duguit belongs along with Walter Lippmann and other notable anti-intellectualists quite evidently among the former class, as an affinity in his treatment of moral questions with that of Dewey might have led us to suspect. On this issue he differs sharply from his sociological master, M. Durkheim, whose ultra-positivism has led him to the dogmatic assertion of the reality of the group person.[40] M. Duguit accepted, as we have seen, the "imposition" idea of morality which Durkheim and Lévy-Bruhl have used as a substitute for the internal obligation of a morally responsible self.[41] But he rejects most heartily any *moi-commun*, existent through association, as the merest fiction. It can not be organic, for want of what Herbert Spencer called a "common sensorium"; it can not be metaphysically real because all metaphysics is speculation about unreal things, that is about questions whose demonstration one way or the other is impossible. The only realities are individual men; the only real wills or minds are the wills or minds of individuals. Corporate personality is a metaphysical and a moral fiction, therefore, and one which in the realm of law is as useless as it is confusing.

"Men in groups form, it is said, a living organic being, thinking, willing, and distinct from the individuals who compose it. But no one has seen it. Volumes have been written in an unsuccessful attempt to prove its existence. Behind these individual wills and consciousnesses, there is, it is averred, a collective will and consciousness, distinct from those of the individuals. It is true that a certain number of men in the same epoch have the same wishes and thoughts but does that make a will or consciousness which is not merely the sum of the individual wills

[40] For an excellent discussion of the points of difference between M. Duguit and M. Durkheim, *cf.* the brief statement given them by A. W. Spencer, *loc. cit., supra,* Note 38. M. Durkheim is illustrative of Jamesian anti-intellectualism in the matter of the reality of the group-self.

[41] Durkheim, *Le suicide,* p. 359, *et passim.*
Lévy-Bruhl, *La morale et la science des mœurs.*

or consciousnesses? . . . We can be sure that an individual thinks and acts; we can be sure of nothing else." [42]

We can be sure, on the contrary, that the indispensable conditions of an individual's thinking and acting are contributed by the ends which he holds in common with a certain number of other individuals associated with him to realize a common purpose. The will which results from such association may not constitute a will distinct from the wills of the members, but it is a will which can not be described accurately as their sum. To what extent does the group act through a representative will? To what extent is its action comparable to that of an organism? To what extent is it purely a mechanical organization of forces under the law of its creation? The answer to these questions will enable us better to estimate the worth of the contribution that *droit objectif*, with its anti-intellectualistic method, and its so-called scientific positivism, has made or can make to an adequate philosophy of the law, and of the state.

If the concept of the legal personality of the state, basic to the entirety of the noble system reared by Jellinek, may be (after some revision) shown to have a legitimate use in combining the representative capacity essential to responsible political institutions, with the concept of a function defined by law, it will prove an adequate foundation for political theory. But it must clearly be a personality, which in Jellinek's own words "is not the foundation, but the result of legal community." [43] The state and the groups within the state alike partake of a nature at once purposive and organic. How shall we do justice to the facts?

Mr. Dewey has given us here the "organic" view of a plurality of groups: "Groupings for promoting the diversity of goods that men share have become the real social units. They occupy the place which traditional political theory has claimed either for mere isolated individuals or for the supreme and single political organization. Pluralism is well ordained in present political practice and demands a modification of hierarchical and monistic theory." [44] That seems a flat enough rejection of legally unified

[42] *Op. cit., supra*, Note 35, pp. 242-243.
[43] *System der Öffentlichen Subjektiven Rechte*, p. 27.
[44] *Reconstruction in Philosophy*, p. 204.

sovereignty. Yet he says in the preceding paragraph: "Political parties, industrial corporations, scientific and artistic organizations, trade unions, churches, schools and clubs, and societies without number, for the cultivation of every conceivable interest that men have in common," have come into existence as voluntary associations to replace compulsory ones, not as a movement toward individualism, but as an associational movement. "As they develop in number and importance, *the state tends to become more and more a regulator and adjustor between them; defining the limits of their actions, preventing and settling conflicts.*" This "supremacy" he likens to that of an orchestra conductor, who harmonizes the whole without making music.[45] His figure is well chosen, but it hardly supports a *political* pluralism. For the orchestral conductor must have disciplinary powers of the most monistic type to hold his musicians in harmony through the weariness of rehearsals, etc. The state as the regulator of the relations of associations with each other, with their members (when these have legal significance), and with itself, needs the right to command that comes with recognition of only one source of law. As a regulator its function is to assure "social solidarity".

The significance of the tremendous growth of associations to modern law is in no danger of being slighted. It has raised the issue of their legal personality and has found in general an affirmative answer. Although M. Duguit and Mr. Dewey do not accept that theory, they have taken an organic view of the state that leads from pluralism to Fascism, because it leaves no place for the political rights of responsible personality but bases its social ethics upon fear and force.

In the matter of groups as persons, Mr. Dewey is once more in substantial agreement with M. Duguit. "It is difficult to see that the collective mind means anything more than a custom brought at some point to explicit, emphatic consciousness, emotional or intellectual." [46] He goes on to speak of "family-custom, or organized habit", and concludes: "Substitute the Republican party or the American nation for the family and the general situation remains the same. The conditions which determine the nature and extent of the particular groupings in question are matters of supreme import. But they are not as such subject matter of psychology [or M. Duguit would say, of a psychological reconstruction of jurisprudence] but of the history of politics, law, religion, economics, invention, the technology of communication and intercourse." [47] The proper approach for social psychology is the study of collective habit or custom.

We have seen to what use collective habit is put to form the "social morality" of Instrumentalism, and the positivistic limits of that morality. Are they not precisely those of the social solidarity and functional interdependence basic to M. Duguit's system of *"droit objectif"*? And is that explanation of society and the nature of social groups any more adequate to explain the facts of purposive association for a common end? In order to do so, Mr. Dewey stretches "habit" into creative intelligence, and M. Duguit makes his rule of law based on "social solidarity" normative in its nature. That is, it seems to me, to abandon once and for all the positivistic basis of a reconstruction which proposes to limit itself to fact alone. Ultimately the purely scientific method of behavioristic solidarism must lead to putting entire moral responsibility in the group, and that is to give the "group-self" a most vicious metaphysical reality, which it does not in fact possess. I say *must* lead, because the "social morality" of both systems refuses to find its origin in the normative moral consciousness of individuals. Norms are group creations, if fear be our moral motive force. They are "collective representations" in which the personality of individuals plays no part.

The matter resolves itself into a logical dichotomy: either we must accept impositional morality and attribute real personality to the group as Durkheim did; or we must reject the "organic" conception of morality along with the unreality of the so-called corporate person. Instrumentalism and *droit objectif* attempt to form a combination of the logically incompatible conceptions of a morality imposed by "social reactions" centered in groups, with a refusal to admit the reality of the groups as moral persons.

The solution does not lie in that direction, it seems to me. Nor can we hope for anything but contradiction from a proposed reconstruction or juristic thought which is confessedly based on

[47] *Ibid.*, p. 62.

such an assumption. The state can not be more profitably reduced to a collective habit, or to the organic manifestation of social solidarity than to a State-Person with a General Will. The importance of the analysis of the notions both of juristic and moral personality in their application to the state and to the associations among which it forms a *communitas communitatum* is sufficiently obvious. Its connection with the real problem of sovereignty is indubitable. So that it may not be amiss here to suggest the outlines of a solution that has characterized the views of such widely separated thinkers as Mr. Ernest Barker, Mr. Graham Wallas, and M. Fouillée: the group is a "moral" or psychic organism in the words of the first of these; [48] its reality is its "organizing idea". The nation state is not a mind but an idea possessed commonly by its citizens. Mr. Wallas by the term "organization",[49] has wished to extend the reality of the group beyond idea to feeling and will as well, as has M. Fouillée in speaking of a "contractual organism," [50] and of *"idées-forces."* All of these thinkers agree, however, in making the reality of the group depend upon the community of purpose existing among the individuals who are its members. They admit the organic structure of group life, but insist that its organic nature is limited and conditioned by the moral ultimacy of its members as individuals.

Until Mr. Dewey and M. Duguit have given the moral implications involved in their own theories a more searching analysis, the proposed reconstruction of legal thought must fail, as all purely descriptive and pseudo-scientific systems do, to do justice to the political aspects of Human Nature and Conduct. The organic social morality which relies upon fear and force to achieve its ends is the necessary apology of Fascism. Pragmatism becomes an economic interpretation of social solidarity that rules out of consideration all ends for the state that interfere with the efficient functioning of the state as a productive organism. That is the philosophy of Fascism.

To put ethical responsibility in organic groups of every sort is, as we have seen, the essential moral basis of syndicalistic

---

[48] "The Discredited State," *Political Quarterly*, Feb., 1915.
[49] *The Great Society*, chapter on "The Organization of Thought."
[50] *La Science sociale contemporaine*, p. 15.

pluralism.   It is to substitute sovereign group for sovereign
state. To put ethical responsibility in the state-organism alone
is the essential moral basis of nationalistic Fascism. M. Duguit's
solidarism, starting out from the former standpoint, has gradually in his writings come to embrace the latter because he, like
Mussolini, has interpreted social reactions and national survival
as imposing organic solidarity upon the nation to the sole end
of functional efficiency in the public services. If this concept of
public services be extended to the whole economic structure of
the nation, as a productive unit which stands or falls together, it
becomes Fascism.   Mussolini has made a quite logical application of *droit objectif* to the Fascist corporative state, with his
syndicates hierarchically "disciplined".

B. FROM PLURALIST SYNDICALISM TO FASCIST SYNDICALISM

In a series of lectures given in 1920-1921 at Columbia University, M. Duguit has given an *exposé* in somewhat simplified
form of the development of his ideas toward an organic solidarity
of society very much the same in kind as Mr. G. D. H. Cole's
Guild Socialism, with Fascist trimmings. Whether the juridical
basis for this syndicalism be called *solidarité* or *Organokratie*
(to use Rathenau's term) the conception leads inevitably
away from an ultimate pluralism to social harmony. M. Duguit
has, as we have noted, based the rule of law on the state of
social interdependence, and the necessity of safe-guarding the
public services. Yet how is this to be made to conform with his
declared sympathy with syndicalism if syndicalism be a revolutionary labor movement? The syndicalist philosophy of Romanticism, at least as it appeared in the revolutionary syndicalism
of M. Sorel and the *Mouvement Socialiste,* was of a very different order from the syndicalism of the Solidarists.

Evidently we must look for a different interpretation of syndicalism in order to square it with the solidarist conclusions.
In M. Duguit's theory we find it: "By this same word syndicalism, one means two things completely different, often without perceiving it. One means at the same time a social fact
of incontestable reality and of an importance which can not be
misunderstood, and also a doctrine which pretends to be based

on facts, but which interprets them badly, which is on the contrary in contradiction with them, and which, on that account, falsifies the normal evolution by the influence it exercises, slows it down or hinders it, and that to the detriment even of those that it pretends to serve and who would profit most from the arrival of the new order of things that would result in the near future from an evolution normally accomplished." [51]

It is naturally the former of these two that he means to accept. Syndicalism is primarily not a labor movement, but a new effort of society to give it stratification into juridical coherence. In the second volume of the second Edition of the *Traité* (now five volumes instead of three) which appeared in 1923, M. Duguit sets this out at length:

"What is to-day called the syndicalist movement is the principal manifestation [of the vast associational movement which fills our epoch.] This movement (as I showed in Volume I, page 509) is not restricted to the class of manual laborers. It is *not*, contrary to what revolutionary syndicalists pretend, the effort of the laboring class attaining self-consciousness in order to concentrate in itself power and wealth and to destroy the bourgeoisie. It is a much larger movement, and a much deeper one. It is not a means of war and social strife; it is, on the contrary, a powerful means of pacification and union. It is not a transformation of the working class alone—it extends to all classes of society and tends to coördinate them in a harmonious *faisceau*. [N.B. the similarity to the *Fascio* of Italian *Fascismo*.] It prepares the constitution in society of strong and coherent groups with a defined juridical structure, composed of men already united by community of social function (*besogne*) and by professional interest." [52]

From M. Duguit's conception of society as a vast work-shop [53] comes a new "fact" which he lays down as enjoining obligations from its very nature as fact. He does not think the day of communism is at hand yet. "The dreadful state into which Russia has fallen—according to all the information which we have from diverse sources that yet are in agreement—is the best proof of the utility *for a long while to come* [my italics] of the capi-

[51] *Souveraineté et liberté*, p. 179.   [52] *Op. cit.*, p. 9.
[53] *Souveraineté et liberté*, p. 162 ff.

talist class."[54] What the new social solidarity of syndicalism means is nothing compromising either to capitalism or national unity, as the *Traité* proclaims. But it does mean that the individuals within the state, reduced to the equality of fine dust by the iron wheel of egalitarianism and the French Revolution, are finding in the syndicalist group principle a new means of building up the complex social structure necessary to the protection of their liberty. This is Fascist Syndicalism at least in theory. In practice the syndicates of Fascism are not protective—as yet.

The revolutionary aspect which the French C. G. T. has given to syndicalism simply horrifies M. Duguit.[55] It is a fact which he rules out, by proclaiming it a theoretical misinterpretation of the meaning of group autonomy. The differentiation of classes inherent in society "because there are different tasks in the social work-shop" [56] does not mean a Marxian class war, but the possibility of harmonious functioning in the social organism through Herbert Spencer's formula, "always true", of social progress from a state of indefinite homogeneity to a state of definite heterogeneity.[57] Historically one may determine that the strife between social classes has been less keen in the degree in which they were more heterogenous and juridically distinct.

"Syndicalism is the organization of the amorphous mass of individuals, it is the constitution in society of strong coherent groups with a clearly defined juridical structure. . . ." [58] But M. Duguit retains his juridical idealism once more by a flat denial of the impositional group morality of Solidarism. He will not have it that this means the absorption or the destruction of individuality. All along he has attacked the idea of the dominant personality of the group-self, although he has refused to accept the contractual basis of purpose offered by co-organic theories like Fouillée. Something of the notion of *"quasi-contract"* elaborated by M. Léon Bourgeois, and by the critical studies of M. Bouglé, serves as the meeting ground for social solidarity and the idea for individual liberty which has been reinforced by the justice M. Durkheim has done to individual resistance to absorption by the group. The quasi-contract represents the

---

[54] *Souveraineté et liberté*, p. 183.
[55] *Ibid.*, pp. 188-189.
[56] *Ibid.*, p. 185.
[56] *Ibid.*, p. 182.
[57] *Ibid.*, pp. 179-180.

organic notion of a social heritage and cultural context that I
have attempted to give its due in the co-organic theory. What
remains, then, in order that the solidarism of M. Duguit pass
over into the idealistic conception of purposive re-arrangement
which that theory insists upon? Notably, the conception of
human personality which holds that the moral self is the irreducible "atom", if one likes, of all purposive activity. And it is
only M. Duguit's dogmatic anti-intellectualism which prevents
him from discarding fear and force in favor of such a normative
will striving to realize genuine moral ends.

"The individual," he admits, "resists [the annihilation of his
will by the group-will] and there results an equilibrium between
the social sentiment and the individual sentiment, and equilibrium
from which will result at the same time a social action, and an
intensified individual action." [59]   But this is merely a return to
the jejune harmonization of social purpose by a "self-regarding"
and an "other-regarding" mechanism of balance in the human
instincts such as we are favored with by much sociological dogma
of an earlier day.

What I should like to insist upon is that the juridical theories
of M. Duguit (as was the case with Mr. Dewey) in their own
practical aspects are becoming increasingly idealistic. He has
been forced to pedal less and less strongly on the bass undertone
of force in his theories, to renounce more and more clearly the
positivistic basis of mere "social reactions" treated as facts, and
to do justice to the moral nature of man that renders society
co-organic to the degree in which it transcends the economic
and pragmatic plane of interest and reaches that of purpose.
In the hands of others the impositional morality of pragmatism
has had an opposite application. The co-organic theory which
I have attempted to offer as a critical reconstruction of anti-
intellectualistic solidarism finds that movement continually
approaching the personalism which a true ethics must consider
fundamental, and in doing so becoming continually less anti-
intellectualistic. It could desire no better statement of the faith
that is in it than M. Duguit's own:

"Without doubt this effort and this realization [the syndicalist movement in its larger meaning of juridical harmonization]

<hr />

[60] *Souverainété et liberté, loc. cit.*

will encounter numerous resistances, but they will be conquered. Without doubt there will be strife and conflict, momentary victories of violence and error, but they will be triumphed over, and, in spite of all, we must believe firmly in the final triumph of reason, in progress by justice and by law, and work untiringly toward that end." [60]

A credo like this is that of the new Liberalism. It repudiates the other strain of M. Duguit's writings which emphasizes fear and force, and social necessity. The philosophy of social solidarity, of the forcible guarantee of the public services constitutes the constructive side of *droit objectif*. If we are to disregard the deterministic and positivistic leads of the theory, we may ask of their author, as we did of Mr. Dewey, "To what goal? Your 'facts' turn out to be in need of a theoretical interpretation of moral tendency which you accept—though it is stated in quite different terms from the professed tendency of your theory. Which way are you to be understood?"

There is one way in which he may be understood. Fascism, in its own structure of the solidarist and public-service state, has clearly chosen fear and force. It has used syndicalist organization not to check and balance the force of the state but to impose the hierarchical absolutism of the Fascist state more firmly on Italy. It has taken the positivistic side of M. Duguit's theories of social solidarity, has accepted, as he has, the nation as their limit in fact, and has drawn the logical conclusion that the use of fear and force is justified by national economic necessity. The Fascist-Syndicalist State, to use the new term proposed by Mussolini and his Fascist theorists, has seized on the pragmatic test of efficiency as the only available one, and has geared up Italy, by a repudiation of all responsibility to critical opinion and representative democracy, into an industrial organism ruthlessly forced to function at its maximum capacity. Wages and hours, prices, rent and even the smaller capitalists such as landlords, are being increasingly subordinated to the collective "necessity" as it is interpreted by a strong-willed Fascist oligarchy which recognizes no rights and imposes all duties. Not only human rights and civil liberties have disappeared. An onslaught has been made on the outer walls of

[60] *Ibid.*, p. 190.

property rights—though the inner citadel of privately controlled big business remains strongly protected against Mussolini as long as he needs working capital and foreign loans.[61]

[61] For an estimate of the economics of the Fascist régime see Appendix B, this volume.

CHAPTER XI

MUSSOLINI, PROPHET OF THE PRAGMATIC ERA IN POLITICS *

What Professor W. B. Munro has called "the Pendulum of Politics" has one of its aptest illustrations in Italian Fascism, most imposing of the European dictatorships.[1] The public press, not only of this country but of England and of continental Europe as well, is full of current prophecies, inspired by Mussolini, that the age of democratic liberalism is dead and done for. It is a phenomenon of curious portent, following as it does upon the heels of the late crusade to "make the world safe for democracy". The immediate aftermath of the war, which saw the expansion of the suffrage reach its apogee and extend even to the newly aroused Orient, saw also the imposition of the dogma of self-determination and of Wilsonian liberalism in international affairs. True, that doctrine underwent some curious metamorphoses in the actual peace settlements, but it none the less leavened the loaf. The League of Nations and the Permanent Court of International Justice stand as substantial witnesses to the power of this liberal spirit in international affairs.

At the same time, however, the unleashed powers of nationalism were beginning to feel their strength and, as Lloyd George put it, "to smash crockery" in international politics as well as in the international market of a *Weltwirtschaft*. First it was tariff barriers; next it was exclusion or drastic regulation of immigration; then it was a series of incidents grouped about the oppresson of racial or religious minorities in the new areas; finally, it was the old economic struggle for exploitation of "backward races", met, however, on their part by a new power

* Reprinted with corrections and additions from the *Pol. Sci. Qu.*, Vol. XLI, No. 2, June, 1926.
[1] See his interesting theory in *Harper's*. May, 1927, and in "Modern Science and Politics," *Yale Review*, July, 1927, and *The Invisible Government* (1928).

of resistance to the domination of occidental control in finance and industry.

With some of these forces the League and the World Court can deal; with others they dare not interfere. But with the most profoundly deep-rooted cleavage of all, the explosive and disruptive forces of Communism, they can not hope to cope. That is a struggle which must be fought out inside the nation, so long at least as Communism does not control enough nations to make a world crusade possible. And within the nation, Communism challenged the old machinery of constitutional settlement by proposing the dictatorship of a class-conscious minority in place of the older machinery of liberalism. Fascism, in combating it, has taken over its methods and its general philosophy of government.

The liberalism that fastened itself upon the parliamentary institutions of most of Europe was the outcome of that absolute faith in reason and logic which passed over into the nineteenth century from the age of prose and reason.[2] The Philosophical Radicals, led by Bentham, were writing a new chapter in the history of government attuned to the first turning of wheels in the Great Industry. They were as convinced that the Utilitarian philosophy of government would assure men liberty through the reign of reason, as they were that the unrestricted march of economic laws made for a sort of divine working out of economic liberty. Give men freedom to elect representatives with limited terms, and the problem was solved. The end of government being the protection of the individual, representatives should be so hedged about with restrictions as to protect individual liberty to the greatest possible degree. Liberalism was an idealistic version of this faith. When Italy won its nationhood after the *Risorgimento*, it assumed as a matter of course the liberalistic parliamentary institutions that were in the very air nationalism breathed. Not Garibaldi, but Cavour shaped the dream of Mazzini into an actual form.

Now all that has passed into the discard in the new Italy

[2] This view, disputed by Carl Schmitt in *Die Politische Romantik*, is interestingly shared by the distinguished Spanish historian and social philosopher, Sr. Fernando de los Rios, in his *El Sentido Humanista del Socialismo*, and in his *La Crisis de la Democracia*. See also the work of Sr. Posada, *La Crisis del Constitucionalismo* (1925).

which has sprung to life under Fascism. Fascism is a repudiation of the old logical Utilitarianism of the English Radicals of
1832 in favor of the older psychological pragmatism of Machiavelli. "Liberalism," says Mussolini, "is not the last word;
it does not represent any final and decisive formula in the art
of government. In this difficult and delicate art which deals
with the most refractory of materials, not stationary, but always
in movement since it deals with the living and not with the
dead; in this art of politics there is no Aristotelian unity of
time, of place, and of action. Men have been governed, more
or less fortunately, in a thousand different ways. Liberalism is
the contribution, the method, of the nineteenth century. . . .
It cannot be said that Liberalism, a method of government
good for the nineteenth century, for a century, that is to say,
dominated by two essential phenomena like the development of
capitalism and the growth of nationality, should be necessarily
good for the twentieth century, which already betrays characteristics differing considerably from those of its predecessor.
Facts outweigh books; experience is worth more than theory.
To-day the most striking of post-war experiences, those that
are taking place before our eyes, are marked by the defeat of
Liberalism. Events in Russia and in Italy demonstrate the
possibility of governing altogether outside the ideology of liberalism and in a manner entirely opposed to it. Communism
and Fascism have nothing to do with Liberalism." [3]

That is, of course, a far more complete break with Liberalism than that involved in the mere repudiation of a party. In
England and in this country economic class distinctions may
increasingly determine what is apparently to be the new party
cleavage, yet there remains a willingness to work through the
constitutional machinery that is so largely the fruit of Liberal
doctrine. The new Germany seems steadfast in its practice of
parliamentary government, under the benign moderation of
Hindenburg. France, too, seems in no mood to give up its par-

---

[3] Fascism does accept the economic motivation of Liberalism—self-interest
and gain, operating through privately owned industry. In practice the
revalorization of the lire has forced a collectivistic control not only of wages,
but of rents and prices. But the profit motive of big industrial organization
has to be carefully safeguarded in order to attract foreign capital for
investment.

liamentarism, despite the exhortations alike addressed to it by the Royalist Right and by the *Chemises Bleues*, and equally by the Syndicalist Left and by the Communists. But Italy and Russia have cast the die. Spain, Poland, and the Balkans have followed their lead; while the remnants of Central Europe waver on the verge. To parallel Lenin's "Democracy is a mere bourgeois superstition", Mussolini concluded the attack on Liberalism quoted above: "Know then, once and for all, that Fascism recognizes no idols, adores no fetiches; it has already passed over the more or less decayed body of the goddess Liberty, and is quite prepared, if necessary, to do so once more." [4]

Is it merely the perversity of intellectualism to suggest that back of this rejection of Liberalism, parliamentarism, and the whole democratic machinery of representative government, lies a philosophic doctrine of a sort? It is the gospel of pragmatism, pushed to the same extremes which Papini, before he popularized the *Life of Christ*, gave to the radical empiricism of William James. The observers who have commented upon Fascism have agreed upon one thing at least—that its method is essentially pragmatic. Although they have not always so named it, and although only its protagonists attribute to the movement a profound underlying idea, Fascism has come to mean to the popular imagination just this application of pragmatism to politics. Mussolini attributes his own intellectual shaping to William James, on equal terms with three great pragmatists in politics: Machiavelli, Nietzsche, and the syndicalist, Georges Sorel.

Now if it be mere vexation of spirit to try to establish any causal relations between ideas and events, we must yet recognize that there is this persistent attitude among those whose profession it is to think. Perhaps we may call it Hegelian, in a broad sense. It is expressed in the efforts that the human

---

[4] Benito Mussolini, *"Forza e Consenso,"* in *La Gerarchia*, March, 1923. I use the translation given for this speech in the English edition of Odon Por's book on *Fascism* made by Mrs. E. Townshend. Fascism seems to have fastened upon the British Liberal Party as the enemy. After the general election of October 29, 1924, in which the Liberal Party was almost wiped out, the Fascist *Idea Nazionale* argued that liberalism all over the world was dead, and Mussolini said with satisfaction: "One section of the international anti-Fascist front has been smashed." (*Manchester Guardian Weekly*, November 7, 1924.)

mind makes to find "ghostly essences" of reason operating in the world of history. "In each epoch of time there is current a certain type of philosophic doctrine," says, for instance, M. Leroy of the Collège de France, speaking for once with the authentic voice of this intellectualistic temper, "a philosophy deep-seated in each one of us, and observable clearly and consciously in the utterances of the day—alike in novels, newspapers, and speeches, and equally in town and country, workshop and counting house." It is the business of historians of ideas, on this reading of history, to make clear the philosophy of an epoch.

One may, indeed, be more than doubtful whether any such philosophic singleness of mind ever characterized any period of the history of man, possessed as he is of a reason so essentially argumentative in its character. But if we permit ourselves the dangerous luxury of simplification, we can certainly speak of the *Zeitgeist* of our own day as an intellectualized distrust of the intellect in its effort to make programs of action. In the area of politics, where theory finds one of its most immediate contacts with the world of history, it is natural that theorists who must be men of action, too, should seize upon the philosophy of pragmatism to deal with affairs in which expedience and concrete solutions have always been desiderata. Statesmen have, apparently from the beginning of political experience, made their appeal to the idealistic nobility of a stand upon principle, most of all when they were unostentatiously pursuing a compromise in fact. The practice of politics has never been other than pragmatic. A stand on principle may be the nobler gesture, may even be a necessary sop to man's compensatory desire to idealize his pursuit of deeply rooted, instinctive interests. But rationalism too often serves only as a cloak for imperative and unreasoned desire. That, at least, is the way the matter looks to the political pragmatists of our own day.

Even where idealism is genuinely disinterested it seems to be hardly able to survive in the inevitable test to which it is put by conflicting economic interests. There is little use in laboring the point while the ghosts of the Fourteen Points still linger in the air, their reality having vanished at Versailles with an imperceptible slowness, like the Cheshire Cat in *Alice in Wonderland*, leaving behind nothing but a feline smile—this time "on the face of the Tiger". If Castlereagh, a century ago, could call Alexander the First's proclamation of the Holy Alliance "a piece of sublime mysticism and nonsense", Lloyd George could be more delicately brutal by utilizing the idea of the League to cover his own opportunism. He rendered lip-service, all the while acting prudently on the assumption that such a thing as a real and powerful agent of world opinion could not and would not exist. Metternich's dismissal of the Holy Alliance as "a sonorous nothing", too, found a match in Clemenceau's exclamation: "Fourteen Points! The good Lord himself had only Ten!"

Politics has never been characterized by too rigid a Platonism in the application, or even in the entertainment of "principles". Yet never before, perhaps, were principles in such disfavor as during the period immediately following the fall of President Wilson from the idolatry in which he had been held at the close of the war. He had seemed to sum up in a single personality the hope of the world in human reason and good will, in their combined power to restore a world "fit to live in" after the four years of nightmare. His failure to accomplish the impossible at the Paris Peace Conference seemed symbolic of the ineffectuality of idealistic principles in the face of conflicts of interest. He had spoken prophetically in his triumphal tour, the tragic prelude to Versailles: "Interests do not unite; interests can only divide men." And he had appealed to that higher community of purpose for which the Allies had professed to have made war as the unity on which they might build peace. But Versailles wrote a different history—and as its aftermath, Mr. Harding came into power in America upon a program that was tantamount to a signed promise to do nothing on principle and to do whatever else he had to, carefully; Mr. Coolidge holds our confidence on a program of thrift. M. Clemenceau went out of power in France largely because he was felt to be a man d'une idée fixe, and so did M. Poincaré. Mr. Lloyd George retained power in England by the most adroit political jugglery, and the most supple bending as the wind blew that even politically minded Britons had seen for some time; and at last even he went into his wilderness. Italy drifted through syndicalism to Fascism with the same facility as it changed front toward the "Fourteen Points". With Latin fervor it had worshipped Wilson; with Latin fervor it now branded him as the anti-Christ. The spirit of these times, politically speaking, was voiced by Mr. Harvey, American Ambassador to the Court of Saint James, in a speech to the Pilgrims at their dinner on May 19, 1921. Mr. Harvey took the occasion to make a statement of the "policy" of the Harding Administration; he declared that he was empowered to announce America's participation in the decision of the Supreme Council on the Silesian question then pending. America's position in foreign relations, as Mr. Harvey interpreted it, was one of opportunistic intervention whenever she conceived her rights or interests to be affected. She would enter into no "entangling alliances" nor would she commit herself to defined policies: "We shall get nowhere until we abruptly put aside academic discussion of theoretical proposals, and manfully face without wincing or mincing, the actual realities." [5] What these actual realities were, other than the ambassador's refusal to commit himself or his country to any lines of policy whatever, hardly appeared from the context. The British members of his audience may have suspected that they were debts and markets. Whatever they were, they were not to be found in the *"doctrinaire"* efforts of an idealism which attempted to put a curb on the play of interests. Those who had tried to interfere with the machinery of things as they were, had just met the rebuke of democracy, or were already in sight of political wildernesses. *Vox populi* had spoken: the Lord's face was turned against "points" and such abstractions. The political prophets preached a new gospel—pragmatism, the reasoned distrust of rationalized solutions.

The very Mahomet of this worship is Mussolini. Ideological programs and a superstitious reverence for the formal democracy of the ballot box had led his Italy to a state of anarchy approximating that before which the medieval republics of the cities had bowed. For the new Italy that had emerged from the Risorgimento, liberalism through its prophet, J. S. Mill, had laid down representative government with all the refinements of parliamentary institutions of which the gospel according to Mill was capable. And Italy had accepted liberalism with the enthusiasm

[5] London *Times*, May 20, 1921.

of a new convert; even, just after the war, she accepted proportional representation. But liberalism, to be workable, depends not alone upon a stable party system based in turn upon a national psychology that is at least the pale shadow of Mill's sweet reasonableness. It depends even more fundamentally upon the hypothesis that the unity of the nation is firm enough to support a constitutional state. And that hypothesis can hardly be fulfilled when poverty and ignorance have laid the basis for turning democracy into class warfare. Before one can understand either the origins or the success of Fascism it is necessary to remember the economic condition and the cultural hopelessness of the Italian laboring classes. Over-population and under-production, aided by superstitious ignorance, are the greatest enemies of Italy. Nor may any one of them be overcome, if it alone is attacked.[6] This is the picture as it is usually painted:

After the war, an Italy badly divided, sabotaged by Communism, grew sicker and sicker under government by blocs, government by unreal coalitions, by log-rolling, and finally by *"decretileggi"*. It all amounted to no government at all. Machiavelli's *Prince* was not more needed, when he wrote, to raise Italy from her divided weakness, than was a dictator, now—one strong enough to seize the reins of governmental power from the lax hands which refused to tighten them on syndicalistic violence. Under such conditions it was natural that Fascism, symbol of united power in a single hand, should gather strength until it swept the slate clean of timid parliamentary equations and inscribed in a bold hand the single word *Force!*

Parliamentary government—we have the high authority of Lloyd George for it—means "government by talk". But, as ex-Ambassador Child put it, "When a spirited people cannot stand it any longer, they act. Talk and party conferences and social theories and sentimentality are luxuries enjoyed by these people who do not face intolerable situations. . . . When a people face an intolerable situation the real ravenous hunger is not for a program, but for a man." [7] This apology for Fascism, broadcast through the columns of the *Saturday Evening Post,*

---

[6] For an excellent analysis of the demographic origins of Fascism see Robert Michels—*Socialismus und Faschismus in Italien* (1923).
[7] *Saturday Evening Post,* June 28, 1924, pp. 157-158,

is accurate enough. Yet it is perhaps worth noting that it is
only these peoples who insist on the luxury of party systems
and the sentimentality of social theories who arrive but rarely
at "intolerable situations"; on the other hand, nations who are
forever in search of the man, not the program, seem to find
almost all situations equally and chronically intolerable after a
trial more or less brief.

As for programs, apparently Ambassador Child was sufficiently
interested in the meaning of Fascism to make some inquiries of
Mussolini, even when the Black Shirt was still a bravado gesture.
This is his report of the interview:

"Well," I said, "what is the Fascisti program? It is easier to
snatch the tiller than to steer the boat. . . ."

"Program?" he said. "My program is work, discipline, unity."
He shot another look at me and saw that I was doubtful about
vague slogans. He said with tremendous conviction, "Programs
are endless. It is the organization—it is the men—it is action,
not talk—it is men!"

There you are: the program of the politics of the period is
action—not talk, not theory. The time, whether or not it be
out of joint, is as impatient of theory as was Burke, who felt
that a society was sick to the degree in which it attempted rational self-criticism. Political activity is only healthy, Burke
held, so long as it is spontaneous. Hamlet is the bogey, as well
of our politics as of our philosophy. It is to the Bismarcks, the
Roosevelts, the Napoleons, the Mussolinis, that the imagination
of politics is turned, away from dreamers and critics. It is a
direction to which William James had already pointed in his
essay on "Great Men and their Environment".

It may quite well be that the reason for this present distrust
of reason is the same that led Burke to his later defense of instinctive conservatism. The reaction which swept the author
of the *Speeches on Conciliation with the Colonies* into his half-
mad hatred of Jacobinism, was inspired by the antics of Mother
Guillotine in her Mob Cap, dancing the wild jig of the French
Revolution. Theories had begot that monstrous orgy. They
were feared with the same superstitition that earlier smelled
witchcraft in the simple-gathering and senile mumblings of village crones—and with more justice, no doubt. It was, in any

case, with shouts of "no philosophers!" that the anti-Jacobin mob burned the house of Priestley over his head, on the unfounded suspicion of his having attended a Reform dinner; and it was the same fear that hounded harmless members of the London Corresponding Society until it had shipped them for treason to Botany Bay.[8]

Something of this distrust of "intellectuals" has been of late in the air. When the world's eyes were drawn toward the spectacle of Communism's red terror in Russia, they beheld theories again at their ghastly work. Liberal sentiment was as horrified by the pranks of Demos in its proper abandon as Burke and his contemporaries had been at Guillotine. The dress now was Marxian red, but the dance was the same. Even the garment's self had undergone no other change than in the shade of the dye.

Burke, whose defense of instinctive prejudice against the rationalistic lure of abstractions and pure logic finds a hearty modern echo in the pragmatism of William James, had led the stampede back to the toryism of his generation. There has been as great a crush, contemporarily, along the path "back to normalcy", and not all the signs say that the rush is past. People, at least up to the last campaign, were beginning to smile at the orators who inveighed against the mildest social reformers as Bolsheviks. But now the governments of the world seem to be shifting back to "Tranquillity", away from what Mr. Punch aptly called "Sidney-Webbicalism" as well as syndicalism. And Mussolini, though he was sadly shaken in his saddle (after the "unfortunate jest" implied in the to-be-regretted disappearance and subsequent murder of one of the opposition leaders, Signor Matteotti), still retains an unrelaxed hold on Italy. He has driven most of the real leaders of the opposition into exile along with Salvemini and Don Sturzo. He has a "Bill of Attainder" against them at his discretion. He has successfully suspended or muzzled all save the Fascist papers, and no man dare criticize Fascism or *il Duce* on pain of his life or health, as Amendola (had he not died of gangrened wounds) and Misuri could testify.

[8] H. N. Brailsford, *Shelley, Godwin, and their Circle*, pp. 39-41. See also F. K. Brown's splendid *Life of William Godwin*.

But how can such a movement have even a claim on pragmatic origins? Pragmatism, in the hands of William James,
was a bracing and rather revolutionary refusal to take logic and
the monistic Absolute too seriously. It has lent itself, however,
to such apostles of political revolt as the apologist of syndicalistic
violence, M. Georges Sorel, and the defender of "direct action"
on the part of groups within the state, Mr. H. J. Laski, as we
have seen. Both of them declare that they are the disciples of
James, the pluralist in philosophy, in their attempts to pluralize
authority, and discredit the state as a court of last resort. They
will have none of the legalistic fiction of absolute sovereignty,
any more than James would of the Absolute's self. William
James is known to Mussolini probably only through the filtration
of Sorel and Papini, his Italian popularizer. Mussolini, great
admirer of American strenuosity and efficiency, accepts this Romanticist side of pragmatism with its repudiation of shams if they
be the shams of rational parliamentarism and its worship of
myths if they be the myths created by a strong will to believe.

On the other hand, pragmatism in the hands of Mr. Dewey, the
foremost of its living exponents, has meant a philosophy of
social synthesis, more and more tending to an absolute science
of society and morals. If he calls himself a pluralist, it is by
no means with James' meaning of pluralism—"the absence of
any singly unifying relationship." Groups have a claim to their
separate existence and rights only from the point of view of
their functions in the organic context of social interdependence
and solidarity. Indeed, without any conscious discipleship on
either side, his own pragmatism has taken him straight along the
road to the philosophy of "solidarism" of the French sociologists
who follow Durkheim and the Italians who follow Pareto.[9]
Solidarism is a "functional" philosophy, one very closely akin to
the "instrumentalism" of Mr. Dewey. In the hands of M.
Duguit, the foremost of the jurists of this persuasion, the realistic
side of this Janus-faced philosophy has become a defense before

[9] Pareto, a sociologist of a rank equal to that which he holds as a mathematical economist, has tried to marry the anti-democratic emphasis of Sorel
on the *non-logico-sperimentale* technique of myths to a functional and scientific philosophy. See, for instance, his *Les Systèmes Socialistes; Fatti e
Teoria, Transformazione della democrazie;* and *Traité de Sociologie
Générale. Cf.* T. E. Wolfe, *Conservatism, Radicalism, and Scientific Method.*

the fact of Mussolini's ends and of the methods actually put into practice by Fascism; for it holds fear and force to be the foundations of political order, and all means to be justified that assure the proper functioning of the public services.[10]

Is it only an accident that this pragmatic philosophy of law has turned syndicalism to its theoretical uses just as Fascism has done in practice? Not if there is a reciprocal connection between the development of ideas and the parallel development of facts. Instrumentalism is the same development away from the radical empiricism of James's doctrines which Fascism represents in relation to syndicalism. M. Duguit claims for his interpretation of law that it is syndicalistic; but his is a syndicalism profoundly conservative in its tendencies, one that aims at creating a more flexible system of law, based upon a contractual régime of group-made laws. The political structure of the future will be "professionalism", or the autonomy of occupational and professional groups. The only constraint upon group autonomy will be the duty of the rulers of the state to assure the functioning of the public services. This is, almost word for word, the Fascist program for the new "Fascist-Syndicalist State". The reservation of all control necessary to assure the public service, however, turns out to be a very important proviso. It means a syndicalism only of form. The real power rests with the rulers of the state. When the French *Confédération Générale du Travail* attempted to make its own law by launching a general strike, beginning with the famous May-Day railroad strike of 1920, the government in power used troops to assure social solidarity—to the vast delight of M. Duguit. In the same manner the Fascist militia smashed the Italian general strike of 1922. It turns out that the nation, through the government actually in power (that is in control of the actual force), is still to have the final decision as to what is law, and the duty of enforcing that law—whether it be the constitutional government or not. Unitary power seems to be a practical, a pragmatic necessity. Syndicalism is merely a convenient method of grouping citizens to assure their complete subjection to "Law and

[10] To understand the connection between Duguit's ideas and Mussolini's it is necessary to study the social ideas of Vilfredo Pareto (*cf. supra note* 9) and Pantaleone—both positivistic sociologists. In particular Pareto, like Durkheim and Duguit, believes in a functional state.

Order" even if that be attained along the lines laid down by Judge Lynch.

The development of the theory of Fascism has been in profound accord with this outcome of "solidarism". It, too, started from syndicalistic origins. It, too, followed a pragmatic progress toward the negation of its premises. Theories of any sort are forced to conform to historical conditions in their application, if they are to realize themselves in events. But there is something peculiarly inevitable about the result of the syndicalist attempt to integrate society by dividing it. The emphasis must be placed at one end or the other. And the result of placing it at pluralistic pole has been, historically, just as sure a swing toward absolutism in fact, as the practice of absolutism has meant a revolutionary reaction toward a reign of feudalistic violence. In the end it has embraced an absolutist philosophy of the state that makes it a crime, under the new penal code, to "offend" anywhere in the world, in Italy or abroad, against the political interest of Italy or the "personality" of the state. This is surely the apotheosis of the sovereign state-person which pragmatism set out to escape.

Let us point our moral, even though that may not adorn the tale. Signor Mussolini, in the days of his youthful adherence to the revolutionary wing of socialism, was one of the most intransigent of the revolutionary leaders of Italian Labor. His apostleship to the gospel of syndicalistic violence and the General Strike Myth cost him the editorship of the *Avanti* and an exile (more or less voluntary) from an Italy in which parliamentary socialism had won. He spent it in Switzerland (contemporarily with Lenin and partly in the same city of Zurich), improving his mind by further reflections on violence. Then he was expelled from Switzerland by the government as a dangerous radical. The origin of Fascism is commonly admitted to lie in those *"Fasci* for Revolutionary Action" which he joined as a leader some time after his return to Italy. They hastened the entry of Italy into the war on the forlorn hope that by so doing they were bringing about the reign of syndicalistic Socialism throughout the world. The gospel of violence preached by such followers of Sorel as Panunzio and Mantica was seized upon by d'Annunzio to bring Italy in upon the Latin (French) side. Mussolini and

the other Revolutionary Socialists who had repudiated parliamentarism, by some twist of the imagination saw in the death-
grips to which Europe had come a situation that meant Marxian
world revolution.[11] They joined d'Annunzio and the Republicans
and the Mazzinists (who were purely nationalistic in their hope)
in bringing Italy into the struggle, staking their socialistic future
upon the correctness of their own diagnosis of social tendencies.
They lost—as socialists. Nationalism, not internationalism, the
dice read when the war was over. But the syndicalistic groupings—the *Fasci*—still survived. Also the gospel of violence, and
the Romanticist myth-worship that had so played into the hands
of d'Annunzio, flourished apace. Just as the nationalistic faith
had absorbed the internationalistic hopes of their socialism, so it
now swallowed up the leaders of the latter movement in the maw
of Fascism. The form of *"fasces"*, taken from the Roman symbol
of lictor's power (the joined band of rods about an ax, borne
before the consuls and magistrates, and signifying the union of
all forces in one) likewise underwent a transformation in the
direction of closer cohesion. In 1919 there came into existence
the *Fasci di Combattimento*, a Latin version of the more strenuous mood of the American Legion, bent upon law and order of
the 100 per cent Italian kind, and with a natural affinity for
securing the fruits of victory which played once more into the
hands of d'Annunzio. Significant traces of the syndicalistic
origins of the movement show in the Guild Constitution which
that fantastic statesman gave his Fiume.[12]

[11] The first vigor of Bolshevism was applied to the hope of world revolution,
too, but it soon turned its attention perforce to consolidating its hold upon
Russia. It has become, since the inauguration of Lenin's "New Economic
Policy", primarily concerned with the government of Russia, as Mr. Michael
Farbman has shown in his excellent studies, *Bolshevism in Retreat*, and *After
Lenin*. Bolshevism, at the present time, has hardly more of an international program than has Fascism, for the latter is equally bent on stirring
up trouble for its neighbors, though not with any idea of a world revolution
or a Fascist international.

[12] The enormous literature on this subject includes Carleton Beals's *Rome
or Death!* and Odon Por's *Fascism*. Among the best treatments of origins
are Don Sturzo, *Italy and Fascismo* (1926), Gaetano Salvemini, *The Fascist
Dictatorship in Italy* (1927), Robert Michels, *Socialismus und Faschismus in
Italien* (1923), Umberto Foscanelli's *D'Annunzio e il Fascismo* (Milan, 1923)
and ex-Premier Bonomi's *From Socialism to Fascism* (1924). Although
William Bolitho's *Italy under Mussolini* hardly does justice to this side of
Fascism, it serves as an excellent counterweight to the mass of hyper-
bolical pro-Fascist propaganda.

After this comic-opera interlude, Fascism proper came into being out of the wreck of the forces that had enjoyed Fiume under d'Annunzio's occupation. Dino Grandi, a considerable Fascist apologist and protagonist, put it this way: "Fascism has been, and is, nothing but the continuation of the 'Interventionism' of 1914-15, just as the *'Fasci di Combattimento'* [bands of ex-combatants] are the representatives and glorious offspring of the *'Fasci d'Azione Revoluzionaria'* of 1915, to whom belongs the credit of propaganda of the war among the masses, not so much as a military necessity, but as the best hope for revolution, as a mystical re-birth for the nation and for humanity." [13]   And Odon Por, who has in his book on *Fascism* given one of the most authoritative statements of the origins of the movement, shows how Mussolini and the other backers of the Fiume venture came to look on Wilsonism and parliamentarism and all the intellectualistic forces aiming at political regeneration of the world as "renunciatory". Still smarting under the Treaty of Rapallo, they declared war on the milksop policies of a government that permitted Italy to be robbed from without and sabotaged from within. The race, from that time on, was between Communist and Fascist violence, as to which would first overthrow the shell of the state.

For a time it looked as if Red revolution had won against Black. The syndicalist program of the general strike, which Mussolini had abandoned for the nationalism created by the war, was actually put into effect. The Federation of Italian Metallurgical Operatives took possession of the factories and plants in which they were employed in northern Italy, but the latter days of 1920 saw the golden opportunity of Italian Bolshevism loom large and then fade away, from want of leaders like Lenin. Mussolini, like the government, was a passive, even a benevolent, spectator; he had encouraged the previous seizure

---

[13] Odon Por, *op. cit.*, p. 29, quoting from *Le Origini e la Missioni del Fascismo*, by Dino Grandi, *Biblioteca di Studi Sociali* (Bologna, 1922). Both Gorgolini, in a book officially sanctioned by Mussolini, *The Fascist Movement in Italian Life*, and Luigi Villari, in *The Awakening of Italy*, bear out this statement; and so do Ferrero's *Four Years of Fascism* (*Da Fiume a Roma*) and G. Prezzolini's *Fascism*. See also J. Marschak, "Der korporative und der hierarchische Gedanke im Fascismus," *Archiv für Sozialwissenschaft und Sozialpolitik*, Vols. 52-53 (1924 and 1925) for a profoundly philosophic analysis. A. Lion's *Pedigree of Fascism* is pure metaphysics.

of the Dalmine plants.[14] In the 1920 seizures of industrial units he had not gauged the true helplessness of Italian labor. Even he made "a dignified request to the Leninists for a truce and, during the occupation of the factories, proclaimed his 'benevolent neutrality' towards the F. I. O. M."[15] He was not yet willing to risk a direct trial of strength between Fascism and Communism. His own program was anti-bourgeois, anti-clerical, anti-royalist, and it called for a "decimation of wealth" by means of confiscation and a capital levy.

But with the fiasco of the occupation of the factories, and the complete failure of the proletariat to organize political control, the day of the new Fascism dawned. The Milanese group of Mussolini was subsidized, it is claimed, by the government.[16] Its full sun shone when it utterly broke the attempt at a general strike in 1922. The main criticism directed against the impotence of the old "parliamentary" government was equally applicable to the workers' control under the "Occupation" of 1920; trains failed to run, factories were idle, business of all sorts was tied up through the failure of the public services, including government. The national organism did not function. Economic stagnation and psychic disintegration—Italy knew both.

[14] Benito Mussolini, *Discorsi Politici* (Milan, 1921), p. 177. According to Por, he referred to the Dalmine seizures as "a creative stay-in strike . . . that does not interrupt but continues production." Por, *op. cit.*, pp. 41-55. See the first program of Fascism which included factory operation by the workers, published in *Il Popolo d'Italia*, March, 1919, outlined by James Murphy, *loc. cit., infra*, note 16.

[15] Por, *loc. cit., supra*. This is further substantiated by Don Sturzo, and by Salvemini, as cited *supra*.

[16] A view, somewhat inaccurate in its details, but not controverted on this point, given by James Murphy, "The Parabola of Fascism," *Fortnightly Review*, December 25, 1925. According to this statement the Prefect of Milan, like some medieval prince hiring *condottieri*, brought in Mussolini's Milanese group of Fascists to smash the socialists who were trying to get control of the Milan Savings Bank through control of the municipal and communal councils. Mr. Murphy asserts that the Nationalist phase of Fascism dates from this period, say 1921, but that Fascism did not finally pass under the control of the Nationalists until it had to fall back upon the big banks for support of the new government, after the *coup d'état* that won Rome. It was consolidated by Volpi with the help of the J. P. Morgan Co. loan in 1925, after de Stefani's failure. See also Mr. Murphy's articles in the *Atlantic Monthly* for January, 1924, and for December, 1925. Mr. Murphy is generally corroborated in his economic interpretation by the correspondents of the *Journal des Débats* and by the *Manchester Guardian*, but his figures on the budget are doubtful. William Bolitho's series of articles in the New York *World* during December, 1925, are now available in book form (*Italy Under Mussolini*, Macmillan, 1926).

Already staggering under a mountain of debt, the state threatened to collapse entirely. The nation, having been led divided into the war, emerged physically untempered and spiritually divided against itself, into the period of reconstruction that everywhere tried nationalism upon a ruthless anvil. Fascism was a call to unity through the integration of groups of men who were desperate and well led. It had been schooled in violence from its syndicalistic origins and further instructed in the long course of war and by the occupation of Fiume. Men turned again to the myth of Machiavelli, after Sorel's syndicalistic myth of the General Strike had been exploded as a means of social reconstruction. Group action was still the core of their practice as well as their theory. But, like the juristic evolution of M. Duguit, it had become group action bound together by the ties of economic necessity, and a gospel of social solidarity summed up in terms of the nation. They clinched their claims to national consideration by running trains, and acting in some communes as a government in the second strike in 1922.

Once in the saddle, however, Fascism has utilized the syndicalist idea to strengthen its hold upon power. Even after the dramatic march on Rome that followed, it did not attempt to destroy unionism entirely, as the more misguided elements of English and American reaction have done. It followed the advice which M. Duguit had been offering all governments, and transformed revolutionary syndicalism into Fascist syndicalism.[17] At Ferrara, in October, 1921, one year after the breakdown of revolutionary syndicalism in Italy through the attempt to follow the vague counsels of Mr. Sorel's Myth of the General Strike instead of the political action of a shrewder Bolshevism, syndicalism as a trade-union movement had already turned definitely away from circuses to a clamor for bread. *La Confederazione Nazionale delle Corporazione Sindacali*, formed in Bologna the following January, parallels in a most interesting way the break of the main wing of the French C. G. T. with the Moscow International. The National Confederation of the Syndical Corporations in Italy was controlled by the bourgeoisie who had found

[17] See also Carl Schmitt, *Die Diktatur* (1921). A very interesting economic interpretation of Fascism from the pro-Fascist side is *Corrado Gini's* "The Scientific Basis of Fascism," *Pol. Sci. Qu.*, Vol. XLII, No. 1, March, 1927, which gives a positivistic and scientific defense.

in Fascism their lost unity of front against the proletariat; but by the end of 1923 it had brought to its membership of over 2,000,000 not only about the entire membership of the "white" syndicates, but most of the beaten "reds" as well. A special convention called in Milan in August of that year renounced all socialistic connections, bent the knee to Mussolini, and accepted a program of national as opposed to class solidarity. Functionalism and solidarism (the program of Fascism) were thus translated, as Mr. James Murphy has shown, into a program of guild organization, deriving its inspiration from the old Roman *collegia* (or control of all labor by the skilled "colleges"), and attempting to rescue from "the twilight of the Renaissance" the true guild spirit. Now, the Fascist trade unions are the only ones recognized by the new law imposing compulsory arbitration and the only means even theoretically possessed by Labor of nominating members to the new Chamber of Deputies. At first they threatened to become a democratic menace, as every official and every laborer must be a Fascist in the state bureaucracy, and as the Socialists tried to capture the other syndicates by swamping them. For some time, however, they have been "purified" by vesting control only in tried Fascists, and by "supervising" their elections and their funds.[18]

It is not of course the medievalism of the guilds that has in fact been reconstructed, in spite of the efforts so to interpret it that are made by Fascist apologists. The entire structure is built about nationalism like a solid structure of reinforced concrete, with nothing of the Gothic except in ornamental architectural frippery. The essence of the guild spirit was decentralized localism, just as the inspiration of the Gothic was a many-spired marvel of detail.

By a decree of the government of February 6, 1924, under the practice of Fascism, all labor organizations had already been made subject to state supervision and control in a degree that

---

[18] Files of the *New York Times*, November and December, 1925. See also a partial summary of Fascism's system of labor control in the special articles of Mr. Wilbur Forrest, *New York Herald-Tribune*, Jan. 25-29, 1926. The text of the law is to be found in N. 624-A, *Documenti, Camera dei Deputati Legislatura*, XXVII (1924-1925). An excellent summary of the new laws is to be found in the *Round Table*, March, 1926, "Fascist Reforms in Italy"; and an able pro-Fascist defense in *Il Carroccio* (New York, January, 1926), "The Fascist State" by James P. Roe.

went far beyond any effort so far made by a modern state. The prefect had power not only to supervise the funds, but to order an inquiry into the activities of the association, "to overrule or set aside its acts, and in cases of a serious nature, to dissolve the administrative council." [19]   But as that did not suffice, Fascism resorted to the same method that Communism attempted in Russia, of permitting representation of labor only by the disciplined élite. All unions recognized by law must be Fascist. Dues paid them are compulsory on members and non-members alike. Their officials must be acceptable to the prefect. In a word, Fascism has tightened its hold upon syndicalism, and has reduced labor in Italy to the organic rôle demanded by Fascist theory.

The National Corporations created by the Fascist Confederation have as their function the "expression of national solidarity", and they exist "as a means of developing production".[20]   They derive, as Odon Por shows, from the lyrical constitution given by d'Annunzio to the Free State of Fiume (under the Constitution of Carnaro) and embrace agriculture, industry, commerce, transport and communication, public and private employees, liberal professions and art—a mystic seven in number. Under the practice of Fascism they include, in fact, "all forms and systems of production and labor", with a view toward taking their control out of the hands of trade unionism or employers' associations, and putting them, finally, under the control of the state. Against the "struggle of classes" they set up "struggle of capabilities". The governing organs of the Corporations were in the original theory to be constituted by a *Corporative Council* of representatives, nominated by the various provincial trade unions (one for each); by a *Directorate*, composed "of as many representatives as there are types of trades, arts, or professions interested in the great branch of industry or labor represented by the

---

[19] *Law and Labor*, August, 1924, p. 228. The latest English compilation of the newer Fascist laws is H. W. Schneider's, "Italy's New Syndicalist Constitution," *Political Science Quarterly*, Vol. XLII, No. 2, pp. 161-202. Mr. Schneider shows how much of this "syndicalism" is mere façade.
[20] Extracts from the original *Statutes of the Confederation of Corporations* available in Por, *op. cit.*, Appendix III. These, of course, are modified and applied by the new Charter of Labor, and by the proposed law which will reform the Chamber, to be functionally organized to represent the corporations.

Corporation"; and by a *Secretariat* (to be elected by the Directorate). The Corporations are supposed to bring together the workers' syndicates (unions) and the employers' federations.[21] The actual control of the unions is completely in the hands of Fascist leaders of these unions who need number (legally) only ten per cent of the workers residing in the district. The leaders may exclude workers at will. "Capability" is imposed upon all workers. They must function for national production. No corporate rights exist when that is at stake. Consequently the Corporations are a mere façade. The actual settlements depend on what Mussolini thinks the industry will bear. The federated employers, too, must accept compulsory arbitration in theory at least. So far wage reductions have taken place wholesale by Mussolini's decree. Only a few resorts to the courts have been had, in one of which the employers were allowed to lock out on account of shortage of raw materials.[22]

In a generation harassed by the incessant industrial warfare between trade unionism and employers, this solution is being eyed with increasing favor. Employers need not fear compulsory arbitration under this system: the result is a foregone conclusion, if any threat of a diminution of production is involved. It is pragmatic in the extreme, for it proposes no other tests than the palpable fruits of productivity. *Function, capability,* these are its watchwords—and its unit is the *Nation,* "an organism embracing an indefinite series of generations in which each individual is but a transient element", in the words of the Fascist program of December, 1921. It sums up the materialistic imperialism of the times by giving it a statement into which all the romantic elements of operatic revolution and patriotism are introduced. It speaks of "the battle of coal" and "the battle of wheat". But once it has caught its hare, it proceeds to skin

[21] See the article of H. W. Schneider, cited *supra*, and the writer's article in the *Survey Graphic*, March, 1927. See also Edmondo Rossoni (General Secretary of the Fascist Corporations) "The Fascist House of Work" in the same number of the *Survey Graphic*, describing the theoretical connections of the thirteen Grand Corporations.

[22] See the interesting analysis of index numbers given in *La Liberta* (Paris Anti-Fascist Journal), 29 Jan., 1928, p. 2. *"Note Sulla Situazione Economica."* Merchant marine operators were not permitted to reduce workers' wages, according to the report of the Labor Court's decision (la Magistratura del Lavoro) given by *La Stampa* (Turin), Jan. 29, 1928. Unemployment is put at about a half million.

him. Italian labor was so heartily sick of the "maximalists" (syndicalistic revolutionists and communists) who had nothing more creative than a general strike to offer, that it readily accepted the guild idea on which the Corporations were supposed to be founded. During 1925 some of the old unions organized "protest strikes" against Fascist control up to 80 per cent effective. But now they dare not even protest. Non-Fascist associations now are outlaws, at the mercy of the prefect. Many ex-socialist leaders came, hat in hand, asking for an absolution of past sins and the privilege of sharing the new control. They gained nothing except immunity from persecution. From now on the struggle will be between the forces within Fascism which propose to give this guild system a fair trial, and those who are only interested in the suppression of the proletariat. The weight of the employers behind Signor Benni of the Employer's Federation and of the great bankers behind Signor Volpi is on the latter side. But the supplanting of Farinacci by the more moderate Augusto Turati, as Secretary of the Fascist Party, may mean a limited triumph for the guild principle. Turati is credited with having sponsored the Fascist labor strikes in 1925 which forced the metallurgical employers to act as a unit in dealing with the Corporations.[23]

Mussolini, from his syndicalistic origins, might be expected to be sympathetic to the former element of Fascism, for that gives it a *point d'appui* with labor, in agriculture as well as industry. But the inspiration of the guild system is not nationalism. It is an altogether different community of feeling, interest and purpose. And the inspiration of Mussolini's Fascism *is* nationalism, and nothing else. Nationalism really made head only when the guild organization of industry of the middle ages was thoroughly weakened.[24] It had, indeed, no small part in

[23] See the *New York Times*, April 1, 1926.

Augusto Turati is not the old Socialist Filippo Turati (now in exile in Paris), as some dispatches and Fascist propaganda indicated at first. He is a young Fascist, supposedly moderate, but responsible for the renaming a peak of Mont Blanc, Monte Benito Mussolini. He is one of the heirs-presumptive to Mussolini. His place at the head of the Fascist syndicates has been taken by Edmondo Rossoni, an old syndicalist exile from Italy who led the intelligenzia of Italian radicalism in this country prior to the war. Rossoni has protested violations of the Charter of Labor.

[24] See J. A. Penty, *Guildsman's Interpretation of History;* Renard's *Guilds in the Middle Ages;* and Austin P. Evans, "The Problem of Control in Medieval Industry," *Political Science Quarterly*, Vol. XXXV, pp. 603-616.

breaking down the guild system of control that feudalism and the régime of mediate and immediate liege cities had fostered under the Holy Roman Empire. Causality, here as elsewhere, is too complex a matter to be lightly ventured upon. But it is certain that the notion of an all-absorptive nationalism is antithetical to the pluralistic spirit of the guild system that must be preserved if the latter is to function as a really creative force.

Mussolini and his Fascism are committed to nationalism with the utmost finality. Therefore they must treat the Syndicates as James I treated his non-conformist subjects, i.e., "make them conform themselves or harry them out of the land, or else do worse"—conform in this case to the state religion of maximum production. If there seem to be other matters, such as the free right of association to protect hours of labor and standards of living, which are just as important in the eyes of the members of the Corporations—so much the worse for them. As long as Fascism is firm in its saddle, it will make few concessions of a radical nature. When it begins to make them, one may reckon that it has ceased to be Fascism and become something else— perhaps Guild Socialism.

But the Guild Socialist element in Fascism is apt to get very short shrift from the Nationalist ministers who are now directing the economic policies of Mussolini's régime. One by one the old Black-Shirt ministers have dropped out under the program of a struggle of capabilities. Their places have been taken by men whose convictions are those of the "Blue-Shirt" Nationalists who were incorporated into Fascism after its successful march on Rome. These Nationalists (or those who sympathize with the Old Nationalist policies of reaction) who furnish four leaders that are now part of Mussolini's real inner council—Volpi, Corradini, Federzoni and Rocco—are what would be known in France as the Royalist Right. They stand for the precise antithesis of Fascism's earlier program, for they are ultra-royalist, ultra-clerical, ultra-bourgeois in financial policies. They agree with Fascism's earlier phase only in finding force handy for repression, and in being equally militaristic and imperialistic. And they have conquered Fascism, through the banks, which are now represented by a seat for the group on the Fascist Grand Council.

Italy's great need of working capital has so far forced Mussolini to come to terms with the bankers. His program of production has forced him to afford every aid and comfort to big industrial ventures, from a strongly protective tariff to special tax exemptions and subsidies from the state.

At first these Nationalists, through Deputy Benni, who is also President of the Italian Confederation of Industries, forbade the extension of compulsory arbitration to employers in industry; then they accepted Mussolini's assurance of December 11 that, "The workman's syndicates are Fascist . . . they must do nothing to diminish the productive efficiency of the nation." Let Signor Alfredo Rocco, Minister of Justice, speak for them:

". . . Briefly, the forces which I have referred to [the opposition to Fascism] and which are directed against the State, we would discipline and include in some way in the central authority we have established and under which this opposition must work.

"It is for this reason that I have refused to accord judicial representation to Fascist syndicates, so that in the end a state within a state cannot be set up which would dictate to the central authority, and it is for this reason that I fight the opposition press." [25]

But he has had to accept the legal status of the Fascist syndicates. So far as the control of the guild spirit is concerned, the Nationalists feel that they have little to fear from a Fascism which controls every expression of opinion, and asks in return only *panem ac circenses*. They may be deceived in the event.

In the orientation of foreign policy, too, there can be no doubt about the necessity of nationalism to Fascism. Mussolini has declared his disbelief in the League of Nations by word and deed.[26] Let Corfu be witness. Fascism represents the last stand

[25] Quoted from an interview given by Sig. Rocco while in Paris at a meeting of the Commission for Intellectual Cooperation, commenting upon Mussolini's declaration that the Aventine Opposition would never be permitted to sit again until they had sworn loyalty to Fascism. *New York Times*, Jan. 19, 1926, p. 4. How successful this subordination has been can be judged from the fact that the general addition of an hour on the working day and each of the general wage reductions has been given out as coming by request from the Fascist syndicates!

[26] The control of the Italian members of the League personnel by the Fascist government has been, by all accounts, a source of great embarrassment. Similarly the International Labor Bureau has not been able to reconcile the declaration of its statute for freedom of association with the acceptance of the Fascist heads of Italian syndicates.

of the theory of the absolute sovereignty of the nation-state. More than that, it represents a revival of Machiavelli in all his saturnine views on human, and especially Italian, nature. S. E., Benito Mussolini has recently submitted an appreciative dissertation upon Machiavelli for the degree of Doctor of Laws.[27] *"Il Duce"*, as he is called by Fascists, has set himself to the modern application of *Il Principe*, a pragmatic application of that essentially pragmatic document. Needless to say, he was enthusiastically awarded the degree, *honoris causa*, by the University of Bologna. Like Machiavelli,[28] he holds no moral values above a united and Imperial Italy: "My ideas are clear," asserts *il Duce*, "my orders are precise. As in the well ordered and powerful days of the first Empire, Rome must again become the marvel of the world." [29]   Like Machiavelli, he believes that it is necessary to expand in order to survive.

To this end, Fascism yokes the methods of the Ku Klux Klan to the service of national production. It can not see behind political obedience any farther than the "fact" of the fear of the weaker for the stronger, and that is an old trail, well enough worn by travelers upon it as far back as Thrasymachus in Plato's *Republic*. The end of it leads to a thoroughly Machiavellian *Politik*, spelled in any language you choose—a conclusion which Benito Mussolini has most heartily accepted so far as Italy is concerned. The youth of Italy, now regimented by Gentile's Fascist education, is singing *"Italia sopra tutto"* with as much lustihood as ever Prussian youth did when it goose-stepped to *"Deutschland über alles"*.[30]   And Mussolini keeps Fascist Italy scanning the horizon for new worlds to conquer.[31]

---

[27] *Living Age*, June 28, 1924, p. 1245, quoting from the *Avanti* (Milan), May 11, 1924. The *Avanti* is now ruined by Fascist suppression. All the great papers of Italy have been tamed or forced into the hands of Fascists by the simple expedient of putting it into the power of the prefect to hold up any issue he pleases, or as many issues as he pleases, and by various devices in the new law governing the press. The *Corriere della Sera*, property of the Albertini brothers, and the best of the Italian papers, was so forced into Fascist hands.

[28] See an interesting article, "Lenin and Mussolini," by H. J. Laski, *Foreign Affairs*, Sept., 1923.

[29] Quoted by Wilbur Forrest, *New York Herald-Tribune*, January 26, 1926.

[30] "Le Présent et l'Avenir du Fascisme," anonymous, *Le Correspondant*, Dec. 1925, showing the incorporation of the youth of Italy in the *avvanguardia giovanili e balilla*.

[31] See his speech in Tripoli, April 11 (*New York Times*, April 12, 1926).

Revolution and reaction, a cycle often enough remarked; in our time the moral is pointed by syndicalism that prepares the way for Fascism. Out of the refusal or the inability to order society by taking counsel together comes the repudiation of the slower methods of constitutionalism in favor of direct action. There are times, no doubt, when Jefferson's sometime preference for revolution by the violent methods of mobs—*piazza*, the Italians call it—may be necessary. But among a culturally and nationally homogeneous population it seems fairly safe to say that permanent results are not won in this fashion. The dead weight of an unconvinced majority is too heavy a drag to permit progress. Conviction won by force is more than apt to be lost in the same way.

The pragmatic desire for progress that is impatient with representative government in any form, that demands facts, not theories, and action, not programs, is quite as lop-sided a view of politics as its intellectualistic antithesis. There is something almost Hegelian in its practical fulfilment, too; for it embraces the actual enthronement of a dictator in the same fashion which it so condemned in rationalistic idealism. It becomes "its own other", its antithesis through the synthesis of force. And now Fascism, like Revolutionary Communism in Russia, is in the hands of the *doctrinaires*. Gentile and the seventeen Solons associated with him are grinding out the new "organic state" philosophy, by imperial decree. Step by step they follow the progress of Leninism to the imposition of an economic dogma by an uncriticizable dictatorship. This time, however, the industrialists and financiers are well pleased, for it is Volpi's brand of capitalism that is enforced. Consequently there is as hearty a welcome for Fascist dictatorship as there was recently hysterical condemnation for Bolshevist dictatorship.[32]

Germany had no monopoly on the worship of force. The Hohenzollerns throve upon the same popular inability to act and think politically that Fascism lives upon. They, too, offered action and imaginative magnificence; they, too, placed their control of the state upon the basis that they made it function with an organic smoothness which tolerated no social waste

[32] See the writer's "The Case against Fascism," *The Forum*, April, 1926, and ex-Premier Nitti's, *Fascism, Bolshevism, and Democracy* (1927).

or lost motion. Word for word, the philosophy of social solidarity through organizing and safeguarding the public services that M. Duguit offers might have served the All-Highest of the German Empire quite as handily as it does Signor Mussolini. One need not quarrel with a people that prefers this organic solidarity as the basis of its law.[33] It has certain compensations which are obvious enough, as well as certain dangers.

Liberalism still has a word to say, a protest though feeble. "The way to good government does not lie by any such shortcut as Fascism," it holds. "Direct action may cut the Gordian knot, but it forges chains that are even more galling to those who like to have at least a free effort to convince others of the justice of their own views. Representative government under a generally accepted constitution is on trial the world over. The necessity of more independent expert administration and advice is obvious. But to throw constitutional government and all idea of representation overboard from the ship of our state will not rid us of Jonah, nor will it propitiate Leviathan for long. Such a Jonah must out; and in the meantime, it is apt to be the pilot we are most in need of whom we thus sacrifice to still the waves that, by the very nature of political seas, are bound to try timbers in any vessel of state."

Very edifying, no doubt, especially when spoken with the Asquithian accent. However it may quite well be that self-government cannot be imposed upon a people whom it does not fit—as the 19th Century seems to have thought it could be. The test of that fitness is surely the success with which representative machinery is worked, and the morality practiced in observing and changing the constitutional forms.

In the case of Italy, though, as well as in the case of many other European countries, the fact seems not to have been so much the failure of all representative government as the failure of one type of parliamentary government—the breakdown of a coalition bloc system rendered doubly inevitable by an unworkable system of proportional representation. In any case, making due allowance for the political development and psychology of

---

[33] Vilfredo Pareto in his *Fatti e Teorie e di Trasformazione della Democrazia* (1920) and in his *Trattato di Sociologia Generale* (2nd ed., 1923) had given, as the *"Avvertimento"* of Giulio Farina declares, a theory of this sort of which Fascism is "the proper experimental verification."

the Italian people, a modified presidential system seems to be much more nearly in line with their needs, although there is much to be said in favor of a parliamentary system like that of England, in view of the strength of the traditional attachment of the people to their monarch. If the present law governing the premiership (with Articles Six and Nine struck out) were actually adhered to, it might offer a very workable compromise for attaining what is practically presidential government in the future. Under it the premier holds office as the leader of the party which goes into office with a parliamentary majority. He depends for his tenure of office, on the other hand, not upon a vote of confidence in the Chamber of Deputies but upon the confidence of the King. Of course the law has no application to the present state of affairs in which Mussolini frankly rules without the least pretence of observing any constitutional limitations that irk him. He still goes before his Parliament to harangue them and to be cheered by the Fascists, or to hurl panegyrics at the tamed Opposition—of which, naturally, the Communists were those who were longest suffered to be present. The Communists afforded a never-failing source of comparison through the retrospect of some years, and an equally stimulating and unresisting object for Mussolini's unrestrained flagellation. They were on display. Of the rest only Giolitti remains.

Under the last proposed reform of the legislature, the Chamber of Deputies is to become a smaller body of 400 members representative of non-political groups, the Fascist Corporations; and the Senate is still to be made up of an undetermined number of senators appointed for life by the King, that is to say by Mussolini. There is to be a single party, the Fascist, and a single ticket, which the nation must accept or reject as a unit. Nominations are to be made by the thirteen great Fascist Corporations made up of the unions of labor and the unions of employers, it appears, if the Grand Council's list is rejected. As this gives at least a possibility of the real political power to the unions, the Grand Council of Fascism has announced "the necessity of a central governmental organism, which on the basis of Fascist doctrine and experience, shall control, coördinate and harmonize the forms of activity of the great labor unions in order to bring about progress in the augmentation of the material and moral power of the nation." This is obviously intended to prevent the democratic tendencies of the unions from getting out of hand. The Grand Council further eliminates any nominees who displease it and adds a number of its own candidates who will represent the interests of the party.[34]

Mussolini having destroyed universal suffrage and limited all representation to Fascism, is not yet prepared to constitutionalize even the question of his successor. It was *lèse-majesté* in Italy to suggest that Mussolini had ever been a sick man or even a man worn out by his superhuman labors, when it was apparently a fact. It was rumored at one period that he had contemplated as successors a triumvirate made up of Farinacci, the "terrorist" of Fascism; of Federzoni, friendly to the Vatican, a bigger man, but not so popular with the old Fascisti; and of General Badoglio, a very capable militarist.[35] That suggests the usual difficulties that beset the ultimate division of the mantle of dictorship. In any case, it does not suggest that Mussolini has any tenderer feelings for democracy than he has shown so far, although he could easily constitutionalize his position if he chose to do so. He looks far enough ahead only to avoid the revival of criticism which this would mean. Now he rules like a Cæsar. In one of his moments of enthusiasm in the course of the important speech to the Chamber of May 26, 1927, he went so far as to declare "My successor is not yet born." He does not propose to rest government upon consent, for that would be to repudiate Fascism. His face is still set toward that "hierarchy and discipline" that offer to his critics only the old "dilemma" he proposed for them in the beginning:

"I declare that my desire is to govern if possible with the consent of the majority; but, in order to obtain, to foster and

---

[34] *New York Times*, April 1, 1926, Nov. 13, 1927, March 18, 1928. Mussolini himself has added this Ministry of Corporation to his load, and proceeded to a summary regulation of wages to outstrip both the revaluation of the lira and the fall of retail prices. He will no doubt treat elections in the same fashion. The election laws are continually changed, unused.

[35] Wilbur Forrest, *loc. cit.* Badoglio is supposed to have been supplanted by Italo Balbo. Farinacci and Federzoni have both been for the time relegated to the background, the former possibly because of a scandalous connection with the failure of the Bank of Parma, the latter as scapegoat for the imbroglio with France over Fascist subvention of Garibaldi as an *agent-provocateur* in the Catalonian revolutionary conspiracy hatched in Nice. The new choice is said to fall on Balbo, Turati, and Rossoni.

to strengthen that consent, I will use all the force at my disposal. . . .

"For it may happen that force may bring about consent, and, if that fails, there is always force. With regard to all the requirements of government, even the most severe, we shall offer this dilemma: accept in the spirit of patriotism, or submit.

"This is my conception of the state and of the art of governing the nation." [36]

Certainly he is right in thinking that governing, especially in Italy, is more an art than a science. But even in an art there are certain principles relating to the scheme of arrangement. It was Rousseau who put one of these most finally in the first book of *The Social Contract:* "The strongest is never strong enough to remain forever master unless he transforms force into law, and obedience into duty." The whole history of unconstitutional government bears him out, even though much of the scheme he devoted to eliciting a "general will' has passed into limbo, and the "general will" itself is under suspicion. But there is about "the consent of the governed" in real democracies an element of moral obligation that force can never compel.

To secure this element of moral obligation Fascism hopes, however, to use the technique of myths, advocated by Plato to keep the lower order of his Republic content with their lot, and by Mussolini's old revolutionary master, Georges Sorel, to stir them up. For pragmatism, a myth is true so long as it works. Mussolini offers himself as the new Cæsar, to lead Italy once more to the day when Rome will become "the center of the world". If he can capture the imagination of Italians and inflame them with his dream, he feels that he can govern with consent. In the meantime, "The second foundation stone of Fascismo is represented by anti-demagogism and pragmatism. We have no

[36] "Speech to the Department of Finance," March 7, 1921 (Por, *op. cit.,* p. 148). Mussolini has promised to leave Parliament, as long as it is made up of loyal Fascists, to act as a cheering corps. "Representative government," he wrote in the dissertation on Machiavelli mentioned above, "belongs to the domain of mechanics, not of morals." And again, out of the fulness of his experience, "To speak of a sovereign people is to utter a tragic jest." The proper mechanics of representation is "deputed functional authority", which is a way of translating *La Gerarchia,* the official organ of Fascism. See Mrs. Townshend's note to Por, *op. cit.,* p. 175.

preconceived notions, no fixed ideas . . ." [37] and again, "Fascism seizes individuals by their necks and tells them: 'you must be what you are. If you are a bourgeois, you must remain such. You must be proud of your class!' " [38]

Let him be rendered his due. He has had the courage and the consistency to say flatly that he did not himself know what the word *normalization* means, even though it used to be the chief stock in trade of Fascist oratory—a frankness to be recommended to the apostles of "normalcy" elsewhere. "All governments," he pronounces, "are for normalization, even those arising from the most violent of revolutions, if that means preserving the form of government which they represent." [39] He has to his credit a veritable slaughter of the bureaucracy, and a stout effort to balance Italy's budget through turning over the state telephonic services to private capital and through increasing taxation by the tariff—even to a tax on salt—and other unremarked means.[40] The cost of living has dropped since the appreciation of the lira but wages have more than kept fair pace. Retail prices have fallen from the peak reached in 1925-1926 about 20% on the average. Wages have been reduced by more than 20% on the average. Over against his budget one may set the reign of terror kept up in some of the Italian provinces, of which the case of the rule of the Fascist *"ras"*, Regazzi, over Molinella in the Province of Bologna is typical. For over a year after a warrant was out for the arrest on clearly substantiated charges of premeditated murder—to say nothing of pranks like that of

[37] *Mussolini as Revealed in his Political Speeches* (Nov. 1914-Aug. 1923), by Barone B. Q. di San Severino, p. 114. The philosopher Gentile has linked this pragmatism up to Mazzini's unity of "thought and action" and to his own philosophy of the "pure act." See his *Che Cosa il Fascismo* and his "The Philosophic Basis of Fascism," *Foreign Affairs*, Jan. 1928. In the latter he has said: "Fascism is not a philosophy. . . . The significance of Fascism is not to be grasped from the special theses which it from time to time assumes. . . . Mussolini has boasted that he is a *tempista*, that his real pride is in 'good timing.' . . . The real views of the Duce are those which he formulates and executes at one and the same time." *Loc. cit.*, pp. 299-300. See Filipo Carli, *"Classicismo, romanticismo e fascismo,"* *Nuova Antologia*, Nov. 16, 1927.
[38] *Ibid.*, p. 317.
[39] *Manchester Guardian Weekly*, Oct. 24, 1924, p. 351.
[40] It is exceedingly difficult to get the truth about the Fascist budgets. The slain Matteoti, in *One Year of Fascist Misrule* (*London*, Labor Press, 1924), produces some interesting figures. See the writer's review of Constantine McGuire's "Italy's International Economic Position," printed as Appendix B in this volume. The prohibitive tariff shows small returns.

leading his Black Shirts in a modernized version of the Sabine Women by assaulting peasant women and then blacking their faces with a mixture of soot and vitriol—for over a year this Fascist lieutenant, in high favor in Rome, could not be found, officially, by the police, although he dined and wined almost nightly in the company of the Chief Commissioner of Police in Bologna! [41]

It was no doubt as much to control the lawlessness of these local *ducini*, and to curb their feudal independence of any control, that Federzoni, with the approval of *il Duce*, brought out the institution of the *podestà* from that period of Italian medievalism when the cities were beginning their long struggle to curb feudal anarchy.   The *podestà* appointed by the central government first ruled without any administrative interference from the representative council in every Italian commune of under 5000 in Italy.   That meant about four-fifths of the entire number.[42] And Rome and the larger municipalities have "Governors" after the same model.[43]   Every municipality now has a *podestà* imposed upon it who acts legally subject only to Mussolini, through the prefect.   That of course is centralization with a vengeance. If it destroys all freedom of local government, the answer is that that freedom had never existed in fact since the dawn of syndicalist and later Fascist violence after the war.   On the other hand, in spite of the obvious abuses of a rigidly centralized rule, it is better than the rule of local bullies.   There are signs from such press information as is possible to get, that the authority of the *podestà* is not yet strongly enough established to rule the local Fascist bosses, but that it is well on its way in that direction with the support of the public, so far as the public dares do anything except remain passive.   Unhappily the "old Fascists" seem to be claiming these *podestats* as the reward of the faithful in most instances.

In short the Fascist dictatorship in its recapitulation of the

[41] *Supra*, note 39.

[42] See the articles of Murphy, Forrest, and the *Round Table*, cited above. See also for the historical origins of the *podestà*, the article by S. K. Born, "What is the Podestà?" in the *Am. Pol. Sci. Rev.*, Vol. XXI, No. 4, pp. 863-871.

[43] The first governor, Cremonesi, was summarily dismissed by Mussolini after an orgy of graft that not even the censorship could prevent from leaking out.   On the censorship see George Seldes' article in *Harpers*, Oct., Nov. 1927.

cycle of government in Latin countries has now reached the point of consolidation. There are many people who feel that Mussolini, having accomplished so much as he has already, may go on with the help of the Fascists to give Italy the same sort of government that Diaz and his *rurales* gave to Mexico— a government capable of satisfying the national pride of his country and a government that will not be ungrateful enough to bite the hand that has fed it. They point to the degree of confidence shown in it quite lately by some well-known international financiers.[44] They urge that it is only under such a government that we can hope to have the Italians pay any substantial part of their debts. If the Italians are satisfied, they say, we ought to be.

The apologists of this realistic stamp go on to show that it is idle to expect the Italian people—even less than the Spanish under Primo de Rivera—to rise and demand parliamentarism again. For not only has Fascism brought a tolerable prosperity as long as foreign loans can be secured. It has restored to an opera-loving people all the fine flavor of medievalism, so far as spectacles and drama go: Mussolini poses in the lion's den; Mussolini evokes "the grandeur that was Rome"; Mussolini metes out a little discipline. No one can deny the necessity of fitting government to the psychology of the governed. Why should other nations venture criticisms on the "domestic concerns" of Italy? Will anyone offer to rule Italy better—outside of the handful of deputies who made a great play of absenting themselves from Parliament as it is run by Musso-

[44] See the remarks of Mr. Thomas W. Lamont and of Mr. Otto H. Kahn in reply to the writer's speech before the Foreign Policy Association in New York, January 23, quoted in the *New York Times*, Jan. 24, 1926. A corrected reprint of the latter speech is to be found in *The Fascist Dictatorship*, published by the International Committee for Political Prisoners, New York City, 1926. See also the economic analyses offered in *The Survey Graphic*, March, 1927.

The recent (December 1927) loan of $125,000,000 arranged by a large group of international banking institutions in many countries was aimed at providing a credit to stabilize the lira on international exchanges. It is interesting that J. P. Morgan Co. again took fifty million of this loan, and that our Federal Reserve System participated to the extent of thirty millions. It is certain that this tightens the bankers' hold on Mussolini: a withdrawal of the credit would sink the lira. It may effectually serve to prevent his becoming too bellicose in the crisis which seems to be developing through his efforts to arm Hungary, to isolate Jugo-Slavia from the Little Entente, and to establish an Italian hegemony over the Balkans.

lini?[45]   Even English memory holds a Cromwell and may hold
another soon.[46]   After all, can anyone be sure of what Edith
Cavell meant when she said "Patriotism is not enough"?   To
pragmatism, the only test of sufficiency is "prosperity"; the only
demand on patriotism is that it must "work".

There are several difficulties with this sort of reasoning. Obviously Italy will have to work out her own destiny. But the
destiny of a government in these days is affected by world opinions. And now Italy's destiny has become momentous for many
countries where democratic and representative government had
won a slender foothold, at least. In its imperialistic program and
in its avowed disbelief in the settlement of international disputes
through any possible machinery of international justice, Fascism
has international implications. It represents a complete denial
of the existence as well as of the availability of any principles
of morality applicable to the conduct of states—except the law
of the survival of the fittest. It is the most serious existing threat
to peace in Europe.

Has Fascism received, then, even the pragmatic sanction of
working? For the moment, undoubtedly. By creating a myth
of patriotism and embodying that myth in the figure of Mussolini, Fascism may succeed for a time in imposing what Plato
would have called "a noble lie" upon Italy. But the actual
operation of a dictatorship can be tested only when the Italian
peasant and worker have had a little longer to gauge the real
nature of "grandeur that was Rome". Even if the worker bears
his load philosophically, the test of the dictatorship can hardly
be said to have been made. It will come when Mussolini, a
tragic and not a comic Pooh-Bah, has to lay down the burden of
his ministries, of his imperialism, and of his dictatorship. The
claim of the supporters of Fascism is that the "Party" will prove
to be self-perpetuating in the same way that Bolshevism has done
in Russia. Perhaps that may be possible, although the state of

[45] The Aventine opposition have all been scattered in exile or are held
as hostages.   Only Giolitti and three followers have remained in the
chamber.
[46] British Fascists clamored for a dictator to deal with the General Strike
in 1926. Baldwin's cabinet had the intelligence to capitalize British love
of law and order by keeping within constitutional bounds—thus strengthening his later position in outlawing general strikes in the new Trades Union
Reform Act of 1927.

political development in the two countries is very different, and even Bolshevism has not held power long enough as yet for a test. Or the test will come earlier, when the imperative need of the imperial, the operatic gesture which Fascism demands, can not be met except by war.

Leaving out of account those liberties that some people still hold to be essential to the development of any real moral values in human life, a Fascism that denies the rights of national minorities even to their own tongue, that talks in official organs of reclaiming all territories that were ever Italian, that provokes suspicion and the other forerunners of war, a Fascism that repudiates the World Court in favor of the old diplomacy of the balance of power, a Fascism that boasts of 3,000,000 effective soldiers in reserve, and a Fascism that strives to control all men of Italian descent abroad, "even," as Mussolini says, "to the seventh generation", is following the old road down which Germany went to ruin. It may prove to be very *un*economical, *in the long run.*

To threaten the preparation of air forces that will darken the sun, of 5,000,000 men to "launch" into the cock-pit of Europe between 1935-1940, "the crucial moment of European History", does not allay fear.

Mussolini's characteristic "Brenner Pass" speech aimed at Germany, and his avowed efforts to form a Latin-Slav bloc, as well as the Italian delegate's ostentatious abstention from expressing regret at Germany's first failure to gain a Council seat at the special session of the League Assembly at Geneva, all point to Italy as a chronic danger-spot in modern Europe.

Irredentist ambitions are encouraged against France in the wild Fascist press, Germany and Austria are flouted over the minority question of the German language in the upper Adige, and Albania is turned into what amounts to an Italian protectorate. The Balkan pot of intrigue and assassination is now stirred from Rome as it used to be from Vienna.[47]

Behind all this feverish "lo-here lo-there," there is a real problem from population pressure which Mussolini aggravates by stimulating breeding through every state device possible. Italy is bound to overflow somewhere, he has said; and it is

[47] See the article of H. Fish Armstrong, "Italy, Jugo-Slavia, and Lilliputia," in *Foreign Affairs*, Jan. 1928.

Fascist policy to keep that overflow Italian, if possible, by keeping it in Italian lands. Hence the endless intrigue over mandates, and the envious eyes on French North Africa. Hence also the Fascist organizations abroad which strive to enroll and regiment all Italians and those of Italian parentage, even those who have become citizens of other countries.

There are various speculations as to the meaning of his foreign policy: Mussolini has proclaimed, among other things, that the destiny of Italy lies on the sea. But he has contented himself so far with gradually building up a navy, relying chiefly upon submarines, and a formidable newly built merchant marine. He has laid his plans so as to avoid antagonizing England too early, and seems to be working out a near-Eastern policy particularly vis-à-vis Abyssinia and the Yemen, in conjunction with the present Tory government of England. Greece, under Dictator Pangalos, had been brought to heel behind its Fascist prototype, and furnished war supplies and naval aid—at a certain price, one imagines, in the matter of future freedom of action in the near-East. Now Pangalos has gone into a madhouse, the situation is hardly as clear. Hard-pinched Italy still finds money to lend out for military use and in order to strengthen its position as against France in the Balkans, notably to Roumania and Albania. But now Jugo-Slavia is ready to fight Italy over the Treaty of Tirana which reduces Albania effectively to an Italian protectorate and bottles up Jugo-Slavia in the Adriatic.

Perhaps it will be Turkey, and possibly her old ally, France, who are to be the prospective victims in the near-East. Smyrna is a tempting objective, and Italy may feel willing to try her hand with Syria, if the opportunity is afforded. As for League resistance—Mussolini does not fear the League, if it is faced with a *fait accompli*, and if the troublesome Turk is the victim. The accord with Spain, followed by Rivera's claims on Tangier, suggests a potential storm brewing over North Africa.

These are speculations, but they are not unreasonably grounded on the past history and performance of Fascism. Mussolini, it is true, has begun to talk less violently of the necessity of colonies for the New Empire, since he has stirred up the fears of France. He now promises that Italy itself will be made to support a nation of 60,000,000 by 1950.

What does Mussolini's pragmatic Fascism offer us in the way
of a test of pragmatic theory? In the first place one must note
that it has become dogmatic as soon as it faced the problem
of holding the power it had won by force. The "Fascist-Syndicalist" state is a concept worked out with the most elaborate
ideology, the basis of which is echoed by every Fascist spokesman: the nation is an organism, in which each individual is a
cell. Authority must be organic, and hierarchical discipline absolute, and the functional stratification of society accepted as an
ultimate fact of social solidarity. The state is based upon an
enforced consent; its rulers are those who are strong enough to
survive in "the struggle of capabilities". The only social values
that it embodies are survival, expansion, increased economic
activity, and the spiritual exaltation of an army being led to
battle—always at war.

The positive value of Fascism lies in the fact that there is an
organic necessity of law and order and economic peace in the
modern state. Nationalism may satisfy a real psychological need
for spiritual exaltation in Italy. Dictatorship may be necessary
where national survival is at issue. The rôle of force is that
attributed to it by Admiral Mahan in *The Effect of Sea Power
on World History:* it is to make possible the development of
morality by assuring order. A dispirited people profits by re-
gaining its self-respect as a nation.

The Greek lawgivers and tyrants came about from the breakdown of previous social institutions; first as Draco, Solon, and
Kleisthenes did in Athens, from the inadequacy of gentilic society
to a new economic setting; later the coming of the tyrants resulted from the unrestrained ochlocracy of the unconstitutional
democracies. Their function as rulers was to prepare the way
for constitutionalism through a needed discipline. Rome under
the Republic resorted to dictatorship in times of social crisis
(as every modern nation did to some degree under the stress of
the World War). But the dictatorship in Republican Rome was
a temporary necessity, resigned of his own accord by the dictator
who had functioned during the crisis. Revolution would have
followed any refusal to do so. Our own war-time dictators were
soon brought low.

Similarly Fascism has taken the short-cut of force to accomplish the unification of Italy, after the interim of chronic syndicalistic anarchy and civil war on a sporadic scale. Opinions may differ as to the necessity of Fascist intervention in the march on Rome. Competent critics feel that the Facta ministry was already showing the possibility of parliamentary adjustment; that Bolshevism was on the run, strikes ceasing to hold attraction to the disillusioned workers; that Italy had reached in late 1922, a position that France has just attained in 1926, where political groups were faced with a situation so desperate as to call forth a ministry of national union. I do not myself think that this point had been reached in 1922 but I believe that it would have been reached without the Fascist *coup d'état* and with far less danger of ultimate catastrophe.

De Stefani's financial measures were merely a continuation of drastic reforms undertaken by the earlier ministries. To date the balanced budget of Fascism has been attained by shifting the burden through indirect taxation to the consumer, at the cost of increasing the price of living tremendously, and without touching the fundamental economic factor of an annual adverse trade balance of over a billion gold lire. The state of the treasury seems temporarily sound, but a persistent fall in the Italian trade balance shows that the remedy is not to be obtained merely by Fascist pressure to increase production. In a land deprived of coal and iron, an industrialization built up about a highly protected heavy industry is artificial in the extreme.[48]

Even if one agrees to mythical heights of heroic salvation accomplished by the "march on Rome" and its consequences, the test of Fascism lies in its ability to fill Italians with more lasting spiritual values than the intoxication of *Roma rediviva*, and dreams of conquest. There is little in the Italy of Fascism, filled with police spies, censorship, and bludgeons, to suggest an elevation of moral stature.

Mussolini has fulfilled, as far as he could be expected to do so, the immediate organic demands of Italy. Economically as well as politically he is likely to suffer from that "vaulting ambition that o'erleaps itself and falls on the other side." Law and order are not ends in themselves. Their too exclusive wor-

[48] See Appendix B and contrast Volpi's statement and the *Carta del Lavoro* (*International Conciliation*, Nov. 1927).

ship means the spiritual regimentation of human life to the service of economic values alone. Unless Fascism constitutionalizes its methods of government, and returns to a responsibility less profoundly demagogic than that of theatrical appeal to cover its use of authority, it will fail to consolidate its gains, and render Italy spiritually a sicker nation than ever. Dictatorship can not forever distract attention from internal failure by foreign "alarums and excursions".

PART IV

THE GROUP AS A CO-ORGANISM

"The group in other words is the embodiment of the differences in the behavior of individuals as group members from their behavior as isolated persons."

"Thus the group is neither an organism nor a phantom. It is an entity which, although composed of individuals, is not only abstractly but concretely distinct from the individuals concerned as non-group members. In short, although the group is created by individuals it, in part at least, recreates the individual. . . . It is the embodiment of the process by which the ever-present and ineradicable self-interest of human beings is slowly permeated by the broader feelings which in the finest individuals grows into loyalty and unselfishness."

E. R. A. SELIGMAN, "The Social Theory of Fiscal Science," Part 1. *Political Science Quarterly*, Vol. XLI, No. 2. (June, 1926.)

CHAPTER XII

THE CO-ORGANIC CONCEPTION OF THE NATURE OF GROUPS *

Any constructive theory of the state which proposes to do justice both to the pragmatic and idealistic nature of experience must test its theory that there are both organic and purposive elements in the make-up of the state, as well as other groups. What is the nature of what we call a *group?* What are its limits? Is it completely organic in structure? Is it purposive? Or both? Can it be said to possess a personality distinct from the personalities of its organized members? Has it in a real sense a mind, a will, and feelings of its own? Can a group be held to be a real moral agent equally in the eyes of the law and in our conception of what constitutes ultimate moral responsibility? Do groups vary too greatly to permit any general answers to these questions either for states or other forms of association? These questions constitute the issue upon which pragmatic political theory has so far divided, though there was a substantial agreement in its pluralistic attack on parliamentarism and on unitary legal sovereignty. Before proceeding to a consideration of the contribution its criticism has made, the positive problem must be faced.

Upon the satisfactory treatment of this problem indeed depends what is perhaps the most far-reaching issue in modern political theory: syndicalism and Fascism divide diametrically as to the function of the state, the former holding it to a position of equality with other groups, the latter treating it as organically absolute. The same questions are demanding solution in all the kindred social studies: in social psychology, in economics, in ethics, in jurisprudence perhaps most pressingly of all, because of

* This essay, in its original form, was awarded the James Hall Essay prize at Balliol in 1921. Acknowledgments are due to the donor of the prize and to the Master of Balliol for permission to withhold its publication until it had reached its present state.

the very immediately important practical aspects that the answers must take on.

How stubbornly the notion of the organic character of group life persists in spite of its many deaths at the hands of critics let contemporary social thinking witness. It is in vain that we reslay the slain. The ghost will not be laid. May there not be some reality which this persistent concept is attempting to describe?

Supposing association for ends of an abiding nature, like those which exist as the *raisons d'être* of states, to possess some common characteristics, what part of the group life is due to economic motivation? What to ethical? How can we explain the psychological entity resulting from association for a common end? In terms of collective representations? Of imitation and like-mindedness? Or of a resulting organic unity and moral personality constituted by a real group will and mind?

In the following discussion I have attempted to show that a normative theory of the relation of individuals to groups, and of groups to each other (including states) depends upon a proper relationship of the economic aspects of the group to its ethical purpose, as well as in relation to its members and to other groups. To make clear at the outset the use of terms: I have started out with Croce's meaning of the ethical and the economic aspects of the practical activity as given in his *Filosofia della pratica*. But I have in the course of the argument broadened the meaning of economic activity from being merely a calculus of efficient means to individual ends by showing that "the economic activity" of group life properly includes what I have called the group's organic aspect: the necessary adjustment of the group through efficient structural organization to meet the given environment in which it exists. Political science as a pure science of technique is occupied with this aspect of the problem of groups. Political theory must consider both aspects as they are inter-related.

We may start out by limiting the use of the term *groups* to enduring forms of association which show a defined structural quality and a division of function, better to accomplish commonly felt needs. The structural organization may be of varying development, but there must be a basic psychological unity in the shared feeling of a common group end, an enduring and shared value.

Every highly organized group, therefore, represents two types of consensus in the ends of its members: first, an organic consensus as to the means of economic activity and the structural organization necessary to the realization of the group end. Cournot has called this the mechanical side of associational life. But it is organic rather than mechanical, for it is concerned not only with the internal problem of technique, but also with finding the complex cultural conditions which determine the survival of the group as a social unit. Second, a moral consensus as to a common value or purpose for which the group stands. To this extent every group has both an economic and a moral (an organic and a purposive) aspect: it must work (1) with the economic (or given) conditions of a socially inherited context, through an organized, functional structure. This organic side of group life consists in a problem of efficient structural adjustment to its environment; it is obviously analogous to the biological functioning and context of an organism. But (2) because the group is a human group, it can and does attempt to bring whatever of leadership and intelligent coöperation exists within its range of attraction to the service of a purposive group end that shapes the structure of the group so far as purpose can control environmental factors. The proper combination of the two elements is the essential problem of politics. I have ventured to suggest for describing this character of groups the term *co-organism,* a term whose defensibility can best be investigated after preliminary examination of the present terminology of group life which is in use among the social sciences. The two elements are interfused in a co-organism as they are in human personality, except that the reciprocal reaction of the economic *given* with the purposive *ought,* never is bound into a functional solidarity in the group that results in a super-personality, conscious of only one individuality as human personality is conscious of its own unity.

The economic element of efficient technique may, indeed, be separated for descriptive simplicity of analysis from the morally purposive element. That is the justification of economics as a science and of politics as a science for the state as a group. As a matter of fact, it is never so separated in the actual life of a group. The cultural totality of group life includes both the active shaping purpose and the limited and restricting malleability of the context as it is acted upon by the functional structure of the group.

A. THE NATURE OF THE CONSTITUTIONAL STATE AS A GROUP AMONG OTHER GROUPS

A constitutional state is the product of a national community of political purpose as to the ethical ends of political association. In a written constitution this element is to be found partly in the preamble and the Bill of Rights; but partly, as in the unwritten, in the usages and the traditional spirit of the constitution. As purpose must work with a given context, politics must deal first of all with the possibilities of institutions and human dispositions and with the environmental facts at hand. These facts are infused with a social heritage of past purposes, and transformed to new meanings by purpose presently operative. But there is a stubborn limit on Utopias: the state must survive among other states and it must assure law and order by an efficient adjustment of representative government to social forces and economic needs.

A nation has only a juridical birth as a state. Its cultural birth is slower, less definite, a precedent condition to successful statehood. It becomes a state when it assumes a constitutionally defined form. In this sense the constitution is, as the Greeks insisted, the life as well as the form of the state. The state can not be created by a fiat of a few wills *ex nihilo*. The "founding fathers", like the great legislators of antiquity, could do no more than find a workable organization to fit the economic needs and the given possibilities of an already existing institutional order into a purposive development which would thenceforth command general assent and inspire a purposively organic loyalty. The development of a nation into continued unity depends upon the maintenance of a shared cultural purpose capable of translating all economic forces into a constitutional community that fits the new areas of group life into federal spheres. When territorial areas are not susceptible of limitation from without by the community of all the members, they achieve definition into statehood of their own, as the British Self-Governing Dominions have outgrown Imperial control. When the communities of group life are not territorial but based on class or economic lines the breakdown of the national community as a superior and limiting basis of law means the bankruptcy of the state's sovereignty and probable revolution.

Organic activity, taken out of this cultural context for purposes of analysis, is the activity rooted in necessity. It concerns itself with the necessary adjustment of means to ends—treating the ends as given. It concerns itself with technique, with efficiency, with functional adequacy of adjustment. But it can not, unless it is erected into a false moral end of its own (as Mr. Dewey's Instrumentalism tends to consider it) escape the critical shaping of moral values which are not concerned with survival or even with productive efficiency, or organic smoothness of function *as ends in themselves.* The moral values which shape group purposes are concerned with economic organization, with survival, with smooth adjustment, only as this technique is brought to bear in making the Aristotelian good life more possible. The proper function of economics and politics as sciences is the shaping of this technique. The function of ethics is a criticism of the values of the ends involved and of the possibility of realizing them in a given situation. The function of political theory, or Aristotelian politics, is both an estimate of present fact and an evaluation of moral ends in the light of all the facts.

The limitation of nationalism consists in the fact that the good life is usually defined in terms only of a single state, not of the more ideal community of mankind. One may make out something of a moral case for nationalism as McDougall has done in *Ethics and Some Modern World Problems.* That is in part a recognition of fact, men being the socially limited animals that they are; but it is in part due to what Plato would have called a "Myth", since socially limited perspective is often treated as a cultural virtue. The result is to define economic goods, the limits of association and of cultural solidarity in terms of the national fellowship alone. Patriotism and loyalty are thus brought to serve exclusive values, with the result that where national ends clash, no community of purpose exists which is even capable of delimiting them by law and enforcing a solution through compromise, arbitration, or mutual consent. The issues, intensified, threaten survival itself, and the nations resort to the organic test of war as the only solution. International law, unless the World Court and the League can furnish it with coercive sanctions, depends upon too slight a community of voluntary values to become co-organic. And the League and World Court can only develop sanctions as their need to limit nationalism becomes strong enough to create a consensus among the nations in accepting the limitations of the new community. It is a vicious circle out of which nations may win only as reason prevails, probably at the dictation of painful experience.

The cultural organization of a world society depends upon a conscious realization that the conditions of the good life can not be attained by an imperialistic and intensive organic nationalism like that to which Fascism is dedicated, or even by a "closed-wall" economic nationalism. The inevitable conflicts which develop out of such a system show that the nation-state can not be a law to itself and depend upon its strength to impose its will upon less developed communities, without perpetuating the pluralism of international anarchy. It is a philosophy ultimately as suicidal to Western civilization as was the city-state organism to the civilization of Greece. It would be worthwhile but not immediately relevant to try to point the moral with considerations of struggles over markets and raw materials, and even the complexities of tariffs, debt settlements, reparations, and colonies. It would be, however, wilful blindness not to recognize that for the present one can only hope for a voluntary recognition of the folly of this pluralistic international society with no effective limits on national duels. Coercion of great powers is not possible, till general consent makes the League an instrument of law. And general consent waits upon the abating of the exclusiveness of nations as cultural communities. In the meantime if the League affords only a settled means of conference, that is still a great step toward limiting anarchy.

Let us take, however, other examples of groups where moral ends are not so apparent as they are in national states. A golf club, to seize on a familiar example used effectively by Mr.

Seligman,[1] seems a neutral sort of thing, morally considered. A, B, C, *et al.* organize it to fulfil a want (that of sport) that is universally human, but not immediately ethical. Where does moral value enter? The organization of such a club is aimed at the most expeditious fashion of making golf possible to its members. Aside from incidental friendships, one golf club of equal technical quality is as good as another. The matter of its organization is morally indifferent to its members. Of course even a golf club wins the loyalty of habit and of cemented friendships, of pride in standing, etc. And in that realm moral values already begin to enter.

The commonly held end of playing golf is itself to be tested, however, as a moral end. To some men—unlucky mortals! it possibly represents only another economic means (in the Crocean sense) either to good health, to advantageous business and social connections, or the like. To these men golf is not an activity enjoyable in its own right, even devilishly seductive. As nearly as is possible the golf club is a purely economic want—as it is to a golf professional. But even with them it represents a choice necessary to a system of implied moral values: golf may be chosen as a business or an adjunct to business but as such a choice it implies an acceptance or a rejection of moral values that hinge on the choice of a business and of business methods. And so far as it promotes any real fellowship it has a positive moral aspect.

In a business corporation, the moral element may seem to be completely absent. The common "want" is profit—as much as possible—and the element of morality is limited to such observances of business usage as are considered to be conducive to long-run profits. The organization and conduct of the corporation are measured in terms of efficiency toward that sole end. If any moral scruples of methods are raised—"do or be done" is the answer. "Business is business."

There is a very real fact underlying this attitude. The supplying of economic wants, *treated as if there were no moral criterion involved or commonly applicable,* is at the basis of unrestrained competition, and of the *laisser-aller* theory of society. Human

[1] "The Social Theory of Fiscal Science," Part I, *Political Science Quarterly*, Vol. XLI, No. 2.

labor is, like all other commodities, grist for the mills of the gods of this deterministic economic theory—and "they grind exceeding fine". One has to have a Benthamist faith in the divine providence behind such competition to accept it as a Law of Nature.

It is true, moreover, that no single business corporation, unless it enjoys a quite improbable strategic position for unusual reasons, can change the conditions of its survival in the face of competition, or refuse to meet them. Therefore, where no common standards are enforceable, business corporations do take on the character of purely economic activity, susceptible only of the pragmatic test of efficiency in the scientific fulfilment of their ends as profit-making associations. That this results in anarchy, just as international pluralism does, is a matter of fact, commonly enough accepted by modern economists.

Ultimately a society in which the economic interests are so unleashed through quasi-mechanical profit organizations must develop other protective institutions and associations, if it is not to be enslaved to material necessity, or destroyed by the blind play of economic forces and the equally blind reactions of balked instincts and moral dispositions.

Our contemporary great industry, which has given rise to the most complex mechanism of credit and exchange and in which corporate activity is the typical form of production, distribution, and partly of consumption, has also mothered the social inventions of the extensive monopolistic trust, cartel, or consortium alongside the organizations of employers and of workers, the chain stores alongside the consumer's coöperative, and a host of variations upon these themes. Collective bargaining has become a recognized institution in industry. There are few employers short-sighted enough to imagine that trade-unions of some sort are not a modern necessity. Competition of a useless and wasteful sort in both labor markets and industrial enterprises has been strictly limited.

While these inventions, like the device of the joint-stock limited liability incorporation, are partly the product of economic necessity, they are increasingly coming to be pervaded with moral values. Chambers of commerce, manufacturer's associations, and business clubs of all sorts are beginning, at least, to work out

standards of business morality. The Harvard Business School
is dedicated to the making of business into a profession, and
the realization of such standards as those laid down for it in
Owen Young's fine statement of a philosophy of business for
America. The trade unions came into existence, on their part,
that men might be enabled to live under the factory system.
They have continued to develop, as Aristotle thought the state
did, in order that men might live the good life more abundantly.[2]
By imposing a moral restraint with some uniformity upon the
"wages-fund" theory as a matter of practice, as much as upon an
"iron" law of wages, they have assisted and even forced the
development of a degree of employer's morality.

On the side of the employers' contribution one may count
profit-sharing, some attempts at enlisting workers in the control
of business policy, and in general a recognition of the ultimate
economic value of high wages and of the human factors in production. Employers in the United States have been able to
demonstrate, with the help of the natural aids afforded them by
America, and its market, the economic possibility (through mass
production and efficient organization) of increasing wages, decreasing hours and prices, while at the same time increasing both
unit-production and profit. But if corporate organization has
brought about some slight introduction of moral purpose into
the realm of industrial competition, it has been through the
communitas communitatum of the state that the greatest progress
has been made in this direction. Monopolistic combination may
in certain instances gouge both unfair wages and unfair profits
out of its unorganized industrial fellows in other trades as Mr.
J. A. Hobson has shown in *The Conditions of Industrial Peace.*
The state must concern itself, both through taxation and supervision of business practices, with the problems raised.

Let it be granted that the state as umpire of the associational
life within it is to some degree a partial arbiter, as Mr. Laski
insists, when there is a question of changing the fundamental
rules of the game involved (whether the social context be that
of a capitalist or of a socialist economy). Not, of course, that
the state is the sole agent of change; still it is largely through

[2] Nowhere is there a finer statement of this development and of its possibilities than in Delisle Burns' *The Philosophy of Labor.*

the acceptance of a politically responsible arbiter who enforces constitutional rules that moral progress toward controlling the clash of purely economic interests has been made without the wasteful methods of revolution, where the choice lay between political and direct action. If the rules are unfair one may choose between political and direct action as a means of amending them—that is true enough. But direct action, whether it be frank revolution or the contingent revolution of a general strike, is, on the witness of the times, not the most really useful pragmatic method, where constitutional means of change exist, for securing a new basis of moral consent and of constitutional morality. Neither Bolshevism nor Fascism chart hopeful directions for a freer state. Syndicalism of the revolutionary sort simply makes one or the other inevitable.

The development of corporate organization both in the world that is called "Labor" and in that called "Capital", if it has afforded some protection from economic necessity, has at the same time forced upon the state the most difficult rôle yet played by political organization. For not only must the state clear the road by legislation to permit the development of moral values in the lives of the groups within it; it must frequently intervene to impose standards of value upon those groups in cases of conflict, as is the case in minimum wage laws and legislation affecting conditions and hours of labor. Even more immediate is the modern necessity, everywhere evident, of adjusting the corporate lives of the groups in conflict to the shell of economic necessity necessary to organic survival, for the state is set in the context of competitive industrial nationalism.

The free *Welt-Wirtschaft* which is the ideal of the "internationally minded" of our generation is sadly removed from the context of economic fact which the state must face. There are glimmerings of future hope in the existence of the League and its Bureaus, and in the World Court. But the dawn of a day of coöperative world control is not even faintly visible. Rather statesmen must face the tough and presently inevitable facts of tariff walls, immigration restriction, national debts, and competitive markets—topped by the unwillingness of nations to share the goods and the natural resources of which they are in fortunate enjoyment without exacting in return all that the traffic

will bear.   There is no means of controlling *national* monopolies
except by agreements, either by private agreements like the Continental European Steel Consortium and the various international cartels; or by public agreements such as are found in trade
treaties, consular conventions and the like.

These facts render utopian any program which slights them.
American labor with its more fortunate conditions may achieve
Owen Young's cultural wage.   But British labor, though it may
be just as interested in a "national minimum" fit for decent
citizens and education, and may bend all its efforts toward such
a redistribution of national wealth as would be effected by the
program, say, of the Webbs, or of Mr. Laski's *Grammar of
Politics,* cannot outstrip economic possibilities.   Therefore the
British Government, unless it can make these schemes square with
economic survival in a world of competitive trade, can not take
them seriously.   It is the primary duty of the state to assure
this organic realm of economic survival.   That is why the
exchange rates of national currencies taken over a reasonably
extended period, are fairly accurate barometers of political
weather conditions, within some limits of psychological error.[3]
In peace, as in war, the issue of survival or even of great economic distress, makes the organic character of the state prevail
over the development of freer purposes.   The condition is pathological, but it is useless to suggest the high duty of martyrdom
except to a community more devoted to other-worldiness than
is any modern national state.   Even established churches usually
prefer a vicarious enjoyment of the blessings of martyrdom.   The
program of any political party must first square with the necessity of national survival.[4]

But once the economic conditions of survival are assured, the
moral values of political liberalism come up.   If survival is the
first necessity, it is not the last.   It is a necessary means to

[3] Although there is something to be said for the other side of the question
as Mr. R. H. Tawney puts it in his fine book, *Religion and the Rise of
Capitalism:* "It is possible that the bankruptcies of Governments have, on
the whole, done less harm to mankind than their ability to raise loans, and
the mobilization of economic power on a scale unknown before armed the
fierce nationalism of the age with a weapon more deadly than gunpowder
and cannon" (p. 77).

[4] *The End of Laissez-Faire* by Mr. J. M. Keynes may be taken, however,
as showing how much of state-regulation is now necessary to a healthy
economic system even from the Liberal point of view.

the real end of the state-justice. Moral ends are at issue in the entire organization of the relation of the state to other groups, including other states. Even economic survival taken without regard to moral values would ultimately require an international rule of law over the state, as well as the rule of law within—wars being as bad business ventures as they are.

Is there not, however, a real difference in the relation of the state to groups within itself from its international relations, taken on the basis of existing communities of purpose? If the League of Nations were, as Mr. Laski thinks it demonstrably is,[5] a super-state, the difference would be merely one of degree. It seems to me that the *Grammar of Politics* overestimates international solidarity and underestimates national solidarity as orders of fact.

The constitutional basis of legal community affords, in the states which rest on firmly grounded historical unity, an obviously more adequate basis for the legal settlement of group conflicts than do the League and its appendages for international disputes. Even where class ·struggles have destroyed constitutional morality, it is not Syndicalism but Fascism or Bolshevism that has triumphed—still limited by nationality. The best that one can hope is the gradual federalization of international power.

In intra-national affairs, the state must, on this reading of facts, assume the rôle of the adjuster of disputes, where economic interests or moral standards provoke serious or chronic conflicts. Here it must proceed by determination rather than by negotiation. Its determinations will not force issues unless the need be great. But force them it must, if its constitutional sphere is seriously challenged, and in the mood with which Lincoln faced Secession. Its business is to allow the development of associational activity freely and without let, unless the developing areas of community impinge violently upon each other, or upon the rule of law necessary for fair play in group competition. Its power over them is neither absolute nor eternal, for the state as well as other groups operates in a world of relative values, in time and in space. Community of moral purpose varies in extension and in intensity in response to given conditions. Italy

[5] *A Grammar of Politics*, pp. 588 ff.

is not England. The British Commonwealth of Nations must follow a very loosely federal development for its autonomous units to fit a scattered co-operative congeries of *states*, not the centralization necessary to constitutional development in the United States. But the state as umpire remains, whether Dominion or Federal Empire, the inevitable condition of all moral development in the lives of its citizens. It must assure the minimum conditions of orderly social intercourse. It should ideally (and always to some extent does actually) offer a cultural direction to moral values which give to it a positive purpose as well as the negative moral function of delimiting group struggles. The rule of law must be realized constitutionally within the state in order to grow beyond it.

Such a theory of the relation of the state to other groups flows from a conception of the nature and functions of group life for which I propose the term *co-organic* as opposed either to the contractual or to the organic conceptions. The functional structure of groups is a matter of economic activity, to be tested in terms of efficiency, but not of efficiency for its own sake. The common ends which groups serve must fall into a scheme of moral values. The associational scheme of any political society assumes a character at once organic, economic, and functional. But the ordering of this functional realm can only assume moral character through a coherent scheme of ideal values.

Each group, then, possesses something of both aspects. What is the reciprocity of relationship in the two phases? What is the nature of the "group self"? It is hardly too much to say that all the social sciences, particularly social psychology, constitute a great theoretical and experimental battlefield on which the issue of the nature of the group self is continually being fought out. It is evident that any adequate solution will go to the depths not only of ethics but of metaphysics itself, for the problem is, as Mr. Ernest Barker has said, "the simplest and most terrible of all problems. It is the problem of universals: the problem of identity and difference." It is all the more easy, as he suggests, "to run into either the nominalist or the realist extremes to the utter loss of the facts. Perhaps the identical in this matter of groups is neither a real person nor a nominalist fiction. Let us call it an idea and see into what dim port we drift with that pilot." [6]

The truth of the matter certainly lies somewhere in the direction thus vaguely charted. At least, one feels, it has been very charmingly expressed. At the same time it is hard to forget that the charm Maitland could throw over the most technical jurisprudence has been largely responsible for the vogue won by the doctrine of the *res præter res*, the reality of the corporate person in its most extreme formulation. It is well to be on guard, then, against "the organizing idea" which Mr. Barker offers as a complete explanation of the nature of so-called corporate personality, if *idea* is to be taken in any literal sense, although ideas which, as he says in true Hegelian fashion, have a pathology, even "hands and feet" of their own, suggest a Platonic reality that comes very near the essence of group life. But just because they are suggestive of so much, as Platonic Ideas usually are, it is imperative to avoid being led too far into the lost regions of mysticism under their guidance.

For the facts of group phenomena in all their cultural aspects compel the admission of other elements in their lives and characters than the bare organizing ideas which give a conscious unity of purpose to their component members. The competition of groups involves more than the "competition of ideas," though it does not, as Mr. Barker is quite clear, involve a struggle of real personalities in any such sense of personality as is applied to individuals. The facts seem to show that a group is differentiated from an unorganized crowd chiefly because it possesses an idea of its end as a group and a common interest which is its group purpose or end. About this unifying idea of a common end, however, grow up traditions and sentiments in the way McDougall has aptly described in *The Group Mind*.[7] Under the growth of this rich background, and with it, grows, too, an entity which takes on, in its more highly organized stages of development, a character which is in many ways analogous to that of the physical organism, even to conscious personality.

The developments of the conception of a social organism and its relations to political theory are too familiar to require sum-

<hr>

[6] "The Discredited State," *Political Quarterly*, February, 1915.
[7] *Op. cit.*, pp. 69-79.

marizing.[8] Professor F. W. Coker has devoted a monograph to *Organismic Theories of the State*, and Professor Seligman in the essay mentioned above has abundantly documented the post-Comtean doctrines. The political use of the term organism has as a rule been merely ideological, although some of the medieval scholastics clearly intended to convey a mystic Platonic realism by their use of the analogy. Mr. Ramsay Macdonald has, however, in our own day used the analogy of the Organism as an apology for Socialism almost as Platonically as Mussolini has made it serve Fascism.[9]

If the group is not a super-organism, or even completely analogous to the organism of biology, it is none the less, in Seligman's words, "responsible for many subtle changes. It engenders a sense of obligation; it subordinates the feeling of self to that of companionship; it creates the idea of loyalty; in short it socializes and in this sense moralizes the individual. Through the satisfaction of common wants something new is born which is more than a mere collocation or assemblage of separate units, and which in this sense, while indeed not an organism, is yet a distinct unity." [10]

[8] Mr. Tawney, in *Religion and the Rise of Capitalism*, has made this conception a key to history. He shows the development from status to contract, from sacramental to contractual relationships in these terms: "What set the tone of the social thought in the eighteenth century was partly the new Political Arithmetic, which had come to maturity at the Restoration, and which, as was to be expected in the first great age of English Natural science—the age of Newton, of Halley, and of the Royal Society—drew its inspiration, not from religion or morals, but from mathematics and physics. It was still more the political theory associated with the name of Locke, but popularized and debased by a hundred imitators. Society is not a community of classes with varying functions united to each other by mutual obligations arising from their relations to a common end. It is a joint stock company rather than an organism, and the liabilities of the shareholders are strictly limited. . . . The State, a matter of convenience, not of supernatural sanctions, exists for the protection of those [natural] rights, and fulfills its object in so far as by maintaining contractual freedom, it secures full scope for their unfettered exercise" (p. 189).

The Co-organic theory of the state is an attempt to formulate a modern theory that combines the virtues of the medieval organic and the eighteenth century contractual doctrines, by avoiding their errors.

[9] Mr. F. W. Coker's study was published as a separate monograph in the *Columbia University Studies in Economics, History and Public Law*. For Mr. Macdonald's views see *Socialism and Society*, Introduction. Odon Por in his interesting book on *Fascism* (Labour Press) has called attention to the resemblance of the Fascist organic theory of the nation to the mystic use to which "A.E." has put the terms in his apology for Irish nationalism, *op. cit.*, pp. 146 ff, quoting *The National Being* of A.E. (Russell).

[10] *Op. cit.*, p. 209.

It is to suggest the nature of this entity, functionally arranged, but purposively limited, that I have suggested the term co-organism as applicable to group life. It is not merely that groups satisfy certain economic or organic wants and that to the end of efficiently attaining such satisfactions they are organically arranged in a functioning hierarchy of members. The wants themselves, one must add, take on purposive moral character when they are made part of each member's complex value-system. Therefore the organic character of the group is limited to its functional arrangement, to what I have called its economic efficiency; but it does not subordinate its members organically to its purposes. The *co* element of the proposed term is used to suggest the ultimate moral responsibility of those who share its life. It is a *societas* in terms of the irreducible character of the individual persons, its members. It is always to some extent dependent for even its organic efficiency upon this moral loyalty freely given. But the moral loyalty, once having accepted the group end as its own, is conditioned by accepting a functional subordination to the organic structure which is necessary to the efficient attainment of the group end. To this degree it is also a *communitas* because it unites its members about a shared purpose. The end, itself, is not static; yet it must be clearly and abidingly present as morally valuable to the members. It must therefore maintain a characteristic identity throughout a continuous evolution.

Actual groups obviously vary in their emphasis upon one pole or the other of what is not a purely logical separation of elements. Some, like business corporations, possess, as we have seen, only indirect moral reference at all. Their activities are so largely economic that they elicit very little moral loyalty. On the other hand there are groups in which the moral end so predominates that the matter of detailed organization is of little importance. A Quaker meeting or any primitive religious community is a case in point. The *co* element here predominates over the *organic*.

The function which the state must fulfil as the assurer of legal stability and economic adjustment makes constitutional morality include satisfying the organic and functional side of the state's life as a group. For the creation of a stable con-

stitution is the indispensable condition of realizing moral fellowship and consensus as to the obligation of reciprocal adjustment.
Without that possibility of *consensus juris,* as well as *utilitatis
communio*—to use Cicero's phrases [11]—the commonwealth is
merely a utilitarian substitute for breaking heads—which is to
say that it is no commonwealth.[12]

An understanding of the integration of these two factors into a
cultural entity—the organic and the purposive in their proper
balance in all the variety of social groups—is the business of
social philosophy; a similar marriage of elements in the state
must be the business of politics. The biological, the economic,
the complete environmental context of human existence forbids
us to stress the purposive character of group life, if we fail to
do justice to what there is of organic necessity in the business
of survival and adjustment. On the other hand, the economic
interpretation of thought and society in terms of quasi-mechanical determinism, is a misapplication of the method valid enough
for the physical sciences. Moral values, for the very reason of
their ideal coherence, tend to grow and develop with the act
of choosing. Group life itself shows us this process of co-organic
development by the presence of conflicting parties within the
co-organic whole that yet unites them.

How then are we profitably to study the different kinds of
groups? Will it be as they emphasize one or the other of these
two factors? That will be difficult, for primarily purposive
groups frequently shift their emphasis to the economic and
organic aspect of their lives in group crises. In the same way
primarily economic groups may become vitally suffused with
moral significance because the means to an end is a necessary
part of realizing the end itself.[13] To a communist, for example,
the capitalistic economic structures have a viciously immoral
character. He sees in them so many objectifications of false
moral values. And of course capitalistic society has manifested
an even more virulent *sæva indignatio* against the communistic
institutions of Bolshevist Russia on the grounds that they make

[11] *De Re Republica,* quoted by R. C. and A. J. Carlyle, *History of Medieval
Political Theories in the West,* p. 4, Vol. I.
[12] See A. N. Holcombe's *Foundation of the Modern Commonwealth* for an
excellent discussion of the meaning of *commonwealth.*
[13] As Mr. John Dewey shows in *Experience and Nature,* pp. 397 ff.

the good life an impossibility through an organic regimentation of personality. It strikes one a little oddly when some of these castigators of Bolshevism have nothing but praise for the even more organic Fascism.

Can we find a better classification of groups in terms of what might be called the natural history of their growth, what Mr. John Dewey proposes as a scientific study of group behavior, the conditions and consequences of various types? [14] Unhappily this, again, will only afford us differences of degree. It is a necessary part of any description; but it is not an interpretation or even a complete analysis. Its chief value lies in its insistence upon the relevance of the context of groups, their history and their setting.

Taine, in his *Notes préparatoires pour les origines de la France contemporaine,* suggested that groups fall into two general types:

"(1) Artificial associations: religious orders, commercial associations and industrial, as well as those of a philanthropic nature, etc. In these, no sort of anterior or innate engagement: the engagement is wholly arbitrary; one only enters by express willingness. First state of will.

"(2) Natural associations, the family, State, religion. In these, there is an anterior and innate engagement, sometimes (family) indestructible insofar as it is psychological. The engagement signifies tendency and desire to remain therein, duty to remain there, in virtue of a debt contracted by the benefits received." [15]

This distinction between artificial and natural associations implies that while in the first the contractual obligation is completely voluntary and revocable, in the second the members are bound by what French "solidarists", following M. Léon Bourgeois, have called a *quasi-contract*—an obligation so deeply rooted in the nature of man and society that it is unescapable. M. Duguit has turned this obligation into organic necessity of a less freely purposive type than that of M. Bourgeois' *Solidarism.*

[14] Instrumentalism proposes this useful behavioristic geneticist account as the *sole* criterion for determining, scientifically, social consequences. That is to leave out of account all the non-empirical factors of morality as Mr. Dewey frankly says we must. *Human Nature and Conduct,* pp. 40 ff *et passim.*

[15] *Op. cit.,* Vol. III, Correspondence, p. 327, cited by Bouglé, *Le solidarisme,,* pp. 72-73.

On the analysis of groups which I have offered, this organic element of society is indeed inevitable, but the form which it takes is at least partly the result of normative moral activity on the part of individuals. Economic activity is the necessary context of moral activity. But moral activity aims, as Benedetto Croce has put it, at lifting the individual and unrelated ends of economic activity into the universalized moral realm of coherently related values.[16] It is the effort of normative consciousness to apply moral direction through a choice of economic means—accepting economic activity as a necessary framework for moral choice.

The state, the family, religion, etc., which Taine treats as natural associations, like all others deeply embedded in the institutional life of a given society, are not indefinitely malleable, nor may they be dispensed with. In some form they are the necessary context of human survival. But while they are not to be dispensed with as readily as the so-called "artificial" associations, they differ from the latter only in the degree of their malleability to conscious purpose. In them, as much as in the corporations of less permanent utility, the developing moral standards of society are shown forth. The family, state, religion, nation itself—none of these are permanent moulds of activity. Their variations in different cultures and epochs are adequate proof of their susceptibility to moral development, as the moral consciousness of their individual members plays upon them. The existence of a nation, said Renan in his celebrated essay, itself implies a daily plebiscite.[17]

Taine based his distinction between artificial and natural groups upon two orders of will:

"(1) Will expressing itself by a vote, a precise action, a yes or no, by the choice of an individual. That is the point of the pyramid.

"(2) The pyramid without point, that is to say the tendencies or profound and intimate desires, which, when they are cleared up, conscious, wind up in such and such an act of will, a choice, a vote which expresses them—but they often don't so wind up." [18]

---

[16] *Filosofia della Pratica (Ethica)*, English translation by Douglas Ainslie.
[17] *"Qu'est-ce que c'est qu'une nation?"* For the vast literature of cultural nationalism, see H. E. Barnes, *Sociology and Political Theory.*
[18] *Loc. cit., supra*, Note 15.

It is profoundly true that the freely contractual element of society rests upon a foundation of institutionalized activity. We are, both for good and ill, the creatures of the past to an extent that makes all purely rationalistic interpretations of society absurd. But the significant point is that what Taine has called natural associations are really in the abstract meaning that he has given to them only social *institutions*, themselves expressive of a morally active social heritage. They limit the range of choice, but they are continually being "cleared up" as he puts it, in associations of a consciously moulded order. The family assumes legal form, and changes with the development of moral standards. The state is outlined by a constitution which is consciously developed. Citizenship may even be changed by the individual from one state to another except in time of war or in the equally organic control of Fascism. Religion assumes organized form in churches which develop both as to dogma and as to their internal polity.

The difference between types of groups, therefore, so far as their "artificiality" is in question, is one of degree. Not even these "natural" associations are organic in their morality. They assume an organic structure, and a functional division of labor. But their members know a moral freedom of choice different from that of the bees, or from even the almost organic society of the tribal and gentilic stages of human institutions. When Solon and Kleisthenes change the basis of Athenian law from gentilic to territorial citizenship, the state becomes the agent of legal protection against the absorption of moral status by other groups.[19] But the state itself is not morally absolute. Antigone opposing Kreon's decree in the name of the natural law of Zeus shows us the individual who has declared moral personality, ultimate in its right to refuse all commands that bear only the sanction of force. Socratic eudæmonism and Kantian moral personality are our indices of social progress.[20]

The dramatic conflicts between the organic needs of a society

[19] Lewis Morgan's *Ancient Society* is now highly suspect to anthropologists, but his chapters on the passage of gentilic into territorial society in Greece and Rome are well substantiated. See also R. H. Lowie, *The Origin of the State*.

[20] See Jerusalem, *Moralische Richtlinien nach dem Kriege*, pp. 30 ff. (Vienna, 1920).

and this eudæmonism form the theme of the most moving tragedies in our occidental literature. Religion may demand an organic conformity of belief as an aid to its social discipline, as the "Grand Inquisitor" did in that magnificent chapter of *The Brothers Karamazov;* eudæmonism may be willing to pay even the price of martyrdom for its spiritual autonomy.[21]

Constitutional government, arising out of a natural-rights philosophy, was aimed from the beginning at enlarging and securing the sphere of moral freedom from the organic realm whose method is coercion. It had a partly economic interpretation in its defence of the "rights" of property. It was often too savagely intolerant of groups within itself. But on the whole it championed personality against organic coercion.

B. The Psychological Analysis of Group Life: Groups as Co-Organic

So that, while we may see an organic analogy in group life, the conception of the social organism even as an analogy must not be pressed too hard or far. The locus of psychological life and the consciousness of that life lies in the separate conscious selves of the group's members. In no matter what degree it possesses the power of subordinating the parts to the whole, that power is always conditioned as a moral force by the necessity of holding it through the individual's consent. In other words, once society has moved from the stage of primitive group morality or the unquestioning loyalty of the animal herd, the individual becomes and must remain the ultimate unit of moral responsibility. Fascism and kindred philosophies of the state are merely retrogressions in moral progress, under economic pressure.

The organized group, or co-organism, resembles the organism of biology only insofar as both can be said to order their lives

[21] Professor Jerusalem finds that "through human association something *überpersonliches* arises . . . of a purely spiritual nature" (*op. cit.*, p. 24). This leads him to question Kant's definition of personality as "freedom and independence from mechanism of every sort", I think correctly, since personality must use an organic necessity to choose within, although personality actively reshapes necessity to norms as Kant thought. Professor Jerusalem himself defines duties as "social imperatives which are deep printed in the consciousness of the individual", and personality *"ein Entwicklungsprodukt des menschlichen Zusammenlebens"* (p. 25), but he admits that morality is not simply imposed by the group.

by division of functions toward a common end with a power of adjustment to environmental demands. In the case of the co-organism the degree in which it functions organically depends upon the degree in which the will to coöperate toward the common end exists in the members: final control of his decisions is retained by the individual. In the physical organism there is no court of appeal from the ruthless subordination of the parts to the demands of the whole.

The necessity of maintaining this distinction has led to a varied terminology for the description of the true nature of purposive groups. Some of the idealistic philosophers, by speaking of a "moral organism",[22] have attempted to do justice to what is organic in the structure of the group life, i.e., to the functionally arranged entity which comes into being through association for a common end and yet keep clear of the vicious tendency to biological analogy pushed beyond this point. With the same purpose in view Mr. Hobhouse uses the term "social mentality" and Graham Wallas has urged the use of the term "organization"[23] instead of organism, to denote the purposive character of group life in its corporate or consciously ordered form; and Fouillée has used the expression "contractual organism" to denote that a particular society is "an organism which exists because it has been thought and willed, it is an organism born of an idea."[24]   A somewhat vaguer although a very suggestive notion is implied in R. M. MacIver's *Community*.[25]

[22] Mr. Morris Ginsberg has given perhaps the most adequate critique of this concept from the negative point of view in *The Psychology of Society*, especially Chapters IV-VI. See also Ernest Barker, *Political Thought in England from Herbert Spencer to To-day*, pp. 62-64, especially for a typical statement of the "moral organism" concept of groups.

[23] L. T. Hobhouse, *Social Development, Its Nature and Conditions*, pp. 179 ff. And G. Wallas, *The Great Society*, p. 235 ff.

[24] *La science sociale contemporaine*, p. 115. M. Fouillée's general point of view as a social philosopher seems to me nearly that suggested here.

[25] Suggestive as Mr. MacIver's conception is (and I am greatly indebted to him for a stimulus toward the present approach), it seems to me that the "areas" or "circles of common life", which are all alike as communities, want more definition in order to be juridically useful. The attempt to turn them all into legal areas has led to Mr. G. D. H. Cole's *Social Theory* of "communes" and "Functional Representation", a political structure that would give citizens no time to be producers as well, and that well-nigh demands that man be *only* a political animal. Professor MacIver himself in his *Introduction to Social Science* has cleared up the term more satisfactorily, and has drawn sound distinctions between associations and institutions, society and state. Such a use of this familiar term, *community*, can hardly make head against popular usage.

Obviously here are several minds with very nearly a single thought; yet the expression of it is in terms dissimilar enough to throw the uninitiated into some confusion. Any of these terms might serve to express the idea which appears to be common to them all, were it possible to strip them of all traditional connotation. I should like to suggest the impossibility, though, of using such words to express a technical term when their meaning has become so diffuse through constant popular usage. What is wanted is a term which should at the same time be exact in its limitations and yet suggestive of the living entity created by group life. Many social scientists have deplored the poverty of our language for the purpose.

The term *moral* suffers particularly from the variety of senses in which it may be used; to apply "moral organism" to such an economic group as the old Standard Oil Company, or to the U. S. Steel Corporation, would be in the vulgar ear at best a humorous contradiction in terms. Mr. Wallas' term, *organization*, aside from its popularly blurred meaning the best of the lot, suggests an emphasis on the formal order of the group which is not always present, even in those groups, such as frontier communities, in which there may be a high order of group sentiment. Organization, again, is generally speaking essential to groups of any permanence; yet "organization" no more than "organizing idea" or "social mentality" does justice to the spontaneous, living force begotten by association for a common end. The power of growth, of evolutionary adaptation, belongs to the true groups. These powers may change both idea and organization as an individual changes character: witness the famous case of the United Free Church of Scotland, or even the transformation of Balliol College from pre-Jowett to post-Jowett character.[26]

As for the notion implied in Fouillée's contractual organism, it seems to me admirably to cover the facts, aside from a legacy of false suggestion which Rousseau left forever associated with

[26] Changes of this sort suggest that purpose may be moulded by powerful leaders, but nothing can be changed greatly from the level of group purpose in the long run. Jowett was the commanding figure of Balliol, but he was hardly more than *primus inter pares* among the other Fellows. Leadership liberates potentialities otherwise lost, but it must have the materials with which co-organic purpose works.

the term contractual. *Contractual* implies an element of rationalization which is absent in any contract which may be said to exist in groups of the environmental type. To speak of a quasi-contractual organism borders upon terminological absurdity.

Jellinek has noted that group life of the state, e.g., represents a unique order of being possessing as it does many of the characteristic modes of action of the organism, even of the person.[27] Yet it is for all that dependent for its own life upon the recognition by its members of a common need. They, in turn, are always conscious of existences which are not exhausted of meaning by their relations with it alone. To convey this unique character of group life it seems to me that we have no adequately descriptive term, either because usage has broken down the particularity of meaning in the words that it is proposed to apply, or because the terms in use were made to fit a false psychology from the beginning. I should urge that a real necessity exists for accepting some agreed upon word, preferably a new term, even though I am sensible to the objections which are brought against debasing further the literary currency by dubious coinages.

But it was Jellinek again, who noted how useful a purpose the word *state* served, or ought to serve, because of its restriction to a meaning which could be set apart. Unhappily no word more than *state* has suffered from a blurred usage. Would not a real purpose be served by an expression to denote the nature of the "self" created by group life? And as the word *state* has broken down in its exactness of meaning from being a word in common use, do we not require for our purpose here a new word, not a worn one?

The immediately apparent advantage of such a word is just this fresh capacity for bearing the seal of a new usage, narrowly defined to cover no more than the technical meaning it is desired to convey. It would obviously be more convenient to handle than any descriptive phrase of adequate length to define this meaning, and its composition might none the less be given the quality of apt suggestion without destroying the conventional bounds of its definition. It could be made in this way a con-

[27] *Allgemeine Staatslehre* (revised edition, 1920), p. 150, also *System der öffentlichen subjektiven Rechte*, pp. 20-32.

ventional symbol for what has been called, for want of a better word, "the group-self", when that "self" is used to indicate the organic quality of group life.

Tentatively and for the purpose of clarifying at least this study of groups, I suggest the term *co-organism*, and as the appropriate adjective, *co-organic;* in its favor I urge that it is a word whose composition does suggest just what I mean to say about the nature of the new entity that comes into being with the group, i.e., an organic arrangement of persons who act as a unit toward a common end or ends, more or less consciously accepted and actively shared by each member. The group has an organic or functional unity without creating through it either a super-organism or a super-self. This organic unity, functional in structure but partly purposive in its limitations and in its development, I shall term a *co-organism.*

The word itself is formed on two Latin roots *co* and *organum,* after the analogy of such words as *coaction, coadjument, co-agency, coalescence, coherency, co-operation,* in which the prefix means a mutual sharing in a common action—not an additional or a joining action or quality as it sometimes does. The word itself is legitimately formed, then, and it does suggest a mutual membership in an organic existence—but an organic life at once created and limited by the reciprocal mutuality of its component members. Instead of a corporate person or a group-self, the nature of the group's life principle is best suggested by saying that it is *co-organic,* not personal or organic.

But why should association not create a super-organism or a self, and why need we search for a better term to fit the resultant entity than "group-self"? This is the question that believers in real corporate personality put immediately. Once grant the existence of an Hegelian *objektiver Geist,* some absorptive spiritual essence behind the related individuals who compose the group, and the way is open to endow this spirit with all the attributes of moral personality.

From what has been said it will appear that what I have called a co-organism is indeed something more than its members taken "as a mere sum". Its unity is rather a resultant than a sum: an effect which reacts causally upon its efficient units. But to treat it as possessed of personality in the same sense that personality is used in speaking of human individuals is merely to vitiate the unique meaning of that term. Personalizing of this sort is a part of the artist's bag of tricks, especially apt for the symbolism of poetry. But the artist has always been a professional magician whose trade is the creation of beauty by illusion. Philosophy, by increasing the poetic suggestion of its terms, risks decreasing its claim to being philosophically genuine—*pace* the poetic Mr. Santayana! [28]

[28] The esthetic naturalism of *Scepticism and Animal Faith* is really as romanticist as the philosophy of William James, in its constructive phase particularly.

CHAPTER XIII

THE CO-ORGANIC THEORY IN JURISPRUDENCE

A. THE CORPORATE PERSONALITY OF GROUPS AS A MORAL FACT

To those who hold the view that only by claiming poetic license can the term personality be used to describe the psychological entity created by association for a common end, it is disconcerting to find a school of close-reasoning jurists using the term for a scientific description of fact. Lawyers, one would suppose, ought to be the last people in the world amenable to the seduction of poetic symbolism in their construction of a systematic jurisprudence. Yet the followers of Gierke, both on the continent and in England, have used the conception of real corporate personality as the very cornerstone of what is perhaps the most noteworthy modern reconstruction of juristic thinking.

Gierke himself, in his celebrated *Das Deutsche Genossenschaftsrecht*, hardly claimed a real moral personality for corporations with the abandon of Maitland, his professed disciple. In opposing the "fiction" theory of Savigny and the Romanists, Gierke was chiefly interested in freeing the Germanic law from the uncompromising nominalism which the Canon law had grafted over the older and less artificial manner of conceiving group rights and duties. Gierke held simply that there was a psychologically real unity in groups which was no *persona ficta* created by the sovereign will of the state, but a definite social entity which law had to recognize not from motives of convenience but of necessity.

Maitland went further: In his often quoted essay he held the personality of corporate bodies to be "no fiction, no symbol, no piece of the state's machinery, no collective name for individuals, but a living organism and a real person, with body and members and a will of its own. Itself can will; itself can act; it wills and acts by the men who are its organs as a man wills

379

and acts by brains, mouth, and hands. It is not a fictitious person; it is a *Gesammt-person*, and its will is a *Gesammtwille;* it is a group person and its will is a group will." [1]

Evidently the *Genossenschaftstheorie* has here assumed ethical and metaphysical proportions, as the context of the brilliant essay in which it occurs and the rest of Maitland's writings on the subject show he intended that it should. Elsewhere he has devoted a famous lecture to show that the corporation is indeed the "ultimate moral unit".[2] If this be true, the co-organism, as I have tried to define it, turns out to be in good sooth an organism of the highest development, with more claims to real personality than the individual, because it and not he, controls his decisions and subordinates him at will to its own needs. I believe it can be shown that this is not the case either in actual law or in the facts with which the law attempts to deal.

What do we mean when we speak of personality? Surely when we speak of human personality we mean the conscious self-hood of a being in autonomous control of all functions belonging to its organic nature. The conception of a person involves even more than a moral self uniting in its acts the intellect, feeling, and will, with its island peak of conscious control emerging from the sea of the unconscious. It implies in A. G. Heath's words, "not merely to be a self, but to have a developed consciousness of self; to realize definitely the existence of an outer world against which the self acts and reacts; to form deliberate plans in which the memory serves to guide and rational criticism to control the will." [3]

Let the rigid behaviorists rage; it is still an unescapable fact that for the human person the self-conscious ego is among the most immediate and unquestionable data of normal consciousness; the self is organic, too, in the biological sense of that term, subordinating every act of every part to its sole ends, but having to fit those ends to meet the need of survival. The parts have no lives independent of its life and no ends to serve save its ends. Is anything like this the case with the co-organism, the so-styled group, or corporate person? The unity elicited for corporate

[1] F. W. Maitland's Introduction to his own translation of Gierke's *Political Theories of the Middle Ages*, p. xxiii.
[2] *Collected Papers*, Vol. III. Essay on "Corporate Personality."
[3] Arthur Heath, *Personality*, pp. 10-11.

action is conditioned always by the degree of importance which the common purpose of the group serves in the various conscious systems of values that are the lives of its members. Their loyalty to this unity is not absolute; it is relative to the usefulness which the co-organism has in each case to the entire complex of purposes of the individual: he accepts its suzerainty and rejects it, in the last analysis, for the same reasons *and those reasons are ultimately his reasons, not the group's*. He may be, and frequently is, a member of several groups of a purely voluntary character at the same time. To none of them is it possible to yield his whole will, for that would mean the surrender of his selfhood.. Even religious bodies (like the monastic orders) which come nearer than any others to absorbing their members utterly, never quite succeed; perhaps one very significant effect of the Reformation can be seen in the rebuke human nature administered to the absolutist world organization of "other-worldliness". What is an effect may conceivably have been as well a cause. Surely the lesson is writ large on many another page of history that a group, be it state, church, or economic corporation, which tries to bind the wills of its members to its "will" when those wills begin to run seriously counter to each other, is resorting to the resource of spiritual ill-health—the use of force. Nor has the decline of that group ever been stayed by such medicament, even in the most heroic doses. Decomposition has set in and death must follow—a lesson Fascism might read from the fate of similar ventures toward absolutism.

The phenomenon of group life is, then, co-organic, not organic. There is not born from it a conscious self, a super-person, for its "will" is dependent upon the wills of the associated individuals, its members; it has no good apart from their good; it is only because it affords the means of realizing their goods in a particular direction common to the individuals composing it, that it exists at all.

If this be true, is the term "group mind" justifiable in scientific works on social psychology? On the whole, it seems to me that it is not, for mind connotes the personality which it is essential to banish before we can ever grip with a sure hold the essence of the group. Can a co-organism, not a self-conscious entity in itself, be said to possess a mind? Only, it is evident, if mind be defined in so unusual a way as to exclude the element of consciousness from among its necessary functions. And this is precisely what a distinguished psychologist has done, in order that he may retain the notion of a group mind. "In this book it will be maintained that the conception of a group mind is useful and therefore valid," says Professor McDougall with pragmatic logic in *The Group Mind*,[4] and a little later: "We may fairly define a mind as an organized system of mental or purposive forces; and, in the sense so defined every highly organized human society may properly be said to possess a collective mind. For the collective actions which constitute the history of any such society are conditioned by an organization which can only be described in terms of mind, and which is yet not comprised within the mind of any individual; the society is rather constituted by the system of relations obtaining between the individual minds which are its unit of composition."

The latter part of the passage was quoted from an earlier work in which it had drawn the acute attack of Professor R. M. MacIver, who had refused to accept the definition of mind offered as adequate.[5] McDougall reintroduces the passage in order to defend it against the contention that "the mind of each of us is as a unity other than that of such a system," i.e., "an organized system of mental or purposive forces"; and he challenges MacIver to say what sort of a unity it is that the individual mind has and the group mind has not. He cites another earlier work of his own, *Body and Mind*, to show that he has himself advanced the hypothesis of such a "unity of soul substance" for the individual, but he dismisses this fertile suggestion by doubting whether "MacIver accepts or intends to refer to this conception".

Surely the issue involved is a more important one than that involved by the personal beliefs of our two disputants. Does Professor McDougall himself mean to urge that a group in some way generates this "soul substance"? Are the inter-mental rela-

---

[4] *Op. cit.*, pp. 11-13. For criticisms see R. M. MacIver, *Community*, and M. Ginsberg, *op. cit.*, quoting from *An Introduction to Social Psychology*.

[5] *Community*, quoted by McDougall, *loc. cit., supra*. Mr. MacIver's essay in the *Political Quarterly* of May, 1914, and his recent *Introduction to Social Science* treat "Institutions as Instruments of Social Control" in the precise spirit that I should desire for the co-organic theory.

tionships, which constitute the so-called collective mind, "mental stuff" of the same sort as the stuff which composes the individual mind, simply because they "can only be described in terms of mind"? I believe this sort of talk results from a confusion of *substance* with the looser use of *stuff*, whenever it is used, or suggested by the trend of the thought—as it is here.

But McDougall shifts his ground to a denial of anything more to the individual mind than what he has allowed to the "group mind": "I do not know how otherwise we are to describe the individual mind than as a system of mental forces." [6] If that be a fit description of the individual mind, and if by mind one means only a "system" that thinks and wills and feels and acts, then it will not be difficult for McDougall to justify his conception of the group as also possessed of such a mind. One may suggest, however, two very serious objections which have been raised in different terms by MacIver and by others.[7]

The first would be that if the individual mind is a system of mental forces, it is a system of a peculiar order in that it forms not *inter-mental* relationships but *mental* relationship within a single self-consciousness. Now McDougall has himself rejected, in the work cited, any such thing as a unified collective consciousness in the group and he has given in a magistral fashion his reasons for doing so.[8] But he says that self-conscious unity "is by no means a general and established function of the individual mind". In defense of this declaration, astounding enough had it come from the pen of a more radical believer in the

[6] *Loc. cit., supra,* Note 4. *Cf.* the interactionist doctrine of Durkheim of the collective mind as "an organization of collective representations" similar to the individual mind in its composition. *Représentations individuelles et représentations collectives,* pp. 274-295.

[7] It is interesting that M. Duguit's theory of the organic, solidarist state yet rejects the conception of the group as a person, although he speaks of the individuals as consciously functioning cells of the biologically organic state.

Mr. John Dewey, also a believer in "group" or socially imposed morality, nevertheless rejects a group mind. "It is difficult to see that the collective minds means anything more than a custom brought to some point to explicit, emphatic consciousness, emotional or intellectual" (*Human Nature and Conduct,* p. 60). He goes on to speak of family-custom or organized habit, and political parties in the same way. Really Mr. Dewey's use of the word *habit* reduces all groups and associations to institutions. But groups are not so uniformly the result of custom. Allowing even for Mr. Dewey's queer use of the term *habit,* they cannot be so described.

[8] *The Group Mind,* chapter on "The Mental Life of the Crowd."

Behavioristic method in psychology than Professor MacDougall in fact is, he produces the facts of the dissociation of personality. Can this appeal to the psychology of the abnormal be seriously considered as disproving the conscious identity of mind in the person? The fact of the existence of "fierce conflicts" within the personality may indeed mean that the "system is by no means always a harmonious system" but it is an altogether different thing to say that it has no conscious unity. In fact the phenomena of dissociation of personalities and of the more severe psychoneuroses offer a convincing testimony that the true mind *is* such a conscious unity; for what results from such pathological conditions is the destruction of the mind, even defined as MacDougall would have it: instead of *a* system, there result *several alternating systems* or no true system at all.

It is MacDougall himself, once more, who has given us the apt criticism of his own doctrine: Dealing in an earlier work with what he has called "the cinematograph method" of describing the mental processes and its consequence of ignoring the agency or activity of the subject, he goes on to say: "We cannot, in fact, get rid of the notion of the subject by substituting for it a collection or a system of ideas; the subject is, at least, that which has and enjoys the ideas and holds them together to form one mind." But having in this satisfactory fashion retained his hold upon the active subject, he prepares the way for turning it loose in the next sentence! Here is all that is left of his warning about substituting systems for thinking subjects: "For if we recognize ideas at all, we must also recognize that ideas considered as things are not scattered about the world as loose and separate existences, but that they cohere in systems, each of which constitutes a mind." [9]

Now the question is as to whether such a system as is constituted by a group of associated individuals with a common end does create a *subject* capable of having and enjoying ideas. Granted that the mental states of the individuals are conditioned by their participation in the action of the group toward its unifying idea, does that in the least establish a mind outside of their minds, above them, beyond them, or in any way separate

[9] *Psychology, the Study of Behavior* (Home University Library Series), p. 77.

from them; or even *a mind* which acts through their minds as channels? The whole construction is the result, it seems to me, either of an unnecessary and confusing distortion of terminology, or the most unscientific mysticism, the sort which mistakes a facile and vague suggestion for divine revelation.

Towards mysticism McDougall has a perceptible sympathy but no scientific leaning, although he writes with great power of imagination. But it is of a confusing use of *mind*, not at all mystic, that I believe another grave objection to his pragmatic employment of the word may convict him. We may fairly say that his search for the subject who *minds*, so to speak, in the group, has still failed to put the Prince of Denmark among the *dramatis personæ* of our *Hamlet*. It is always the individuals who think and will and feel and act, even though they do so together. May one not ask, then, whether to speak of *a* mind which permits the group to do all of these things is not equally as inadequate to account for the facts as it is to speak of the organizing idea as the group's whole essential being? McDougall unceasingly reproaches the Idealists with the intellectualistic fallacy of assigning to inanimate ideas the living power of action; yet has he not been guilty of the equally vicious anti-intellectualistic failing of treating whatever behaves *like* an object of known character as being conceptually identical with that object?

For certain purposes this is, as he says, "useful", at least in the pragmatic sense of promoting an end already determined upon. But conceptual logic, with all its limitations, was created for the sole purpose of preventing a confusion in thought of which this pragmatic treatment of concepts is a typical instance. To see that a group acts in a way that is closely analogous to the behavior of individuals is not sufficient ground for the assumption that the group is itself a person, or that it possesses an individual mind made up by the *collectivité*. So to assume is to fall into the disposition common among the anti-intellectualistic philosophers to treat all laws, even those of thought, as a merely convenient system of what James called "conceptual shorthand" to enable us to describe. Convenience is a matter of degree, however, and that which is immediately convenient for a chosen end may turn out to be most troublesome in the long run. Shorthand notes may save time for the present operation but involve an inaccurate transcription that ultimately will render the whole enquiry scientifically misleading.

A description of mind which leaves out the unity of the thinking self seems to me to involve just this error. To say that the organized system of forces formed by group association can only be described in terms of mind is one thing; to say that it is itself a mind is another and a very different other. Mind is organic; the group thinking of associated individuals is co-organic. It is always they who think, etc., though they do so conditioned by membership in a group whose aims they have accepted to the degree at least of belonging to it.

The very fact that a society may be said to have a collective mental life, and a distinctive individuality which persists and changes even though its members themselves pass, is significant of its co-organic nature. It is the *social usefulness* of the group end which perpetuates it through generations. Members may fall away from it of choice, too, but so long as its end serves a living purpose in the common life of its social setting, so long will it exist as a group. It may gather momentum until it seems eternal and irresistible as did the Roman Empire or the Catholic Church of the Middle Ages. But when its day of use has been outlived or when it has attempted to absorb all social activity into a maw that engulfs man's whole loyalty, it has vanished so as to leave no more than a poet's wonder; or it has learned and survived because of the chastening lesson.

Dr. Rivers, in *Psychology and Politics*, written just before his untimely death, develops the analogy between society and the physical organism in reply to the objections so ably raised by Mr. Morris Ginsberg in *The Psychology of Society* by pointing out that the pathology of each is very similar. "Every case in which we are able to demonstrate the value of the knowledge derived from the medicine of the individual in the treatment of social evils adds another link in the chain of evidence in favour of the view that the relation between society and organism is not merely a pleasing analogy, but has a reference to an underlying community of nature." It is established, he thinks, that the phenomena of repression are similar and equally necessary in each case. The unity of the physical organism is not what it was supposed to be in an antiquated biology. He points his moral with the familiar phenomena of the dissociation of personalities.

Surely, however, the most modern of biologies or psychologies —and they succeed each other with a speed terrifying to a layman—can hardly deny that the physical organism, even with the complexity of the nervous system taken into account—maintains a physical unity of function so long as it survives as an organism. If the digestive system suddenly chose to take over the functions of the brain, or if red corpuscles—like sinners who would be saints—suddenly determined upon conversion into "whites", there would be an end to all that is organic. Within societies there is a constant and arbitrary change of function by individuals, and we define freedom in terms of the possibility of such change. As for the higher plane of responsible personality, Mr. Ginsberg pointed out "that the analogy between society and the organism may tend to obscure the uniqueness of the position of the individual within the social organism, with the possible practical consequence that a belief in the unity of the social group may tend to weaken the sense of individual responsibility which every member of the groups should possess." But, thinks Dr. Rivers, "this practical difficulty . . . cannot be allowed to interfere with the concept of similarity of constitution if, on other grounds, this can be shown to exist."

Is the difficulty not theoretical as well as practical? Can any such responsibility be vested in the group "person" without overlooking the facts of man's moral nature, and their logical implications in theory?

The intensity of co-organic life in a given group, like all community of interest and purpose, is a matter of degree and one that varies with the type of group in question. Loyalty to a political party is not the same as loyalty to one's kin or to one's nation; again loyalty to a stock-company in which one may be financially concerned is not of the same importance as loyalty to church or to profession or trade union. This suggests that not only is there a difference in the nature of groups which makes the more permanent, the environmental and racial, broadly speaking the more important, but that there is also a difference as between the members of the general classes of consciously organized groups, as well. Every individual becomes for this reason the center of a system of memberships which compete in certain fields for his loyalty. In the long run it is he who must decide between them, though admittedly his history as a πολιτικὸν ζῷον has made him more susceptible by what Aristotle called "nature" to some than to others. Out of their strife is sown a questioning of their respective values, however, and out of that questioning comes the necessity of choice preceded by reflection. The associational life of the individual is to some extent an index to his value system.

Ultimately, therefore, the individual must be the unit of moral responsibility, because only in the individual does there exist the true selfhood, the personality without which neither mind nor the capacity for moral action can be. If I have insisted on examining at some length the conception of the group mind advanced by McDougall, it is because that conception was arrived at in a fashion common to many thinkers who proclaim themselves in revolt against the sterility of intellectualism. In the name of a pragmatic gospel of works, they have widely adopted the method of treating the co-organic activity of associations as the manifestation of a real personality.[10] In the name of these super-persons too, they have attacked the authority of the national state, demanding that it derive its sovereignty in every individual act by the consent of groups which represent a more real life than its own, wherever there is a clash involving their interests. The volume of their outcry against the state is made up by the one insistent refrain of writers led by Maitland, Figgis, and Laski: "Let not the dead hand of tradition be laid on the living bodies of church or trade union," the assumption being that the state person is of an order too artificial to be given

[10] A typical example is that of Miss M. P. Follett, whose *New State* and *Creative Experience* have aimed at Hegelianizing the pluralism of James. Miss Follett quite correctly points out that James himself in his latest philosophical phase did not rest content with discrete pluralism. He found that the "all form" and the "each form" were not incompatible. She might have added that nothing else was allowed to remain incompatible by this amiable reconciler. Groups each have a real personality, but "true federalism" is attained by James' "compounding of consciousness"—according to Miss Follett, for the tendency to "seek others" is the nature of groups. As a juridical principle this Hegelian total relativity in undivided oneness offers no tangible outlines; although it aims correctly at defining groups in terms of moral purposes, it ignores their organic character. See the *New State*, especially chapters on Pluralism and Federalism.

precedence and power over such vital growths as religious or occupational bodies. To Professor MacDougall, on the contrary, the most real group mind is to be found in the nation, not in these other groups. His more recent works on *Ethics and Some Modern World Problems,* and on *The Indestructible Union* err if anything in treating the nation state as organic rather than as co-organic. He hardly does justice to the real loyalties evoked by other groups.

Something there is, evidently, to justify the claim that such organizations represent a more real hold on men's loyalty than does the state. Their claims might be put under two quotations: for the churches, "Man does not live by bread alone;" and yet for the trade unions, "Bread is the staff of life." Still, if the relative claims of the organizations within the state are to be weighed among themselves and even against the state's self, some more satisfactory standard must be found than the claims that they advance of possessing Platonic reality. For it is into this Realism, oddly enough, that we shall be led if we accept the behavioristic test of the nature of personality which the anti-intellectualists have proposed. On the other hand, if we start with the assumption that all group life is co-organic in its nature, we shall be prepared to test all the claims in conflict in terms of the ends which they serve. That this will straightway necessitate for our constitutional state the construction of a system of social values is at once evident. It will be in the light of Professor Hobhouse's rational social utility, with the state as umpire and rule maker, then, that the various groups must be judged, if they are to be judged at all; otherwise we must leave them to prove their right to their interests by the test of survival in a match without an umpire, what Mr. H. Laski has been pleased to call the "ceaseless striving of progressive expansion", created by "group competing against group".[11] Law is to be arrived at by "negotiation" between the interested parties, as if they, too, were states.

The contention has already been advanced that out of any such striving comes the common need of a justice-dealer which finds its unvarying expression in one form or another of the sovereign state. To escape the rulerless rule of anarchy, society has found

[11] *Problem of Sovereignty,* p. 23.

only the one means of establishing the rule of law, enacted, administered, and interpreted by definite branches of a recognized government—in its developed form, under constitutional restraints. My point is here only that the state, too, is a co-organism, and that its right to command results from the end it serves; and this right need not be tested, as our pluralists hold, in every individual act as to whether it be the result of a more "real" or more intensely expressed and held will than that of any association that may be involved. On the other hand, the very existence of the state is conditioned by the extent to which the need for political organization is created by the problems arising out of the conflict of these group "wills", many of which are so real, co-organically, and so vital to the members, that a clash means bloodshed. The state is the condition of peaceful intercourse in society, and the willingness of a community to submit even to the rule of Fascism rather than be exposed to the feudalism of a weak state is evidence of the recognition of this fact.

That this body of generally accepted law may, and at times undoubtedly does, conflict with the dictates of the individual conscience is an unescapable and a tragic fact. Law is not co-extensive with morality, though there is normally the closest reciprocally causal relationship between the two. Korkunov has given the distinction a fine statement in his *Theory of Law:* [12] "Morality is a rule for the individual, law a social rule" . . . "the latter is the delimitation, the former the evaluation of interests." Logically there is always in political obligation something of

[12] *Op. cit.* (Korkunov), p. 54. See also Stephen C. Pepper, "The Boundaries of Society," *International Journal of Ethics*, p. 421, June, 1922. "A society is a unit of co-operation." Mr. Pepper in his very interesting division between "concentric" and "intersectional" social structure suggests that the former type may be illustrated by the inclusiveness of the State, while the latter may be represented by purposive voluntary associations which group their members without regard to area. The former has the power of constraint but not authority over the latter. It can tell them what *not* to do, but not what to do.

Mr. Pepper draws the conclusion that sovereignty and morality (of the impositional sort) may be equated. This may stand for legal sovereignty. The boundaries of sovereignty are therefore the boundaries of imposed morality. But surely coöperation itself is capable of federalized expression, which may take a *political* form of a voluntary nature also. The States of the world may *voluntarily* federalize the community of purpose which they hold in common into a limited League—though the community formed may lack the sanction of legal statehood.

the nature of a social compact, or general compromise, whatever be the historical origins of the state. The politically organized community maintains a government to serve the interests of all its members as possessed of certain common rights as individuals, in opposition to their particular interests as members of certain groups. These rights have sometimes been enumerated (as they are in the Bill of Rights which forms a part of almost all State Constitutions in the United States) to include a guarantee on the part of the state of equal protection to every man in life, liberty, and property; but the foundation upon which they all rest is the power of the state to coerce, if necessary, the parties to a dispute endangering social order and welfare to submit their differences to its arbitration instead of settling the issue by recourse to violence. Rights reciprocally imply obligations, a truism as much neglected by pluralists as the converse is by Fascists.

To guarantee this reciprocity the state must monopolize force. Because of its primary function of umpire, it can not escape from the lurking bogey of force that is behind the power of its decrees. From the serious abuse of this force, the ultimate appeals must lie in extra-legal sanctions, in the amenability of government to the constitutionally organized and politically effective public opinion to which it is ultimately responsible,[13] in the last resort to revolution. Under modern conditions of politically responsible government the program sanctioned by a majority constitutionally agreed upon remains the only "will" that can be politically arrived at. Unsatisfactory as it undoubtedly is from many points of view, it remains also the best working compromise for securing stable government, when the rights of minorities to consideration are given the proper safeguards. Law exists to assure these, and to compromise conflicts that are in the nature of things inevitable, in accordance with principles of justice which are no respecters of persons, even if those "persons" be powerful corporate groups. If these groups are politically able to change laws, there is better ground for believing

[13] President Lowell of Harvard University has called this ultimately sovereign agreement in public opinion political "consensus" (*Greater European Governments*, p. 158). Mr. Walter Lippmann has outlined its function in *The Phantom Public*, although with too complete a skepticism of the possibility of a "consensus" in opinion based on the merits of the actual issues.

their cases are just than if they attempt to exploit economic power through direct action.

B. The Corporate Personality of Groups as a Legal Concept

It is important, at the outset, to arrive at an understanding of the fact that law represents only the morality of the social sanction, and not of that immense realm of moral choice which is beyond the reach of positive legal rules, in order to do justice to the fundamental difference in meaning which the term personality may have for the two systems of law and of morals. Only persons in the sense of self-conscious and autonomous beings may be said, as we have seen, to possess moral responsibility. But in law terms must be taken as historically developed parts of the entire system, i. e., of course, unless we are prepared to scrap all existing law in favor of rationalized codes taken from purely *a priori* considerations of the nature of justice, or some such conception as an automatically registered Law of Nature. Among the most basic of the legal conceptions of an historical nature is that of the "person in law"; and the legal personality which is its derivative.

"In law, a person," says Pollock in the *First Book of Jurisprudence,* "is such, not because he is human, but because rights and duties are ascribed to him." "In fact not every human being is a person."[14] To distinguish a corporation from an individual person by calling the former artificial, the latter natural, has come therefore to be considered in some modern jurisprudential theory as a distinction of very little pragmatic value. If a person in the eyes of the law means, as it is universally defined, "the legal subject or substance of which rights and duties are attributes",[15] then corporations for practical lawyers, as well as legal theorists, possess *legal* personality in the same sense that individuals do. But this extension of the use of personality is done merely in conformity with the principle of convenience in usage, in recognition of the obverse side of the truth of Mr. Balfour's celebrated retort in parliament, that he could "talk English" without talking "law". If it might be extended to corporations because they acted like persons well enough for

[14] *Op. cit.,* p. 114.   [15] *Ibid., loc. cit.*

legal purposes, there was no reason why legal personality might not be extended to unincorporated groups such as trade unions by precisely the same reasoning.

The revolt of Gierke's school of legal thought in Germany, and that of his followers like Maitland, against the "Fiction theory" of Savigny and the Romanist jurisconsults is based on much deeper objections.[16] It has risen from the conviction that what I have called the co-organism of a corporation is really an organism, in a sense biological, possessed of a moral personality not different from that manifested in the individual. This conception of real moral personality led Maitland to declare that legal personality is "no fiction, no symbol, no piece of the state's machinery, no collective name for individuals", but that the corporate body is indeed "a living organism and a real person, with body and members and a will of its own". It is not strange that accepting this as true, Maitland finds "the ultimate moral unit" in the corporation, as indeed he does.[17] Let us consider now, however, the *Genossenschaftstheorie* (as Maitland interprets it) purely from the standpoint of its legal implications.

To begin with, what were the reasons which induced sound thinkers like Maitland, Geldart, and Dicey in England, Dean Pound in America, A. Mestre, G. Davy, and to some extent Hauriou and Michoud [18] in France to adopt this view (to greater or less degrees) as to the nature of corporate personality, coming as it does from Germanistic origins? I think we may not put altogether out of mind the fact of the ascendency of the Neo-Hegelian school in philosophy, led in England by thinkers like Green and Bosanquet—so far as Maitland was concerned, at least. Still there were more obvious and more practical reasons as well. The most weighty of these was, no doubt, the unsatisfactory nature of the position in which corporations were kept by any "fiction" theory, that made their right to act in all

---

[16] *Cf.* Gierke's *Genossenschaftsrecht*, Introduction. See also p. 32.

[17] Introduction to Gierke's *Political Theories of the Middle Ages*, and *Collected Papers*, Vol. III. Essay on "Corporate Personality in Morals and Law."

[18] Nearly all of these distinguished jurists have qualified their acceptance of Maitland's extreme Platonic realism by restricting corporate personality to the realm of law, although M. G. Davy (*Le droit, l'idéalisme, et l'expérience*) has accepted the metaphysical implications of Gierke's doctrine, and has reproached M. Duguit for his failure to base *droit objectif* on this metaphysically real personality of groups.

ways as legal persons dependent upon legal "dodges", to use an expressive Americanism. The Roman Law doctrine had, as Savigny pointed out, attempted to give personality to the *universitas* which corresponded to our modern corporation by the institution of Guardianship, ingeniously seeking to supply through the *pupillus-tutor* relationship the deficiency created by the fiction theory—the theory, i.e., that the corporation, itself having no personality, cannot act of itself. Similarly English law won to the freedom of personal action on the part of corporate bodies by climbing, as Maitland happily phrased it, "up the back stairs of the institution of Trust" to what it could not obtain by way of the front stairs of corporation. Gradually, however, along with the remarkable growth of corporations in number and importance, certain aspects of their development pointed to the necessity for permitting to them wider scope for the exercise of rights almost completely analogous to those of individual persons, and for requiring of them the same legal responsibility for duties.

Together with this desire to simplify the question of corporate right and obligation by making the status of the corporations in law conform more closely to a pragmatic interpretation of their capacities for personalized action went the kindred need of finding for them some satisfactory legal category. Such a category had first of all to fit the growing complexity of functions which associations with a high degree of corporate organization, whether they had been legally incorporated or not, had begun to fulfil. The "fiction theory" of the Canon Law which Pope Innocent IV had announced and which Savigny had revived from what he held to have been its still earlier origins in Roman Law, gave way to the "concession theory" whose modern success is perhaps mainly attributable to Ihering: The law could not create the power to act as a responsible unit by granting incorporation, but the law did bestow on an association its standing as a legal person, and the law could revoke what the law had given. The medieval doctrine of the *fictional* personality had been enunciated by Lucas de Penna: *"Solus princeps fingit quod in rei veritate non est."* [19] And the concession theory agreed with this in ad-

---

[19] *Cf.* Maitland's "Introduction to Gierke's *Political Theories of the Middle Ages* on Lucas de Penna, p. xxx.

mitting artificiality of the corporate person which the prince created, created at least so far as the law was concerned by recognizing with due process the ability of an aggregate of persons to sue and be sued as one. Evidently if it be the sovereign power of the state alone which can entitle an association to corporate personality, no association which has for any reason failed of legal incorporation has standing as a legal person. It was in conformity with this doctrine that in the Seventeenth Century a body of men might be cited in contempt for venturing to act "as a corporation". Even so late as 1886 Lord Bramwell maintained the classic doctrine of Blackstone that a corporation could not commit tortious acts in the famous *Abrath vs. North Eastern Railway Co.*, in language that made it evident he held the corporate self to be the merest legal fiction, and that he found legal necessity to fasten responsibility on more real shoulders.[20]

To understand this change we may follow a trail already well-blazed by Mr. Laski in *The Foundations of Sovereignty*. The immense growth which unincorporated bodies such as churches and trade unions have attained in quite recent years has forced a reconsideration of the legal status of such bodies, so abundantly possessed of "bodiliness" in every other capacity for action. The famous Taff Vale case definitely committed English judicial law to the recognition of legal personality wherever the capacities of personality exist, as the decision held they did exist in trade unions. True enough the unions still enjoy a quasi-corporate character and are exempt from actions in tort alleged to have been committed in trade disputes, and even "in respect to any tortious acts alleged to have been committed by or on behalf of the trade union", but that is a privileged position granted them by special dispensation of parliament, in the Trades Disputes, Act. 1906 (s. 4. subsec. I).[21] The Clayton Act in the United

[20] Quoted by J. H. Laski, *Foundations of Sovereignty*, p. 146. See the chapters on "The Personality of Associations," and "The Early History of Corporations in England" (from the articles previously published in *H. L. R.* XXIX and XXX). *Cf. Atty.-Gen. vs. Great Eastern Ry. Co.* (L. R. 11, Ch. D. 449-503, 1879) also quoted by Laski, *op. cit.*, p. 141. See also Woodrow Wilson on "Corporate Personality" in W. Z. Ripley's *Main Street and Wall Street*, Chap. I.

[21] *Cf.* Geldart, "The Present Law of Trade Disputes and Trade Unions," *Political Quarterly*, May, 1914, especially p. 34 ff. Baldwin's ministry, especially through Churchill's efforts, has repealed many of the statutory exemptions accorded to Labor and the Trade Unions. Since the General

States aimed at a partial dispensation, but its liberality has been pared down by a series of court decisions, particularly by the *Duplex Printing Press Co.*, the *Hitchman Coal and Coke Co.*, and the *Coronado Coal Co.* cases. The *obiter dicta* in the last cases present a view strikingly analogous to the Taff Vale case. In the United States it is the legislature and not the courts which must give way. The *dicta* as to the corporate liability of unions for tortious acts committted during the course of an authorized strike still stands in the United States.[22]

But there is a further difficulty with either the fiction or the concession theory; if personality be the fiction of the prince, as de Penna stated, then the prince can destroy even as he has created, *à son bon plaisir*. It was, I do not doubt, a great anxiety to protect from this state absolutism the personality which he felt really existed in corporations, not as the gift of the legal sovereign alone but as a living thing, that led Maitland to insist on bringing them under the shielding wing of the English common law conception of personality. For no other legal system has ever had so basically embedded in it the full protection of

Strike the Chancellor of the Exchequer has forced through a bill to prevent civil servants from affiliation with the Congress of Trade Unions, to make picketing illegal, to outlaw general strikes, and deprive labor of political levies made in blanket fashion through the Union. *Cf. Duplex Printing Press Co. vs. Deering*, 254 U. S. 443 (1921) ; *Hitchman Coal and Coke Co. vs. Mitchel*, 245 U. S. 229, 65 (1917) in the United States, and Francis Sayre, *Cases on Labor Law.*

[22] In America, two recent cases have fixed the principle of liability for torts as a corporate body on the trade union :

The first, *Coronado Coal Co.* case (259 U. S. 344), denied federal jurisdiction in cases involving mining of coal or iron (*cf.* Hammer vs. Dagenhart), but laid down none the less as dicta the principle of corporate liability of the labor union, as well as maintaining individual liability (Danbury Hatters Cases).

The second, *American Steel Foundries vs. Tri-City Central Trades Union Council*, brought under section 20 of the Clayton Act.

These two cases are set forth in their more important outlines by Edwin S. Corwin, *American Political Science Review* for November, 1922, "Constitutional Law," 1921-1922. Mr. Corwin points out that in the first mentioned, the Taff Vale decision was cited by the Supreme Court in its decision. Since the Debs case (158 U. S. 564) "government by injunction" had been tried and found wanting as a means of coping with the labor unions as unincorporated bodies. These two decisions mean an escape from that unhappy effort :

"Unquestionably these two decisions signalize a new era in the effort to extend the rule of law into the field of industrial controversy," says Mr. Corwin (p. 628). "Government by injunction which sprang full panoplied from the judicial bosom in the Debs case has not proved a success in all respects ; yet the only tolerable escape from it is the one which the Coronado decision opens up, to wit legal responsibility on the part of organized labor."

personal liberty and the safeguarding of those rights to unhindered self-development that liberalism holds to be essential to social health. The Scotch Free Church Case is an example of just what Maitland wished to avoid; he said of the decision of the House of Lords which held that the Church had not the right to alter its original articles, that it was "the dead hand being laid upon the living body with a resounding slap", for he saw in the Church something more than a mechanism with the stamp of the Crown upon it.

It is apparent in such cases as this that there is an injustice done to the nature of the corporate body if it be considered as granted the right to maintain a continuous life only at the price of remaining forever fixed in the status of its creation. Certain types of highly organized associations do develop in a fashion analogous to the responses made by the human individual to environmental needs constantly changing. This reasoning led lawyers in many instances to hold with Maitland that it was by no fiction that these organizations were spoken of as having wills of their own. Their acts were proof enough of their unity; the power to adapt themselves which these acts manifested was rightly thought of as, behavioristically considered, the very essence of will. And so, to a great part of jurisprudential reasoning, it came to be regarded as a useless metaphysical subtlety to hold that analogy in this instance was not adequate ground for assuming identity of type. The associations behaved like persons; therefore, they were persons.

Obviously, as the judicial learning of a New York judge found, they "can not eat, or drink, or wear clothing or live in houses;" [23] nor, he might have added, can they marry or be given in marriage, beget children, divorce or be divorced. These, however, were characteristics of human personality which the law did not attempt to enforce even on those beings capable of showing them. So that the corporation, in spite of escaping thus the greater part of fleshly ills, at the negligible cost of missing as well the pleasures, could generally be said to show a unity of will in its acts; and legal personality presented the only general status under which it could be reached where that will was affected. To the law, which was most of all interested in fixing

[23] *Darlington vs. Mayor, etc., of New York*—31 N. Y. 164-197 (1865).

liability, the corporate person was quite adequate to reach the individual members where their interests were common. Though the courts refused to permit in the indictment of a corporation under the English Lottery act the terms "rogue and vagabond",[24] they held that it might be a "respectable and responsible person" within the meaning of the usual proviso in a lease limiting the lessor's right to object to an assignment by the lessee.[25] A number of cases have established that a corporation may be held responsible for having been "actuated by such motives as would be malice in law, were they the motives of a private person".[26] So long as personality was for law, prior to this, only a name to express the sum of the members, responsibility could be logically treated as distributive among them.   One can detect visible traces of embarrassment in certain early decisions of jurists puzzled by the problem of what to do with a thing which had "neither a body to kick nor a soul to save".   They were, as has often been noted, inclined to agree with Hobbes: "From corporal penalties nature hath exempted all bodies politick," an opinion that gave point to his comparison of corporations in the state to "worms in the entrails of a natural man".   American law dealt hardly with individuals in the *Danbury Hatters* cases.   In the *Coronado Coal Company* case it announced its intention of finding a body to kick wherever the unions could be shown to have sanctioned tortious acts, even though they were not legally incorporated.[27]

Even after the preliminary difficulty of legal liability had been arranged, in a fashion, by attributing *artificial* personality to the corporation, still other problems led jurists to question whether the personality so grudgingly admitted were not as real as that of the natural persons it had always recognized.   Lord Lindley had in several leading decisions emphasized the fact that there was no need, as he put it, "to introduce metaphysical subtleties

[24] *Hawke vs. Hulton and Co.*, L. R. (1909) 2 K. B., 93.
[25] *Wilmott vs. London Road Car Co.* (1910), quoted by Vinogradoff, *Common Sense in Law*, p. 80.
[26] *Cf.* Vinogradoff, *op. cit.*, *loc. cit.*, note 25, *supra.*, quoting Justice Darling, *Cornford vs. Carlton Bank*.
[27] Hobbes, *Leviathan*, Chap. 22.   For the Danbury Hatters cases see S. Blum, *Labor Economics*, pp. 92 ff.   For a full discussion of the first *Coronado Coal Co.* case see E. B. Tolman, "Review of Recent Supreme Court Decisions," *American Bar Association Journal*, July, 1922.   In the second *Coronado Coal Co.* case no attempt was made to apply the *dicta* of the first.

which are needless and fallacious". But he held none the less in the important case, *Citizen's Life Assurance Co. vs. Brown:* "If it is once granted that corporations are for civil purposes to be regarded as persons, i.e., as principals acting by agents and servants, it is difficult to see why the ordinary doctrines of master and servant are not to be applied to corporations as well as to ordinary individuals." [28] Neville, J., in *Bath vs. Standard Land Co.* went as far as holding that the directors of a company are more than mere agents: "the board of directors are the brains and the only brains of the company which is the body, and the company can and does act only through them." [29] To take an interesting and important example of this idea in legal progress: The fiction theory would deny to a trade union the right to act as a legal person and hold its members guilty of contempt or conspiracy for so doing without incorporation. The concession theory would hold that only if incorporated could the union be held collectively liable for its acts. The theory of real personality would hold that the association acted like a legal person, and could therefore be treated as one despite its failure or its refusal to incorporate.

If the corporation is an organism it follows naturally that the law need not look beyond the corporation as a legal person in all questions of crime and tort. In tort this finds pragmatic justification. The corporation does indeed furnish an entity capable of bearing the burden of liability because the corporation does represent the interests of its members in all those purposes for which it was organized. In all questions of tort the members may best be dealt with through the corporate body. Both as to its rights and its duties, then, the corporation is for tortious acts personally responsible.

But the question of criminal liability involves a more difficult point, the determination of the *mens rea*, as Mr. Laski has adequately shown. Not only does law hold that a corporation cannot commit those crimes peculiar to natural persons: murder, incest, adultery, etc., but that in the words of Pollock, C. B., it cannot even "sue in respect of a charge of corruption, for a corporation cannot be guilty of corruption, though individuals composing it may." Methods of certain corporations in the

[28] Case cited, A. C. 423-426 (1904).   [29] Case cited L. R. 2 ch. (1910).

United States at least have made it clear that if it is the individuals who do the corrupting, it is as agents of the corporation that they do so, and in its interests. The corporation in such cases, it seems, might well be held liable for their acts as employers, proved to have acted through agents, on the principle laid down in the decision of Neville, J., quoted above; though the individuals concerned ought not to escape their responsibility too. The liability of the corporation, *quâ* corporation, ends with a fine, or in extreme cases dissolution; for its punishment can go no further.

It will be readily seen that if the doctrine of real personality be carried to its logical conclusion, however, the individuals responsible would be shielded under the broad cloak of the corporation; for if the corporation represent in truth the ultimate moral unit, the individual is no more responsible for his particular act than a man's hand is for the dagger thrust it delivers. Evidently then no such authority can be recognized over the individual as takes from him the freedom of his choice. To do so would be to make criminal law a futile effort to weigh various social determinants and to leave it nothing but ghosts to grapple with.[30]

Is it, indeed, possible to speak of the corporation itself as guilty of murder, for example? If so, in what degree? English and American law have generally held that it is not capable even of manslaughter as a legal unit; there is in the corporation no *mens rea* separate from the individuals who direct it, a self which can be held responsible for crime. Law, as well as morals, recognizes the individuals here as ultimate. A railroad may be held liable for damages for an unlawful shooting by one of its agents. But the ranger who did the shooting is the one corporally punishable.[31]

[30] *Cf.* the declaration of the French authorities in the Occupation Army of the Ruhr to the effect that they proposed to hold the directors of the big industrial companies personally responsible for any acts contrary to French interests committed by their companies. The conviction and sentence of Herr Krupp von Bohlen and his associates shows how a government forced to deal with the practical exigencies of controlling such corporations thinks it must proceed in order to fix responsibility. Whatever one may think of the justice of such rough and ready methods, they indicate that there are others beside Justice Neville who think that the "directors are the brains and the only brains of the company which is the body, and the company can and does act only through them."

[31] The case is *St. Louis Southwestern Ry. Co. of Texas vs. Hudson* (Court of Civil Appeals, Texas, 282 Southwestern, 257 (1926). *Cf. Queen*

Another difficulty of a similar but even more serious nature opposes itself to any attempt to carry the application of unqualified legal personality too far. It occurs in the form of the question, What acts are *ultra vires* for corporations? In the United States the corporation was, until recent decisions, held to be merely a person within those limits of action described in its franchise, ever since Chief Justice Marshall declared it to be "an artificial being, invisible, intangible, and existing only in contemplation of the law" . . . "it is precisely what the act of incorporation makes it." [32] The chief aim of the Sherman so-called Anti-Trust law was to restrain corporate action within such limits. Recent legislation on the other hand has attempted to aid corporate development.[33] In England, too, the necessity was earlier seen to be only, in Lord Bramwell's words, to hold "a registered company to its registered business".[34] Though Common Law Corporations (those created by Charter from the Crown) have all the contractual capacity of individuals, it was held in the famous Ashbury Railway Carriage Company case that they must not go outside the purpose for which they were chartered.[35] Even when a very wide latitude of interpretation is allowed for the scope of acts incidental to the purpose of the company, it is at once evident, as another leading decision put it, that, "Where a corporation has been created for the purpose of carrying on a particular trade, or making a railway from one place to another, and it attempts to substitute another trade, or to make its railway to another place, the objection is to its entire want of power for the new purpose; its life and functions are the creation of the legislature and they do not exist for any

vs. Great Western Laundry Co., 13 Manitoba Rep. 66 (1900), cited by Laski, *op. cit.*, p. 155 n. and a recent New Jersey case in which a corporation was held liable criminally for manslaughter and punished by a heavy fine. 90 N. J., 372; see also 92 N. J., 261, and 94 N. J., 171.

[32] *Dartmouth College vs. Woodward*, 4 Wheaton, U. S. 518-636, 1819.

[33] The Clayton Act (1914), The Webb-Pomerene Act (1919), and The Esch-Cummins Railway Transportation Act (1920). *Cf.* M. Ed. Lambert, *Le gouvernement des juges et la lutte contre la legislation sociale aux États Unis*, however, for the "elimination by construction" of the more rigid features of the Sherman Law as a weapon against the trusts (p. 140). The ineffectuality of the Clayton Act as a charter for Labor is well pointed out by S. Blum in *Labor Economics*.

[34] *Atty.-Gen. vs. Great Eastern Ry. Co.*, L. R. 11, Ch. D., 449-503 (1879).

[35] *Cf.* Vinogradoff, *Common Sense in Law*, p. 80, and *Ashbury Ry. Carriage vs. Riche*, L. R. 7 H. L. 653 (1875).

other than the specified purpose. For any other the members are merely unincorporated individuals." English business still complains of being hampered by a too narrow construction of charters.[36]

However, if no such distinctions be drawn, how is law, after all, to decide what groups are corporate persons, where "bodiliness" begins or ends? What limits can it put upon corporate activity? These very real difficulties, the determination of the *mens rea* and questions of what is *ultra vires*, constitute what seem to me permanent grounds for refusing to the corporation even unqualified *legal* personality; for though a corporation may express a consensus of wills which is a social reality and may possess a united entity which demands legal consideration, it exists for only those purposes toward which its members created it; and these purposes are of necessity limited in a way that the individual's are not. The distinction implied in *"artificial"* personality turns out to be useful, after all. As for granting to the corporation full moral personality, that is still wider of the mark. Maitland, in urging this doctrine, uses the fact that law has found it necessary to set up a separate personality in joint stock companies, for example, against which every member has rights. He argues that this personality is moral in its nature, and possesses the ultimate responsibility for its acts, because it can be treated as a separate entity. But consider the very example he has chosen. Is such a personality even analogous to the individual self? What would happen to that self if functional parts of it could advance claims against it, as of right?

As a concrete illustration of these difficulties, let us consider the example Maitland gives as clinching the claims of the corporation to be "the ultimate moral unit", the case of Nusquamia, any sovereign state, which owes money to various creditors: "What is it that really owes you money?" he asks. "Nusquamia. Granted, but can you convert the proposition that Nusquamia owes you money into a series of propositions imposing duties on certain human beings now in existence? The task will not be easy. Clearly you do not think that every Nusquamian owes

[36] Coleridge, J., in *Mayor, etc. of Norwich vs. Norwich Ry. Co.*, 4 E. & B. 397 (1855). The serious confusion of English law is indicated by Mr. Laski, *op. cit.*, p. 149.

you some aliquot share of the debt. No one thinks in that way. The debt of Venezuela is not owed by Fulano y Zutano and the rest of them. Nor, I think, shall we get much good out of the word 'collectively' which is the smudgiest word in the English language, for the largest collection of zeroes is only zero." [37]

Any such treatment of Nusquamia's debt seems to me to indicate a fundamental misconception of the nature of *moral* responsibility. Legal responsibility is a matter of practical convenience, and legal theory must meet that need in assigning liability. So far as law goes, it is at once easier and more practicable to hold the Nusquamians responsible through their government than as individuals. But let us not for one instant forget that this pragmatic legal personality, though it is founded on a socially real entity, a co-organism, nevertheless does not mean there actually exists a person Nusquamia who makes and contracts debts independent of its member citizens. It commands no credit apart from their collective willingness and ability to undertake the obligation it contracts. A sensible reduction in their number, through war or pestilence, would reflect itself in the extent to which their government could borrow. Its credit depends upon their known constitutional morality, or upon their habitual capacity to bear being squeezed. In the last analysis, credit is based on the extra-legal obligation which "Fulano y Zutano and the rest of them" feel and acknowledge by paying taxes to that end. Whatever the esthetic qualities of the word "collectively"—smudgy or otherwise—the principle of collectivity, of individuals' willingness to create a co-organic means for concerted action and to bind themselves constitutionally to its support by a morality which is extra-legal, is the principle upon which the entire structure of public credit is based. There are no sanctions within the domain of courts of law to go beyond the bounds of the corporation in the case of the sovereign state, and generally very limited means in the case of joint stock companies, incorporated for limited liability. Yet it is because the collectivity Nusquamia is a co-organism composed of a collection of individuals capable of wealth production, and not a collection of zeroes (reduced individually to zero only if they are absorbed into a corporate "moral" personality) that it can

[37] *Collected Papers, loc. cit., supra,* note 17.

command credit frequently incomparably greater than that accorded to an individual of equal wealth and resources. Credit of any other sort is extended only from ulterior imperialistic motives with the hope of collection by external force.

International law, indeed, does recognize the responsibility of individuals for the acts of an unrepudiated government, insofar as is practicable. Were our mythical Nusquamia to prove dishonest or recalcitrant about paying debts it had justly contracted, a concert of powers might arrange to take over its custom-houses, and levy thus indirectly on Fulano y Zutano *et al*. The same facilities for collection are wanting, it is true, among the great powers. Yet, because future credit depends upon the states' paying their debts, none of them dare repudiate their obligations. They bear even the galling burden of war debts for this reason. Nor is a people allowed to escape either its legal or moral responsibility by changing its government, wherever that government acted without fraud in what were tacitly sanctioned by its retention in power as the interests of the commonwealth. German reparations at the present time present a case in point, though one which is complicated out of any such simplicity by many other contributory facts. As a general doctrine, however, "perpetual succession" is the corner-stone of corporate obligation as well as right, among the nations.

With the creation of new states partly by the *fiat* of a general conference of the Allied victors, the doctrine has received some dubious stretching. Many of these "succession states" certainly represent somewhat artificial personalities, although they none of them exist only by and for "the pleasure of the prince" who brought them into being from the wreck of the older empire. They are perhaps no more artificial than it was. In any case, are all the obligations contracted by the "corporate person" now deceased to be wiped off the ledger, or do they form to some extent a just claim on the estate which has been so much divided among the heirs? Obviously the answer is beset in any direction with many practical difficulties, but it remains true that certain classes of public debt, from which the now separate communities have actually profited, should in equity remain a charge against their resources, even though the "state-person" in whose name they were contracted is no more. The allocation of this responsibility, difficult as it will be, frequently impossible in the face of bankruptcy, must normally proceed along the line of determining *to what extent the new co-organisms have shared the purpose which created the obligations.* Contract relative to degrees of shared responsibility remains basic to the co-organic conception of legal obligation, and it has so been wrought into the difficult problem of liquidation.

But it is not only in the matter of corporate responsibility for debt that the state-person proves itself susceptible to very important accusations against its ability to satisfy the facts as well as the needs of theory. In terms of the nation any absolutism of the "divine State" type which sanctions the transfer of responsibility to the mythical personality "higher up" translates itself in fact to something very different from the Hegelian *"Gang Gottes in der Welt"*. More near the truth is "exploitation by special interests", the prostitution of the power of a great people by all too human individuals to their own ends. The "divinity that doth hedge" the kingship of the State-Person is often no more than a convenient cloud drawn about the doings of very real persons indeed, marshalling the State's mechanical citizens from the mysterious regions of "aboveness". Until Fascism really constitutionalizes consent, it cannot escape this charge.

Apply the notion of the co-organism to the State, on the other hand, and we are free at the instant from the Fascist *étatisme* which is so impossible an attempt to revive the ghost of Louis XIV in the complex federal structure of society from which the modern state must derive its life. At the same time we escape the infertile individualism of anarchy, and its scarcely disguised kinsman, pluralistic syndicalism. Since the existence of co-organic unity is dependent upon the will of the individual members to the realization of a common purpose—based, it is true, upon common wants, but wants that have in constitutional states the moral character of ends with an ideal value—the nature of a co-organism is not exclusive, but interpenetrative. Its separation from the other associations will always be a matter of the degree to which there is a community of purposes, or a conflict. But as the existence of law is an essential to the existence of all associations, the co-organism which is the state will always have a province necessarily *about* the purposes of other associations, so to speak. It does not exhaust the purposes of the Great Society which forms the air in which it itself breathes. But it does form the indispensable condition for assuring that all may breathe that air without unjust hindrance. When the state has achieved constitutional responsibility it has a real moral claim to legality.

Because it is a co-organism, however, it possesses no geographically or temporally absolute body. The will toward maintaining its life is dependent upon the service which it renders to the citizens who compose it: the degree to which it performs their purpose in what may be called the state-direction. And that, one must remember, is relative to a complex whole of purposes that determine within the peculiar historical settings the life and the death of nations. The possibility of moral purpose is sadly but actually conditioned by an historical context of economic necessity.

What is true of the state is true on a smaller scale of the co-organisms within it. Each of them has its disciplinary rules and organic law. But the community of will which is the condition of every one is always a matter of degree, relative in the case of each individual to the purpose of moral continuity which we have seen to constitute selfhood. In some cases it may be of an intensity which subordinates every other value to the one represented by a particular co-organism, be it the fatherland, the church, or a body like a trade union. In any case where a real co-organism exists, there must have been elicited a certain loyalty, for the nature of association in which a common purpose exists begets a voluntary spirit of coöperation.

At this point we must face, however, a question of whose relevance there can be no doubt, and one which seems at first sight to demand a revision of all that has been said as to the moral and purposive nature of co-organisms, i.e., at least, if we intend to apply that term to all associations organized for the pursuit of a common end. Are there not, one may demand, certain types of purely economic associations which exist indeed for common ends, but into which no really moral quality whatever enters? Does not, for instance, the modern business corporation constitute a case in point? It operates for certain distinct ends laid down by the articles of incorporation, but these ends are purely economic. Do they not rather mould men's wills than show them forth objectified?

Does not the same reasoning apply to the state in times of economic stress? Is not Fascism the only form of government capable of ruling a capitalistic society in which class war is inevitable under democracy?

C. ORGANIC SURVIVAL AS IT AFFECTS THE STATE AND ECONOMIC ASSOCIATIONS

To take these questions up in order, what of the contention that business corporations are purely economic organisms, designed to fulfil [38] wants into which no moral purpose enters? The contention was advanced earlier that no associational activity can escape moral implications, even those most nearly neutral in their ends. It may be argued, however, that the individual can make no effective protest against the type of economic activity prevalent in a given society, that he is caught up in the wheels of a capitalist or a communist economy into which he must fit or go under. But this is only true of the prophet born out of his times, or of the crank, or the outlaw. My contention has been that where political organization is possible it permits to the individual, through party groups and propagandist associations, the power at least of moral protest against this helplessness. Unless he is hopelessly out of touch with his times—a crank, a genius, or an unheeded prophet—it permits him to make his weight felt, to share in control through political persuasion. My assumptions have been (1) that the constitutional state, in its attitude toward property rights and social obligations, reflects the prevalent view in a given society as to the proper means of controlling economic activity; and (2) that constitutionalism offers the best means of educating values through co-organizing society.

[38] The most effective opposition within business to this idea came from Walter Rathenau in Germany, a figure in many ways unique in our times, so far as a combination of executive ability with the most idealistic social vision went, or perhaps comparable to Owen D. Young in the United States. The German General Electric Company assumed something of the same moral significance under his direction that co-organized business may ideally strive for. See Gaston Rafael, *Les idées sociales et economiques de Walter Rathenau* (Paris, Payot, 1921).

There seems to me to be small doubt that business corporations do tend to assume the survivalist ethics of "natural selection"— if they are left unhindered. The state exists, in T. H. Green's phrase, precisely "to hinder the hindrances to the good life"—in other words to impose moral restraint upon the results of blind economic activity. I have already argued that other associations assist in this rôle, and that by doing so they make possible the realization of a code of business ethics, even the exhibition of an honesty not based upon policy.

There is, however, this value in differentiating economic corporations from cultural associations: the former impose only a morality of limitation; the latter propose to their members a positive loyalty to an ideal standard of right. Henry Ford and Son may claim to infuse a spirit of "square dealing" (for profit) through a huge vertical trust. They can hardly hold up an ideal of the good life as a church or a college can. The Ford policy toward labor during the 1927 adjustment was hardly ideal.

Much of the theory of social reform which proposes a guild socialistic or a syndicalistic reorganization of society is based upon the assumption that democratic administration of industry is the only means of infusing a moral element into economic organization. This assumption is equally, I think, behind the diverse proposals of the Webbs, Mr. G. D. H. Cole, and Mr. Laski. They all feel that the present organization of economic institutions limits the rôle of trade unions to that of a fighting association and engenders class war—and that feeling is at least partly justified by the facts.

It is true that trade unions do at present function from primarily economic motives. Marx's condemnation of the "cash nexus" of unrestrained competition is just, so long as labor is treated as a commodity like others. A great banker like Owen D. Young sees that as much as any Marxian. But would giving labor of every sort voting control of industry change its attitude about getting all the profit that it could? Is it not rather necessary, first, that the state, organized to represent citizens of every economic category, should be able to regulate the possibility of all economic gain? In order to limit the "get all you can" attitude that knows no bounds, the state must be able to control labor anarchy as well as capitalist. Second, is it not necessary to ask whether democratic control of industry can not be adequately maintained without sacrificing the entire dynamic of private enterprise to the hypothetical benefits of such a voting control of industry as Guild Socialism proposes? Every reflective critic recognizes the necessity of a variety of forms of production in modern society as well as some degree of labor partnership in industry, both as to profits and as to control over the conditions of production.[39] But the complexities of economic structure preclude any simple democratic solution. The structure of industry must be infinitely various to fit economic to moral needs workably. Craft unions can participate in control of transport, technical processes, and manufacture requiring a high degree of skill, in a way that would hardly be possible to apply to unskilled "gang" labor. Has industrial unionism either the will or the skill to rule? Even craft unions can hardly hope for more than the degree of partnership which Mr. Laski accords to them in the *Grammar of Politics*,[40] unless the fetish of the ballot box is substituted for the dynamic of productive efficiency that centres in the state regulated but privately managed variety of industrial control.

Laisser-faire is done, but that does not mean that Fascism or Communism is to succeed it; or that all competition is done and that Syndicalism or Guild Socialism will supply the unique technique of modern industry. Industry even under a preponderantly collectivist régime must embrace, as Mr. Laski has himself shown,[41] a variety of productive forms. Probably men in fact will remain willing to test those forms by their productive efficiency and by their social satisfaction. By both tests a high standard of real wages will not be the least criterion. If state control and high wages prove to be better attained without voting in every work-shop than with voting, society is apt, pragmatically, to choose to sacrifice voting to efficiency—leaving ultimate control to the politically democratic state. If voting in industry proves to contribute a dynamic as well as a control

[39] See the excellent treatment of D. H. Robertson, *The Control of Industry*, Cambridge Economic Series, and J. M. Clark, *Social Control of Business*. For an historical treatment of origins see J. & B. Hammond, *The Rise of Modern Industry*.
[40] *Op. cit.* Chapter on "Economic Institutions," Part II.
[41] *Ibid., loc. cit.*

it will come about experimentally, because no economic dogma can stand against the urge to increase production.

It is essential that unions should assume other functions than those of combat units. To some degree, where there is wise leadership, they are doing so.[42] To the laborer they represent a fellowship that increases individual power as well as individual self-respect. Even in the unskilled and semi-skilled lines of employment they are beginning to afford him, too, the gregarious satisfaction of club association, and the protection of the mutual assurance societies. In the more skilled trades they are creating standards of craftsmanship and are taking pains to provide adequate apprentice training. Above all there is the promise of better things in the workers' education movements, wherever they are found. Labor must be made ready to rule before it can hope even for its fair share.

If the unions, as well as other economic associations, are to cease playing a combative rôle, they can only do so through the state's assuming a rôle of its own which it has not dared to attempt under the present patchwork of a *laisser-faire* philosophy of government. The rôle of the state must not be to intervene to punish or even to threaten the parties to industrial warfare. The state must be able to intervene to *prevent* industrial warfare wherever that struggle assumes critical proportions to what M. Duguit has called "the assurance of the public services". The conditions of urbanized existence are too organic to permit an organized exploitation of this interdependence by threats of general strikes or by appeals to "property rights".

But what do "crucial proportions" mean? What *sort* of prevention ought the state to apply? Does the existence of a crisis,[43]

[42] The A. F. of L. in its recent conventions has stressed the need of craft educations, apprenticeship, and labor partnership. Even if one is not so optimistic as Professor T. N. Carver, one must admit the force of his figures on Labor ownership of industry through the investment of wages. See his *The Present Economic Revolution in the United States* and *The Economy of Human Energy.*

[43] In the New York Emergency Rent Law Cases the Court of Appeals practically held that an emergency existed wherever the people through their representatives were sufficiently roused to declare that one existed. (*Marcus Brown Holding Co. vs. Feldman*, New York Court of Appeals, 1921.) A doctrine like that would go a long way toward pulling the teeth out of Judicial Review under the 14th Amendment. It was sustained by the Supreme Court of the United States, but without reference to the lower courts' sweeping definition of "emergency" (256 U. S. 170). See also the

such as war or prolonged economic stagnation and misery, afford the justification of Fascist methods? Are there times when the state is forced to assume an organic ruthlessness, suppressing all free criticism and constitutional liberty?

On the face of history we must, I think, admit that the state does do these things whenever its survival is in question or even when it is economically too hard pinched. The League of Nations is an attempt to put a rule of law over international anarchy, in order to afford a surer basis for international morality. Until each nation can feel safe from the aggression of such realistic disciples of Machiavelli as Mussolini, it is idle to ask it to disarm. The League, shaky as its sanctions are, does tend to secure, in some degree, the basis of confidence that reposes on security from attack. It must be strengthened before it can be really relied upon, to what degree the recent sessions of the League have shown. It dare not inquire into Mussolini's doings in Albania or Hungary, and it was almost disrupted by the question of Germany's entry to a Council seat.

Even, however, if one omitted all consideration of wars as making a nationally organic morality necessary, what are we to say of social and economic crises? Under the Republic, we are told, our antique Romans used to call forth a dictator in great social crises, who held plenary powers until he had seen the crisis through. Then he resigned. Ought that to be our method of meeting crises in the modern state? It is on that assumption that the continent of Europe is being largely ruled. Is not industrial society at present undergoing a prolonged crisis, owing to the disruptive tactics of communism, and to the staggering post-war burdens of debt? Need our modern crop of dictators ever resign, then?[44] Is not Fascist dictatorship, resting upon an oligarchy of fighting, patriotic youth, the natural government for these times?

Certainly Fascism will be the residuary legatee of any such

language of Justice Holmes in *Bloch vs. Hirsh* (Washington, D. C., case), 256 U. S. 135: "A declaration by a legislature concerning the public conditions that by necessity and duty it must know is entitled at least to great respect." Similar reasoning has marked the upholding of zoning laws of the most comprehensive type as in the Euclid case (1927), 272 U. S., 365.

[44] The list of them happily does not include Poincaré. France seems to have reached a recognition of her plight that makes a parliamentary solution possible.

bad botches of governing as the old order of politicians was making in Italy, although it is in the long run the worst possible solution. Better a much more incompetent and less patriotic dictator than Mussolini, says that galled jade, the Public, if the alternative offered is chronic civil warfare and national disintegration. Modern communities depend so strongly upon the essential public services that democracy must find a way to secure them, or democracy will have been found wanting. It is to be hoped that Mussolini may have taught that lesson to those who wish to discredit the state.

But that does not mean that Fascism is a necessary answer. Democracies, decently led, may willingly tighten their belts to meet crises; they cannot safely be given a blanket mandate of all power to a dictator. Otherwise they may find that the right to resume political control and free criticism is denied; and that they are delivered over to the dubious virtues of government by an oligarchy of bankers and industrialists; or, through revolution, to Leninism. Constitutional assent may increase willingly the grant of powers to a government; but there must be retained the power of enforcing political responsibility for mistakes. Otherwise nations find themselves being led helplessly to war by the grip upon their noses which they have afforded to their dictators. It is not otherwise now with Italy under Mussolini—unless his whole foreign policy is one of colossal bluff.

England, to seize upon the archetype of a constitutional state, seems at the present moment to be in as tight an economic plight as the democratic leader of an Imperial hegemony [45] may be, and still survive. If we believe prophets like the gloomy Dean Inge, it is an open question whether democracy can through constitutional machinery afford leadership to the nation adequate to make it accept economic necessity. If it can not, the organic demands of national survival will ultimately bring desperate remedies to bear, either the swing to Communism, or to Fascism, perhaps both, one after the other. But that need only occur if misery increases out of all proportion to present conditions, and if no way is found either to recapture markets or to get rid of

[45] *Britain's Economic Plight* (1926) by Mr. Frank Plachy, Jr., is journalistic and dogmatically "American" in its solution, but the figures are interesting. For the Imperial aspects of the problem see Richard Jebb, *The Empire in Eclipse* (1925).

surplus population. The constitutional morality of England has been demonstrated as lately as the General Strike of 1926. Where Fascism or revolution would have sprung up in many continental countries, through the lack of confidence in peaceful measures, or from sheer panic, Englishmen kept their heads. It is this preference of political action to revolution that makes the purposive element so strong in England's co-organic statehood. Constitutionalism requires of a people that its organic demands must be subordinated to political discipline until reasonable means of solution have become hopeless. In the long run, it believes rightly, constitutional morality offers better solutions than those leapt at from fear.

It is necessary, then, to do justice to the realm of organic necessity in the state, as well as in other group life. Economic processes, if they are kept in view as means to moral ends, still can thwart or aid the realization of those ends to the degree that they are inefficient or efficient. Business corporations ought therefore to exist as efficient means of realizing socially desirable production, whereas under a policy of haphazard state intervention they are often neither efficient nor controlled. The critics of *laisser-faire* say that when unregulated competition is the only law, neither long-run efficiency nor morality is possible. They insist that business corporations then become ends in themselves. The criticism is a valid one. Not only business corporations, but other associations, among them the state, from time to time under unrestrained competition cease to represent an association that is a means to the fulfillment of a common purpose, and become ends in themselves. Economic nationalism requires the curb of a real League. It becomes absorptive to the point of organically subordinating its citizens.

Such periods in the life of a co-organism would be, on the reading of social health that I have offered, pathological and ultimately self-destructive if they be prolonged beyond great crises, for the very reason that they do tend to absorb the freedom of individual personality into a life that is for the time that of a controlling super-organism—a Fascist state, a Jesuit order, an army. A society in which desires, or interests, or ends,—call them by what name you will—are subject only to the pragmatic criticism of survival, or self-fulfillment, will always be a society in which groups take on, so to speak, the veriest flesh and blood. It is apt to be a society in which they have, at the same time, a spiritual life denuded of all value by a rigidity of tradition and custom that can only be called impersonal, and by a motivation that is purely materialistic. Look where you will into religious or secular history and wherever you see a group life that is organic rather than co-organic you will see a society which contains within itself the seeds of disruption. For the human soul is not content with any loyalty required of it as if it possessed no power to accept or reject that loyalty. Where its full consent is given, there it is faithful; but force its consent and you evoke the most formidable phenomenon with which authoritarianism has to contend—the spirit of martyrdom and of resistance to the death.

That is, it may be, one of the reasons for the profound spiritual apathy which religiously inclined critics discern existing in the midst of the disillusionment and materialistic hardness of modern society. "Business" has become a god, say its critics; not Baal nor Moloch was more terrible. Science, by satisfying the more immediate demands of man upon his environment, has rendered religion less necessary to mere existence. But it has not filled the void left by the disappearance of faith. Materialism is quite as basic to Fascism as it was to Leninism, although Fascism has seen fit to supplement the religion of production with the myth of *Roma rediviva,* and the religion of patriotic loyalty to the organic state. But materialism is rather a symptom than a remedy, in our present social ills. The state, if it be turned into a *mere* organism of production, either Communist or Fascist, is a monster.

The co-organic theory of associations admits readily that the degree to which the common ends of association are moral is in practice a thing relative to the standards of morality which obtain in a given society. Where, for various reasons, to gain wealth and power is regarded as an end in itself by the social conscience more or less articulated in prevailing opinion, business organizations will naturally operate on the dogma of "business first" and on the theory that "the end justifies the means"; just as what war-time feeling taught us to regard as purely a "Prussian" absolutism will characterize the state where the social conscience accepts the state as an end in itself. Only to the degree that the ends for which organizations exist become consciously and critically accepted as moral purposes by the individual members, does a co-organic society come into existence. The co-organism, like the moral personality of the individual, has its ideal side: it aims at the realization of a community, always to some extent marginal and ineluctable, between the moral aims of the persons who compose it and its own. It is never possible, as I have suggested, for the co-organism, whatever its nature, to exhaust the moral purpose of the real selves of human beings capable of so many and such various contacts with group life. On the other hand the individual is indubitably enriched by participations in the co-organic purpose which he shares with the others of his group. His values are clarified, are defined, are to some extent formed, by each co-organism of which he is a member part, and by their bearing, each on others.

Yet if what I have said about the moral ultimacy of the self may be considered valid, those values are only in part imposed upon him by the necessity of "joining" some fellowship. If the power of comparison, and of reflective choice have any meaning in our acts, then the self is continually being educated to take an autonomous part in the co-organization of society. Membership in groups is not entirely voluntary with men. It is impossible to avoid joining some. But transfers of allegiance and the dialectic of choice educate the ends of groups through constitutional competition, and educate the individual personalities who shape the groups as well as being shaped by them.

The theory of the co-organism has something more to say for itself than to offer merely another term, with a seductive vagueness of implication, to be applied to the perplexing order of phenomena that arise out of human association. It offers a way of regarding society differing from organic medievalism as much as from "joint-stock company" *laisser-faire* conceptions. Indubitably human societies differ from those of the animals, or those of the ants and the bees, as well as from those group phenomena of plant life which in their accommodation to animal and insect habits are technically summed up under the name of *symbiosis*. But at the same time they possess many of these structural characteristics. To the degree that normative purpose, subject to individual criticism, characterizes human groups we must look for a contribution which is unique from the human personality. To that degree, too, human society may be said to be co-organic, for it has evidently introduced into association something which can not be explained either in terms of instinct or habit or of both in combination. The conscious self-direction of the human person toward ends which it evaluates in accordance with moral norms always to some extent ideal: that is what gives to human groups, on a plane of society above that of the primitive, a constantly increasing purposiveness incapable of being described in terms either of mechanics or of biology.

The co-organization of society, once under way, gathers power as the complexity of phenomena (partly resultant from it) grows and expands. No *organic* or *mechanical* responses are able to cope with conditions for which they were not evolved unless they undergo a long period of adjustment. Yet within a generation of such industrial progress as it seems already possible to predict, the responses of human society, and of the human individual, must be made to conditions almost inconceivably changed. Were we stripped at the present time of only a small part of the means we have found for the transmission of what Graham Wallas has called *Our Social Heritage,* we should be put to the most hopeless difficulties, with a real danger of social break-down and retrogression all along the line. Even with the flexibility which conscious adaptation and direction gives to our institutions, we are hard pressed enough.

To escape catastrophe, society has protected itself, in part unconsciously, by means of the co-organic life of such institutions as churches, states, cultural institutions of all sorts— through which it manages to provide a continuous vehicle of transmission for the tremendous burden of knowledge and of social discipline which even the humblest individual must take up. It must seem, to the critical observer, at all times terribly inadequate to the task imposed on it; and yet, because it is a co-organic life, it is capable of adjustment to purposes that must change with changing conditions. It has an element that is in some sort organic and functional: the framework, the structural *cadre* around which the common purpose of a group is gathered and through which it finds expression. By means of institutionalized forms part of its life is thus reduced to the plane of organic action, non-spontaneous. The true significance of its activity is to be found not only in this stored-up heritage of institutions but in the spontaneous character of those acts into which its purposive nature enters, contemporary efforts to shape new instruments, for it is here that the group becomes an instrument of social progress—the expression of the moral will to coöperate. Through the constituent power to develop and to change their constitutional structure, groups possess purpose.

One must frankly admit the fact that this morally creative and directing purpose actually operates in a very small, though a very important margin of the abundant group activity which characterizes our age. Much of the scientific and technical activity of our age is devoid of moral ends. The institutional life out of which particular co-organisms grow is apt, moreover, to resemble the huge realm of habitual and unconscious activity in the individual life. Social energy is conserved in these reservoirs of experience, and the forms which co-organic activity will take may be to some extent predicted by its necessary continuity with the stream that has filled them. But while it is true, for example, that the characteristics of a reservoir remain largely the same as they were in the days of cliff-dwellings, or of Babylonian or Roman systems of aqueducts, the water supply of a modern city is a vastly different affair in its complexity and greater technical efficiency. The change there, as in modern institutions, may be scientifically regarded as due to the gradual growth in number and in complexity of human wants; but the scientific attitude which attempts to interpret the growth of civilizations in this descriptive fashion can hardly do justice to the real change involved. That can only be treated adequately by giving its due to the power of the human mind to find the means of satisfying its desires, and of evaluating them. And this power, in turn, demands the recognition of an order of normative consciousness uniquely human and moral, capable of co-organic purpose.

This is the setting, I should urge, of all human association: an eternal and universal school of morality, whose education no thinking being may escape, set within the context of present economic possibility.

What conclusions of real usefulness grow out of the co-organic theory of human associations? If the theory be accepted in its large outlines, it will affirm that the individual is the ultimate unit of moral choice, and yet it will affirm at the same time the unique order of being constituted by human association for a common end. It will deny the applicability of the term organism to the common life so constituted, and deny also the springing into existence of a "group mind" or moral personality transcending or absorbing into itself the minds or personalities of the members. Yet it will see in the association of men for the realization of a shared purpose the possibility of a moral community, and in the existence of such co-organisms the only source of authority which carries with it ethical obligation. It will not accept the economic individualism that makes of the state a mere joint-stock company; neither will it recognize in the state a Super-Person.

It is evident that this is to reserve the term personality to the human individuals who are capable in varying degrees of exercising the responsibility of self-direction; but that is not to say that the co-organism is no more than the aggregate of their wills. Membership in the co-organism involves the acceptance of its ends and the structural arrangement by which those ends may be attained. Applied to the state, this means the preference of constitutional to "direct" action. Any co-organism shapes, in subtle ways, the values which each member holds, because it embodies his interests. This inter-personal play of interests, however, is just the thing which prevents the group from ever assuming that aspect of completely absorptive unity which the doctrine of the real personality of groups maintains. The contacts which an individual must make with the society in which he lives, the interests which pull at his will, are too various to permit any set of them to dominate entirely. Insofar as he becomes an organ, so to speak, of the co-organism, it is by a consent which is far from fictional in beings who have become capable of deliberate action. That fellowship in purposive groups of a high order elicits our greatest loyalty, let church and state witness.

In the end, the co-organization of society means the utilization of the mechanical resources of structure through which energy may be multiplied and conserved, with a thoroughgoing recognition, too, of the part that the inherited and unconscious mechanism of the self must play. But it means even more emphatically that the purposive character of human groups must be recognized to the degree in which purpose exists. The first rule of constitutional states must be to permit free association in order that values may be chosen in a free competition for moral loyalty. Purpose can not be imposed on men in the long run by controlling all associations through a hierarchical state, whether its masters claim the divine sanction of caste or the pragmatic sanction of efficiency. Society can not be forced to be free—even by Fascist methods.

Purposiveness in the group context of the individual life must be aimed at as the ideal toward which society strives continually, if the social order is not to fall victim to blind forces which are generated within it. No age, perhaps, has been fuller both of the promise of a happier and richer life for humanity, and the same time of apocalyptic presages and threats of a general *débâcle* of civilization. To go back, as revolutionary anti-intellectualism bids us, to the blindness of the instincts, or to trust ourselves to the sweep of the "natural" forces which have cast up man out of their deeps upon an island of consciousness—that is a solution unworthy of the times. To yield "reason" at the behest of this mystic and revolutionary romanticism is to drift toward a shore already sufficiently strewn with the wrecks of cultures and of racial achievements. It is equally folly to apply the remedy of reaction toward "efficiency" and try the regimentation of humanity by Fascist methods. Unless the civilization which we know as European is to follow the cycle of degeneration which many have thought to descry as the law of historic civilizations,[46] the remedy for its social pathology must lie first of all in the scientific study of social ills, and their elimination by

[46] Oswald Spengler's *Der Untergang des Abendlandes*, the most pretentious exposition of this thesis in our times, cannot be dismissed with a shrug. In spite of errors, it commands the respect of historians like Eduard Meyer. Its deterministic thesis has undoubtedly caused it to treat history as Procrustes did his guests; its psychological background in the pessimism of a post-war Germany accounts, no doubt, for much wishful thinking in it. For all that it is no mere phantasia, and it offers food for some solid reflection on the forces within democracies which evoke Cæsarism. The Roman analogy is of most dubious application to the other types of civilization, particularly the modern European. But there are some indubitably suggestive likenesses.

assuring the conditions requisite to health. We have great need of those "good physicians", as Plato called them, who can tell us the conditions not of cures alone, but of social health. Our need is equally great to educate ourselves morally into the co-organic attitude of loyalty: to accept with good will the necessary subordination of our wants to community of purpose, but to insist upon the freedom of individuals to weigh that purpose in every group. Only by the protection of the rights of free moral personality can the creative forces of the human spirit be loosed.

PART V

THE CO-ORGANIC THEORY OF THE STATE

"There can never be a truthful science of government; for human pre-science can never foresee and provide for all the new circumstances that may arise. . . . Wise statesmen will always act experimentally, tentatively, and pathologically, accordingly as change of times, manners, morals, surroundings, and varying circumstances, internal and extraneous, may dictate."

GEORGE FITZHUGH, *De Bow's Review* (New Style) III, p. 377, April-May 1867.

"The demand for abstract justice is seldom as abstract as it appears. It accepts the valuations of existing society, and demands that the things at the production and preservation of which society seems most to aim, should be available to all members of society. If the demand fails, the failure is the condemnation of the ends. The demand for abstract justice is the touchstone of the purposes of any given society."

A. D. LINDSAY, *Karl Marx's Capital.*

"The constitution is the form of the state."

ARISTOTLE'S *Politics.*

"The constitution is the life of the state."

ISOCRATES.

CHAPTER XIV

CO-ORGANIC PRAGMATISM IN POLITICS

Let us set briefly the problem with which all modern political theory is faced: the sphere in which autonomy may be and should be permitted to what English political theory has termed *voluntary associations*, that is to say, the relationship in which they must stand to the state. The revolt which we have been studying, much of it aimed at curbing the power of the state over other associations, has been characterized throughout by a distrust of the ideas of the French Revolution as they found application in the legal sovereignty of the democratically organized Nation-State. It has been called the "Eighteenth Century error" to believe that the state or any other social product could be regarded as the result of a reasoned agreement among men: the jurisprudence founded upon Rousseauism resulted in reducing the individuals it was supposed to protect into a powder of equal impotency under the iron wheel of the state. The aim of the anti-intellectualist revolt in politics has been to substitute for the State-Idea a group reality, capable of giving structure to the legal mass of atomistic individuals treated as citizens only. Syndicalism or Solidarism (according to M. Duguit the two things are one), it has attempted to find a new legal unit in the group, and a new legal structure in group federalism. But through revolutionary syndicalism and its attempt to discard the state, syndicalism has been delivered into Fascist hands.

No doubt can be entertained that pluralism is a most deeply rooted growth in trade unionism. The state has not been able to claim the loyalty of labor in much of the world. The General Strike has been used even in England. In a larger sense of Syndicalism, that in which it has been used by M. Duguit, and by Mr. Cole, its significance may be seen more markedly still in the acceptance of the principle of collective bargaining in industry as the basis of binding contracts between employer

423

and employee, often with legal sanctions back of these voluntary agreements. When the London *Times* can speak in an editorial of a blow at collective bargaining being a "Blow at Trade-Unionism", and deprecate the unwillingness of a member-union in a Labor Federation to be bound by agreements made for the whole trade, the change of public attitude toward the principle of collective bargaining may be assumed to have moved very far in the direction that M. Duguit has predicted.[1] But is not the legality of such covenants still to be determined in the last resort by the rule of law? Is it possible to declare that they derive their legality from the autonomy of the groups—in this case the acceptance by the unions? That is what syndicalist theory holds, as we have seen it put forth by both M. Duguit and by Mr. Laski. But does not the existence of employers' groups as well as trade union groups render the seal of the state necessary to any juridically applicable basis of contract upon which collective bargaining may be enforced? And even under a Guild Socialist régime in which the organic unity of industry which Syndicalists dream were arrived at, would not the problem of the federalization of authority still make the state a necessity in its function of law-declarer?

For instance, in the case of the refusal of the Boiler-Makers' Union to accept the terms negotiated by the General Federation of Engineers and Shipbuilders of which it formed a part, the case alluded to in the *Times* Editorial of April 29, 1923, cited

---

[1] For M. Duguit's prediction see *Souveraineté et Liberté*, pp. 197-198, or Traité, 2ᵇᵐᵉ ed., Vol. I, p. 509, Vol. II, p. 9. *Times* quotation from Editorial April 29, 1923. The dispute, a jurisdictional dispute, is quite typical of the difficulties necessarily to be faced by any functional organization of society, making legal sovereignty as necessary for a soviet or guild socialist state as any—witness Russia. I quote also the *Times* Labour Correspondent, May 2, 1923:

"The Boilermakers' leaders assert that the executive of the Federation acted contrary to the constitution of the Federation when it concluded the agreement with the employers. In these circumstances the boilermakers declined—and the decision was approved by the delegates of the society in London last week—to be responsible for the consequences of the signing of the agreement."

For American conditions see *Jurisdictional Disputes Resulting from Structural Differences in American Trade Unions*, Solomon Blum, *University of California Publications in Economics*, Vol. III, No. 3 (1913).

The solidarism of M. Duguit is much less pluralistic in its implication than is that of its greatest popularizer, M. Léon Bourgeois. See the latter's *La philosophie du solidarisme*, and also the critical analysis of M. Ch. Bouglé, *Le solidarisme*.

above, is there not a real difficulty as to the locus of autonomy and legal responsibility which would persist under any system of economic federalism? Mr. Cole has admitted the necessity of the state as the final legal authority; M. Duguit, in the end, denies it the right to command, but only to impose command upon the rulers as a duty,[2] and upon the ruled through fear and force. So that we may say that the revolt against legal sovereignty, in so far as it escapes mere Romanticism and protest, turns out in the end to be aimed at making legal sovereignty correspond to degrees of interest. Decentralization is the key offered, decentralization along the lines of community of interest. But when this decentralization is pushed to the pluralistic extreme which would take the actions of syndicates out of the competence of the courts, or put them beyond the reach of corrective statutes, the rule of law is at an end. If pragmatism is to be taken at its own word, and tested by consequences, the result of any such pluralism as this, which Mr. Laski has in effect proposed, can only be legal chaos that provokes Fascist remedies.

Many observers, notable among them Dean Pound and Professors Frankfurter, John Dickinson, Ernst Freund and Mr. A. A. Berle, Jr., in America and Mr. Ernest Barker in England, have set forth and criticized a sufficiently evident tendency in administrative competence to be extended in practice beyond the practicable cognizance of the courts.[3] The extension to

[2] The organic theory of command is based upon a solidarity of duty conceived by M. Duguit in terms so analogous to the biological organism that he expresses it thus:

"The Solidarist doctrine considers that individuals are like the cells composing a living body, which cannot live without the activity of the cells composing it, the latter being no more able to live isolated. From this interdependence is born the natural law which imposes on each one of them the duty of working in its sphere of activity, in order to assure the vital activity of the body that they compose. It is exactly the same with individuals, members of the social body." (*Souveraineté et liberté*, pp. 145-146. The obligations of the state to *"réglémenter"* the life of society are thus tremendously increased, and along with the obligation goes an equal increase in power (pp. 159 ff.). Sovereignty becomes organically absolute, and practically unquestionable, so long as it is directed toward maintaining public services, and the smooth functioning of the social organism. There could not be a completer statement of the Fascist idea of the state.

[3] See Mr. John Dickinson's *Administrative Justice and the Supremacy of Law in the United States* (1927, Harvard University Press), and Mr. Berle's article in the *Harvard Law Review*, e.g., on "The Expansion of Administrative Law" (*H. L. R.* 30—1916-1917), p. 430 ff:

guilds or unions or any professional associations—even medical
or legal—of the same legislative finality that already causes
so much difficulty in *ad hoc* and permanent commissions would
serve simply to make an end of the possibility of legal unification
which the co-organic theory holds to be the essence of the state-
purpose. Federalization of an administrative nature, as well as
of a legislative, is a modern necessity, because of the continually
increasing complexity of social and economic structure. Our
own Federal Reserve system has hoped to find the requisite
balance in its Regional Districts. It ought to correspond to the
ordering and sub-ordering of function which the organic aspect
of co-organic society demands. In practice the old centralization
of banking power has been creeping back since the Harding
régime. But one may admit the principle of federalism as
applied to function and community of interest without extending
it to the destruction of that ultimate community of purpose
which is represented by the unified law of the state. Federalism,
more than any other form of government, demands an accepted
constitutional system of synthesis.

"As we have learned to use these commissions they have made their own
law. Put epigrammatically . . . administrative law has expanded coinci-
dentally with administrative machinery." He points out further that administrative law, because it is juristically taken, the law governing "the
transmission of the will of the state from its source to the point of its
application," has perforce unified the theoretically divided powers of government in practice through its specialized instruments. The Interstate Commerce Commission has been held to have quasi-judicial, as well as administrative and legislative powers, and to serve a special function that excludes
the participation of the general organs of government in its field. (*Interstate Commerce Commission vs. Cin., N. O., etc., Ry. Co.*, 64 Fed. 981, 982,
1894.) It was held later that the same Commission can "inquire into judicial
questions, *though not to the exclusion of the courts*" (my italics). *Missouri
K. & T. R. Co. vs. Int. C. C.*, 164 Fed. 645 (1908).
   See also President Goodnow's classic text, *Administrative Law in the
United States*, and Ernst Freund, *The Police Power*.
   Mr. Ernest Barker has treated the same growth of administrative law
and the necessity for it in an article called "The Rule of Law" in *The Political Quarterly* for May, 1914. He urges the necessity for bringing the principle of State-responsibility for governmental acts into the English Law,
and suggests a system of administrative law of the nature of the Prussian
Verwaltungsrecht rather than the French *droit administratif*.
   The fact is being borne home from all directions that the common law
system as it is at present applied in both England and America leaves much
to be desired, both as to flexibility to the particular needs for justice in petty
or technical matters and as to the responsibility of the state in the "acts of
state". But there is a necessity for keeping the extension of legal agencies
in contact with the rule of law based on constitutional sovereignty.

The great appeal which Fascism undoubtedly makes to the imagination of this generation lies in its recognition of the necessity of state-control. If the Fascist-Syndicalist state rested upon political responsibility and not upon the dictatorship of the Fascist Oligarchy, it might represent a tolerable working solution of Italy's difficulties. Of course the answer is made that its authority could never have been realized by political means: that had it depended upon votes and not clubs it could never have so disciplined Italy. There is, however, reason to believe that it could have accomplished the unification of Italy and even the control of labor disputes by relying upon political authority, once it was in power—had it avoided violent reprisals like the killing of Matteoti. A leader of Mussolini's type would have been able to hold political power by consent, although he would not have achieved the complete and dangerous irresponsibility that he now possesses through having disposed of all political opposition. Even had he failed, Italy would have come out of its post-war slump as France has, constitutionally. The crest of the wave of difficulties had been passed. The breakdown, rather than the threat of Bolshevism, provoked the desperate Fascist coup of the March on Rome with the connivance of the militarists.[4]

The virtue of Fascism rests in its organization of law so that the economic and social life of the community is assured. Its vice lies in violently centralizing authority to such a degree in the state that no other groups may claim a right to their own development. It is organic, not co-organic.

The conceptual systematization of law at the hands of constitutionally accepted branches of government is the mark of the unity of purpose which constitutes the developed political community that may be called a co-organic state. As a system, law must be made as flexible to social needs and to group interests as is possible without taking it out of the realm in which courts may test it for its agreement with the purpose of the community. One may view with great hope the development of business arbitration and the conciliation of labor disputes by advisory commissions. Federal government we may hope to see extended

[4] See Gaetano Salvemini, *The Fascist Dictatorship in Italy* (1927), Chapter 3.

both as to regions and as to functional interests, but with constitutional unity under the rule of law, where legal sanctions are necessary. Voluntary action is always preferable where it is possible.

I make no pretence that such a declaration of principle offers the solution to practical issues that must be met in the concrete instance. But I insist that it remains the formal necessity for the rule of law, and that the concept of legal sovereignty which it states is of pragmatic value because, without it, coherent construction, in juridical theory and practice alike, is an impossibility. M. Edouard Lambert has devoted a recent volume, *Le gouvernement des juges*, to the American application of this theory of legal unification by judicial control of the constitutionality of laws.[5] It may be true that we possess a judicial oligarchy. It rests, however, upon consent. Federal government demands a supreme umpire of the federal system. If judges go too far by intervening in matters of legislative policy there is always the amending system to curb their power. The development of constitutional law shows them to be responsive to any genuinely matured public opinion in permitting a liberal exercise of the police power. The extension of public regulation and control of business and labor meets few serious obstacles from Chief Justice Taft's Court.

So long as the practice of the rule of law attains to formal unity, as it does equally in the English system of parliamentary sovereignty, the co-organic nature of the State is the same. For it is to the practice of the constitution that we must look for its meaning, the theory of the constitution being no more than the expression in conceptual form of the unity of purpose really operative in all responsible government.

[5] M. Lambert has called his little volume (based largely on the articles of Professor T. R. Powell) on the control of legislation by the American judiciary, *la lutte contre la législation sociale* to show how the courts have aimed at defeating class measures, particularly labor measures—a reading of the meaning of some recent covert legislation that is not unjust. But if we are to escape "government by injunction" in labor disputes, the courts must find some other way to hold the Unions legally accountable. The *Coronado Coal Co.* Case (cited in Note 27 to "The Group as a Co-Organism") apparently opens up a new vista of decisions in American courts, for the Unions were held to be liable in their corporate character for tortious acts, and suable whether they were legally incorporated or not. For a judicious estimate of the possibilities of legal settlement of labor disputes see John Dickinson, *op. cit.*, *supra*, pp. 214 ff. and 228 ff.

The nature of the co-organic State appears in the conformity of government to this unity as it is embodied in a constitution accepted by citizens and applied by public servants. A State whose practice tends to personify government with the endowment of a non-responsible and controlling will, to treat the force it holds as bearing an automatic moral sanction, becomes organic, a Fascist state. The community of purpose becomes lost in the realization of a despotic unity of control and in the conception of the *Machtsstaat*.

But the reaction of revolutionary Syndicalism against the *Machtsstaat* has offered simply to transfer the locus of power and ultimate authority from the state to the syndicate. War between states is the translation of the self-sufficient state-person idea into the world of act. States that know no higher moral standard than that of self-interest can accept only the law of force. Would syndicalist self-interest as the juridical basis of society result in the rule of the same law of survival?

Utilitarianism is a protest usually against futilitarianism. That may go far toward explaining the solidarist conceptions towards which we watched Syndicalism steadily taking its anti-intellectualistic way. The stock Idealistic conception of the state talked in terms of morality where obviously "ought" had too scant concern with the limitations imposed by "is" for any proper understanding of political reality. The Kantian conception of "rights", inherited in so large a measure from Rousseau, presented a juridical theory which remained formally self-consistent, but which failed signally to grapple with the growth of groups and associations as entities in law. From *la loi de La Chapelier* and the French Revolutionary interdiction of corporations within the state, this individualistic conception refused to permit any group to come between man and the state, in as absolute terms as the Reformation had used to deny intervention between man and God. Yet it is obvious nowadays,—so obvious that the most backward systems of law have had to recognize it—that the corporation must be admitted to a definite legal status, one that I have called co-organic because of the impossibility of treating it as that of complete legal personality. Even unincorporated groups must take on co-organic responsibility under law. On the other hand, it is just as obvious that the

reconstruction of society along such purely functional lines as
Solidarism or Fascism would have us attempt, is as inapt as the
atomism of individualistic "rights" which it is meant to supplant,
and is quite as savagely opposed to free groups in a free state.
Dean Pound has declared that the Utilitarian criterion of Bentham, "How far does a rule or doctrine or institution conduce
to or promote human happiness?" "might well have been used
to break down the individualist idea of justice" had the age
of Adam Smith been farther off.[6] And that is what the organic
conception of social solidarity does for the notion of subjective
right, by a very similar dialectic.

But is the notion of functional obligation which it proposes to
substitute any more adequate as a basis for the rule of law?
Only, it is apparent, for such a law of fact as M. Duguit proposes.
Purpose and morality are lost with the loss of responsible selfhood in the individual. Solidarism, like Fascism, would "seize
individuals by the neck", as *il Duce* says. The constitutional
state must permit freedom of association and the unity of
purpose that constitutes the only effective means of social self-
expression. But it must offer a responsible control through an
adequate party system of the clashes between interest groups.
To functionalize representation in parliament would be to inten-
sify differences of interest and to prevent the coördination of
policies which a political cabinet now accomplishes.

For historic reasons of great complexity, the intellectualistic
side of Utilitarianism dominated the theory of the nineteenth
century to a remarkable degree.[7] Even the Historical School of
law strengthened the *laisser-faire* side of its theory by discovering
metaphysical principles operating in Hegelian fashion throughout the evolution of the law. The net effect was to discourage
legislative zeal and to restrain the action of the state, until
Utilitarianism became futilitarianism in its turn. Collectivistic
regulation was dictated by the economic and social context. One
may see, perhaps, in the activity of the Sociological School of

---

[6] Dean Pound, *The Spirit of the Common Law*, p. 159.

[7] *Cf.* W. L. Davidson, *The Utilitarians from Bentham to J. S. Mill*, Political Thought in England Series (Home University Library) and Leslie
Stephens, *The English Utilitarians*. The aptness of the classical economic
theory of the Utilitarians to a century of expansion through the liberation
of vast natural resources by individual enterprise", and through the coming
of the Great Industry, has often been noticed.

Jurists at the present time a reaction toward the voluntaristic and pragmatic side of the earlier Utilitarianism. In any case, the general tendency which we have remarked in political anti-intellectualism of revolt has been only nominally in the direction of an anti-state movement—so far as it has reached a more respectable plane than the advocacy of blind destruction. The effort has been directed against "Victorian" democracy, against "parliamentarism" and against "sovereignty", but it proposes simply to substitute the functional state for the representative state-person, and to extend law as widely as authority of any sort is a social fact. It has become, in short, a positivistic pragmatism, an Instrumentalism.

With the pragmatic side of this movement which insists on the social relevancy of government as the organ of law, and upon the necessity of decentralizing the agencies of legislation and of administration to conform to community of interest, the co-organic theory is in accord. That is, in Crocean terms, the economic aspect of the practical activity of the state, its organic arrangement. It is therefore one part of the business of politics. Without it, unity of legal rule remains merely formal. But with the positivistic program of functionalism which challenges the unified rule of law, which challenges the necessity of any other but a functional representation, which attacks the special legitimacy of state power and of law, the co-organic theory takes sharp issue. Law as a mature system demands a special province for the state, if the state is to be the expression of a consensus of will about a unifying purpose. The representatives of the parliamentary organ of the State must represent not "interests" but "state-purpose", if parliaments are to serve as something more than a battle ground on which the alignments of classes and conflicting groups are more and more clearly drawn until the scene of conflict is moved to more real war. Party politics and local constituencies are perhaps not ideal vehicles upon which to bear in the perfect legislator to power; but they are a better practical medium for obtaining a community of purpose than would be obtained by occupational representation. The "Grab it for the constituency" interests of the legislators would be multiplied and intensified, and even such community of purpose as is represented by the political programs of parties campaigning for office would be lost in the demagogy of appeals to particular interests. Local and sectional particularism are perhaps preferable to interest-group and class particularism, and easier to unite on a workable legislative program. For representation on a territorial basis makes it imperative for political parties to reconcile sectional with national interests if they are to survive.

Naturally "interests" can not be kept out of politics under any system of representation. But if legislators are to ask themselves the "right question", as Rousseau called it, that is what is best for the "general will" (the co-organic purpose) of the community, they cannot be the mere puppets of interest-groups. At the present moment in all large democratic states we find political organization responding in some measure, however, to the pressure of group-interests, either through the existence of political *blocs* within the legislatures, or through lobbyist organizations and interest groups of voters of perhaps greater power. Almost all countries have similar problems in more simplified terms, usually centered about the industrial and agrarian problems.[8] Always it is a question of political power corresponding to a very large degree to the strongest interest, or group of allied interests. Is this not to accept the economic interpretation of politics offered by Instrumentalism, to become pragmatically a "realist in politics" after the fashion of M.

[8] Professor and Mrs. Beard, in *The Rise of American Civilization*, run that thread, evident in the McNary-Haugen Bill, through all American history.

Balkan governments have more than once ridden into power on agrarian shoulders. Denmark is perpetually vexed by agrarian problems. In large powers, too, there is a growing tendency to division between the interests of the farming sections and the interests of the manufacturing sections. Russia remains an impossible experiment from the Communist viewpoint, because of its stubbornly individualistic peasantry. Mussolini attempts to balance agricultural with industrial development and talks of preventing the dangers of urbanization.

Mr. Hilaire Belloc has even proposed a complete system of peasant proprietorship under a sort of protective Guild System, in his *Servile State*, as the remedy of our collectivist evils. He and Mr. Chesterton wish to go back to a "Distributive State".

For the actual laws of agrarian tenure see "Die Agrargesetzgebung der Europäischen Staaten vor und nach dem Kriege," by W. Schiff, *Archiv für Sozialwissenschaft und Sozialpolitik*, 1925, pp. 87-131, 469-529.

The recent International Economic Conference (1927) at Geneva showed that agriculture the world over had been subordinated to industry since the War. See its reports and also the Bulletins of Economic and Social Institutions of the International Institute of Agriculture at Rome.

Duguit and Mr. Laski? Are not these the very facts that led the latter to speak of the survival of groups in competition, "Darwin-wise"? Ultimately will they not lead us to choose either the discredited state, or its Fascist alternative?

Not altogether. The very existence of government under law instead of a universal feudal *régime* of petty groups, knowing no other arbitration than the right of might, shows to what a degree the state-purpose is real and operative in modern society. In the dialectic of history, Fascist is more apt than pluralist syndicalism to survive. In the constitutional state one wants control, limited and responsible. Nor is law in a constitutional state merely a camouflage for social force, as the "realist" view holds it is, unless social force be taken in a very much wider sense than the power of material constraint. The "interests" are at work in the making of the law, but they are themselves constrained to accept law as the expression of a wider community of interest than any interest of their own, and one that is always to some extent informed with moral purpose. There are limits to "log-rolling" where parties must answer for their records. In the American federal government there are also the President and the Supreme Court. Where "interests" invade the realm of accepted social morality, where they begin to hinder the realization of the good life,—as, e.g., the liquor and saloon interests did in the United States—they meet a rebuke that is moral, not economic, sometimes a rebuke that is fanatical in its repudiation of human nature.

Miss Mary P. Follett's *The New State* is an interesting attempt to decentralize with the neighborhood group as the unit, giving recognition to the part the occupational group must play also. Although she is an advocate of federalizing authority, she is opposed to the political pluralists, who misinterpret James. It was, she thinks, through the "compounding of consciousness" that James found unity in the self, and it is to the same principle in the life of real moral groups that she looks for the unifying state, in the chapter on "Political Pluralism". The community principle of the neighborhood group she hopes to make the unit of political association, though it never quite appears how "the true Federalism" is to be brought about, except through the analogy of the relation of the Community

Council with the Council of National Defense. Her subsequent work on *Creative Experience* carries this problem further by a psychological analysis of the nature of group coöperation.

The use of war-time analogies to treat the creation of a "general will" surely underestimates the difference in peace-time feeling. In the one case, the "principle of wholeness" to which Miss Follett looks for "the social law; the law which connects neighborhood with neighborhood", is actually realized in the phenomenon of a nation almost organic in its war unity. In the other, the separate interests of different groups tend to pull against each other, and the neighborhood community itself has interests which differ according to whether one lives in Boston, in proper Back Bay or around Scollay Square.

The group principle has been more correctly interpreted by the pluralists perhaps than by Miss Follett's pragmatic and somewhat Romanticist Hegelianism, so long at least as economic interests are consulted as the test of the intensity and validity of group life. Miss Follett says that "the local units must *grow* sovereignty" through a "process of life, always unifying through the interpenetration of the Many-Oneness an infinite goal." [9] But natural growth depends upon many other things than what might be called "the will to grow it", and until the neighborhood community takes on a character of more real social unity than at present characterizes it in either urban or rural life, men must find in the party-system the chief organ of unification on national issues.

The groups like Women's Club Federations and the League of Women Voters (for the Women Voters have become suddenly something to be reckoned with politically) the various Civic Clubs (Rotary, Kiwanis, etc.) extending throughout the nation, have become instruments of forming opinion in the United States that have the greatest political significance, in spite of their non-political character. Labor Unions and Chambers of Commerce have a tendency to educate their members politically after the fashion of the Jesuits: to indoctrinate them, in opposite directions, of course, in the two cases.

The whole structure of modern society is associational, even

⁹ *The New State*, pp. 284 ff.

where its political methods tend to run to "mass democracy", to the initiative and referendum, as they do in some Western States. To "put over" a popular vote on a measure, means to get great interest groups "behind" it. The traditional Jeffersonian confidence in the *vox populi* has operated to put the election of senators and even of judges in the reach of universal suffrage, and to extend the area of popular decision through a ballot referendum on important questions of public policy. In California, for example, an elector is frequently called upon to decide several very complicated issues on one ballot: e.g., anti-Japanese land laws; additional taxation for public improvement, education, etc.; state-ownership of water-power; and proposals of various sorts, amounting in 1914 to forty-two separate decisions.

This may be taken as showing, in a different direction, the tendency and an obviously exaggerated tendency on the evidence of the times, to limit the general sphere of legislative activity by popular intervention, in contrast with the growth of special commissions, and *ad hoc* bodies which relieve representatives of detailed legislation. In the areas in which the co-organic purpose of the entire community is at stake, and where the electors can reasonably be supposed to have educated opinions, the mandate sought by government may be a direct one. But the difficulty of putting proper limits on the type of referenda seems insuperable. The American experiment in constitutional conventions is especially interesting for the problem in co-organic organization of purpose-expression that it offers, for here a separate organ is created to organize the fundamental law by which the legislature must be bound. Experience has shown the electorate of the average American State to be quite as conservative as the electorate of Switzerland, even in the referenda on questions of accepting the work of constitutional conventions.[10]

The co-organic theory of the State sees the only possible remedy for the acute conflicts of interest, not in turning the legislature into a battle-ground for the realization of group ends by political means, nor, on the other hand, in allowing the con-

[10] For modern literature on the Initiative and Referendum see Haines and Haines, *Principles and Problems of Government* (revised edition).

flicts to settle themselves "Darwin-wise" in the presence of a passive state as a mere onlooker. The upshot of that attitude is to make life so intolerable that Fascism is welcomed by contrast as the lesser of the two evils. The remedy lies rather (1) in taking out of the sphere of general legislative interests the special problems of groups, those of internal organization and autonomy, by means of liberal charters reserving mainly the right of ultimate judicial review, and (2) in retaining within the legislative competence the power of co-ordinating group ends by limiting their use of force and by evaluating their ends in terms of the co-organic purpose of legal community which they serve. As a concrete instance of the first problem, that of administrative and legislative decentralization, it is only necessary to point to the tremendous growth of home-rule in local and regional authorities within a federal framework of law, to committees and commissions, to such industrial experiments as advisory arbitration bodies for labor disputes, legally organized trade-boards, industrial councils, and the Whitley Report; to the newer attitude of English and American law toward legal corporate personality; and to business arbitration and the growth of unions and professional associations setting their own standards. Each type of group has a function of education and of social integration; it is impossible to overstate its real importance to modern society; but that function is not to absorb the individual either morally or juridically. To prevent just such an absorption is the function of the rule of law which has been stated under the second of the problems of the state in terms of the "co-organic purpose of legal community". Without the integrating power of legal sovereignty, unified by judicial review in accordance with the constitutionally defined purpose of the State, or by the High Court of Parliament (under the English system now a legislature) the rule of law degenerates into a battle-royal of interests.

Obviously this is to attribute a fundamental importance to the judiciary, as well as the legislature, in modern governments. But the power of judicial review, under the co-organic interpretation of the State, is not a separated power, so much as the means of coördinating power. There is a tendency, often remarked in the American judiciary, to use its power of consti-

tutional interpretation with legislative freedom.[11] Statutes are
not so much brought into constitutional conformity as "controlled" into thinly disguised judicial enactments by limitation.
There is, of course, a large historical justification for particular
cases of the exercise of such power, particularly under a government in which the pioneer distrust of office-bearers has bred a
system of checks and balances which sometimes checks into
static equilibrium, and balances in impotence.

The natural result, however, has been to draw the judiciary
into politics. Election of judges has spread as far as the Supreme
Bench of the several states and the recall of judicial decisions,
the popular election even of federal judges, and "judicial recall",
as it has been termed, or the power to remove judges from office
by a popular vote as a rebuke for unpopular decisions have
seemed at several periods of our history about to threaten the
independence of the bench upon which much of the ·successful
working of the bold American experiment in democratic government has been based in the past.[12] Actually even the elected

---

[11] Burgess called the governmental system of the United States "an aristocracy of the robe" (quoted by T. R. Powell, *Political Science Quarterly*,
Vol. XXXIII, p. 439). The elder La Follette before the campaign of 1924
for the Presidency, provoked a great deal of political agitation by proposing
that the two houses of Congress be empowered to make a law constitutionally
valid by repassing it by a two-thirds majority, as they are able to do in the
case of the President's veto. Theodore Roosevelt in 1912 went so far as
to advocate the "Recall of Judicial Decisions" by popular vote. La Follette
also proposed to make the Federal Judges subject to popular election for
ten-year terms.

The literature on the subject of the power of the judiciary to enact covert
legislation under the cloak of judicial review and constitutional control is
endless. An interesting treatment of the origins of the idea is to be found
in A. C. McLaughlin, *The Courts, the Constitution, and the Parties*. Perhaps the work of Professor Thayer has established the historic development
of this power from its assumption by Chief-Justice Marshall in the famous
Marbury vs. Madison (*Legal Essays*) most definitively. *Cf.* also C. A.
Beard's *The Supreme Court and the Constitution*, and E. Lambert, *op. cit.*
(for a very complete documentation). E. S. Corwin's monograph, *The Doctrine of Judicial Review*, and C. G. Haines, *The American Doctrine of Judicial Supremacy* are limited surveys supplemented by Charles Warren,
Congress, the Supreme Court and the Constitution, and the first volume
of his monumental three volumes, *Supreme Court in United States History.*

[12] *Cf.* Dean Pound's warning to the men of the law, Introduction to *The
Spirit of the Common Law*. Roosevelt's Progressive Party, taking up many
of the old Populist ideas, was sponsor for much of the movement toward
a more direct democracy.

As early as 1812, the prophetic voice of Chancellor Watties of South
Carolina had been raised against the attempt of the judiciary to legislate:
"The intervention of the judiciary in legislative acts," he said, "if it was

judiciary in the states is still fairly independent. But the real function of the judiciary is not legislation cloaked under the interpretative robe of the law, most of all where there is a rigid constitution to be applied. It is perhaps of some significance to note that in France, as under the less rigid and unwritten constitution of England, no such liberties have been taken by the judges with statutes duly passed by a Parliament legally absolute in its sovereignty, possibly because of tradition, but possibly also because the courts are legislatively created. The proper judicial function, assumed with a success none will deny by the British judiciary, is that of unifying the law of the land in practice, by dint of that "artificial reason and judgment of the law" which Coke boldly opposed to the will of James I. Judicial interpretation is not, of course, like the operation of a slot-machine, as Dean Pound has shown so pithily.[13] But judicial empiricism can not be carried into covert legislation without over-stepping its proper bounds. The common law and legitimate constitutional review in a federal state possessed of a Bill of Rights, offer a sufficient field for judicial discretion without intruding upon statutes on the grounds of reasonableness.

A real necessity exists for making justice practically available by the same process of decentralization applied to the judiciary that operates in modern legislation. Much is being done and well done, in business, labor, and trade arbitration outside the

frequent or for dubious causes, would be the source of so great a jealousy against this power and of a prejudice so general against it, that it would provoke measures leading to the total destruction of the independence of judges, and thus of the best safeguard of the Constitution" (quoted by M. Ed. Lambert, *op. cit.*, p. 60).

The real "balance of power" in the American government is often found in the Supreme Court. Victor West showed in the *Illinois Law Review* (Vol. VIII, pp. 571-575) that of the fifty-five cases cited by C. W. Collins in *The Fourteenth Amendment and the States*, in which the Supreme Court of the United States had admitted recourse against the state statutes on account of violations of the 14th Amendment, only twenty-four had been unanimously decided, and of the rest, many of them only by five to four votes. In Labor decisions, the *Coronado Coal Co.* case presented the almost unique spectacle of a court unanimous in its decision. Five to four decisions against federal laws are few in number but of the greatest importance—e.g., *Pollock vs. Farmer's Loan & Trust Co.* (1894), which had to be overridden by the 16th Amendment.

[13] *Cf.* his "Social and Legal Justice." *Proceedings of the Missouri Bar Association*, 1912, p. 455, and the chapter on "Legal Philosophy" in the *Spirit of the Common Law*, as well as "Law in Books and Law in Action." 44 *American Law Review*, p. 12, and *Introduction to the Philosophy of Law*, and his *Interpretations of Legal History*.

regular courts. Courts, especially commissions with mixed functions of a quasi-judicial character, have followed the march of legislation toward specialization of function. But wherever they have escaped the unification of the legal sovereign, they have had to be brought back by judicial review into the realm of the rule of law.[14] In the courts, indeed, lies the sole available means of harmonizing into the rule of law the growth in power of the executive branch of government to an extent that practically dominates the legislative. It is commonplace in these days to remark the accretion of real political power to the President and his advisers in the United States, and to the Cabinet and its ministers in England. Although there have been unmistakable signs of a disposition to "balk" like a stubborn and overdriven mule, lately manifested by both Congress and Parliament, the dominance of the executive over the legislative program is still sufficiently marked. In France the power of the executive in this direction, much more curbed by a multi-party system and by the Parliamentary commissions in its legislative initiative, if not in the latitude permitted it in the exercise of its administrative duties, has brought with it a compensating increase in administrative responsibility. The *Conseil d'Etat* has served some of the functions of a supreme court, and administrative law has tended more and more clearly to fix administrative responsibility for its acts upon the government. In this manner the courts are serving to bring all *actes de gouvernement* within what Duguit, Jèze, and Berthelémy have shown to be an increasingly harmonious rule of law.[15]

The point is often made that, as a matter of fact, constitutional government under modern conditions is no longer so much a matter of separate expressions in each act of a popular mandate (as the intellectualist construction of representative expression of a general will assumed) but a matter of expert administration and formation of policies under a mandate of popular confidence. And up to a point that is quite true. France has finally awakened to the organic necessity of setting her finances in order. The powers granted to Poincaré's ministry were willingly given at last. A mandate to experts is, indeed, what the co-organic theory would lead us to expect wherever the community purpose

[14] *Cf.* note 3, *supra.*   [15] *Law in the Modern State,* Chapter 5.

has found articulate means of expression. But what limits of policy may we impose upon experts? The organic arrangement of the state is no mere mechanism with the function of registering mechanically the decrees of automatic social reactions, nor is it the completely rationalized creation of an infallible general will. Mr. Walter Lippmann has shown that "public opinion" conceived as an organic will is hardly more than a phantom. The state is the expression of a purpose not always clearly self-conscious, any more than purpose is in the individual. The acts of those who control its policies are tentative and experimental, sometimes hesitating and half-blind. But wherever a really co-organic political community exists, with party systems and a rich associational life to form opinion, the law is a consciously directed effort toward clarifying those acts, and rendering them coherent. The direction of administration and the formation of policies can only be entrusted to men, politically expert and politically as responsible as is possible under the given circumstances. What is the technique of representative control? How far is it necessarily *ex post facto?*

CHAPTER XV

THE POLITICAL STRUCTURE AND FUNCTIONS OF THE CONSTITUTIONAL STATE

Any normative approach to the problem of authority must be prepared to offer a fruitful technique for the organization of co-organic responsibility as well as an orientation for the problem of the moral basis of authority. I have spoken of *constitutional* responsibility. May that not exist wherever the ruler *does* in fact satisfy the ruled? Are fixed and fundamental laws or customs needed? Need we demand limited terms of office and representative control? What means of translating purpose into fact ought to characterize the constitutional state? The criticism of Mr. Laski's ideal solution has already given many hints as to points of agreement with his fertile theories, as well as points of difference. It will be useful, perhaps, to add a final word on the nature and technique of the responsible state in order to make more explicit some of the implications of this critique of pluralism and Fascism.

In the first place it is manifestly impossible to offer a general formula for the distribution, functioning, and limitation of powers that would apply to all states, even if mankind were more racially and culturally homogeneous than it is, and at more uniform stages of industrial development. Huge, heterogeneous, cultural areas such as exist in the United States and in other countries of similar character demand federal institutions, a division of powers, and some supreme arbitral body to determine the constitutional use of powers. It is often urged that if the judiciary's right of passing on the constitutionality of laws is susceptible to arbitrary abuse, the amending system must be rendered adequate to correct judicial absolutism. In 1924 Mr. LaFollette proposed to vest the power in Congress as well as the courts (in fact above the courts), and to elect the federal judges for ten-year terms. At the same time, the necessity

441

of rigidity in the fundamental bases of federal association is such that the amending system ought not to be rendered a legislative agency. Better correct the method of selecting judges, the tradition of judicial interpretation, or the policy of putting some of the property provisions of Bills of Rights in their hands, particularly of property rights under sweeping provisions that permit arbitrary interpretation, if we are to restrain the judges from what amounts practically to a veto of social legislation—better this than tamper with the amending clause to render it more flexible. For according to the coörganic analysis, the constitution is the permanent basis of political co-operation. If it become the spoils of a bare majority of the federalized nation after an election victory, it ceases to have value as a federal instrument, or as a permanent basis of moral consent. Protection through judicial review for federal purposes, for a proper separation of powers, for the protection of personal liberty in itself educates a nation to political morality because it demands respect for the rule of law. Judicial review serves to hold the administrative and legislative elements in a proper relation to the constitutional basis in a way peculiarly valuable in a federal state. The technique of political responsibility through parliamentary control is perhaps more effective in the smaller unitary state.

For if diversity of sectional interests tends to prevent highly unified party-control and to make the separation of powers more apt to secure a working balance in the federal state, the same principles do not apply to a closely knit, homogeneous nation like England. There is not the same necessity for protecting the diversity of federal areas, unless one thinks of England in relation to the Dominions. And the Dominions have passed beyond a federal and into a national status of their own. In the United Kingdom, "devolution" of any federal nature is a doubtful virtue, so far as regional legislatures with protected areas of competency are concerned.[1] Deconcentration of administrative functions is a matter of arrangement on the basis of

[1] See Wan-Hsuan Chiao, *Devolution in Great Britain*, Columbia University Studies in History, Economics, and Public Law, Vol. CXXIV, No. 272, and H. J. Laski, *Grammar of Politics*, Part II, Chap. 1, for a criticism of devolution. See also the extracts on Devolution in Sait and Barrows, *British Politics in Transition*.

the most efficient government possible; but legislative unity is
necessitated by the interweaving of foreign and domestic policy.
No scheme of further dividing parliaments by a functional arrangement—either guild socialist, Sydney-Webbicalist, or other
—can work which forgets this primary function of coördinating
all policy into a coherent administration.

We may conclude then, that other things being equal, the
historically developed system of parliamentary government with a
flexible constitution, dependent for its safeguards upon a spirit of
constitutional morality, fits the United Kingdom just as a legally
rigid functional separation and a federal division of powers is
necessary to the United States. The former has the advantage of
being a quicker, stronger, less wasteful, and more responsible
form of government for a small, closely interdependent nation.
It is possible that the future development of national solidarity
of culture in the United States may bring with it an increasing
fusion of powers by making majority rule more possible, and
with it a limited responsibility of the executive to the legislature.[2]
Such a responsibility already exists *ex post facto* when Sena-
torial investigations force resignations of cabinet officers.

What, however, of the machinery of representation necessary
to insure constitutional responsibility? It may, of course, be
varied tremendously to fit different states and different stages of
political development as it is in the rich social laboratory of
the British Empire. Universal suffrage is not logically implied
except in highly educated nations. In general, I accept Mr.
Laski's ideas as to the defensibility of the present parliamentary
system, with especial emphasis upon the greater flexibility of
control from national rather than local motives, possible in
practice only where non-resident candidacy strengthens the
national party leaders. Politics offers a career under the English
system that a young man may choose without paying too great

---

[2] There is a real need of a modern treatise on Federal Government to
supplement J. A. Freeman's *History of Federal Governments* and A. V.
Dicey's *Law of the Constitution*, and the classic passages of the *Federalist*.
For discussions of advantages and disadvantages see Freeman, *op. cit.*,
Chaps. 1 and 2. For a comparison of parliamentary sovereignty with fed-
eralism, see Chaps. 3 and 4. Dicey, *op. cit.*, 9th ed.

Walter Thompson's *Federal Centralization* examines that particular tendency in the United States both in legislation and administration, without
noticing any tendency toward a breakdown of the functional separation of
powers as a concomitant. See also A. F. McDonald, *Federal Aid.*

a price of subservience to local interests, and with some possibility of making it the job of a life-time. Leadership, under a system of non-resident candidacy, is developed among the active representatives and parliamentarians, and not among bosses of local areas operating behind the scenes. The hands of representatives are strengthened by the greater independence that chances of election in another constituency give, whereas a single defeat is often disastrous to the congressional career of any except the second-rate, small-town lawyer, under the American system. Of course, such a tradition can not be created by fiat, and it is particularly hard to implant in a federal country wedded to the custom of local delegates whose merits are judged in terms of their raids upon the national "pork barrel" in the interests of their constituencies. It can be brought about in the United States only by developing within the states the importance of national issues. In this connection proportional representation might have real merits in the United States.

The party system, with territorial representation, seems to be proved by such social experimentation as we have yet had, to be the best primary means of securing democratic control of policy. There is no valid reason why universal adult suffrage should not be tempered by educational and intelligence tests. Conceivably a publicly educated democracy may demand educational qualifications for candidacy to public offices. In order to secure the simplicity requisite for responsibility there is an obvious necessity for decreasing both the number of elections and the number of elective officers. On the whole the initiative or referendum as a democratic remedy seems to be a confession of the bankruptcy of the representative system. The remedy lies in curing the weakness of legislatures rather than in taking over the onus of decision through direct popular votes. When we begin to take our political problems as seriously as befits their importance and our national status, we can create a better tradition of public duty and of office-holding. But a change of heart is often vastly assisted by a change of machinery that removes the voter's feeling of impotence.

As the efficiency of government is also a consideration of primary necessity, public administration bulks always larger in importance in the modern state. Whether one likes it or not, the major part of actual government is in the hands of a bureaucracy of civil servants.[3] No code, no common law, no statutory enactments, or executive ordinances are self-executing. It goes without saying that the organization of the commissions, the departments and the civil service, which coördinate and transmit the actual application of all social purpose of a legal character, must insure continuity of service, personal efficiency, and administrative responsibility. Even legislation depends for the greater part of its detailed bulk on the civil servant.

General indications of attitude have been given already on this question. Continuity of service must be maintained by denying the right to civil servants to strike as an organized threat. I accept the position of Duguit on this as sound, agreeing generally to organization for purposes of protest and for the representation of grievances and the improvement of morale, but not for the purpose of directing an organized stoppage in the public services. There is also a serious question as to whether public servants ought to ally themselves with national trade unionism, when the latter is a political organization as it is in England. Baldwin has answered this by a dogmatic negative. The civil servants are politically so numerous and so important an element in the community that they do not lack means of making themselves heard and felt. And if government services are to enter into group competition by means of strikes to increase wages, we shall soon have a state like that of pre-Fascist Italy. Poincaré has recently called attention again to the danger to free institutions in France from a plethoric and powerful bureaucracy. Baldwin's government is depriving civil servants of the right to join general Labor Unions. Coolidge became Vice-President of the United States largely because of an historic sentence that expressed the extremest form of this view. "There is no right to strike against the public safety by anybody, anywhere, anytime," he said to the Boston police.

As for personnel efficiency and the technique of administra-

---

[3] For an interesting and profound interpretation of the historical relations between bureaucracy and representative legislatures, and the modern bearing of the problem on European parliamentarism see *The Crisis of European Democracy* by Moritz J. Bonn (Institute of Politics Addresses, Williamstown, 1925). See also Carl Schmitt, *Politische Romantik* and *Die Diktatur;* A. Weber, *Die Krise des Modernen Staatsgedankens in Europa.*

tion, it is sufficient to note that most of our present difficulties
have flowed in the past from three sources, each of which seems
to be in a fair way to be ameliorated: (1) lack of scientific
study of administrative problems, and particularly a lack of
means of pooling information.[4] This is a condition rapidly
disappearing in this country before the organization by states,
colleges, and the Federal Government of proper facilities for research, and for encouraging qualified researchers. It would
be impossible to overestimate the potentialities of the independent foundations for research in the social sciences, if they
are themselves wisely administered. At present, the danger seems
to be rather a lack of fruitful methods than a want of facilities
or of researchers. (2) The continuance of the spoils system even
in the appointment of the most important bureau chiefs [5] and
ubiquitously in the appointments of state and local officials
where government comes nearest home to the ordinary individual. (3) The assumption that the state can "hire a Daniel
Webster for forty dollars a month", as one old Tennessean
whom I knew used to put it. Executive talents, as well as technical, command such sums from private companies that government is hard put to it to equip even its most necessary
control commissions,[6] with qualified experts, or to keep them
away from the lure of private firms, sometimes interested in
removing them from quite immediate and obvious motives.

---

[4] For a survey of the agencies now existing for such research see the Report of the American Council of Learned Societies, *Survey of Research.*
H. D. Hall in *The British Commonwealth of Nations* has called attention
to the great need for subsidiary conferences and special agencies for this co-
operative pooling of information in the Empire, partly in process of realization at the present time.

[5] See the exposition, all the more trenchant for being dispassionate, of
the present policy of appointing and retaining "Bureau Chiefs in the National Administration of the United States" by Arthur W. MacMahon, *Am.
Pol. Sci. Rev.*, Vol. XX, Nos. 3 and 4 (Aug. and Nov. 1926).

[6] As a former member of the Railroad Commission of the State of California (meant to regulate all public utilities of state-wide significance) once
put the matter to me: "When we have an engineer who is really capable,
the big corporations snap him up at double the salary, usually at some critical time in our decisions. Even if the offer is not openly made then, he
knows his fate depends on his attitude. The technicians who are left are
usually so incompetent that they are browbeaten by the experts of the
corporations, and accept whatever estimates are offered." Every student of
public administration will be able to supply a wealth of similar cases from
his own knowledge. See O. C. Hormell's study of *Maine Public Utilities*
(Bowdoin College Bulletin No. 164, Feb. 1927).

It is of fundamental importance to build up an *esprit de corps* in the Civil Service and then to make its expertness really available to the Legislature. The separation of powers often defeats this aim, and that is perhaps the most serious criticism of a legislative machinery like ours in the States of the United States where this coöperation is rendered difficult.

Administration is like the nervous system of an organism, carrying and interpreting messages throughout the whole. In the modern state, simply because the economic efficiency and organic security of government bulk so large in daily life, good administration is fundamental to any realization of the state purpose. A change of attitude toward it is already apparent that may give us a better tradition, more like England's. It has long been pointed out that our civil service examinations attempt to find already acquired fitness for positions rather than to test general capacity—with bad results in the upper classifications.

Responsibility for administrative acts has been somewhat discussed in the critiques of M. Duguit and of Mr. Ernest Barker. I need only add my conviction, even though it differs from that of so competent authority as Mr. John Dickinson in the matter of administrative law and its development by courts, that the common law needs to develop a special administrative jurisprudence and a properly qualified and flexible system of administrative courts, particularly to deal with the responsibility of the state in law. Here as elsewhere in administrative matters, modern Germany offers a remarkable example. Professor Dickinson has offered a more conservative estimate of remedial needs [7] in his attempt to restate the governing principles of administrative justice under our American common law practice in the well-documented study already noticed. While he takes a pragmatic view that the courts can never draw sharp lines between law and fact for the criteria of "fair" return in administrative valuations, he appears to feel that the courts ought to leave facts as much as possible to experts.

The relation between executive and legislative bodies, and the

---

[7] *Op. cit.*, Note 3, Chap. XIV. *Cf.* A. Merkl, *Allgemeine Verwaltungs lehre*, Vienna, 1927 (Springe). The older works of Otto Mayer and Jellinek are out of date, but still remain the fullest accounts.

extent of legislative control through committees or commissions, or through a cabinet system responsible to parliament must differ with historical conditions, racial tempers, cultural and economic homogeneity of population. In general federal governments seem to rely more effectively for stable conditions upon a more politically independent executive than the pure parliamentary system affords, one who can enforce a limited discipline over his legislature through party leadership, and over his administration by liberal powers of removal, as well as of appointment to offices of a political nature. More compact states can with profit centralize responsibility in a parliamentary system, although the parliamentary system, when it is not based upon a fairly stable party grouping, has certain marked disadvantages under the rapidly changing conditions of modern life through interrupting the continuity of governmental policy with undue frequency.[8]   However, in some instances, interruption is a positive virtue and four years is a long while to wait for it. Senate investigations really enforced an individual responsibility on the Harding *régime*. If, by having the recognized right to question representatives of the executive

[8] Various proposals have been made for lessening the seriousness of an overturn of governments, or for making them less frequent. Some of them have been incorporated into presidential features. (See C. E. Martin, "The Growth of Presidential Government in Europe," *Am. Pol. Sci. Rev.*, Vol. XVII, No. 4). Mussolini, in so far as he has a constitutional position, has what amounts to presidential tenure at the King. of Italy's legal pleasure, not the chamber's. For English opinion see Willoughby and Rogers, *An Introduction to the Problem of Government*, pp. 234-262, and E. M. Sait and D. P. Barrows, *British Politics in Transition*, pp. 123-157.

The Constitution of the Irish Free State attempts a combination of responsible and non-responsible ministers in the same executive council and without much practical difference in the working of ministerial responsibility. See Stephen Gwynn, *Ireland*.

Up to 1926 in the Dominions the practice of the Governor General as well as the Governors in Australian States had been to refuse dissolution to a defeated government under certain conditions. (See A. B. Keith, *The Constitution, Administration, and Laws of the British Empire*, pp. 209-211.) This will probably no longer take place even in the States after the Imperial Conference of 1926. The new status of Royal Governors is Vice-Regal, with the Crown's position having become purely ceremonial and symbolic. For Canada see especially H. A. Smith, *Federalism in North America*, pp. 38 ff. The most recent and important exercise of the power was Baron Byng's refusal of dissolution to Mackenzie King and the Liberal Cabinet in February, 1926.

The best brief critique in English of the difficulties of Parliamentarism is perhaps Herr M. Bonn's *Crisis of European Democracy*, cited *supra*, Note 3.

departments, the Senate might forestall instead of punish, we should have a judicious mixture of presidential with parliamentary government. Probably such a right would involve the reconstruction of the Senate upon a regional basis of representation. It is hardly conceivable that the House of Representatives should exercise this power without a complete shift of emphasis on its function.

The chief difficulty with any system that would make our executive department in the Federal Government politically responsible to the Senate for its tenure of office—either individually or collectively—is that the control would be irresponsible itself. Unless the executive had the power to dissolve the Senate and to force the development of a responsible opposition ready to take over the administration, we might merely exchange our presidential system for a shifting coalition cabinet system like the French.

On the whole the parliamentary systems of England and of France seem to be accommodating themselves to the contemporary situation through a realization that any government must have a mandate of confidence for a certain period of experiment. It may be more a change of heart and of psychology that is wanted, on the part both of representatives and of the electorate, than a change of machinery. The duration of M. Poincaré's "ministry of national union" in France will be widely regarded in Europe as a test of the ability of parliamentary institutions to accommodate themselves, under the continental system, to the hard exigencies of national stability in finance during a dangerous period.[9]

The advocates of Fascism (open or camouflaged) as "an economic solution" of all difficulties really reckon on getting government by practical economic experts, which in modern times means government by bankers.[10] Now bankers ought to have a

---

[9] This is clearly evidenced by the almost hysterical acclaim with which the French press hailed the Poincaré ministry in 1926 and by that barometer of confidence, the exchange value of the franc.

[10] Mr. H. G. Wells, in *The World of William Clissold*, wants the bankers without the Fascists. He has consistently opposed Fascism where G. B. Shaw has inconsistently upheld it. See the lucid exposition and critique of Fascism as a historical phenomenon in a capitalistic society in M. J. Bonn, *op. cit., supra*, pp. 88 ff. Wm. Bolitho's *Italy under Mussolini* professes to show, with perhaps unjust cynicism, the puppet character up to

large say-so in any co-organic state, for no profession is better qualified to direct economic reorganization, and no profession has, really, a more direct interest in the enduring prosperity of the community. But not all bankers take a long view of the situation. Some of them, who stand to gain whatever way the financial current sets, see things naturally in terms only of an immediate and exorbitant return to themselves. And some of them are politically short-sighted in their attitude toward labor. It is this very fact that is making so dangerous the severance of corporate control from corporate risk, through control by directorates swayed by the representatives of investment bankers who are often only self-interested manipulators. The golden rule of capitalism is the association of risk with control. Corporate finance by losing that thread (and even the ordinary stockholders' meeting may hardly hope to follow it or regain it), has made imperative state regulation, or at least state inquiry into and supervision of all economically important corporate finance.[11]

Fascism as a philosophy does not have to be imported from Italy. Insofar as it proposes to turn over the reins of government to the super-organic control of a financial hierarchy, supported by an uncriticizable oligarchy of well-tamed private servants, but ruthless public masters, it is a philosophy indigenous to any state that is dedicated to maximum productivity, whether from choice or necessity. The pressure of post-war financial problems on the continent of Europe threatens to seduce hard-pressed states away from the luxury of liberalism—the protection of a free public opinion. That means the end of responsible government and a return to the days that made podestats

1924 of the chief Fascist protagonists and their relations to the *Banca Commerciale*. Professor Salvemini, however, attributes control to the militarists rather than to the bankers. See *The Fascist Dictatorship in Italy*.

[11] D. H. Robertson's *The Control of Industry* is a little classic of economic exposition particularly based upon English conditions. See also A. C. Pigou, *Economics of Welfare*, and Marshall's classic, *Industry and Trade* (edition of 1919).

In the United States, Professor W. Z. Ripley has more than once unsettled the hectic "bull" movement of the stock market by his published analyses of the dangers of non-voting stock control and the interesting devices of holding and managing companies by the stock manipulators and certain types of investment bankers. See *Main Street and Wall Street*, Introduction. Professor Ripley also offers some remedies, which critics rarely bother to do in these days.

necessary. If the experiment fails economically, the power of control is gone, even the power of protest. Fascism becomes the only judge of its own success, so long as it can satisfy its militia of mercenaries.

That this is ultimately a short-sighted policy, even for financiers as a class, frequently does not impress the pragmatically minded. They want *"results"*, results that they can see at once: and social "discipline", trains running on time and factories actually at work are such results. It does not appear to them worth considering, even if it be true, that the best discipline can only be maintained in the long run by enlisting the consent of those under discipline. Consent that is free must have the right to think itself out through public criticism, and the right to enforce that criticism through constitutional responsibility. Consent that is forced to conform (though it may not protest) can be bottled up—for a time. But unless industrialism has changed the hearts of men radically, few nations can be reduced for long to this slave morality. To cork them up by Fascist methods is to invite ultimate explosion. What Fascist methods are doing is to render Communism a long-run aid. To lose respect for revolution because one has seen the backs of revolutionists and because there is an appearance of tranquillity, is simply to ignore history. Revolution is too many-headed a monster to tame by the bastinado method, or even by the added refinement of castor-oil.[12]

Those who urge the organic and anti-democratic state of economic solidarity base their claims upon two grounds: the first is that any attempt to elicit the popular will by ballot-box methods is vitiated by the rationalistic hypothesis of popular sovereignty. The second is that only organic government is efficient.

"To speak of a sovereign people is to utter a tragic jest," says Mussolini. Government is always by the few. Under democratic methods, it is a government by demagogues or by hirelings, and it is in either case not government for the people but misgovernment of the people. Get a devoted and efficient dictator, who will rise to his position in Fascism through the will to

[12] For a statement of the ideal possibilities of a free world of labor see Delisle Burns, *The Philosophy of Labor.*

govern and the "struggle of capabilities". Then do what he says without question or murmur, if you wish for economic salvation. Otherwise your Phantom Public is called upon, like the gods of old, to save you from natural disaster—and it has no magic.

A. PUBLIC OPINION AND THE PHANTOM PUBLIC

Now there is little use in disputing some of the real truths stated, although they do not imply Fascism as a permanent remedy. In the United States there has been an almost mystic belief in the value of mere "publicity". Public opinion cannot act executively, as Mr. Walter Lippmann has finally concluded.[13] The range of decision is so great that even a small and compact group of individuals like a cabinet has infinite difficulty in bringing unified decision to bear upon them. Mr. Lloyd George put it during the *vi et armis* period: "You can not make war with a Sanhedrin." And he proceeded to cut his inner War Cabinet down to five. Nor can there be any reality in the conception of a general will operative over the vast range of legislative decisions, certainly still less in the complex business of judicial determination of legality. Even Rousseau limited his general will to a small city state. Mr. Lippmann's conclusion is that this whole way of thinking of public opinion tries to grapple with a ghost, although, aside from its rationalism, it is somewhat like his earlier own way of thinking of *Public Opinion* (as *clichés*, "pictures in the mind" or "stereotypes") brought to bear by individuals on all large issues. The only possibility of a real consensus in opinion in a large political community is one that demands only that "a settled rule" be applied in all acts of government, and to the solution of all social "problems". In other words, public opinion can only be valid to enforce con-

---

[13] *The Phantom Public*, a revision of his previous views as to the possibilities of an educated public opinion, given in *Public Opinion*. See in *The Phantom Public* on executive activity, especially Chapters III and IV. Mr. Lippmann's change of heart is especially interesting in view of the fact that his *Preface of Politics* was widely hailed as the manifesto of pragmatic anti-intellectualism in American political thinking. His idea of *Public Opinion* in the work of that name was, as has been wisely remarked, the notion of "private opinions on public questions". Some reflection on the limitations of this anti-intellectualistic conception have apparently led him to a restatement of public opinion simply as the equivalent of constitutional morality. Both of these conceptions miss the nature of the real public opinion which President Lowell has soundly analyzed in his classic work.

stitutional activity upon social groups in conflict. It can establish an equilibrium that forces settlement by consent. It can not intervene on the intrinsic merits of the situation, because as an outsider it is "external" to them.

The pragmatic answer of Mussolini to this chastened statement of democratic function would be simply that there are no settled rules. The times are in flux. A mandate must be unconditional. Any attempt on the part of the public to demand settled rules really implies ignorant intervention, usually that of conservative traditionalism. Rules are changing, and must change perpetually. Settlements that wait for consent are never made. One must decide and command—and enforce obedience.

Naturally the coörganic theory of the state is sympathetic to Mr. Lippmann's point of view, because it maintains that the rules of social conduct, even in changing, do not leap out of their skins. Constitutional continuity, through a mandate to responsible political leaders, is a surer way of social progress than the saltatory reconstruction of Mussolini, although the latter may be necessary where the former is not available. And it is worth remarking that Fascism, in becoming organic, has more and more accepted the necessity of settled social institutions, although it has denied the validity of public opinion to pass judgment on their change or development.

It is obviously where rules are challenged as "defective",[14] to use Mr. Lippmann's terminology, that it is impossible for the public to keep hands off or even to establish "an equilibrium" that will force a settlement by consent among the combatants —as he counsels opinion to do in cases where the settled rule is not challenged. The equilibrium of the old rule is not adequate, e.g., to the settlement of industrial issues where communism demands its change. It is the constitution itself that is in question, just as it was when the Dred Scott constitutional decision brought the issue of the extension of slavery to Civil War.

What Mussolini has said, with justice, is that where the basis of public opinion is shattered by a fundamental divergence, the issue is one of force. That is certainly the case where communism becomes revolutionary and powerful enough to defy

[14] *Ibid.*, Chap. XI. *Cf.* John Dewey's just published *The Public and Its Problems.*

the capitalistically organized constitutional state. But what Mussolini goes on to say is only justifiable in particular breakdowns: he holds that democracy is not, under the conditions of modern industrialism, an adequate conduit for social forces; that the change of rules necessarily implies a choice between communism and Fascism.

It is evident, however, that if this is not to be true there must be a public opinion, capable of expressing its merits on general issues that are either acute and universally important, like war; or chronic and annoying, like coal and railway strikes. On such issues there develops a public opinion that is not ghostly but real. What is the possibility of creating such an opinion? If it can not exist, Mussolini, and not Mr. Lippmann and his brother editors, will decide what people shall accept as settled rules or will change the rules to order: There is no use for the Labour Party in England to appeal to the electorate on an issue like nationalization of coal mines because such issues are "external" to the public and can not be filtered to it.

Mr. Lippmann's pessimism arises from the assumption that "Education for Citizenship" expects somehow to create an omnicompetent citizen. Some sorts of education, usually hailed as "for citizenship", obviously have a mystic faith in such a myth. Mr. Lippmann himself has neither faith in the individual's capacity nor in the capacity of collective groups of individuals to achieve effective purpose. I believe it is because he misinterprets the nature of the group activity which depends upon individual personality but which magnifies and educates and makes the individual effective in manifold degree. Like Duguit and the rest of our positivistic anti-intellectualists, he holds that groups (including the nation) are abstractions, not realities; although, like them also, he admits that groups are the basis of modern social organization and social conflict. He is so struck with the "deep pluralism" of individual and of society, that he says "Society is not the name of a thing, but the name of all the adjustments between individuals in their things; it is the individual who thinks, not the collective mind; it is the painter who paints, not the artistic spirit of the age; it is the soldiers who fight and are killed, not the nation." [15]

[15] *Phantom Public*, p. 172.

But, as we have seen in examining the co-organic nature of groups, the individual in the group is a different individual from this atomistic concept. If he thinks, and not the collective mind, his thinking must be colored, moulded, and limited by the group life which he shares; as an artist he derives inspiration and technique from a group and a tradition, as the history of art abundantly shows; as a soldier he dies not for himself but for the nation which has helped to produce him, the citizen.

As a citizen, therefore, although he is not individually adequate to its problems, he is a member of a co-organic state: he acts within and upon a rich variety of associational life. As leader or follower, he shapes in various degrees the attitude of these groups. As a member of a political party, in particular, he shares in the formation of party programs by the filtering processes of representative government. His function is more negative than positive; he protests more than he projects; he is not atomistically adequate. But he may be raised by the education of his co-organized activity to effective citizenship, through learning to throw his weight effectively behind the leaders whom he critically supports. The public opinion of the nation will reflect this composite focus through the resolution of all the foci brought to bear with varying intensity by different groups. Public opinion is therefore real because it is composed, not atomistically as an aggregate of isolated individuals, nor organically through a super-personality, but co-organically through the constitutional integration of many groups. Representative government and the party system still seem about the best method of evoking this active focus of group ideas. An adequate party system is responsive to group needs and group leadership without being at the mercy of an organized interest group. In the modern state this demands a centering of final responsibility in parties.

It is Mr. Lippmann's unwillingness to concede anything of reality to this co-organic filtration of purpose through the utilization of democratic leadership and constitutional divisions of power to conform to the area of purpose federally affected, that lies back of this cry of despair against majority rule. If majority rule is not institutionally filtered and federally restrained by constitutional morality, he is quite right in attacking it as an impossible demand upon public opinion to register itself automatically by merely counting heads. That is the fault of the initiative and referendum, used indiscriminately for all sorts of issues.

"A vote," says Mr. Lippmann, "is a promise of support. It is a way of saying: I am lined up with these men on this side. I enlist with them. I will follow. I will buy. I will boycott. I will strike. I applaud. I jeer. The force I can exert is placed here, not there." [16]

But what Mr. Lippmann does not allow for is the purposive element of each choice, and of the total grounds for partisanship. It is true that "the action of a group is the mobilization of the force it possesses", but it can not mobilize or possess force without satisfying the critical demands of its members. Its members are not perhaps as critical as Mr. Lippmann. Neither are its actions so reasoned as his, perhaps. But its members in following leaders, in applauding and jeering, exercise the same prerogative of choice; and in that sense the public does *share* in "selecting the candidate", "writing the platform", etc.

Mr. Lippmann really recognizes that this constitutional morality implies a powerfully active national culture. "The Ins may have favored certain manufacturing interests; the Outs may favor agricultural interests. But even these differing tendencies are very small as compared with the immense area of agreement, established habit and unavoidable necessity. In fact one might say that a nation is politically stable when nothing of radical consequence is determined by its elections." [17]

But what are we to do where problems *are* disturbing and where alternative solutions of the greatest importance must be chosen, as they must in England? Mr. Lippmann interprets satisfactory adjustment to mean the absence of outcry and effective opposition. On that basis the Republican Party in this country could justify Harding's *régime* as long as it "got by". It is valuable, and in thorough accord with our theory of constitutional sovereignty to insist upon the virtue of constitutional morality. But the focus of opinion on problems depends to a large degree upon the effectiveness of editors like Mr. Lippmann and upon propagandist groups and parties, who air public problems. Otherwise the galled jade may wince in vain; for the

[16] *Phantom Public*, p. 57.　　　　[17] *Ibid.*, p. 128.

public withers go unwrung. Opinion organized through interest groups, through parties and groups of publicists who make themselves felt, depends upon the ability of leaders to bring a satisfactory percentage of national issues within the range of John Citizen's comprehension, and to impose a public policy toward them that "hangs together" in the face of events. John Citizen can not run these affairs himself. But as a member of many groups, he takes attitudes that count. And education can raise the level of his effectiveness by making him critical of his values and armed against stampede by slogans or by the perversion of his instincts of fear, or by similar familiar manipulations of "public" opinion.

Times of economic stress under conflicting social philosophies may rend constitutionalism to its core. Mr. Lippmann's own formal test for judging the "new rule" which comes with the necessity of constitutional amendments implies that public opinion must always be united by constitutional morality. But the issue may shatter that unity. "To judge a new rule the tests are three: does it provide for its own clarification? for its own amendment by consent? for due notice that amendments will be proposed? The tests are designed for use in judging the prospects of a settlement not by its substance but by its procedure. A reform which satisfies these tests is normally entitled to public support." [18]

As a sound maxim of constitutional morality, the tests for amending constitutions are excellent. But as a test of the consequences of concrete proposals for change its value is purely negative. It outlines some methods of settlement that would rule out the Fascist solution where constitutionalism is cherished more than any of the different interests that produce the conflict. Where the consideration of the intrinsic value of the proposed change is concerned, however, it offers a procedural device as a test of the merits of a concrete measure—a queerly intellectualistic proposal from a pragmatist. Shall England, for instance, accept nationalization of industry as a policy simply because it is proposed in such a way as to conform to these tests? Or shall we revoke in the United States, through a constitutional amendment, the Supreme Court's finality of decision

[18] *Ibid.*, p. 138. John Dewey, *The Public and Its Problems*, takes a different view.

as to the constitutionality of congressional acts, supposing these issues to have become vital enough to be "problems"? It is obvious that the settlement of issues which demand the change of a settled rule, because of a challenge to that rule, must be made by "judging the prospects of a settlement . . . by its substance"—contrary to Mr. Lippmann's view of the limits of public opinion.

What, then, is the true function of public opinion? Mussolini says: to support its masters. Mr. Lippmann says: to hold the ring for social contestants. But I imagine that the constitutional state must view both methods as only partial solutions. The function of opinion is to organize purpose. The party system under the stimulus of the press and of interest-groups is its proper vehicle for a workable program, and representative government its machinery. A party is held responsible on its general record tested by the way its consequences fit the dominant way of thinking in the state. It is warned in particular acts by press and propagandist utterance. It must convince a constitutional majority that it is the better choice of alternatives, which may both be regarded as partial evils, but which do afford a vehicle for social protest and reform. Public opinion is that resultant of all active opinions that gets itself accepted as binding, in President Lowell's words, on the minority as well as the majority. It depends upon constitutional morality—which is what Mr. Lippmann now calls "public opinion"—but it is not so fundamental as constitutional morality. Public opinion can change things within its sphere by a legislative majority. To change the constitutional basis for registering opinion should and does require more nearly unanimous consent.

Here, however, we face the most serious charge brought against democratic control. It is interesting that it is a charge made most determinedly by those editorialists extraordinary of *The Saturday Evening Post* who have sung the praises of Fascism.[19] Democratic control through party government and the agency of a constitutionally settled majority is not a fact, the charge goes, so long as propagandist associations, multiplying the volume of their outcry by all the devices of "loud speakers" known to pro-

[19] See the articles of Kenneth Roberts and Richard Washburn Child, *The Saturday Evening Post*, 1925-1926-1927.

fessional "organizers", can intimidate legislators into thinking that they hear the rumblings of the popular voice, their master. Add to this the disproportionate weight attaching to "bloc" methods in legislative assemblies and you get government by highly organized minorities, just as much as you do under Fascism. The difference is that these minorities use representative government to further their sectional or group interests, whereas Fascism thinks only of national interests (as interpreted, of course, by its benevolent autocracy).

It is indubitably true that the absence of a strong party system, caused by electoral devices such as Proportional Representation and by a political temperament that prefers to split into an endless and fissiparous grouping about minor differences of political belief, can bring about parliamentary impotence.[20] It is also true that a federal government even where as in Canada and Australia it is also parliamentary government, almost inevitably makes for an increase in particularism and log-rolling, and the formation of blocs of economic interests. Occupational or functional representation aimed at displacing territorial representation would, I believe, tend to increase this trend.[21]

Really, however, the situation is not so black as it is usually painted—even on the continent. The differences of interests are inevitable. Public opinion is not a general will. It is not even a consensus of purpose except as to the constitutional rules under which the game must be played out. What happens under representative government is simply this: the conflicting interests in

[20] What is ordinarily merely an annoying feature of parliamentary methods, their dilatory attitude toward financial issues, can under the stress of class war and social conflict become a breakdown for lack of decisive and swift action. Dr. Bonn paints a graphic picture: "Moreover, the preponderance of economic interests has brought about a state of affairs of parliamentary deadlock. The interests of the working classes and the interests of the capitalists are facing each other. No permanent majority can be formed, and as no permanent homogeneous majority is available there really is a deadlock. The government is paralyzed. . . . Nothing happens for the parliamentarians, supported by the bureaucrats, have learned only the art of how to stop action, not how to bring it about. . . . The nations are dissolved into economic fragments fighting each other bitterly in a purposeless economic struggle. They are in danger of losing their national consciousness." (*Op. cit.*, p. 89.)

[21] See the convincing critique of both occupational and of proportional representation under a parliamentary system, with cabinet responsibility to a single popular chamber by Mr. H. J. Laski, *A Grammar of Politics*, pp. 84 ff. and 315 ff.

a community are forced to seek a political solution instead of one based upon force. It is idle to expect groups not to seek special privileges.[22] But is it not better to make them limit their search through restricting the possibilities of settlement to constitutional action, in which public inquiry and open confrontation of interests bring about resistance by the community of groups to exploitation by any one group? Does not this mean a real influence by public opinion? Or do the opposing methods—pluralistic group competition in an impotent state, or Fascist reduction of all groups to rule by one—afford more hope of a happy combination of organic stability with the free play of purpose?

Those who bewail the blocs of a sectional nature in our own federal legislature usually mean simply that they would like a highly protected industrial East to be left to the peaceful exploitation of a farming minority in the West and South. South and West apparently cannot agree on a permanent political coalition which would unite them into a party. West wants "special privilege all around"; South until recently could not see that there ought to be so many "special" privileges, having usually had less possibility than the East for tariff privileges, being chiefly an exporter of cotton and raw materials. Now, however, the South is bound to feel the equally solid privileges accorded to the new and largely industrialized South.

Regardless of the economic merits of the "McNary-Haugenism" which temporarily united West and South—and they are, aside from a probably temporary dependence of agriculture upon the export market, not far from a par with excessive protectionism in industry [23] —bloc methods have not disrupted the republic nor defeated really essential legislation. They possibly afford a warning which the Republican party cannot much longer ignore,

[22] The best examples in general form of realistic analyses of legislative acts are Bentley's *The Process of Government* and Haynes' *Social Politics in the United States.* Professor A. N. Holcombe's classic interpretation of *The Political Parties of To-Day* has been supplemented by particular studies like Stuart Rice's *Farmers and Workers in Politics,* and Senator Arthur Capper's *The Farm Bloc in Congress,* and by E. P. Herring, *The Representation of Organized Groups in Washington.*

[23] For the usual hostile analysis see the President's Veto Message—*The United States Daily,* February 26, 1927. But see also the earlier Report of Sir Josiah Stamp rendered at the request of Vice-President Dawes, who seems inclined to champion the farmers—no doubt because he is genuinely impressed by the tremendous number of contemporary small bank failures in the West, and the alarming drift of farm population to the cities.

that the Republican West must share Republican spoils; and that the country really faces a serious problem in the passing of the independent farmer. They simply force consideration of minority interests within a great party. If they win a majority it is because party lines have ceased to represent real cleavage or leadership has afforded no alternative policy, and probably also because many doubtful votes secretly counted upon a veto.

The fact seems to be that a politically minded people finds means through representative government to get all sides of questions, economic and moral, considered and reconsidered. Procedural limitations including all types of closure are necessary to the plethoric lower chambers of modern states.[24] But they must not be drawn so tight as to make the legislature the rubber stamp of the caucus. Government must have the flexibility to tighten or relax control as the area of community involved is vital or non-vital. The *bloc* system, on the record of the past Congress, seems to have introduced a valuable flexibility into our party system without destroying its essential strength. The way to destroy that strength, infallibly, is to try to tighten up control in order to stifle political outcry from minorities. Mr. Coolidge was canny enough as a politician to understand that clearly. He permitted the outcry to cry itself out, and then vetoed the result.

But the existence of *blocs*, and of powerful lobbyists and propagandist organizations do indicate the intrusion upon the political sphere of group *opinions*, of group interests impinging at every point upon the unfortunate legislator of these times. He can never entirely duck ultimate decisions. That is his job. He can, however, be rendered helpless by the fanatical opposition of associations organized about some one single interest who "knife" a representative for opposition to their program no matter how good the rest of his record. It is the job of citizenship and of an enlightened press to evaluate a representative's service as well as a party's, on his whole record—not on a single minor issue. This is particularly true where we have not the device of general

[24] See Bryce's *Modern Democracies*, Chapter on "The Decline of Modern Legislatures"; and H. Finer, *Representative Government and a Parliament of Industry*, Part 1.

See also Congressman Robert Luce: *Legislative Procedure*, and J. A. R. Marriott's rather cursory *Mechanism of the Modern State*, 2 vols.

elections to decide crucial public issues. Public opinion, operating through elective machinery, cannot escape (though it may badly perform) this evaluative function in each elective area. Let Mr. Lippmann bewail it as a phantom if he will. His whole editorial career is aimed at making that ghost walk—and walk righteously. The "education for citizenship" which he regards as monstrous must be itself educated into an adequate method.

Happily leadership of opinion is a fact. We do not entirely depend upon the intelligence of the average citizen to judge the complex issues with which his representatives are confronted. We depend upon the effectiveness of well-led groups. We depend upon that "education for citizenship" which Mr. Lippmann so contemns, in order to get the members of those groups to judge the character of the results of governmental acts, and to distinguish the falser prophets from the truer, even if we despair of an absolute answer to Pontius Pilate's question in matters political.

Political scientists have with general accord accepted one maxim: "The more simple the machinery of democratic control, the more effectively it can be exercised." As a maxim this is probably as true as any other. But the assumption generally made by the advocates of the "short ballot" that democracies can best assure control of modern governments through centering their efforts on the selection of a responsible executive with plenary powers over the whole administration is sometimes used to excuse local electorates from carefully watching their legislative representatives. There is a real question as to whether following the Roman precedent of separating powers and then relying on the popular tribunes may not lead us to Cæsarism. Parliamentary indirection of representative control often escapes this danger. Reliance upon the executive is too often the old "We-want-the-man-not-the-program" attitude that means the end of active public opinion.[25]

[25] H. J. Ford's *Representative Government* is one of the most interesting studies and adequate criticisms of this tendency. Woodrow Wilson in his earlier works, particularly in *Congressional Government*, felt the need for an extra-constitutional parliamentarization of the rôle of American executives, particularly the President. While it is true that a strong Governor frequently carries his points, he does so despite the unwieldy technique of our separation of powers in the State governments.

A radical proposal for reconstructing our system is to be found in W. MacDonald, *A New Constitution for a New America*.

There is this reason for believing that in the State Governments and even more in the city governments of the United States we have followed the wrong institutional path in taking over the colonial practice and the revolutionary dogma of a separation of powers. The Jacksonian period of our pioneer democracy fastened the emphasis on the executive firmly upon us. The result has been to weaken the development of real issues for the formulation of state-wide opinions, and the fastening of state political parties as illogical appendages to the national parties. Furthermore the existence of two chambers in state and even city governments has added another useless reduplication and a positively vicious means of escaping the assumption of political responsibility. There is small doubt that bloc methods and pressure by propagandist, lobbyist, and interest groups is more felt and less easily brought under party programs in the States of the United States than in the provinces of Canada or the States of Australia.[26] There is a much smaller importance attached to the Lobby in these Dominions. It exists, no doubt, but it exists as an outlaw and not on open sufferance. The legislative body offers an opening to a political career toward an executive beginning—say as a mayor or as a member of the governor's "official family". Our public men are less public and our lobbies more powerful for the lack of centralizing both executive responsibility and political control ultimately in the legislature. The perpetual condition of a governor and his legislature at loggerheads is not conducive to a coördinated program.

A comparison between our elaborately checked and balanced and politically irresponsible municipal systems with the simplicity of council-controlled municipalities upon the continent of Europe and particularly in England, is a source of constant humiliation to those who study political institutions scientifically. In order for any community to achieve a co-organic political life

[26] This very important fact seems to have escaped the notice of our enthusiasts for "majority" government who still believe in the separation of powers—such as R. W. Child and the other popularizers of party regularity and anti-bloc activities. Lobbies are less effective in the British system for two reasons: (1) more effective concentration of responsibility for a legislative program in the party leaders in parliament with a consequent strengthening of party discipline and power, (2) more effective committee investigations aided by the available expertness of a civil service in liaison with the legislature.

its internal structure must be scientifically adjusted to secure responsible control and at the same time make possible administrative experts. The board of directors idea must be for that reason imported into our governing processes.

To examine concrete questions of effective social structure in the light of the context and the values to be realized through organization is a genuinely pragmatic task. But a political pragmatism that takes into account the co-organic character of groups will examine purposes as well as present facts. Its method in fact-finding and questions of technique must be scientific so far as objectivity is concerned. But its ethical postulates must transcend those of romanticism and of instrumentalism in asserting the ultimate value of moral personality in individuals, and the necessity of a social structure that will protect it.

B. Pragmatic Jurisprudence in the United States: Dean Pound and Justice Holmes

In this way we come back to the really fruitful part of James' doctrine, a part not original with pragmatism, but as old as the realist spirit in philosophy: the *Denkmittel* of experience, he admitted,[27] "are now a part of the very structure of our mind. We cannot play fast and loose with them. No experience can upset them. On the contrary, they apperceive every experience and assign it to its place.

"To what effect? That we may the better foresee the course of our experience, communicate with one another, and steer our lives by rule. Also that we may have a cleaner, clearer, more inclusive mental view."

Pragmatism, thus rid of its anti-intellectualist bias, is the spirit of the living law. For in politics, as in all life, we have great need of the willingness to experiment and to profit by our experience. So long as Instrumentalism, too, remains normative and purposive, instead of descriptive and positivistic, it can serve us well. How well, indeed, the jurisprudence of Dean Pound and the decisions of Justice Holmes have proved.

Dean Pound has phrased his own pragmatic criterion thus:

---

[27] *Select Papers on Philosophy,* "Humanism and Truth," p. 224 (Everyman ed.).

"The moral criterion by which to try social institutions and political measures may be summed up as follows: the test is whether a given custom or law sets free individual capacities in such a way as to make them available for the development of the general happiness or the common good. The formula states the test with the emphasis falling upon the side of the individual. It may be stated from the side of associated life as follows: the test is whether the general, the public, organization and order are promoted in such a way as to equalize opportunity for all." [28] He adds that the "interests of personality" are recognized and defined, not created by law. "There is so much truth in the old theories of natural rights."

This is a different pragmatism from that pragmatic functionalism represented by De Maeztu, e.g., "Rights do not rise from personality. This idea is mystic and unnecessary. Rights arise primarily from the relation of the associated with the thing that associates them. . . ." [29] The pragmatism of Dean Pound is really a sort of critical Social Utilitarianism, as he would, himself, be the first to say. The same thing is perhaps true of the ethical *attitude* of pragmatism in James and in Dewey, distinguished from their ethical theory. Professor R. B. Perry has said of them: "The instrumentalists, like many radical theorists, are protected against themselves by their adherence to the traditional idea of collective human happiness, but in principle they are open to the same charge as that which may be brought against the more revolutionary exponents of irrationalism. They encourage the view that it does not make so much difference where man is going, as long as he is on his way." [30]

It is this same traditional principle which prevents the constitutional decisions of Mr. Justice Holmes from expressing in fact that hard gospel of survivalism which he has expounded at times in theory: "I used to say when I was young," he says in a delightful essay on "Natural Law", [31] "that truth was the majority vote of that nation which could lick all others . . . and I think

---

[28] This moral criterion he quotes from Dewey and Tufts, *Ethics* (pp. 482-483). The quotation is taken from an article in *H. L. R.* 28, pp. 343-344.
[29] *Authority, Liberty and Function*, p. 250.
[30] *The Present Conflict of Ideals*, p. 347.
[31] *H. L. R.*, XXXII, pp. 40 ff. Reprinted in *Collected Legal Papers*, p. 310.

that statement was correct in so far as it implied that our test of truth is a reference to either a present or an imagined future majority in favor of our view. If, as I have suggested elsewhere, the truth may be defined as the system of my (intellectual) limitations, what gives it its objectivity is the fact that I find my fellow man to a greater or a less extent (never wholly) subject to the same *Can't Helps.* . . ."

This is a true pragmatic ultimacy of values, and Judge Holmes clinches the matter by saying, "Deep-seated beliefs can not be argued about—you can not argue a man into liking a glass of beer—and therefore when differences are sufficiently far reaching, we try to kill the other man rather than let him have his way." As against those who believe in Natural Law, then, he urges that there are no *a-priori* moral obligations generally recognizable: "The jurists who believe in natural law seem to me to be in that naïve state of mind that accepts what has been familiar and accepted by them and their neighbors as something that must be accepted by all men everywhere . . . the question remains as to the *ought* of natural law." And it is Dewey's morality of social imposition at which he logically arrives. "I see no *a-priori* duty to live with others and in that way, but simply what I must do if I wish to remain alive. If I do live with others they tell me that I must do and abstain from doing certain things or they will put the screws on me. . . . I believe that they will, and being of the same mind as to their conduct, I not only accept the rules, but come in time to accept them with sympathy and emotional satisfaction, and begin to talk about duties and rights." This is not juridical realism in the mouth of a theorist like M. Duguit. It is the pronouncement of one of the most influential justices of the Supreme Court of the United States. If he really decided cases on this moral basis, it would be echoed in decisions where pragmatism assumes the most immediate and far-reaching consequences. It is Justice Holmes who says: "But for legal purposes law is only the hypostasis of a prophecy—the imagination of a substance supporting the fact that the public force will be brought to bear upon those who do things said to contravene it, just as we talk of the force of gravitation accounting for the conduct of bodies in space . . . but that does not seem to me the same thing as the supposed *a-priori* discernment of a duty or the assertion of a pre-existing right. A dog will fight for his bone."

It is with this psychological background, very similar to that remarked in M. Duguit, that a Supreme Court Justice says he approaches the problems of "controlling" the legislation aimed at settling the "dog-fight" between "Capital and Labor" over their eternal bone of contention. Mr. Laski, who can say "Moreover, it is not greatness of purpose that seems important so much as the capacity to secure intensity of affection. This . . . is surely the attitude of those who resist the state," naturally finds great comfort in the decisions of Justice Holmes.[32]

Mr. Felix Frankfurter has analyzed "The Constitutional Opinions of Justice Holmes"[33] to show the pragmatic fruits of this attitude: "In all the variety of cases the opinions of Mr. Justice Holmes show the same realism, the same refusal to defeat life by formal logic, the same regard for local needs and habits, the same deference to local knowledge. He recognizes that government necessarily means experimentation, and while the very essence of constitutional limitations is to confine the area of experimentation, the limitations are not self-defining, and they were intended to permit government."[34] And there really is this admirable quality in Justice Holmes' opinions. In the famous *Lochner v. New York* case[35] his dissenting opinion went far toward making good his declaration that "The Fourteenth Amendment does not enact Mr. Herbert Spencer's *Social Statics*", by showing the developing context within which rights must be interpreted. But the very Kantian morality at which he has poked pragmatic fun, is implied in his philosophy of the law, and really underlies his decisions to a far greater degree than Survivalist ethics and the Fear-Theory. Let Mr. Laski take note of his dissenting opinion holding that congress had the power to legislate in regard to industrial relations on inter-state railways as a means of securing industrial peace[36] in order to see what store he sets by state-purpose. Justice Holmes is not a pluralist in that respect, or in respect to the ultimacy of federal control:

[32] Problem of Authority, pp. 15-16. Cf. Preface also.
[33] *H. L. R.*, Vol. XXIX, p. 683 and supplemented in Vol. XLI, No. 2.
[34] *Op. cit.*, ff. 692.
[35] 198 U. S. 45-75.
[36] *Adair vs. U. S., 208 U. S.*, 161 (1908).

speaking on the Interstate Commerce Clause, he said: "I do not think that the United States would come to an end if we lost our power to declare an act of Congress void. I do think the Union would be imperilled if we could not make that declaration as to the laws of the several states. For one in my place sees how often a local policy prevails with those who are not trained to national views, and how often action is taken that embodies what the commerce clause was meant to end." [37]

The pragmatic philosophy of law, in the hands of its American exponents, has tended in spite of its fact-loving and realistic temper, toward the same juridical idealism which we observed in the practical recommendations of M. Duguit. No one has better pointed out this tendency than Professor Morris Cohen. The social solidarity which it assumes is one of purpose, and a purpose based upon the ethics of personalism and universalism which it, like the pragmatist philosophers proper, takes for granted. As a practical philosophy, pragmatism presents the paradox of approving what its theory condemns. Pragmatic practice contradicts, happily, pragmatic preaching in these jurists. For it discovers in community "interest" something not purely economic, but purposive and moral. Its state turns out to be not pluralistic but unifying; not organic, but co-organic.

The attitude of such a pragmatism, illustrated in Mr. A. D. Lindsay's theory of the Constitution as the nexus of constituent and legal sovereignty, is both a philosophy and a method, and not one merely of revolt. It is willing to test consequences themselves by the reason that is in us. It does not remain rooted in the anti-intellectualism of instinctive revolt, but sets about the construction of a new order with full consciousness of the organic connection which the new must have with the old. In its application I have suggested that it must attack the problem of groups so central to modern theory neither in the spirit of the ultimate pluralism of real group persons which Mr. Laski once advanced as the pluralists' standard, nor in the anti-metaphysical positivism of the Solidarist doctrines of M. Duguit. William James himself has given a statement to the faith that is the necessary concomitant of any co-organic purpose, one that, applied to the

[37] *Speeches and Essays*, 98-103, "Speech at a Dinner of the Harvard Law School Association of New York."

state, contrasts oddly with the distrust of his professed disciples in politics:

"A social organism of any sort whatever, large or small, is what it is because each member proceeds to his own duty with a trust that the other members will simultaneously do theirs. Wherever a desired result is achieved by the coöperation of many independent persons, its existence as a fact is a pure consequence of the precursive faith in one another of those immediately concerned. A government, an army, a commercial system, a ship, a college, an athletic team, all exist on this condition, without which not only is nothing achieved, but nothing is even attempted." [38]

The co-organic or constitutional State must be the result of this faith, a faith that can only result from the demonstrable belief that government under law is the expression of a shared moral purpose toward an ideal of the good life. That is a purposive community, it is true, which cannot be conjured up by rationalistic legerdemain; but it is certainly a community which does not thrive in an atmosphere of stimulated distrust of men's power to secure justice through the rule of law. Wisdom in ordering the political life of the community, like wisdom in the entire realm of human conduct, may lie, after all, in that Aristotelian mean which assures an attitude of mutual tolerance, and a spirit of coöperation in the achievement of those broad moral ends common to all morally mature persons.

[38] James, "Will to Believe" (*Select Papers in Philosophy*, Everyman ed., p. 119).

Faith and loyalty are given to an organization, if my analysis of the co-organic nature of such groups as command them is correct, because it represents a common moral purpose. The members of such a group feel that they become "somebody" through sharing its common life and purpose. The laborer finds his self-respect in the very real democracy of the trade union, just as an undergraduate joining a college begins to share the feeling of its corporate life. The sense of purpose is there ; however dimly conscious it may be in the individual, it is always operative as a moral stimulus. The more conscious the members become of the part they play in its realization, the more co-organic the group.

From this standpoint it is impossible to overestimate the value of Workers' Education Movements, and the potentialities of the Unions themselves, if they can ever escape the necessity of being primarily fighting units bent on attaining security. "Man does not live by bread alone," but a hungry belly knows no law.

CHAPTER XVI

JURISTIC ASPECTS OF THE CONSTITUTIONAL STATE —INTERNAL AND INTERNATIONAL

Is it also fair to ask what will be the effect of this pragmatic modification upon constitutional and international juristic theory, once we have accepted it for politics? While it is obvious that this is not the place to undertake a detailed survey of juristic concepts such as Professor W. W. Willoughby has given in his valuable *Fundamental Concepts of Public Law,* it is perhaps possible to offer some suggestions in bare outline. To fill in the details requires historical citation to actual states in accordance with cultural contexts. For what we have accepted of pragmatism dictates that juristic may no more than political science remain purely formal. Its concepts must be fitted to the structure of political facts.

In the first place, a co-organism, like the orders of organic life, must adapt itself to the prevailing requirements of its environment. The fact that this adaptation is normative means that it will not be content merely with survival nor will it make the group of any sort an end in itself. The co-organic state must attempt to secure all the conditions of economic and political survival, but it will attempt to impose as much of ideal purpose upon those conditions as lies in the power of its resources of intelligence, social discipline, and leadership. For the very reason that the conditions of national solidarity, of culture, of economic development, of religion, and of race differ enormously, it is impossible to do more than offer a general orientation to all political development toward constitutionalism as the basis of our juristic theory and then come, as Mr. Dewey insists, from *the* state to concrete cases of actual states for our test by application.

470

A. Sovereignty

It is already clear that a legally unifying sovereignty is regarded, under the co-organic theory of the state, as the primary organic condition of political efficiency for the nation. It is equally clear that in some states efficiency must often give way to lack of cultural community. Such sovereignty, legally treated as absolute in the *de jure* government of the state, exists in varying degrees as a fact, dependent upon economic as well as purposive community.

Even while jurists were most rigidly affirming the absolute legal sovereignty of the British Crown in Parliament over the entire Empire, the facts had long since given this fiction the lie. The British Empire would perhaps be economically more efficient as a partially federalized system of imperial preference, from the point of view of England, at least—possibly also from the Dominion standpoint, in the long run. But the natural areas of cultural community are not those of a single co-organic commonwealth, where the good of the numerical bulk of the people of the "white" Empire could be legally registered by a single legislative organ into such a system of imperial exchange. The Dominions have long refused to share their good things with Great Britain, or to accept a full share of its heavy tax burden. Great Britain naturally uses her less autonomous dependencies to her own advantage. Sovereignty over an Empire as a fact rests in the power of England to control only England's smaller dependencies and the home realm; in India and in Egypt the same anomaly of partial control exists as in the mandates system, a control subject to limitation in the former case by internal rather than by world opinion. But a very real and now fairly complete autonomy is vested in the new nationalism of the Dominions. The limits of legal community are created rather by a complex nationalism than by economic laws. In fact it is the nationalism that makes the unit of economic law.[1]

But is Willoughby's State-Person juristically adequate as a theoretical basis for sovereignty in a world so politically relative

[1] For an economist's impatience with this state of affairs see F. Delaisi, *Political Myths and Economic Realities*, English translation, N. Y. (1927).

and complex? Or can we accept Kelsen's theory of pure law that would make only international law real law? Legal sovereignty is formally useful and actually a working description of facts in the internal law of homogeneous nation states. The concept is false if applied out of its proper context. And it does not rest even as a concept upon a state-person, but upon a co-organic constitutional system.

The second point about sovereignty as a fact is that though it can not be based permanently upon fear and force, it may be as absolute a present condition as force can make it, and hence juristically as valid as constitutional sovereignty. As a fact, something like Fascist sovereignty is far more complete than is the fact of group resistance to law, in any state that Mr. Laski chooses to consider. Not only as a normative ideal but also as a long run condition, satisfactory to civilized society, neither Fascist sovereignty nor pluralistic impotence can characterize the state. It may be politically a sound prediction that legal sovereignty, or the monopoly of organized force, can only be vested for long run utility in a constitutionally responsible government. But for juristic purposes the sovereignty of the Fascist government is unquestionable. Legal sovereignty need only be functionally adequate to its legal end; that is, it must be capable of preventing any resort to force for the settlement of group as well as individual conflicts. Such conflicts may include strikes or lockouts of any nature that acutely endanger the most vital public services or chronically disturb the necessary sources of all production.

Furthermore, legal sovereignty must be organically self-sufficient in any fully developed state. That is, it must have a division of the powers of government so legally determined that there can be no ultimate conflict of laws or of jurisdiction. A system of law demands coherence of juridical structure, as well as the ultimacy of the legal validity vested in the process of constitutional amendment. At its basis must be the constituent sovereignty of fact based either on constitutional morality or upon existing and recognized force. For juristic theory it is only necessary that the existing government be recognized internally and internationally as that which actually acts upon its subjects with the possible sanction of all the state's force behind it. In international law it need only be able so to speak as bearing the *personam* (or from its Latin derivation, the *mask*) of the nation sufficiently to guarantee the forces of its treaties and international obligations.[2]

B. The Federal State and Federal Representation

It is clear that the complexity of political control, taking a world view, is not so simple as this, *de facto*. How shall we account, juristically, for those political groups that are real units but not full juridical states? The *organic* theory of the state that issues in the juridical theory of the State-Person cannot recognize any degree or area of community protected from the sovereignty of the state. Yet such degrees and areas manifestly do exist. Fascism is as savagely opposed to group federalism, territorial or functional within the state as were the men of the French Revolution under the inspiration of Rousseau, or as was even Hobbes himself. Every association must be Fascist. Yet even the Leviathan's maw of Fascism can not and dare not attempt to engulf the Pope.[3] The relation of the Pope to Fascism bears some analogies to the position of a strong protected state toward a "protector" whose power over the protected is dangerous if exercised.

The strictly *pluralistic* theory of the state is equally as absolute in its contention that the federalism of regions and functional associations must be ultimate, and that the state must possess no powers that will permit it to intrude upon group autonomy. It insists that the pluralism which characterizes international society also marks national authority.

[2] A good statement of this point of view in international law is to be found in David J. Hill, *World Organization and the Modern State*. It has been generally accepted by English and American writers on international law, Lawrence, Hall, Hershey, G. G. Wilson, etc. It has been savagely and acutely criticized on the continent by Hans Kelsen, *Das Problem der Souveränität und die Theorie des Völkerrechts* (1920), and by Nelson, Pillet, Krabbe, Borchard and others. For the literature see Crane, *The State in Constitutional and International Law*, and the very interesting critical analysis of "The Limitations on Sovereignty in International Relations" by James W. Garner (Presidential Address before the American Political Science Association), printed in *Am. Pol. Sci. Rev.*, Vol. XIX, No. 1 (1925).

[3] The very interesting overtures by Mussolini aimed at placating the papacy in its opposition to the extreme *étatisme* of Fascist practice in education and indoctrination have gone so far as to suggest the revival of a limited temporal power for the Pope, extending perhaps over the old Leonine city. Naturally the Pope has not taken the bait.

The co-organic theory of the state attempts to do justice both to unity and plurality. It finds in the constitution of the state the real basis of legal sovereignty, supported by a constituent sovereignty—the active loyalty of citizens to the constitution—sufficient to ensure its acceptance and enforcement by the great bulk of the people. But as constituent sovereignty means only loyalty to the constitution, it does not preclude a "rigid" division of the exercise of legal powers either to territorial or to functional areas of community, nor does it deny the limits of loyalty in *fact*,[4] even where they are denied in law.

The state, if it is a state in the full sense of the term, is a people organized for law on a definite territory. If it is to be a federal state and not a confederation of states, the constitution must contain a definite and generally accepted means of legal amendment not requiring unanimity, as well as provisions that afford the power to the central government to act if necessary directly upon individual citizens within the scope of its most important functions. If these two powers are absent, as they are in the relations between Great Britain and the Dominions, there is no federal state but a league of more or less formally confederated states. The political facts may be a compromise between a confederation and a federal state that no juristic category precisely fits.

On the other hand a confederation may be formally complete, as was the first government of the United States in the period 1781-1789; but it is not a co-organic state in the full sense of the term, even though it may be a formal confederacy of states. For nullification and secession are, theoretically and practically, disputed powers, depending upon the good will of the members, or the vigor of the leading states of the confederacy. The history of the period of the Articles of Confederation is proof enough of that, without turning to the Netherlands or to the Greek Leagues.

---

[4] Few even of the analytical jurists professed to be describing an absolute reign of automatically enforceable law as a fact. They merely insisted that jurists must have a logically coherent and integrated hierarchy of legal powers in order to avoid conflicts of laws—a legitimate assertion. It was only when they began to erect this legal structure into the assertion of an equivalent metaphysically absolute sovereignty that they ran seriously aground—so long at least as national systems of law were the limits of legal conventions. See John Dickinson, "A Working Theory of Sovereignty," *Pol. Sci. Qu.*, Vol. XLII, No. 4, and Vol. XLIII, No. 1.

It is obvious, however, that while there is a tremendous practical difference between a confederation and a federal state, and a theoretical distinction of equal necessity, there is none the less present a common purpose toward a limited degree and area of community of action in the confederacy. To a smaller degree the same thing is true of a League, even though the members reserve the right to be judges of their obligations to the League. Allied states during a war offer another instance of temporary community of purpose. To formal juristic theory all these must fall into rigid and separate categories. But is the whole question of statehood, then, one simply of degree? What is one to say of the nature of the member units of a federal state, where, as in the United States and in Australia, they have surrendered only certain enumerated functions to the central (or so-called federal) government? Or what is one to say of the even more difficult cases of countries like Egypt, proclaimed to be an independent state "with reservations" on the part of a "protecting" sponsor like Great Britain?[5] Are these, too, not states? Do they not meet half the Austinian test by possessing autonomous control over their subjects and is that not enough to meet Jellinek's full test of auto-limitation? Or may we not apply the term state to a political grouping of states like the British Commonwealth of Nations that fulfils the other half of Austin's requirement by being, as a group, independent of external control? And what of the "divided sovereignty" of the League Mandates System?

Let us deal first with the difficult problem of leagues and confederacies and their similarity to the federal state. It is clear that in external relations they approach our criteria for statehood in hanging together as a co-organic unit. May one not say that in this relation and for this purpose a confederation must juridically be considered a state? It is only when we approach the question of internal supremacy of the central body on questions that do not bear on external relations that the power of unified action disappears: a confederation is a state only

[5] For a brief description of the legal side of British control in Egypt see A. B. Keith, *The Constitution, Laws and Administration of the British Empire*, pp. 290-293. For details see George Young, *Egypt* (1927). A detailed study is still wanting of the new Empire: perhaps because it is still too much in the making, for positive statement. The recent study, *Empire to Commonwealth*, by W. P. Hall (1928) partly supplies this lack on the historical side.

for certain purposes. The objection to this relativity in juristic construction is that external independence may depend in fact upon an internal supremacy not actually existent. Formally, nullification may be legally impossible. Practically the experience of confederacies indicates a strong probability that in order to have unity in external matters, coercion of member states must be possible internally.

I think it is clear that there is in the federal state an extension of the range of unity also to internal affairs by a determinate amending process, not requiring the consent of each member which can alter the whole character of the distribution of powers. The relation internally is no longer contractual. The states are not final judges. This process protects the members in a way in which they are not protected as areas of local government in a unitary state, but it makes the members no longer final judges of their own acts. In a truly federal state, that is—while the consent of the members as units is required, not merely the consent of a majority of population taken without consideration for the federal units [6] —there is none the less a legal finality vested in a process above the separate states. Usually a Supreme Federal Court is vested with ultimate powers of federal judicial review.

Usually the consent of more than an ordinary majority of the members is required to alter the federal constitution which protects the members. That is not the case in a unitary state in relation to the powers of local government. There the consent of the territorial areas is not taken by units but by bulk of total population, without regard to distribution. Devolution, decentralization, deconcentration do not mean federalism, unless the powers of altering the status of the smaller areas be taken out of the control of the central government. This much formal definitions can do for us and still not do violence to facts. When

---

[6] A study of the amending clauses in federal states will bear this out. The Union of South Africa is *not* a federal state, and the Dominion of Canada really requires practical unanimity of all the great provinces to amend the constitution, so long as the legal process is in the hands of the British Parliament. See note appended to British North America act of 1907. (W. P. M. Kennedy, *The Constitution of Canada*, p. 450.) Future amendments will have to be accepted by both major parties in all probability; whether the formality of then submitting them to British Parliament will be gone through with is doubtful.

we examine particular cases we must see whether the facts *really* do fit our definition, however.

There is, then, in any federal state, a determinate process not requiring unanimity of the members by which the whole constitution may be altered. Therefore the state has assumed a character of legal self-sufficiency, both internal and external, with the locus of ultimate sovereignty not in the individual members, but in an extraordinary majority of them acting according to a constitutionally accepted process. Nor do the members remain judges of their own obligations or final jurisdiction, as they do practically in a confederacy, and theoretically as well as practically in a league. Once a federal state is created in fact, there is no legal right to nullify its laws or to secede. On the other hand, the federal balance of representation may be quite rigidly maintained *in statu quo.*

Therefore the co-organic theory insists that organic self-sufficiency under a constitution amendable by a specified majority is the characteristic, juridical and actual, of the complete state, federal as well as unitary, if the state is considered both in the context of its internal supremacy and external independence.

The protection of the local autonomy of certain areas from interference by the federal government is, though, a fact of great importance.[7] The federal state is different from the unitary state in the degree of its organic homogeneity. While the unitary state is based upon a co-organic constitution in which the indi-

[7] It cannot be juristically reduced to the same status as the right of local government without falsification of the facts. In the very subtle juristic analysis of Professor W. W. Willoughby, the difference between federal government and unitary government is for juristic purposes a difference simply of degree, not of kind, as it is when approached from the conception of Jellinek or Kelsen. For the comparison of the two views see Willoughby, *Fundamental Concepts of Public Law,* Chapters XIII, XIV, and XV. Professor Willoughby is perfectly correct in saying that the member states only possess "limited legal competence" (p. 196 n), but that legal competence, even though limited, is self-derived in a way quite different from the rights of local governments lumped together. As it is more simply put in terms of the co-organic federal state, where areas of community correspond to areas of historically grounded cultural and economic integration, the federal areas of states have autonomous rights. Failure to recognize this relation and its grounding in historical processes gets Professor Willoughby into the usual logical dilemma over the constitutional issues that led to the Civil War. See especially pp. 240-244 and 251-253, *op. cit.* Force, organically necessary in this case of the breakdown of community of constitutionally workable purpose as in others, completed an evolution that juristic processes could not solve without force.

vidual citizen is regarded as the unit of political equality, as well as of actual co-operation and legal right, the federal state is based upon the balance of a co-organic relation among states, as well as among individuals. The unit of equality for many important powers (as in those of the Senate of the United States) is the state, without regard to population. Federalism is therefore an attempt at retaining the relative permanency of a limitation on the federal government, through a constitution not alterable by a simple majority of the federal legislature. The community of purpose among the member states is a limited community. In its fundamental basis of equality of states in a Senate it may be a community limited in change to consent by each State. The possibility of changing its constitutional basis in any respect is limited to a majority of an unusual order, an extraordinary majority of the states as equal units. The State-Person can hardly explain the facts of federalism on any simple theory of a unitary will.

I. Federalism and Representation

The truth of pluralism lies in its insight, in theories like that of Mr. Laski, into the fact that federalism based upon a working division of powers to fit areas of community is the key to a workable means of political association in international as well as in national society. International society may not be able to set up anything more than the League, but a league may exert real powers under constitutional limitations without possessing the sovereignty of the full juridical state. To the degree that its coercive sanctions for its limited purposes become real, its members as well cease to be juridically full states. The new juristic order will admit the possibility of a co-organization of legal community to fit the focus of purpose.

Even in the federal state, the matters that concern all the member states, as a community of purpose which they share with each other but not with other and foreign states, is vested in the central government. The control of the central government over matters of common defence is given in terms usually the most absolute, because a common organic need has created it; yet that does not involve a similarly absolute federal police power. The control over economic standards common to the entire group of states is usually less complete, with a gradual tendency to grow more extensive and more uniform as economic interdependence develops. The history of the United States (or of any other federal state) may be cited. There remains, however, a cultural sectionalism that forms the true basis for state control of the bulk of the police power in regulating ordinary morality and the standards of legislation affecting it.

Ought not this cultural federalism to be extended as far as possible to other than territorial areas? If upon the free and spontaneous growth of cultural differences, protected by the free development of all varieties of groups, depend the conditions of creative activity which human personality must share in order to realize its full moral stature, there seems to be a case for federalizing the internal autonomy of other than territorial groups, by giving them a constitutionally protected status from legislative interference with their chartered rights.

The point that Mr. Laski's theory emphasizes is that there is a place for such federalism, based not only on territorial but on functional groups, even in the unitary state. He advocates a rigid constitution in which the limits of state power should be set forth as to individual rights but, curiously enough, not to group rights. Practically, the end of protecting other than territorial areas of community is perhaps better attained in the legally unitary as well as the federal state by a tradition of constitutional restraint. Unless the functional groups are to be made units of political representation they have less need for the rigidity of federalism. England has not been less successful in protecting the rights of individuals as well as of both territorial and functional groups under her largely unwritten and legally flexible constitution than have other countries under rigid constitutions. Quite possibly she is more successful in this protection though not legally federal or even rigid in her constitutional protections of group and individual rights.

Whatever success Mr. Laski is willing to credit to British constitutionalism in the protection of groups within the state he thinks is due to the spirit of resistance. He urges that the juristic problem can not be stated without this *addendum*. That, as I have urged, is to misinterpret the technique of constitutional restraint. It might be used to describe the struggle for the suffrage and for parliamentary reform. But under universal suffrage it is rather because the British party system is fairly balanced and imbued with a respect for constitutional practice, and because the oppression of any group or individual offers the opportunity for political protest through a change of party loyalty and of governments. It is most of all because the accepted "myth" of constitutional restraint has proved its value throughout the last two centuries of British history that what amounts to a real federal protection can be accorded to groups within its legally unitary sphere. So long as resistance to oligarchic control was necessary, political action could not alone secure the rule of law. But constitutional democracy obviates the necessity of direct actions.

The fact is that a constitution, whether its rigidity be due to tradition or to mechanical difficulties thrown in the way of amendment, does attempt to treat group autonomy as having a protected sphere of development, and hence does introduce into any constitutional state the co-organic aspect: limitation of community of every sort to conform to a defined area of purpose arrived at by *political* competition of groups for their rights, within the limits of constitutional morality. The state itself is limited in sphere because it represents not the whole purpose of society as Fascism assumes, but simply the purpose to create workable rules in restraint of settlement by force. Within its area of community, broadening with the increase in social solidarity and intensifying whenever there are threats against its life, the state is supreme. A constitution, written or practiced, is the attempt to co-organize the state in terms of community of purpose. Its very nature as a legal co-organism restricts its application of force by constitutional rules. There is, therefore, in such a state the idea of the *Rechtsstaat* as its basis, with a real limitation to conformity with a *Rechtsidee* that sanctions only constitutional procedure. This is the point of juristic connection between legal and constituent sovereignty. No juristic theory of sovereignty can escape the effort to marry constituent to legal sovereignty without being merely formal and tautological.

Actually, even in the unitary state, the apportionment of representation is not rigidly mathematical. Historically integrated areas are retained undivided to secure real areas of community. Country is weighted against town, to make up for the greater compactness of urban political organization. The English borough and county system and American state apportionment are familiar and often exaggerated examples. This weighting of electoral areas is already a step in the direction of the technique of the federal state.

Are we not carried a further step by the representation of various cultural and economic interests in second chambers, or actually in third chambers of an advisory nature?[8] The principle of economic and cultural group representation on a nonterritorial and undemocratic basis of selection cannot be sanctioned, as we have seen, as a means of securing final representative control. But as a means of securing advice and restraint, might it not become a valuable adjunct to the legislative machinery? Would it help to preserve a co-organic relationship between the state and the great social groups which comprise it? In the modern state such groups are certain to make themselves felt. A proper federalization of authority might keep them from making themselves felt simply by threats to legislators, or against the community's public services, but would enable them to be heard where all may command equitable attention and fair play. This is the principle on which modern states are trying to turn lobbyists into advisers who must come into the open with their proposals. It is the kernel of the case for advisory economic councils and commissions. The experiment is as yet in

[8] For descriptions of the various devices of group representation in second chambers see H. B. Lees-Smith, *Second Chambers in Theory and Practice*, with special reference to the Irish Free State.

For the literature on advisory economic parliaments, see the article of A. Bergsträsser in Schmoller's *Jahrbücher* (1925), *"Neuere Literatur zum Berufständischen Gedanke."* An excellent historical survey is given in Georg Bernhard's *Wirtschafts Parlamente* (Vienna and Leipzig), 1923.

For a strong case against advisory or other economic parliaments and in favor of Parliamentary Commissions of advisory aspects see Mr. H. J. Laski, *A Grammar of Politics*, chapter on "Political Institutions," especially his use of the *Report of the Machinery of Government Committee*, and pp. 84-139, pp. 349-352.

For an early estimate of the Provisional Economic Parliament in Germany, see H. Finer, *Representative Government and a Parliament of Industry* (1923).

For France see Edith C. Bramhall, "The National Economic Council in France" (*Am. Pol. Sci. Rev.*, Vol. XX, No. 3, Aug., 1926).

For Italy see Schneider, "Italy's New Syndicalist Constitution," *Political Science Quarterly*, Vol. XLIII, No. 2, June 1927, and Chapter XI, this volume.

its beginnings. But no modern legislature can perform its duties without expert advice to assist its committees. The most efficient organization of that advice is, however, a political not a juristic problem.

C. Semi-Sovereign States, Dependencies, and Mandates

To understand the position of these political groups in relation to the co-organic theory of the state, it is first necessary to come to some conclusions as to the nature of international society, if our juristic concepts are to be adequate to fit the facts.

In the first place, it cannot, I think, be denied even by the League's best friends that international society of the present time is pluralistic rather than constitutional or organic. As a state the League of Nations and the World Court represent exactly that "Discredited State" which syndicalistic pluralism desires within the nation. The League is able to justify itself as the super-state which Mr. Laski oddly believes it to be only if the constitutional state is treated, as he treats it, as internally lacking coercive finality. Simply because in "the ceaseless striving" of national group competition there is not yet a sufficient trust in it as an arbiter to endow it with coercive powers, negotiation and a "Darwin-wise" struggle still characterize international intercourse, on the patent witness of the times. The League is a beginning in the effort to put a stop to international anarchy. Actually it constitutes about the same authority in the modern feudalism of international society that the king's authority did in the area comprising France of, say, the Thirteenth Century, with perhaps some addition of the moral suasion of the Pope. The League has, theoretically, large powers of sanction, economic, military, and moral. But it has not the force at its own disposal to check this modern feudalism, any more than had the King of France of that period to hold his own greater vassals in order. Any comparison to our own impotent government under the Articles of Confederation would be vastly in the latter's favor, so far as control over its members was concerned.

It is as a settled method of conference on international problems that the League has real value. Aside from that the League can proceed only to coöperative welfare work, because it is limited to matters commanding unanimity. That is not ideal; that is not, one hopes, a permanent condition. There are signs, indeed, that the sanction of the moral disapproval of such intertional community as already exists is becoming a real restraint on the more blatant types of international bad morals and worse manners. But the absence of final legal control is a present fact. And it is in the light of the fact of an international pluralism, with only a small realm of securely sanctioned law, that we must approach the nature of semi-sovereign states, dependencies, and mandates. A settled method of conferring about the issues which they provoke is a great step forward, but it is not a constitutional state above them.

The tremendous complexity of actual political organization is nowhere better illustrated than in the British Empire with its Commonwealths of Dominions, its Empire of Colonies, protected states, protectorates, mandates, and spheres of influence. It is obvious that the co-organic theory implies as a normative ideal the principle of self-determination for really national units, with the ultimate hope of an internationally federalized and co-organic society, when a sufficient strength of world community shall have developed. But how shall juridical theory determine the sufficiency of national units to co-organic completeness and statehood, in the absence of a real international control?

In the first place, one aspect of juridical theory is, as Professor W. W. Willoughby has put it, not interested in ideals.[9] Its business is simply to describe the facts. A descriptive theory of the state can only say that if internal supremacy and external independence are characteristic of the great powers and of a large number of juridical entities to which the term state is applied, some addition must be made to that description, such as the word *sovereign*, if it is proposed to treat states that are not possessed of both internal supremacy and external independence as also being *states* within the juridical

[9] I do not contest the legitimacy of such a juridical discipline, or the utility of its conceptual analysis. But I agree with Mr. Laski and other pragmatic critics in demanding that the description of facts shall also make allowance for the moral tendencies and economic forces upon which facts are based; and shall not conceive that its concepts, however useful, are more than working approximations of political reality.

meaning of that word. Or, as an alternative, some qualifying word must be added to the word state, when it is applied to the latter category, to indicate the incompleteness of status— a word like semi-sovereign, or non-sovereign.

There is a real and practical difference between the two types of so-called states—the independent and the dependent. Italy is in fact finally its own judge of its obligations and commitments to the League. It can withdraw; or it can resist with all the force at its command, any interference by the League. India is not its own judge, ultimately, of its inter- national relations, for that control rests finally in the British Parliament, until (if ever) the British army in India shall go. Similarly Egypt is not its own judge, nor even completely its own director, as the shadow of the British lion falls heavily athwart its path to any independence that would permit foreign interference with the relations of Egypt and the British Empire, or of Egypt and the Soudan. After the murder of Sir Lee Stack, the Sirdar, England did not go to the League for permission to put the screws on Egypt.

It is largely a matter of practical convenience as to whether jurists prefer to speak of the sovereign state whenever they talk of Italy and similarly independent states, and apply the simple term state to all groupings that possess, as Jellinek insisted they must, political authority over all their citizens in their own right, even though that authority be limited by some more powerful state; or whether, on the other hand, they reserve the term state for those political groups both internally sovereign and externally independent, and add the term non- sovereign to other autonomous groups as a modifying qualifi- cation of their statehood. The advantages of the latter as a stricter juristic usage are perhaps counterbalanced by the wide current use of the term state, without qualification, in speak- ing of the State of New York, or the State of Mysore, or of Egypt as a state.

From the point of view of the co-organic theory one may regard the distinction as largely verbal, because of the actual confusion in current usage of the word state, both in consti- tutional and in international law. As a normative matter it would be better, no doubt, to accept the Austinian logic, for it is hardly conceivable that a state dependent upon another state, even simply in its foreign relations, should not be influenced deeply in its internal supremacy by ramifications of foreign policy—particularly in economic matters. "Influence," said Washington, "is not government", speaking with the bitter experience of the Articles of Confederation in mind. But in Egypt influence is often tantamount to government, and it certainly is the larger part of government in the Indian Native states and the Protected States and Protectorates of the British Empire. And who shall say that our "missionary interest" and influence in Nicaragua is not government?

The Englishman has learned the value, in dealing with people whom he is trying to "influence" (particularly when they are not of his own skeptical blood), of calling things by pleasant names. "A rose by any other name would be as sweet." Yes, but there's virtue in a name if it can save face by parading a cabbage as a *chou-fleur*, or something more delicate. For that reason the keen psychological insight of British statesmanship has called upon the classical erudition of its Empire-holders to find words like *dyarchy, condominium*, and the like. Even the term Commonwealth is rather the adumbration of a wish than the description of a state of fact.

The co-organic theory must face the fact that this various shading of political influence is also government of a sort—perhaps the most practicable sort. Even in these days when it is fashionable to sneer at the motives behind "the white man's burden" attitude, any but the most short-sighted would deplore the sudden withdrawal of the British red thread of unity and the rule of law dependent on it from all the tangled skein of Empire, or our own relinquishing of the Philippines to the *politicos* of the Islands, without international supervision. Chaos would certainly result in many parts of the world (possibly in the Philippines) and an indescribable increase in human misery. The areas of purpose stable enough for real self-determination, and constitutionally responsible government in Africa and the Orient are not many. And it is only in such areas that the organic completeness of constitutional government is possible. Even in Eastern Europe and in Asia independent rule is far from implying even a pretence of democracy or constitutional government. In other areas one must choose between pluralism amounting to civil anarchy, as in China, with the hope of some livable unity eventually resulting; or dictatorships and the rule of local tyrants such as India knew prior to British rule; or finally, the introduction of order by a foreign state which has itself won to some degree of constitutional morality. Apparently the world has reached a point in the development of racial and national consciousness where political intervention by single states is increasingly impossible, and where withdrawal will be increasingly necessary. But withdrawal is in many cases both a political impossibility and a moral futility, or worse, unless provision is made for external aid to internal stability in the region quitted.

It is at this point that the mandates system, with its three classes of governmental control, offers a new hope to solve the difficult problem of partial political control over savage, semi-savage, and politically immature communities. The future will probably see a gradual extension of the mandates principle to all colonial dependencies, or it will see the usual bankruptcies of imperialistic control. Political extension of colonial boundaries, or even retention of existing dependencies is becoming practically very difficult without some new basis of political authority over colonial areas. Sarikat Islam is arousing the racial consciousness even of the hitherto easily exploited Malay archipelago.[10] What the situation is in India, in Egypt, in the Philippines, in Korea, in Morocco, is too well known to require comment.[11] The same leaven is working everywhere.

Of course the League and the World Court, or a Pan-American substitute for both, would have to be resorted to rather than a mandate system for the Central American countries. Any intervention there in the future should be sufficiently international to remove the suspicion of "Yankee plotting".

Even where the political intervention has been opportunistic and sporadic, and economic exploitation has been practiced without more than casual aid from battleships and marines, there are

[10] See the interesting description of the pervasive influence of Sarikat Islam in the Pacific in the Articles of Samuel E. Blythe, who is not an anti-imperialist, in *The Saturday Evening Post*, March, 1926.

[11] *The Re-awakening of the Orient* by Sir Valentine Chirol, Tsurumi, and Sir Edgar Salter, gives a partial picture supplemented by *The Political Awakening of the East*, by G. M. Dutcher, and by *China: an Analysis* by Frank J. Goodnow, and *China* by Bertrand Russell.

signs of dangerous ferment. China is like a dismembered dragon clawing and clutching at its own vitals. There seems to be a danger that it may be rewelded by nationalism and hatred of foreign imperialism into the brazen unity of Mars. A million and a half armed men cannot forever be supported by brigandage and factional strife, especially when there is such a flame fanning up as the Chinese resentment against foreign control seems to indicate.[12]

Nor is the situation in Central America more promising for the permanent applicability of what is obviously a new conception of the Monroe Doctrine, as dangerous because it is more economically inevitable, on the lines of our present policy, and less blatantly absurd than Olney's talk of fiats.[13] The results of our economic penetration and political supervision of some of our southern neighbors have not been solely in the interest of banking houses and trading companies, as those who assail "dollar diplomacy" assume. A careful analysis of the facts does not betray any such political slavery as enthusiastic radicals like to cry out upon,[14] although they do show a most dangerous coöperation of the bankers and the State Department.

The facts do show that any interference with other countries is suspect by those countries and by all the Latin brotherhood to the south of them. And the facts further show that even the prosperity of the countries which we have undertaken to supervise does not take the sting out of supervision nor remove a just suspicion that our government has created profitable monopolies for American trade and finance. We can hardly exert our "moral mandate" to continue choosing governments for Nicaragua without making it a protectorate.

The only possible way in which a colonial empire, political or economic, may now be held without perpetual violence and re-

[12] For a temperate estimate see Sir Frederick Whyte, *China and the Foreign Powers;* a more general picture is to be found in Paul Monroe, *China, A Nation in Evolution.*

[13] An extreme statement is to be found in *Dollar Diplomacy* by Scott Nearing and Joseph Freeman. A more balanced and briefer survey is contained in *International Relations* by R. L. Buell. See President Coolidge's speech to the United Press of April 16, *New York Times*, April 17, 1927.

[14] See the interesting analyses in *Current History*, Jan., Feb., and March, 1927; also the speeches of J. Fred Rippy and D. Y. Thomas before the First Annual Conference at Louisiana State University on Foreign Affairs and American Diplomacy, *Proceedings*, pp. 11-44.

pression, is under the actual practice of a trusteeship for the peoples who make too painful a botch of the job of governing themselves. And trusteeship implies accountability to a third party—an outside tribunal. Otherwise the disgruntled intellectual classes of such countries, for whom government has been a class monopoly, are all turned into revolutionaries. And the more intellectuals the government over them makes by encouraging education, the more revolutionists it has on its hands. Witness the revolutionary agitation of most of the educated classes in India, led by many "failed B.A.'s" and our own similar experience in the Philippines; witness the student backbone of Southern China's demands on the foreign communities to give up extra-territoriality and customs control. Can this situation be avoided?

Obviously not entirely. But the difficulties might be ameliorated if the great colonizing powers are willing to pay the necessary price. No change can be made so long as the principle of exploiting colonies as economic monopolies guides colonial administration. That principle demands a Roman peace; and no amount of moralizing, or even of pretty names, can disguise the necessity from the natives themselves. It is not the theory of the mandates as applied by General Sarrail in Syria nor the French methods in Morocco that are needed for solution, for they are simply thinly disguised colonial exploitation.

In order to introduce an acceptable basis for a community of purpose between the colony and the colonial rulers, their relations must be co-organized. Here the purely descriptive aspect of juridical theory is useless for normative remedy, unless it supplies the conceptual key to fact necessary for a practicable remedy. It makes small difference that the mandates are under the joint sovereignty of the mandatory power and the council of the League of Nations, as they are in legal theory,[15] unless that theory succeed in introducing a truly functional subordination

[15] For a legalistic view of the mandates question see ex-Secretary Lansing's Austinian monograph on *Sovereignty* and the question which he raises in *The Peace Negotiations*, pp. 151-153. The legal aspects of the title to the mandates are in the usual confusion of disputed titles under international law. Does title still vest in the Allied and Associated Powers? We claim a share under the latter category and have made good the claim by treaty rights. On the origin of the mandates see Pitman B. Potter, "The Origin of the Mandates." *Am. Pol. Sci. Rev.*, Nov. 1922. For an interesting contrary view see David H. Miller, "The Origin of the Mandates System," *Foreign Affairs*, Jan. 1928.

of the mandatory power to the League's Council and its Permanent Mandates Commission. Otherwise, the interest of the mandatory as an exploiter cannot be curbed into limits that permit a real growth of purposive community between the mandated area and the mandatory. The League exists already in a formal way to create that possibility. But Mr. Lansing, as a jurist, was not so completely mistaken as some pluralists thought him in insisting on the lack of clarity in the concept of the mandates from the point of view of locating sovereignty. There is a practical significance to unifying legal reference in one body. South Africa has, to all intents, defied the League to intervene in such obvious abuses as her ruthless suppression of the Bondelzwart "Rebellion" in former German South West Africa, a Class C mandate.[16] France has gone on her way almost as unchecked in Syria (a Class A mandate) as she has in Morocco, although she made the pious and somewhat unjust gesture to world opinion of offering up General Sarrail's official head upon a platter.[17] And in the Urtaz Springs Case, brought up in the Palestinian mandate by the native Arabs, the British Empire has obviously decided that finality in determining the obligation of the terms of the mandate rests with His Majesty's Judicial Committee of the Privy Council, and not with the League's Commission or Council.[18] Furthermore, in the administration of Irak, Great Britain by her own authority transformed the status of the mandated territory from a Class A mandate to a state leagued with England by treaty—in short a protected state; though the Mosul award [19] of the World Court has given a sort of League sanction to the arrangement.

These facts indicate that the workings of the mandate system,

[16] See the Reports of the Permanent Mandates Commission of the League Council, *Official Journal of the League of Nations.*
For a general view of the mandates question among others, see W. E. Rappard's *International Relations Seen from Geneva* (1925) and his article, "The Present Status of the Mandates," *Journal of the Royal Institute of International Affairs*, 1925. A more popular treatment is John H. Harris' *Slavery or "Sacred Trust?"* (London, 1926).

[17] See T. P. Moon, *Imperialism and World Politics*, pp. 481-492.

[18] For an analysis see Quincy Wright, *American Journal of International Law*, Oct., 1926, and "The Palestine Problem," *Pol. Sci. Qu.*, Sept., 1926.

[19] See Q. Wright, "The Government of Irak," *Am. Pol. Sci. Review*, November, 1926, and Cmd. 2370, Great Britain Treaty Series, No. 17 (1925).

as of all the rest of the League's actual machinery, have resulted so far only in moral pressure through publicity, inquiry, and resolutions of condemnation being brought to bear as a sanction upon sovereign states. Where nations can be persuaded to accept the jurisdiction of the World Court, the sanctions are usually adequate.[20] But nations do not accept the Court's jurisdiction on essential issues so far. The United States, for instance, seems greatly to fear any arbitration, even at the Hague Tribunal, of matters affecting control of the Canal or Mexico's assertion of the right of eminent domain over our citizens' oil or land holdings. The Court will probably win confidence before the League does. As yet international law has not been able to organize sanctions sufficient to insure international security from war or protect "backward peoples" from exploitation at the hands of the "forward".

That was to be expected, in the backwash from the tidal wave of "international mindedness" that broke in early 1919. The League and its World Court can gradually assume the functions of a real co-organism, endowed with coercive strength, only as they prove their necessity to a new world order. They cannot achieve control before the necessary confidence exists in the possibility of a co-organic world society of states, linked into a truly federal state. But they can develop that control by degrees. The conception of sovereignty can not be made absolute in the nation-state. The necessities of world intercourse, the cruel uselessness of wars, may bring a modification of it, sooner or later. The hope of the early triumph of civilization lies in the fact that human nature is purposive: a co-organic state is assisted in its growth by the conscious adaptation of purposive coöperation, once a common end becomes clearly visible, and once men have found "a moral equivalent", as William James called it, for the catharsis of war. The existence of the United States for a century and a half under a constitution that preserves to each state inviolably its equal representation in the

[20] See the objective studies of Manley O. Hudson, *The Permanent Court of International Justice* (1925), and *Current International Co-Operation* (Calcutta University 1927 lectures).

For a pro-Court view see F. de Bustamente, *The World Court*, and for an anti-Court and pro-reservation view see Vol. II of *International Security*, the *World Court and the United States Senate* by Frances Kellor and Antonia Hatvany.

Senate shows the possibility of international organization in which the sovereignty may be assigned by a constitutional agreement to fit the limits of the international community of purpose.

The mandates system, under the final sovereignty and supervision of a workable League, is the ultimate ideal of colonial organization. Then the question of the ripeness of mandated areas for self-government and independence will no longer be one for bitter strife between the natives and their rulers. It will be determined by a community of states all interested in the orderly progression of political development. And this can only come about if it is possible to substitute the rule of law for imperialistic force in a feudal society of nations. It is necessary for progress toward this ideal to be gradual because of the artificiality of the present League structure as a real organ of political control.

That there is no immediate possibility of translating that solution into fact does not prevent its being an ideal toward which a co-organic society must turn. The United States cannot much longer, without endangering its whole international future, depend upon its isolated supremacy and superior economic development. Our dismal and totally unnecessary intervention in the Tacna-Arica dispute shows what way the excesses of the "New Monroe Doctrine" lead.[21] Much of South America, powers not yet sufficiently reckoned with by the diplomats who think only in terms of battleships, might conceivably be turned against us with Europe, already our suspicious and envious debtor, and with Asia, an equally unfriendly area of immigration controversy, and commercial rivalry. Some of our statesmen, in thanking God publicly that we are not as other men, match a testy suspicion of the good faith of all other countries with the most naïve assertions of our own spotless motives. Psychology counts in politics.

A mandatory supervision under the League of the Philippines and Porto Rico, and perhaps Haiti and San Domingo and the assumption of our proper status in the League along with the rest of the world, would have changed our relations to Haiti, and San Domingo, as well as to the states of Guatemala, Costa Rica, Nicaragua, and Colombia. Failing that, the Pan-American

[21] See H. Clay Evans, *Chile and Its Relations to the United States,* and H. T. Collins, *Current History,* March, 1927.

Union could be more genuinely utilized.[22] We have little of any permanent value to lose by willingness to accept the World Court's jurisdiction over Central and South America and over our relations with them. Our interests of a legitimate nature are protected and we might have had League sanction for any just intervention. But if we fear Europe we must at least work in harmony with South America. We have everything to lose by a crabbed isolation that invites suspicion as to our good faith, as well as to our own confidence in the merits of our case. If we reject the World Court we had better look well to our military and naval preparedness for the imperialistic alternative.

The League of Nations and its organs, the variety of political structure found in the British Empire, ought to be for our purpose examples enough of the diversity of political facts. Formal juridical theory cannot do more than describe these facts. It cannot possibly subsume them even for purposes of juristic description as Professor Willoughby attempts to do, under one principle of authority, the legislative will of a State-Person, because the principles of authority are various—ranging all the way from constitutional consent to unabashed force, military and economic.

But juristic theory has never succeeded in remaining formally descriptive because it must, for the sake of its own peace of mind, arrive at a description of facts in other than behavioristic terms. Professor Willoughby himself leans heavily upon a theory of the general will operative "in the law-making bodies". [23] Yet it is clear that in Egypt, for instance, there is a perpetual adjustment of two "wills" involved, just as there is in the wide varieties of imperial control elsewhere. And it is clear that the "general will" as it operates through law-making bodies is subject in rigid constitutions to limitation by a fundamental law that co-organizes the state.

[22] *The Pan-American Union* by L. S. Rowe. The present possibility of carrying our points or avoiding discussion of them in the Pan-American Congresses has just been demonstrated by the skilful diplomacy of Hughes at Havana (1928). That does not obviate the need of providing more adequately for future needs. For a constructive suggestion see R. L. Buell, "The United States and Latin America," Foreign Policy Association Information Service, Vol. III, No. 4, Jan. 1928.

[23] *Fundamental Concepts of Public Law.* "The Situs of Sovereignty," and "The Juristic Theories of Krabbe" in the *Am. Pol. Sci. Rev.*, Vol. XX, No. 3, 1926.

The term *will*, as we have seen, is not applicable to constitutional sovereignty. It is formally valid, no doubt, to say that all acts of government are an exercise of sovereignty; this is true but of no practical value. Jurisprudence has to establish a theory as to the moral validity and social origin of laws in order to explain constitutional structure, and the origins of legal sanctions. Otherwise it remains a mere manipulation of terminology, with no critical attitude toward the adequacy of its terminology to the concepts it is describing, or of the relations of those concepts to political reality.

For that reason, the co-organic theory which approaches political phenomena from the normative explanation of the community of purpose actually present in a given society offers, it seems to me, a more fruitful approach to political theory, in both its juristic and its ethical aspects. Relying neither upon Bosanquet's "real general will", nor Herr Krabbe's "feeling for right", nor upon Duguit's positivistic "social solidarity", it interprets political community as the resultant of a consensus of moral purpose varying in the degree of its organic integration with the economic and cultural variations in actual societies. It admits both pluralism and solidarism (or Fascism) as facts more or less characteristic of actual states. But it also demands the recognition of the fact of constitutionalism where that exists, and it holds the constitutional state, responsible through representative government, to be the normative ideal of political society.

Because it sees in political community a conditioning purpose, dependent upon the intelligent resolution of environmental forces, the co-organic theory is flexible enough to account also for the growing degree of international community. It sees in the League in Professor Hudson's words "a settled method of conference between nations" and a promise of something more. It explains the limits of that community by pointing to real problems not susceptible of purposive international solution because of the lack of applicable common cultural values as a basis for representative control. But it sees in the purposive nature of political community in every human society, the hope of a peaceful organization of international society, winning for itself consent as it proves its necessity to a moral world order. States that represent community of purpose are not mutually exclusive in their areas of community. And this overlapping may be given its own legal form in the League and the Court. The fact that community varies in the source area of its purpose from cultural (including economic) conditions and in the focus of its purpose according to the intensity of the realization of a need, permits a gradual overflow of integrating forces, limiting the finality of national sovereignty to varying degrees in fact, until the League be adequately supported with sanctions.

CHAPTER XVII

SOME CONCLUSIONS AS TO POLITICAL IDEALS AND THEIR EFFECTS ON POLITICAL STRUCTURE, NATIONAL AND INTERNATIONAL

It is of fundamental importance for any theory of the state to establish its method: normative, romanticist, or behavioristic; idealistic, pragmatic, or positivistic; co-organic, pluralistic or organic; constitutional, syndicalist, or Fascist. The everyday activity of citizens is shaped, more or less consciously, by their own attitudes toward these alternative views. An age, a culture, a nation, takes on much of the color of its dominant philosophy, just as the philosophy speaks in the accents of its times. What shall be our philosophy of the state? It will have an important bearing on what our state is to be.

If this examination of pragmatism in politics has demonstrated its premise, it will have shown that the pragmatic attitude toward the state offers an easy, popular apology for the attacks on constitutional and representative government that dominate contemporary political phenomena; but it will have shown that pragmatism is too easy a gospel to be a true one. On the assumption that ideas, too, are social forces, I have attempted to test pragmatism, so far as evidence offers, by its social fruits. Just as Marxian doctrine, preached as a gospel, with its apocalyptic vision of the crash of capitalism in a general strike, has had sufficient grip of reality to shape the whole course of labor tactics all over the face of Europe, so a philosophy like pragmatism, with its romanticist and its instrumentalist sides, has offered many political theorists a handy key to social problems in these times of confusion. Like most philosophies that base themselves on the inadequacies of the preceding period of intellectualism, it has been adopted not simply because it fits the economic disruption and drifting institutions of an era of change, but because, most of all, it is spiritually congenial to men's ways of living and

495

easy to "get hold of". It is congenial to the times because it comfortably assures us that the lack of religion, and the moral emptiness of science do not matter: there are no norms except those of convenience, and of survival. Therefore, in the midst of rapid social transitions, even when the institutional mechanism of society is hopelessly inadequate, pragmatism as a lay philosophy carries comforting assurance that whatever happens will be pragmatically right, and that the "scientific" attitude is to take the line of least resistance, or quickest solution, to go from "consequence" to "consequence" with regard only for the immediate situations.

In politics that attitude spells an impatience with representative and constitutional government. It gives the strength that a popular philosophy always lends to action already historically favored by forces that have largely escaped social control—the forces of monopolistic consolidation in industry, of urbanization, of class solidarity, of economic nationalism, of overpopulation, of war.

If it is possible to correct and master these forces by understanding them, then we shall have a true pragmatism capable of fruitful application, one that fits the melioristic morality of James' faith to Dewey's objective scientific willingness to learn from experience. But it will not be an easy gospel that can be applied with magic efficacy either by willing to believe, by scientific description, or by intellectualistic naming. There is virtue in names if they are transformed into ideas-as-tools, and if the concepts for which they stand can be shown in practice to fit the deep moral needs of human nature. That is the truth of pragmatism as a philosophy. The co-organic theory of the state, therefore, must also accept the pragmatic test. As a word alone it has no more virtue than *abracadabra,* or *hey, presto!* But if it can be made a working idea that is consistent with the profound urge of human personality toward fellowship in the highest possible moral community, then it will work because it is true. It can be made to serve the dynamic purposes of Sorel's "social myths" without being afraid of critical examination.

Has it not, in fact, had the test of practice wherever constitutional morality exists as a reality? Does not the survival of the constitution of the United States as an organic core of moral purpose adequate to permit the shaping of political practice to developing conditions, prove the value of constitutionalism, even on the pragmatic test of social satisfaction and survival alone? Who will say that British parliamentarism, with its offshoots over the whole world, has not given pragmatic proof of the value of a purposive arrangement of organic law, moulded by gradual social contrivance to a continuous and peaceful constitutional evolution? The same thing might be said of Switzerland and the Scandinavian countries, of Republican France and of contemporary Germany. Are these not pragmatic proofs of the value of the constitutionalism that is the essence of a co-organic state?

Social attitude, the outward sign of social morality in any community, is of the most fundamental importance to any theory of the state. The attitude promoted by holding fast to constitutional morality under the discipline of the rule of law is too valuable to be junked simply because unusual pressure is brought to bear in crises. England, for that reason, can bear a burden under which other states would sink into anarchy, Bolshevism, or Fascism. There are limits to all endurance. But if reason is permitted by the party system to operate, and the facts of economic necessity are recognized, constitutionalism offers a basis of moral strength that is lacking to shortcuts by the route of direct action.

The co-organic theory of the state, therefore, repudiates pluralism and Fascism alike as ideals for the state. They can, indeed, claim to be facts; but they are not facts sanctioned by anything like the weight of examples, or the pragmatic and proved utility over long periods that constitutional government can claim. And they can lay no claim to satisfying both the purposive and the organic elements of association demanded by human spirit; for pluralism fails to take into account the need of organic law to fulfil shared purpose; and Fascism denies the right of the individual as well as the group to a purposive attitude of his own toward the organic state.

Yet each of the two philosophies has its virtues, if corrected by the other. That is precisely the value of constitutional government among a people politically capable of working its institutions: it assures the benefits of a strong state, one capable of economic survival and commonwealth. At the same time, after assuring the stability of a workable public opinion through its party system, by the protection of free criticism and of minority opposition under majority rule, it permits the growth of consent and commands and strengthens loyalty by justifying itself in practice.

If constitutionalism has these virtues, and if the idea of the co-organic state is a correct interpretation of constitutionalism, then that concept is practically valuable. Plato was not wrong in believing that political authority springs from the citizens' acceptance of a common belief. He was wrong only in thinking a myth could be imposed that did not fit their needs and that reduced them to unquestioning subjects rather than free citizens. The hold of Marxian doctrine upon the moral imagination of its followers is in one way what M. Sorel thinks it is, for it is the hold of a social "myth". But it is the myth of a united and free world of labor, not the myth simply of the General Strike, that inspires the real heroism of Labor.[1] The hold which Mussolini keeps upon Italy springs not only from his control of force, but also from the fact that enough of the youth of Italy believes religiously in the myth of a New Roman Empire to make Fascism secure so long as their imaginations are captured. Such a myth must be tested by time to lose its hold, where free criticism is denied by force. But a great "myth", capable of winning and holding consent in crises, must be able to stand free criticism.

That is really the main function of leadership: to create and to embody a popular belief, a Platonic mythos, in a co-organic group. The leaders of a nation are the measure of its ability to put its myths into practice, just as the myths themselves are the measure of its character and intelligence as a people. For myths imply not untruths, but simply belief. The *mythos* of constitutionalism is a true myth, worthy of belief and proved so. Leaders arise if there is nobility of imagination, and courage in action enough in a racial stock under the stimulus of the times to call them forth. Every leader to be effective, must embody the vir-

---

[1] See the Master of Balliol's beautifully just study of *Karl Marx's Capital* (World Primers Series). See also H. J. Laski, *Karl Marx*, and Werner Sombart, *Sozialismus und die Soziale Bewegung* and *Der Moderne Kapitalismus* (especially Vol. I and Vol. III). For a general bibliography there is Professor H. E. Barnes' useful *Sociology and Political Theory*.

tues of so co-organic community. Washington, Lincoln, Wilson, all spoke the words of their followers and their times. If the community be infused with a high purpose and a conscious realization of that purpose by its members, that community, be it college, church, army, nation, fraternity, labor union, or international association for propagandist purposes, will make its weight felt out of proportion to mere numbers. It will survive to the degree that its organic roots as a group are thrust deep into the cultural soil left it by the past. It will flourish as its present purpose is nourished by these roots and is made more vigorous through adequate leadership and the conscious realization of the potency of its ideal. Constitutionalism is a "myth" (in the sense of a social belief which stirs men to moral action) that has proved its claims to being true and worthy of continued acceptance.

Every social gospel impels its believers to realize dimly or clearly this secret of its power, for every social belief must meet this test. A realization of this strength underlies the faith that constitutionalism, even under the strain of war and misery, will not yield to syndicalism or to Fascism, because we have seen it tested before. Its spiritual values are superior. In the long run it will survive or rise again, even where it goes under temporarily beneath the organic pressure of blind forces not adequately understood and controlled.

That greatest of modern "myths": "Peace on earth; good will toward men" may one day itself bear fruit through an extension of the notion of constitutionalism to the relations between nations.

APPENDICES I

APPENDIX A

M. DUGUIT'S REVISION OF HIS JURISTIC POSITION *

Traité de droit constitutionnel, 2ème éd., tome III, *La théorie générale de l'état (suite et fin)*. By Léon Duguit. Paris, E. de Boccard, 1923.—800 pp.

The appearance of another volume in M. Duguit's *Traité* (2ème édition) expands the series now from the projected three volumes to five, the last of which will deal with those problems of public law and the descriptive treatment of French political organization originally proposed for the third (and final) volume. Actually the third volume is an expansion of Volume Two, in which M. Duguit found it difficult to compress the entire theory of the state, as he had planned. His method from the beginning of his fruitful authorship has been to elaborate in the minutest detail and with endless reiteration his own approach to a positivistic philosophy of law: the three volumes of the second edition which have so far appeared have added a wealth of interesting material, drawn chiefly from the decisions of the *Conseil d'État*, to the main theses supported in the original edition of two volumes (1911). They have expanded the polemic in which M. Duguit has engaged against the German theorists and their *"Machtsstaat"*; they have also led to some important changes from the earlier positions, although to none which M. Duguit regards as in any way crucial. He remains steadfast in his contention that organic social solidarity, and not the expression of a general will, is the necessary source of law; that the guaranteeing and assuring of the public services is a more useful conception for jurisprudence than the idea of the sovereign state; and finally that law must be stripped of all metaphysics, and reduced to a scientific basis, in which group obligations replace individual rights and the rule of law is based upon a proper sociology.

These conceptions have come to have more than academic interest since M. Duguit first wrote, in 1901, *L'État, le droit objectif et la loi positive*. He himself points, by way of example, to the jurisprudence of the *Conseil d'État*, to the Great War, and to the developments of syndicalism in the direction of forming the basis for a new juridical order, in which men shall be treated in their associational capacities, not as the individual bearers of legal rights, but

* From *Political Science Quarterly*, Vol. XXXIX, No. 4 (corrected).

as functioning members of groups, legally obligated to preserve "social solidarity". He might point to the decisions of the United States Supreme Court, e. g. those recently handed down on the validity of the Esch-Cummins Act of 1920, to show how important a place the public services, and the conception that the first duty of government is to assure their proper functioning, have come to occupy in American legal doctrines. Or he might have illustrated by a wealth of examples other than the familiar one of the failure of the French general strike of the railway workers in May, 1920, how the face of government is set against syndicalistic attempts to interrupt those services. At a time when "government by injunction" is frequently heard from in America, when even the Liberals in England have come to demand government intervention to prevent stoppages on the London tubes etc., and when Canada is forced to heroic measures to prevent postal employees from disrupting the mail service by strike, the concept of the security of the public services has become fundamental to government. Fascism and the movements akin to it make their bid for the solid support of the bourgeoisie on the ground that they are the saviors of the country from industrial as well as social disintegration. And they have been no more unblushing in their use of force to inspire fear in their political opponents than M. Duguit would have wished. Indeed, M. Duguit has given the same clear-cut formulation to the movement of reaction that M. Sorel, in his *Réflexions sur la violence*, gave to the movement of syndicalist revolt.

The third volume takes up in successive chapters the continuation of the theory of the state as it is concerned with *"les agents publics"*, *"le patrimoine de l'État"*, and *"l'État et le Droit"*. Public servants, according to M. Duguit, can be divided into functionaries (all office-holders as well as civil servants) and employees of the state: the former participate in the functioning of the public services in which the state is engaged in "a permanent and normal manner", whereas the latter participate only "temporarily and accidentally". He thus attempts to extend to the law relating to the organic rules of government services and to state responsibility for the acts of its agents the same separation by *function* which has been so adequately discussed by Mr. R. K. Gooch in a recent article in the *Political Science Quarterly* as it relates to the traditional "separation of powers".[1]

French administrative law has come, on the whole, to very satisfactory solutions of the problems of state responsibility in the actual decisions of the *Conseil d'État*, as even Dicey was forced to note in the last edition of his *Law of the Constitution*. But the actual *arrêts* cited by M. Duguit do not depend on such a system of *droit objectif*,

---

[1] R. K. Gooch, "Modern French Views of the Separation of Powers," I and II, *Political Science Quarterly*, December, 1923, Vol. XXXVIII, No. 4, and March, 1924, Vol. XXXIX, No. 1.

founded upon the necessity of guaranteeing the public services, as he lays down. The jurisprudence of the *Conseil* is much richer and less academic. If it lays emphasis on juridical obligations instead of subjective rights, it none the less retains the conception of legal rights as the necessary reciprocal to that of legal duties. In the main it follows the lines which M. Jèze has plotted much more closely than those to which the arguments of M. Duguit would limit it. And the division of acts of power into M. Berthélemy's *"actes de gestion"* and *"actes d'autorité"* is by no means so foreign to it as M. Duguit would wish.

As in all modern law, the trend of French administrative law flows away from the older individualistic constructions toward conceptions of the public interest. But public interest is not to be interpreted, as M. Duguit would read it, in terms of group functions alone. There is still basic to all legal systems the conception of the general legal rights of citizenship, paramount to all other public interests. Some of M. Duguit's efforts to reduce this general category to the specific relations of membership in professional groups are fairly Procrustean. Obviously civil servants stand in a peculiar relation to the state—M. Duguit likens them to soldiers. But even in bureaucratic France they are still permitted some liberty of association by the statutes on civil servants as revised to June 1, 1920, a fact which M. Duguit has some difficulty in recognizing and incorporating in his system. (*Cf.* his correction of the first edition as to the unilateral character of adhesion to public services, pp. 116-117, and pp. 147-262 *passim*.)

He is forced, too, to fall back on something very like legal sovereignty to explain the impossibility of enforcing responsibility for certain acts of the judiciary and other public servants. Of what use is it to quarrel with the legal conception of *l'État-personne*, if all the legal attributes of such a conception be granted to the state through its agents? There may, indeed, be a gain in emphasizing the fact that we are dealing with "legal" personality, not moral, and that legal personality is only another name for a corporate aggregate of functions. But the gain is lost if we see rulers only as "men holding power".

The same motives which have led to a refusal to use the classic terms in dealing with the separation of powers seem to prompt M. Duguit to reject the civil law distinction, current since the introduction of the *fiscus* into Roman law, between the state acting as the final source of legal authority (*l'État-personne*) and the state in those activities in which it assumes the same rôle as any other business entity (*l'État-fisc*). The practical consequences he is forced to draw from his own doctrines of the public-service state admit most of the distinctions aimed at (albeit imperfectly stated) by the older theory. Some acts of the agents of the state remain subject to no review by the courts, because they are what the Supreme Court of the United States has consistently held to be "political" in their nature. As the administrative functions of government increase, it is natural that greater emphasis be laid upon the accountability of governmental agents for *ultra vires* acts, and that the state assume increasing responsibility for actual faults of its services, or injuries inflicted through its acts. "Due process of law" has included this conception to a growing degree ever since proceedings against the Crown were admitted into English law through "petitions of grace"; and the Court of Claims meets the same requirements in our Federal Government. But the very foundation of the "Rule of Law" is the unquestioned finality of constitutional acts of government. There is no conceivable remedy, e. g., for an unjust decision of the Supreme Court, except before the bar of public opinion or by an amendment to the constitution. And for "political" acts of the other branches of government, political, not legal, recourse must be sought. It is not to the jurisprudence of the courts that we must look, ultimately, for constitutional morality.

Indeed, M. Duguit's conception of the relations of the State to law is no more novel than the consequences he draws. The idea of the *Rechtsstaat* has been elaborated by civil, as well as common law jurists. Its roots lie very deep in political theory, as far back as the vaguest gropings for a Law of Nature, superior to what analytical jurisprudence calls positive law. A *"règle de droit"* based on social solidarity and the interdependence of a differentiated modern society is a more sophisticated formulation of this *ius naturale* than, e. g., that of Blackstone. But it is an effort in the same direction, and one that is subject to the same limitations in application. It fits much better our industrialized society, but it is equally ideal; and the difficulties of defining just what services are to be considered "public" remain undealt with in any but the most hazy fashion.[²]

The *Traité*, in spite of its background of scholarship in continental law, particularly in French and German jurisprudence, is a vast polemic, and it suffers consequentially when it is placed beside so balanced a work as that of Jèze. Particularly for students of modern French legal theory, though, it remains a monumental contribution, not to be dispensed with, as much because of its inexhaustible mine of information as because of its theoretic importance. Not only the jurisprudence of France, both of the courts and of the theorists, but the whole array of nineteenth-century German theorists

---

[²] "Public Services," according to M. Duguit, are simply those social activities which are considered by a given nation at a given time as so important for the maintenance and development of social interdependence that there is a positive obligation on the rulers to assure their functioning (Tome II, § 8, and Tome III, p. 7). The exact determination of details is left to *"la conscience juridique"*. *Cf.* his article, "The Concept of the Public Services," *Yale Law Journal* (March, 1923).

are passed in review. With the latter, indeed, M. Duguit's method is summary: he treats them in much the same fashion in which the Queen, in *Alice in Wonderland*, dispensed justice to her guests at croquet.

To those who are looking for the "New State", the "New Society", and a new heaven and earth—not too altogether different in matters of fact from the old—M. Duguit's "system" may appear to salve the wreck of the past. To those who are skeptical of intellectualistic reconstruction of civilizations, in gross and in detail—even though these be guaranteed strictly non-metaphysical—*"droit objectif"* will no doubt seem another monument to the French genius for ideas, both in seizing the *Zeitgeist* and in giving it new names.

It remains to be added that he has possibly restricted his consideration to problems of French law to a degree that renders the work less broadly useful to American scholars than it might otherwise have been. His acquaintance with English and American law seems limited to the broad outlines offered by Dicey and Bryce, although his visits and lectures in this country render that an obviously false hypothesis. Limitations of space have no doubt prevented more frequent use of examples apt to his hand in both systems of law. He does draw lessons in favor of a Supreme Court (pp. 669-681), and makes frequent reference in passing to the principle of federalism, which he distinguishes from decentralization by calling federalism "a voluntary abandonment on the part of the rulers who monopolize power at a given moment of a part of the prerogatives of government, and in that way the constitution on the same territory of a new group of rulers" (p. 68). A single sentence could not better illustrate the limitations of M. Duguit's "realism".

He has had the misfortune common to all who suffer from typographical monstrosities begot from foreign words—the poor devil of a printer whom we always blame! On the pages 679-680 there are no fewer than ten minor errors of spelling or date in the bibliography offered on the American doctrine of judicial supremacy.

APPENDIX B

THE ECONOMIC FACTORS IN FASCIST ITALY

*Italy's International Economic Position.** By CONSTANTINE E. Mc-
GUIRE. (New York: Macmillan. 1926. Pp. xviii, 588.)

The purpose of this useful addition to the publications of the Institute of Economics is, according to the author, "to determine what
factors affect the wealth-producing and the foreign-debt-paying capacity of the Italian people". It offers a careful survey of the basic
and abiding factors which limit the wealth-producing power of Italy—
physical geography, lack of coal and iron, and population pressure on
the subsistence level. As an economist, and not as a political scientist,
Mr. McGuire adopts what might be termed an attitude of benevolent
neutrality toward Fascism, and proceeds to examine the economic
aspects of the present situation by showing their roots in the past,
as nearly as possible without taking into account political factors.
Doubtless that was the only legitimate attitude in such a study, undertaken under such auspices; but the results show the impossibility of
attaining the purpose proposed without taking into account the stability of the regime and the trustworthiness of even economic information
where all information is controlled and where no hostile analysis of
official data or conclusions is possible.

The economic analysis of known permanent factors, however, is
sound and well done. The picture is clearly presented of a nation
having to import around ten million tons of coal and around two-thirds
of a million tons of petroleum, thus increasing the cost of these fuels
by about fifty per cent over their cost to competing industrial nations.
Add to this the necessity of importing in round figures a million tons
of scrap iron and steel, and one wonders where there is to be found
any basis for the development of the heavy industries artificially stimulated by the war and nursed along since by high protective duties and
government subsidies to ship-building. It is true that there has been a
steady development of hydro-electric power on the program already
under way when Fascism seized power. About two million kilowatts
were available in 1925, with another quarter of a million in prospect in
the next three years. But this development had to serve an equipment
with a gross capacity of nearly eight billion kilowatt hours per annum

* From *American Economic Review*, Vol. XVII, No. 4 (Dec., 1927).

into which six billion lire had been poured.[1] As Mr. McGuire shows, there are very definite limitations to the possibility of hydro-electric development, dictated by the exhaustion of economically exploitable sources. The only prospects for fuel relief lie in the distillation at low temperature of the considerable lignite deposits by means of the new German process now reported to be commercially feasible.

Agriculture appears to be hopelessly incapable of supplying the present population, to say nothing of Mussolini's projected sixty millions whom he would hold in the hive by shutting off emigration and by encouraging even more rapid breeding. The total area of tillable land can be increased by little more than four per cent beyond the 1923 figures of 46.9 per cent of the total area of all lands. That has meant, and failing an agronomic revolution of technique will mean, the importation of at least thirty per cent of the total amount of cereals consumed.

From these figures it readily appears that Mr. McGuire's scepticism as to any prolonged improvement in the 1925 adverse trade balance of about eight billion paper lire (one and one half billion gold lire) is thoroughly justified. One is only tempted to question his optimistic estimate that "The expenditure of tourists must have amounted to fully 700 millions gold" (p. 45) in estimating the invisible service items of Italy's trade balance. Even allowing the maximum figure of 1,600 millions gold for Italy's income, Mr. McGuire shows that interest charges would make a yearly deficit of about 300 million gold lire which would have to be borrowed. In short, Italy continues to be, as she has been for at least fifty years, increasingly dependent upon international economic developments. Her own inadequate supply of liquid or working capital makes her industry more than usually subject to its precarious strategic position.

Fascism can claim to have managed its budgetary and currency problems well, according to this analysis which accepts Fascist figures *en bloc*. Mr. McGuire, in common with most foreign critics, hardly does justice to the heroic retirement of war charges and the internal loans by the governments preceding Fascism. It was generally thought by Italian economists that the program of the parliamentary governments would have produced a balanced budget by 1924 or by 1925. Aside from the disappearance of strikes, a phenomenon by no means limited to Fascist Italy in the years of increasing sanity, 1923-1925, Fascism offered little change in the general current of economic life except in the direction of an increasing paternalism that attempted a perhaps too rapid industrialization and that has not stopped short at fixing either wages or prices; and in the direction of a resolute effort at deflation that has shunned the perils of debauched currency only at the price of a very considerable increase in bankruptcies and industrial stagnation, which Mr. McGuire thought possible when he wrote. Even

[1] *Op. cit.*, p. 142.

in 1926, within the period included in this survey, a remarkable drop in the value of internal public securities and private shares had occurred (before the rise in the lire) that was relevant to the state of Italian finance. No analysis is here offered.

The situation in Italy is developing and shifting so rapidly that not even a somewhat snap survey of contemparary conditions could hope to fix the currents. Since Mr. McGuire wrote, the attempt at a gradual revalorization, then the fixed stabilization of the lira has changed the aspect of the industrial situation, at least superficially. He shows that a check on foreign borrowing, a moderation of tariff protection and immunity from war are fundamental requisites under any conditions— none of them particularly well seen by Mussolini.

It is unfortunate that the investigator of Italian economic and financial conditions is forced to rely so largely upon an exposition of data as suspect as that of the Italian Debt Funding Commission, even though Mr. Moulton, editor of the series, professes to speak for the Institute of Economics in declaring that no reason has been found for suspecting that the figures of the Italian Government (in spite of their quantitative inadequacy) are less accurate than those of other European countries. The appendices, which occupy about half the volume, are often hardly more than notes from which the text has been previously abstracted for the main work, although their elaboration is occasionally useful and even necessary to support previous methods and conclusions. In the final appendix is printed, without critical commentary, a memorandum of the well-known Italian economist, Professor Corrado Gini, which was presented in connection with the negotiations for the funding of Italy's foreign public debt both to the United States and to England.

APPENDICES II

APPENDIX A

THE PRAGMATIC REVOLT IN POLITICS: TWENTY YEARS IN RETROSPECT*

The editors of the *Review of Politics* have asked me to do something that is indicated by the title of this informal essay. It is something that I have long had in mind. Substantially I am asked to assess after the passage of almost twenty years the thesis laid down in *The Pragmatic Revolt in Politics*. Ordinarily the biography of a book or of a writer's ideas had better, in good taste, be left to others. But I hope that I may be forgiven some notes on the nature of that work, because of their relevance not only to this return to the subject, but because of their relevance as well to what seems to me to be a general change in scholarly attitude toward a central problem: the place of ethics and the place of science in that study which Aristotle named by one word, *Politics*. It is pecularily a pleasure to contribute this revision of a position to a journal devoted to the high cultivation of that Aristotelian conception. The distinction already achieved by the *Review of Politics* is in itself a witness of the changed temper of contemporary thought to a deep concern with political *values*.

During the world war, that is now sometimes called, a little prophetically, the First World War, I became interested in trying to determine the meaning of pragmatism by a pragmatic testing, i.e., in terms of its fruits. The result was a work written at Oxford in the years immediately following the war and published piecemeal in reviews, finally as a book in 1928. Since it is quite probably unknown to many readers of the *Review*, I may be permitted to outline its thesis. In doing so to avoid the first personal pronoun would be both awkward and at times misleading. I have chosen a directness that I hope may be forgiven me in this matter.

It was a necessarily immature book with many faults, obvious to the kindest reviewer. But it had the merit and the good fortune to point in the right direction: it tried to answer the question, What is the common ground between the direct action of pluralist syndicalism and the fascist totalitarian state? Written before the terminology of "social myths," "ideologies," "symbolism," etc., had become by-words, the book left a

* From *The Review of Politics*, Vol. II, No. 1 (January, 1940). Copyright 1939, © 1967 by William Y. Elliott.

strange impression of unfamiliarity on American students. It seemed, as indeed it was, a hesitant and somewhat incoherent "feeler" in a direction new to most American thought and quite out of keeping with the dominant "scientific" trend of the purely materialistic interpretation of politics then being popularized by Beard, Bentley, Holcombe, and others. Its insistence on the legitimate, even the necessary effort of evaluating politics in the light of the moral norms, and of understanding scientifically the part played by the ethical character of human behavior ran head on into the current efforts in American circles to study politics as a science by the methods appropriate to the physical sciences.[1] It owed a great part of its tone and temper to my old tutor at Oxford, A. D. Lindsay, to the study of Kant under him, to the *Theory of Knowledge* of E. Walker, S.J., and to long arguments with Alexander Meikeljohn and with Father Martindale at Oxford.

It is not surprising, therefore, that it was a defense of reason if not rationalism, and that it dealt with a vigor often more earnest than judicious with the shortcomings of pragmatism as a philosophy. In spite of disclaimers contained in the book, a fair-minded reader might well have come away from its reading with the impression that William James and John Dewey represented in the author's mind two types of an allegedly philosophical attack on metaphysics and intellectualism which were responsible for the aberrations of Sorelian and Laskian syndicalism on the one hand and for the Fascist corporative and totalitarian syndicalism on the other.

James was used to typify the revolt against reason in the name of satisfying total emotional urges: the psychological approach to determining what was meant by "a working test of truth." Consequently James' school of pragmatism, which I called "Romanticist," seemed to me to furnish the groundwork for those theories of revolt against the rationalized systems of constitutional democracies of which George Sorel, by his own confession of discipleship, represented the extreme development.

Dewey, on the other hand, essentially a positivist and a logician, though not quite what we now call a "logical positivist," set up criteria

---

1 See for a characteristic attempt at giving a theoretical base for these efforts the earlier works of G. E. G. Catlin.

For an idea of the extent of this movement in the U. S. A. one has only to turn to the Proceedings of the various conferences on Methods in Political Science, supported by the Social Research Council, with the interested sponsorship of C. E. Merriam, Arnold Bennett Hall, and many of the school of what I may call "Public Administrators." The Committee on Method in the Social Sciences, sponsored by the same Council under the chairmanship of Professor R. M. McIver, took a more comprehensive view of the problem of methods, as might have been expected from its chairman, a soundly trained philosopher. However, the dominant tone may be seen from *A Case Book on Method in the Social Sciences*, edited by Stuart Rice. See especially my critical essay on W. B. Munro and G. E. G. Catlin in this volume.

for working in terms of social behaviorism. He ruled out any principles of a general and certainly of an absolute character, and based his theories of society on a combination of anthropological, psychological, and sociological theories of human nature, essentially biological in method and emphasis. Survival, it seemed to me, was his real test for social habits and social character.[2] I was concerned to show that this was the real philosophical basis for that "organic" type of "social solidarity," used as the foundation for law by such jurists as Leon Duguit, and for the superstructure of the Fascist corporative state.

James, in short, remained essentially a passionate individualist in his pluralism, though his thinking might be used by the group pluralists of syndicalism to attack the unifying concept of a constitutional state and its "sovereignty." Dewey, though professing a leftist type of social democracy, made a philosophical case for the organic reactions of nations considered in terms of biological survival. His premises, though not his reservations, led straight to that type of "complete social planning" which the totalitarian state has ushered in. For planning, an instrumentalist conception was to be judged only in terms of operational logic (Percy Bridgman's term) or scientific method, i.e., not in terms of any ultimate moral criteria but according only to the successful adjustment of men to the plan and the plan to men in a world guided by social "morality," a compound of the Sophists' "pain-pleasure" calculus, of sheer materialism, appetite, and the lust for power or of approval in a context of necessity. Mr. Dewey himself has spoken so often and so slightingly of alleged moral personality as to make his point clear.

A look backward on this brash effort to link political movements with ideas severely tests one's faith in any such simple application of Platonism—or at least in what is understood by Platonism: the shaping effect of archetypal ideas on action. It is clear that no such elementary thesis can encompass any such institutional upheavals as have produced the present enduring crisis of our western culture. James and Dewey are merely visible objects borne along by the general flood of anti-intellectualism. The positive effort that *The Pragmatic Revolt* made to capture an Aristotelian balance by applying a "co-organic" conception to associational life is hardly more adequate to such a colossal task.

Yet today I am astonished at how well the general analysis and the positive thesis of that book still hold up in both its predictions of tendencies and in its values. Mr. Laski and Mr. G. D. H. Cole, with whom I broke so many academic and theoretical lances, would like to forget those earlier aberrations of syndicalistic pluralism that then

2 That this view is quite commonly accepted by Mr. Dewey's own disciples and partisans may be verified by reading Mr. Eliser Vivas' essay on "John Dewey's philosophy" in the *Partisan Review*, Vol. VI, No. 3 (Spring 1939)

occupied their whole attention. Mr. Laski, after a brief transitional period of passionate "League of Nations" internationalism, has fallen back on what he repeatedly calls a "grim" view of social predestination, indistinguishable from the orthodox and doctrinaire Marxism that has been buried without honor even in Russia—though its ghost is still agitated and serves to advance Stalin's own ends. The "United Front" or "Popular Front" serves only tactical uses. Mr. Cole has become a foremost "planner," without quite answering (or even raising) the question of what sort of political control goes with such *étatist* and total economic planning. The stubborn facts of national community disturb them both but get no place in their thought.

Whereas I am left still concerned to find the moral basis for free constitutional agreement within nations as a pre-condition of going beyond nationalism in much the old terms: an Aristotelian balance that retains on the one hand the ultimacy of moral personality and free individual choice (with the state as its guarantor) of *all* group loyalties. This I have called the shared purpose of the *"co-"* element of human associations. On the other hand, the balance must allow for that necessity which I called "organic," of the total environmental and institutional context. The organic includes (1) a selfcompleting and coherent legal system (sovereignty), (2) a state adequate "to promote the common defense and the general welfare," and (3) through its internal organization and separation as well as integration of powers, a state adequate for survival. If it be constitutional or co-organic it must so organize these powers as not to become totalitarian in spite of the professions in the Bill of Rights, the Preamble, or whatever other "fundamental law," written or practiced, contains the basic social myth.

Ends and means, purpose and organization, values and techniques —however this dualism is stated it must be resolved in actual living and in all human association. This is the meaning of the co-organic theory.

The pragmatic pluralist would have resolved it by making the organic needs of groups each absolute in terms of the only criterion he recognized: the facts of needs or interests, i.e., demands for satisfaction: The state as one group among the others had no "general will," and no free contractual basis of consent for subsuming this play of group interests to a general scheme of values and public interest. It had to hold the ring for these "insiders," in Mr. Walter Lippmann's terms.[3] Public opinion had itself no other public interest or public right than to insist on procedural regularity.[4]

Under such circumstances and such a theory, what Cicero called a

---

[3] *The Phantom Public*, passim.

[4] This notion naturally derives from the conception of morality as being "disinterested" *(Preface to Morals)* and it is further developed in the trial-by-lawyer technique of the common law advocated in *The Good Society*.

consensus juris is limited to the maintenance of constitutional morality. That is, indeed, its deepest role, and there its operation transcends the bare majority principle and depends upon a *general purpose*, an accepted *mythos*, rather than a general will.

Must this level of shared purpose demand universal acceptance by all citizens? My colleague Professor C. J. Friedrich is bent upon showing that dissent is possible within the constitutional state even at this deep level.[5] He urges that a fundamental pluralism of beliefs can be tolerated that would permit presumably fascists and communists to be protected by the very constitutional structure that they seek to destroy. To support his argument he adduces the protection of religious freedom as a proof that the deepest differences are reconciled in fact in healthy constitutional systems. But, passing by the analogy between spiritual, religious beliefs and étatist mythologies of the totalitarian order—a very suspect analogy—one may argue that a *real* religious cleavage as to the ends of human life and society can not be sustained in a constitutional state. We are apt to forget that the basic tenets of our Western Christianity and even of Judaism all support the belief in the ultimate moral responsibility of human personality. The consequences which flow from this conception support, as Stoic doctrine did in a less mature form, the *rights* of moral personality. They can not tolerate *coercion* of belief or forced loyalty to any association. When a church sets up institutions that are so widely at variance with the accepted family morality as did the Mormon Church of an earlier day, the answer was not one of tolerance.

Democratic faith, under a true constitutional system, requires that there should be no suppression of *ideas*, but it does not have to countenance *acts* hostile to its very survival. Strategy may dictate a wide latitude of tolerance of crank movements or of demagogic intolerance, trusting to the good sense of citizens. It becomes a dangerous strategy if it permits any other association to challenge the monopoly of force exercised by a responsible government under law.

But the pluralism of Mr. Lippmann in certain of his works, at least, is interested only in preventing a majoritarian public opinion from acting (1) so as to prevent the formation of future majorities on a *free* basis. It is only when he rules out the possibility of an opinion, genuinely public, and operative (2) on the policy-forming level through majoritarian forms, and (3) assessing the *intrinsic* merits of issues on the asumption that *public interest* makes the public take sides, that his pluralistic analysis challenges the facts. The constitution itself provides a framework of reference for all governmental action by relating all public *interest* to public *purpose*. Within that framework the public

5 See his "Democracy and Dissent," *Political Quarterly* (October, 1939), retracting his earlier views in *Constitutional Government and Politics*.

operates (1) through extraordinary majorities to decide, *and on the merits of the question raised,* the amendments of the constitutional rules. It operates (2) at the governmental level, majoritarian but checked and balanced by a separation of organs, to register opinion on public interest. The creation of commissions to regulate economic issues may serve to illustrate. Party mechanism is the method of *generalizing* purpose to superimpose public interest on the conflict of special interest. The public visibly reacts when issues affect the whole community at some vital level, either acutely as in wars or chronically as in, e.g., prohibition.

Today pluralism and the Jamesian emphasis on the total satisfaction of emotional urges have ceased to give comfort to syndicalists. Group pluralism is represented in no more extreme form than the theories of Mr. Lippmann or the behavioristic approach of Bentley's *Process of Government.* In terms of psychological description, always James's strongest point, group pluralism may study fruitfully the attitude of pressure politics in the American system and to some degree in all free democratic sytems. But the need for a method of arriving at a conception of public interest as the basis of public policy is generally recognized as a necessarily normative attitude.

Not that the pragmatists of James's persuasion are without champions. Professor R. B. Perry is rephrasing today the older pragmatic calculus of what he used to call "The Moral Economy" in terms of what he now calls "practical agreement." He is still trying to put "the will to agreement" on quantitative rather than Kantian terms.[6] But, in spite of treating personality as "the organization by which the several interests of one human individual are brought into agreement with one another,"[7] it is clear upon close analysis that the whole calculus rests upon the Kantian (and the Christian) ultimacy of moral personality. Practical agreement must in short be *real* agreement, i.e., free agreement. Professor Perry does not recognize Hitler's method of securing agreement as *practical* in his sense of the word.

The pluralists may have their day if order is ever introduced into the world so that there will be less organic pressure for solidarity of interests in the interests of survival—a national survival that conditions in the present conflict with totalitarian systems the survival of the very basis of all free human values. But today the winds of doctrine do not blow with them but against.

It is today the Fascist threat to the purposive order of human society that must be met. This fact, for fact it is, leads me to acknowledge how completely I missed the shape of things to come by failure in *The*

6 See his "The Moral Norm of Social Science" in *The Journal of Social Philosophy* (October, 1939).
7 *Ibid.,* p. 21.

Pragmatic Revolt to assess the "organic" as well as the mythical aspects of Nazism and Communism. Of the first, I can only plead that one who had seen Germany fight back through the inflation period to what seemed to be national sanity, might well have missed the importance of Nazism at the time. It seemed to be a feeble imitator of Mussolini's successes and methods as he to some degree had been an imitator of the Russian communists. But in spite of student days spent during Oxford vacations in the very birthplace of Nazism—not only in Munich but, I regret to admit, some of them in the very beer hall so recently blown up—I did not take seriously at that time that Locarno was being set up as a new European mile post, the disease then being propagated by the prisoner who had just finished writing *Mein Kampf*. Today many others have documented the essentially Machiavellian type of pragmatism which makes that work and the movement that grew about its "leader" perhaps a fitter study than was Mussolini, for my purpose.[8] There is little need to recapitulate the profound anti-rationalistic cult of violence, the use of myths and as sophisticated a sense of mass reaction and propaganda as a pathologically gifted demagogue has ever shown in writings, speeches, and acts. The solidarity of race is substituted for the Italian "organicism" of the nation, but they come to the same end.

In a more extensive essay it would be appropriate to do more than merely point out how the essentially Spartan elements of Nazi totalitarianism dictate not only a different end than the divine justice of Plato's *Republic* but characteristic differences, too, in the means of state organization. Hitler's state, like Mussolini's, has no moral end beyond itself. That self is the changing will of a man who identifies the national or the racial being with his own desires or fears. It is, par excellence, the survival theory that is appealed to as a test; no other "moral" standard. Words like "honor" become an obscene mockery. And until the day of catastrophe, no criterion of Mr. Dewey's Instrumentalism may say the leader-principle nay. It works, it handles, it plans, it survives—in short, it is Instrumentalist.

Communism, too, came to fit the pragmatic mold in a way that I understood little when I wrote. The imposing facade of rigid Marxian doctrine always had behind its Utopian statelessness a possibility of anti-rationalism. Perhaps a closer study of Marx and Engels themselves

---

[8] Out of the wealth of such studies one might suggest as of especial interest for this purpose Frederick Schumann's *The Nazi Dictatorship;* Stephen H. Roberts, *The House That Hitler Built*, pp. 11-58; Melvin Rader, *No Compromise—The Conflict Between Two Worlds;* and Rauschning's *The Revolution of Nihilism*, passim.

Of these Mr. Rader's recent work most nearly places both Italian and German Fascism in the perspective that I attempted, though with too great positive reliance upon "science" to find moral values. Rauschning's brilliant work is interested in proving too much, though it fits my thesis peculiarly well.

might have shown me this. Certainly in the hands of Lenin and how much more in those of Stalin, this pragmatic warping of the dialectic to practical survival led straight toward fascist totalitarianism: one-will, one-party, power. The imposition of economic equality as an end in itself produced a queer evolution to the imposition of the most complete autocracy of history, with the most flexible doctrine and subservient propaganda, in the interests of purely materialistic planning. If Mussolini's theories of totalitarianism have been happily belied in practice by the independent power wielded by the House of Savoy and by the Church, and Hitler's absolutism has never quite achieved the complete suppression of opposition in the *Lebensraum* that he has acquired or by the Churches within Germany, Stalin has been more successful. "Orthodoxy" is his latest wish, in every sphere, in the party, in religion, in education, in science and the arts. And the changes are so rapid that even the most devoted Bolshevist heads must fall to accent the pace.

But the most serious weakness of *The Pragmatic Revolt* lay, it seems to me now, in not connecting the vulgar conception of "science," positivistic science as the be-all and end-all of human knowledge, with the threads of doctrine that were being unravelled. Science in the sense of an objective view of the world of physical causality and mathematical relations has a high calling that can produce humility and a sense of the truth and values of religion, as can also that philosophy of which it is a sister in method and attitude. But positivistic science which assumes that the method appropriate for handling and manipulating *things* is the only human tool for *knowing* and *living* the values which Aristotle called "To *eu* zen." Positivism I should call vulgar science—an impostor. Yet it is this impostor which puffs up mankind with "hybris," making it vain glory in its triumphs over space and time, and forgetful of the stark tragedy involved in the loss of man's true selfhood.

Against this false "rationalism," among others, William James, with an artist's appreciation of man's fuller nature inveighed feelingly and well. But he himself offered no other criterion than feeling. Against this falsification of reason's role in the realm where "science" is alleged to give the grounds for "total planning" of man's whole existence, constitutionalism is a defense. For a truly constitutional state protects the ultimate *moral* pluralism of the person, who must create communities of free belief.

Yet this "science," which aims only at adjustment and manipulation is erected into a method for determining all moral values by such "operational" logic as that of Professor Bridgman.[9] And such a tool, turned to the hand of the planners of society, often can be plausibly used to fit the totalitarian pattern.

[9] See his article in *Harper's* (December, 1933), in addition to his *Logic of Modern Physics* and its application in later works.

It is of course true that insofar as this or any "science" means free inquiry it is incompatible with dictatorship and must presuppose a free system in order to flourish. But scientific method of the type applicable to test tube and laboratory can never demonstrate anything more than the relativity of moral values. It is neutral to any true morality. Since it would weigh and measure and handle, it is as doubting as Thomas of the deepest verities of human experience. And this measuring cast, so-called "scientific" thought, has been laid over the world, with a heavy shadow of materialism as its result.

The physical sciences are cultivated instrumentally, by all dictators as the essential means of maintaining their power. For an understanding of the nature of belief and of obedience and loyalty they rely upon a "scientific" Paretian view of human nature apt to their purpose of treating human beings as indefinitely manipulable. The soul of man has always given the lie to those who treat it so. Man is a little thing, of small freedom, whose institutions are partly grounded in organic necessity. But the vision of divine perfection given for his imitation frees him from totalitarian necessity and the worship of Caesar as God. That vision never came from the positivists and sophists of this world; though there is always a possibility that through suffering it may one day be seen by them, even as it was by Saul of Tarsus.

APPENDIX B

THE CO-ORGANIC CONCEPT OF COMMUNITY APPLIED TO LEGAL ANALYSIS: CONSTITUTIONAL AND TOTALITARIAN SYSTEMS COMPARED*

The emphasis that has been put in the very learned and useful effort to relate the nature of community to the coercive necessity for legal systems by Mr. Huntington Cairns seems to me very persuasive and not really subject to the main strictures that have been brought to bear on it. As I understood his intention, it was to illustrate the fact that all types of communities had at least one common characteristic: they produced an overriding necessity for a systematic statement of the rules governing the application of force in the community. In any mature community, this statement depends on the character of a legal system. I would like to add a note on the need for balancing purpose with this organic must for law.

Legal philosophy can approach the study of legal systems from two main points of view: (1) The ethical problem of why men should obey law, and what constitutes "legitimacy." This takes law beyond the analytical and positivistic method. It asks what is the moral foundation for authority and obedience. (2) The roots of legal systems may be traced in the sociological conditions of cultures and in the compulsion of some alleged necessity. The latter compulsion leads to a limited type of positivistic or analytical jurisprudence, running through Hume and positivistic sociology on the one side; or from Hobbes through Bentham to Austin on the analytical side. This last school generally finds its summary in some statements of law as a command.

But even Austin had to put into his classic definition of sovereignty that the person or persons who were to be called sovereign must not only be independent of any necessity to yield obedience to any other sovereign, but must "receive the habitual obedience of the bulk of the people."

This qualification inserted into Austin's definitional analysis is in itself a sufficient entanglement. The problem of what is the source of the "habitual obedience of the bulk of the people" can produce all the subsequent schools of jurisprudence—the historical, the metaphysical,

* Developed from comments at the meeting of the American Society for Political and Legal Philosophy on the Nature of Community, December 30, 1957, and published as Chapter IV of *Nomos II: Community* ed. by Carl J. Friedrich (New York, 1959). Copyright ©, 1959 The Liberal Arts Press, Inc. Reprinted by permission.

and the sociological—which, of necessity, all look beyond the limits of purely "positive law," as defined by Austin. "Habitual obedience of the bulk of the people" even raises the question of the ethical basis of obligations to obedience.

The thing that is most difficult, however, is not simply to ground law on what Professor Lon Fuller has spoken of as the compulsion of its "external sanctions," or its referential relations, by which I take it he probably means to include relevance to the facts of a given culture. This grounding of law in a community's culture is a prerequisite, it is true, to any adequate jurisprudence. It was the main insistence of my old master of studies at Oxford, Sir Paul Vinogradoff, in his magistral *Historical Jurisprudence.* It was also precisely the failure to bring the formal system of law—which Hans Kelsen calls a pure theory of law— into relationship with any actual system, in order to establish its real roots, that makes Kelsen's jurisprudence so sterile of any useful applica- tion. There can be no doubt about the need for relating law to those sources which David Hume would have treated as exhausting the nature of law.

But beyond that region of fact, i.e., the relations of law to the traditions and customs of a society, developed through pressures, as I believe Mr. Cairns has shown, in large part determined by the very nature of social needs (for which I have used the term "organic"[1]), there lies the need to account for the effort of law to claim what is more often called "legiti- macy." Another way of stating this is to say that every mature system of law asserts that the rules under which the monopoly of force is exercised by government can be morally justified because they rest on that legitimate basis for which Cicero used the term *consensus juris.* The word *"jus,"* from this Roman beginning traced through nearly every European language, has had the intentional ambiguity of meaning both "law" and "right." From it we derive "justice," of course, and it is the claim of law to embody justice on which an appeal for a moral obligation to obey generally rests. This is the meaning of "moral" legitimacy.

It is true that positivistic systems of law, even though they may talk, as Austin did, of "positive morality," rule out the relevance of any discussion of the moral validity of law. Hans Kelsen himself is quite ambiguous on this point, but he cannot logically import a moral test into a system of purely abstract norms, developed as he has developed his theory of law.[2]

---

1 See *The Pragmatic Revolt in Politics,* W. Y. Elliott (1928), especially Part IV, "The Group as a Co-Organism," for an analysis of the difference between the "organic" and the "organismic" conceptions of the nature of groups, especially political communities.

2 One of Kelsen's most interesting efforts to escape his self-imposed limits was his article in *The Journal of Social Philosophy and of Jurisprudence* (July, 1942) on "Value Judgments in the Science of Law."

All systems of jurisprudence which profess to be limited to what *is* law rather than what *should be* law leave out the most powerful factor in establishing the binding quality of law, and one essential to the understanding of its true nature. It is, after all, the greater part of the philosophy of law, even if that be taken in the most objective and scientific terms of describing the facts of experience, that has gone into the struggles over social myths that try to establish legitimacy in terms of obligation. Even Marxism claims to do this. This, in short, is the purposive character of law which relates it to ethical norms to give it validity. The various forms of social contract theories, the appeals to natural law or natural rights, all look in this direction.

In terms of a moral community, shared purpose is what binds together the political unit into a legal community. It is a purpose which, to form a legal system, must be superimposed on those facts of history and the requirements of a given culture that belong to the realm of the organic. This purposive sharing is suggested by prefixing *co* to *organic*, suggesting a combination of purposive organization and control, to meet given and required needs. The prefix also suggests *sharing*, in a group effort, as many cognate uses would illustrate. The balance of necessity and purpose is necessary if law is to represent both order and the legitimacy of moral justice.

This morally purposive side of the law goes far toward explaining, at least in constitutional systems based upon the consent of the governed and their active participation in the process, why the "habitual obedience of the bulk of the people" is in fact forthcoming. Hume can put this fact of obedience down to habit and custom. But in a system in which the law-making activity has achieved the stage beyond customary law and entered into genuine legislation involving conscious purpose, habit is no longer an adequate basis for the acceptance of the moral obligation to obey, and, hence, for the ultimate legitimacy of law as representing a consensus on the nature of justice (*consensus juris*). In *The Pragmatic Revolt in Politics* I attempted to outline this co-organic theory of jurisprudence[3] in such a way as to distinguish it from any of the organismic analogies. The *co* was intended also to suggest the ultimacy of the individual moral personality, never absorbed by any group in a society that had matured beyond the primitive.

Totalitarian society challenges absolutely this conception of moral ultimacy in the individual personality. It, perforce, substitutes for a *consensus juris*, freely and critically arrived at, a social myth carefully indoctrinated and supported by all the weight of totalitarian controls and, ultimately, by terror. But even a totalitarian system attempts to secure the "habitual obedience of the bulk of the people" by conditioning responses to loyal obedience, utilizing rationality in the high levels of

3 Elliott, *op. cit.*, Parts IV and V.

propaganda at least, and in the quasi-theological explanations and revisions of the basic mythology.

It may be observed that this, too, produces a system that calls itself law. Professor Berman at the Harvard Law School has so described the Soviet system, and admired many points in its claims to superiority as setting out the objectives of the system. In a formal and analytical sense it would certainly meet Austin's criteria. But one need not take the late Dr. Vishinsky's praises of the social and moral objectives, as professed, at face value. Even as a formal legal system, Soviet law would not, however, meet what I understand to be one of the main criteria which Professor Fuller proposed for a true system, in that it is not coherent with its own logic and assumptions as stated. It is subject to quite arbitrary invasion by power from sources not acknowledged by the legal system itself—extraordinary courts, party terror, actions involving the use of force not contemplated in the formal statement of the sources for applying law or its sanctions.

It is significant, however, that even a totalitarian system erects a highly rationalized constitution, that it pretends to act by settled rules, and that it erects, as Vishinsky did, an elaborate cloak of legalism even for its trials and for the most obvious violations, in fact, of the formal legal norms of the system. There are few apologists who claim that the Soviet constitution protects the rights it professes to establish, except in terms of double talk and double think, where the words mean what they do to Tweedledum in *Alice in Wonderland*.

Any such totalitarian community is a community that rests upon coercion. The community of shared opinion as to justice, on the witness of the outbreaks in the satellite countries, at least, and the Chinese repression of the "hundred flowers" that sprang too quickly after Mao Tse-tung's invitation to differ, dare not be left without an instrument of coercion, all-pervasive and all-controlling in the society. The struggle which Khrushchev is presently undergoing to maintain his hold on the party mechanism and his Stalin-like purges of his competitors for power up to this point indicate that the logic of totalitarianism can never permit dangerous divergencies or different, even differing, roads toward Communism. Let Tito take care. Deviations destroy the nature of the system, and freedom becomes its poison. If we must cultivate our garden in the totalitarian manner, only prescribed flowers will be allowed.

Such a system, if it is to persist, must maintain not only an organic but an organismic, i.e., a "corporative" control that approaches the organismic analogy even to the degree of having a common directing center and a controlling nerve system through the one-party mechanism. Law in such a system is entirely different from law that subjects itself to the appeal to a free moral conscience. There is not, in this sense, any genuinely co-organic basis for law in any totalitarian system, or even in one of an absolutist character. The purpose is infused from too narrow a center of control and, generally speaking, from and by a single center of control, through a logic that leads to a choice of words like *Führer, Duce,* and the use by Stalin (to describe himself in his last phase) of the phrase "Great Leader," after he had tried out and found wanting variations on other themes such as "Generalissimo" (already pre-empted by Chiang Kai-shek!).

On the other hand, the nature of community in any free and constitutional system of law which depends upon the protection of the rights of individuals to both political and civil liberties and on a genuinely shared consensus requires embodying in some fundamental law rules as to the making of law. This fundamental law, written or practiced, has the unusual sanctity ascribed to a constitution.[4] It is the operation of this framework of accepted rules embodying objectives like those in Preambles and Bills of Rights that permits the allocation of power by its separation and division both along functional and territorial (Federal) lines. The areas of community can be appropriately defined in a legal system by the degree to which the sharing both of purpose (the *co* element) and the compulsion of the *organic* facts of defense and survival and economic need (common defense, common welfare, taxation, interstate commerce, and the like) have to be combined in areas of legal outline, for both policy formation and the administration of law and justice.

This is the realm in which political philosophy can be of some assistance to legal philosophy in determining the difference between systems of law which genuinely meet this test in the interests of searching for a moral validity acceptable to the members of the community. Even on the most elementary basis of classifying legal systems, it offers a very useful clue.

But for the classification of legal competence within the framework of the community which we call the state, there is a further very useful basis for the co-organic concepts that I have suggested—a co-organic analysis of the relations of subordinate systems of rule making to the ultimate testing of the final source of legal authority. Federalism in this sense cannot permit the devolution of really autonomous powers to groups that conflict with the legal finality of the political community organized on a territorial basis. This type of pluralism, much vaunted but never closely formulated by the late Harold Laski, turns out to be a contradiction in terms, not only because of the organic and organizational requirements of legal systems, understood by Hobbes and Austin and better explained today by Mr. Cairns and Professor Fuller. A system cannot permit *many* final sources of legal authority. Moreover,

---

4 See, for best general analysis, C. J. Friedrich, *Constitutional Government and Politics,* supplemented by W. Y. Elliott and Neal McDonald, *Western Political Heritage,* for theoretical and historical development of the concept.

if the system itself is to have moral authority to coerce, it must monopolize that power to use force, or go down before anarchy. But it can
protect areas of moral and cultural *autonomy* where the membership
in these groups is freely accepted (including the right to withdraw),
and no coercion by force is permitted to any other group than the state.

Bare as this outline is, it may serve to suggest the combination of
the essential qualities which a legal philosophy must attempt to ascribe
to a mature system of law, if that system aims at justifying obedience
in other terms than that of an indoctrinated myth. If men are to be
free to give their loyalty not only on a basis of voluntarily shared community of purpose, but also because of common need (the latter Cicero
called "the binding together of a republic"—*utilitatis communione*),
then even the description of law must allow for a moral and purposive
factor in which shared civil action is the creative factor in both shaping
and changing the *organization* of the state. The common defense pre-
cedes the general welfare; both are necessary for the "blessings of
liberty." The founding of constitutions is no longer a matter for the
great legislator endowed with divine wisdom, and often accepting his
guidance from the Deity. It is a matter of rational effort and discussion,
guided by commonly shared moral values and objectives for human
life and society. The source of law, therefore, cannot neglect the ethical
aspects of human nature unless it denies to all law any concern with
justice, so defined.

*Can Systems of Law be Classified in Terms of Their Emphasis on the
Purposive as Opposed to the Organic Aspects of Law?*

Most positive jurisprudence, taking off from Austin's concept of its
purely analytical functions, limits itself to describing systems of law in
terms of some characteristic that it holds to be common to all of them.
Austin's celebrated definition of sovereignty, noted above, has had its
usefulness in describing a common characteristic of the national sov-
ereignties which comprise the groundwork for international organization
and on which the accepted practices of international law have hereto-
fore been built. The essential point that he made about sovereignty
was that no person or persons deserved to be called sovereign, even if
they were in the position of receiving the "habitual obedience of the
bulk of the people," unless, in turn, this sovereign was independent
and did not yield any like obedience to any other sovereign. In other
words, Austin was describing the state that existed in a period of
nationalism, admitting no limits to the legal competence of any state,
and making all international organization dependent upon treaty rights
which the state could denounce at will. International law rested ultimately on comity, good faith, convenience. It allowed some degree of
necessity for *pacta sunt servanda*, if nations were not to deserve too
truly Hobbes' immortal phrase about their assuming "the posture of

gladiators" on their respective boundaries, in a way that fitted his description of the state of nature.

The Constitution of the United States, in its statement of the supreme law of the land, has, it is true, made treaties parallel to statutes and to the Constitution itself in their claim to supremacy, when they were made "under the authority of the United States." But any statute passed subsequent to the ratification of a treaty may denounce or undo the treaty by its legislative content. In other words, the sovereign can take back what the sovereign has yielded in the way of international obligations. It is this theory of the finality of legal sovereignty that the Bricker Amendment wishes to make certain and to extend to protecting, in the Federal system, the rights of states against treaty encroachment or by a form of "international legislation." Even those who oppose the extreme position of the Bricker Amendment nevertheless agree that Congress can override a treaty and could presumably at any time withdraw from the United Nations or any other international obligations. The President might protect his opposition to such an act by his veto, but in this respect he is a part of the legislative process, and the veto could be overridden by the requisite majorities.

Now, Austin's theory, on the whole, correctly described the behavior of really independent states. As long as there was any reasonable basis in fact for the doctrine of equality of states in international law, the international community was thus precluded from coming into anything more than limited existence as shared purposes and for specific points. This sharing rested upon the voluntary consent of each and, in that sense, a kind of alliance or strictly limited federation among its members. The veto power of the so-called "Big Five" in the Security Council which was written into the Charter showed inequality, but also sovereign finality. Even among "equals" this finality of sovereignty, however, was paralleled to some extent by the ability of all states to withdraw from the United Nations. A state could and did deny the legal competence of the United Nations to coerce it if the issue were pushed to a conclusion. Such an issue would arise in a purely hypothetical case involving United Nations action to coerce some sovereign power, if, for example, South Africa considered the matter to be within its domestic jurisdiction protected by Article II, Sec. 7 of the Charter. The legality of any proceedings by the U.N. against the Union, to deal with laws enforcing *apartheid*, would be extremely moot. Only in a very clear case affecting the peace of the world would such coercion by the U.N. have been alleged to have any genuine legal status.

In other words, the political nature of world community has not rested, to date, on a *consensus juris* sufficiently strong to embody powers of executive coercion or legislative competence in the United Nations like those of even a Federal union; or of anything in the way of a juristic union beyond an alliance, that could be denounced and repudiated as a source of law by the members severally and independently. The behavior of members who simply "took a walk" from the Assembly, *à la* Moscow or Communist Hungary, threatening but not wanting to carry out a final withdrawal, has given some testimony on the degree to which the United Nations, in effect, can exercise coercive powers. Indeed, given its composition, where the currency is being increasingly debased by the introduction of states of as doubtful international character and responsibility as Yemen or Ghana, perhaps it is the part of wisdom to limit the assertions of the supernational and superstate nature of the United Nations as those of a legal entity. The United Nations is not co-organic because in fact its powers cannot be used coercively with success—an organic factor; and this fact, in turn, rests on the absence of the elements of a truly shared common set of moral values for law.

In this matter it is not only a question of the degree to which there is a genuine sharing of the sense of justice and moral values on which law must ultimately rest, if it is to form a true legal community with powers of sanctions. The danger of mistaking an ideal hope for a present reality might lead to very grave disillusionments, through vesting powers in the U.N. to extend its powers to operate. Even limited by the legal requirement to operate under the required majorities, such an extension might one day conceivably result in an attempt to coerce the free world's dwindling bastions in some of the most basic areas of security. So far this danger has been no more than a possibility; but there is a limit to the degree to which the U.N. can have its membership increased among these small and relatively powerless states who are still given prospective voting privileges, without raising this possibility. Many of these states cannot even produce stable government, free from infiltrated control, much less responsible behavior.

The organic ties that unite the international community have not, up to the present time, included sanctions that could be applied against the members of the United Nations to coerce them under the guise of law. But there is a growing demand to achieve such a world order, backed by force, from those people (like the World Federalists) who misunderstand the possibilities of controlling such force and applying it against an aggressor. Most of all they misunderstand the degree to which there is a *consensus juris* that would protect free institutions in that part of the world where they genuinely exist because they have been *won*, not bestowed. The Soviet Union, the most probable aggressor and the one whose indirect forms of aggression characterize the protracted political war in which it is engaged with the free world, cannot be safely or effectively coerced by the U.N. In consequence, the writ of the U.N. does not run behind the Iron Curtain or even behind the Bamboo Curtain.

This raises a serious question as to the use of the U.N. for limiting national action on domestic issues arising within constitutional states, or even in their self-defense. The reason for this caution is that the operation of its moral influence, backed by forces like the U.N.E.F. in the Suez crisis, can operate only against those who are willing to concede moral validity to collective action. The sanctions do not and cannot operate, without the risk of provoking World War III, to coerce the Soviet Union itself.

Of course there are those who maintain that, since the moral basis of law is the ultimate test of its legitimacy, judged in standards of ideal justice rather than expediency, really determined efforts backed by a show of real force might have forced the evacuation of Soviet troops from Hungary. And so, they say, the rule of law could have been enforced in both directions. Would they fight a general nuclear war to establish this sanction? If not, bluff is either dangerous or humiliating, and a humiliating backdown can itself be most dangerous.

This kind of judgment, however, enters the realm of political decision and has only the relation to the ordinary conception of a community under law that the idea of *bellum justum* had in the late medieval period to the inception of international public law as a system.

Any genuine analysis of the nature of community must, nevertheless, emphasize both its organic, that is, its determined and given character, its organizational "musts," the forces of tradition and habit, and the analysis of the capabilities of physical force on the one hand, and, on the other, what possibilities there are of imposing co-organic, i.e., moral purpose upon these given factors in order to change their operation and apply a purpose to the direction of force that will prevent it from operating blindly.

It is in this sense that the developing demand of an international community for its collective security obviously looks toward an ultimate control by an effective form of such a community over the type of destructive weapons which now are, in practical terms, possessed by two (or at most three) members of the world community of nations. But this ultimate ideal cannot be used as a means to put a monopoly of such power in the most ruthless hands, through either sheer force or sheer funk.

A Basis for Classifying Constitutional Legal Systems as Against Totalitarian

Ultimately, the usefulness of the co-organic relations of law to community suggests that where purposive factors are controlling and are freely shared by the bulk of the community, the system may genuinely be called constitutional; that is, founded upon and constructed in its organization of forces around the principles of moral responsibility of the individual and the protection of these rights through the recognition of corollary duties. This is the whole aim of a system of public law that practices what Jellinek called, in his *Allgemeine Staatslehre,* "auto-limitation," or self-limitation. Such a community can accept external limits on its sovereignty, voluntarily, in the interests of realizing areas of common purpose.

On the other hand, a totalitarian system can never admit the possibility of any outside organ determining its own conduct, even by consent. There can be no area of genuinely shared purpose, since the aim of totalitarianism is to bring all other systems under its own rubric of force and under its grand design. Its purpose is not a shared purpose, but a monopoly of all purpose.

In this sense Immanuel Kant was surely right, in the essay *Eternal Peace*, in saying that the moral basis for international order under law could be achieved successfully only by states that he called "republican," that is to say, constitutional states. To the degree, therefore, that the purposive aspect of community is emphasized, a nation may be said to be what the Germans used to call a "Rechtsstaat"—pretty much the same concept.

It is clear that to Austin's type of analytical jurisprudence there is no particular distinction which can be made between a system of law that in its internal character at least professes to be consistent with its own premises, such as Mr. Vishinsky's interpretation of the Soviet law; and, on the other hand, the constitutional public law of a system like that of the United States or of Britain. Each can be treated, for analytical purposes, as a command structure, if it has sanctions. Indeed, the operation of the hierarchical principle is simpler in the Soviet design.

It is true, as Professor Fuller has noted, that close examination of the operations of the legal system may break down this apparent consistency. The Soviet system does have contradictions within the framework of its courts and operates in the application of punishment and legal sanctions quite outside the professed framework of law. The protections of constitutional rights as written in the public document known as the Russian Constitution are known to be illusory. So that even on the external evidence of fact and on the internal consistency of the system, analytical jurisprudence may raise some questions. But, since analytical jurisprudence can never really check by a higher standard of moral law (some version of natural law), it can never really draw a distinction such as the co-organic theory does offer as a basis. For between law founded on a conception of justice based on moral responsibility, and a system of law that rests upon compulsion, at best claiming legitimacy through some form of indoctrinated social myth, there is a very wide gulf of tragic fact. If an analytical treatment cannot, consistently with its own assumptions, account for or even discern this gulf, it proves to be pragmatically blind to the most important order of legal and moral fact. Certainly we do not wish to exchange our present freedom for the slavery urged by Lord Russell as a better alternative than human destruction. There is a much less obsessive view than his of the false dilemma: we do not have to commit suicide to retain freedom, nor can we be sure that the Communist masters whom he would accept might not themselves be the ruthless and reckless source of an internal struggle for power which would loose the ultimate destruction upon all humanity while they were fighting over world mastery of some future Kremlin, with all the savagery of the gangsters whom the system breeds.[5]

[5] For an expanded treatment of the moral limits of law making and enforcement by the United Nations see the author's concluding chapter in *The United States and the United Nations*, ed. by Franz B. Gross (Univ. of Oklahoma Press, 1964).

APPENDIX C

PUBLIC ASPECTS OF PRIVATE ASSOCIATIONS:
THE NATURE OF GROUPS

AS THEY BEAR ON POLITICAL ACTION IN FREE SYSTEMS

Some Definitions and a Setting for a Theory of Voluntary Groups in Politics

Political science, for reasons natural to its development, has in the United States of America taken on a behaviorist character. Its effort has been to achieve an "objective"—i.e., what is termed "positivist" or "scientific" and analytical approach to politics. "Scientific" method may by this easy definition, merely by limitation not by tested assumptions, consist either in a sociological approach in the Comtean tradition; or in any one of the other dissecting methods that seek and generally profess to find a magic formula showing what makes human beings "tick." This approach has led to a primarily sociological emphasis on the role of groups in political processes as if it were the peculiar discovery of the twentieth century, pioneered (in the general estimate of the prevailing American scholarship in this field) by the thinking of people like Arthur F. Bentley. It was Bentley who wrote the study on *The Process of Politics* in the first decade of this century, centered on voluntary group action (i.e., "Private"), which later on became subsumed under the term "pressure groups." The groups that depend on *voluntary* action, even political parties, are thus private in origin though they obviously affect public policy.[1]

Bentley, sweepingly and obviously limiting his analysis to the contemporary scene of Western political institutions, primarily American, attributed an ultimate political reality in the formation of governmental

---

[1] Happily, a balanced critical review of Bentley's work that makes unnecessary a repetition of my own Bentley summary in *The Western Political Heritage*. This is Bernard Crick's *The American Science of Politics* (Berkeley, Univ. of California Press, 1959), especially Chapter VII: "The Science of the Group Process in Politics: A. F. Bentley." Dr. Crick develops with a great skill and judgment the critique which he cites (p. 120, Note 2) also from my *Western Political Heritage* (pp. 880–882). His whole book would, along with W. R. Dennes (later cited) serve as philosophical background for sustaining, balancing, and extending with improvements, my own theoretical earlier insights. I should also cite R. M. MacIver and especially Francis Wilson as theorists, whose views I find obviate reiteration of my own first stated in *The Pragmatic Revolt* (1928).

action and policies, and indeed of all forms of political influence, to what he lumped with quite unscientific lack of classification as "group process," or "the pressure of interests," assuming group freedom from state control. Of course, this was in itself an assumption based upon a limited view of political science since it was rather peculiar to democratic and constitutional processes that are, historically speaking, the exception, not the rule. The nature of groups varies greatly. They flourish as voluntary growths particularly in a "permissive" type of society which not only allows the free evolution of groups but encourages them. Totalitarian and even merely authoritarian societies start off with Hobbes's typical attitude toward groups, which he lumped under "corporations" [artificial bodies]: "Corporations in the body politic are like worms in the entrails of the natural man," said that original "Old Curmudgeon"!

The French Revolution's first monument of basic legislative change was the famous *Loi des Associations*, expressing Hobbes by abolishing some private groups (e.g., the Jesuits and other orders), whom the Jacobins felt were really not "private" in origin or intent.

Bentley's analysis of groups did not contribute very much that was fundamental to any truly scientific (objective) analysis of voluntary groups, either as to their nature or effects, because he did not get to the basic problem of *what* a group was. Like most pseudo-scientific "group" analysis, he leaves out not only what causes groups to "tick," but what *kinds* of groups existed for different moral or other ends and purposes. His definitional activities were extremely limited. One has only to read the book once more to find that he does not even get as far as the science of botany did in the days of Linnaeus, i.e., to the stage at least of *classifying* the different kinds of groups. He did, however, misunderstand the botany of his own day, as Bernard Crick shows.[2] He is singularly apt to lump all kinds of group activity together—a mistake avoided by Aristotle in looking to group "ends" in the *Politics*, building up to the state from the family through *phratry*, tribe, and *deme* to the *polis*. Unlike Aristotle, Bentley does not really distinguish in the working of political groups those which are serving in a broader purpose, subsuming to it diverse private- or sub-group differences of interest, from those which are promoting more limited economic and functional interest as their distinctive bond of unity.

British, German, and for that matter Continental social sciences in general have been much more structurally inclined than was Bentley in the typical analysis of groups from the eighteenth- and nineteenth-century beginnings of political sociology. By not trying to formulate the distinctions between the responses of "groups" to the different kinds of environmental pressures, or to cultural contexts, he could not show the

2 *Cf.* Crick, *op. cit.*, Chapter VII, p. 114.

difference between the groups that filled functional needs (mainly "interest" groups) and those that filled what one might call "purposive" needs, to be true to their broader nature and objectives.

This step depends on the soundness of a philosophically basic distinction between *interest* and *purpose*—one of my earliest contributions that I have tried to keep alive in today's political philosophy. The necessary analytical tool was the "co-organic" concept of all really free political action. Constitutionalism, to be truly understood, is in fact organized for *both* moral objectives deeply shared in a fundamentally purposive *consensus juris*, and *also* for essential interests—organic functional stability: defense, economic welfare, and adequacy—the organic realm of *utilitatis communio*, to use Cicero's terms from *The Republic*. I refer (for the sake of people who are no longer familiar with a book that has been out of print for a good many years) to the first book that I wrote,[3] *The Pragmatic Revolt in Politics: Syndicalism, Fascism, and the Constitutional State*.

This was, essentially, an effort to deal with the "revolt" which had taken place in both academic philosophy and more popular circles (including both Georges Sorel and Benito Mussolini!) against the stereotypes of absolutism, and of metaphysical politics of a highly abstract order which refused to take into account the realities, the *data* of our relevant human needs. Pragmatism lent itself to solidarist functionalism, Sorel's myth-making and Duguit's jurisprudence of *droit objectif*. I thought it was necessary to concede the organic need of proper tests for relevance and correpondence, including testing by experience, to the pragmatic call for this reform in philosophy, though without conceding the jettisoning of systematic logic, metaphysics, and ethics: these situational realities must take into account the functional and the organic contexts of societies—the *given*, if you like. All experimental science shows this necessity by *checking* its *data*. Any society has to analyze its basic assumptions by this testing, and any philosophy of history has in some way to explain and accept its results. Those, like Marxism, which most profess to the "scientism of the magic formula" most violate scientific method by disregarding all evidence that does not square with the basic dogma of the master's *ipse dixit*. Thus they exhibit all the faults Marx attributes to ideologies—always *other's* ideologies, of course.

What is it that determines the limits of a man's freedom, if he has freedom? And what kinds of freedom is he permitted in the midst of so much that is obviously necessary and determined by what he finds as a biological creature in a given environment and at a given period of history, culturally grounded in the past?

3 Essentially a reworking of my Oxford D.Phil. thesis, done under A. D. Lindsay—of happy memory—the Master of Balliol, the Vice Chancellor of Oxford, and my tutor for the years after World War I.

How does this moral ultimacy of individual choice—the prerequisite of any freedom—square with the manifest objectives, purposive goals that can be freely accepted in all organized and enduring groups? How do such groups differ from the syndicates of the Corporative State of Fascist theory? Obviously, the latter are judged and directed by a central control, whereas voluntary groups that do not challenge the basic constitution of a free state are allowed to develop their own ends.

My point in this book (now quite ancient but, I am happy to say, still well regarded) was to sketch as a philosophical method the development of what I called a "co-organic" nature of group life. This analysis I have reviewed in the second volume of *Nomos*, on *Community*, which contained a condensed contribution, brought up to date, on the legal and juristic aspects of political community, treated from this purposively organic point of view. The "co-organic" philosophy is intended to explain and make clear the implications, moral and political, of the difference between the totalitarian and constitutional views of politics, very badly understood on the generally available present evidence of intellectual default, if not defection.[4] Human behavior at its deepest levels of dynamics shows this clash to be rooted in conflicting religious and ethical faiths—symbolized ultimately on "religions" whose affirmations are grounded on assumptions of quite opposing moral universes of value. Cultural history has shown in the whole human past[5] the epic struggles of the world's great "co-organic" culture myths. The rise and fall of civilizations can be best understood in these, rather than Spenglerian, Toynbeean, Nietzschean, Petriean, or other terms.

To meet our first test let us examine the twentieth-century treatment of the nature of groups themselves to give better perspective to the problem today: obviously, it is beyond the limits of an essay of this compass to give a catalog or an evaluation of all the contributions to this vast body of writing that may conveniently start with the summary W. R. Dennes laid out in his *Method and Presuppositions of Group Psychology*, and then pay some homage to Georg Simmel, Werner Sombart, Max Weber, and a dozen other Germans of note and worth, since the exaggerations of Bluntschli attributed sex differences to such groups as church and state. I am mindful, personally, of the early days of our own American Social Research Council (in which I served for a few years on a "Committee on Method in the Social Sciences," in the period when such methodological study was first encouraged, especially

---

4 Once called by Julian Benda *Trahison des Clercs*.
5 Herman Schneider, *The History of World Civilizations*, 2 vols. (New York, Harcourt Brace & Co., 1931). Translated from the German, and treated in the Introduction and *passim* in *The Western Political Heritage*, W. Y. Elliott and Neil A. MacDonald (New York, Prentice-Hall, 1949). See also Herman Schneider, *Religions and Philosophy of History*, 2 vols (not translated).

in the latter part of the 1920's by the early Rockefeller Foundation). Edmund Day was the presiding and representative genius, our true benefactor, who essayed a novel foundation-man's role—alas today, not often so openly and frankly revealed—it was in fact one of being the chief guide and mentor of our sessions! Today McGeorge Bundy seems to be reviving, about as frankly, this early tradition, applying it for the first time to the Ford Foundation. Day was himself also a scholar and a thinker of some parts; not just an economist, but a mind of wide-ranging interests. I remember particularly the benefits I had from serving on this Committee on Scientific Method in a happy association with R. M. MacIver, our great contemporary Scots "moral philosopher" in the great tradition, who had already written a philosophical and sociological book on *Community*, and another which soon followed, *The Modern State*,[6] somewhat along the lines that I treated in *The Pragmatic Revolt in Politics*, about the same time.

The essential approach of our "moral philosophies" was that there was room for *both* purpose and, if you like, something like a large weight of the past's determinism. Scientific analysis of uniformities of behavior could usefully draw on these "organic" factors, not only to describe but to predict or at least to deal with causes and types of action, habitual or heavily weighted by those uniformities based on the cultural patterns and institutions which were historically "given": one could, however, never rule out innovation, adjustment, purposive growth and therefore unpredictable novelty.

These data (the "given" in the context of interests, needs, and functions of group behavior) were the factors that impinged on human beings which had to be treated in what I called their "organic" context, because organic suggested first the idea of "functional"; then the problem of survival for a common end through central control that subordinated its parts; next, collective community or lesser group action for common ends, adjusted to an environment sometimes hostile—never without challenge, with a view not only to survival but to growth. *The Pragmatic Revolt* structured the whole problem crudely, both for politics and jurisprudence, but systematically, in the last two sections of the book, which dealt with the nature of the group as a "co-organism." It was an effort at the purposive marriage of idealistic logic to realistic ethics, and equally of this moral purpose to pragmatic realism, in a balanced political and juristic theory. Its importance lay in the effort, at least, to structure the whole value system of ethics to a more realistic politics than the tradition of Willoughby, Garner, and even the historical surveys of W. A. Dunning. At the same time it demanded a sterner philosophical seriousness of pragmatism, and a less simple solution than

6 MacIver's definitions of "associations" and "communities" as group class-ifications, as opposed to "institutions" as modes of behavior, still are most useful.

the economic interpretation generally favored by Charles A. Beard and A. N. Holcombe.

Some Other Pioneer Origins for Twentieth-Century American Group Theory

About 1925–30, a new look at this problem of groups came from many other students of the "realistic" treatment of the political role of many differing types of voluntary groups. In applying the theories of groups from the works of Dewey, Dennes, Charles Merriam, MacIver, Elliott, and others, Peter Odegard's study of moral and propaganda special-purpose groups like the W.C.T.U. led to adding other devices to the questionnaire method in the use of statistics for measuring group solidarity.

Many of these pioneers later on became quite famous in their several ways through variations, like Harold Lasswell, who drew on all sorts of sources—from *Psychoanalysis and Politics* to the simpler *Politics, Who Gets What*. I joined with E. Pendleton Herring, who was just finishing his doctoral thesis at Johns Hopkins on *Group Representation Before Congress* (later published as a pioneering book), in putting out two articles on *"Le Role Politique des Associations aux Etats Unis"* in the *Revue des Sciences Politiques* (1929, Volume LII) in France.[7]

Even a very spotty selection from great names of continental sociological theory in the history of the development of the theory of groups, such as those included in *The Pragmatic Revolt*, illustrates that the main currents of the twentieth century took for granted a considerable amount of ballast and did not treat as too ancient history to be relevant some of the more respectable surviving theories that were derived from classical history.

The Germans remained much more categorical in their analysis of groups from the older line of Gumplowicz and Ratzenhofer, not forgetting Ostrogorski and some prophetic Slavic analysts of group theory in politics. The wide variety of sociologists (whom I will not take the trouble to list at this time) includes later giants like Max Weber, whom Talcott Parsons and others have refurbished. The classic historians, of whom perhaps the last were Werner Jaeger and Jacob Burckhardt, also included those who were of the persuasion of Otto von Gierke in their efforts to deal with some of the realities of the roots of Germanic institutions. This school affected Maitland in England more than it did Gierke's own later compatriots so far as treating the group as the unit of real moral personality went. It affected later even the more legitimate

---

[7] *Revue des Sciences Politiques* (1929, Vol. LII), France—two articles by E. Pendleton Herring and W. Y. Elliott on *"Le Rôle Politique des Associations aux Etats Unis"*—is still a most useful catalog of the nature and role of groups in the contemporary politics of the United States, though Parties now bow to labor more than business, and to racial and religious minorities than to most propaganda and special interest (economic) pressure groups.

Hegelians, who had their own way of spinning out history through the *Gesammtperson;* or like F. Tönnies in his version of *Gemeinschaft und Gesellschaft.* But the Hegelian tradition also, like Gierke's, disposed British disciples, e.g., Bernard Bosanquet, to go to some lengths in the "idealistic" logic of history which Charles Beard and the pragmatists Peirce, James, and Dewey, and American sociologists like Sumner and even Ward, very much opposed.

Original Group Theory of Our Founders

Charles Beard himself was at one phase very much in the sociological vein, although he did not call it that: He called it "the economic interpretation" of history, not Marxism—but flavored as Arthur Holcombe and a host of allies, if not disciples, did by finding (often with some justice) the prime mover of political party backing in the broad base of sectional or other economic interests. Beard's was essentially an effort to find in this "economic interpretation," *à la* Seligmann, not Marx, a magic formula for explaining party loyalties, and human motives—Hamilton's formula too, though slanted with quite different class values.

The Founding Fathers themselves had some room for at least analyzing the nature of groups as "factions," based on interests primarily, which Madison hoped the Union would be broad and deep enough to submerge, as he showed in the "Tenth Number" of *The Federalist.*

Faction, specifically, was an "interest-group" type of analysis. It was that phase of Bentley's group analysis that pleased the Beard school, who were looking for economic interests as the main motive power of democratic politics.

This analysis also gave rise to the theory that a considerable part of the dynamics of any free democratic society was the result of pressures for the realization of specific types of interests.

But today, Beard's *Economic Interpretation of the Constitution* is generally conceded to be vastly overdone. Even the historians and sociologists who stress pressure groups stress not only economic interests. They would agree rather with Charles Pinckney of South Carolina, again as an example from our Founders' period, who made a very notable analysis of the three natural regional divisions of major *basic* occupational and economic interests in the colonies that had to be taken into account and which were, in some ways, the background for many of the most important compromises of our constitutional system. But Pinckney, like modern historians, e.g., Samuel Eliot Morison, stressed the ties as well as the division on the broad basis of human nature's differences that later separated the Federalists from the Jeffersonians.

We started our historical development with a mature political theory— never better expressed—in which groups were recognized as playing an essential role, a divisive, as well as uniting one—a formative and a conserving role. The group work of the Founding Fathers themselves from their earlier days of holding together the Committees of Correspondence during the Revolution, on through the Annapolis Convention, the Philadelphia, and then the State Ratifying Conventions, showed how very important they were as "general purpose" groups, in the minds of the men, like Madison and Wilson, who had worked in this context and knew something about its realities. Compromise, yes—but held together by broad fundamental consensus on the Preamble and Bill of Rights, as well as on the machinery for respresentative responsibility and the organizing, dividing, and separating as ways of limiting, but also of building an effective use of power, under a rigid Constitution—not at the mercy of bare "one man, one vote" majorities. Ours was a government of "corporate," i.e., community representation at least in one of the two Houses, even *in* the states, themselves federations through territorially workable communities of purpose.

Voluntary group organization is, after all, one of the oldest and best recognized strengths of any type of British-derived democracy. Voluntary groups are also one of the classic ways of getting a variety of political viewpoints taken into consideration for both representation and for the formation of policies. The multi-faceted types of interests and purposes with which contemporary British politics are concerned have been treated in more depth by Sam Beer of Harvard probably, than by any other single contemporary scholar. The British capacity to organize themselves to pursue their interests and purposes by small groups forms the basis for the excellent analysis of this trait of character in A. D. Lindsay's little classic on *The Essentials of Democracy* and his more substantial *The Modern Constitutional Democratic State*.

Parties Role in Group Theory and Practice

But what about parties? Are they not just larger pressure groups? They are surely public in effect but private in origin. What role does purpose play in this governing transmission belt between people and legislative policies, as well as for the administration of resultant programs? V. O. Key and Pendleton Herring among many others have shown great sophistication on this theme. Schattschneider and J. M. Burns have probed deeply into the need for public policy protected against pressure raids—and so, hopefully, have I (e.g., in *The Need for Constitutional Reform*, 1936).

On more classic authority, Madison himself really gave to party a much more substantial role than in fact he give to "faction." Although he did not stress it so much under this term (party), since parties in England in spite of Burke still had a bad name as self-serving cabals, Madison assumed that the very great need for federal union was to get a sufficient and general (if not universalized) need to put into policy something that was larger and more ethically structured than interest, in order to produce a national purpose, though again he did not call a unity for principles by that name. That is, party's duty was to reconcile and structure interests. And what Madison foresaw, Jefferson took over from the Federalists and practiced, though with a different political set of values.

Edmund Burke, if you like to go back to the source of the more favorable view of party, said as wise things about the nature of party as anybody has ever said—as he did about much else, e.g., the state as a "partnership in all virtue," not just a compact for limited liability like a joint stock company. Party was not for promoting just special interests. Party was to promote the general or common purpose—even though they, as we, often spoke of public *"interest,"* when they meant purpose— the public policy for arriving at something that was good for the nation. Burke accepted not only the necessity that parties should exist. He thought that they must and should serve and preserve the public good. His classic definition of parties has been often quoted in that regard.[8]

No politician who is going to be a political leader of any broadscale community can afford to neglect the wisdom of Burke's insight, because he must in some sense be not only a "broker of interests." He must find a platform to expound party purposes that transcend interests and force a resolution without conflict, through new and less limited goals which give a new direction permitting reconciliation of lesser interests. That is the true *art* of politics, which is more than and better than a "pseudo" science. Since men are not robots it works through human adjustment, including compromise within a uniting framework of purposive principle.

In other words, parties are not just interest groups, although they no doubt do have their roots very deeply—as all political realities do—in the interests that spring from the community's organic needs. Needs help to produce the direct prompting of interests as the expression of attitudes devoted to dealing with efficiency of functioning and the basic appetites and drives that keep men going and growing.

Group Classifications from Aristotle On: Purpose, Functionalism— "Organic" Need—The Co-Organic Theory of Politics: Consensus and Necessity Combined

This analysis offers a clue at least to a philosophical ground, a *fundamental* basis for classifying groups, which I think has been singularly neglected among political scientists. Such a need is increased by the pulls of our contemporary speed-up in a technology that makes purposive integration of policies and programs for a *res publica* ever more essential to save human beings from repeating the *finished* evolutionary pattern of the ants and bees. It is a basic need, beginning to find some recognition.

---

8 "A political party is a body of men united for promoting by their joint endeavors the national interest, *upon some particular principle on which they are all agreed."* (Italics mine; and I read this clause to mean "common purpose" since that is the precise nature of national interest so qualified.)

It is capable of being rephrased in a larger, more normative form: We do not lack evidence that this is a sound lead, for if we go into ancient history, we can find this trail going back far into our classical past: Plato rejects the whole idea of the basic organization of society only on the interest group used as the organic adjuster of function: This rejection comes *after* he has very poetically sketched the first "division of labor"— indeed what we may call the first "functional approach to politics"—in *The Republic*. There must be a perfectly coherent functional organization of this productive group life as the basis, at the origin of any polis. But immediately he goes far beyond that by saying this would be only a "city of swine," to use Glaucon's term.

Functionalism could give no more than basic satisfaction of the *needs* of life. It would not provide the way of organizing these needs, of subordinating or uniting them, for developing civic morality, the loyalty that produces leaders and follows them, understands justice and willingly obeys it; above all, develops in its arts and its happy virtues what Pericles claimed for Athens: the School of Hellas. So Socrates tries to show that Justice lies deeper than mere organic need. It is the purposive arrangement or organization, to which function is merely ancillary. It is that quality which leads Aristotle to say that the constitution is not merely the arrangement, balancing of power and structuring of functions; it is the *form* and, Isocrates would add, the *life* or "spirit" of the state.

Fundamentally, Aristotle uses both in the *Nicomachean Ethics* and in the *Politics* this same order for developing a *polis* from families, although he goes still further into the origins of group life by a broader genetic treatment of cultural groups. He is very specific in making the family the first group in the point of the genetic build-up of anything leading toward a political union. But he also shows that beyond the family lie the *gentes*, and *phratries*, the religious and kinship organizations, and finally the tribe. Beyond that, later, comes the organization on a *polis*, based on a *demic*, a territorial ordering. By this Solonian period tribes are no longer the best units for uniting people. Now more complex loyalty requires some kind of *mythos*, a "demic" unity that he calls a "constitution," for the *politea*, the mixed and balanced powers as the best form for the state. This evolves by a natural history going back beyond Solon's four-class Athens, but finding its mythos in the persuasion by Pallas Athena of the Furies to become instead the *Eumenides*, leading them to become the happier ordering Laws of Athens, a pretty and a profound myth which Aeschylus used to wind up his great trilogy of *The Oresteia*.

To find what legitimizes law one must understand *why* every association, as Aristotle says, has for its end "some good" for the association— "The state, being the highest association, has the highest good" is the usual translation. This is not quite correct. The state, being the most comprehensive association, he really says, has the most inclusive good, or at least that is what I take the Greek to mean: the most broad-ranging and necessarily inclusive community as the fundamental grounds for law-making. Constitutionalism teaches this as the matrix of all order, the guardian of all civic responsibility, therefore, the "highest good" among all *associations*, because necessary to the existence of all others than the state.

This reasoning leads on to the development of what I would call "the myth of the social contract," of which the earliest form perhaps can be found already in Glaucon's small exchange on this theme in *The Republic*, or in Socrates' rejection of this as the sole basis for the state. Community by the mythos of contract rests on the idea that all voluntary obedience is implicit. It is the notion of an *implicit* contract binding individuals to obedience to a state so composed as to be based on natural law, and to protect the natural rights of man, as Stoicism foreshadowed and Roman Law developed. Probably the best formulation of that ideal is what Cicero stated as the foundation for the "Commonwealth"—*The Republic*. Quite early along he says, "The state, or the Commonwealth (the *res publica*) is not just any sort of "coming together" of men, but one bound "*consensu juris*." [9]

The word "jus" obviously means both law and right—therefore, bound by a fundamental agreement on what is right law. Its ambiguity is not unintentional. It expresses the Western political demand on law that it should also have a moral content of justice or "rightness" which imposes a sense of its voluntary obligation on the people whom it protects. That is the main thrust of the whole later social contract theory.

To this framwork for purposive loyalty—not mere Hobbesian necessity —Cicero also adds an equally important binding force to the community. He specifically speaks, in this instance, of *communione* (by a sharing). Community is a good word for sharing, i.e., by a shared community "of utility," *utilitatis*. Now this shared utility is what I call the organic side of the state, one of the needs that the Preamble of the Constitution of the United States covers so effectively, when it talks not only about a more perfect union (in itself the necessary condition for any organic effectiveness) but of the setting up of a constitutional system by which we, the people of the United States, can "establish justice," then "insure domestic tranquillity." There in themselves are both sides of law, the purposive (justice) and the organic (tranquillity). Justice is the right-ness of law, its purposive value. But domestic tranquillity is something more immediate—and one may say a prerequisite which we seem to be in danger of forgetting in our concern for the superiority of the rights of criminals or of demonstrators who are really violent, as against the pro-tection of the rights of innocent, responsible and virtuous citizens. Do-mestic tranquillity is the Hobbesian side of the "public business," an "organic" necessity for all order on which justice hangs: The stability of

9 See Appendix II B, pp. 522ff.

the state is the prerequisite for free development by all other groups in it.

Justice in this sense requires the immediate necessity of establishing the decent order that prevents crime being treated as a normal social pattern —"to insure domestic tranquillity." Justice makes no sense, unless we have an order in which there is a monopoly of force in the hands of a government which can and does exercise adequate authority to keep order, under procedures that are certain and sure and with adequate sanctions which, as Austin said, command "the habitual obedience of the bulk of the people." That is minimal sovereignty for a "rule of law."

You will note that the very next thing in the Preamble of our Constitution is "the common defense": "to provide for the common defense and to promote the general welfare." General welfare has an additional ambiguity in that it suggests, and was intended to suggest, not just a welfare state such as has grown into the weeds of "The Great Society," but a true *well-fare* that would permit spiritual and moral growth, as well as the capacity for individuals to provide for decent family life, not just on a basis of general state support by the Roman mobs' demands for *panem ac circenses*. Pressure groups demanding the right to stipulate and then control the distribution of their own state-provided bounty do not create *true* welfare but destroy the self-respect and incentives on which it rests. Certainly when the Constitution of the United States was being hammered out in Philadelphia and ratified by the state conventions the Founders were talking about welfare in a much broader sense that included a moral sense too. There is no question about that moral quality (purposive) when they go on to talk about ensuring "the blessings of liberty to ourselves and our posterity." These phrases sum up the whole concept of individual moral responsibility as the only basis for any real rights or dignity, and for constitutional morality, and the only true happiness rooted in liberty that comes from a life of dedication to something more meaningful and sustaining than mere gratification of appetites. Governing groups are needed to check, *by law,* the growth of demands whose only basis is a need that cannot be happily met except by hard work and one's own efforts.

In short, this division of interests and purposes is woven into the framework of the United States Constitution, which was an effort at stating the very things that Cicero was talking about in his *De Republica*. It is also the foundation of all really genuine constitutionalism, because it means protecting those aspects of life for which *order* must be assured as a prerequisite, but under conditions where justice is also a limitation on the exercise of governmental power to bring it into line with "due process" of law with its essential protection of genuine civil liberties and of our earned political liberties which, by the way, are necessary privileges for loyal citizens who support a true community—but are not the *universal* necessary protection for all men to be able to live and work well and freely under our law what we mean, and the Romans meant, by *civil* rights and liberties.

This Preamble serves as a framework for the organization of political and legal relations for subsuming functional types of voluntary groups because, within its enumerated ends (above), the relation of groups to each other and to the political community has an agreed way of being worked out by a legally coherent process, with protection for the citizen's free choice of belonging or not belonging to any group. These processes must be tested by courts that can raise issues which show the kind of relevance and correspondence to reality that is the essence of any sound political theory—*and what are*, also, *its basic assumptions.*

There is a real question whether a society basically atheistic or otherwise divided as to the nature of its fundamental values *can retain* a true *consensus juris.* Differences of religion must be protected. But first the *free exercise of religion* is the foundation of public morality—not spurious and misguided "activism," under a false mask. To take away this right to practice *voluntary* prayers because any sort of even self imposed and publicly sanctioned abstention is alleged to be "exclusion" from voluntary common worship and "offends" those who do not acknowledge or testify by conduct to a common faith, really prevents "free exercise" by those who do.

An "agreement on fundamentals" was the way the Founding Fathers stressed this matter; and a "frequent recurrence to fundamentals" was talked of in most of the early state constitutions, just as a matter of habit. They felt that it was essential to get back to these from time to time in order to remind themselves of what their basic purposes were, as well as what were the nature of those political units which, certainly on the very narrowest view, were *general* in their purposes, though not claiming exclusive authority or universal validity. Federalism itself showed this by dividing powers in terms of territorial units of community—as well as sharing them.

Can the constitutional state be capable of being, or of justly claiming to be, universal in its purpose? Not as long as it is a *limited,* i.e., a *truly* constitutional state, not as long as it equally does not profess that *its* law must be supreme and enforced on the whole world. Universal purpose for the state was only claimed when totalitarian states came into being —taking the place of quasi-totalitarian theocracies, if indeed there ever were any, i.e., religious systems that asserted as of divine right a complete (totalitarian) control over *all* human behavior, requiring control over the machinery of law and the state by an unlimited and all-inclusive scrutiny of all the ends and the total behavior of all human being. It is only through such a claim to be—what manifestly it was not—a world-dispensing reign that the question of a universal purpose group ever arose. In fact, if not in some fanciful and totally unenforceable claims, totalitarianism has only been made organically possible quite lately by modern technology. The Pharaohs and Genghis Khan could not possess nor exercise such power, even had they desired to claim it.

World Law and Consensus—Plus the Logic of Force versus Lord Russell's False Dilemmas

In theory, a system of world law, even if it were set up with completely coercive powers and a nuclear monopoly, would have to claim at least a sufficiently universal purpose to put the chain of command in the hands that were commonly enough agreed on to support such force with an effective *will* to world law, even at heavy cost. That would have to find means of enforcement that seem so far to escape even Mao's communism—and whose lack has long been apparent to Moscow—so long as our nuclear deterrent holds good.

It is precisely the lack of any such unifying common purpose fully *prepared* to coerce recalcitrants, that makes one-world rule a utopian suggestion at any present stage of human society. It is alleged to be a logical necessity by some disciples of Lord Russell. But he himself refuses to accept (certainly to face) the full force of his logic. We find it too difficult—and we have found it on a world scale substantially impossible—to get a sufficiently agreed purpose to set limitations on nuclear weapons or enforce them in an effective way. We have found, alas by sad experience, how unenforceable even "agreements" with the Russians are, not to mention with the China of the Red Guards, under (?) Mao: a one-hundred-megaton (claimed) test in violation of our "no air burst" testing agreement with Russia has had more recent repeats, to say nothing of the blatant attempts at paralyzing our deterrent capacity by putting large medium-range missiles in Cuba, in the past few years. Certainly any such nuclear agreements with the Chinese, even if they were signed (as they will not be), would be *more* unreliable as protections in fact, even were there any thought that they would ever be willing to so much as discuss such agreements. Yet we go on repeating the delusions of our past "treaties."

This stubborn gulf between our basic objectives for human happiness and "theirs" has rendered the anarchy of the international order in this respect distressingly absolute so long as the facts of such rooted all-out ideological assaults on our freedom to choose our own values exist; and so long as we are not either willing, able—or both—to deal with this in the way that Bertrand Russell in 1949 suggested that we should deal with Moscow to force an acceptance of no further independent development of nuclear energy on their part—even if an ultimatum, *which we meant*, was needed.

Now, almost two decades since his proposal, after the Soviets got nuclear power and we did nothing to prevent it, long after he wrote a book on *Power* to suggest that all conquerors got soft, he hopes that we still might have some freedom in the long run—not quite the thousand-year-Reich period of Nazism, but a good long span of time of perhaps several centuries. He now suggests that we should in effect surrender rather than run the risk of nuclear war—a view known as the "rather be Red than Dead" approach popularized by the disciples of his Pugwash propaganda. Maybe he changed sides so quickly because we did not take that golden opportunity, as he then regarded it, to give them an ultimatum and wipe them up if not out; at that time he seemed to be calling for action—whatever was needed to convert them if they did not accept our proposition for international control of nuclear weapons, so that there would not be a further spread of this apocalyptic threat. He *assumed* then what he now writes off: that there could and would be a genuine binding and enforceable "international control," the *how* not spelled out. Of course, Russell's weakness always has been and is in the unreality of the relevance, and the lack of correspondence to the facts, of his assumptions. The idea that there ever could be a universal *responsible* world control, certainly without totally disarming all the totalitarians, was itself an assumption of a very pathetically wishful order.

But his logic was faultless, if given his assumptions—i.e., if his false dilemmas were the only alternatives. It is just that he has never been in the habit of dealing with anything but dilemmas, or propositions of dichotomies, alternatives that are absolutely exclusive by their "either-or" character, or something quite like it.

Unfortunately, being mortals, not Pucks like Lord Russell, we have to proceed on somewhat different lines of reality: the whole nature of to-day's world is a witness to this fey character of the false world of Russell's imagining—a realm in which he is not even a gifted amateur but an opinionated scold, who would like to revenge himself on foolish mortals by a complete Pugwashing of humanity. His proposals, seriously and malignantly intended, to bring the President of the United States to trial in Paris—of all places—before a squalid collection of his chosen judges, adequately dispose of him as anything but one who—after the United States and the U.N. would *not* accept his counsels to *force* Moscow to forego building nuclear power and *force* internationalizing it (a not feasible even if wise 1949 ultimatum)—gave up hope in us and went to the other extreme: *our* surrender by degrees. Logic without realistic and relevant assumptions can suffer from a tragic excess of virtue.

The politics of groups involves this fundamental question of legitimizing power—the question of proceeding from the basic constituent sovereignty which we obey not from fear but by a deeper consensus freely given—to the level of governmental sovereignty that we allow in operating within the Constitution, i.e., for the Legislative body, for the Executive, and also, n.b., for the Judiciary. If we examine closely the organic role and the purposes of all those branches, separated in some

major degree, they are concerned to impose policy—by coercion if need
be—that will govern and limit the actions of all groups other than those
who form governmental organs. This power of government to decide and
impose limits on voluntary actions, in order to get common policies by
law, must be within the framework of the powers granted by the Constitution, i.e., as they are there separated, divided federally, limited in
many ways by bills of rights and other specific or general limitations
and, most importantly, protected against amendment by anything except
the extraordinary majorities stipulated in the amending process. These
are all protections against unconstitutional usurpations of power, if I
may call them that. They go beyond the routine prevention of unintentional abuse of powers which the courts can correct as *ultra vires*—
by statutory interpretation, by common law extension, or by equity
procedures.

Real usurpations of power are things that Locke perpetually feared
in thinking that governmental abuse of basic rights might have to be
met in the last analysis by the "right of revolution," reserved to cases
where it violated the nature of the fundamental agreement that men
had, he thought, set up in the social contract establishing both civil
society and its government. It ought to be so manifestly to the interests
of those vested with this power and duty to protect rights that they
would not fall into serious dispute about their nature or limits. Alas,
history has not written that record in terms that would be compatible
with Locke's faith in the rationality, the Stoic concept of the rationality
of natural law and its effect on natural rights. Need for a "common judge"
which was his own initial reason for the contract, was indeed to ensure
reason. But his answer to *quis custodiet custodes ipsos* is not more clear
today—and the right of revolution still looms in the tragic background.
It is a tribute to our system that when the claim to the right of
revolution was once entered upon by the Southern states it failed to
destroy our own Union.

We have had to support, reluctantly, in the new so-called "states"
coming out of colonial status, political constitutions that fail completely
to meet the very large arena of contests, so-called "wars of liberation"
that are really outside-guided revolutions from systems that assert an
absolute, that is to say universal, "organic" type of rule in the totalitarian
state. These revolutions are really take-overs which once in power
destroy all freedom for the future, by which parties can develop that
are at best mandated for *general* purposes. Any really free parties in
truly constitutional systems *cannot* aim at violent overthrow or sub-
version of the legal system which must permit the existence of other
parties with general purposes, providing they all accept a common
purpose that can be summed up as constitutional due processes and procedures, effectively implemented.

No Universal Purpose Groups are Possible in Free Societies

This analysis at least sketches the framework for strictly limiting claims for the political universality of groups. Such claims are simply incompatible with constitutional freedom, the source of any political growth and responsibility in personal as well as national character. But, obviously, there are many other groups that assert values of a *general* character, many of which *can* come into conflict with the same laws of the state and *do* come into at least moral conflict with the government under parties whose ruling purposes and values they fundamentally oppose. Often groups with an extensive international base, e.g., or a doctrinally compelling social philosophy at variance with freedoms defined by the state's constitution, do challenge a part or even the whole basis of the state. Communism is not the only challenging revolutionary totalitarian set of values.

For instance, the struggle between church and state is too well known as a part of history from the medieval period up through the Renaissance and the Reformation to require much documentation at this time to make this point. And this is a perpetually reviving struggle. It can take new and quite different forms through the effort of the church to adjust itself to totalitarian systems by doing what the Catholic Church appears to be doing today—by bargaining with a totalitarian state which exerts powers that the church is unable to reason with, by urging other people —states and faiths—to sacrifice some of their preciously held free ground in order to permit "the church" to "negotiate," or to get some sort of a "placating program," if I can put it as brutally as that. The papacy qualifies for this citation in its pressure on its "all" Christians to extend *its* influence for its secular ends in Red areas, especially Russia and its satellites.

In my view, it is on that line that we are being urged to seek peace in Vietnam at what amounts to "all costs," forgetting Lincoln's injunction that we "do all that may achieve and cherish a just and lasting peace among ourselves with all nations" as well as his other injunctions that we should not only consider this, first of all, "with malice toward none, with charity for all" but, as he goes on to say, "with firmness in the right as God gives us to see the right, let us strive on to finish the work we are in." Presumably, this Lincolnian injunction, which states as clearly as any utterance what I should take as a national credo, aims to protect the grounds on which we are responsible for our own freedom, at a very minmum. This much "firmness in the right," in point of fact— given the fact that our nuclear deterrent is the sole shield of that freedom —is the only way that we—or anyone else—*can* protect the freedom of the world. This makes our own "common defense" the shield of the world's true "welfare."

One might almost summarize the entire problem, and the dilemmas that result from it by saying that if we lost our nuclear deterrence, we would lose the world's freedom. Any just and lasting peace requires at least that safeguard. It now appears that we could be tricked into this simply through a treaty that we signed and kept that would give no assurance of the Soviet system keeping its pledges, e.g., in the space treaty recently ratified. If violated, as it could be, practically with impunity, it would permit them to steal a decisive march on us by installing orbital space weapons that could fire from a distance close enough to our earth targets to be practically unanswerable by anti-missile defense—until too late.

Given the peculiar properties that these satellites in orbit would have, it would be impossible *really*, without the gravest risks of setting them off, to inspect or detect their perhaps booby-trapped mechanisms in spite of any agreement to the contrary we think we have negotiated. In the second place, we are now asking for only the *same* "sacred word"— to prevent the fatal discrepancy of what would happen to our present safe margin of retaliatory deterrence which could in a few years be created by a widespread Russian adoption of anti-missile ballistic missiles at this time, now being widely installed by Moscow. Are we again relying only on our hopeful, wishful thinking that mere acquiescence on our part to treat agreements, to protect us against this step-up which would produce after a very short time a perhaps hopeless gap in our own net missile capabilities? It might then really put us in a position where Bertrand Russell's logic would become a description of fact: it would no longer be probable, or at least likely, that one could be Red and Dead in the Kremlin, because the chances of our deterrent capabilities might be very much minimized. We might find his advice based on a really relevant lack of alternatives by our own acceptance of his counsels.

A few examples will show that any such purpose as his that is too naïve or innocent of evil can be misused by the deluded, if it misconceives its assumptions of the real "net capability" analysis, of weapons systems in war-gaming terms; or if it forgets the hard facts of the moral gulf in the present international "order." Up to now we have repelled the threats to our survival in freedom not by unilateral concessions but by sternly being willing to take not gulling words but fair and clear deeds as tokens of good faith. No real "opening up" of the Soviet Union is even remotely in prospect in spite of, or perhaps now even more because of its growing difficulties with Red China. Mao in power will *not*, if his system survives even if he does not, mean a more relaxed set of Soviet rulers—though the division may still be better for world freedom than a single Red monolith. *These examples show that organic necessities of defense may underpin all hopes of preserving our entire free system of political values.* The safety of the world may depend on our general purpose *political* system protecting the possibility of free choice for all others—no coercion into the totalitarian universalism.

General Purpose Groups Versus *Interest Groups in Politics*

A further distinction between general purpose groups and universal purpose groups might not apply at all to pure interest groups, because of the fact that it would be very difficult to conceive of any universal *interest* group. The idea would be a contradiction in terms. There is no such thing as a *universal* interest. Unqualified to that point, it would necessarily become a *purpose*. One *could* propose to make a Marxian definition of class the basis of an interest as well as a purpose. But the illogic of its assumptions would be proved by any effort to apply them. Class is certainly meant to define a group, which both in its original application and in practice is a political, not an economic nor even a materialistic matter. In practice, Marxism puts the monopolistic nature of class, *without limits on its control over the instruments of production, so defined,* in the hands of *state* capitalism. If ever achieved, this would create in fact the most extraordinary world monopoly that could ever be dreamed, with total monopoly certainly brought about by Marx's remedy —not because of or at the hands of any of the various systems of public and private capitalism practiced in so relaxed a way by the free world. State-controlled capitalism, as in the present stage of Red rule, is in every sense rule by an interest group since it consists in "who gets what" in the simple terms that Lasswell and others who have applied *"Politics, Who Gets What?"* to it. Its professed purpose may appear to be anarchistic communism—"in the sweet bye and bye—Pie in the Sky"—as the Wobblies used to sing of it.

In all fairness it must by now be clear that *the nature of the totalitarian system requires government as a group to control everything*—so long as it has not been corrupted, as Russia already *in some measure* has been by market economics; and as a large part of Red China seems struggling *not* to be. That means to control *all* purposes, including basic interests, and to lump them all together under an ideology that Marxism does not admit to be an ideology, because its magic formula, alone of all such, is the only absolute *truth.* Nevertheless, such a regime must and does certainly function with the absolute ruthlessness of a dictatorship, imposing its pattern on the entirety of humanity that it is able to reach and hold. In that sense, any true world communist system—even if only in aim— must surely be a "universal purpose" group which attempts also to control every conceivable type of interest and bring it to this single measure and test: the criterion of the Marxian philosophy, for instance, is absolute for communists though they are forced to act in the manner that Orwell has satirized in both *Animal Farm* and in *1984* in their efforts to square history with doctrine, when and where doctrine's "science" does not in fact control *actual* history at all. Of course, communism may be relaxing some controls in Russia. But they can be reassumed, if a monopoly of power is still held by the party leaders.

Development of Groups from Interest to Purpose

Now the same parallel is not true to the degree that special interest groups, and general interest groups can change by a natural growth. This natural evolution may in fact produce genuine communities, even if in the beginning they do not aim to be such. In one respect, even as interest groups they are concerned with the needs of *their* members, first of all. They do tend to test everything in public policy by what these members *think* they get out of it. Some Negro and other lowest-income groups in cities tend to repudiate the general community's concerns even about basic national strategy and defense if it interferes with the benefactions required to satisfy repeated promises of their Great Society, or even those made by their own special minority-interest leaders, CORE, SNCC, and SNACC.

In this sense, the largest range of "pressure" groups in the United States has in the past tended, with exceptions like the PTA and the service clubs, on the whole to act mainly as interest groups. They are set up to meet *limited* needs—limited to their clientele. They may claim that these needs fulfill the public purpose—but their acts show where their hearts are.

It has been very instructive to me to find that there is a very different trend away from pressure group "special-interest" tactics today in the Conference of National Organizations, of which I have been an honorary member for several years; its list of members includes the most various types of organizations, some of which I shall select as examples for voluntary group classification.

What shall we call the American Bankers Association—is it just an interest group? To start with—yes. But it now has developed and publicly professes a well-articulated and more defensible general philosophy. In that respect, it has a way of looking at the problems of humanity which exposes them to something that has at least as much basis for a general philosophy (or purpose) as the labor union groups have[10]—I believe more.

Members of the groups comprising the present C.N.O. meet without any fanfare or publicity twice a year for a couple of days. They have extended exchanges of views, and very useful dialogues or dialectical discussions by noted experts of large public issues, often from very different points of view. One can certainly say that there are several "general purpose" groups here that transcend the mere special interests of their members, and that a common attitude on hitherto disputed issues often emerges from discussions by the C.N.O. group of delegates.

For example, when we examine the National Education Association, it may and does have the interests of the teaching professions and educa-

10 The labor union groups, by the way, withdrew from this Conference of National Organizations because they did not like to submit their claims today to any review by the other groups, even for discussion.

tional administrators generally, very much in mind as a starting point. The Conference, however, is made up of many other people with very much broader ranges of interests and of purposes. Its generally expressed attitude toward the relation of education to society shows that N.E.A. is not just an interest group. It must consider its purpose to be mainly one of the shaping of Americans, as part of humanity's values, and of our total nature, both as a society and as individuals. The N.E.A. is a clear instance of a group that does have a general purpose as well as both a general interest and a specific interest. In other words, it transcends the specific needs of a merely professional order of its clientele—in ways that are also reflected in other professions: law, medicine, accounting and, more and more today, banking, retail manufacturers associations, insurance companies, transportation, and public utilities.

The whole effect of the Conference of these national organizations (in the time I have been a part of and seen about three years of its work) is to make all of its members more and more able to act as *purpose* groups relating their ends to national policies. The discussions for several years have reflected the types of programs which have been carefully selected for useful general discussions.[11] They clearly show a growing effort first to inform their members and, second, to bring to bear the weight of other opinions (after discussion) in ways that show up in publications reaching all told about sixty million or more people regularly. These topics include crime in the cities, for instance; the place of the computer and automation in our society, and what it is doing to human behavior; the bearing that our national balance of payments has on our total economic power structure; or the weakening of private organizations as we put more and more burdens on the states and federal government, e.g., in social welfare and medicine.

The American Medical Association, obviously, comes into play with an especial interest in the question of the growing heavy hand of public control over hospitals, doctors, ethics, licensed drugs, and the squeezing out of private medical responsibility for publicly acknowledged dependence on tax-supported and more publicly-controlled hospitals, with Medicare as a vanguard. The unwillingness of many groups to support a stronger fight against "public encroachment" may disappear as the Great Society ceases to be regarded as a panacea (there are signs of a reverse

---

11 Recent Programs of the Conference of National Organization meetings:
Education and the Demands of Our Changing World
Urban America—Today and Tomorrow
Our National Responsibilities: Public and Private (with emphasis on health and medical care, education, housing, urban renewal)
Cybernetics in Perspective: What Has Automation Done to Us and For Us?
Balance of Payments Problem Today, Long-Term Aspects, Points of View (including British and French representatives)
USA Economic Opportunity 1965, especially Role of Government, Role of Non-Governmental Agencies.

swing of this pendulum). But a studied change toward professing national purpose, not just self-interest, has already taken place—most easily discerned in the American Bar Association, National Association of Manufacturers, and in the Chamber of Commerce.

There are those who think that the American Medical Association is a purely defensive organization, much like some of the Manufacturers Association's behavior used to be—say, ten or fifteen years ago—when it was really defensive to a considerable degree. All these groups had natural attitudes much like the labor unions' general theory has been: labor's first concern was to advance the rights and the privileges and the interests of their members by protective "labor-oriented" laws; also to protect their rights in bargaining processes to the point where nothing could resist them. They would regard with hostility any change in the Clayton Act's exemption of union action from restraint as a monopoly, which it often is to a painful degree. Even a judicial fiat holding this exemption to be an unconstitutional imposition of inequality on management would be regarded by labor as tantamount to declared war on the labor unions. So, also, to abolish the right-to-work laws in the states where they are legal becomes a chief test of the unions' political success.[12]

In short, labor unions tend to develop also general purposes (shown by public attitudes) as well as general interests. They certainly have to transcend the interests of any single union if they are going to be successful in setting up not just one big union, but even anything like really purposive collaboration between the several really big unions. There are still four or five in the field today besides the A.F. of L. and the C.I.O. which have, themselves, never gotten together in any kind of real organization where they have balanced off the craft and the industrial unions in a way that secured united action, except on some aspects of protecting their rights of collective bargaining. This protection includes not having any weakening of the exemption from antitrust procedures which they enjoy under the Clayton Act. That act, in my mind, is an *un*equal protection under the law, if ever I saw one.

If the present Supreme Court really took equal protection seriously, it would strike down the Clayton Act, as well as require the states to change their laws that now operate to disfranchise all the voters who do not help to carry at least a plurality in the state's votes for party candidates in the Presidential Electoral College representatives. Our national election system, by present state-vote distribution of Electoral College votes to plurality winners means that a popular minority-chosen President is still quite possible. It is far from a reasonable application, in its representation of "one man, one vote," though the present Court has refused to entertain state suits based on this effect of the present Electoral

12 "Memorandum of Dissent" by William Y. Elliott, in *The Public Interest in National Labor Policy* (New York, Committee for Economic Development, 1961) pp. 140 ff.

College laws without real argument, hearings, or decisions based on legal principles.

The point is that the labor unions are not in any sense able to bring in the Railway Brotherhoods or the Pullman union or, for that matter, the Transport Workers, the Longshoremen's union, or, above all, the Truckers. In spite of the fact that Mr. Hoffa is now in jail, he appears to be successful in directing his union, somehow keeping control over his successors, etc. He certainly is not playing ball with the other unions in any kind of way that makes a more moderate union bargaining position for them easier in any way whatever or, for that matter, to ease the built-in inflation of their present annual "pistol-to-the-head" demands.

Here unions have developed more than merely general purposes. They go beyond the British Labour Party in special purpose power just because they do not have full party responsibility. They tend to become almost totalitarian in some of their attitudes in the pursuit of their special labor programs. They are insistent upon attacking not only the right-to-work laws and maintaining special exemptions from control over campaign funds. They are getting what amounts to a real monopoly over most large production industry. They are in a position which, if pushed far enough, might give them a monopoly of at least a lease on controlling political power in this country too by unionizing all bureaucrats.

As consumers wake up, this past trend is encountering a resistance that is increasingly strong, and one hopes it will become more effective as retired people, other nonorganized or white-collar sections grow disenchanted with the inevitably painful effects of union-produced inflation. The organizing power of the unions and their use of "check-off" funds—in spite of any legislation purporting to deal with the way political funds for party support should be managed—seems to be almost unlimited. No legislator in normal constituencies—now rendered more vulnerable by "one man, one vote," which increases easily organized city pressure groups' powers—no legislator can afford to take on an open fight with labor as a political organization. This gives labor a more than equivalent political control, measured by its deliverable votes.

These are just selected samples from the roster of great voluntary groups with a political goal and a hand in the administration as well as the party politics which represent very great political pressures in this nation.

One could extend the generalization of a trend toward general purpose groups to the veterans' organizations, all of which certainly have a special interest group concern in protecting the rights of veterans. But very definitely they do take a more generalized interest even in doing that, and they have to struggle with each other as to how general that interest can be. It is fortunate, therefore, that we have more than one veterans' organization. The same thing is true of the farmers' groups. The Farm Bureau is a rather conservative organization. But, as is well known, many of the other farmers' organizations run the whole gamut to the New Left and even those that go beyond the New Left, whatever and wherever that may be.

Conclusion: From Interest Groups True Community Must Broaden Beyond Even Parties, to Consensus

To conclude, let me both illustrate scientific efforts at classification and relate them to co-organic group theory by reviewing a number of other examples in which the theories of politics have been forced to concern themselves with political action groups.

First focus: the nature of universal political values, if there be any, which the totalitarians alone assert at this time. These systems are finding conflicts among themselves quite significant and disruptive to any thought that they may impose this coercive system to produce a real world unity, unless they do it by the simple device of having a nuclear monopoly and being ruthless in its exercise. China's example may demonstrate whether even such ruthlessness will not eventually—maybe soon—defeat itself. People grow tired of perpetually whipped-up youth demonstrations and Red Guard anarchy as a substitute for orderly civic progress. The take-over by the army seems almost inevitable.

The second proposition is that parties are in essence a more limited projection of the agreement that is found in every constitutional system, but at a less general level than the Constitution itself. The parties operate *within* and *under* the Constitution: this method is used for uniting people in the pursuit of those common purposes which party platforms at least represent in some degree, over which battles are often fought over genuine differences as to what the true moral basis of humanity may and should be. People who insist that *"the Good and Great Society"* means delivering everybody from all want are in some measure conceding to the communist utopia its magic: i.e., the removal of wants and of the need for any "requirement to work" discipline for unwilling labor, leading one sweet day to enjoying the right to eat, to appropriate any other needed goods freely, and participate fully in society, without assuming one's own load, simply means that an elysian form of human nature can—without any coercion or even self-discipline by a market economy geared to a wage system, gauged by payment for useful and exchangeable products—be created in which there will be no real compulsion by the state in any form and no need for it. At the very least, utopian communism means that this compulsion would in fact then take the form of only equalizing things so as to get out of the well-provided the necessary flow of stuff for the ill-provided, and to put the burden of those who can't, won't and don't on the backs of those who can, will, and do.

This is a formula that, even heavily disguised under the O.E.O., is not having very great success at the present time in the United States, though proposals that go as far as a general compulsory minimum family income, not related to effort, above $3,000 are being added to the bait.

Where is the alternative of communism proving more successful even in simply feeding humanity? It has, I think, singularly misjudged real progress in terms of values that the projected image of the end to "poverty" in the "Great Society" did promise as a goal. This was because it assumed that by removing all hardships, and the incentives of possible suffering for noncooperation in production, still more by producing mere "easement" for all human wants, state action could render human beings by satisfaction of basic needs capable of becoming noble and great. This form of the communist ideal of the Great Society would (by hypothesis) *automatically* result in just what men want, and all the ideal characteristics of heaven at no hard price. Even if proverty could be diminished or removed, for instance by a guaranteed wage and a right to everything called "needs," the American dream of a Great Society would fall flat. There would then be a standard of living of whatever the figures in a perpetual inflation had to be boosted to: $3,000 (now considered too low a floor) was quite recently regarded as a rather substantial differential from poverty, particularly in a society which gives so many benefits to its members free anyhow, and leaves increasingly still others to be taken by constant petty theft without real punishment. Check at any store where customers are allowed to collect their own purchases, particularly on youthful shoplifting by mere children, let run wild: prices go higher!

Other Effective Purpose Groups

But passing by that idyllic picture of an illusion which hides the ugly real prospect, the next problem is *to get at how much general purpose is present in what other groups*. It certainly is present in churches, in some forms of organizations which have the broadest possible basis for reforming society as well as in political parties, with claims for exercising a general purpose to shape the broadest levels of society. Sometimes the state seems to be pushing allegedly spiritual values while the churches— most of them—are outdoing the politicians in an "activism" that seems by applying coercion to charity to be quite un-Christian in character and moral meaning. It is on this kind of misplaced and quite unqualified shift of the sources for right judgment that political issues emerge in their most clear form—out of disappointment in promises from both sources. Conflicts over political programs originating from such groups, as for instance the "activist" churches with pacifist doctrines, show that those that have an ideological base like these "New Left" churches; or demand, as some do, an ideological change that is even more sweeping and absolute, are merely trying to outbid the communists in utopian promise. Perfection through the magic of collectivism means uses of force that are bound to conflict with constitutional responsibility and the more painful progress produced by self-discipline and hard work at really useful tasks for ends not corrupt that do provide useful exchanges on market terms.

Such a constitutional political system cannot be run by demonstrations led by hate-mongers—even if organized, led, and directed in the name of Christ, falsely used. It must, to remain morally sound, develop and maintain in control citizens devoted to a true and continuing community with past virtues in order to shape future leaders. Claims that "black power" is developing a new social dignity by renouncing responsibility for "violence" but using any power for "black" interests only must, if continued, destroy moral community. True constitutional consensus operates for limited but general purposes all based, first of all, on the fundamental agreement of a greater than majority base for the principles of a co-organic constitution, as applied by parties that struggle to secure alert citizen cooperation, to get and support the necessary representative majorities that are implicit in the system, whether federal or otherwise. The organization of a Citizens Union, pledged to support such a program for maintaining a community dependent on such a real consensus and to protect it from betrayal, by opposing anyone willing to buy special interest support on blackmail terms, might prove a powerful protection and an antidote against poison by minority block pressures demanding the answer only to one question: "Will you give us what we demand?" Even the power of "political labor" can be over-matched if out-organized.

It is precisely in this support of consensus, voluntary, by citizens general-purpose groups that we raise a crucial issue about the functions and nature of a number of groups that do not have really *general* purposes, but still show *special* purposes that are very different in character from just their special interest. They too may be enlisted to preserve community against "gimme and grabby" one-interest blocs. Take for instance the propaganda groups. To single out a few of those that are or can be very important:

First, we can or should remember how powerful were the propaganda groups that put in the prohibition amendment—where membership was obviously very widespread and effective. These prime movers of sweeping reform were not just interest groups; they were not people who were trying to make money out of abolishing the whisky business, even though they undoubtedly thought that their lives would be safer and better if they could get rid of "demon rum" in his various forms. It is very interesting that this Eighteenth Amendment, though put into the Constitution by the required majorities, failed in its effort to reform Americans by banishing all transportation and sale of "demon rum," i.e., alcohol consumed as a beverage. It was ultimately repealed because it went too far in trying to coerce human nature, as many very good and often long-suffering people were then moved to do in their fight against alcohol and alcoholism—certainly a prime source of much human misery and crime.

Consensus or Crime—Protection of Virtue

Today we do not get much argument about the outlawry, at least, of poisonous or narcotic drugs, although we have great difficulty politically in enforcing this process, and British law is quite permissive—too much so to lessen addiction. To my mind, the most serious weakness in our whole criminal system is in failing to take the drug traffic seriously and to make the punishment fit the crime. If preventions are to be adequate really to establish protection against the destruction of souls as well as bodies on the massive scale in which this is being done, especially to the young—even to children—sanctions must be drastically severe and the true sources of supply really controlled. This is one more reason for not giving Red China a U.N. seat as the reward for cooperation toward a better world, a world which Peking—a main source for the illegal narcotics banned by world treaties—systematically aims to debauch in every way possible.

The recklessness that the pandering to the dangerous psychedelic craze shows it to be—openly advocated and practiced—as well as what the widespread use by mere children of marijuana and other new drugs is now doing to their futures—to say nothing of the well-established addiction drugs that have been a curse to humanity for so long, all show that our present struggle with the drug trade under any form of international control has been impossible to win—so far. Yet it must be at least not so hopelessly lost.

To deal adequately with drugs law must be predicated on an aroused active judgment that they are in fact worse than any curse of alcohol— bad as that is—or of cigarettes. This is because these abuses of drug habits may, in fact, *take away any hope of moral responsibility*—the great sin against man and God, as black as any in the Book. To squash drug addiction would require a special purpose kind of organization, but it ought to go along with a declared broader kind of purpose: "To protect by all means those who are really helpless to protect themselves." We are sacrificing many people to exploitation by ruthless masters, simply because of the fiction that the victims are adequately prepared to live in city jungles because they were born a number of years ago in some part of this "enlightened" country and should have learned how to cope with this tough and complex world on adult, i.e., responsible terms. But to thrust this burden on children, even before high school, shows criminal negligence by all responsible citizens, and a breakdown of all basic moral concern for true protection for our young. It is the product either of criminal negligence and willful ignorance; or of cowardice in protecting our homes that masks often as enlightened tolerance or moral *laissez-faire*.

Certain types of social and political actions by some preachers or chaplains from some churches are particularly to be noted as encouraging a moral confusion worse confounded: many of the extreme "civil liberties" forays, calling for demonstrations and protests that inevitably invite violence, are being made at least in the name of and with the alleged support of high-purposed organizations sanctioned by churches, often in an atmosphere of complete ignorance of the stern realities, or of the really possible remedies for the sad situations that they are dealing with. This type of preacher, priest, and theologian shows no willingness to study deeply the limits of cultural background, the lack of any real capacity to act effectively, the absence of possible moral motivation, and of how best—in the light of these stern truths—to create the saving self-help of cooperative *responsibility* in the people they are working with. To accomplish immediate social "cures" they shift the burden from Christ's miraculous healing power to discredited economic nostrums and "magic formulae" for education that make up generations of backward motivation by burying in plenty. God's help is the last light they bring to this problem which they propose to solve by drastic redistribution of wealth, through destructive taxation—disguised. They have manifested the same reckless haste and social ignorance in planning the antipoverty crusade and its related nostrums which could not by any amount of "give-away" charity have dealt with the real problems of motivation, moral training, and hard work needed to create true personal dignity, not just an arrogant assertion of false pride, hatred, and violence that tears down but builds nothing on the ruins.

It is noteworthy that the substitution of this kind of falsely based "social reform" for the genuine religious transformation by turning in prayer for God's guidance of man's feelings toward other men, through the introduction of Christian love into the processes of our own personal history, is such a popular cult with ministers who are busy burying God with the other hand, as their theological contribution to our too little faith. They no longer even profess a belief in the dead deity— though oddly enough they profess a religion based on the deification of His Son—still calling themselves Christians.

Burying God: The Theologian's False God—Taking Away by State Action All Human Testing by Hardship—Is This Truly Christian Charity? Or Justice?

A miscarriage of real faith into the activism of political or direct action that spells an end to all social order can pervert the channels for our really possible and genuine spiritual revival. It can destroy any true effectiveness for the Christian church, so organized and used, if pursued as a substitute for the deeper spiritual insights and moral firmness—not the mere permissiveness—which the church is weakly affording to humanity at this most testing time. This is not Christian leadership, but shepherds turned into sheep.

One might note as a final summary of group differences, the same sort of differences between types of special interest groups that appear now in their professed conceptions of the right public behavior for almost any of the national organizations that tend to attain to a general rather than merely special interest. This shows more clearly wherever they have to reconcile the natural differences of goals in the perspectives of sizeable numbers of their most active members.

One could exempt from this type of analysis—because it is inapplicable to them—the so-called service groups, like the Lions Club, the Kiwanis, the Rotarians, and others of that useful and truly devoted sort, which have different and compelling reasons from their founding purposes and their methods of recruitment, not only for their professed objectives but their public interest types of performance.

These service clubs (from their origins) have professed and pursued a general purpose as well as the general interests of their members, even for selected types of memberships. They are made up of people who have sufficiently broad differences in their special interests. Therefore they have to achieve, in order to survive, some general interest reconciliation, at least, that accounts for the broad nature of the special purposes which they tend to emphasize. The Kiwanis Clubs, for instance, stress national concern about fundamental values, like religion, the development of youth leaders, and good ends of that sort. As a natural outcome, this commitment carries an attitude of moral campaigning for business— service to the community and the various forms of community action, by doing good works that take into account the preservation of the community—which has always been a basic point also for the Rotarians. I would judge that the same thing is true for nearly all the other groups of a similar order. Some of them have more strongly emphasized the problem of the welfare of their members through insurance and special services of this sort. It is very interesting to note what effect the increased supplying of social services and the kind of things that the welfare state is beginning to insist upon thrusting on people may have for fraternal organizations, and other groups of that sort which used to be a way of taking care not only of funerals and family care but of forms of health insurance and comparable advantages now performed for less immediate cost by the government—always on a poor actuarial basis that causes great deficits now, and leaves arrears to be made up later, or inflated out. Even the Community Givers Funds groups are affected.

Particularly interesting combinations in emphasis on both general interest and general purposes mark characteristic groups like the Federation of Women's Clubs or the Parent-Teacher Association, under Mrs. Jennelle Moorhead's leadership at this time. Of course there is a genuine and general interest in improving in every way the education of their children. Naturally, they stress national educational problems from the point of view of the philosophy of education, and study some very basic problems that affect the whole moral life of the child and the schools in the community. Perhaps they could go further to encourage greater depth in other studies, e.g., by foundations and the Department of Health, Education and Welfare. For these reasons they are far from being limited just to questions of the technical aspects of whether or not, e.g., to follow track systems in the lower grades, or whether to emphasize one form or another of school activities, and alternative ways of shaping educational disciplines—more emphasis on vocational or other training methods for jobs. They are raising the most basic questions about the values as well as the techniques of our public school systems.

Generally, they take quite strong lines about using school buildings for voluntary prayers, for example—and more power to them for doing so! They are concerned to protect the free exercise of religion, as well as to prevent any real threat of the establishment of religion. The Supreme Court of the United States, because so far it seems to have come down almost entirely on the dangers to somebody's emotional upsets in not being "included in," so rule that no public school prayer decisions tend to exclude everybody *out*—"include" them all out, as the celebrated Hollywood motion-picture producer's *bon mot* put it, when he said "include me out." It is right and proper to exclude people out, *on request*. But all bona fide religious groups ought to insist upon the protection of their own rights to the free exercise of individual rights to practice their religions in public buildings, if not in conflict with school exercises. Conscientious atheists cannot impose their view, I think, on other people without exercising a corresponding and unconstitutional *dimunition* of the liberty of others. And this is one of the things that free group activity is very essential in protecting: a primary role for the Citizens Unions. The whole tone of society depends on its active exercise of this right *not to be coerced by some fancied emotional strain claimed by a nonconformist*. Non-conformists of any value do not shrink so painfully nor inflict their alleged woes on others. They are more robust!

The Poison of the Spirit

Note particularly what kind of groups are concerned with the impact of the poison now being dripped into the human soul by media like television, the movies and a spate of literature from the most suspect sources by interests of some sort who are turning the output of pornography into a profession. Profession is not the right word—into a racket is nearer the truth—a very lucrative racket, alas, with a very free "go" sign from the courts and no effective way for the community to combat it except by organized disapproval of movies or programs and by parent's boycotts. This makes organizations of national scope, like the Federation of Women's Clubs or the churches, very important centers for rallying opinion of this kind. The League of Women Voters used to be concerned with such matters, but their overwhelming conquest by a peculiar sort of liberalism (that somehow seems always to ally itself with the "New Left") has somewhat changed that picture. The old League of Women Voters, not so initiated in these phony "barrel load" forms of political salvation, was an important factor in this sort of real moral struggle. So were the churches. Now ministers and chaplains vie with each other to urge "let yourself go." It seems to me that the same hope for enlightened, tough-minded political analysis—with more hopeful prospects for useful civic action—could be said of the Association of American University Women, which has time and talents, and should devote them to general interest and purposive matters that concern the whole moral tone of the community, not just the more esoteric concerns of cultural interests of college graduates. The various women's clubs have a similar possibility.

A Round Table for the Republic

In conclusion, may I make a special plea for a type of group that I do not think we have today—as a nation. I am influenced by a memory that goes back to my young manhood, even to my boyhood in Nashville, Tennessee, when the most respected group of citizens belonged to a sort of super dining-and-discussion club, called "The Round Table." There used to be a tone-setting group of this kind of "leading citizens" in many communities. Is it still true today? I believe something like it still goes on in Nashville, Tennessee: A highly selected group were co-opted somewhat in the manner of the Business [Advisory] Council, which is another example of a high-level group that has maintained (since its inception during the New Deal) a high standard by the device of holding up a sense of duty, honor, integrity and service to the country as a measure for choosing the level of special character, so that for membership it was not enough just to run a very big business. In the Business Council, over nearly all if its thirty-odd years of national service, active current members carefully sought to improve, if possible, in their new members these high qualities. To be chosen, one must have a well-tested patriotism and also show a willingness to serve his country in any proper way, at local and state as well as national levels.

No doubt I am first prompted to propose the grander-scale Round Tables ("For The Republic" and "For Freedom") because of the great influence of the old "Round Table" that existed in Nashville in the period after World War I. This august body, to whose sessions it was a great honor to be invited as a young man, included two ex-Supreme Court Justices, Chancellor Kirkland of Vanderbilt (a very remarkable educator and philosopher), the Dean of the Law School, the Dean of the Medical School, the President of the American College of Surgeons, and other worthies of that sort, including some of the best professors and writers of the period: only a few of my brethren in *The Fugitive* (Poets) Group graced it, even at a later time. But then poets have never been held to serve in the first line of "wise councillors"—even in the South!

They are apt to be people who are taken as *not* representing the most all-round court of conscience of mankind, in spite of the fact that they have been called the "unofficial legislators of the world"!

My point is that these two groups, by their tone and influence, one on a local, and the other, the Business Council, on a national community basis, showed broad moral purpose and helped to give members an influential, even a national voice—by prestige, service, and example. There needs to be some voice for the fundamental values that are really meta-political, that transcend the things which daily politics must deal with on deadlines, that parties cannot deal with because they lie too deep, that tend to have to run the gamut of human testing in a broader way than the churches are dealing with today—because the churches in too many cases have interested themselves too strongly in only one side of liberty and one side of responsibility, and have defined freedom only as freedom from all material want. They do not take into account the witness of God by stern duty in the testing of character and Christian doctrine. This is a point of view that may sound heretical to some who are neither good preachers nor, above all, good teachers. I think it is very sound criticism in the light of the doctrines of the Gospels themselves; and can be defended in terms of either the Old or the New Testament, with texts adequate to any occasion.

We must find ways to produce some high purpose groups like a non-political, nonparty, Round Table for the Republic, chosen on a co-opted basis, selecting those people who best represent the best principles—the truest, best-tested values of our society. We must find funds which our thousands of foundations could amply provide, privately, and ways to supply them with a staff of young men who would themselves be potential members of this highly honored and motivated group: They would be particularly fit for the honor if, after being tried out and given missions to perform, they really succeeded in holding together the community and the consensus on which community rests—justly, wisely, and with honor and dignity, with self-effacing service and heroic willingness to undertake missions no matter how dangerous or difficult. This is what the Round Table of the Arthurian legend suggests. It is a very important symbol, I think, from the standpoint of our future unity as a people and our adequate leadership. We need an epic symbol to develop, and better use our epic leaders—who teach most by their examples.

No doubt I shall be told that this proposal, after all, is itself utopian if we do not have a popular, i.e., a democratic political base. In some measure this may be true. We cannot neglect or abandon our struggle for political power to protect as well as to foster good ends. I would hope that Round Tables could be spread on an international base by a parent Round Table for Freedom—chosen in the manner I suggested in a speech[13] at the Bruges Conference that actually set up a sort of proto-type in the Atlantic Institute—so regarded for the cultural side of the

Atlantic Community, at least. We should aim ultimately to bring in Japan and those nations of the Far East and other continents that have a sense of honor and decency and courage, and are willing to join us in protecting the free world so that we would have a high-level world court of conscience in our Round Table for Freedom. We had the makings of something like this on a lower-level model in the well-chosen representation of the Harvard International Summer Seminars (set up during the ten years in which I ran the Summer School, and with Henry Kissinger as the prime guide for it through most of its life). For years it produced a really distinguished magazine called *Confluence* that still has a legacy in that its editor, Stephen Graybaud, has gone on editing *Daedalus* since then for the American Academy of Arts and Sciences.

Now I think this business of a high model for excellence is of very great importance. If we can grow in that direction, we can spread to the regional and local levels. We can deal with the problems of cities on an entirely different basis from what they are being dealt on today. Now, more often they are the crucial center for social conflict than for cultural unification and creativity in our civilization. We cannot go on doing housing in the way we have been doing it; we cannot go on dealing with poverty by wholesale and slipshod ideas and magic-formula methods that encourage the very evils they are supposed to remedy.

If we are going to deal with the impact of technology on our times, it must be not only in the media of mass communications. But that is the first area needing attention because of the poisoning of opinion it has achieved—to an extent of damage that is almost incalculable in lowering the tone of entertainment, of public discussion, of the molding of immature minds, perhaps of all minds. Children themselves are the most helpless against it. These things are of great seriousness, and they are just as serious (probably more although they are less direct) as those things that I have been agitating and never cease to lift my "barbaric yawp," like Walt Whitman, "over the roofs of the world," as long as I have voice left to do it: namely, the pollution of the air, pollution of the water and, ultimately, the pollution of the sea and the destruction of its other great resources on which one day man's food supply may well depend as much as on all other sources.

A Meta-Political Court of Conscience

Our companions of these Round Tables, Free World and National, must be able, as accepted missions, to seek, to find and to deal effectively with those deep, often hidden, issues which transcend the ordinary purview of politics. These are the "meta-political" problems that require anticipation, sensitivity, openness to planning for them years and years before one can make most busy and apathetic people aware of them,

13 *Orbis* (Summer, 1958), pp. 221-235.

by mobilizing opinion and of getting action—tying on these groups to the interest groups and to the action groups that are national, at least in scope, and broadening these to the community. They must be able to analyze and improve our basic moral and other principles to strengthen the faith of our nation in its mission—the best way to set and raise our tone—especially by their examples.

Perhaps the ultimate range of this proposal is too far ahead to talk about at this time in any effective way. But time is running out for us. I see it as a necessity for tomorrow—not the day after. Must we wait on world sorrow?

There is a need for another grouping for patriotic community action, for which I have just proposed the term (for lack of a better one) of "Citizens Union." We need to organize our citizens nationwide on a non-partisan but unifying basis for the protection of our citizenship in all aspects of true *community,* for the protection of real equality of *liberty,* so that we cannot be coerced into a *leveling down* process that takes away our greatest liberties; namely, to be our best selves—not a common denominator of mediocrity. We cannot have our children picked up and used as pawns for somebody's sociological theories about "busing" them, and making equal racial numbers the false solution of the basic problem, which is one of securing real liberties and privileges, by the equal protection of *all* genuine rights, especially the right to grow to one's highest self. This reverse racism of cocktail-shaking—either for competition of races or forced melting pot—is an invasion of liberty of so gross a character that the Supreme Court is itself in danger of decreeing the violation of the most fundamental liberties of our system. Its acts show something deeper in error, that I think we need to address ourselves to, particularly in the nature of what the Court has come to be in the last twelve years—a constitution-making body—not merely a censor or a legislator—undoing the past with reckless fiats in spite of Article V.

It is at this deepest level that the Citizens Union must be alerted and find unifying ways to protect the rights of citizens as *citizens.* It must protect the rights of those colored men of the best possible will and behavior and views and moral character and everything else that marks our best and most soundly loyal Americans, who need protection against the destruction of their own true position by violent agitators and people who, posing as class champions turn against what their own best produces. It is these racists, whether openly or not fighting for black power, who are getting nearly all the publicity—and, unfortunately, much of the support of the churches—instead of these solid citizens who are going on doing their duty, raising their families well, and trying to protect the community and serve in it. One Senator Brooke is worth a thousand demonstrators. Not only Senator Brooke—but behind him in the long line of (to my mind) the highest distinction, the greatest Americans that we have produced—men like George Washington Carver.

Thank goodness, there are some of them not only in public but in private life who are beginning to demonstrate this kind of character. It is the kind of true dignity of service to all men on which a true *American* community, instead of a community that exists on "my rights" and "my privileges" as being the sole basis for voting, and for everything else. Black racism is just as wrong as white racism—and at the present stage of urge to violence and of slogans like "burn, baby, burn" far more dangerous in inciting counterviolence.

I would go so far as to say, at the end, that we must establish some criteria for determining how general a constitutional *consensus juris* must be, if it is to be tested, as it is by such strains as the Court has opened it to. For instance, if a man burns his draft card, should he then enjoy the privilege of voting, should he enjoy the protections of a passport and the rest of our system, of full citizenship in it, whose lawful protection he has by his act denounced and repudiated, and which he is in effect destroying if his own action is an indication of his feelings about it? Can he claim a Moslem religious base for actions that do not reflect any concern for the true Mohammed or the Koran—just the false Mohammed, whose feet are not alone of Clay? This becomes a very real issue. A Citizens Union could keep alive and distinguish true from false issues of this sort; and do it without complicating them by injecting party issues, along divisive lines. If some groups are organizing to protect only their one special interest, or their minority demands for privileges, which they miscall "rights," for a special position in society that exempts them from duties and responsibilities, then it becomes necessary to remind them that they cannot share the benefits of that community which is dependent upon their participation in it truly, and with full recognition of their responsibility and willingness to carry its burdens as well. If they repudiate all but their own interests in that community, and *their* demands on it, and require only that the community protect *their* special privileges as interests, they are not *of* that community to share it or protect it, or to draw on its resultant treasures. Responsibility is the price not just of freedom, but of the political privileges that we call political liberties.

This is, I think, one of the true shibboleths that is fairly easy to apply: I believe it should be the duty of a Citizens Union to get guidance from a court of conscience like that of a Round Table for the Republic in giving an extended study to the fundamentals of such proposals as those made here—and then giving them support to the degree that they command support on a local basis by a nonpartisan (bipartisan-group) in every community of this country, aimed at protecting the true Constitution in its application to the *consensus juris* as well as what Cicero added —the *utilitatis communio*, i.e., the shared organic needs (utility) which our republic now demands to meet its perils, internal and external, never more seriously threatening our security and our world mission as the sole real bastion of the world's freedom and its economic strength.

INDEX

"A. E.", *See* Russell, A. E.

Abrath vs. North Eastern Railway Co., 395.

Absolute Idealist School, determinism in, 43.

Absolutism, 17, 20; repudiated, 45; and moral liberty, 168; Duguit's theory results in, 266; Mussolini's theory of, 335.

Action, as program of politics, 321.

Acton, Lord, quoted, 167.

Adair vs. U. S., 467n.

Adams, B., on sovereignty, 181; *Centralization and the Law*, 181n.

Adams, H., quoted, 21, 36, 37, 54, 55; *The Education of Henry Adams*, 36n, 39.

Adamson Act, cited by Laski 155.

Administration, political, regional movements for, 12ff; responsibility of, in United States, 98, 447; importance of in modern state, 444; public servants in, 445 Dickinson on faults of, 447.

Administrative agencies, powers of, 425.

Administrative bodies, functions of, 97.

Administrative law, 426n; development of, 447; in France, 504.

"Age of Reason," 15.

Agrarian problem, 432n.

Agreements under law, 295.

Agriculture, Laski's omission of reference to, 170.

Ainslie, D., 371n.

Alazard, J., *Communisme et "Fascio" en Italie*, 140n; 158n.

Aliotta, A., *The Idealist Reaction Against Science*, 42n.

Allgemeine Elektrizitäts Gesellschaft, 209. *See* Rathenau.

American Council of Learned Societies, *Survey of Research*, 446n.

American Federation of Labor, attacks on state's authority by, 3; "moral personality" of, 109; use of bloc system by, 156; demands of, 191.

American Steel Foundries vs. Tri-City Central Trade Council, 396n.

Anarchy, evolution toward despotism, 293n, 294n; state of in Italy, 319; rule of law as means of escape from, 389-390.

Angell, N., "The Political Theory of," 107n.

d'Annunzio, G., imperialist influence of, in Italy, 325-326.

Anonymous, "Deputato al Parlamento," 127n.

Anti-intellectualism, 10; growth of, 26; dangerous aspects of, 37; attitudes of, 53; in politics, 69-85; Duguit's doctrine of, 251-255;*See also* Intellectualism.

Antonelli, E., *La Russie Bolcheviste*, 137n.

Arbitration, compulsory, in labor disputes, 188-191; in Fascist industry, 332.

Aristophanes, 59.

Aristotle, 8, 80, 141, 264; *Politics*, 152n, 421; on moral ends of state, 152n; meaning of politics, 217; concept of social morality, 239.

Armstrong, H. F. Jr., "Italy, Jugo-Slavia, and Lilliputia," 346n.

Articles of Confederation, 284.

Ashbury Ry. Carriage vs. Riche, 401n.

Askwith, Sir George, as chairman of the Industrial Council, 197.

Asquith, Herbert A., *Fifty Years of Parliament*, 69.

Associations, artificial and natural, 370-371.